COLLEGIUM

CHRISTI REGIS

FROM THE COLLECTION OF

GEORGE SCHNER, S.J.
1946 - 2000

The Genesis of
Heidegger's
Being and Time

The Genesis of Heidegger's
Being and Time

Theodore Kisiel

UNIVERSITY OF CALIFORNIA PRESS
Berkeley   Los Angeles   London

University of California Press
Berkeley and Los Angeles, California

University of California Press
London, England

Library of Congress Cataloging-in-Publication Data

Kisiel, Theodore J., 1930–
    The genesis of Heidegger's Being and Time / Theodore Kisiel.
     p. cm.
    Includes bibliographical references and index.
    ISBN 0-520-08150-1 (alk. paper)
    1. Heidegger, Martin, 1889–1976.   Sein und Zeit. 2. Ontology.
3. Space and time. I. Title.
B3279.H48S46633   1993
111—dc20   92-33888
                                                   CIP

Printed in the United States of America

1 2 3 4 5 6 7 8 9

Wir haben gedienet der Mutter Erd'
Und haben jüngst dem Sonnenlichte gedient,
Unwissend, der Vater aber liebt,
Der über allen waltet,
Am meisten, daß gepfleget werde
Der veste Buchstab, und bestehendes gut
Gedeutet. Dem folgt deutscher Gesang.

We have served our Mother Earth
And lately the sunlight,
Unawares, but what our Father
Who reigns over all
Most loves is that we keep the letter
Fast with care and well interpret
What abides. Which German song obeys.

—FRIEDRICH HÖLDERLIN, CLOSING LINES OF "PATMOS"

CONTENTS

vii

* Note that there is *no* Appendix A. See Introduction for explanation.

FIGURES

KEY TO ABBREVIATIONS AND NOTATIONS

WORKS (SEE BIBLIOGRAPHY FOR FURTHER DETAILS)

BT   *Being and Time* (cf. SZ below). The English translation of *Sein und Zeit* includes the German pagination in its margin.

BZ   *Der Begriff der Zeit* (talk to the Marburg Theologians on July 25, 1924).

FS   Heidegger, *Frühe Schriften* (Frankfurt: Klostermann, 1972).

GA   Heidegger, *Gesamtausgabe*, followed by volume number, page number/page number of English translation; for example, GA 20: 7/5.

GA 20   *History of the Concept of Time*, lecture course of SS 1925.

GA 21   *Logic*, lecture course of WS 1925–26.

GA 24   *The Basic Problems of Phenomenology*, lecture course of SS 1927.

GA 25   *Phenomenological Interpretations of Kant's Critique of Pure Reason*, lecture course of WS 1927–28.

GA 26   *Logic (Leibniz)*, lecture course of SS 1928.

GA 29/30   *The Basic Concepts of Metaphysics: World, Finitude, Individualization*, lecture course of WS 1929–30.

GA 56/57   = ZBP

GA 61   *Phenomenological Interpretations to Aristotle: Introduction to Phenomenological Research* ("Einleitung"), course of WS 1921–22.

GA 63   *Ontology: Hermeneutics of Facticity*, lecture course of SS 1923.

GS   Emil Lask, *Gesammelte Schriften*, volumes 1 and 2 (Tübingen: Mohr, 1923).

Ideen I   Edmund Husserl, *Ideen zu einer reinen Phänomenologie und phänomenologischen Philosophie, Erstes Buch.* (First published in 1913; there are two extant English translations of this book.)

Ideen II   Ibid. *Zweites Buch.* (First published posthumously in 1952 as Husserliana IV, this book is now available in an English translation by Richard Rojcewicz and Andre Schuwer.)

Logos-essay   Edmund Husserl, *Philosophy as Strict Science*. First published in
              the neo-Kantian journal *Logos* in 1911.
LU   Husserl, *Logische Untersuchungen (Logical Investigations)*.
Oct. 1922   followed by the pagination of the 51-page typescript sent to the
              Philosophical Faculties of Marburg and Göttingen in October
              1922. It was intended to be the "Einleitung" (Introduction) to
              a never-published book on Aristotle. Full title:
              "Phenomenological Interpretations to Aristotle: Indication of
              the Hermeneutic Situation." Available in both German and
              English.
PW   Karl Jaspers, *Psychologie der Weltanschauungen*.
SZ   Heidegger, *Sein und Zeit* (Halle: Niemeyer, 1927, [7]1953).
US   Heidegger, *Unterwegs zur Sprache* (Pfullingen: Neske, 1959).
ZBP   Heidegger, *Zur Bestimmung der Philosophie*. GA 56/57
              (Frankfurt: Klostermann, 1987). This volume contains the
              following lecture courses of 1919: KNS 1919, *The Idea of
              Philosophy and the Problem of Worldviews*, pp. 3–117; SS 1919,
              Phenomenology and Transcendental Value-Philosophy, pp.
              121–203; SS 1919, *On the Essence of the University and Academic
              Studies* (Oskar Becker's transcript), pp. 205–214.

METHOD

BCD   Biography Chronology Doxography [the philological trinity that
      provides the facts for this Genesis Story: why there is an Appendix
      B, C, D, but *no* Appendix A]

SEMESTERS

KNS   Kriegsnotsemester (War Emergency Semester): Heidegger's course was
      held from February 7 to April 11, 1919.
SS   Summer Semester. Typically held from May through July.
WS   Winter Semester. Typically November through February, with a
      month off around Christmas.

"HEIDEGGER" NOTATIONS (A CONVENIENT PERIODIZATION OF HIS CAREER, AS A UNIVERSITY STUDENT FROM 1909 TO HIS DEATH ON MAY 26, 1976)

The young Heidegger   Up to 1919.
The early Heidegger   1919–29.
The later Heidegger   The thirties to the fifties.
The old Heidegger   Late fifties onward, as he gets more
                      autobiographical.

Introduction

"And so you remained silent for twelve years," remarks the Japanese visitor to Martin Heidegger in a quasi-factual dialogue, as they discussed the linguistic problems broached by Heidegger's habilitation work on Duns Scotus (1915) and a subsequent lecture course, which antedated the publication of his magnum opus in 1927, *Being and Time* (= BT).[1] Well over a half-century has passed since Heidegger virtually exploded upon the larger philosophical scene with the publication of BT, achieving with it an international acclaim and notoriety which has not really waned over the intervening years. The difficulty in comprehending this classic of twentieth-century philosophy has since become legendary—"like swimming through wet sand," remarks one perceptive commentator. The fact that Heidegger published absolutely nothing in the decade preceding BT compounded the difficulty immensely, so much so that one was forced to regard this complex work as something that sprang full-grown, like Athena, from the head of Zeus. Herbert Spiegelberg's description of BT, "this astonishing torso," which alludes especially to the absence of its projected Second Half, can be applied as well to its initial "fore-structure," the dearth of publications before 1927.

This at least described the situation of the reader of BT for decades. That situation is now rapidly changing. After a half-century of having absolutely nothing but hearsay regarding the decade of publication silence between Heidegger's habilitation work and his masterwork, we will soon be faced with a wealth of documents which promise to show us how this great work came into being. Heidegger's *Gesamtausgabe* (Collected Edition), launched a year before his death on May 26, 1976, has from the start included editions of previously unpublished lecture courses from his Marburg period (1923–28). Thus, the initial draft of BT em-

1

bodied in his course of SS 1925, "History of the Concept of Time," has
been available to us in a faulty German edition since 1979 and an improved English translation since 1985.[2] The recent decision by Heidegger's literary executor to publish the earliest of the Freiburg lecture
courses (1919–23) will serve to steadily fill in much of the rest of the
gap.

However, for the long-felt desire for an unbroken overview over this
hitherto uncharted stretch of Heidegger's way to BT, such "original
sources" are not enough. For one thing, some of these are missing. Instead of the early[3] Heidegger's original text, a student transcript of a
course in SS 1919 has had to be published, and the same will be done
for the all-important course of WS 1920–21 on the phenomenology of
religion. For another, the editorial principle of an *Ausgabe letzter Hand*
(a "last-hand" edition: in practice, a deadhand edition),[4] instituted two
years *after* Heidegger's death, yields editions made from course-manu-
scripts as Heidegger last left them, making no distinction between the
course as it was presented at the time and material added afterwards,
sometimes years later, which thus serves to distort the public chronological record of Heidegger's actual development. Furthermore, the same
editorial principle sometimes makes editors hesitant to draw from student transcripts—clearly not of Heidegger's now nearly infamous
"hand" but rather of his voice, as he departed from his prepared text
to clarify his points—even to fill in obvious gaps in meaning in Heidegger's own manuscripts. Finally, even with an optimal editorial policy, the
publication of the separate courses in the Collected Edition would still
provide only a disjointed picture. Heidegger's teaching was an integral
part of his development toward BT, but only a part. The published
courses are not enough for a truly unbroken overview of this developmental history, which should also include, for example, important seminar exercises whose transcripts will probably never be published. And
it turns out that two of the most pivotal documents in this development
are, so to speak, "extracurricular." Finally, philosophically pertinent evidence for such a Story can also be drawn from Heidegger's correspondence and various university "acts" and documents, which are just beginning to come to light.

This book has as its aim just such a full and reliable story of Heidegger's development from 1915 to 1927, on the basis of the most complete
documentation that can be mustered, including student transcripts, correspondence, and university documents. It is basically a Book of Genesis
of a great classic, perhaps the most important, of twentieth-century philosophy. It seeks to relate the in-depth philosophical story which would
track the discovery and development of the conceptual constellations
that constitute the early Heidegger's response to the problems posed by

his hermeneutic situation in those formative years. It is a conceptual story, a *Begriffsgeschichte*. It would establish why and how the various conceptual Gestalts take shape and are sometimes undone and replaced or reshaped, eventually finding their place within the fabric of BT. But it is also a story of conceptual threads severed only to be picked up later, leads and projects totally abandoned, author's intentions left unfulfilled or modified for other purposes, dead ends encountered along the way. These too should be noted, in order to offset the retrospective distortions that accompany the fact that we already know how the Story ends, namely, in BT itself. For part of the Story is that BT itself is a failed project, and that Heidegger then returns to earlier insights left unpursued in order to begin again. This is the real meaning of his self-professed and much discussed "turn." The Story should therefore conclude—at this stage it will not, for practical reasons—by going beyond BT in order to assume a larger perspective upon the decade that preceded BT, to assess its significance for Heidegger's entire thought, to determine whether, for example, it already contains *in ovo* everything essential that came to light in the later Heidegger's thought.

There is, at any rate, a certain rawness and freshness of first discovery in those early works of the Ur-Heidegger circa 1919, when he first found himself, when he first became *Heidegger*, and before those newly discovered ideas underwent a kind of scholastic complexification in BT itself. That is in part why the conceptual genealogy imparted by this Story should help to throw light on the still opaque concepts and contexts that continue to baffle readers of BT, by providing the historical axis of interpretation as an approach to this systematic work. This is in fact the interpretative approach recommended by the old Heidegger himself, who at the end of his life coined the motto, "Ways—not Works," for his Collected Edition, and from his early years insisted that the systematic cannot be understood without the historical dimension of philosophy.

There is more than one good reason why this Story should be a *conceptual* history, sensitive especially to the emergence and development of the fundamental concepts and conceptual schemes that enter into BT. Heidegger's peculiar genius and forte lies in his ability to expose the "root" concepts that "seed" a field of study. This uprooting "deconstruction" is, more often than not, followed by their replacement with new conceptual τόποι of Heidegger's own making, as the traditional categories are displaced by existentials in BT. From the very beginning, Heidegger's entire way is marked by this traffic of concepts: the category problem in Duns Scotus, his doctrine of the transcendentals of being, how it is "said in many ways" through categorial intuition, the formally indicative "concepts" which try to catch experience in its incipience and latency, the search for the fundamental concepts of the West emerging from their pre-Socratic roots. "In the end, the business of philosophy is to preserve the *force of the most elemental words* in which Dasein expresses itself" (SZ 220).

And yet, as helpful as this might be, we would still have but a shallow and static doxography if we were to be satisfied merely with the parade of interlocking concepts emerging in rapid succession at different points along the way, for example: the historical I (1919) to factic life experience (1920) to Dasein (1923), its movement as motivated tendency (1919) to passionate action (1924) to thrown project (1926), its temporal structure as retention-protention (1919), appresentation (1925), and ecstatic schematization of horizons (1927). Thus, Appendix D, which summarizes the chronological rise and sometimes the fall of Heidegger's basic concepts at this time in a Genealogical Glossary, should be used with a bit of caution. A true conceptual *history* must probe below this doxographic surface to the motivating problem situations which prompt these concepts and the hermeneutic situation of inherited presuppositions which shape them. Once again, it is Heidegger himself who notes the "searching" character of his concepts and points to the need to "work out" the question itself from the interrogative situation which prompts it, in order to ensure that the very "terms" of the question themselves become transparent to us. Beyond the litany of rapidly changing concepts, therefore, there is the motivating unity of the problem situation to which they are a response. The question then is whether this situation itself still remains constant as it becomes clear and develops, like a "guiding star," or whether it too is subject to dimming or disappearance and, as a consequence, radical displacement by another.

This conceptual genealogy and flow constitute the philosophical core of our Story. But in order to relate this Story, at this early stage of research in this area, it was necessary to correct many a factual error in the BCD—*B*iography, *C*hronology, and *D*oxography—of this hitherto relatively uncharted stretch of Heidegger's Way. These three intertwining strata have since Theophrastus constituted the minimal philological aids necessary for any reliable record of the story of philosophy. But in our case, they have fallen into disrepute in part because of the negative attitude toward philology assumed, in a wrongheaded imitation of the Master, by the over-seers of Heidegger's Collected Edition. Thus, in addition to its central interpretative philosophical thrust, this book incidentally also fills the need for a reliable record of these subsidiary factual threads of our Story. Regarding the doxographical thread, for example, Otto Pöggeler recently remarked: "Regrettably, even today there is still no reliable overview of Heidegger's early lecture courses based on the extant student transcripts and Heidegger's manuscripts."[5] This book, in its Story and Appendixes, will seek, to the extent that this does not obscure its central interpretative thrust, to fill this especially glaring lacuna in Heidegger scholarship.

But of course we want more than just to set the doxographical record straight: We wish to enter each course, seminar, or written text as its own conceptual universe not only with the doxographical questions, "What does it say?" and "What is its basic intent?" but also with the intertextual questions of "Where does it come from?" and "What does it lead to?" dictated by our genealogical and diachronic concerns. The synchronic pause is conceptually essential, and so lengthy, especially at the critical turning points in the Story. But synchrony is often "brack-eted," as necessary, to do a diachronic framing of certain key concepts, like ex-sistence and angst, in order to examine them backwards and especially forwards into BT, at the tender early spot at which something new develops. The strands into BT are thus explored directly into BT long before we reach that terminal stage of our Story. And because we are first telling a Story, where BT itself will turn out not to be the goal but just one more way station, we shall never find the time to gather the strands together even at that particular central station. The Story to that extent does presuppose some familiarity with BT itself. But even those who are quite familiar with BT will find, I believe, that approaching it by way of this genealogical track makes us look at its passing landscape in a way that is quite different, traveling against the grain of many an old interpretation.

The temptation is always great in such a philosophical account to inter-ject an excess of "interesting" biographical details in order to keep the story line "light and lively." And the question of the relation between Life and Thought has become especially acute of late in the "case of Heidegger." But the critical reader should perhaps not be too quick to judge as philosophically irrelevant, say, the repeated allusions to Heideg-ger's difficult writing style which led, among other things, to his being denied a university appointment and to his having an article rejected for publication. This biographical infrastructure is in fact fraught with philosophical (or, more precisely here, "metaphilosophical") significance. Take, for example, the seemingly bland and straightforward statement of biographical fact of our opening citation, "And so you remained silent for twelve years." The "And so" takes us to the very heart of Heidegger's philosophy: his naming of a topic for himself which had traditionally been regarded as "ineffable," his early struggles to develop a hermeneu-tics to express this topic at first on the basis of the phenomenological principle of "self-showing" intuition, thus his development of the linguis-tic strategy of "formal indication" out of the context of the Aristotelian-scholastic doctrine of the analogy of being and Lask's "logic of philoso-phy." This is but one instance in our tale, insofar as it resorts to philosophical biography, in which it strives to pay close attention to a much-discussed and still unresolved general question in the metaphilosophy of the historiography of philosophy: What exactly are the revelatory and intrinsic links between the life and the thought of a thinker? The question applies especially to a thinker who prided himself on the ontic "roots" (*Boden*) of his ontology, taking pride in the claim that he was the first in the history of philosophy to declare openly the inescapable need for such roots.

A related question at the interface of biography and philosophy arises especially from the old Heidegger's autobiographical statements. We are here treated repeatedly to the story of his boyhood years in the gymnasium and the gift of Brentano's dissertation on "the manifold sense of being in Aristotle," which has triggered a small industry of articles analyzing this text in its relation to Heidegger's thought. Such work demonstrates the eagerness of scholars for reliable biographical clues to Heidegger's development more than the actual relevance of Heidegger's selective reading of his own life to the main lines of his thought. Why this attempt in his old age to revive the ties with his Catholic past, his early relationships with Father Conrad Gröber and the Thomistic philosopher, Carl Braig? Why do we hear absolutely nothing about those dark war years of 1917–19, about which almost nothing is presently known, when he broke with his Catholic past and clearly emerged as a "free Christian" in his first postwar lecture courses? At any rate, Heidegger's own autobiographical statements, which of course cannot be ignored, must themselves be carefully weighed, counterbalanced, and so corrected against all the archival evidence that can possibly be mustered. This is what I have sought to do here, in order to establish a reliable, complete, and relatively uninterrupted story of this entire period of Heidegger's development. It has dictated the correction and demystification not only of the autobiographical Heidegger but also of Heidegger's literary executors, who have established a track record of factual misstatement and chronological distortion in the composition of their Collected Edition, as well as of the more nebulous constellation of tenacious anecdotes from diverse quarters, for example from the literary genre of "Conversations with Heidegger," which have fused together over the years to give us the Legend of Heidegger. Particularly in the area of autobiography and reported "table talks," the authority of the old Heidegger has been found to be insufficient and at times even contradictory, thus hardly above question, contrary to the natural tendency to accept that authority.[6]

In view of these tasks of completion and correction, the appeal to Theophrastus is by no means so farfetched. For the state of Heidegger scholarship at the "BCD" level is still very much like that of our factual knowledge of the Pre-Socratics. An accurate and reliable reconstruction of the problematic *situs* or conceptual τόπος out of which Heidegger develops his ideas requires a background knowledge of the elements of βίος, χρόνος, and δόξα which constitute that situation. By way of an introduction, an example from each arena of philosophy's BCD which will play a telling if not crucial role in our Story may suffice:

Biography. We have it from the old Heidegger that it was his "theological provenance" which put him on the path of thinking (US 96/10). But we also have a much more immediate expression of the concrete direction in which this provenance was taken in the early Heidegger's personal letter to Karl Löwith on August 19, 1921: "I work concretely and factically out of my 'I am,' out of my intellectual and wholly factic origin, milieu, life-contexts, and whatever is available to me from these as a vital experience in which I live. . . . To this facticity of mine belongs what I briefly call the fact that I am a 'Christian theo*logian*.' "[7] The entire letter is in fact an application of Heidegger's own philosophical "hermeneutics of facticity" to himself and so testimony to Heidegger's own sense of the intrinsic importance, rooted in his own philosophy, of the biographical element in the autochthonous "hermeneutic situation" out of which a philosopher speaks.

Chronology. Comparison of the published *Ausgaben letzter Hand* of the Collected Edition with extant student transcripts uncovered a number of chronological distortions which such "last-hand" publications introduce into the public record of the early Heidegger's development. The most important of the resulting chronological corrections in turn produces a different setting for the genealogy of one of Heidegger's best-known concepts. Contrary to the impression given by the published editions, Heidegger was sparing in his use of the language of existentialism then in vogue until the very last draft of BT. His resistance to the popular jargon was breached not for existentialist but for "formally indicative" reasons, by his discovery at the last minute of the "ecstatic-horizonal" structure of temporality, thus etymologically connected with "ex-sistence," in part perhaps through his reading of Aristotle's *Physics*.

Doxography. This ancient art of establishing what a philosopher actually said comes into play here in correcting error-ridden editions and filling in the gaps left by the Collected Edition. I shall, for example, provide an extensive paraphrase of Heidegger's course of WS 1920–21 on the phenomenology of religion based on student transcripts, in view of the fact that there are no plans at present to publish this course, since the manuscript of the course from Heidegger's hand has not been found. Extant but unpublished transcripts of Heidegger's seminar exercises are also sometimes important in bridging certain gaps in the public record of development. But in a letter to Löwith shortly after the appearance of BT in 1927, Heidegger warns his student during these first postwar years of development toward BT that "the work cannot be judged simply by what was said in the lecture hall and the seminar exercise. . . . To tell the truth, I am not really interested in my development, but when the matter comes up, it cannot be put together simply from the sequence of lecture courses and what is only communicated in them. This short-winded consideration forgets the central perspectives and impulses at work both backwards and forwards."[8] The search for clues to Heidegger's development must accordingly be extended to the then private record, to Heidegger's correspondence and personal notes, for example. Especially important for the Story of this development are certain major documents which were privately circulated at the time and are now belatedly beginning to come into the public arena: the review of Karl Jaspers's *Psychologie der Weltanschauungen*, first drafted in the summer of 1920 and published in 1972; the Introduction to a projected book on Aristotle written in October 1922 in support of Heidegger's candidacy for a chair at Marburg and Göttingen, recently discovered in Göttingen in its entirety; "The Concept of Time," the lecture to the Marburg Theologians in July 1924 and the longer journal article of November 1924 with the same title, which amounted to the very first draft of BT, but was never published in that journal because of problems with its length and style.

It is in fact only in the last several years that the three most pivotal documents that mark the three giant leaps forward, the three *Ur-sprünge* (original leaps, or leaps *from* the origin), toward BT have in fact come into the open. These three critical junctures where the development makes an abrupt surge forward in fact mark three different geneses of BT, ranging from the remote to the proximate. They offer us, as it were, three different magnifying lenses or prisms through which this still opaque systematic masterwork can be viewed along its historical trajectory. In the language of the maxim which the dying Heidegger affixed to his Gesamtausgabe, BT can now be viewed through these prisms not as a work but as a way. In brief, the three geneses are: BT as a topic, as a program, and as a text.

Accordingly, a full doxographic record, chronologically corrected and set straight, naturally divides the course to BT into three phases marked by three major academic events of breakthrough in Heidegger's early career:

Part I. War Emergency Semester 1919 (KNS), when the returned "veteran" becomes Edmund Husserl's assistant and advocates a radicalized phenomenology understood as a *pre*theoretical science of origins differing from any other (i.e., theoretical) science. For its subject matter is not an object at all but the already meaningful "stream of life" in which each of us is already caught up. How to approach this topic without "stilling the stream" (Paul Natorp's objections to phenomenology), how to articulate this non-objectifiable "something" (*Es*) which contextualizes (*Es weltet*) and temporalizes (*Es er-eignet sich*) each of us? With this response to the double question of the accessibility and expressibility of the immediate situation of the individual, traditionally regarded as ineffable, Heidegger has in fact named his lifetime topic. (*Das Ereignis*, the event of "properizing," will become the old Heidegger's very last word for archaic Being, *Seyn*.) The courses of 1919–21 constitute an initial phenomenological elaboration of this topic in the hermeneutic language of life-philosophy and in continuity with the young Heidegger's project of a phenomenology of religious experience. [Chapters 1–4]

Part II. Die Aristoteles-Einleitung, October 1922: This version of an Introduction to a projected book on Aristotle, written to secure a chair at the University of Marburg, concentrates for the first time the interrelations familiar to us in BT as the double task of 1) a fundamental ontology based on an analysis of the "human situation" (Dasein) and 2) a concomitant deconstruction of the history of ontology aimed at retrieving the Greek conceptuality of that situation rooted especially in λόγος, φύσις (especially its κίνησις), and ἀλήθεια. The project of BT thus takes shape in 1921–24 against the backdrop of an unrelenting exegesis of Aristotle's texts, especially *Nicomachean Ethics* Z, from which the manifestly pretheoretical models for the two Divisions of BT, the τέχνη of ποίησις for the First and the φρόνησις of πρᾶξις for the Second, are derived. (The νοῦς of these two more practical dia-noetic virtues—as well as of the two theoretical virtues—is in BT replaced by the "lighted clearing" *[Lichtung]* of ecstatic temporality, in marked contrast with the "eternal" νοῦς in Greek philosophy.) [Chapters 5–6]

Part III. "Der Begriff der Zeit" (July 1924), the talk to the Marburg theologians, inaugurates the writing of the three drafts of BT: 1) the hermeneutic draft, the article likewise entitled "The Concept of Time" and rejected by a budding young journal, seeks to found the problem of historicality raised in the Dilthey-Yorck Correspondence; 2) the phenomenological-ontological draft, the course of Summer 1925 on the "History of the Concept of Time," is introduced by an extensive exegesis of Husserl's Sixth Logical Investigation and for the first time analyzes Dasein as the being which questions being; 3) the Kantian more than the "existentialist" draft, reflecting the last-minute development of the temporal apriori as an ecstatic schematization of horizons. [Chapters 7–9]

Three intertwining phases groping their way to BT, toward a hermeneutics of the Fact of life (1915–21), deconstructing Aristotle's ousiological ontology by way of his anthropology (1921–24), and redrawing the classical question of being directly out of the temporal dynamics of the human predicament (1924–27). Despite the first two drafts, BT itself, composed in its major lines in a single month, in March 1926, constitutes a massive step forward in its innovations. Perhaps too far forward, Heidegger will eventually conclude. He later observes that "perhaps the fundamental flaw of the book BT is that I ventured forward too far too soon" (US 93/7). The seeds of self-destruction are thus planted in BT itself. A full genealogical account of BT can be claimed only after we have also traversed the steps leading to its demise, the sequel to the Story of the genesis of BT. Γένεσις καὶ φθορά belong together, they are equiprimordial. This tale of foundering must be left to another occasion. The Genesis Story traverses a far less known path, where much of the evidence is yet to be published. And without this Genesis Story, the story of the foundering of BT cannot really be told in the fundamental conceptuality that it requires. That is why I have belabored the initial halting steps toward BT, perhaps more exhaustively than some readers would wish. I did so with the growing conviction that these "juvenilia," as the old Heidegger came to regard them when the question of their publication was posed, for all their rawness and crudity perhaps contain the key to all of Heidegger. At the very least, they certainly throw a great deal of light on the later Heidegger's development by demystifying much of its mystagogic language into more ordinary terms. This may seem a surprising statement to make, especially in view of the initial bafflement that the book BT posed when it first appeared. We have indeed come a long way in our understanding of what Heidegger is really up to.

My way of telling this Story is thus deliberately "bottom-heavy," dwelling as it does on Heidegger's first fumbling steps toward his insight. Perhaps a genesis story is by its nature slow to start, slow at least in carefully deliberating its start. Slow to come to its climax which, when it comes, is there all too abruptly. A rather unpopular "ontic" ideal of narrative sexuality in this impatient age of sitcom "quickies." The reader is forewarned, and may want to adjust according to his or her own desires. But there is also a documentary reason for its deliberative pace. In addition to the need to deal in depth and detail with the most pivotal documents, studded with "firsts" and "for the first time," there is the need to inform the reader in some detail concerning unpublished documents which may not be published in the near future, or at all. The course of WS 1920–21 is a case in point, where the autograph is missing, and a handy edition of the five extant student transcripts is not acceptable to an "edition of the last hand." In such cases, I have provided a relatively complete English paraphrase to bring the reader abreast.

This is a good point to inform the reader of the BCD Appendixes. (To accentuate the methodology of fact-gathering sketched above, there is deliberately *no Appendix A*.) The goal of Appendix B is to establish the precise titles of the courses, seminars, and lectures held by the teacher

Heidegger at the time that he gave them, say, on the opening day of the semester, which is not always the same as the title pre-announced in the university catalogue, or the title bestowed upon them by the GA-executors. Its indispensable starting point is the initial list authenticated during Heidegger's lifetime through the scholarly efforts of William Richardson, who composed it strictly from university catalogues. For our present purposes, however, from the standpoint of the more factually biographical criterion being applied throughout this book, this list, which has served us well over these many years (even the administrators of Heidegger's Collected Edition at first relied upon it almost exclusively!), now stands in need of correction. Appendix C provides a bilingual chronological documentary of the events leading to the premature publication of BT, where the facts once again serve to supplement and correct as well as confirm the well-known anecdote told by the old Heidegger. The galley-by-galley story of the internal composition of BT is moreover one more aid in coming to regard BT itself as a "way" instead of a Work rendered almost sacred by being frozen in time, as Great Books are wont to become. Appendix D combines doxography with chronology in trying to establish the precise time frames in which the early Heidegger conceived, applied, and, at times, abandoned some of his key concepts. As a by-product of our tale, this record of development may also be of use to translators of Heidegger, for example, in the vexed question of whether his terms can be rigidly translated in a strict one-to-one fashion. This Genealogical Glossary also indicates how rapidly Heidegger developed in this period, casting off one conceptual scheme after another, but always in conversation with the tradition in which he found his ground, and so his ground concepts.

The Bibliography is somewhat lean, restricting itself by and large to published works actually cited in the body of the Story. This is also due to the virgin territory being explored, with much of the material still unpublished. In these circumstances, I could entertain the vanity of keeping myself untainted by sources that seemed extraneous, uninformed, or otherwise unripe: "Away with the secondary literature, back to the archives themselves!"

For that very reason, this book has been long in the making. It found its start in 1981 from the need to examine the underlying documents of Heidegger's course of SS 1925, in order to correct the error-ridden German edition before translating it into English. I wish again to thank Dr. Hermann Heidegger for permission to do so and Walter Biemel for assistance to this end. This first venture into the archives made me see the signal importance of such unpublished material for understanding this most crucial period of Heidegger's development. I wish first to thank the entire staff of the Deutsches Literaturarchiv in Marbach (first Bernhard Zeller, then Heinrich Ott, Directors) for their cooperative spirit and friendly assistance over the years, especially my good friend Joachim W. Storck for sharing his wealth of knowledge of the Heidegger papers throughout the project, and for his advice in locating material accessible in other archives throughout Germany. These archives and personnel are likewise gratefully acknowledged: the Herbert Marcuse Archive in the library of the University of Frankfurt, to begin with, Barbara Brick, who first compiled the papers in Marcuse's literary estate in 1986, and Dr. Gerhart Powitz, its present administrator; the Erich Rothacker Archive, University of Bonn (Dr. Hartwig Lohse, Library Director); the Paul Natorp Archive, Marburg University (Dr. Uwe Bredehorn); Hessisches Staatsarchiv Marburg (Dr. Inge Auerbach); the University Archive in Göttingen (Dr. Ulrich Hunger); the Engelbert Krebs Archive, the University Archive in Freiburg (Dr. Dieter Speck); Dilthey Forschungsstelle, Ruhr University of Bochum (Frithjof Rodi, Director); the Husserl Archive in Leuven, Belgium (Samuel IJsseling, Director); the Rudolf-Bultmann-Archiv at the University of Tübingen (Dr. Friedrich Seck, Chief Archivist), with special thanks to Antje Bultmann-Lemke for access to that portion of her father's papers pertaining to the early Heidegger, and to Dr. Klaus Müller, European caretaker of these papers, for smoothing the way; in this country, the Simon Silverman Phenomenology Center in the Duquesne University Library (Richard Rojcewicz, Executive Director, and Andre Schuwer, Co-Director). Of the many private archives I consulted, two that were especially important at crucial junctures in the work were the collections in the possession of Ernst Tugendhat (the transcripts of Helene Weiss) and the late Ada Löwith, succeeded by Klaus Stichweh. Scholarly assistance came from colleagues in Europe and America too numerous to mention, but let me especially thank Otto Pöggeler for unwavering support and advice over the long and diffficult haul. Tom Sheehan has been generous in sharing the unpublished results of his own "detective" work, done years before I came onto the archive scene and took over where he left off, and in his role as reader of my manuscript. My teacher and advisor in things Greek has been Gerald Hawthorne (Wheaton College). Funding for this decennial project came from numerous agencies: the Alexander von Humboldt Foundation, the Fulbright Commission of the Federal Republic of Germany, the German Academic Exchange Service, the National Endowment for the Humanities (Research Materials Division and Travel to Collections), and Northern Illinois University (Graduate School, College of Arts and Sciences, Department of Philosophy). Last but not least, my everlasting gratitude to my wife, Marie, for her patience on the home front, enduring support and supportive endurance in the cycles of preoccupied presence and overseas absence.

PART ONE

The Breakthrough to the Topic

Where exactly does Heidegger's Way clearly begin to point to BT? There is something abrupt and arbitrary about any beginning, and a great beginning involves an especially violent burst of creativity. In retrospect, there is a tendency to dispute its intrusion and heal the breach in history by pointing to the precedents latent in the situation of departure. Anticipating this tendency, the historian wishing to recount its story must himself arbitrarily name his beginning and justify it as a beginning within and against the surge of precedents that then follow and, for the first time, become identifiable as precedents.

In the case of the early Heidegger, his philosophical departure from the tradition is underscored by an interruption in his teaching career during the war years coupled with a personal change in religious orientation. His abrupt philosophical beginning is clearly identifiable in the public record, but the burgeoning precedents leading to it less so, especially those that may finally be rooted in the private conscience. That this religious conversion was associated with a fundamental transformation of "my philosophical standpoint" is testified by Heidegger's letter of January 9, 1919, to his friend, Engelbert Krebs, a Catholic priest: "Epistemological insights extending to the theory of historical cognition have made the *System* of Catholicism problematic and unacceptable to me—but not Christianity and metaphysics (these however in a new sense)."[1] Thus we know that Airman Heidegger came home from the front philosophically transformed and, as Edmund Husserl's assistant, from that moment launched a revolution in his chosen arena of philosophy, in phenomenology.

The external trappings of public reputation, typically spread by hearsay and rumor, also serve to date our starting point. The retrospective account of Hannah Arendt is well known, but here quite apropos:

> . . . *the beginning* in Heidegger's case is neither the date of his birth (September 26, 1889, at Messkirch) nor the publication of his first book, but the first lecture courses and seminars which he held as a mere *Privatdozent* (instructor) and assistant to Husserl at the University of Freiburg in 1919. For Heidegger's "fame" predates by about eight years the publication of *Sein und Zeit* in 1927; indeed it is open to question whether the unusual success of this book—not just the immediate impact it had inside and outside the academic world but also its extraordinarily lasting influence, with which few of the century's publications can compare—would have been possible if it had not been preceded by the teacher's reputation among the students in whose opinion, at any rate, the book's success merely confirmed what they had known for many years. . . . in Heidegger's case there is nothing tangible on which his fame could have been based, nothing written, save for notes taken at his lectures which circulated among students everywhere. . . . There was hardly more than a name, but the name traveled all over Germany like the rumor of the hidden king.[2]

The rumor reached Hans-Georg Gadamer in Marburg as early as 1920 that Heidegger in a "highly original, profound and revolutionary lecture course used the phrase, 'it's worlding.' "[3] This was in fact the very first course that Heidegger gave after the war in the first months of 1919 in an extraordinary "war-emergency semester" (*Kriegsnotsemester* = KNS). Now we know that Heidegger also innovated upon the phrase, *es er-eignet sich* (it's happening, properizing as it "takes place"), in this extraordinary KNS. This second innovation adds further credence to Gadamer's thesis that the groundwork for all of Heidegger's later thought after the "turn" was already being laid in KNS 1919.[4]

Upon first elaborating the phenomenon of the world in the book BT, Heidegger remarks in a footnote "that he has repeatedly presented this analysis of the environing world and in general the 'hermeneutics of the facticity' of Dasein in his lecture courses since WS 1919–20" (SZ 72n). In point of fact, both themes were first broached two semesters earlier in KNS 1919. It was accordingly in this very first semester after the war that basic elements of BT first began to assume clear-cut shape. The Ur-Heidegger had found himself and was on his way. It is here that we find the zero point of Heidegger's development toward BT. Across the gulf of seven decades, the original fascination reported by the auditors of this first course after the war (many of them "returning veterans") can still be sensed, especially by reading the student transcripts. For Heidegger and his students, it must have been like the discovery of a new continent. And indeed it was. The importance of this groundbreaking course, in all its vital rawness and freshness pointing the way to all of Heidegger, in my view cannot be overestimated. For here he first clearly identifies and names his subject matter, his lifelong topic which, even in those early years, rapidly assumed a series of names: the primal something, life in and for itself, factic life, the historical I, the situated I, factic life experience, facticity, Dasein, being. Even though the phrase "hermeneutics of facticity" does not surface until 1922, it can well serve to characterize what is already assuming clear contour in the KNS, namely, Heidegger's lifelong topic of thought and how it is to be approached.

The course bore the title, "The Idea of Philosophy and the Problem of Worldviews," and so reflects the goal of Husserl's program expressed in his Logos-essay (1911) to further "Philosophy as a Strict Science." But upon discovering and naming the subject matter of philosophy, Heidegger transforms this into an almost contradictory goal: Philosophy as the primal science is like no other science, since it is to be a supra- or pretheoretical science, in short, a nontheoretical science, which forces us to the very limits of science. Thus, for the next ten years, Heidegger vacillated between the two poles of whether philosophy is to be the primal science or no science at all. Already in WS 1919–20, he remarks that philosophy as the science of origins, in view of this ambition to overtake and keep to our vital origins, is not really a science in the true sense of the word, but "more." And in the very next semester, he traces this "more" back to the original motive of philosophizing, the "unrest" that resides at the heart of life. A decade later, when he definitively abandons the project of making philosophy into a strict science—which is one mark of the "turn"—he observes (in WS 1928–29) that philosophy is not a science not out of lack but rather out of excess, since it springs from the ever superabundant and ebullient "happening of Dasein" itself.

For an expeditious survey of the breakthrough course of the KNS in its main thrust, the naming of the subject matter of philosophy, and the determination of how it is to be approached, it will be necessary to supplement the published edition especially in the brilliant and dramatic concluding hour of the course (April 11, 1919). For the version there (ZBP 114–117) is quite dense, and—as the student transcripts indicate—especially here in this two-hour course Heidegger spoke "off the cuff" to explain and expand upon his difficult points. The printed text, for example, lacks Heidegger's significant concluding words on the difference between philosophy and worldview, which serve to clinch the task expressed in the course title:

> Phenomenology is the investigation of life in itself. Despite the appearance of a philosophy of life, it is really the opposite of a worldview. A worldview is an objectification and immobilizing of life at a certain point in the life of a culture. In contrast, phenomenology is never closed off, it is always provisional in its absolute immersion in life as such. In it no theories are in dispute, but only genuine insights versus the ungenuine. The genuine ones can be obtained only by an honest and unreserved immersion in life itself in its genuineness, and this is ultimately possible only through the genuineness of a personal life.[5]

Philosophy: neither theory nor worldview, but rather the plunge into life itself in its authenticity. This resolution is reminiscent of the oft-quoted Eckhartian lines in the Conclusion (1916) of Heidegger's habilitation work, that the most authentic vocation of philosophy is to go beyond the theoretical attitude as well as the attempt to spell out reality into a worldview, so that the "living spirit" may aim at a "breakthrough into true reality and real truth" (FS 348). The quest for a breakthrough to pretheoretical life is carried over into 1919. But its "true reality and real truth" has in the interim changed with Heidegger's radicalization of phenomenology, as we shall see, by purging it rather thoroughly of its earlier elements of scholastic metaphysics and neo-Kantian philosophy of culture. The first task of the 1919 courses is to set phenomenology off as sharply as possible from neo-Kantianism, especially the branch with which the young Heidegger had closely allied himself called "transcendental value-philosophy" (so in the title of one course in SS 1919), the "Southwest German School" of Wilhelm Windelband, Heinrich Rickert, and Emil Lask. Since the habilitation work was dedicated to its supervisor, Rickert, and its foreword gratefully recalls Lask "in his distant soldier's grave," the 1919 courses clearly also represent for Heidegger a personal exercise in self-deconstruction and the breaking of old ties.

But for the Story being told here, there is another reason to go back to 1916 from KNS 1919, in order to measure the leap of the intervening three years. In SS 1925 Heidegger pays homage to Husserl and the phenomenological "breakthrough" he brought about at the turn of the century through his *Logical Investigations* and its three central ideas: intentionality, categorial intuition, and the new sense of the apriori ensuing from these two insights. The history of phenomenology and the gloss of the Sixth Logical Investigation presented there are somewhat formal, suitable perhaps for course presentation. But we get very little inkling of how Heidegger himself actually took up these three terms and adapted them to his own brand of phenomenology. This adaptation is already in full swing in the years 1915–19, especially by way of the application of Husserl's *Logical Investigations* that the young Heidegger found in Lask. Lask for him, moreover, not only mediated between Rickert and Husserl but "also sought to listen to the Greek thinkers" (FS X).

Eckhartian meditations on intentionality and categorial intuition—to be discussed in chapter 2—serve to complete Heidegger's transformation of phenomenology in this early period. But the allusions to Eckhart in the habilitation, the need to counterbalance scholasticism with the ideal of religious experience presented in "mysticism"—so in 1916 (FS 352)—are but the calm before the storm. The tumult of the war years is matched in tempo by the young Heidegger's religious tumult in 1917. Though the wording in his letter to Krebs is (perhaps deliberately) ambiguous—"*diese* allerdings in einem neuen Sinne" can refer to just "metaphysics" or to "Christianity" as well—the context gives the plural the edge. By 1919, the young Heidegger had had a radical change of heart and mind in both, which in a deep sense are linked, perhaps even one. Whence the symmetrical structure of the four chapters of this opening Part, alternating between "metaphysics" (phenomenology) and "Christianity," trading off each other in their progressive unfolding. Heidegger's breakthrough to his lifelong philosophical topic is inherently tied to a personally felt religious topic, in ways we have yet to "divine."

This same deep structure of interchange and transformation at once yields the startling relevance of the habilitation. It all began in KNS 1919. This main thesis acquires historical sustenance from its auxiliary or precursor thesis: it all began in the habilitation work of 1915. There are certain developments in the breakthrough of 1919 which necessarily take us back to the habilitation of 1915 and its concluding chapter of 1916 (FS 341–353). With the publication of KNS 1919, this earlier work on "The Doctrine of Categories and Meaning in Duns Scotus," after a dormancy of seven decades, now assumes new significance in more ways than we have so far mentioned. That the prehistory to a "hermeneutics of facticity" must include the habilitation work finds corroboration in the already-cited letter from Heidegger to Löwith in August 1927, shortly after the appearance of BT. Löwith had found the "ontological formalizing" of Dasein in BT not particularly helpful in his own habilitation work on an "ontic" anthropology, and expressed a preference for the more concrete "hermeneutics of facticity" which he had learned from Heidegger's courses and seminars in the earlier years from 1919. In the context of underscoring the ontic founding of ontology as one of his most important discoveries, Heidegger finally remarks:

> The problems of facticity exist for me no less than in my Freiburg beginnings, only much more radically, and now *in the perspectives* which even in Freiburg were guiding me. That I was constantly concerned with Duns Scotus and the Middle Ages and then back to Aristotle, is by no means a matter of chance. And the work [BT] cannot be judged by what was simply said in the lecture hall and the seminar exercise. I first had to go all out after [*extrem losgehen auf*] the fac*tic* in order to make fac*ticity* into a problem at all. Formal indication, critique of the customary doctrine of the apriori, formalization and the like, all of that is still for me there [in BT] even though I do not talk about them now. To tell the truth, I am not really interested in my development. But when the matter comes up, it cannot simply be put together from the sequence of lecture courses and what is communicated only in them. This short-winded consideration forgets the central perspectives and impulses at work both backward and forward.[6]

Heidegger's own brief sketch of his development toward BT, shortly after its appearance, puts the finger on *the very first* impulse which led to it, namely, the full identification of the factic and the means to get at it ("formal indication"), and locates the beginnings of this impulse in his work on Duns Scotus. Indeed, a close examination of the habilitation work will show that it is totally governed by the tendency toward facticity, or what Duns Scotus himself called *haecceitas* (thisness). The very choice of Duns Scotus as a dissertation theme was dictated by the fact that "he found a greater and finer proximity (*haecceitas*) to real life, its multiplicity and potential, than the scholastics before him" (FS 145). But to this, Heidegger also adds an appreciation of Scotus's logical acumen. For it is the coupling of the two senses, the feel for formality and concreteness at once, which comes into play in Heidegger's own breakthrough in KNS 1919. What happened here was in fact a double breakthrough, not only to facticity but also to the "formally indicative" approach to that facticity. The very idea of "formal indication" in fact finds its first stirrings in the Scotian version of the Aristotelian-scholastic doctrine of the analogy of being. Regarding the Scotus dissertation as a precursor brings out the elements of a "hermeneutics of facticity" already operating in filigree in what Scotus might have called his "speculative formal grammar of thisness." It is simply a matter of staring at the dense jungle of the tired old habilitation long enough, and in the right places, until a gestalt switch occurs which brings its overgrown hermeneutics of facticity out into the open. And, like a "formal indication" from beyond, we have it straight from Heidegger, in his letter to Löwith in 1927, that the effort is guaranteed to succeed.

ONE

Phenomenological Beginnings: The Hermeneutic Breakthrough (1915–19)

Where does BT really begin? For decades, this question could only be answered literally, by beginning with the opening page, with the abstruse question of being raised by the Eleatic Stranger in Plato's *Sophist*. A verbal question versus the concrete Fact of life from which BT really begins. The textual clue for that is buried in the footnote (SZ 72n) which places the beginning of BT, two semesters too late, in the first analyses of the environing world within the context of a "hermeneutics of facticity." It all began in KNS 1919, in the upshot of the effort "to go all out after the factic" by finding a method to approach it. The breakthrough to the topic is a double play of matter and method, What and How, drawn to a point where they are one and the same: a hermeneutics *of* facticity.

This double breakthrough first becomes dramatically manifest in the very last hour of the course of KNS 1919, when the upshot of this last lecture, and so of the entire course, is made transparent by a four-part schema which Heidegger doubtless sketched *by hand* on the board in the middle of the hour. This overview scheme, which immensely clarifies an otherwise dense presentation, is not to be found in the so-called "readable" and "last-*hand*" published edition of the course but only in the student transcripts. This "KNS-Schema" is presented at this point as a guide to the following analyses and an efficient means for discussing the entire course.[1]

[KNS-Schema]

I. The pretheoretical something
/ \

A. *preworldly* something
(basic moment of life as such)

B. *world-laden* something
(basic moment of particular spheres of experience)

primal something

genuine lifeworld

Kriegsnotsemester 1919: "Die Idee der Philosophie und das Weltanschauungsproblem"

Heidegger GA-Band 56/57, Zur Bestimmung der Philosophie, vom Anfang bis S. 117.

1. Ergänzung zu S. 116 aus den Nachschriften von F. J. Brecht, Gerda Walther und Oskar Becker:

I. Das vortheoretische Etwas

II. Das theoretische Etwas

A. Das vorweltliche Etwas

B. Welthaftes Etwas

A. Formallogisches gegenständliches Etwas

B. Objektartiges Etwas

(Grundmoment des Lebens überhaupt)

(Grundmoment bestimmer Erlebnissphären)

(motiviert in Ur-etwas)

(motiviert in genuiner Erlebniswelt)

Ur-etwas

Genuine Erlebniswelt

2. Mein Überblick über die Vorlesung durch die Folge der Impersonalien:

es gilt (29, 50), es soll (34), "es wertet" (46) -- "es weltet" (73), es er-eignet sich (75)

Erster [Neukant.] Teil

es gibt (62) -- "es weltet" (73), es er-eignet sich (75)

Zweiter [Phän'log.] Teil

Figure 1.

II. The theoretical something
/ \
A. *formal-logical* objective something   B. *object-type* something
(motivated in primal something)   (motivated in a genuine
lifeworld)

What this scheme identifies and distinguishes allows us to pinpoint the double breakthrough of the course to 1) the ontological question of the "It" which worlds and thus properizes itself, here characterized as the pretheoretical and preworldly "primal something" (*Ur-etwas*). In the following year, in SS 1920, this primal something will for the first time be designated by the abstract neo-Kantian borrowing, "facticity." The related question that Heidegger in particular wishes to raise through the schema is 2) the methodological question of the potentially fruitful relation between the pretheoretical primal something (I.A) and the theoretical "formal-logical objective something" (II.A) which is "motivated" in It, and so provides access to It. This relation, crucial for Heidegger's phenomenological method, two semesters later will for the first time be called the "formal indication." Thus we come to some of the questions which will have to be clarified in the following analysis of KNS 1919: Why precisely does factic life call for a formally indicative approach? What is this facticity which dictates the formal indication? It will be necessary to arrive at a point where we can see that a formally indicating hermeneutics and a dynamically understood facticity belong essentially together in a close-knit unity; whence a "hermeneutics *of* facticity."

A final word about the convention of terms like "something" or "It" prevalent in our discussion. The convention antedates Heidegger, who simply adopts it from the neo-Kantians in his habilitation work as an alternative way of talking about "being." The frequency and endless variety of the impersonal sentence in the German language seems to be behind it (e.g., the popular child's Christmas poem, "Es weihnachtet sehr," "It is really Christmasing"), and Heidegger will exploit this to the utmost. Already in the KNS, he adds two new coinages of his own as he exploits a number of already extant possibilities. In fact, the entire semester can be summarized in terms of the developing movement of German impersonals, from the neo-Kantian First Part through the Husserlian-Laskian thought experiment of the 'there it is' into the phenomenological Second Part:

First Part: *es gilt* (29, 50), *es soll* (34), "*es wertet*" (46)
Transitional Thought-Experiment: *es gibt* (62)
Second Part: "*es weltet*" (73), *es er-eignet sich* (75)

With his very first coinage, "It values" (ZBP 46), Heidegger indicates that he understands such impersonals more in terms of the intransitive verb instead of the substantifying "it." "It" is a sheer action, both subjectless and objectless. "The value *is* not, but simply 'values.'. . . . In the experience that is 'worth taking,' 'it values' for me, for the worth-experiencing subject." It is only through formalization that "valuing" becomes an object. But to call it an object already leads us astray from the initial experience. Heidegger concludes by noting how even such language is not "up to" the "new typology of fundamental experience" that he wishes to express (ZBP 46). This would include an "eidetic genealogy of primary motivations" which would trace experiences like "it values" back to the more primary ones of "it worlds" (ZBP 73).

This linguistic lineage found its start in the young Heidegger's fascination with the neo-Kantian formula with regard to judgmental truth as validity and its proper ontological place: "it 'is' not, rather it holds" (*es gilt*, it is valid or in effect). While in 1919 he still clearly wishes to retain its insight into an "ontological difference" between being and beings, Heidegger is already busy deconstructing what he in 1914 regarded as a "felicitous expression" belonging to the "linguistic treasure" of the German language (FS 211, 111), seeking instead to found validity in a more basic pretheoretical dimension of experience (ZBP 50f.). In BT, validity is in the end denounced as "this word idol" (SZ 154). The rational power of pure validity, the timeless realm of pure logic, yields to the primacy of the more concrete temporal apriori of a dynamic facticity, which is still an impersonal, nonobjective realm which 'is' not, but instead simply worlds, properizes, values.

The German impersonal continues to play a central role in Heidegger's terminology to the very end of his career. Out of German neo-Kantianism, and more basically out of ordinary German and its vast pool of impersonals, Heidegger has found his very first and most perduring formally indicative grammatical form. Like "It's raining!" in English, "It" points to a most singular, unique, and comprehensive Event happening now. What is this mysterious It, no longer a substantifying It but a sheer Event, when it is directed to the sheer fact of life, of being, of being here and now? How are we to talk about It, even name It in its simple but comprehensive happening, find a language for It, such that we are not constantly seduced by the substantifying tendency that the very term "It" itself brings with it? Ontologically different from things, subjectless as well as objectless, how to return to this obviously primary but mysterious "something" of life and sheer being which "takes place," happens to me, like a Big Bang or sudden onslaught of being (*Es blitzt*, "it flashes like lightning," already in 1914: FS 126)? Life befalls me, anonymously, impersonally. I am of It, I find myself in It willy-nilly, already under way in existence. This is the pretheoretical "hold" that Heidegger is giving already in KNS to the wholly theoretical neo-Kantian "It holds," the It that empowers theoretical judgments in their truth, as he backtracks phenomenologically, with Eckhartian overtones, to the more primal empowering It of life and Its truth, Its ontological difference from beings. Throughout his long career, Heidegger will never seek to surpass this central insight which gives priority to the impersonal event enveloping the I *which* "takes place" in that Event. He will never in any way moderate or mitigate this lifelong fascination with the impersonal sentence which proliferates in the German language, this German infection which he picked up in his early neo-Kantian years. The original something is an original motion, the facticity of our being is an event or happening, the facticity of Time itself. And the most direct, indicative, way which Heidegger finds to simply name this It which happens to us, to point to its sheer action, to attempt to describe its character and basic tenor, is the German impersonal sentence.

HARBINGERS IN THE HABILITATION

We shall take our first bearings for our Story from the habilitation, which is the very last work that Heidegger published before BT. The gap between 1915–16 and 1927 has always been too broad for interpreters to leap, itself indicative of how much and how rapidly Heidegger modified and deepened his orientation over the intervening years. But there is a connection. And the recent publication of the courses of the early Freiburg period has enabled us to some extent to divine it by way of a retrospective reading. And yet the key to detecting elements of a "hermeneutics of facticity" operative in filigree in the habilitation text has been available almost from the start. But although Heidegger, both young and old, repeatedly singled out the influence on him of the youngest of the neo-Kantians of his day, Emil Lask (1875–1915), no one has thought of reading the habilitation work, where the influence of the neo-Kantians upon Heidegger was at its peak, specifically through the eyes of Lask. For who nowadays reads Lask? One who had, Heinrich Rickert, teacher of both Lask and Heidegger, observes in his final report on the habilitation work—he was the director, the *Doktorvater*—that Heidegger "is in particular very much (*ganz besonders viel*) obligated to Lask's writings for his philosophical orientation as well as his terminology, perhaps more than he himself is conscious of."[2] For Heidegger cites Lask a scant half-dozen times in the work. And yet any reader also steeped in Lask will note how not only its central, but also countless incidental, terms bear the stamp of Lask.[3]

The basic problem of the habilitation work is a medieval version of the "category" problem, the problem of the articulation of the field of being into its various domains of reality and the fundamental concepts that describe them; consequently also their unification in "transcendental" concepts like being, one, true, and good. This theme of scholastic logic and ontology is to be examined by the means of modern philosophy and its logic. For the young Heidegger, this means the focus provided by the confluence of neo-Kantianism and phenomenology in Lask's application of Husserl's *Logical Investigations* to the "logic of philosophy." Lask's distinction between the *constitutive* categories, which pertain to the matter of the domains of reality, and the more formal, general, and so "empty" *reflexive* categories, will serve to orient our discussion of the harbingers of a hermeneutics of facticity in the habilitation.

We pick up the first clues of *facticity* in Heidegger's discussion of the transcendental *verum* (the true), where the extrovertive (noematic) side of the relationship of truth first leads to the discovery of the "principle of the material determination of form" specifically within the *constitutive* category. On the other hand, the first stirrings of the *formal indication*, central to Heidegger's hermeneutics, occur in the discussion of the transcendental *unum* (the one), at the point where the *reflexive* category is related to the medieval doctrine of the analogy of being. Lask's distinction thus plays a catalytic function in both components of Heidegger's later breakthrough. While Lask will serve to mediate other insights in this complex equation of "Heidegger–medieval transcendentals–Lask," our basic terminological interchanges in what follows are accordingly 1) facticity–*verum*–constitutive matter and 2) formal indication–*unum*–reflexive forms. The fruits of these interchanges in Heidegger's own "logic of philosophy" will be far-reaching, inasmuch as the eventual descendants of such revamped transcendentals will be called "existentials" in BT.

A Categorially Charged Facticity and Haecceitas

How do we know that there are different domains of reality? How are such differentiations articulated? The young Heidegger's answer is, in its simplicity, a paragon expression of the basic phenomenological conviction in the possibility of description: such differentiations can only be "read off" from the reality itself (FS 197, 257, 263, 346).

> That there are different domains of actuality cannot be proved a priori by deductive means. Facticities can only be *pointed out*. What is the sense of this *showing*, this de-monstrative display? That which is shown stands before us in its selfness and, graphically put, can be immediately apprehended, it needs no detour across something else; the *single* thing that can be pointed out holds the view fast. In practice it is our duty only to look, to grasp actually all there is to grasp, to draw out the pure self of what

is offered. Over the immediate there can be no doubt, probability, and delusions. For as immediate it has, as it were, nothing between itself and the apprehension (*simplex apprehensio*). (FS 155)

That the differentiations of meaning stem directly from the domains themselves (implying that they are already "categorially" structured [FS 196–198]), that they therefore need only to be "read off" from such "facticities," already amounts to a "hermeneutics of facticity" ensuing from the young Heidegger's commitment to Aristotelian-scholastic realism: simple apprehension espies the analogical distribution of an identical meaning (*ens commune*) differentiated "in each case" (*je*) in accord with "the inherent differentiation of meaning coming from the domains of reality themselves," and so "determined by the nature of the domains" to which the meaning is applied (FS 198f, 229). A few years later, the small German distributive *je*, so easy to ignore (it often is by translators), becomes the veritable "indicative" mark of the facticity of Dasein, which is "in each case (*je*) mine."

This phenomenological construal of "facticity" constitutes a radical reversal of classical neo-Kantianism, which coined the term. The abstract term "facticity" first appears in Fichte, who uses it to describe our encounter with the "brute" face of reality not amenable to rational thought. The factic is the irrational par excellence, the sign of the insuperable irrationality of the "matter" *given* to thought. In the Kantian tradition, Fichte was the first to explore its various polar pairs in terms of the "hiatus irrationalis," the abyss between the empirical and the apriori, the individual and the universal, *quid facti* and *quid juris*, intuition and concept, in short, between facticity and logicity.

But what if our immediate encounter with facticity in all of its "logical nudity" involves not just an empirical intuition but also a categorial intuition? This is the step that Lask, following Husserl, took beyond traditional Kantianism. Lask's expansion of Kant's transcendental logic beyond Aristotle's categories of empirical reality dictates that such categories must themselves have categories if they are to become objects of knowledge. But this possibility shows that there is already a precognitive moment in which the initial categories or forms first present themselves as simply given in experience before they are known. This immediate experience of living through the forms in order to mediately know the cognitive object, the matter, is the moment of categorial intuition in every cognition. Thus, the nonsensory form is at first not known but only experienced or lived (*erlebt*). This constitutes the immediacy of human life fraught with meaning and value (= form). Only the factic experience of the pure sensory manifold is absolutely irrational (GS 2: 78). In a fascinating but elusive chapter on "Living and Knowing" in his

Logik der Philosophie (GS 2:190ff.), Lask describes, in a somewhat 'mystical' vein, this immediate experience of the nonsensory in its first occurrence "as a pretheoretical something" (cf. the KNS-Schema!) in which we first simply live before we know it. In brief summary: our first experience of categories is such that we are "lost" in them in "pure absorption," for example, in aesthetic, ethical, or religious "dedication" (*Hingabe*: GS 2: 191; but also 56, 85, 103, 129, 132 *et passim*), in which we already find ourselves simply "given over" (*hingegeben*) to the given form, meaning, value. Contrary to traditional Kantianism, this is the life especially "deserving" of philosophical study, "not brute factic life but rather the sphere of immediate experience replete with value, of life already made worthwhile" (GS 2:196).

In KNS 1919, Heidegger will adopt this favored word *Hingabe* (submission, self-abandonment, devotion, dedication). Lask uses it to describe the tacit intuition of the categorial dimension, and Heidegger extends it to also include the more overt working intuition that the phenomenologist (not Lask) seeks. More on this "mystical element" in the following chapter, which Heidegger here actually picks up directly from Lask, who in turn simply betrays the fascination with Eckhart within neo-Kantianism itself (another German infection, like the impersonal sentence?).

Lask had already found this higher level of facticity, clearly the one that already interests the young Heidegger, in his dissertation on *Fichte's Idealism and History*.[4] For the middle Fichte had already distinguished between the extremes of two facticities: on the one hand, the minimal epistemological sense of individuation which starts from the multiplicity of "bare" sense data; on the other, the fuller cultural sense of the factic individual in history. Paradigms of the historically individual in its fullest manifestations of humanity include Kant's "genius" understood as a "value individuality," the hero, artist, scientist, saint, in short, those who "have had a decisive impact on the progress of humankind" (GS 1:17, 196, 206). At the end of this series stand the deeds of the Divine intervening in history in an "irrational" revelation, like the Word made flesh in the person of Jesus. Such acts of God's grace constitute a "breakthrough" of absolute values and a unique "influx into history of the ever fresh and new" (GS 1:226f., 240f.), in what has since been called a *Heilsgeschichte*. These more surcharged manifestations of "irrationality" or "brute facticity" (Fichte's word for them: GS 1:173, 284) thus mark the entry into human history of the unexplainably new, unprecedented, and creative.

The trailmarkers of the young Heidegger's swelling interest in this higher level of facticity of "the historical in its individuality" (FS 204) are clearly recorded: in July 1915 he delivers his formal "test lecture" on "The Concept of Time in Historical Science" (FS 357–375). His Conclusion of 1916 calls for a thorough revamping of the category problem by centering it upon the pretheoretical "living spirit," which is a "historical spirit in the broadest sense of the word." Accordingly, "history and its teleological interpretation along the lines of a philosophy of culture must become a meaning-determining element [i.e., a form-differentiating matter, a reality principle] for the category problem" (FS 349f). While history as the arena of value formation and worldview ultimately points to the value-laden "transcendent primal relationship of the soul to God," this means that it ultimately rests in the inner personal life of the individual. Accordingly, this primal value-relation must by analogy "be compared to the back-and-forth flow of the stream of experience in selective spiritual individualities" (FS 351f.).

Compared to this lavish metaphysics of history of the habilitation's Conclusion, the more methodological test lecture, while still couched in the neo-Kantian trappings of value and culture, is a paradigm of soberness. It owes its basic insights to Rickert's works on concept formation in the "individualizing" science of history. The basic idea: the uniquely individual (and so "irrational") events of history receive significance, and so can be conceptually represented, through their relation to value. Accordingly, in contrast with the quantitatively uniform time of the natural sciences, historical time is qualitative and selective, in accord with the event's significance. To exemplify the value-ladenness of time, one need only to think of an especially significant Event (*Ereignis*): the founding of Rome, the birth of Christ, the Hegira (FS 374). But even here, there is much to deconstruct (the neo-Kantian starting point in extant sciences, the teleology of value, etc., where "history" is already prejudged) before the phenomenological backtrack in KNS 1919 to the "properizing" (*Sichereignen*) of the "historical I" (the first precursor to Dasein) can take place. One finds more promising harbingers in the habilitation corpus in the young Heidegger's attempts to describe the matter of history from which its categorizing must necessarily start. For when irreducible ultimates are invoked, the only recourse that is left is phenomenological seeing: "To give a schoolbook definition of it will not be possible, since it is an ultimate, something which is last. Its essence can only be described, pointed out (*notificari*)" (FS 189), "read off " from the actuality itself.

Rickert describes the reality of history as a "heterogeneous continuum" (FS 195-198, but also ZBP 171ff.), which makes it irrational. For utter heterogeneity or absolute multiplicity is a limit concept that lies at the outskirts of any category theory. With any category or form, there is at least a minimal order, which "lifts" the utter dispersion (FS 197). The continuum of history is its absolute flux, "the continuity of uninterrupted transition and change" (ZBP 171), such that every part of its actuality is absolutely different from every other. Such a continuum can be conceptually grasped only when it can be found to be homogeneous in its entirety or in a discrete portion of it, in short, when it is formed. We already know Rickert's teleological solution of a value relation. Heidegger by contrast, when he first gives his own in KNS 1919, will couch it simply in the minimal terms of the above description of the very matter of history, in terms of the differentiating indifference of the flux.

Such deceptively simple terms hide a complex intertwining of homogeneity and heterogeneity which he first learned in the medieval description of the real world in terms of the order of analogy (FS 199). "Nevertheless, the complexity of the historical person, its uniqueness, its relativity and manifold bearing, its involvement with its surroundings, the idea of historical development and the problems related with it, all these are present to the medieval mentality only in a very inadequate conceptual specificity" (FS 206). Yet Scotus's *haecceitas*, the very form of individuality, shows promise, since it invests each individual with its own "this-here-now" (Dasein!) and so brings out a rich categorial structure that underscores the decisive function of time (FS 195). Nevertheless, since each individual is an "irreducible ultimate," does not such a "form" reduce the immediate givenness of reality to the chaos of "boundless multiplicity"? By no means. By following the various strands of "the guiding thread of givenness (*modus essendi*)" (FS 263) within the Scotian texts, especially those on speech significations, Heidegger finds that the concrete universality of *modus essendi* (the order of being, i.e., factic reality) is centered in the fullness of the historical individual which is "consciousness," precisely through the unity of its intentional correlation with all that is "given."

Intentionality

At this point, it might be noted that the operative concept of the entire habilitation work is intentionality, operating there through the coincidence of the conceptual pairs noesis-noema, form-matter, *modus activus et modus passivus*. What Heidegger finds astonishing and fruitful, in the interpretation of a key Scotian text, is that even the "order of being" has an active mode, that there is a *modus essendi activus*, which is self-evident for the orders of knowing and signifying (speaking). In their passive modes, these latter two orders converge upon and coincide with the *modus essendi*, from which they receive their "passive" objects.

What precisely is the "order of being"? "The *modus essendi* is whatever can be experienced and lived (*das Erlebbare überhaupt*), in the absolute sense whatever stands over against consciousness, the 'robust' reality which irresistibly forces itself upon consciousness and can never nor again be put aside and eliminated" (FS 260). The overriding sense of facticity emanating from this passage—"robust reality" will soon turn out to be the historical—has been building ever since Heidegger had mentioned the *fact* of different domains of reality, whose very difference cannot be proven but only pointed out, shown. "Whatever gets pointed out stands before us in its selfness and, graphically put, can be grasped immediately . . . Regarding the immediate there can be no doubt, probability, and delusions. For, as immediate, it has, as it were, nothing between itself and the apprehension (*simplex apprehensio*)" (FS 155).

But by now, it should be evident that the young Heidegger is also working at cross-purposes with his mix of mentors, both scholastic and neo-Kantian, regarding the basic "noetic" character of this rudimentary level of givenness and meaning, reflected in terms like simple apprehension, direct acquaintance (*Kenntnis*), pre-judicative cognizance, and now "lived experience" (*Er-leben*). Is it living or knowing, or perhaps both at once? What exactly is the *modus essendi* **activus** (FS 262; my boldface) analogous to the active noetic correlate in the orders of knowing and signifying? What is the character of the immediate experience corresponding to immediate givenness? This question concerning a potentially rudimentary "understanding of being" is at least speculatively "mirrored" in the remarkable "backtracking" into the Scotian text (or, if you will, "re-duction" or "deconstruction" of it) which we have been following. The crucial pages (FS 259–262) bear closer scrutiny, inasmuch as they are invariably missed or botched or balked by virtually all commentators, much to their detriment, especially in understanding the much-remarked Eckhartian footnote in the Conclusion (FS 344), which refers more or less explicitly back to those pages. In the words of one commentator, "it would make no sense to speak of a *modus essendi activus*" apparently because, when it comes to the given, all that one can ultimately say is "that is how the things themselves are."[5] But *brute* facticity à la Fichte is not the last word for medieval man, who can always go on to say, "God made it that way"; likewise not for the young Heidegger, who is still operating wholeheartedly out of the medieval worldview (FS 351; his *Vorhabe* in common with "Scotus"). And it is precisely those allusions to the ultimate baseline of medieval experience, namely, to that "distinctive form of inner existence anchored in the transcendent Ur-relationship of the soul to God" (FS 351), God's intentionality, that he now draws out of the Scotian text.

Heidegger begins his final "backtrack" here by observing that all three modes (*cognoscendi, significandi, essendi*), though *they* converge noematically by being one in their matter, nevertheless differ in form, in the regard in which that matter is taken, where he clearly includes the *modus essendi* among *them* (FS 259f.). What then is its form, especially if we recall that "forms are nothing but the *objective* expression of the various *ways* in which consciousness is *intentionally* related to the objective"? (FS 261)

What is striking here is that "Scotus," even though he never explicitly speaks of a *modus essendi activus*, nevertheless invests this mode with a particular *ratio*, thereby making it "approach the character of a determinateness of form, which must correspond to the character of an act." What then are "the acts in which immediate givenness actually becomes conscious"? (FS 262) The answer can no longer be put off:

> The *modus essendi* is the immediately given empirical reality *sub ratione existentiae*. There is something significant here which must be noted: Duns Scotus characterizes even this empirical reality as standing under a *"ratio,"* a point of view, a form, an intentional nexus [*Bewandtnis*]; this is nothing less than what is nowadays being said in the following terms: Even "givenness" already manifests a categorial determination. (FS 260)

In Rickert's words, what we have here are the "most rudimentary logical problems" which force us to "draw even 'prescientific' knowing into the sphere of our investigation" (FS 260). Or in our terms, the immediate experience corresponding to immediate givenness is that of "a categorial determination," it is a categorial experience. In short, it is what Husserl calls a categorial intuition.

Links With KNS 1919

With the invocation of intentionality, we are now one further step removed from a brute facticity and toward the comprehensive sense of an encompassing factic domain which becomes the concrete starting point in KNS 1919. We are getting a sense of the global magnitude of the "primal something," the irreducible ultimate from which phenomenological seeing must take its point of departure. Perhaps still lacking from this categorially charged and now intentionally structured immediacy of life and experience is a true sense of its temporal character implied in terms like "living spirit" and "historical individual." But the still static structure of intentionality can now be developed in two directions: 1) as a rich form-matter relation, which yields the constitutive category, and perhaps is a precursor of "worlds"; 2) as a bare subject-object relation, which yields the more "subjective" and formal reflexive category. The distinction in categories is Lask's, so let us have him introduce the levels of discussion, which at once anticipate the levels of the KNS-Schema:

> A something stands as logically naked and preobjective only before the "immediate," unreflected, and theoretically untouched dedication and surrender [I.A. in the KNS-Schema]. By contrast, it always confronts reflection as an object. . . . Of course, only a minimum of objectivity needs to be involved in such reflecting [II.A]. In such a case, the matter needs to be legitimized theoretically merely as a "something" which "is given" or "is there" ("es gibt"). It remains to be seen what the precise relevance of this

bare "reflexive" category of merely "being there" ("Es-Geben") may be. (GS 2:129f.)

With this initial introduction of the reflexive category, Lask then proceeds to distinguish it from the more substantive constitutive categories, which articulate the hierarchical domains of the sensory, nonsensory, and suprasensory something. The distinction coincides with the two types of the "theoretical something" in the KNS-Schema, between the unhierarchized formal-objective (II.A) and the hierarchized objective something (II.B). And what Lask here calls the logically naked, preobjective, pretheoretical, and immediate something accessible only through submissive dedication is the "primal something" (I.A), the categorially charged, intentionally structured global concretion of immediate experience which we have just finished discussing under the Scotian rubric of *modus essendi*, the pretheoretical order of being. The fact that Lask's broad distinction between a theoretical "something in general" in the order of knowing and a pretheoretical "primary something" in the order of being (life, immediate experience) fails to isolate, under the latter heading, a world-laden something (I.B), may suggest precisely where Heidegger found his decisive insight in his hermeneutic breakthrough beyond Lask.

The Constitutive Category

However, even Heidegger's discovery of a preobjective, pretheoretical world (I.B) as the meaningful context for things may have been suggested by Lask's hylomorphic way of describing the intentional relation. Since we live immediately in the form in order to know the matter mediately, we, as it were, live in categories as in contexts through which we experience the things included within them. The relation of form to its matter is thus one of "environment" (*Umgebung*). Matter is encompassed, embraced (*umgriffen*), surrounded or environed (*umgeben*), bordered (*verbrämt*) by the form; it is enveloped (*umhüllt*), enclosed (*umschlossen*) in the form (GS 2:75f.). Lask's exploratory metaphors here may have been one of the lines of suggestion that prompted the early Heidegger to make the leap from category to world, more specifically to the environing world (*Umwelt*), which is a central thrust of his first major breakthrough.

This form-matter relation is in turn used to reinterpret the intentional relation in the context of comprehending the transcendental *verum*, being as knowable or intelligible. This is not the truth of judgment, truth as validity, but the truth of simple apprehension,[6] truth as meaning, that of the simple encounter at the interface of the orders of knowing and being, "the essential union of the object of knowledge and the knowledge of the object" (FS 344, 208), intentionality at its most direct. It is the truth of simply having an object as "a meaning independent of judicative characterization. . . . The truth is consummated in givenness and does not extend beyond it" (FS 210). Material givenness, and not judicative forming, plays the major role on this rudimentary level of truth, where the categorial forms of thought are dependent on the matter of being for their meaning. This "principle of the material determination of form," which permeates the habilitation text (FS 252–263, 344–350 but also implicitly 193, 198, 206f., 222, 229), in language and content is clearly an outgrowth of Lask's "doctrine of the differentiation of meaning" (GS 2:58ff., 102, 169).

"Form receives its meaning (*Bedeutung*) from matter" (FS 193). It accommodates ("tailors": GS 2:59) itself to a particular matter such that it is itself particularized by meaning. Meaning is thus the particular fruit of the union of form and matter. Meaning is that very union, which is why the ultimate answer to the question "whence sense?" cannot simply be "matter" but rather "by way of matter," "relatedness to matter." The "moment of meaning" is the "relatedness of the validlike to the outside" (GS 2:170). The answer is not at all surprising, in view of the operative concept of intentionality which governs the analysis. From the standpoint of "pure" form, meaning is an "excess" arising from its reference "to a something lying outside of it." Lask, as a Kantian, views this inescapable "reference" to matter as a kind of fall of pure form from the realm of "pure" validity into a "lower" realm mediating the univocal homogeneity of the logical realm (FS 224) with the "multiplicity of all that is alien to validity," with the "opaqueness, impenetrability, incomprehensibility" and "irrationality of matter" (GS 2:59–61, 77). Form accommodating itself to the multiplicity of matter yields the "impure" middle realm of meaning. The "moment of meaning" is accordingly the "principle of individuation" which particularizes and differentiates forms, the "principle of plurality in the [otherwise homogeneous] sphere of validity" (GS 2:61), multiplying forms as it specifies them.

Especially important for the coming years is the young Heidegger's express desire to make history, though here still burdened by a neo-Kantian interpretation, into a "meaning-determining element for the category problem" (FS 350). This historical facticity of meaning reflects Heidegger's choice from among the options of the transcendental philosophies of the time. Not an ideal and theoretical realm of validity but a "transcendental" realm of pretheoretical meaning flowing from life itself. Lask called it a "panarchy of the logos" (GS 2:133) in which I already "live in truth" (i.e., intelligibility, meaning). This phrase taken from Lask's aletheiology will be repeated in BT.[7] But aside from a brief and unimportant cameo appearance of ἀλήθεια as unconcealment in KNS, it is noteworthy that Heidegger is virtually silent on the problem of fundamental truth for six long years after the habilitation, from 1916 to 1922, when it makes an abrupt and dramatic reappearance. Instead of aletheic terms, it is the kinetic and dynamic terms of "life" or the "living spirit" of the historical individual, the precursor to Dasein in 1916, which will dominate Heidegger's concerns in the intervening years. Or to put this dynamism more "logically," what is emphasized is the differentiating power of the "matter" of life in articulating the meaning that is encountered in the truth of apprehension. Immediate experience, the irreducible ultimate with which phenomenology begins and ends, is not a surd, a chaos of sensations, but rather a global concretion at once categorially charged (the truth of simple apprehension) and intentionally structured (*modus essendi activus*).

Thus, through Lask's mediating of the neo-Kantian tradition in the direction of Husserl and Aristotle, the two earliest philosophical influences upon Heidegger, he has developed a sense of intentionality and categorial intuition which allows him to move toward a new sense of the apriori, that of the facticity of historical meaning, which finds its norms in experienceability instead of knowability.

Let us sum up this point. The habilitation already betrays its phenomenological proclivity of backtracking to facticity in three clearly identifiable ways: 1) in the shift in the locus of truth from judgment to simple apprehension, with simple apprehension already understood not just as an empirical but more basically as a categorial intuition, or in Lask's more nonvisual term, categorial immersion (*Hingabe*); 2) in the movement from a *modus cognoscendi activus* to a more rudimentary noetic form of intentional consciousness on the level of life itself, a *modus essendi activus* (the scholastics sometimes called this precognitive noetic act of immediacy, which is correlative to the immediate givenness of reality, *intellectus principiorum*, an immediate understanding of the primary intelligibles of being, one, true, good; it is clearly the precursor to Dasein's preontological understanding of being); 3) in the movement from form to matter or, more precisely, to the more basic "principle of the material determination of form." Look carefully at PMDF, of matter determining and differentiating form. It is simply a specification of the maxim of phenomenology: "Away from forms, back to the matters themselves." What forms? What matters? Forms of thought, like "values." Matters of life, like history. This at least will be the direction in which Heidegger applies PMDF three years later, in the opening hours of KNS 1919, in order to free phenomenology itself from its residual neo-Kantianism, beginning with his own.

The Reflexive Category

Lask not only contributes to a new sense of facticity, but also to the problem of how to express this precognitive realm of lived meaning, to that special language which Heidegger will soon call "formal indication." In this vein, Lask's treatment of the reflexive category appears in the habilitation text expressly in the section on the doctrine of speech significations. But it had already appeared unannounced in the earlier section on the transcendental *unum*. While the constitutive category plays a central role in the differentiation of the domains of reality, their regionalization into various material logics, the role of the reflexive category is that of their unification, in a logic tending toward the most general and formal of considerations. Its utter generality suggests that it is the emptiest and most abstract of categories. But Lask's account of its genesis at the very outskirts between knowing and being, in the very first stirrings of taking thought and reflecting upon an initially amorphous absorption in a homogeneous experience, suggests instead a proximity to the concrete whole of being itself (GS 2:129f.). Thus, Heidegger in KNS 1919 can say that the formal objective "something in general" (II.A) of the reflexive category is "motivated" in the undifferentiation of the primal something of experience (I.A).

The medieval discussion of the categories expressed this primal indifference in the concept of *ens commune*, about which one can indifferently say, "it is." "Aliquid indifferens concipimus" (FS 156). If this indifference is thought to its extremity, "the 'general' here loses all meaning" (FS 159), and *ens commune* can no longer be made subject to predicative subsumption according to the hierarchy of genera and species. Because it is beyond such hierarchical generalization and has its own unique universality, being is called a "transcendental." In the language of neo-Kantianism, something in general, the object pure and simple, is not an object at all but rather a homogeneous continuum. This "indifference of the on-hand (*Vorhandenheit*)" surfaces in a surprising number of places in BT, alongside the limit of indifference of everyday absorption in the world.[8]

The reflexive category thus arises at this utter limit between the indifference and difference of being. For the starting stuff of the reflexive category is this (?) "something in general" and its initial form is "there is" (*es gibt*). Put otherwise, the very first reflexive category is "persistent being" (*Bestand*), sheer presence. Out of this indifferent identity arises the categorial pair of identity and difference, which belong together in the relation of heterothesis (Rickert's term for it) or the transcendental *unum*. It is at this point that an object clearly becomes an object. "There is (*es gibt*) no object, no object is given, when the One and the Other is not given" (FS 173 citing Rickert). "Why is the something *a* something, *one* something? Because it is not an other. It is a something and in being-something it is not-the-other" (FS 160). Being an object at all, being identical with itself and being different from something else are "equally primordial" (gleich ursprünglich: FS 172, 323; also 158, 166), in the very first use of this important term in Heidegger's thought, here associated with the "convertibility" of the transcendentals ens and unum (FS 160). In the proximity of the primal indifference, basic terms tend to converge. What this basic convergence yields is the most minimal order (form, determination) necessary to apprehend an object at all; Rickert would add, necessary for anything whatsoever to be thought at all: for a pure monism without opposites cannot even be thought. The apparent tautology ens est, "a being is," necessarily already involves a heterology. In an account of the difference in function between the noun ens and verb esse in this sentence, which already calls to mind his later reflection on the ontological difference between being and beings, the young Heidegger writes: "Equally primordial as the object in general is the object's state of affairs; with every object there is an 'intentional nexus' (Bewandtnis), even if it be merely that it is identical with itself and different from another" (FS 323). Thus, in BT (SZ 114), the key term "equiprimordial" first appears in conjunction with formally indicating the I-Other relation.

The ordinary-language examples from Heidegger's account of a speculative grammar (Scotus) or apriori logical grammar (Husserl) illustrate what the reflexive order of categories promises for him: logical insight into the structural resources in a living language which would abet especially the "logic of philosophy." In the present jargon, one might even call it a "gramma(on)tology." Lask too alludes to this connection between logic and language. At one point in his defence of the seemingly ethereal and remote reflexive categories, he poses the rhetorical question: what would we do with a language without words like "and," "or," "one," "other," "not"? (GS 2:164). Accordingly, such hyperreflective categorial artifices, which buy transparency at the price of depleting the constitutive categorial forms upon which they are parasitical (GS 2:158, 163, 68), still have their concretion. For the reflexive categories draw their moment of meaning-differentiation from the subject-object duplicity rather than from the form-matter relation (GS 2:137). In its own way, therefore, the reflexive category constitutes a formal skeletal structure of the intentional structure of life itself. Lask thus describes the panarchy of the logos as a "bundle of rays of relations" (GS 2:372). The reflexive object is the pure ob-ject as such; in relation to subjectivity, it is a "standing over against" (GS 2:72f.). Its being "is stripped down to the bare reflexive being of the shadowy anything whatsoever, to the naked something of the 'there it is.' " (GS 2:229).

The young Heidegger sees the need here to supplement Lask and finds that the medieval theory of speech acts and their contents already "manifests a sensitive and sure disposition of attunement to the immediate life of the subjectivity and its immanent contexts of meaning" (FS

343), especially in sorting out the signifying functions of univocity, equivocity, and analogy, "which originate in the use of expressions in living thinking and knowing" (FS 277). In the same vein, Heidegger tantalizingly suggests that the variety of domains in any category system, even though they are differentiated primarily in objective accordance with the actual domains themselves, at least to some extent receive their identity-difference relations from the "subjective side" which finds expression in the reflexive categories (FS 346). This side is at least partly met by the concerns of medieval speech theory for privations, fictions, and other nonentities or *entia rationis* (FS 254f.). In coping with such articulations, linguistic forms, in contrast with empirically oriented constitutive categories and much like the reflexive categories, develop a peculiar dilution and indeterminateness which make them amenable to 'anything whatsoever," the very matter of reflexive categories (FS 256f.).

It is precisely these resources of a living language which philosophical discourse must draw upon in order to perform its comprehensive tasks; in short, not so much upon empirical metaphors but more upon structural considerations already latent in the comprehension of being by language. The young Heidegger's interest in the impersonal sentence and the distinction between genitive objective and genitive subjective exemplifies this quasi-structuralist sense of language. The perennial embarrassment of philosophical language to attain its goals might well be lessened by a fuller explication of the formal-reflexive schematization of intentionality already operative in our extant language. This accounts for the importance of Lask's distinction between the reflexive and the constitutive category. It coincides with the medieval distinction between the unique universality of being and the stepwise hierarchical generality of beings (cf. SZ 2), Husserl's distinction (*Ideen I*, §13) between formalization and generalization, and the one in the KNS-Schema between two kinds of the "theoretical something." In KNS 1919, in the face of phenomenology's embarrassment to express the primal something of life, this distinction will yield the method of "formal indication" as a way of approaching a subject matter which borders on ineffability. The expanse opened up by the reflexive category between the extremes of homogeneity and heterogeneity, indifference and difference, will serve as Heidegger's initial space of articulation of that ineffable domain of our being.

KNS 1919: THE IDEA OF PHILOSOPHY AND THE PROBLEM OF WORLDVIEWS

In order to achieve the goal of "Philosophy as a Strict Science," Husserl in the closing pages of his programmatic statement of the Logos-essay (1911) calls for a radical break with any philosophy which is even remotely oriented toward a worldview. On the opening day (February 7, 1919) of his course, therefore, Heidegger observes that the reigning neo-Kantian philosophy, even though it regards a worldview to be the personal affair of the individual, understands itself as the critical science of values which, "based as it is on the basic acts of consciousness and their norms, has in its system an ultimate and necessary tendency toward a worldview" (ZBP 12). And breaking with his own earlier desire for a metaphysical "optic" (FS 348) as well as with the entire tradition of philosophy, he proposes with Husserl, as an opening thesis, that philosophy and worldview have absolutely nothing to do with each other. The course thus places itself in pursuit of "a brand new conception of philosophy . . . which would have to place it outside of any connection with the ultimate human questions" (ZBP 11). And if philosophy is still to be the Ur-science, this would necessarily entail an entirely new conception of origins and ends, the first and the last things. Philosophy itself now becomes a problem especially in its starting point, its primary subject matter, and consequently in its method and goal. What then is The Idea of Philosophy?

In 1919, a sharp contrast between neo-Kantianism and phenomenology was dictated by the very proximity of the two schools. Both approaches in particular lay claim to the venerable ambition of establishing philosophy as the "primal" or "original" science (*Urwissenschaft*). Both seek to determine origins and ultimates, the first and the last things, the underived from which all else is derived, which can only be "shown" or "pointed out" but not "proven," thereby inexorably implicating the original science in a circle, assuming in the beginning what it wishes to find in the end. What then is the beginning, the "primal leap" (*Ur-sprung*: ZBP 24, 31, 60, 95; also 160, 172, 247 in the habilitation) of thinking or knowing, the point from which it gets its start? For Heidegger, such a starting point will stem from the pretheoretical, and so would have to allow for the problem of the very "genesis of the theoretical" which he finds already operative in Lask (ZBP 88).

As he promised in his Conclusion of 1916, the 1919 course moves, albeit slowly and laboriously, to displace the neo-Kantian starting point in the "fact" of knowledge and science with the phenomenological starting point in the "primal fact" of life and experience. Situating the original domain of philosophy beyond the theoretical in a "pretheoretical something" at once overcomes the circularity of presupposition and proof which characterizes the neo-Kantian Idea of philosophy. The principles and structures developed in 1916 play a large role in this movement of displacement. The following selective summary of the course[9] will first focus on the strategic use of those principles and structures in that deconstruction and regression toward the original domain of the "environmental experience" and of "life in and for itself."

First (Neo-Kantian) Part

The Principle of the Material Determination of Form emerges already in the second hour in delimiting the very Idea of the primal science. As a Kantian Idea, as an infinite task, it must be left open to further definition. Any further determination of the Idea depends on the content of the object of the Idea, that is, on the "regional essence" or categorial character of the object which motivates the search (ZBP 15).

The problem of material determination thus gradually but inexorably displaces, and so reverses the orientation away from, the teleological determination which the "forms and norms of thought" provide. In order to found the laws of thought in an ideal and normative manner rather than in actual fact, the teleological method is at first sharply set off from the genetic-psychological method. But in order to offset the abstract constructivism of the early Fichte's "dialectical-teleological method," the "critical-dialectical method" allows for, in fact is in need of, a "material clue" or "guideline" (*Leitfaden*: ZBP 37 = 263 of the habilitation!) simply to find the points at which the goal of reason is "realized." For example, philosophy "borrows" from psychology the material distinction of psychic functions into thinking, willing, and feeling, on the basis of which it then articulates the normative domains into the true, the good, and the beautiful. But in the end, psychology still offers only the formal characteristics: "The real content, the formations of rational values, is first shown in history, which is the true organon of critical philosophy. The historical formations of cultural life are the real empirical occasion for the critical-teleological determination" (ZBP 38). The quotation recalls the young Heidegger's third task for a "cosmos of categories," of factoring in the Material Determination of "history in its teleological interpretation along the lines of a philosophy of culture" (FS 350).

Psychic and historical matter provide the "impetus" which "motivates" the bestowal of norms. The operative concept of intentionality is clearly in evidence as the early Heidegger gradually draws the givenness of matter and the giving of normative forms into an indissoluble intentional unity. The noetic side involves a first attempt to unravel the neo-Kantian tangle of validity, value, and oughtness. A few results: "In the end, validity is a phenomenon constituted by its subject matter, presupposing not only intersubjectivity but the historical consciousness as such!" (ZBP 50f.). And the *es soll*, oughtness? "How does an ought give itself at all, what is its subject-correlate?" (ZBP 45). Is its object-correlate always a value? Clearly, the reverse does not always hold. The value of the "delightful," for example, gives itself to me without a corresponding experience of the "ought." This entire tangle of experiences calls for an "eidetic geneal-ogy of primary motivations" to set things right (ZBP 46, 73). For that matter, even to call the valuable an "object" is already wrong. Like validity (*es gilt*), the valuable is best expressed in an intransitive impersonal sen-tence, as a sheer verb, subjectless and objectless. "The value *is* not, but simply 'values'. . . In the experience that is 'worth taking,' 'it values' [*es wertet*] for me, for the worth-experiencing [*werterlebende*] subject" (ZBP 46).

With this tangle of impersonals which represent the basic constitutive categories of neo-Kantianism, one of them of his own coinage, Heidegger in 1919 is already finding that language is not "up to" the "new typology of fundamental experience" that he wishes to express. The fact that they will be separated at this critical juncture from the impersonal constitutive categories of hermeneutic phenomenology (the Second Part of the course) by Lask's formulation of the reflexive category par excellence, *Es-Geben* (ZBP 67, 69 = Lask, GS 2:130, 142, 155, 162ff.), gives substance to the methodological claim we discovered in the young Heidegger (FS 257): in those instances when language fails us, the very indeterminacy and dilution of reflexive categories can play an indispensable role in developing more suitable descriptive categories. The thought experi-ment that Heidegger now performs is first of all designed to break the tyrannical predominance of the theoretical represented by the psychol-ogy of his day, both hypothetical-inductive and descriptive. Considera-tion of the latter will lead to a kind of psychologistic parody of phenome-nology itself.

The Transitional Thought-Experiment

The issue leading up to this critical juncture is in fact the material deter-mination of the forms and norms of thought by their psychic matter. The joining of the issue begins when the matter and the ideal norms are drawn so closely together that Heidegger can entertain the anti-Kantian question: Is the giving of matter perhaps also the giving of ideals? For in a certain sense, "everything *is* psychic or mediated *by* the psychic." Can we perhaps arrive at an "objective level" within psychic matter upon which the ideal norms could be grounded? What is an objectively given "psychic matter?" According to psychology—here extrapolating its quest for facts to its extreme—the psychic manifests the continuity of a tem-poral process which is analyzable into sensations and representations. Can psychic processes be so regarded such that they at once give the ideal? Do they constitute the level of origin, the primal leap of the primal science we are seeking? How is the psychic itself as a total sphere to be given? (ZBP 60f.). "We can only get at the sphere by pure dedication and submission (*Hingabe*) to the subject matter." Without bringing in assumptions or theories, we must fall back upon a description "pointing out the facts befitting the 'thing itself.' " Just the facts (*Tatsachen*) of the thing (*Sache*) itself, of the psychic? Description? "But description itself is a psychic phenomenon [and thus also] belongs in the thing itself. What is that supposed to mean, to have one thing describe another? Is description really a way of connecting things?" (ZBP 61). "We are thrown from one thing to another, which remains mute like any thing" (ZBP 65). Can we even speak of things when there are only things? Heidegger summarizes his experiment in terms of the staple term then current among neo-Kantians,[10] *es gibt*, "there is": "Is there even one thing when there are only things? Then there would be no thing at all, not even *nothing*, for with the total domination of the thing itself there is not even the 'there is.' Is there the 'there is'?" (ZBP 62). Or as it is almost derisively put in the student notes, "Gibt es ein 'es gibt,' wenn es nur ein 'es gibt' gibt?"

Thus, the quasi-naturalistic neo-Kantian route through the "fact" of the science of psychology likewise dead-ends in a kind of paradox: if there are just facts (givens), then there are not even facts (givens). But we have already seen that even that tradition had developed a facticity other than that of the *factum brutum*. Going far beyond what Windelband and Rickert ventured to do in their "transcendental empiricism" (ZBP 40), where matter is a mere appendage to the teleological method, Lask gleans the following description of the material realm from Fichte's middle period, in his most extreme "positivism" (GS 1:148): "The 'really real' is what you 'really live and experience,' the givenness which happens to you, 'filling the flowing moments of your life,' the self-forgetting and immersion of dedicative intuition." This is life at ground level, "raised to the first power," so to speak; put in reverse, it is "the sinking of consciousness to its lowest power." "Whatever occurs in this sphere is what is called 'reality,' 'facts of consciousness,' or 'experience' (*Erfahrung*)." Are we describing the mute life of the dullard, "the limiting case of dull abandon to the given" (*dumpfes Hingegebensein*),[11] or is it the immediate contact with the very source of life, the first stirrings of meaning in human experience?

In short, is this immediacy mute or meaningful? The first alternative applies if we rule out the possibility, as Kantians of the Strict Observance do, that our most immediate experience is already "categorially" charged. The second option is clearly the early Heidegger's direction of interpretation, reflected in his continued use of Lask's language for categorial intuition in his own descriptions. "The only way to get at this original sphere is by pure dedication (*Hingabe*) to the subject matter" (ZBP 61; 65). "Let us immerse ourselves again in the lived experience" (ZBP 68). To escape unwarranted opinions, free-floating theorems, and speculative excesses, "the philosophers . . . throw themselves into history, into robust reality" (cf. p. 260 of the habilitation!) and "give themselves over to its richness and its movement" (ZBP 135). For this primitive level of direct acquaintance or "taking cognizance" is already "characterized by a pure and undivided dedication to the subject matter. It operates first of all in the very stuff of natural experience." It is subject to different levels of clarity and so can be improved upon. It can become the propae-deutic form of the theoretical but also the "primal form in the religious" (ZBP 212).

It is in fact toward this boundary issue of immediacy ("Mute or mean-ingful?") that Heidegger now, at the very fulcrum of the course, directs his thought experiment, which aims to reduce everything to the level of the *es gibt* (there is, it gives; thus, "the given"), to the level of "brute" facticity, of the sheer and naked "there it is . . . and nothing else": Is there something? Is there even the "there is"? Everything is now made to hinge on such boundary questions reminiscent of Leibniz's famous question. "We are standing at the methodological crossroad which will decide the very life or death of philosophy; we stand at an abyss: either into nothingness, that is, absolute thingness, or we somehow manage the leap into *another world*, or better: for the first time into the world as such" (ZBP 63).[12] This marginal comment in fact prematurely anticipates the sense of world as meaningful context. The first leap to be made here is simply from mute thingness to a "categorial" that is, meaningful, context. Is Heidegger here perhaps alluding to another leap he has tacitly made, his intuitive leap from Lask's environing form or category as a creative bridge to his environing world? Or is he suggesting the difference be-tween his thought experiment and Husserl's, which it recalls, where Hus-serl leaps from an annihilated world to a worldless subject? Let us exam-ine how Heidegger here recovers from the naturalistic devastation of the total reification of experience.

What is left after the absolutizing of thingness? There is still the inter-rogative movement itself, "Is there . . . ?" What does the interrogative *experience itself give* us? If we simply immerse ourselves in the experience itself, in its *movement toward* what motivates it and nothing else, and now diligently seek to avoid stilling the movement through the blatant reifica-tion of our previous reflection, we really do not find anything either psychic or physical. The "object" of our present reflection is a living experience and not a psychic process, not "a mere entitative occurrence." It is even questionable whether we have an "object" here. "The living-out of an experience is not a thing which exists in brute fashion, begin-ning and ending like an encountered process. The 'relating to' is not a piece of a thing attached to another piece, the 'anything.' The living and lived of experience are as such not like entitative objects stuck together" (ZBP 69f.). Intentionality is not an entity.

In fact, this particular experiencing is itself not only nonobjective but also impersonal. For is it really I myself, in full personal involvement, who asks, "Is there anything?" Not really, precisely because what is asked about (*Gefragtes*) does not touch me personally. The experience is related to *an* I (no matter who) but not to *my* I (ZBP 69). It is the remote theoretical I, the "pure ego."

Finally, what is asked about, that toward which "I" live in the experience, the content of the question or its "hold" (*Gehalt*) and so its "hold" on me. For in any experience, intentionally understood, there is a "pull" (*Zug*) toward something, such that the noematic pole, in its directive sense (soon to be termed the *Gehaltssinn*), motivates the experience. In this experience, something is asked about something in general. What is being questioned (*Befragtes*),[13] the matter of the question, is "anything whatsoever." What is asked about, what stands in question, the form that the question takes, is the "es geben." In both form and matter, the question "Is there anything?" contains the emptiest, the most general, the most "theoretical" of the reflexive categories. From Lask, we have learned that "givenness" is the very minimum that can be said about the most minimum. It is so devoid of substantive meaning that we have a tendency to fill in the phrase with examples. This very "pull" reflects a certain dependence of the phrase on something more concrete which itself will have to be explored. Even apart from its interrogative quality (which in fact proves to be irrelevant in this context), this experience both noetically (the empty ego) and noematically (anything) points beyond itself to another experience, with a fuller sense, upon which it depends and (presumably) from which it arose. "The sense of the anything, as primitive as it obviously is, in its very sense proves to be the motivator of an entire process of motivations." "Where is the sense motivating the sense of the 'es gibt' to be found?" (ZBP 67f.).

Second (Phenomenological) Part: The Environmental Experience
We are now well on our way into the Second Part of the course. Having performed his thought experiment of total reification and having arrived at the bare bones of a world governed strictly by the subject-object duplicity, Heidegger then rather abruptly introduces an entirely different experience, the environmental experience, which by contrast is far richer in content than the skeletonized structure of the reification experience. For the experience of looking around (*Umsicht*) and "seeing my desk" is very much *my* seeing, individual to the utmost and not at all a depersonalized experience. It takes place in a context of orientation thoroughly freighted with meaning-content, the very opposite of a formalized expe-

rience. By way of contrast, Heidegger will now say that the previous skeletonized experience of the "I-remote" theoretical subject is an unliving, unworlding, designifying, and dehistoricizing of the seeing experience, which itself is fraught with the meaning drawn from its context. The environmental experience is not so much "of " as "out of " the immediate world around us (*Umwelt*).

The descriptive emphasis in this very first of a series of environmental analyses will be more on looking around (*Umsicht*) rather than the later "getting around" (*Umgang*). Looking around for an example, Heidegger selects the mundane, habitual, common, and yet in its way individualized experience of walking into class and "seeing your desk." Such a seeing 1) always takes place "in an orientation, illumination, and background"; "in an orientation" means "laden with a meaning." 2) It is always "*my* seeing [and so] individual to the utmost" (ZBP 71f.). If we "reduce" the more current theoretical constructions as we describe, what I see are not brown patches on rectangular shapes, or a box which I eventually construe *as* a school desk: I simply see my desk at once, quickly noting also at once anything that might be out of place or unusual about it, a book on it, and the like. Others more or less familiar with things academic will also see "this pupil's (or teacher's) desk."

Even a total stranger to such things, say, an African aborigine suddenly transplanted into this classroom, will not see "a something which is simply given" (reflexive category) but perhaps something to do with magic or a good defense against arrows or, at the very minimum, a something "which he does not know what to make of or do with." In this limiting case, therefore, what is experienced is not so much logically contradictory as it is contrary-to-sense, such that this sense-alien experience of the useless still belongs to the same class as that of the meaningfull desk. (ZBP 71f.: This example of "instrumental alienation" is already reminiscent of the "broken hammer" experience in BT.)

All these things (books, pens, cars, campus, trees, shade, etc., etc.) give themselves directly out of the immediate context of meaning encompassing us which we tend to call the "world." Much like Lask's objects known only through the constitutive categories in which we live, such things receive their significance from that meaning-giving context encompassing us, whose activity can then be described as "worlding." If we then take our campaign against reification one step further, then the true locus of our experience is not in objects or things which "in addition are then interpreted as signifying this or that," but rather in the signifying element itself, the "it" which "worlds," a milieu which in conjunction with Lask has already been called the "transcendental realm of meaning (intelligibility, truth)." The conclusion, which will echo its way through and beyond BT: "The meaningful is the primary, [for] it gives itself

immediately, without any detour of thought across the apprehension of
a thing. Overall and always, it signifies to me, who lives in an environing
world, it is wholly worldlike, 'it worlds'" (ZBP 73, 71ff.).

But is this impersonal *es weltet*, this completely constitutive *es gibt*, so
to speak, really an impersonal experience? Contrary to the reflexive *es
gibt* with its abstract I, my own and temporally particular I is in some way
wholly present "with" the worlding experience. In fact, in the "seeing"
involved here, my I goes out of itself completely and immerses itself in
the world in total absorption. This impersonal experience of the historical I wholly "given over" to its world is thus the opposite of that of the
theoretical I almost totally remote from its objectified *es gibt*. The latter
experience of the indifferent I is only a rudiment of the "living through"
(*Er-leben*) of experience in the full sense; it is in fact an un-living (*Ent-
leben*) of experience. All that is left is an "impoverished I-relatedness
reduced to a minimum of experiencing." Correlatively, the object is removed (*ent-fernt*), extracted from its authentic experience. The objectified occurrence, a psychic *process* (*Vor-gang* = going-by) for example,
simply passes the cognizing ego by, immobilized like a thing. By contrast,
"in seeing the desk, I am there 'with it' with my whole I, the I resonates
with this seeing in total harmony, we said, it is an experience properly
(*eigens*) for me." It is my proper experience because it appropriates me
and I, in accord, appropriate it. I am It, I am of It, It is mine. This
experience is accordingly not a process but rather an event proper to
me, a properizing event (*Ereignis*). "This living-through does not pass by
before me like a thing posited by me as an object; rather, I myself properize it to myself and it properizes itself (*es er-eignet sich*) according to its
essence." Such an "event" is something entirely new, outstripping all talk
of psychic and physical, subject and object; even "inner" and "outer"
make no sense in this context. "Living experiences are properizing events
insofar as they *live out of the proper* and life lives only so, in accord" (ZBP
75; 73ff.).

There is thus the sharpest contrast to be drawn between living-
through (*er-leben*) the worlding which properizes my full historical I, and
the un-living (*Ent-leben*) of the "there is" before the remote theoretical
I. It is the difference between the fullness of the *Er-eignis* and the impov-
erishment of the *Vor-gang*, impoverished of sense, unworlded and dehistoricized. It is the contrast between the pretheoretical and the theoretical.
The primacy, the absolutizing, of the theoretical is now breached. With
the contrast, it is now possible to make the theoretical itself into a problem. The problem of the genesis of the theoretical would be one of the
tasks of the pretheoretical science, the science of lived experience as
such. One of the most difficult would be the problem of the transition,
the boundary crossing from environmental life to the initial objectifica-

tion (ZBP 91). It is a problem intertwined with the very possibility of a pretheoretical science, which itself would want to keep itself free of the objectification that would destroy its unique essence and make it once again into another theoretical science.

But how is a pretheoretical science of experience at all possible? For its "object" is the "experienceable as such" (*Erlebbares überhaupt*: ZBP 115f.) which is not an object at all. This formula for the primal something was already used in the habilitation work to describe its form-determining material guiding clue, the "givenness" (FS 263) of the *modus essendi*: "The *modus essendi* is the experienceable as such, is in the absolute sense whatever stands over against consciousness, the 'robust' reality which irresistibly forces itself upon consciousness and can never nor again be put aside and eliminated" (FS 260). What is put aside in 1919 is precisely the rigidifying language of consciousness-over-against-object to characterize the primal realm of experience. Heidegger now emphatically rejects the characterization of the environmental as "given," regarding that as a kind of theoretical infringement, albeit the slightest. "Thus 'givenness' is already quite probably a theoretical form" (ZBP 89). Already for the young Heidegger, the discovery of a *modus essendi* **activus** was a source of much excitement and astonishment, now intensified by the discovery of other aspects of the "in-itself of the streaming experience of life" (ZBP 116). But his newly heightened sensitivity to his basic terms now extends even to terms like "life" and "lived experience." "The word 'lived experience' is itself nowadays so common and diluted that it best would have to be put aside were it not so relevant. It cannot be avoided, which is all the more reason to come to terms with its essence." In the same context, Heidegger even begins to experiment with another impersonal, "It lives, and moreover it lives toward something," for his basic experience, without following through any further (ZBP 66).

Natorp's Double Objection

The problem of a pretheoretical science thus ultimately becomes a problem of language: how to approach and articulate the dynamic, and thus elusive, facticity of life? We are now nearing the climactic last hour of the course. The problem of a nonobjectifying language comes to a head in Paul Natorp's simple but ingenious objections against Husserl's phenomenology, which Heidegger now makes his own.[14] Put at its extreme, phenomenology claims to be able to get at and articulate the pretheoretical realm of life in a pretheoretical way, and so to achieve the unique status of a pretheoretical science, the virtually contradictory limit-case of an Ur-science. This is the upshot of Heidegger's radical reformulation of Husserl's program to make phenomenological philosophy into a strict science. His response to Natorp's pair of objections as they apply to his own endeavor gives birth to the solution of a formally indicating language and hermeneutics.

1. How is the nonobjectifiable subject matter of phenomenology to be even approached without already theoretically inflicting an objectification upon it? How are we to go along with life reflectively without de-living it? For reflection itself already exercises an analytically dissective and dissolving effect upon the life stream, acting as a theoretical intrusion which interrupts the stream and cuts it off. "For in reflection the life-experiences are no longer lived but looked at. We ex-posit the experiences and so extract them from the immediacy of experience. We as it were dip into the onflowing stream of experiences and scoop out one or more, which means that we 'still the stream,' as Natorp says" (ZBP 100f.). This is Natorp's first objection against phenomenology, against the intuitive access to its chosen subject matter.

2. Phenomenology claims merely to describe what it sees. But description is circumscription into general concepts, a "subsumption" under abstractions. The concrete immediacy to be described is thereby mediated into abstract contexts. There is no such thing as immediate description, since all expression, any attempt to put something into words, generalizes and so objectifies (ZBP 101, 111). This is Natorp's second objection against phenomenology, against the expressibility of its immediate matter.

First, a distillation of Heidegger's response that shortcuts to the end of the climactic last hour. Is immediate experience inaccessible and inexpressible? In response to the first objection, Heidegger will point to a non-intuitive form of access which hermeneutics calls understanding (Lask's *Hingeben* versus *Hinsehen*), a certain familiarity which life already has of itself and which phenomenology needs only to repeat. This spontaneous experience of experience, this streaming return of experiencing life upon already experienced life, is the immanent historicity of life. Instead of objectifying con-cepts which seize life and so still its stream, this spontaneous access that life has to itself provides the possibility of finding less intrusive pre-cepts or pre-concepts which at once reach back into life's motivation and forward into its tendency. Such a precursory pre-conception or provisional indication which at once repeats and fore-runs life's course accordingly stretches itself unitively and indifferently along the whole of the life stream without disrupting it. Thus, the response to the question of accessibility is at once an answer to the objection against the expressibility of immediate experience: *Verstehen*. Instead of the abstractive objectifying universal which is not only extractive but also subsumptive in character, thus subject to the schema of form subsuming matter, Heidegger points to the nonobjective option of a more concrete indicative and intentional universal stemming directly from the very temporal intentional movement of finding oneself experiencing experience. The problems of intuition and expression are therefore transposed into the possibility of a 1) nonreflective understanding and 2) the nonobjectifying conceptualization that it itself provides, that allusive universal called the formal indication. These are the two new mainstays of Heidegger's more hermeneutically oriented phenomenology.

Now to the step-by-step movement toward the last hour. For it is actually in answer to this double methodological problem of "intuition and expression" that Heidegger will develop the four-part KNS-Schema which guides him to his solution of the "formal indication." In response to this single methodological problem divided into two parts—how to approach and articulate lived experience—Natorp, Lask, indeed Husserl himself, sought a theoretical solution, Heidegger on the contrary a supratheoretical one. For Natorp, the immediate is the subject that determines everything and thus lies "this side of all determination" and so itself is not immediately accessible. His solution is to resolve the subject, in the spirit of mathematics, in an infinite series of admittedly objective determinations of thought from which it can again be asymptotically reconstructed into its original subjective unity (ZBP 102ff.). Similarly, Lask's "logic of philosophy" involves an ever-increasing series of forms of forms of forms etc. Even Husserl here speaks of a descriptive reflection upon an initially reflectionless experiencing of experience which is repeatedly reflected upon "into infinity" (ZBP 99). In every case, the immediacy of intuition is lost in the mediacy of expression and the initial unity of intuition and expression is rent asunder. It is well known that the phenomenological "principle of all principles" gives the primacy to intuition. Less noted in this context is the inseparable intentional relation between intuition and expression, that is, between intuitive fulfillment and *empty* intending. All of our experiences, beginning with our most direct perceptions, are from the start already expressed, indeed interpreted.[15] This Diltheyan emphasis of the intentional structures described by Husserl in *Logical Investigations* is the seminal insight of Heidegger's hermeneutical breakthrough in 1919, leading to a pretheoretical solution to the problem of intuition and expression, and thus to a more radical conception of phenomenology as the original science of origins than hitherto conceived. Intentionality itself already contains its own solution to the problem of expression. As we have already noted, in being already intentionally structured, immediate experience is itself not mute but "meaningful," which now means that it is already contextured like a "language." In view of this articulation inherent in intentionality, the problem of "intuition and expression" may perhaps now be more cohesively formulated: How can appropriate expressions be "read off" directly from experience and developed in order to enable rather than to obscure intuitive access to it? Where can we find philosophical expressions which serve this intuition instead of preventing it? The answers hinge upon a proper understanding of both the structure and the dynamics of intentionality.

The Climactic Last Hour: A Formally Indicating Hermeneutics

A final objection, an outgrowth of the first two, will serve to test our understanding of intentionality. The objection spawns a torrent of surprise developments in the very last hour of the course. In view of this complexity, it will be convenient to take the upshot of its formulation of intentionality in terms of each of its two parts: *Verhalten zu etwas* (ZBP 112), a comportment relating itself to something.

The final objection against the purportedly nondistorting intuitive access to life is broached: in this phenomenological intuition, there must surely be at the very minimum a *something* which "gives itself." Is this sheerest something not the anything in general which represents the very epitome of "unliving" ensuing from the process of theoretization? Up to now, this has been *formaliter* so in our account. But now, a fundamental division must be made within the theoretical, which in turn will lead to the exposition of an analogous two-part division in the pretheoretical realm; ergo, the four-part "something" of the KNS-Schema already outlined above in anticipation of this moment.

In sum, the objection is answered by distinguishing between formal theoretization (*Vergegenständlichung*), which yields the "anything in general" in one fell swoop directly from primal life, and the actual theoretization (*Objektivierung*) which occurs stepwise and typewise from the environmental experience: desk, brown, sense datum, physiological reaction to the physical, cause-effect relation, wavelength of aether vibrations, laws relating their simplest units. At each level, in each type of objectification process, one can always say, "it *is* something" (and not "es gibt etwas"!), indicating that the formal something is not bound to these steps of objectification, thus not motivated by these object-domains (ZBP 113). As we have seen from the habilitation work, its compass is far broader: sensory and nonsensory, real and possible objects, even nonbeing. Noteworthy is the fact that it is not tied to theoretical comportment, to the scientific lifeworld, but is to be found also in atheoretical comportment, in the aesthetic, ethical, and religious lifeworlds. Even in religious experience, "something" is given. This suggests that the formal-objective something first has no connection with the theoretical process, that its motivation out of life is qualitatively and essentially different.

It extends to whatever can be experienced, lived (*Erlebbares überhaupt*: ZBP 115 = p. 260 of the habilitation). And *this* is the phenomenological "primal something" (*Ur-etwas*). *It* is indifferent to any particular world and especially to any particular object-type. It is not yet differentiated and not yet worldly; ergo a preworldly something. And this "not yet" is the "index for the highest potentiality of life." This potentiality is the basic "trait" (*Zug*) of life, to live out toward something, to "world out" (*auszuwelten*) into particular lifeworlds. Life in itself is motivated and has tendency, it has a motivated tendency (= "thrown project" in BT) and tending motivation. "But this means that the sense of something as that which can be experienced implies the moment of "out toward" (*auf zu*), "direction toward," "into a (particular) world"—and in fact in its undiminished "vital impetus." (ZBP 115).

"It is out of this preworldly vital something that the formal objective *something of knowability* is *first* motivated. A something of formal theoretization. The tendency into a world [that of *es weltet*] can be theoretically deflected *before* its demarcation and articulation as a world. Thus the universality of the formally objective appropriates its origin from the in-itself of the streaming experience of life" (ZBP 116). In short, the universality of formalization has the direct access to the flowing "primal something" which phenomenological intuition wishes to have. The reflexive categories derived from formalization are not "parasitical" upon the constitutive categories of the world, as Lask thought (GS 2:162). Their contentlessness reflects a freedom from the genera and species generated in the theoretical generalization of the world, a freedom which makes them philosophically useful, as we have seen more than once above, especially in those methodological impasses where language seems to fail us. Traditionally, what philosophy seeks is at once comprehensive and fundamental. And the pure and simple universals of formalization come closer to that than the mundane order of strata caught up in a complex web of genera and species in ever-increasing "subsumption" and generalization.

Pure and simple as it is, however, the form of formalization nevertheless tends toward an object, which, as Lask already noted, "at once alludes to the 'standing over against' in the relation to subjectivity" (GS 2:72). Add to this the "heterothesis" essential to isolating one object from another, and the phenomenological ambition to "go with the flow" of original life and to describe this "living out toward" from the inside out, as it were, is simply thwarted by the escalating diremptions of formalization (ZBP 111f., 117). Why should formalization then be regarded so positively? What does it really contribute to phenomenology's own, enormously difficult category-problem, that of finding the right words for its pretheoretical sort of descriptions? Looking beyond this "minus," the prejudice of diremption, we have in fact come upon a third "plus" which we can now add to our list. In addition to its proximity to the comprehensive uniqueness of life and the methodological flexibility and freedom offered by its contentlessness, the formal category of "object in general" in fact magnifies its relation to subjectivity, what Heidegger will soon call the relational sense (*Bezugssinn*) as opposed to its content sense, what it "holds."

Phenomenology needs only to improve upon the schematization of formalization and expand it into the full intentional movement dictated by the phenomenon of life. Small wonder, then, that Heidegger will shortly (WS 1919–20) call the "open" methodological concept that points the way and guides the explication of phenomena without prejudice, that is, without falling into standpoints and regional limitations, the *"formal* indication" (*formale Anzeige*: in BT, "existence" is the formal indication; in 1916–19, it is what hitherto has been called the "operative concept" of intentionality; for Lask, it is perhaps "matter-needy forms." Each in fact schematizes the same "tendency"!)

The pluses and minuses of formalization and its noematic "formal-logical objective something" may now be applied to the "primal something" to bring out its full character. Both are indifferent in regard to all differentiations, reflecting the hollow dilution of the medieval concept *ens commune* which indifferently applies to everything. But surely there is a difference between theoretical and pretheoretical (i.e., factic) indifference. The step into factic life is the step from the leveling "not" of indifference to the "not yet" of potentiality, therefore "the index for the highest potentiality of life" (ZBP 115). In particular here, factic life has not yet devolved into a world, it is not yet worldly; it is "preworldly." The KNS-Schema thus distinguishes, on the pretheoretical level, a worldly from a preworldly something, and describes the latter as the "basic moment of life as such." It is "life in and for itself" and not a "genuine life," that is, life in a "genuine lifeworld" (ZBP 115f.: What does "genuine" mean here? Heidegger provides no clarification). The distinction serves to divide the e-vent of world-ing into its two parts, as two sides of the same coin, and gives primacy to the suffix, to the (structuring, articulating, thus meaningful) dynamism of life in and for itself, "the in-itself of the streaming experiencing of life" (ZBP 116). This dynamic center of life is now to be enhanced and amplified by formal considerations. How? By investing it with the formal schematism of *intentionality*.

So far, this dynamic center has only been isolated (i.e., formalized) through negative terms, placed on the outskirts of "genuine" worlds and yet—and here is the positive turn—charged with the potential for worlding. The "not yet," this more pregnant "not" of dynamic undifferentiation, contains within itself the power to differentiate worlds; it is a differentiating indifference or, in more Kantian language, a determinable indetermination. The indifference can do something. And *this* is the primal something. How to conceptualize and define this "deed"? For the Kantians, all concepts have the function of determining. According to our already established precautions, this is to be a purely formal determination rather than the hierarchical determination of genera and species. Heidegger finds such a formal determination in the potentiality of intentionality. Within the undifferentiated dynamism of the primal something, in its undiminished "vital impetus," there is the bare intentional moment of "out towards," "in the direction of," "into a (determinate) world" (ZBP 115). The student transcripts add another formulation: the tendency to "world out" (*auszuwelten*) into particular lifeworlds. Put another way, this character of being toward something is "life in its motivated tendency and tending motivation" (ZBP 117). The primal something may be undifferentiated and unformed, but it is not the "amorphous irrational X" (Rickert) of brute facticity, inasmuch as it contains within itself the tendency toward differentiation and determination and so has an intrinsic directional sense.

With this positive development of the undifferentiation, we get a clearer picture of how Heidegger means to overcome the final objection against a pretheoretical science, namely, that a diremption between knowledge and its object always remains, inasmuch as every intuitive comportment is inescapably a comportive "relation toward something." His answer is at once simple and genial: With the primal something, the "something" is the relation (*Verhalten*) as such, it is not an ob-ject at all but instead the intentional moment of "out toward," what Heidegger two semesters later will structurally distinguish as the relational sense (*Bezugssinn*) of intentionality. This is in actuality the *nonobjective* formalization read off from the intentional structures of life. It involves a phenomenological modification of traditional formalization in order to efface its proclivity toward diremption. All formally indicative concepts aim, strictly speaking, to express only the pure "out toward" without any further content or ontic fulfillment. From the relational sense of "out toward," for example, the formal indication of "object in general" becomes the pure "toward which" (*das Worauf*)[16] instead of Lask's reflexive formulation of "standing over against" (*Entgegenstehendes*), which takes the object more from the side of its content sense, and so is still too-objectively formulated. In this sense, formal objectification, even though "motivated" in the primal something, is still not near enough to life's origin, to its "primal leap," for Heidegger's formally indicative concepts. Despite Heidegger's effort to revive it, formal objectification is finally still an unliving in its rigid duality of the subject over against the object, which must be dismantled and revivified by the unified relation of motive to tendency, which is at the "heart" of the intentional movement here. The conceptual pair motive-tendency (later the pair thrownness-project understood as equiprimordial) is not a duality, but rather the "motivated tendency or tending motivation" (ZBP 117) in which the "outworlding" life expresses itself. Expression, articulation, differentiation arises out of a core of indifferentiation which is no longer to be understood in terms of subject-object, form-matter, or any other duality. What remains of the old objectification is the indifferent continuum of the toward-which on the noematic end, and the tending motivation on the noetic.

This simple "concretum" (ZBP 68) of the "in-itself of the streaming experiencing of life" is moreover, as intentional, not so much subjective as "I-like" (so in WS 1919–20). *It* is my life, my full historical I is there in a peculiar way where the personal borders on the impersonal (Bergson's and Merleau-Ponty's terse formulation is apt here: *j'en suis*, "I am of it," "I belong to it"). Life, world, history, all of which is my experience: perhaps now one can appreciate the complex of proximate realities that dovetail and asymptotically withdraw into this undifferentiated concretum, this all-inclusive X of my experience, the It which worlds and properizes. This is the *Ur-sprung*, the primal leap which the early Heidegger makes into the subject matter of phenomenology and wishes to articulate, in defiance of the classical maxim *individuum est ineffabile*.

Already in WS 1919–20, the primal something in which I live is described as an indeterminate something concerning which one does not know what it is, so that it can take on a threatening and disquieting character. This uncanny life, however, stands in a particular horizon of significance which allows it to be determined. Such a primal something plays a great role in the genuine lifeworlds, for example, as the *mysterium tremendum* in the religious lifeworld. It is therefore not to be confused with the formal-logical something.[17] (Clearly, the KNS-Schema had already provoked quite a bit of discussion among Heidegger's students, who had already begun to circulate his course-transcripts among themselves.)

Not at all discussed is the differentiation of worlds, which appear in the plural in the schema, where they are characterized as "particular spheres of experience" (under I.B.). They clearly refer back to the primal something, which is the "experienceable as such" whose "indifference with respect to every genuine [does "genuine" thus mean "particular," "determined"?] worldness and especially every determinate object-likeness" contains within itself "the highest potentiality" for differentiation (ZBP 115). The typification of lifeworlds at this time simply follows the neo-Kantian division of values and so commonly includes scientific, ethical, aesthetic, and religious lifeworlds. Clearly, *es weltet* is here still connected with *es wertet*. The real concern is with the active *es* and how to describe It in its own terms, purely and simply. The entire schema is geared to this process of "abstraction" from regional problems, of the formal isolation and identification of the dynamism of facticity, along with the resources already indigenous to it which allow It to be described "in itself " from itself. Life is sufficient unto Itself, Eckhart already said. The trick is to get to this level and stay with it, thereby reaping the harvest of its self-expression. For factic life also gives itself in the deformation of objectification, which must first be dismantled in order to get to its initial moment of articulation.

This was even true of Heidegger's chosen route through formalization. The formal indication must find its motivation earlier than formal objectification, in the more incipient moment of life "in its motivated tendency or tending motivation." Since the grasp of con-cepts intercept life and "still the stream," phenomenology must find less intrusive, more natural ways to get a grip on its subject matter, which remain in accord with the "immanent *historicity* of life in itself" (an ad lib in the last hour not in the edition). This smoother entry into life's historicity in order to tune in on and read off its self-expression is described as a "hermeneutic intuition" (ZBP 117). Such an intuition immersed in "the immanent historicity of life" must reach back into its motivation and forward into its tendency in order to form those special con-cepts which are accordingly called re-cepts (retrospective grips, *Rückgriffe*, of the motivation) and pre-cepts (prospective grips, *Vorgriffe*, of the tendency), without of course lapsing into old-fashioned objectifying concepts (*Be-griffe*). Heidegger will later improve upon this dualism suggested in the hermeneutic type of concept by having the single term pre-conception (*Vor-griff*) imply both retrospection and prospection, which unitively and indifferently stretches itself along the whole of the life stream. In the same vein, a formal indication is sometimes also called a "precursory" (*vor-läufige*) indication that "foreruns" the stream without disruption. Springing from life's own sense of direction, from the indifference of its dynamics only in view of its incipient differentiation, the formal indication wishes to point to the phenomena in extreme generality, indifference, and contentlessness, in order to be able to interpret the phenomena so indicated without prejudice and standpoint.

In the closing minutes of the course, Heidegger alludes to the unique eidetic universality needed to grasp the "world-character of experienced experience." He does not quite get around to explaining clearly enough that this "experienced experience," this streaming return of life back upon itself, is precisely the immanent historicity of life, a certain familiarity or "understanding" that life already has with itself and that phenomenological intuition must simply "repeat." And what is this understanding, whether implicit or methodologically explicit, given to understand? The articulations of life itself, which accrue to the self-experience that occurs in the 'dialectical' return of experiencing life to already experi-

enced life. In WS 1919–20, he calls this return a "diahermeneutics."
Once again, life is not mute but meaningful, it "expresses" itself precisely
in and through its self-experience and spontaneous self-understanding.
"The pre-worldly and worldly signifying functions have in themselves
the essential character of expressing features of the properizing
event. . . . They are both prospective and retrospective in their grasp
and reach, that is, they express life in its motivated tendency or tending
motivation" (ZBP 117). From such accounts, terse as they still are, one
begins to espy the justification for identifying intuition with understanding, phenomenological with hermeneutical "intuition." "The experience
of experience that takes possession by taking itself along is the understanding intuition, the *hermeneutic* intuition, the originary phenomenological back-and-forth formation of re-cepts and pre-cepts from which
all theoretical-objectifying positing as well as transcendent positing falls
out" (ZBP 117).

Summation: In the Proximity of Husserl

The last citation suggests Heidegger's own version of the "phenomenological reduction" that he had been developing in previous hours in his
critique of the "transcendent positing" of "reality" in realistic and idealistic theories of perception, in order to justify the circumspective seeing
that is entailed in the experience of the environing world. And his allusion to an indigenous "experience of experience" within the life stream
(its immanent historicity), that is, a "reflexive" dimension built into life
itself, is clearly an attempt to salvage, amplify, and deepen Husserl's
sense of "reflexion as a basic peculiarity of the sphere of experience"
(*Ideen I*, §77; ZBP 100) in opposition to Natorp's criticisms. But now he
avoids the term "reflection" because of its objectifying visual connotations—"The experienced experiences become looked-at experiences"
(ZBP 99)—and instead attempts to reinterpret intuition in more kinetic
and vitalistic ways. This nontheoretical, nonobjectifying "intuition" is var-
iously described as a dedicative submission to life, sympathy with it (ZBP
110), immersion in it, in all, a form of life which outstrips the cognitive
connotations of the word "intuition" and suggests the later total attitude
of authenticity (*Hingeben* versus *Hinsehen*). The laboriously achieved
practice of intuition is more a matter of cultivating a basic habit or attitude of life, "and this is not achieved by any conceptual system so far
constructed, but by phenomenological life in its increasing intensification
of itself" (ZBP 110). This is what the "strictness" of the science of phenomenology really refers to.

In taking the "principle of all principles" to be nontheoretical in nature, Heidegger concedes that he is going beyond what Husserl had
explicitly said, but claims it to be an implication. That the reduction leads

to a radically nontheoretical science is also presumably something that Husserl had not got around to saying.[18] Heidegger observes that Husserl's Logos-essay did not go far enough in only blaming naturalism for the distortions of objectification that prevent philosophy from reaching its goal of strict scientificity. The fault lies more broadly in the tyranny of the theoretical as such (ZBP 87); *prote philosophia* lies this side of all theorizing and "transcendent positing" of the "real," the "given," and the like. In speaking of the hazards of the slightest vestiges of objectification, Heidegger notes that even Husserl's investigations tend to situate themselves first in the sphere of things (a note from the transcripts not in the edition). Thus Heidegger begins to hint that the problem with Husserl's philosophy lies not only in a few infelicities with the choice of a language still contaminated with objectification. It was not Husserl but Lask who was the only one who had gone far enough to even see the problem of the theoretical in its essence and genesis (ZBP 88). That the goal of the reduction is a sphere of experience which is not thinglike or real, that the immediacy of the experience of the meaning-yielding lies at the heart of intentionality, is nevertheless still a lesson to be learned from Husserl's studies of "inner-time consciousness," which Heidegger is already drawing upon in his own descriptions of the "stream of experience." The Husserlian vocabulary of "primal impression," "primal apprehension" (understood as an incipient interpretation!), and much more, in describing this primal source (*Urquell*) of experience, clearly suggests Heidegger's "primal something," which even in its most hermeneutical moments of articulation here still trades off from Husserl's retentional and protentional scheme of temporality.

Even the hybrid of "phenomenological hermeneutics" which, as Heidegger notes in the very first hour of the next semester, "lifts" the distinction of the "systematic" from the "historical" in philosophy (ZBP 131f.) may not have been regarded by Husserl as a departure from his own work. Husserl's task-setting letter to Heidegger of September 10, 1918, mentions the convergence with his ongoing work on *Ideen II* of an article by Dilthey's student, E. Spranger, on the "theory of understanding." In SS 1919, Husserl gave the very first of a series of courses all entitled "Nature and Spirit," in which Dilthey's hermeneutic approach plays an essential role.[19]

For Heidegger's part, the months immediately after his return from the front were the most philosophically fruitful phase of his intimate association with Husserl.[20] Heidegger in his courses at this time conveyed to his students a clear sense of joining forces with Husserl while he was at the same time striking out on his own. That such an alliance did not exclude an open and public critique is testified by the "field campaign" launched by Husserl's students against the "pure pole" of a transcendental ego in their regular Saturday discussions with him: "Dr. Heidegger is taking a mediating position by asserting that the primal I is the qualified 'historical I,' from which the pure I is derived by repressing all historicity and quality. Such a pure I can only be a subject of theoretical acts and oriented to things."[21] In KNS 1919, the full historical I finds itself caught up in meaningful contexts so that it oscillates according to the rhythmics of worlding (ZBP 85, 98), it properizes itself to the articulations of an experience (ZBP 75, 78) which is governed by the immanent historicity of life in itself. For the primal It of the life stream is more than the primal I. It is the self experiencing itself experiencing the worldly. The ultimate source of the deep hermeneutics of life is properly an irreducible "It" which precedes and enables the I. It is this unity and whole of the "sphere of experience" understood as a self-sufficient domain of meaning that phenomenology seeks to approach, "understandingly experience" (ZBP 115), and bring to appropriate language: ergo, the intertwining problems of facticity (immediate experience), intuition, and expression, which determine the Idea of phenomenological philosophy and so emerge time and again in the semesters that follow. In BT, this intertwining triad becomes disposedness—understanding—discursiveness, the modes of in-being.

Clearly, the students common to both Husserl and Heidegger sensed a difference in what Husserl's precocious assistant had to say, but did they sense it as a radical difference? Doubtless not, at least not at first. Breathtaking as it is, that phenomenology could be regarded as a uniquely nontheoretical science is but an implication of the epoche taken to its limit of bracketing out all objective formations. Both were saying that the reduction stops at an intentionally structured life stream and not in the sheer flux of a pure sensory manifold, and that the dynamics of this life-context can be understood in terms of a motivational context (*Ideen I*, §47). The "it" of its facticity could be compared to the "anonymously functioning intentionality" of the transcendental ego. That this facticity includes a structure of self-experience reminiscent of the peculiar doubling of the retentive-protentive temporality of the lifestream gave the hermeneutically slanted descriptions a Husserlian flavor. That this historical self-experience dictated a departure from the Cartesian model of "reflection" found resonances in Husserl's efforts to overcome the form-matter dualism in his descriptions of the consciousness's reception of the "primal impression" of the life stream. In SS 1920, Heidegger criticizes, not Husserl's, but Dilthey's conception of "immanent perception" in his search for alternatives to describe this inherently historical self-experience (soon it will become the call-response relation of the situational "conscience"). And Heidegger's overriding interest in the "robust reality" of history allowed Husserl to concentrate his teaching in his preference of systematic philosophy.

After the KNS, with 19 students, Heidegger's classes regularly tripled and on occasion quadrupled in official enrollment, with a large following of unofficial attendees. Many a student came to Freiburg to hear Husserl and followed Heidegger instead, often at Husserl's recommendation! The old founder himself sanctioned Heidegger as a major spokesman of phenomenology. "Phenomenology: that's Heidegger and I—and no one else," Husserl then proclaimed, according to an oft-repeated anecdote. As far as he was concerned, Heidegger was truly "doing" phenomenology.

Whatever Heidegger was doing, it remained consistent to the seminal ideas of facticity, intuition, and expression implanted in the KNS, which is literally the beginning of the Way. In fact, it was in this semester which inaugurated his phenomenological decade that he first discovered the root metaphor of the "way" to describe his very kinetic sense of philosophy. Philosophy is not theory, outstrips any theory or conceptual system it may develop, because it can only approximate and never really comprehend the immediate experience it wishes to articulate. That which is nearest to us in experience remains farthest removed from our comprehension. Philosophy in its "poverty of thought" is ultimately reduced to maintaining its proximating orientation toward the pretheoretical origin which is its subject matter. Philosophy is accordingly an orienting comportment (*Verhalten*), a praxis of striving, and a protreptic encouraging such a striving. Its expressions are only "formal indications" which smooth the way toward intensifying the sense of the immediate in which we find ourselves. It is always precursory in its pronouncements, a forerunner of insights, a harbinger and hermeneutic herald of life's possibilities of understanding and articulation. In short, philosophy is more a form of life on the edge of expression rather than a science. That phenomenology is more a preconceptual, provisory comportment than a conceptual science, that the formally indicating "concepts" are first intended to serve life rather than science, becomes transparent only after the "turn." As Heidegger observes at the end of his phenomenological decade: "The content of such concepts does not directly intend and say what it relates to, it gives only an indication, a pointer, so that those who understand this conceptual connection are called upon to bring about a transformation of themselves into the Dasein [in themselves]" (GA 29/30:430, 428). Philosophy is "philosophizing" (1921–22), being "on the way to language" (1959)," ways—not works" (1976).

SS 1919: PHENOMENOLOGY AND TRANSCENDENTAL VALUE-PHILOSOPHY

The critique of transcendental value-philosophy and of its cultural "system of teleological idealism" (ZBP 121) continues relentlessly and without pause in the following semester, a scant month later in this postwar year. Heidegger now hopes to apply the developed apparatus of the previous semester in what, from the introductory statement—for the most part not presented in class! (ZBP 121–126)—promises to be a full-fledged "phenomenological critique" of that historical stretch of philosophy whose waning moments he experienced at first hand as a student and involved participant. The promise is breathtaking in its scope and "ruthless radicalism" (ZBP 127: the first class in fact began with this statement "On the Goal of the Course"). The promise is not fulfilled, beyond this brilliant statement—the very first by Heidegger—of the method and intent of phenomenological critique or "destruction" (so named first in WS 1919–20). The subsequent exegesis of the texts of Windelband and Rickert displays some moments of depth and insight, but is by and large shallow and pedestrian, especially when compared with later similar efforts like the Kant-book. And unfortunately for our Story, Heidegger never gets to Lask's texts, as he apparently intended. So we never get a real sense of how this elaboration of the nineteenth-century "situation of intellectual history" (ZBP 137), as the problem situation which led to the "philosophy of culture" to which he himself gave brief allegiance, bears upon the "hermeneutic situation" which prompted Heidegger himself to make the radical moves he had just made in the KNS. There is not one hint of the poignantly Spenglerian disenchantment with such things as "culture" and "value" prevalent then in postwar Germany, which Heidegger will invoke in later courses. In this first of many courses which we have from Heidegger on the history of philosophy,[22] he outlines a new and powerful method of "critique" (ZBP 125-128) which promises to go more deeply into intellectual history than the old-fashioned factual history of surface "influences" (128), and then by and large gives us precisely that (141f.)!

The importance of this course for our Story thus lies more in its preparation of such Heideggerian mainstays as "deconstruction" (WS 1919–20) and the "hermeneutic situation" (SS 1922: cf. Appendix D) than in their actual application and illustration in the history of philosophy. Both find their foundation and criterion in the historically dynamic "primal structure" of the "primal level" of "life in and for itself in the eidos" (ZBP 183, 121, 127, 125) which Heidegger had just discovered in the KNS. "For there is no genuine historical understanding without a backtrack to the original motivations" (ZBP 125). Such a regress to the pretheoretical stratum is essential in order to exhibit the theoretical in its very origins, such as that of a philosophical "doctrine." In an ad-lib summary (only in the student transcripts circa ZBP 181) of the KNS, Heidegger observes that philosophy as a strict science has no proofs to offer to a standpoint philosophy, since such a philosophy is itself not committed to a radical return to the ultimate dimension of the originary giving. At this level, there is only the most basic act, the seeing of seeing, in which anything whatsoever gives itself, but which cannot be "proven."

Phenomenological critique (= "destruction" in WS 1919–20) is no mere contrasting of standpoints in order to demolish the opposing one, pointing to its logical deficiencies or inner contradictions and marshaling counterproofs to defend one's own. Phenomenological critique can never really be negative. "It overcomes and points behind confused, half-clarified, and false problems only *in pointing to* the genuine sphere of problems." Critique here is "positive attunement to the genuine motivations" and original tendencies operative in the stated problems of a philosophy, in order to take them back "re-ductively" to "their genuine phenomenological Ur-stratum (life in and for itself)" from which their immanent sense originates. Genuine critique is in fact only set in motion by those philosophical intuitions which already in some fashion are traversing "fields of genuine problems." Phenomenology itself can only profit from such critiques of intellectual history, gaining further insight into the "principles of all intellectual life" as well as into the very "principiality" of all principles which ultimately is its one and only interest, the "quale of phenomena which is the genesis and terminus" of all inquiry (ZBP 121–128). Thus, upon this primal stratum which is the common meeting ground of what are erroneously called standpoints, where there is no such thing as standpoints, even the traditional philosophical distinction between the systematic and the historical is "lifted" (ZBP 132, 125).

The historical reduction is thus from doctrine to problem to motivation. The parallel course of SS 1919 introduces the notion of situation for the first time and defines its underlying structure in terms of motivation and tendency. In short, motivations in historical context are not psychological but situational. As in KNS, the primal something is understood predominantly in kinetic terms. We get glimmers of its impending "aletheic" description (gradually, from 1922 on) in formulations like this: "The phenomenological criterion is nothing but the understanding evidence and the evident understanding of experiences, of life in and for itself in the eidos" (ZBP 125). The traditional doctrine of the truth of judgment is broached in this course in conjunction with Rickert's doctrine of the "feeling of evidence" (ZBP 184–189). The backtrack to the prior truth of simple apprehension had already begun in the habilitation work, and the privative ἀ-λήθεια, interpreted as un-concealedness (only in the transcripts), makes an insignificant cameo appearance already in KNS 1919 (ZBP 49). Given these anticipations, the delay in developing this aspect of the phenomenality of the primal phenomenon is significant, and the situation motivating its development worthy of close scrutiny.

Only the opening statement (ZBP 121–125)—not presented in class—gives us a powerfully concentrated insight into the motivational situation of the twentieth-century type or eidos "philosophy of culture." There, Heidegger targets three groups of problems for reduction to the Ur-stratum of motivation from the "system (III) of teleological (I) idealism (II)": the problems of (I) value, (II) form, and (III) system. Lask is mentioned in conjunction with all three problems, but a remark relating to the first problem is of particular interest to our Story: "Lask discovered in the ought and in value, as an ultimate experience and experienced ultimate, *the* world, which was not thinglike, not sensorily metaphysical, as well as not unthinglike, extravagantly speculative, but rather was factic" (ZBP 122). This sentence seems to acknowledge Lask as the source of Heidegger's own breakthrough to the worldly character of immediate experience. Moreover, it finds the motivation for Lask's discovery in the threat of absolute reification posed by nineteeth-century naturalism. By indirection, then, we are given the proximate historical motivation for Heidegger's systematic thought-experiment of absolute reification in the KNS, as well as why he sees in it the either-or of the abyss of nihilism or a leap into the world as such (ZBP 63). The tendency toward a nonsensory Platonic "world" from Lotze (ZBP 137) to Lask is thus motivated by the desperate struggle to salvage meaning against the scientific worldview reducing all to causal determinism and brutally factic necessity. This motivating situation in turn shaped the specifications of the "world" thus developed, which enabled a worldview which would harmonize natural science with the "life of the spirit" (ZBP 122).

To this source of Heidegger's discovery of the environing world, we might add Husserl's often suggestive descriptions of the "The World of the Natural Attitude: I and my Environing World" (*Ideen I*, §27): "Therefore this world is not there for me as a mere world of things, but with the same immediacy it is a world of values, a world of goods, a practical world. . . . Things in their immediacy stand there as objects to be used, the 'table' with its 'books,' the 'glass to drink from,' the 'vase,' the 'piano,' etc." None of this is intended to detract from the originality of Heidegger's insight. Heidegger's leap from the oriented consciousness to situated existence can easily be compared with the "paradigm switch" which takes place in times of scientific revolution.[23]

In the course itself, the antipathetic relation between critical value-philosophy and phenomenology appears most clearly in the opposition between evaluative and descriptive sentences (ZBP 152f) drawn by the former, which at once epitomizes its overriding epistemological orientation (the nature of judgments dominates the course). For Rickert, the description of reality is an impossible undertaking, inasmuch as reality is a heterogeneous continuum, an irreducible multiplicity. The irrationality of historical reality can be overcome only by judging it in relation to value (ZBP 171–174). One sees the same proximity and distance between the two philosophies in what each regards as its "principle of all principles": for value-philosophy, it is the primacy of practical reason (ZBP 144), for phenomenology, the primacy of originary giving and so of "intuition." The promising step made by value-philosophy toward the pretheoretical level of life is, however, obviated by its "critical" thrust, which deflects its assessment of that reality back toward the epistemological.

SS 1919: ON THE ESSENCE OF THE UNIVERSITY AND ACADEMIC STUDIES

In the bleak month of February 1919 in a defeated Germany, with revolution rampant in all walks of life and cries for university reform rife in his own, Heidegger begins the first hour of the KNS with his own thoughts on the "renewal of the university" (ZBP 4). It is the first of a series of such statements, addressing the issue of the relation of life to science in a radically phenomenological manner, which would culminate in his rectoral address of 1933. In all instances, he was addressing students, sometimes also faculty, that is, those involved in the scientific lifeworld of the university, with a special interest in acquiring and maintaining the personal habit and "genuine, archontic form of life" of science. Heidegger's stress then on science as an originally vital process, both personal and historical, rather than a finished theoretical product, antedates by almost a half-century the same stress in recent decades by the "new philosophy of science."[24] The uniquely phenomenological solution to maintaining "the vitality of genuine research" is the "awakening and the enhancement of the life-context of the scientific consciousness" by renewed "return to the genuine origins of the intellectual life," to its "motivational context," in order to stay in touch with the "effective action of the originally motivated *being* which is both personal and impersonal" (ZBP 5). In short, the aspirants to the scientific life—for Heidegger, this means philosophy above all—must cut through the verbiage of already extant theoretical structures in order to find the "nerve," "cutting edge," or "vital impetus" which motivates their disciplines as an ongoing way of life. Even in the particular sciences, science is not theory but an active comportment to its subject matter in its motivating problem-situation. All true scientists must cultivate a phenomenological sense of their motivating origins.

In terms of our Story, the most prominent feature of the course of SS 1919 is its introduction and abundant use of the term "situation" to characterize the primal stratum of the life-context and the relationship of the various sciences to that context. Quite probably, Heidegger received impetus in this direction from a first reading of Karl Jaspers's *Psychology of World Views*, which had appeared earlier in the year. Jaspers's notion of "limit situation" will play a crucial role in the ensuing years in the shaping of Heidegger's fundamental ontology of Dasein. What is called the "situation-I" in 1919 is a clear precursor to Dasein, which can easily and accurately be translated by the phrase, "the human situation." We shall examine Heidegger's review of Jaspers's book in greater detail in chapter 3. Heidegger's course manuscript is no longer extant, so we shall make do with the published transcript of Oskar Becker's "excerpts" (ZBP 217; 205–214) out of the course. Becker's overriding interest in the philosophy of science led him to excerpt out the connections that Heidegger was making with the nature of the university, so we shall supplement this summary of the course with notes drawn from the unpublished transcript of Gerda Walther, who was especially interested in "social communities" at the time.[25]

Heidegger never quite says so, but the *raison d'être* of the university is evidently the "Idea of science," and the previous semester had already rooted that in the Idea of philosophy as the primal science. No matter at what end one starts, the basic issue is the relationship between life and science, including the problem of the motivation of science in life—"the genesis of the theoretical"—and the tendency of any developing science to depart from life ("unliving"). Is it possible to show how the Idea of science functions as a motive in any life-context? This question is freighted with the double question, what is the Idea of science? and what is a life-context? Instead of resorting to a worldview or to the sciences of "life" (biology, psychology) for an answer, Heidegger proposes to begin with a detailed example of his students' everyday experience of the confluence of the two poles taken out of the thick of the scientific life-context of the university, in the environs of books, lab instruments, lecture halls and seminar dialogue, to wit, the experience of "going to class" (shades of last semester! Cf. ZBP 205 and 70f.). The intentional odd mix of street sights and sounds, a stop at the bookstore, chance social encounters, entering the classroom, recollections of the last class, and the like strung along this life-continuity, ultimately seeks to underscore the point that the whole of this motley continuity nevertheless possesses the self-contained unity of a *situation*. Even the most disparate things, say, what now lies on my desk, are held together in the "relative closure" (ZBP 206) of "my situation." Whatever happens, we say, has its "context." And the experiential context gives itself as a situation, a certain unity already in experience prior to all theorizing. What is the character and basis of this unified whole called a "situation"?

To begin with, the experiencing I is thoroughly steeped in its situation and flows with it, immersed in its tendency. Even though this I does not particularly stand out, it is clearly there in deep involvement. For it is *this* I which gives the situation *this* character; the walk would be different for another student. The I plays a role in defining the tendency of the situation, but in turn is defined by the underlying motivations driving the situation. The historical I of the previous semester can now be called the "situation-I," whose own tendencies help to define the duration and closure of its situations, while it in turn is being motivated by them.

And the situations themselves? The I does not go from one situation to another as if they were a series of sharply defined points. Instead, the situations permeate one another, as they act upon one another and so together constitute the I. Each situation has its time, but its duration does not exclude other situations. Each is defined by its motivated tendency, which is connected with the motivational possibilities of other situations. "Life experience is an ever-changing coherence of situations, of motivational possibilities. The pure environing world is thus experienced as a mixed hybrid. Nevertheless, its structure can be described quite precisely" (ZBP 208).

Thus, the situation itself is not an objective process that passes me by but a properizing e-vent that defines me in my very motivations: "Das Ereignis ereignet sich *mir,* ich mache es mir zu eigen, es hat Bezug auf mich" (G. W.). "The event of situation happens *to me,* I make it my own, it relates to me." "It radiates [*strahlt*] into my own inner being" (ZBP 206). This impersonal It, this Event, is thus the motivational ground of my most personal being. One needs only to take "situation" and "event" out of the plural in order to see here the motivational ground of the later Heidegger: the concrete universal, "jeweils" (each while), that is already beginning to take shape in this course (G. W.).

What happens when the situation-character of experience is dampened or extinguished? Experience loses its contained unity, things fall apart, stripped of their former meaningful relations to one another, and stand in isolation as "bare" things. The self is torn out of its absorption in its situation, its vital ties suppressed; it is "dehistoricized" (ZBP 206). The intentionality of pure experiences is impoverished and atrophied to that of a bare directedness of a bare I toward bare somethings. Husserl has taught us that such modifications yield a qualitatively different intentional act. And when it comes to the intentionality of this theoretical attitude, "the range of this modification is without limit, it dominates the entire sphere of pure experience" (ZBP 207), which itself is an absolute sphere.

Applying Dilthey's distinction between the explanatory and the understanding sciences, Heidegger finds two basic types of this modification of the experiential to the theoretical attitude. The explanatory type of science involves a maximum of theoretization and the utmost eradication of the situation, and the understanding type a minimum of theoretization with the greatest possible retention of the situation, say, in the experience of the artwork or the pious experience of Jesus as viewed by the historian. The basic problem of the latter type: how to unify theoretization with its explication of the experiential context of such different lifeworlds? At the end of this series: "Intuitive eidetic phenomenology, the primal science of philosophy, is an understanding science" (ZBP 208: G. W. here adds her own comment: "Aber nicht bei Husserl!" "But not in Husserl!").

Examining the intentionalities more closely, Heidegger now develops some refinements on the two types of sciences and their genesis in terms of the distinction between experienced experiences and the experienced contents of experiences. The former lead to an intensification of life and are apropos of the understanding sciences. The latter become the focus in exploding the unity of a situation and reducing it to its fragmented contents. But such contents externalized out of the situation still retain their fullness of content and so are not the empty something of formalization. We do not stand before a mere multiplicity of bare objects but rather before "states of affairs" (*Sach-verhalte*, literally "thing-relations") which are to be explained in terms of a nonformal heterothesis, say, the identity-difference of cause-effect relations. "Such coherences bear the character of a specific unity, which means that one cannot proceed arbitrarily, but is restricted to a certain domain. Proceeding from any state of affairs, one comes to a 'natural limit': one cannot start from a mathematical state of affairs and arrive at a religious problem" (ZBP 209). Heidegger thus gives his own rendition of the eidetic reduction and the ensuing regionalization which yields a "typology of states of affairs." But he has not yet finished borrowing from Husserl.

Following the promptings of its states of affairs, theoretical comportment is itself thus a process following the lawful teleology contained in them. "Each state of affairs is inherently a problem ($\pi\rho\delta\beta\lambda\eta\mu\alpha$), literally something 'thrown before' as a provocation. . . . It prefigures the direction of the process of theoretical comportment. The direction is *method* ($\mu\dot{\epsilon}\theta o\delta o\varsigma$), the *way* toward constituting the context of states of affairs" (ZBP 210). Theoretical comportment is therefore motivated by givennesses posed as tasks (*Auf-gaben*), which define a new situation with its own teleological tendency.

1. So much for the forward thrust of the genesis of the theoretical. If we again glance backward toward the continuity of situations from which it arises, we find that the life stream contains a ground level which characterizes the entire life-experience in its motivation. This is its necessary relation to corporeality, what philosophers sometimes call the sensory level. Through corporeality everything has a relation to the histori-

cal I in its social context. All this constitutes the "natural life-experience" (ZBP 210) which conditions the genesis of the theoretical, insofar as it must constantly "tear itself away from the natural attitude" (ZBP 211) in order to renew itself. Much like the religious ascetic, theoretical man must free himself from the burden of this basic stratum of experience and reshape his emotional ties to it.

Theoretical comportment is thus a process on two counts, both in a backward glance and a forward thrust. "Theoretical comportment is first a process insofar as it flows through the chain of groundings that it performs, but also because it tears itself out of the life-context in ever renewed spontaneity" (ZBP 212).

2. Another look at the genesis of the theoretical can be made in terms of the two levels of cognitive comportment that underlie and motivate scientific research, the overt search for knowledge. Both direct acquaintance and overt acknowledgment involve dedicative submission (*Hingabe*) to the subject matter, and both attitudes stand or fall by the need for absolute honesty and veracity. But direct acquaintance, the forerunner of the theoretical, operates strictly in the natural life-experience, though it is subject to different levels of clarity. Open acknowledgment, on the other hand, is already a habit and disposition of the scientific will to know which has freed itself from every life-context. It is sensitive to regional distinctions and operates strictly in its chosen domain. The habit of absolute veracity in relation to the subject matter now epitomizes the idea of scientificity and becomes an obligation, freely chosen, upon which membership to the scientific community stands or falls. One begins to see the mature form of life and the organization needed to maintain scientific purity and stringency, and the strict adherence to the subject matter that lies behind the scientific *profession*.

3. The cultivation of this attitude is subject to three labilities. a) Since the theoretical attitude must constantly be detached from life in the environing world, the researcher constantly suffers from and so must endure the contrast between theory and practice. And since he must always go back to the first spontaneity of his origin for his insights, he is always subject to this temptation of "eternal youth" (ZBP 214). b) Given the regional character of the theoretical attitude, the disarray and confusion of lifeworlds is always possible, both through easy identification and oversharp distinction. c) There is the constant tension between the higher receptivity of acknowledgment and the critical productivity of research. True critique arises from the immediate sense of the problems, such that new domains and horizons of problems are won. The overly critical spirit only produces false problems.

These labilities, which always belong in the fragile balance of true science, also give rise to the deviant forms of scientific life. The specialist, the greatest danger to the university today, fails to return to the primal problems by remaining narrowly in a particular field. The false genius has an opinion on all fields high and sundry. He is a "cultural philistine" and actually has a genius for worldviews.

The book on university reform by the future Prussian minister of culture, Carl Becker (ZBP 214), in the face of such problems, stresses the need for synthesis of the will and ethos into the intellectual life. If this means a return to basic origins or a unification of the various lines taken by the particular sciences, then this is clearly the task of philosophy. But until recently, philosophy has one-sidedly sought to be an epistemology. However, now that it has found the courage to do metaphysics, it has also degraded itself into providing ready and finished worldviews. But it is important for philosophy never to be finished, and instead to provide as many open horizons and problems as possible. The task of philosophy in the university is to deepen the consciousness of both science and life. It is the obligation of each individual to form his own worldview. Philosophy can only awaken the critical consciousness which would put not only worldviews, but also the very process of forming them, to the test of life.

TWO

Theo-Logical Beginnings: Toward a Phenomenology of Christianity

We still stand at the very beginning of the Way: 1915–19. The reader must be patient. Small seeds are being planted which will flourish in the most subtle ways in the coming years. The impatient reader may want to skip forward to where the road more overtly points to BT, in order to cultivate her wonder for the more remote sources of Heidegger's path. For we shall have occasion to recall this double beginning time and again. But we are still twelve light-years away from BT. And an even more remote source of BT must now be cultivated, although the crossovers between phenomenological method and "mysticism" have already begun to take place. So perhaps this beginning is really only one: "Christianity and metaphysics (*these* of course in a new sense)."

We have it from the young Heidegger himself that the fundamental shift in his philosophical orientation during the war years was coupled with a change in his religious conviction. In the letter to Engelbert Krebs on January 9, 1919, announcing this religious-philosophical conversion, he at the same time reinforces his continuing high regard for the Catholic values in which he had been nurtured with the following remark: "My investigations into the phenomenology of religion, which will draw heavily upon the Middle Ages, should bear witness to the fact, in lieu of any discussion, that I have not allowed myself to be driven, by reason of this transformation of my fundamental position, to put aside the objective excellent opinion and high esteem of the Catholic lifeworld for the embittered and barren polemic of an apostate."[1] Indeed, we find the initial stirrings of such a project of a phenomenology of religion in the still "Catholic" habilitation work of 1915–16, which concludes with a panegyric of the medieval worldview.

But then the public record of the religious dimension in Heidegger's philosophy breaks off until WS 1920–21, when he first taught his course on the "Introduction to the Phenomenology of Religion." Until recently, we have had only the old Heidegger's assurances that "without this theological background I would never have come onto the path of thinking." He makes this statement in his quasi-factual Dialogue on Language to show that the use of the term "hermeneutics" in his early Freiburg courses was no mere accident, but rather stems from the fact that he was still quite "at home in theology" owing to his earlier studies as a Catholic seminarian in 1909–11. "At that time, I was particularly excited by the question of the relation between the Word of Holy Scripture and theological-speculative thinking. In short, the relation between language and being. . . . Later, I met the term 'hermeneutics' again in Wilhelm Dilthey in his theory of the historical human sciences. Dilthey's familiarity with hermeneutics came from the *same* source, his theological studies, especially his work on Schleiermacher" (US 96/9f.). General as it is, this remark on the "later" encounter with Dilthey and his work on Schleiermacher is really the only substantive clue that Heidegger himself offers us to the core-period which is of special interest here. Specifically, we are referring to that obscure and virtually unknown Interregnum (1917–19) in Heidegger's development from which he emerges as a "protestant apostate" and breaks through to his own lifetime thought. Heidegger himself describes this crucial Interregnum in the opening sentence of his letter to Krebs in January 1919: "In the past two years, in an effort to arrive at a fundamental clarification of my philosophical orientation, I have laid aside all particular scientific projects. This has led me to results for which I could not have preserved my freedom of conviction and academic freedom, had I any commitments beyond philosophy itself." In order to fill the gap in our Story made by this crisis itinerary, this pause in Heidegger's public development, it will be necessary to fall back on assorted private sources (correspondence, diaries, reminiscences, loose notes, etc.) which are just beginning to be made public. These are sometimes sketchy even in the facts they provide, but at times also richly allusive in philosophical content, like Heidegger's letter to Krebs in early 1919. Since the evidence is uneven and the documents are sparse, this chapter of our Story will be somewhat disjointed and tentative in character, at times simply presenting bibliographies, for example. But this at least permits us to get a glimpse of what Heidegger was reading at the time, on the basis of which his religious-philosophical development during this Interregnum can be at least partially reconstructed. Since some of Heidegger's notes then on a phenomenology of religion have recently surfaced, it is now possible to reconstruct this most glaring gap in Heidegger's record far more fully than ever before.[2]

THE RELIGIOUS-PHILOSOPHICAL ITINERARY (1915–22)

The project of a phenomenology of religion has its birth squarely in the young Heidegger's efforts to make the tradition-hardened medieval worldview more tractable to the modern world by demonstrating that the same perennial problems are operative in both worlds. At the end of the Introduction to his habilitation work, he proposes two specific areas which he would want to subject to this incipient version of destruction: 1) the history of scholastic logic in the Middle Ages, a project which will surface again in Heidegger's deconstructive efforts of 1922 focused on Aristotle, and 2) a parallel history of scholastic psychology which would display its nonpsychologistic character by focusing on the medieval discovery of intentionality. At this point he adds: "For the decisive insight into this basic character of scholastic psychology, I regard the philosophical, more precisely, the phenomenological elaboration of the mystical, moral-theological, and ascetic literature of medieval scholasticism to be of special urgency" (FS 147). In short, what is needed here is a phenomenology of the full spectrum of religious experience ("the living spirit") of the Middle Ages. "It is by such means that we shall first penetrate into the vital life of medieval scholasticism and see how it decisively founded, vitalized, and strengthened a cultural epoch" (FS 147f.). The Conclusion reiterates the need for such an investigation of the "fundamental correlation of object and subject," and so "of 'verum' as one of the transcendentals," and singles out "Eckhartian mysticism" as a particularly fruitful philosophical vein to explore in this direction, which Heidegger "hopes to be able to show on another occasion" (FS 344). For the medieval lifeworld, the "form of its inner existence," is anchored precisely in the "transcendent primal relationship of the soul to God" (FS 351). Which is why "scholasticism and mysticism in essence belong together for the medieval worldview" and so mutually offset the extremes to which each might be carried. "Philosophy as a rationalistic system detached from life is *powerless*, mysticism as an irrationalistic experience is *aimless*" (FS 352).

Thus, on the threshold of his religious crisis of 1917, we find Heidegger already keenly interested in the phenomenology of religion, looking to it for insight into the notion of intentionality—which after all is first of all a medieval notion—as a vehicle for bringing a fossilized philosophy back to life. But at this point, the public record of such a project breaks off and we must now resort to a biographical chronology in our search for clues to fill in the gap.

1916

Heidegger finalized the habilitation work for publication in September of 1916, having written the Conclusion for it a year after the dissertation itself was publicly defended in mid-1915 (FS 133). On vacation the month before, he had written a poem, "Eventide over Reichenau," replete with Eckhartian sentiments, for the *Bodenseebuch* (1917): ". . . From eternities / a heaviness beyond sense—Mine in the gray wasteland / of a great Simplicity." The vacation was more than usually necessary to recover from the shock of not being named to Freiburg's chair of Catholic philosophy in late June 1916, which he had been anticipating for several years.

1917

1917 was the year of turmoil and crisis in Heidegger's inner life. On January 7, he writes to thank the Catholic medieval scholar Martin Grabmann for "your friendly card . . . for me the most valuable spur for further work in the area of medieval scholasticism and mysticism."[3] In February, he completed his third and last semester of teaching as temporary appointee in the department of Catholic philosophy. On March 21, he was married by Father Krebs in a Catholic ceremony; his wife Elfride later reported that already at that time his faith was undermined by doubts.[4] Hermann Süskind's book, *Christianity and History in Schleiermacher*, was an Easter gift in April (the 20th) from Heidegger to a friend.[5] For a belated celebration of Elfride's birthday at the beginning of August, Heidegger gave a moving talk on the Second Speech from Schleiermacher's *On Religion* which his student and friend, Heinrich Ochsner, recalled for the rest of his life.[6]

These slim clues from 1917 may now be fleshed out by presuming that the advice Heidegger gives in the following year to Elisabeth Blochmann on how to read Schleiermacher for her dissertation approximates Heidegger's own encounter and reception of Schleiermacher in the previous year. Heidegger recommends that she first read Schleiermacher himself, especially his juvenilia, the Speeches on Religion, *Christmas Celebration* and the *Soliloquies*, and his correspondence in the Jonas / Dilthey edition, *The Life of Schleiermacher in Letters*. At first, all the secondary literature should be avoided except for Dilthey's genial first book, *Life of Schleiermacher*. Only toward the end should she concern herself with the "literature." Out of this, Heidegger singles out some works on Schleiermacher's philosophy of history, like that of Wehrung and Mulert. But the best one is by Süskind, "the docent in theology from Tübingen who unfortunately was killed at the beginning of the war."[7]

Süskind, Mulert, Wehrung—Weinel is named in a later letter—were all Protestant theologians active in a nondenominational movement then loosely characterized as "free Christianity." Its basic tenets, as articulated by Ernst Troeltsch in *Logos* 1 (1910/11), are 1) freedom of conscience and 2) development of the inner life.[8] Husserl regarded himself as a "free Christian." In a letter to Rudolf Otto on his two "religiously oriented"

students, Ochsner and Heidegger—"in Heidegger the theoretical-philosophical interest is predominant, in Ochsner the religious"—Husserl
writes: "I have not exercised the least bit of influence on Heidegger's
and Ochsner's moves over to the ground of Protestantism, although I
can only take great satisfaction in them as an 'undogmatic Protestant'
and a free Christian (by which I mean that someone has set an ideal goal
of religious longing for himself and understands it as an infinite task)."[9]

One might guess that the young Heidegger was predisposed to such
ideas ever since he left the seminary. His "modernist" leanings, reflected
in his modernizing approach to scholastic philosophy in the work on
Scotus, clearly flared in mid-1914 against an antimodernistic papal pronouncement on the strict adherence to Aquinas in Italian seminaries.
His bitterly cynical response to his confidant Krebs: "Perhaps you as an
'academic' could propose a better way, for those to whom it occurs to
have an independent thought, to have their brains removed and replaced
by Italian salad. To meet the demand for philosophy, for example, we
could set up automats in the train stations (gratis to those without
means)."[10] Such early attitudes are only intensified by Heidegger's voracious reading of more experiential approaches to religion like those of
Schleiermacher and his followers. By mid-1917, he no longer believes
in the corrigibility of the "dogmatic system" of scholasticism by authentic
religious experiences like those of medieval mysticism, as he had suggested in the habilitation's Conclusion in 1916. That his thoughts on this
at the time verged on the "embittered and barren polemic of an apostate"
is reflected in an undated note which he made for himself on the neo-
Kantian problem of the "religious apriori":

> And dogmatic and casuistic pseudo-philosophies, which pose as philoso-
> phies of a particular system of religion (for example, Catholicism) and
> presumably stand closest to religion and the religious, are the least capable
> of promoting the vitality of the problem. One is at a loss even to find
> the problem, since such philosophies are not familiar with anything like a
> philosophy of religion. For one thing, in the environment and complex of
> such systems the capacity to experience the different domains of value,
> the religious in particular, stagnates, owing to a complete absence of an
> original consciousness of culture. For another, the structure of the system
> has not accrued to an organic cultural doctrine. Hence, the inherent worth
> of the religion, its palpable sphere of meaning, must first be experienced
> through a tangled, nonorganic, dogmatic hedgerow of propositions and
> proofs which are theoretically wholly unclarified, which as a canonical stat-
> ute with police power in the end serves to overpower and oppress the
> subject and to encumber it in darkness. In the end, the system totally
> excludes an original and genuine experience of religious value.
>
> This is already implicit in the heavily scientific, naturalistic, and theoreti-
> cal metaphysics of being of Aristotle and its radical exclusion of the influ-

ence of Plato's problem of value, a metaphysics which is revived in medieval scholasticism and sets the norm in the predominantly theoretical. Accordingly, scholasticism, within the totality of the medieval Christian lifeworld, severely jeopardized the immediacy of religious life and forgot religion for theology and dogmas. This theorizing and dogmatizing influence was exercised by church authorities in their institutions and statutes already in the time of early Christianity. [In a situation like this,] an experience like that of mysticism is to be understood as an elementary countermovement.[11]

The young Heidegger looks to the mystical experience to "loosen" the subject from the System and to bring out an entirely different "motivational context in the experiencing subject" which would bring into view "the structural character of the unity of object and subject." This could then be resistant to the "rationalistic conquest of this atheoretical sphere" by the psychology of knowledge and metaphysics of the object operative in scholasticism. Except for the abandonment of all hope of revitalizing the System of scholasticism, such thoughts, in their concern for the experience of "value" in the context of "culture," in the sharp dichotomizing of rational and irrational ("What is the specific irrationality of this mysticism?"), still stand close to the very neo-Kantian Conclusion of the habilitation work, taking their cues from the "transcendental value-philosophy" of religion of Windelband and Troeltsch.

We also get a passing hint here of the young Heidegger's shift in interest from the medieval lifeworld to that of early Christianity, apparently also inspired by Schleiermacher and Dilthey. Dilthey authored not only *The Life of Schleiermacher* but also *The Story of Hegel's Youth*, that is, the story of Hegel's studies of the "positive religion" of early Christianity. What Heidegger took from this multifaceted inspiration is summarized in his own account in SS 1919 of the rise of the historical consciousness in the nineteenth century: "Schleiermacher saw for the first time the uniqueness and proper value of community and communal life and the special character of the Christian communal consciousness, he discovered primitive Christianity and influenced in a decisive way Hegel's youthful works on the history of religion and indirectly the whole of Hegel's specifically philosophical systematics, in which the decisive ideas of the German Movement came together as in its culmination."[12] A sense of the historical consciousness and its unique distillations, especially in primitive Christianity, the loss of its purity over the centuries, the close connection between theology and German philosophy—as Nietzsche put it, "contaminated by theologians' blood"—all of this throws some light on Heidegger's still cryptic explanation in his letter to Krebs: "Epistemological insights extending to the theory of historical cognition have made the System of Catholicism problematic and unacceptable to me—but not Christianity and metaphysics (these however in a new sense)." With these new readings, the thematic of a phenomenology of religion is assuming a much broader scope and depth in both philosophical and religious denomination.

Clearly then, Husserl is almost a year behind when, in a letter of October 8, 1917, responding to Natorp's question on whether the young Heidegger might be unsuitable for a position in Protestant Marburg because of "confessional narrowness," he writes that Heidegger indeed has confessional ties, since he had been proposed the year before for the chair in Catholic philosophy at Freiburg precisely because of his "appropriate religious affiliation." But Natorp's query itself, along with the news from the front that Husserl's assistant before the war, Adolf Reinach, had "fallen" (on November 16, 1917), may well have prompted Husserl to try to get to know Heidegger better both professionally and personally. Heidegger by then had broken with his neo-Kantian mentor, Rickert, and was "trying to come to grips with phenomenological philosophy from within."[13] Over two years later, Husserl feels compelled to write Natorp again in order to correct the false impression he had given of Heidegger in his first letter: "Allow me to inform you that, although I did not know it at the time, Heidegger had already freed himself then from dogmatic Catholicism. Soon after that he drew all the conclusions and cut himself off—unequivocally, energetically, and yet tactfully—from the sure and easy career of a 'philosopher of the Catholic worldview.' In the last two years he has been my most valuable philosophical co-worker."[14]

1918

1918 thus marks the year in which Husserl draws closer to Heidegger in a "συμφιλοσοφεῖν" (so in cards to Heidegger on January 30 and March 28) which ended in his nomination of Heidegger as his "phenomenologist of religion" (letter to Heidegger on September 10). It is probably through Husserl that Heidegger in June gets access to one of the typescripts (prepared by Edith Stein, then Husserl's assistant) of Reinach's fragments on the phenomenology of religion, written in his last months near the front lines.[15] For by this time, Husserl is grooming Heidegger to fill the gap left by Reinach's death. In turn, it is probably Heidegger who directed Husserl's attention to the phenomenological dimensions of Rudolf Otto's book, Das Heilige, which had appeared the year before. In the letter of September 10, Husserl writes: "I read . . . Otto's book on the holy with great interest; it is indeed an attempt at a phenomenology of God-consciousness, bold and somewhat promising in the beginning, but soon disappointing. Too bad that you have no time to write a thoroughgoing critique."[16] On the very same day, behind the front lines in France, Heidegger is reading Bernard of Clairvaux's Sermons on the

Song of Songs. He had also brought with him other books out of the mystic literature, like Teresa of Avila's *Interior Castle.* Months before, he had read Deissmann's studies on Pauline mysticism and the grammatically oriented question of what it means "to be in," in this case in the context of the biblical formula "Christ in me, I in Christ."[17]

1919

1919 Heidegger's letter to Krebs in January concludes with a profession of faith which is clearly accentuated by the tenets of "free Christianity": "I believe myself to have the inner call to philosophy. By fulfilling this call in research and teaching, I wish to do all that is within my powers for the eternal vocation of the inner man—and only for this—and so to justify my existence and my work itself before God." In the same letter, Heidegger notes that his studies in the phenomenology of religion, which will draw heavily on the Middle Ages, would demonstrate his continuing high regard for the "Catholic lifeworld." But as we might guess, this high regard is more for the religious-mystical tradition of the Middle Ages rather than its "scientific-theoretical lifeworld." In April, he concludes his course of the War Emergency Semester with an account of Husserl's "principle of all principles" which is charged with Eckhartian nuances of a dedicative submission (*Hingabe*) to the subject matter and an "intuition" which is not just knowing but more a "phenomenological life in its growing intensification of itself" (ZBP 110). Upon completing this first semester of teaching as Husserl's assistant, he describes his working life to Blochmann: "My own work is quite concentrated, fundamental, and concrete: basic problems of phenomenological methodology, disengagement from the leftover residue of acquired standpoints, ever new forays into the true origins, preliminary work on the phenomenology of the religious consciousness, disciplined preparation in order to attain an intensive and qualitatively high academic effectiveness, constantly learning in my association with Husserl."[18] From this we gather that Heidegger is now getting serious about putting his sundry notes of 1917–18 together into a full-length treatment of the phenomenology of religion. In August, with the end of the summer semester, he begins work on his two-hour course announced for WS 1919–20 with the title, "Philosophical Foundations of Medieval Mysticism." At the end of the month he writes to the dean requesting that it be replaced by another two-hour course entitled "Basic Problems of Phenomenology." The reason given is the lack of time to prepare for it in an already crowded academic year.[19] The early hours of the replacement course abound in examples drawn from the history of Christianity: Luther's personal copy of the Epistle to the Romans, whose marginalia turned out to be the notes for Luther's courses, to illustrate the sudden access to a past world; the lives of Jesus and Luther as examples of a self-world explored by biographical research, and then the "history of research into the 'life of Jesus' " (a veiled allusion to the then popular book by Albert Schweitzer) or the history of Luther research.

Heidegger concludes this particular course-hour with an extended example which will prove decisive for the coming years, by noting that the very emphasis on the self-world in the factic experience of life takes its starting point in the history of ideas from the experience of the early Christian community. But this Christian insight into the inner life of the self in pursuit of a Kingdom "not of this world" was from the start subjected to distortion and concealment by the "worldly" categories of ancient philosophy or "dogma" (Harnack's thesis). It therefore had to be constantly renewed and reasserted, as in Augustine, Luther, and Kierkegaard. Medieval mysticism can only be understood in such uniquely Christian terms. Augustine's *Confessions* penetrates much more deeply into the self-world than Descartes, for example, who takes his starting point from modern science. Augustine's *inquietum cor nostrum* (our restless heart) gives life a distinctly different accent. His *crede ut intelligas* (Believe so that you may understand) means that the self must realize itself in the fullness of life before it can truly know.

One thing that Heidegger does not tell his class is that this brief reading of the history of ideas comes in large part, sometimes almost word for word, from two short chapters of Dilthey's *Introduction to the Human Sciences*.[20] Heidegger returns to these pages in his course on Augustine in SS 1921 to note the second discovery of primitive Christianity which surpasses Greek philosophy: In addition to providing a model for the inner life of the Christian, the personality of Jesus possesses a new, historical life of its own. The fact that God reveals himself as a historical reality in a "redemptive history" (*Heilsgeschichte*) takes Him out of the merely theoretical transcendence of Platonism and places Him in the thick of history. Christianity therefore gives rise to the "historical consciousness" in the West as well as to our sense of a self-world.

1920–21

The two religion courses—WS 1920–21: "Introduction to the Phenomenology of Religion" and SS 1921: "Augustine and Neoplatonism"—mark the culmination of Heidegger's efforts toward a phenomenology of religion. After the second course, Heidegger makes a "confession" to Karl Löwith which provides a revealing self-portrait of his fundamental orientation during this entire phase of religious concerns of 1915–21. Löwith had just finished his second year of study with Heidegger and took the occasion to assess his relationship to Heidegger in contrast with Oskar Becker's, then also an advanced student: While Becker especially appre-

ciated Heidegger's emphasis on science and method in phenomenological concept-formation, Löwith preferred the "existentiell pathos"; in
short, the "subjective" side of Heidegger rather than the "objective" aspects. Heidegger responded by noting that each takes something from
him which is not of the essence, since the two aspects belong together
in a deeper motivation of his factic existence which neither sees or would
ever accept:

> I work concretely and factically out of my "I am," out of my intellectual
> and wholly factic origin, milieu, life-contexts, and whatever is available to
> me from these as a vital experience in which I live. . . . To this facticity of
> mine belongs what I would in brief call the fact that I am a "Christian
> theo*logian.*" This involves a particular radical personal concern, a particu-
> lar radical scientificity, a strict objectivity *in* the *facticity;* in it is to be found
> the historical consciousness, the consciousness of "intellectual and cultural
> history." And I am all this in the life-context of the university.[21]

Heidegger a "Christian theo-logian"? The underscoring of "-logian" in
fact shifts the focus to the philosophical foundations of theology in the
fundamental experiences which phenomenology aims to explore.
Whence the importance of the phenomenology of religious life and consciousness at this stage of Heidegger's development. This involves not
only the "personal concern" brought to its extremity in his personal crisis
and break with the religion of his youth, or the "radical scientificity"
of phenomenology's return to origins. Both are closely linked to the
consciousness of an "intellectual and cultural history" in which philosophy and theology have been deeply intertwined, in which philosophy
(Greek, scholastic, modern) had contributed to a degeneration of the
original Christian experience while at the same time nourishing itself
from that experience. His reading of Dilthey, Schleiermacher, Augustine, Eckhart, Luther, and Kierkegaard had taught Heidegger how deep
the interchanges between philosophy and theology really were up to his
day in their common concern for the "problem of Christianity,"[22] in
particular in its relationship to history and the historical consciousness.
With his special background, Heidegger must have felt uniquely drawn
to a history of philosophy that just happened to be thoroughly permeated
by Christianity. Yet the letter says almost nothing about his being Christian, but instead returns again and again to the stress on scientificity,
objectivity, conceptual labor, the life of research and inquiry, which in
turn is then equated with the personal pathos springing from his own,
very historical and temporally particular facticity. In this autobiographical context of distinguishing himself from his two top students, one
senses Heidegger's growing sense of the unique radicality of the objectivity (*Sachlichkeit* versus *Objektivität*) of the phenomenological way of doing

philosophy. The second half of the letter returns again and again to the difference between an "in-itself objectivity" and one's own temporally particularized facticity:

> You each take from me something other than what is of the essence, what I do not separate, what for that matter is never in a state of equilibrium, namely, the life of scientific research—working with theoretical concepts—and my own life. The essential way in which my facticity is existentially articulated is scientific research, done in my own way. Accordingly, the motive and goal of philosophizing is for me never to add to the stock of objective truths, since the objectivity of philosophy, as I understand it and by which I factically proceed, is something proper to oneself. This however does not exclude the strictest objectivity of explication; that for me is implied in the very sense of my existence. Objective strictness does not relate to a thing but to historical facticity. . . .
>
> Even in the destruction I do not want or dream of an objectivity in itself. It is my facticity which is "foisted" thereupon, if you will. It is simply a matter of whether a purportedly impersonal stance accomplishes more than going after the things directly, where we *ourselves* must obviously *be involved*—otherwise there is no engagement. We are then objectively one-sided and dogmatic, but philosophically still "absolutely" *objective and strict*. . . .
>
> It is only crucial that we agree that what counts is for each of us to go to the radical and utmost limit for what and how each understands the "one thing necessary." We may be far apart in "system," "doctrine," or "position," and yet *together* as only human beings can really be together: in existence.[23]

The drift of this personal letter is of import for Heidegger's thought in many ways, not the least of which is the "an-archic" sense of philosophical community sounded in the last paragraph. In the light of this "proper" sense of phenomenological objectivity, Heidegger will in the ensuing years articulate, for example, the unique occasionality or insuperable "temporal particularity" (*Jeweiligkeit*, in SS 1923) of Dasein and the inescapable ontic founding of ontology (*Being and Time*, 1927). But this particular letter is also of utmost importance for the Tale being told here. For it tells us that, in telling the tale of Heidegger's philosophy, we cannot in principle afford to dismiss the biographical element as fortuitous and so irrelevant, contrary to the pronouncements of would-be purist Heideggerians. For Heidegger himself tells us here that his thoughts stem directly from the deepest motivations of his *own* factic situation, in short, that his thought stems from his life and that one can therefore not divorce the ontological (his philosophy) from the ontic (his biography).

At the beginning of his Way, we must therefore take into account this reciprocity between biography and philosophy and seek to understand philosophically Heidegger's peculiarly personal engagement with his

Christianity, marked by the three autobiographical statements available to us near the beginning and the end of his career: "Epistemological insights extending to the theory of historical cognition have made the System of Catholicism problematic and unacceptable to me—but not Christianity and metaphysics (these however in a new sense)" (1919), "I am a 'Christian theo*logian*'" (1921), and "Without this theological provenance I would never have come onto the path of thinking" (1959). From this, I would suggest that the three experiential parameters motivating Heidegger's problem situation by 1919 are Christianity, history, and radical phenomenology, to be understood as one. At this point, Heidegger will not be satisfied with a mere phenomenology of religion; he is really after a phenomenology of Christianity in its historical particularity, whose experiential logos is to be explicated through the radical questioning dictated by the phenomenological approach. His "Concluding Remark" at the end of his one course on the Phenomenology of Religion is especially revealing in this regard:

> Genuine philosophy of religion does not originate from preconceived concepts of philosophy and religion. Only a *particular* religiosity (for us the Christian) yields the possibility of its philosophical apprehension. Why precisely *Christian* religiosity constitutes the focus of our reflection is a difficult question, which can only be answered by a solution to the problem of our *historical* connections. It is the task of arriving at a *genuine* relationship to history, which is to be explicated from our *own* facticity. The question is what the sense of history can mean for us such that the "objectivity" of the historical "in itself" disappears. For there is a history only when it stems from a present, our present.[24]

Heidegger's personal pathos for his own Christian facticity is still clearly in evidence here. A year later, a new phase is inaugurated when the more formal pathos of *radical questioning* ("skepsis") as such wins out over any specific content or "worldview," especially the Christian, and that passion is itself called the "fundamental atheism indigenous to philosophy." Some years later, we come full circle when the very same pathos of "atheism" or "skepsis," which is rooted in the ever-provisional and temporally particular character of the matter under question by phenomenology, is called the "piety of thinking."

RELIGIOUS EXPERIENCE AS A PHENOMENOLOGICAL PARADIGM (1917–19)

Our first task here is to fill in the above biographical framework with philosophical substance, to the extent that this is possible from the available archive material. To begin with, we are interested in summarizing the drift and specifying the most salient points, from the sparse evidence available to us, of the virtually unknown initial phase (1917–19) of Heidegger's reflections on the phenomenology of religion, culminating in his abandoning plans for a course on medieval mysticism in WS 1919–20. It is a period marked first by the divestiture of "acquired standpoints," most notably Catholicism, which the religiously oriented young Heidegger (an orientation in which, as Husserl put it, "the theoretical-philosophical interest predominates") practically identifies with scholasticism; and second, by the neo-Kantianism of his student years. More positively, it is a period of the radicalization of Heidegger's sense of phenomenology and the phenomenological structure of immediate experience with the help of the atheoretical paradigm of religious experience, beginning with the mystical experience. Our biographical chronology has yielded some clues into the young Heidegger's philosophical progress during this period of divestiture. We wish now to provide a more conceptual account centered upon the young Heidegger's extant notes of 1917–19 toward a Phenomenology of Religious Consciousness and Life, in a thematic continuity which is more or less chronological in progression, to the extent that this can be ascertained.

Scholasticism and Mysticism

The problem of remotion from life through theory, whose tendency toward "un-living" (*Ent-leben*, a term coined in KNS 1919) phenomenology seeks to counteract, is already clearly identified in the habilitation's Conclusion. Heidegger's proposed antidote for a "theory divorced from life" (FS 350, 352) in 1916 is a return to the "living spirit" in the fullness of its accomplishments. Specifically, this means a return to its history, understood in neo-Kantian fashion as a teleology of culture manifesting itself not only in the theoretical domain but also in the nontheoretical domains of ethical, aesthetic, and religious value. The charge of theoretical remotion applies "to some degree" to medieval scholasticism, but Heidegger's entire dissertation on Duns Scotus—selecting him rather than Aquinas is already symptomatic—was designed to show that there was more involved here than the abstract logic and grammar of the Schools. "The very existence of a theory of speech significations within medieval scholasticism manifests a refined disposition toward a direct attunement to the immediate life of the subjectivity and its immanent contexts of meaning, without however arriving at a sharp concept of the subject" (FS 343). In fact, Heidegger's discovery of a *modus essendi activus*, of a subject or an act character on the level of immediacy in the Scotian texts, is to provide the basis for a deeper study of the "fundamental correlation of object and subject" (FS 344, 262) within "Eckhartian mysticism" (FS 344n). Such a study would take us to the heart of the medieval lifeworld, which is based on the "transcendent primal relationship of the soul to God" (FS 351). At least Scotian scholasticism and Eckhartian mysticism can thus be reconciled, and their pairing does not coincide with the opposition "rationalism-irrationalism" (FS 352). Both belong together and cannot do without each other in the medieval worldview. As a "Catholic phenomenologist," the young Heidegger is clearly content to work within the System, despite the obvious problems with scholasticism, which so often seems like a "rationalistic structure divorced from life" (FS 352).

Months after writing this Conclusion, Heidegger allows the latent discontent that it harbors toward scholasticism to take the upper hand. What reasons does he give for going against the System? In view of its dogmatic inflexibility, the System has over the centuries failed to adjust to cultural history and thus stagnated. It is therefore incapable of responding to the history of a problem in all its vitality, especially to the problem of religious experience. Its exaggerated orientation toward the theoretical makes it forget religion for theology and dogmas. Such an attitude constitutes a hazard to the immediacy of religious life. Rather than a cooperation, Heidegger now sees a competition and antagonism against mysticism on the part of medieval scholasticism, which was accordingly bent upon "the rational conquest of this atheoretical sphere." This built-in tendency toward theorizing and dogmatizing stems from Greek philosophy, which in the hands of institutional clerics had already wreaked havoc on the genuine insights of primitive Christianity. The System in fact is not only alien and oppressive to the religious subject; it simply has no sense of that subject at all.

In a situation like this, it is necessary to suspend the System and to bring a new context into play, one that belongs immediately to the subject and is open to the full scope of its accomplishments. The heart of such a motivational context of the experiencing subject is to be found in the "*structure* of the subject of mysticism." What exactly is the "*structural* character of the unity of subject and object" in mysticism? In view of the notoriously inchoate unity of the *unio mystica*—"I am He and He is I," he observes in the same context—Heidegger chooses the "rational" word "structure" quite deliberately. What then is the "specific irrationality" of such a mysticism? What is the "mystical-theoretical superstructure" of the "immediacy of religious experience, the unrestrained vitality of dedicative submission to the holy, the divine"? The answer is to be found in all that is involved in Eckhart's concept of "detachment" (*Abgeschiedenheit*), which describes the movement—in no way a theoretical process—of formation of the mystical subject by way of the return to its ground, origin, and root, and so to the ever increasing vitality of its inner life. The analogy of this movement to the intrinsic tendency of phenomenology is already apparent, and will soon become more so.

It is purportedly the "formless" character of mysticism which makes it irrational. And yet detachment, the movement of return to the intimate root, the vital origin or ground of the soul, does not deliberately seek to exclude form. Instead, it is a process of progressive suspension of multiplicity, particularity, and specificity. The process is essentially related to the ethical telos. For multiplicity disperses and thus makes for vacillation and unrest, which is unworthy of an ethical life. Since the religious life seeks the most worthy object of all, it must exclude all variety, opposition, and particularity. This evacuation of all particularities from the form is accordingly a movement toward the general, the universal. The primal object par excellence—the Absolute—is accordingly an empty form, or "the God-ignited emptiness of form," the indefinable free of all determination. The form of objectivity as such becomes the absolute object. The absolute value coincides with absolute oppositionlessness, devoid of all determination. "The fewer distractions offered by its content to the apprehension that captivates and leads us astray, the purer and more worthy the object."

According to the basic principle that "the like is known by the like," what then is the mystical subject correlated with this absolute object? "You can only know what you are." In the movement back to its ground, the subject itself undergoes a de-particularization, and its particular powers are no longer taken in their particularity. Accordingly, the problem of the priority of the intellect versus the will, which Eckhart himself still tried to resolve, no longer belongs in this sphere. What happens, for example, to the "problem of the universals" in this atheoretical sphere, whose motivational context derives from the vital religiosity of the living subject? For the "abstraction" of religious detachment outstrips that of the theoretical. The scholastic psychology of knowledge and its concomitant metaphysics of objects, in its quest for rational conquest, here encounters its limits. The here and now, space and time, are the forms of multiplicity and opposition, and so do not prepare a place for the supratemporal "eternal now" (*nunc stans*). Sensibility thus does not belong to the subjective correlate of absolute objectivity, nor does the judging intellect in its diremptive activity. We are here at the intimate "heart and core" of the union of intentionality. The absoluteness of object and subject yields a certain reductive unity in which "I am He and He is I," and both God and the soul's ground are "rootless," without origin.

The young Heidegger tries to come closer to this vital center of intentionality, reflecting on the "primal sense of spirituality in its central vitality,"[25] by a reading of two of Meister Eckhart's tracts, "The Signs of a True Ground" and "On the Birth of the Eternal Word in the Soul." He makes note of only three of the twenty-four "sensible signs": right countenance (*rehte minne*, the first sign), letting all creaturely things "stand by themselves" (no. 13), and the fact that the masters of the higher wisdom "have few words and much life" (no. 17). For God's birth "releases the spirit from the storms of creaturely unrest into His still and silent unity." But what interests Heidegger most is the question of the place (*stat*) or power in the soul in which the eternal Word is most truly born. Is it in the reason, which is most like unto God? Is it in the will, which is a free power of the soul? Is it in the soul's spark, which is nearest to God? Is it in the concealment of the heart (*gemüet*), which is most at home in the mystery of God? Meister Eckhart opts for a fifth place. The Word is born in the innermost essence of the soul, where all the powers of the soul are preserved essentially "in a divine taste," where the reason has entry into the divine good, free will tastes the divine good, the soul's spark is a light of divine likeness which at all times inclines toward God, and the concealment of the heart is a gathering of all divine goods and gifts in the innermost essence of the soul. The soul itself is here, in this *stat*, a bottomless wellspring of every divine good. Finally, does the spirit have a knowledge of God's activity in it? There are sensible signs, as already noted, and yet in the birth itself, "the spirit is alienated from all the signs of creatures and stands (*stât*) in a naked intuition of the first truth."

Wilhelm Windelband

This birth of the Word, for the soul a rebirth which brings it to its vital center and still point, is Eckhart's famous experience of "breakthrough." The term was often invoked in a philosophical milieu thoroughly steeped in the works of this precursor "master" of the German language. Heidegger himself invokes it in the habilitation's Conclusion to characterize the ultimate aim of philosophy as "a *breakthrough* to true reality and real truth" (FS 348). One therefore cannot discount the possibility that such a conception of the teleology of philosophy is in fact the religious apriori then sought by neo-Kantian philosophy. At first, of course, philosophy for the neo-Kantians is not metaphysical but instead "critical," such that the breakthrough that it seeks is not toward reality but toward reason. It is not after what actually is but what ought to be, those normative values in each of the spheres of human activity—cognitive, practical, emotive—which are universally valid even when they are not in fact so acknowledged. Thus the "fundamental fact of philosophy" is the "conviction" (!) that "there are" (*es gibt!*) such norms. "Philosophy is thus the science of the normative consciousness. It searches through the empirical consciousness in order to establish the points of saliency within it where such a normative universal validity 'leaps out.' " Working on the basis of the conviction that "here and there" within the movements of natural necessity of the empirical consciousness a higher necessity "now and then" appears, "philosophy looks for those points at which such a necessity breaks through."[26] Thus, Windelband's teleological conception of the history of philosophy, which the young Heidegger makes his own, is oriented especially toward such occasional breakthroughs to the consciousness of universal norms.

It is the later Windelband's essay in the philosophy of religion, "Das Heilige," which in its idealistic way first "lifts" the distinction between being and value, what is and what ought to be, the metaphysical and the critical. The holy is here identified as the goal, norm, and ideal of religion, the absolute telos which comprehends all the other values. It is moreover not just the unity of the true, the good, and the beautiful, but also their reality. "The holy is thus the normative consciousness of the true, the good, and the beautiful experienced as transcendent reality." Religion is transcendent, meta-physical life. Thus, at the very limits of the reflection carried out by the critical sciences of values (logic, ethics, aesthetics), there emerges a belief in the really real, "the conviction that the norm of reason is not our invention or illusion, but rather a value which is grounded in the ultimate depths of the reality of the world."[27]

While noting the overly rational tone of these formulations, which move in the direction of the Platonic metaphysics latent in neo-Kantianism since Lotze, Heidegger nevertheless quotes such passages with approval. However, he cautions against taking the holy simply as a summation of the normative achievements of the three psychic functions of intellect, will, and feeling (religion has no psychic function of its own!), namely, the true, the good, and the beautiful. Such a tendency is implicit in some of Windelband's formulations, for example: "The holy . . . is to be defined by the totality (*Inbegriff*) of the norms which guide logical, ethical, and aesthetic life. . . . These are holy . . . as the value-contents of a higher rational reality."[28] In retrospect, it is odd that Heidegger does not mention Windelband's emphasis on the "conscience," the "divided consciousness" which is the locus not only of religion but of all critical philosophy, while citing passages like the following: "This antinomic coexistence of the norm and its contrary [natural necessity] in the same consciousness is the primal fact, which can only be pointed out but never conceptualized: out of it, all the problems of critical philosophy arise. . . . It is the problem of all problems as well as the springboard of the philosophy of religion."[29]

As promised in the essay's subtitle, "Outline for the Philosophy of Religion," Windelband then proceeds to sketch, on the basis of the religious apriori of the holy, the full gamut of problems of this discipline within a clear-cut Kantian schema of dialectics. It begins with the "aesthetic" of the "transcendent feeling" of "utter dependence" (Schleiermacher), develops four types of "transcendent representation," and culminates in "transcendent willing." After Rudolf Otto later that year published his book bearing the same title, *Das Heilige*, Heidegger in his projected review planned a comparison of it with Windelband's essay. For Windelband's outline of groups of problems is based on almost the same spectrum of religious phenomena as Otto's, all of them to be centered in the holy. Such a structural comparison presumably would have highlighted the uniqueness of the holy over against its interpretation as a composite of the true, the good, and the beautiful.

A Historically Oriented Phenomenology of Religion

A curious aftereffect from his neo-Kantian years is that Heidegger, long after he had weaned himself away from Windelband's simple teleological conception of history oriented toward reason alone, still retains the neo-Kantian division of values in the form of a plurality of "lifeworlds," the scientific, ethical, aesthetic, and religious. Religion, like any lifeworld, can acquire its shape and structure only in the historical consciousness, whereby it comes to a totality (not universality) which bears the unique sense of its particular domain of value. The historical is accordingly one of the most significant *founding* elements of meaning in the religious experience. The religious lifeworld is in its originality (i.e., irreducible to a theoretical theology) centered in a uniquely great historical figure, in the historical fullness of a personally efficacious life. Accordingly, the concept of a unique revelation (and so of a unique intuition) is constitutive of the essence of religion.

More precisely, the few great unique figures of living religion are to be evaluated with the elements of sense and experience that belong to the religious consciousness and not according to extrareligious or even "scientific" standards of "universal validity." The religious experience has its own intentionality, world, and so value, with its own requirements. The religious life must be maintained in its own vitality and not threatened by so-called "scientific worldviews." Even philosophy can hardly provide a legitimate standard of criticism.

For example, to analyze the nonintellectual phenomenon of faith (πίστις), one would separate and phenomenologically evaluate the material available from primitive Christianity and from the history of dogma. One would thus arrive at the phenomenon of "trust" (*Vertrauen*) and the specific sense of "truth" that it yields. It would still be a rationalizing of the religious experience of faith if the idea of the transcendental apriori is merely diluted in its theoretical nature by the addition of the idea of an "atheoretical validity." The phenomenological orientation is maintained in its radical moments of experience only when *intuition is not theoreticized* and the concept of essence is not rationalized in the direction of the idea of universal validity. One must reject the opinion that the suprahistorical sphere of essences, given in intuition, is an inherent enhancement of the particular experience. The experience is realized only in its particular experiential form, where the intuited itself assumes its fully novel and genuine world-character corresponding to its particular subjective comportment.

The fusion of the historical consciousness with phenomenological eidetics thus suggests a disciplinary organization in terms of historical worlds rather than the psychic functions of reason (Windelband). The religious lifeworld in particular, with no distinct psychic function of its own, serves to breach the old Kantian organization. Moreover, by late 1917, Heidegger's project of a phenomenology of religion is no longer restricted to the religious texts of the medieval lifeworld, but now covers the entire history of Christianity, with a decided preference for the period of primitive Christianity and a growing interest in the Reformation. Heidegger's reading list now includes studies on primitive Christianity by Bousset, Norden, Pohlenz, Weinel, and J. B. Weiss, and Jülicher's study on "The Religious Value of the Reformation."[30]

Faith

Two notes of Heidegger's readings on the phenomenon of faith are symptomatic of his first steps in this combined historical-eidetic approach. Seeking orientation in the available encyclopedia articles on "faith," he finds that the combined historical-systematic approach is already a staple in the Protestant theology of the day. The article in *Die Religion in Geschichte und Gegenwart* (2:1425–1461) in particular provides food for thought. Citing a passage in the Old Testament which identifies faith with unshakable trust and secure expectation, he makes a note to himself to read the psalms of trusting faith as opposed to the psalms of lamentation (1425f.). He likewise singles out for further study the two sections written by Ernst Troeltsch which relate faith to dogmatics and to history (1437–47; 1447–56), "where the analysis is to be sure quite deficient." Troeltsch begins by singling out, from the "totality of subjective religiosity better designated as 'piety' " (1437), faith as the "cognitive element of piety." Faith is "an act of trust and surrender (*Hingeben*), but to a reality comprehended in ideas" (1438f.). It is first faith in the hero who is the bearer of the revelation, then it becomes acceptance of the cognitive world whose revelation he embodies. Accordingly, Heidegger cites, "Faith is a mythic-symbolic-practical and uniquely religious way of thought and knowledge issuing from a historical and personal impression. It is a way of thought which believes in the mythos for the sake of the practical religious powers which it conveys, and which knows how to express, objectify, and communicate these powers only through the mythos" (1440).

To understand this complex of faith, Heidegger at this point appeals to some Husserlian notions borrowed from *Ideen I* (§§ 103-105, 139). Faith comprehends a manifold of modalities which cannot be put on the same plane like the species of a genus. Moreover, among these there is to be found an outstanding mode, a protobelief (*Urdoxa*) to which the others intuitively refer back in a specific way. Such modalities of belief are in turn correlated to modalities of being.

Troeltsch also notes that Protestantism makes faith central as the practical knowledge of God and so the source of all ethicoreligious impulses and ideals, whereas Catholicism separates belief as "holding for true" from practical, ethical, and sacramental comportment (1439). Heidegger makes the same distinction in similar terms in a remarkable note—it is the only one in the entire file to which he affixed his signature!—in 1919: Faith in the two denominations is fundamentally different, noetically and noematically radically distinct experiences. The "holding for true" of the Catholic faith is founded in a totally different way than the *fiducia* of the Reformation. The religious contexts of meaning in primitive Christianity are again qualitatively different, where the development of theology and its relationship to faith is motivated in a different way.

The other note from 1917–18, entitled "the *giving* character of the phenomenon of faith," in fact takes us back to early Christianity, and records Heidegger's fascination with Adolf Deissmann's work on Pauline mysticism.[31] The key to Paul's piety is his communion with the living Christ, described by him in the formula, "Christ *in* me, I *in* Christ." The question here—what does it mean to be "in"?—recalls later developments in Heidegger. Phenomenology would ask what sort of intentional relation this is. Deissmann answers by invoking the pneumatic Christ "*in* the Holy Spirit," how this works "*through* Christ," how the "faith *of* Jesus Christ" transcends the distinction of genitive subjective and objective toward a unique "genetivus mysticus." Faith then becomes the giving source of " 'Christ-power' flowing through Paul and radiating from him" (p. 93). Heidegger resolves to study the entire dynamics and structure of "Christ-faith" and to compare the piety of "Christ-mysticism" with that of Greek mysticism (by way of Reitzenstein's work).

Hegel

Clearly, faith in the unique historical personage of Jesus yields a protobelief far removed from a faith in the universal validity of reason central to the Kantian tradition. The young Heidegger notes in particular the decisive influence of Kant on "Hegel's original and earliest position toward religion, and its consequences." Hegel follows Kant in ruling out from the start an immediate relationship to religion, one founded upon an original experiential relation to the holy. The Enlightenment had already distinguished a rational religion from a positive religion, "which receives its sanction from the authority of its founder," and Lessing had provided its major premise: eternal truths cannot be authenticated by historical traditions. Thus the young Hegel, in his tract on how Christianity was transformed from a rational religion into a positive religion, writes: "Eternal truths are of such a nature that, if they are to be necessary and universally valid, they must be based on the essence of reason alone and not on phenomena of the external world which for reason are mere accidents."[32] Revelation in religion comes not from above or the outside but from the "moral law within." Accordingly, "the aim and essence of all true religion"—its protobelief—is "human morality," and all the other goals that it contains must be evaluated in terms of this one. To understand Jesus, one must first see that he sought "to raise religion and virtue to morality."[33]

For the young Heidegger, this degradation of the immediacy of religion to a means is decisive for Hegel's entire further intellectual development, which accordingly must be traced and critically depicted along these degenerative lines. Also to be explored is the question of the extent to which the problem of the historical is thus forced to take a certain course, such that its originality must itself become a philosophical problem.

It is Hegel's older contemporary, Schleiermacher, who keeps the question of the immediacy of religious experience alive for future generations to explore, especially in its more e-motive aspects.

Friedrich Schleiermacher

The need to appreciate religion on its own terms and so the necessity of isolating the specifically religious element of experience makes Schleiermacher's Second Speech, "On the Essence of Religion," a prime early example of a proto-phenomenology of religion. The "cultured" have come to "despise" religion because the complications of culture itself have transformed religion into something which it in essence is not. Religion has come to be regarded 1) as a form of thinking, a belief, a way of contemplating the world which culminates in a metaphysics; and 2) as a way of acting which develops into a morality. But these are but its external trappings. Neither its inherent theoretical nor its practical accompaniments exhaust the phenomenon of religion which in fact constitutes their underlying unity. Piety in essence is neither belief nor morals, neither metaphysics nor ethics. By way of this "sharp contrast," "religion provisionally renounces all claims to everything that belongs to science and morality. It wishes to give back all that it has borrowed from them, all that has been forced upon it, in order to take possession of its own original domain and disclose its peculiar character." Heidegger regards this as a form of ἐποχή which serves to "switch off" and so sort out the various "teleologies" normally operative in and with religion. "For the measure of knowledge does not match the measure of piety" (German 183f/English 35).[34] In the young Heidegger's neo-Kantian framework, these "teleologies" have different "criteria of value." Religion aims not at the true or the good, but at the holy.

Simply from what he excerpts from the text, it is clear that Heidegger especially approves of severing religion from every vestige of the metaphysics of God known from nature, where He is "posited as the ground of all knowing and that which is known." "And yet, even without having anything in common with such knowledge, the essence of religion is known. . . . This is not the way in which the pious have God and know him. . . . For contemplation is essential to religion, and you would never call anyone pious who went about in impervious stupidity" (184/35f.). What is this "contemplative" knowledge which is proper to piety? Schleiermacher's answer in the Second Speech is as direct as it is startling: "The contemplation of the pious is but the immediate consciousness of the universal Being of everything finite in and through the infinite . . . to have life itself and to be familiar with (*kennen*) it in immediate feeling only as this Being, that is religion" (185/36). This is equivalent to two other formulas used in the Second Speech, where religion is described as the "sense and *taste* for the infinite" (cf. Eckhart above) and as the "immediate life in us of the finite as it is in the infinite." Schleiermacher deliberately chooses the vague formula "infinite Being" in order to hold in abeyance any consideration of the various ways of conceiving the relation between God and the world, "which does not belong here and would have only limited the horizon in a harmful way." This for Heidegger is but another example of the phenomenological bracketing of an alien teleology, suspending perhaps the most dangerous theoretical tendency of them all.

But in order truly to comprehend the unity and difference of religion in its relationship to metaphysics and morals, it is first necessary to

descend into the inmost sanctuary (*Heiligthum*) of life. . . . There alone will you find the original relation of feeling and intuition, from which alone this identity and difference is to be understood. But I must direct you to your own selves, where you must apprehend a living movement. You must know how to listen to yourselves in advance of your own consciousness or at least reproduce this state for yourselves from it. What you are to notice is the very becoming of your consciousness and not to reflect on a consciousness which has already become. Once you have made a given activity of the soul into an object of communication and contemplation, you are already within the separation and your thought can only comprehend what is separated. . . . Only a slight trace of the original unity could then be shown. But even this I will not despise, as a preliminary. (191/41f.)

In KNS 1919, Heidegger will make this seemingly impossible task of describing the original unity and movement of life the central task of phenomenology and defend its accessibility against the objections of Natorp. For the time being, he recommends the highly rhapsodic pages that follow in Schleiermacher's Second Speech, including the "love scene" passage, on the "first beginnings of consciousness" which in its immediacy is "raised above all error and misunderstanding" (191–194/41–44). The first task is to disclose an original life of consciousness, that of feeling, in which religion as a particular form of life realizes itself. Religion is the intuitive and affective relation of every experiential content to an immediate whole. Each individual is a part of that whole, the "universe," the "fullness of reality" experienced in its uninterrupted flow and activity in a "moment, charged with mystery, of undivided unity of intuition and feeling. For one is nothing without the other."[35] In the immediacy of that supercharged moment (*Augenblick*), every thetic character, every assertion of being is lacking in the noematic content of the experience. Since nothing is yet decided, the experiential fullness stands in a certain neutrality, no object has priority over the other. This is the specific "infinity" of the religious experience.

From the remainder of the Second Speech, the young Heidegger singles out two terms which will loom large for him in the ensuing years. *Hingabe*, dedicative submission, a term favored by Lask which Heidegger in KNS 1919 will use to describe phenomenological "intuition," is only by implication central in Schleiermacher. But Heidegger glosses one of its infrequent uses in the Second Speech in some detail, understanding it as "allowing oneself to be stirred by the originally unrestrained influx of fullness." Schleiermacher sees all of religious life to consist of two elements, "[1] that man surrender (*hingebe*) himself to the Universe and allow himself to be stirred by the side turned toward him, and [2] that he internally transmit this stirring, which is only one particular feeling, and incorporate it in the inner unity of this life and being. The religious life is nothing but the constant renewal of this process" (212/58). The religious life is therefore not governed by momentary feelings but by their integrity in the inner life, out of which action springs of its own accord "as a retroactive effect of feeling; but only action as a whole is to be a repercussion of the totality of feeling," while individual actions will still depend upon momentary feelings. It is not really a matter of "acting from religion or being driven to action by religion. . . . Piety and morals each form a series by itself and are two different functions of one and the same life. We must do everything *with* religion, not *from* religion. Without interruption, like a sacred music, the religious feelings should accompany our active life" (212f./59).

The second term of importance for Heidegger is Schleiermacher's sense of history, which "in its most authentic sense is the highest object of religion." "History in the most authentic sense is the richest source for religion, not because it governs and hastens the progressive development of humanity but because it is the greatest and most universal revelation of the innermost and holiest. But surely in this sense, religion begins and ends with history [and vice versa]" (238/80). All true history had a religious purpose and proceeded from religious ideas. History is always religious, and religion historical. Heidegger's veiled reference to the ambiguous version of this passage from Schleiermacher's first edition, readable in either direction ("mit ihr hebt sie [die Religion? die Geschichte?] an und endigt mit ihr" [100]), once again registers his fascination with the rise of the "historical consciousness" in nineteenth-century thought and its deeper roots in the rise of Christianity as a historical religion, a theme familiar to him first from Dilthey. He will soon have occasion to criticize Schleiermacher, along with many of his peers of the Enlightenment and, later, the neo-Kantians, for their overly Platonic interpretation of this relationship between history and the "religious apriori."

One sees the beginning of Heidegger's critique taking shape in an extended note on Schleiermacher's *The Christian Faith* §§ 3–4, which postdates the above selective reading of the Second Speech (by all accounts in the summer of 1917) by at least several months.[36] Here, Heidegger wishes to correlate the historical consciousness with Schleiermacher's characterization of piety "considered purely in itself . . . [as] a determination of immediate self-consciousness" or, as a contemporary had described feeling, as "the immediate present of the entire undivided Dasein" (8/7). As pre-objective, this unmediated self-consciousness lies at the basis of all our knowing and doing (13/11f.), and thus circumscribes the very sense of personal existence.

But what precisely constitutes the core of unity and continuity of such a personal consciousness, described in § 4 as the "self-identical essence of piety . . . the element common to all its ever so diverse expressions"? "Common to all those determinations in which a receptivity affected from somewhere predominates is a *feeling of dependence*" (15/13). But for Heidegger, this formulation comes too close to theoretical objectification, to a going outside of oneself in order to ascertain the relation of this objectified self to another. The direction suggested by "utter dependence" is too theoretically crude, taking us toward a rationalist theory of objectified being. That consciousness is "affected from somewhere" is only possible on the basis of a veritable openness (*Aufgeschlossenheit*,

Geöffnetheit) to value and primary meaning, a kind of "love" [care!] at the vital center of the personal existent. It is just such a personal being—and not a blank tablet, a filled ego, or a punctual self—which is capable of being developed, fulfilled, and elevated. The primary relationship of the soul to absolute spirit and vice versa must be interpreted dynamically, so that we arrive at a structure invested with possibilities of fulfillment of the most manifold kind. The "changing determination of ourselves" (14/12) means that our living consciousness is a constant succession from one situation to another. But even this is too much like a characterization of natural science. The connections are really built up from the basic structure and center of consciousness.

Here is where Husserl's concept of "founding" is an extraordinary step forward into the real connections involved. Situations can alternate on the basis of the contents of consciousness and its immanent contexts, or can be motivated by the particular stage achieved. Situations become more immediate when the particular experience achieves an originary and independent fulfillment of the stream of consciousness, thereby achieving a vitally rooted historicity. Consciousness is historical only in this moment of fulfillment (*Momenterfüllung*), and never in the reflection of the pure ego.

The pure ego is the constituting dimension, the form of the possibility of being affected and fulfilled. It is not a value-free affair, but it is also not a good, a valuable object. It is instead the primal form of openness to the worthwhile as such, stemming from an eternal nobility, an absolute honor in the order of the apriori of forms. Its essence is by no means to be found in the two elements of Schleiermacher's "temporal self-consciousness," that of "being able to posit itself" and of "having come to be from somewhere" (14f./13). Its ownmost primal ground is at once and in truth eternal call (*Beruf*) and vocation as the absolute constituent of spirit and life. As in Schleiermacher's schema, it is likewise "from an other" or "by an other," namely called, but whether it has "come to be" or how is really secondary—*anima naturaliter religiosa!* Accordingly, "having come to be from somewhere else" is not opposed to the consciousness fulfilled by norms. Rather, the pure I is the possibility (not logical but vocational) for a fulfilled consciousness to be historical. Fulfillment can be interpreted phenomenologically but not metaphysically, not in terms of the being of "having come to be." That there is something like this at all belongs to the essence and "possibility" of the living consciousness. It is in these terms that the concept of *intentionality* receives its truest interpretation as the primal element of consciousness. It is here first of all that any possible "having not posited itself thus" and accordingly "being affected from somewhere else" find its *ground*.

Adolf Reinach

The desire to preserve the intentionality of historical consciousness from metaphysical distortion also manifests itself in Heidegger's critique of Reinach's fragment on the phenomenology of religion. Reinach's front-line conversion in 1916 prompted him into a reading, in his spare moments from military duties, of texts in the philosophy of religion which included Schleiermacher's *The Christian Faith*. As a trained phenomenologist, he sought to articulate the range of religious experiences into the fundamental and the founded, for example, gratitude, veneration, and prayer derived from the fundamental feeling of utter dependence; or trust in God derived from the feeling of being sheltered by Him (note of May 19, 1916). We have already seen that Heidegger takes such founding relations to be essential aspects of the historicity of personal existence. Reinach's efforts toward a phenomenology of religion culminated in his most sustained fragment, written in late 1917, in which he sought to describe this experiential field of relations between man and God in terms of the metaphysical categories of the finite and the infinite, the relative and the absolute. A typescript of this fragment, which bore the title "The Absolute," came into Heidegger's hands in June 1918.[37]

Reinach begins with a crucial distinction. Among humankind, love, goodness, gratitude, and trust are subject to degrees. One can always imagine a love greater and stronger than it actually is . . . except for the love of God. Already in the direction of the act of gratitude toward God, there is an absolute difference when compared with gratitude toward humans. Compared with earthly love, which "stretches toward infinity," the love for God already "holds infinity within itself." No longer a relation between equals or toward inferiors, possible among humankind, the man-God relation is always that of an "absolute below" to an "absolute above." "Our position to God is decisive in providing the direction for our experiential comportment to Him." But what does "position to God" mean here?, Heidegger asks. For he finds the talk of "under," "over," and "next to" too ontic. Rather, he says, it is our experiential comportment to God which provides direction for the religiously specific constituting of "God" as "phenomenological object." Accordingly, the particular senses of this absolute are to be uncovered only in the specific structures of the constituting experiences, and shown with experiential character for the logical and ontological moments that disclose the element of being and the element of "no longer increasable." Concepts like "absolute," "highest measure," and "measure as such," developed by the constructive methods of rationalist metaphysics, are at first unsuitable for a genuine sphere of experience, unmethodologically applied a priori as if from above. The absolute is definable only within its particular sphere of experience, receives its full concretion within that sphere only by manifesting itself in its historicity, in the specific worldness of the religious sphere of experience.

Despite such methodological discrepancies, Reinach always lets the "weight of experience," varying in accord with the functional context, prevail. "Reality-taking is contained immanently in the experiential sense itself" (610). And in distinguishing three types of absolutes—God is given in absolute height; religious experience is directed toward absolute height; finally, the complete fulfillment of such formal absoluteness in the experiences of trust, gratitude, and love—Reinach speaks of "internally motivated transitions" among these experiential senses rather than some logically theoretical development. The phenomenon of motivation is thus clearly fundamental to the constitution of the historical consciousness. Here is also the real validity and significance of the "knowledge" already contained within religious experiences. The distinctive and wholly novel sphere of religious experiences must first be regarded in its own right, and not in analogy with the aesthetic sphere or any other domain of value. In particular, its primary sense of the historical consciousness must remain untouched by all "epistemological" skepticisms. In this context, Heidegger finds Reinach's distinction between explicit knowledge and experientially immanent (*erlebnisimmanente*) knowledge to be of special value, and copies the entire passage, as it applies to religious experience (but not the aesthetic introduction in square brackets), for future reference:

[The enjoyment of an artwork is not knowledge, but forms the basis and dispenses the knowledge that a picture is beautiful. Of course, one can always ask: Does not the knowledge "it is beautiful" have its own intuitive basis? We regard a perception differently in its relationship to a knowledge of reality, since such knowledge must always refer back to the perception for its confirmation. And yet the perception also contains a holding-for-real which is not really knowledge.] The feeling of security in God contains such a taking for reality in a very different way. Logically, it would be a presupposition for such a feeling. But no one would draw such a logical conclusion. Holding-for-real is instead immanently contained in the experiential sense itself. We must thereby separate two things, the knowledge of being secure and the knowledge of the existence of God, that is, an immediate and a mediately immanent knowledge. Only a mediate knowledge inheres in the experiences of gratitude and love; as attitudes, they are in a certain sense derivative experiences.

I experience my absolute dependence on God. Insofar as I myself take part in this experienced relation, the state of affairs does not stand before me. Instead, I experience myself in this relation, which naturally then cannot be objective for me. Thus also, when I perceive an object, the corresponding relationship between perception and object is not objective for me. To be sure, there is then a distinction to be made: In perception, there arises for me through reflection on it the knowledge that "I perceive." In the experience of dependence, I find myself dependent without needing a reflection, which in fact could also only lead to the knowledge that I feel myself dependent. . . . Absolute dependence, absolute security is not a "fact." (610f.)

Rudolf Otto

Otto's *Das Heilige* (1917) bears the subtitle, "On the Irrational in the Idea of the Divine and Its Relationship to the Rational." The way in which the distinction of rational and irrational is to be applied to the divine or holy is explained in the first two chapters, the only ones to which Heidegger's note refers.

The tendency of religious orthodoxy and even scholarship, say, in comparative religions, to explain the divine completely in concepts has caused us to lose sight of what is unique to the religious experience, even in its most primitive manifestations. If the holy is taken to be "a category of interpretation and valuation peculiar to the sphere of religion" (p. 5),[38] then the Kantian tendency to apply it in a moral (and so rational) sense to a "holy" will, and to speak of the "sanctity" of duty or law, is wholly derivative. The term "holy" indeed includes such moral connotations, but it also includes a "surplus of sense," which in the ancient languages was its only connotation. But since our present "feel" for the word "holy" necessarily includes moral connotations, Otto feels compelled to invent a new term to connote the "unique original feeling-response" proper to religion, as an aid in his "endeavor to suggest this unnamed Something to the reader as far as we may, so that he may himself feel it" (p. 6). Accordingly, the "numinous" is chosen to designate that "special element" in the holy, *minus* the moral and rational moment.

Admirable as he finds Otto's quasi-phenomenological attempt to single out the "thing itself" proper to religious experience, Heidegger in his "preliminary work toward a review of Otto, *Das Heilige*" now begins to express reservations about the neo-Kantian distinction which makes the irrational parasitic upon the rational, a distinction which he himself had used the year before in approaching the mystical experience. This "principle for posing the problem" is itself problematic when it comes to considering the religious domain in its originality and unique constitution. The irrational is still a "counterthrust" which concedes "who knows what" prerogatives to reason and "rational criticism."[39] The grafting of the irrational onto the rational must be resisted and shunned. A sounder methodological approach first requires true insight into the living consciousness and its original worlds, which are completely originary and yet have a common, albeit polyvalent rootedness in the basic sense of a genuine personal existence. Thus, in conjunction with the problem of the irrational, Heidegger wishes also to raise here the problem of the historical consciousness, "the consciousness of personal existence and its fulfilled originary sphere of life and, from there, the pervasive and predominant form of constitution as this relates to the remaining constellation of worlds," presumably the theoretical, ethical, aesthetic, and religious lifeworlds.

On the basis of the methodological foundation of the "historical consciousness" divested of the rational-irrational distinction, Heidegger then makes the following proposals: The holy cannot be problematized as a theoretical noema, or as a not yet theoretical, irrational one, but rather as a correlate of the act-character (noesis) "faith" (not the more intellectual "belief," as Otto discusses it), which in turn can only be interpreted in terms of the basic experiential context of the historical consciousness. Contrary to Otto, this does not mean that the holy is to be explained as a "category of evaluation" (*Bewertungskategorie*: pp. 5, 7). Instead, what is primary and essential in the holy is the constitution of an originary objectness subject to its own formal and functional categories. The purely holy must be distinguished from these already constituted worlds and their objects. If the numinous is the special element in the holy minus the moral and rational moments, do these nevertheless somehow belong to the originary structure of the numinous? What then would be the basis for such connections?

Bernard of Clairvaux

In the field near the front in September 1918, Heidegger finds time to scribble a phenomenological meditation on Bernard's *Sermons on the Song of Songs*, making use of only a few lines from Sermon 3.[40] He takes his phenomenological cue from the opening sentence, "Hodie legimus in libro experientiae" (Today we shall read from the book of our own experience), "Today we wish to move by way of apprehension in the field of personal experience." Each of us must return to his own life-sphere of experience and hearken to the testimony of his own consciousness. The articulations of one's own consciousness are granted exclusive worth and power in one's own religious experience. The claims of religious experience, the struggle for the presence of Jesus, can come only from a basic experience. One does not come to such experiences by the observance of ecclesiastical prescriptions. "Knowing" them in their essence comes only from actually having experienced them. Such an experience truly takes effect only in a closed experiential context and stream. It cannot be conveyed and awakened by description. "Est fons signatus, cui non communicat alienus" (It is a sealed fountain to which no stranger has access).

Moreover, "qui bibit adhuc sitiet" (he who drinks thirsts for more).

In other words, the noetic context of religious experience is constituted "historically." The basic experience is thus primary not only in time (this perhaps need not be the case) but in its founding character. The sense of direction and form of such a founding are essentially "historical," which does not yet imply that it is ultimate. But it is certainly independently primary. It therefore cannot be linked to the founding relations of theoretical acts, but must get its beginnings from primary origins. Methodologically, this *necessarily demands insight into the universal radicality of phenomenologically intuitive description and its presuppositionlessness.* But this itself, in view of the simplicity and directness of such an attitude, is for phenomenology the problem par excellence within the field of constitutions.

Four days later, Heidegger picks up his meditation where he had left off: What is the basic phenomenon within the entire field of historical knowing and formation? How is the sense and goal of its specific constitution of objects to be achieved? To be taken into account here are the constitutive elements of memory and its functional value in the objectifying process of historical knowing. This is connected with the originary constitution of values and their function and meaning for the "historical." The moment of excellence, rank, and advancement is not like a theoretical and indifferent object. Accordingly, the noetic moment of originary relatedness to this noematic moment points to a specific constitution of religiously primal experiences. There are immanent essential connections of levels: "Nolo repente fieri summus, paulatim proficere volo. . . . Citius placas eum, si mensuram tuam servaveris et altiora te non quaesieris" (I do not wish to be suddenly at the heights, my desire is to advance by degrees. . . . You will please God more readily if you live within the limits proper to you and do not set your sights on things beyond you). The superior, the "higher than you" should not be pulled down to oneself. The experiential realities of the religious should instead be allowed to grow steadily outward, letting the immanent connections take effect in themselves.

Before proceeding to the next note, which brings the series of loose notes during Heidegger's war interregnum to an initial climax, we might pause to reflect on the central theme which has been building since early 1917. Religious experience is "historical" because of the soul's progressive intimate movement of founding itself toward its religious heights. Even when this movement was first described by Eckhart's master term of "detachment," Heidegger was not unaware of the multiplicity of religious phenomena involved in this core movement. Some prefatory remarks on these at that time, in early 1917, will also serve to measure the distance he has now traveled from that starting point. Silence as a religious phenomenon is to be understood in connection with the problem of irrationality. The holy is encountered in rapt amazement and wonder (*ad-mira-tio*), adoration, silence, and ineffability. In the face of something which is "set off " [con-templated], all of these phenomena are phenomenologically related to a "higher than." Being thus raised up out of nothing and made to stand in the relief of being, each Dasein is bathed in a kind of brilliance. We thus move toward a *concept of primary brightness* (*Helle*), primary, that is, in terms of an order of value. How then is the problem of irrationality connected with the problem of being?

Although his positive orientation toward value will continue for a time, Heidegger has by now weaned himself from a sense of the irrationality of personal historical existence, especially in its connection with religious "mystical" experience, to what might be called its "hermeneutic rationality," as we shall see in the following note, which approaches the language of the course of KNS 1919.

Teresa of Avila

This brief meditation on Teresa's *Interior Castle* (*Seelenburg*, Las Moradas) is concerned especially with the phenomenon of inner composure and concentration in the "mystical site" of silence, its motivations and tendencies, in short, the problem of the "I-relation" in its history. Its solitude is a phenomenon of personal historical existence as such.

The basic tendency of life is toward "more-life." We start with receptivity, which itself is a "nothing which has become." We regard it as the originary activity of the religious world. On this basis, we can then determine the motivations of sense which enter into meditative prayer, which for Teresa is the door of entry into the interior castle. An originary phenomenon here is the process of constituting the "highest present" in the "stages of prayer." The first series to be analyzed is concentration, meditation, and prayer. Analysis here really means the *hermeneutics already at work in the historical I*. Life as religious is already there. The stream of consciousness is already religious; at least it is so motivated and "tended." It is not to be analyzed as a neutral objective consciousness. Rather, its specific determination of sense must be "heard out" (*herauszu-hören*). The first problem to be acknowledged accordingly is that the intuitive eidetic, as *hermeneutic*, is never theoretically neutral, but already contains "eidetically" (not a geometric eidetic) the "harmonics" (*Schwingung*, "swing") of its genuine lifeworld.

Since the stream of consciousness is already religious, Teresa, as a mystic, already sees phenomenologically. But she is too close to see eidetically, and so does not see the specifically religious eidetic. The soul is "somehow" the place for God and the divine (cf. Eckhart's *stat*), God's abode, and the point of the primal motivation of life. For Heidegger, therefore, the phenomenological Teresa is to be found in her master metaphor of the soul's relationship to God. He is obviously taken by the Eckhartian parallels of this extended metaphor of the interior castle of the soul and its many mansions, which Teresa introduces in the opening pages from which Heidegger cites.[41] "If any of you does not believe in such things [like the essence of God in the soul, the religious and holy as such: *sic* Heidegger], she will never learn it from experience. For the Lord has so ordained that no bounds be set upon his works" (203). Even so, "what I wish to explain to you is very difficult and obscure unless you have had personal experience" (205). We tend to be more interested in the outer wall of the castle, our bodies, and so do not enter the site which is ourselves. Our situation is more like the person who was asked who she was, and had no idea who her mother and father were and from what country she came. "At least we seldom take to heart the great goods there may be in our soul, or Who dwells in it, or the precious value it has" (202). Finally, she who enters the site of the soul must not imagine that its mansions are arranged in a single row, but must fix her attention on the innermost chamber occupied by the King of the castle, from which chamber she, in her inward journey, receives the comprehensive view of the whole (207f.).

There is scattered evidence that Heidegger continued to peruse the traditional devotional literature in his studies of the essential historicity of the religious experience. He makes passing reference to Francis of Assisi's *Regula* and *Fioretti* in his course of SS 1919 (ZBP 211), and Löwith reports that his Christmas gift from Heidegger in 1921 was Thomas à Kempis's *De Imitatione Christi*.[42] But Heidegger's reading of Augustine's *Confessiones* and his other works in mid-1919, prompted by Dilthey's reading of Augustine's role in the history of philosophy, takes him into a much more sweeping historical context, and to the historical origin of the paradoxical connection between Christian inwardness and the historical consciousness.

Dilthey on the Christian Experience

Ever since his days as a theology student, Heidegger had developed the habit of copying long passages from the then widely scattered works of Dilthey's opus.[43] The influence of especially the hermeneutical Dilthey upon the young Heidegger's reflections on Schleiermacher, on the hermeneutic character of the stream of experience, and so on is therefore a likely, but by and large still an undocumented, hypothesis. We get only occasional hints from this period of Heidegger's avid reading of Dilthey as a corrective to his former neo-Kantian mentors (ZBP 123, 125), especially on the distinction between the explanatory and the understanding sciences (ZBP 163–165, 207f.). It is therefore fortunate that we have Heidegger's excerpts from a scant two chapters of Dilthey's *Introduction to the Human Sciences* which, as already noted above,[44] overtly influenced his choice of themes and his reading of the history of philosophy in his courses of the next several years. The two chapters, on early Christianity and Augustine, are part of Dilthey's quasi-Comtean history of the progress from a "metaphysical" to an "epistemological" foundation of the human sciences. They characterize the "breakthrough" of Christian experience, with its emphasis on 1) the inner self and 2) the historical consciousness, which serve to breach the limitations of Greek cosmological categories (251/229). The early Dilthey still speaks here of an "epistemological" rather than a "hermeneutical" foundation in reference to this twin discovery made by Christianity, which was subsequently obfuscated by a relapse into Hellenic categories. This may also explain why Heidegger at that time might still point to *"epistemological* insights extending to the theory of historical cognition" as the source of his disenchantment with the *"System* of Catholicism." And the need for repeated renewal (*aggiornamento*) in Christianity, in figures like Augustine, Luther, and Kierkegaard, may have also been an early key alerting Heidegger to the need for a "destruction of the history of ontology," as portrayed by Dilthey precisely at its Greek and modern Cartesian junctures.

What was the original experience of Christianity, in contrast with that of the Greek cosmos and its human microcosmos? The kingdom of God is not of this world. The will is no longer satisfied with an artistic counterpart of the cosmic order projected in external political works, but instead goes back into itself. Lived experience itself became the focus of interest and new object of knowledge of the new communities. They sought the knowledge that grows from inner experience, from "becoming intimate" (*Innewerden*) with all that is given in the person, in self-consciousness. This awareness of self, of the inner experiences of the will and heart, and especially of the change occurring in the profoundest depths of the soul, is filled with a certitude which excludes all doubt. Heidegger here cites Dilthey's expression of regret that the medieval period, overwhelmed as it was by the "preponderant power of ancient culture," fell back on the objective cosmological categories available from the Greeks to express its new insight. It therefore never developed a human science based purely upon the self-certitude of this inner experience of religious life (251f./229).

It is also important to note from the start, against our ever-present Cartesian predilections, that self-certitude here first refers to the self-assurance of faith and not to the self-certainty of knowledge. "This intimate awareness includes not only thinking but the totality of my person" (260/234). Accordingly, the object of self-certitude is not knowledge but life, historical life, the totality of human experience. Moreover, from the beginning, Dilthey alludes to the self-renouncing tendency of the

Christian consciousness in contrast with the self-assertive drive of the modern consciousness, oriented as it is to scientific mastery. For Spinoza and the Greeks, divine/human perfection is the personal power that is already reflected in the starry skies above. In the Christian experience, the perfection of the deity itself is instead tied to servitude and suffering (251/228). God's kingdom is not of this world. This independence from all natural conditions of existence, this inner freedom attainable by all through faith and sacrifice, is to be distinguished from the inner freedom of the Stoics, which "was attainable only by the wise" (253/229).

These different movements which compose the common struggle to go beyond nature toward the inner freedom of faith—"self-sacrifice, recognition of the divine in pain and in lowliness, and sincere renunciation" (255/231)—are only some of the components of the historical consciousness which originated in Christianity. "Corresponding to all this were the notions of a genealogical continuity in the history of humankind and of a metaphysical bond which unites human society" (253/229). Heidegger composes his own list from this context: "kingdom of God, brotherhood of man, Christian community, sacrifice, inner freedom through faith [and finally the crucial one], God caught up in the historical life of Christ." "God's essence, instead of being grasped in the self-enclosed concept of substance of antiquity, was now caught up in historical vitality. And so *historical consciousness*, taking the expression in its highest sense, first came into being" (253f./230).

This was Paul's basic experience and his crisis of conscience, where "Jewish law, pagan consciousness of the world, and Christian faith clashed with one another" (254/230). He managed to fuse them together by reliving their history in himself, in such a way that the Jewish and pagan revelations were subordinated to the Christian as its preparatory stages. Heidegger cites:

> The struggle of religions with one another in the Christian life fulfilled by historical reality had produced the historical consciousness of a development of the entire life of the soul. For the perfect moral life cannot be represented to the Christian community in the conceptual formula of a moral law or a highest good; it was experienced by the community as an unfathomable living element [*ein unergründlich Lebendiges*] in the life of Christ and in the struggle of one's own will; it referred not to other propositions but to other figures of the moral-religious life who existed before it and among whom it now appeared. And this historical consciousness found a fixed external framework in the genealogical context of the history of humanity created within Judaism. (254f./231)

What is this "unfathomable living element" which constitutes the facticity of Christianity? "The deep mystery of this religion lies in the relation of the experience of one's own states to God's activity [1] in the heart and

[2] in destiny." Heidegger cites: "Everywhere we find revealed faith woven into the religious life to which, in the inner experiences of the will, God is given as will, person to person" (256/232).

Christianity's discovery of an "unfathomable living element" at the heart of self-examination (*Selbstbesinnung*) is at once the key to its break-through beyond Greek thought. For it exceeded even the insights of that master of self-examination, Socrates, whose method necessarily drew its universal concepts and its goals from the public life of the Greek people. "It does not dawn even in Socrates' self-examination that the external world is a phenomenon of self-consciousness, in which a being and reality is given to us, the knowledge of which for the very first time discloses an unassailable reality to us. . . . In his self-examination, there is still no inkling of an enormous reality emerging in self-consciousness, indeed the only one of which we are immediately and intimately aware; still less is there an inkling that every reality is given to us only in our lived experience" (178f./184f.).

This breakthrough contained within the Christian experience, espe-cially in the life of the heart and the will, was first made explicit by that later master of Christian inwardness and self-examination, Augustine. "Here at last an enormous reality emerges in self-consciousness, and this knowledge swallows up all interest in studying the cosmos. Hence this self-examination is not merely a return to the epistemological ground of knowledge, and what derives from it is not merely theory of knowl-edge [as in Socrates against the skeptics]. In this awareness, the very essence of *his self* occurs to a human, and his conviction of the reality of the *world* is at least assigned its place; above all the essence of *God* is apprehended in that awareness, indeed it seems to half uncover even the mystery of the Trinity" (260/234f.). Thus all of reality is accessible in and through the focus of lived experience. This is likewise the focus and central topic of Dilthey's lifelong labors and, after him, Heidegger's, who at that time (1919) was calling it "factic life-experience," and later, Dasein. Both Dilthey and Heidegger continued to be at a loss for words to name this "unfathomable living" dimension first discovered by Christi-anity, this "enormous reality emerging in self-consciousness." How to gain access to this immediate experience which is at once total and full reality, which in its immediacy precedes thought and is not even "given"? For to make lived experience a datum of consciousness is to interject the distinction between subject and object and so to destroy its immediacy. This is why the "living" is at once "unfathomable," why what is closest to us, what we experience most intimately, is at once most remote and alien.[45] The paradox is that this outwardness of inwardness at once makes it accessible. The "reality of the inner world" (257/233) is that it is at once a historical world which as such can be understood. At this point in his development, of course, Dilthey had not yet found his hermeneutic framework—also inspired by Christianity—of a life which is understandable because it always spontaneously expresses itself; instead, he still speaks in epistemological fashion of the need "to go back to an analysis of the facts of consciousness" (ibid.). This residual Cartesianism which Dilthey (e.g., in his notion of immanent perception) never completely shook off will be roundly criticized by Heidegger in his "destruction" of Dilthey in SS 1920.

It is important to note that the historical world is not the same as the natural world, which is the direction toward which some of the other Church Fathers inclined in order to explicate the Christian experience. And this other direction was the predominant one. Heidegger quotes:

> It has been the tragic fate of Christendom to remove the holiest experiences of the human heart from the quiet of a personal life and to make them part of the motive forces of world-historical mass movements, and to evoke mechanistic morality and hierarchical hypocrisy in the process. On the theoretical level it succumbed to a fate which weighed no less heavily on its further development. If Christianity wished to bring the content of its experience to full consciousness, it had to assimilate that content into the conceptual framework of the external world, which ordered it according to the relations of space, time, substance, and causality. Thus the development of this content [of inwardness] in dogma was at once its externalization. (258/233)

Dilthey thus portrays the genesis of a Christianity under the guise of an objective "authoritative System proceeding from the will of God" against which the young Heidegger had already rebelled. He notes its double source in the Roman spirit of legal formulas and the Greek genius which conceived the world in cosmological terms. Each provided its own tragic distortion. Christianity thus came down to us as a "new objective metaphysics" which in fact was but a "counterpart to antiquity." Such a repetition distorts the historical continuity of Christianity with its past by obfuscating its uniquely new insight which breached that past. Augustine's genius provides hope in restoring the lost uniqueness of Christianity, even though he too was subject to the same cultural forces, and so "marks the extreme limits of what was achieved in this [patristic] period" (ibid.).

One may now begin to see the importance of these few pages in Dilthey for Heidegger's immediate development. He summarizes them in his own way in the early hours of WS 1919–20, attributing to Christianity the discovery that factic life experience comes to a focus in the "self-world." His seminars of SS 1919 and WS 1920–21 deal with Descartes's *Meditationes*, with special attention to its religious significance.[46] A sudden change of plans in mid-course in WS 1920–21 finds him glossing, on a moment's notice, Paul's letter to the Galatians describing his crisis of

conscience divided between Judaic faith in the Law and the new faith
in Christ, along the lines already suggested by Dilthey. SS 1921 deals
with "Augustine and Neoplatonism," where the title-theme is concerned
with Augustine's eventual relapse into Greek cosmological categories.
But first, Heidegger glosses the Tenth Book of the *Confessiones* around
the central theme of "concern" (*Bekümmerung, cura*) over one's own life
as the fundamental drive of human life, a theme to which Dilthey only
alludes tangentially toward the end of his own gloss of Augustine (265/
237f on *Lebensdrang*, "the vital drive which motivates Augustine's affective nature"). Thus, as early as WS 1919–20, Heidegger supplements
Dilthey's epistemological focus on Augustine's *crede ut intelligas* with the
more bio-graphical and vitalistic theme of *inquietum cor nostrum* which
dominates Augustine's *Confessiones*, and "which gives life an entirely new
accent." And in SS 1925, upon introducing care as the basic structure
of Dasein, Heidegger recalls that "it was seven years ago, while I was
investigating these structures in conjunction with my attempts to arrive
at the ontological foundations of Augustinian anthropology, that I first
came across the phenomenon of care. Of course, Augustine and ancient
Christian anthropology in general did not know the phenomenon explicitly, nor even directly as a term, although *cura*, care, as is well known,
already played a role in Seneca as well as in the New Testament" (GA
20:418/302). Accordingly, correcting Heidegger's chronology slightly,
we find him already in mid-1919 gradually going a bit more deeply into
Augustine's regress from intellectual understanding to the life of faith,
from secure knowledge to restless life, "behind which thought cannot
go," from the theoretical to the pretheoretical—certainly more deeply
than Dilthey's more epistemological orientation, concerned as it was with
finding secure foundations for the human sciences in the self-certitudes
of lived experience, allowed him to do. While Dilthey insisted that the
human sciences be based on the full range of life-experience, especially
the religious experience (contrary to Comte), and was wary of the
transgressions of transexperiential meta-physical conceptualization uprooted from life in describing such experience, his very orientation toward the immediate knowledge of the "facts of consciousness" certified
by the self-assurances of faith lent itself to metaphysical distortion. In
short, Dilthey was much more concerned with the final cognitive achievements yielded by the Augustinian "religious-moral process of faith" (260/
235) rather than with the "facticity" of the process itself, that is, of the
"quest" for those assurances of faith and the initial interrogative situation
which prompts that quest.

Augustine on Faith-Understanding
Heidegger's reading of Dilthey's gloss on Augustine is accompanied by
a wide-ranging exploration of his own of Augustine's works, from which

he excerpts certain key passages beyond those noted by Dilthey, which on the whole suggest the direction of his own interests in Augustine. Thus, he gravitates toward chapter 10 of *On the Trinity*, which emphasizes the vitality of the conative or "erotic" aspects of the mind seeking to know itself on the basis of already being certain of itself and its desire to be and to know itself, a vitality which persists even (perhaps especially) when that knowledge is being tried by doubt. For "if he doubts, he lives; . . . if he doubts, he wishes to be certain; if he doubts, he thinks; if he doubts, he knows that he does not know. . . ."[47] And in the passage from *The City of God* (11.26) that Dilthey himself makes central, the most important, that is, the most vital, of the trinity of certainties is the third, the "erotic" element: "I am certain that I am, that I know that I am, and that I love to be and to know." With this deeper reason in mind, Heidegger can readily concur with Dilthey's conclusion that Augustine's self-certainty is more profound than Descartes's: "This intimate awareness (*Innewerden*) includes not just thinking but the totality of my person. Using an expression both profound and true, Augustine calls the object of self-certainty *life*" (260/234).

In the same vein, Heidegger cites the following passage from Dilthey: "The famous *crede ut intelligas* says first of all that the full range of experience must be present to analysis if it is to be exhaustive. The distinctive element in the content of this Christian experience lies above all in humility, which is grounded in the seriousness of the conscience when it passes judgment" (261f./235). Heidegger finds two texts of special interest regarding this prerequisite to understanding. *The City of God* 9.20 begins with 1 Corinthians 8:1: "Knowledge puffs up, but charity edifies." This means that knowledge does good only in company with charity, the humility of God in Christ. But the souls of men failed to realize its greatness since, inflated by the impurity of self-exaltation, they are like demons—if not in knowledge, at least in pride. The second text is from *Confessions* 5.5: By way of self-exaltation, men "say many true things about creation, yet they do not seek the Truth, the Artificer of creation, with piety, and so do not discover Him." Thus, in the section on the affects in BT (SZ 139n), Heidegger comes to cite a more succinct Augustinianism: "One does not enter into the truth except through charity." Charity, piety, and humility finally all unite in Augustine's affective sense of the happy life as a "joying in the truth."

Nevertheless, it cannot be denied that happiness has a theoretical component insofar as it culminates in "the truth." Is this eternal truth? Only when we turn inward, away from the world of the senses. "But when it is a question of things we behold with the mind, namely, with our intellect and reason, we give verbal expression to realities which we directly perceive as present in that inner light of truth by which the inner man, as he is called, is enlightened and made happy" (*On the Teacher* 40). This is first of all the truth of the mind itself. "For the mind knows nothing so well as that which is present to itself, and nothing is more present to the mind than it is to itself" (*On the Trinity* 14.7; p. 419). But this first self-certainty is not yet universal and eternal truth, but the individual and mutable truth of the doubting and often mistaken self, shareable with others only indirectly. "When the human mind, however, knows itself and loves itself, it does not know and love something immutable. . . . It is therefore obvious that what a person sees in himself is one thing, for another does not see this but believes what the speaker tells him; but what he sees in the truth itself is another thing, for another can also behold the same thing; the former is changeable in time, while the latter remains steadfast in its unchangeable eternity" (*On the Trinity* 9.9; pp. 278f.). The crucial move to "eternal truth"—already a "Platonizing concept"—is in the mind's turning from the world to God. Dilthey sketches two routes taken by Augustine, both ending in a Platonic metaphysics. Heidegger notes only the objective route of Neoplatonism, which projects the world of ideas into the mind of God (262/236). We already know that he is attracted by the second, "interior" (and mystical) route of tracing the soul back to its "unchanging ground" in God, without, however, interjecting the metaphysical concept of "substance" to describe this ground (263f./236f.). Under these influences, even the volitional path, which emphasizes practical over theoretical comportment and subordinates knowing to the willing of faith, ends in a metaphysics of the Highest Good, even while it seeks to fathom the "vital relationship of God to mankind" in and through history (264/237).[48]

For that matter, even the most secularized philosophy of history is notoriously prone to posit a "metaphysical substance" like universal reason, world spirit, or society to account for the unity and goal of history. Philosophy of history more than any other metaphysical discipline shows that its roots lie in religious experience (98ff./135f.). Comte's ultimate fate, in spite of his law of three stages, betrays the fact that religious life is not a passing phase but the "persistent underground of intellectual development" (138/159). Accordingly, history itself, the arena in which we come to understand our life-experience, is in its "inner depths" governed by the "living power" of religious experience. This inner connection between lived experience as such and religious experience, first uncovered by Christianity, found its first modern proponent in Schleiermacher (138ff./160f.), as we have already seen in earlier notes. The early Heidegger clearly stands in this tradition of Schleiermacher and Dilthey when he makes his breakthrough to his own lifelong topic in KNS 1919, to the ineffable "life in itself" in which we already find ourselves, which he then describes in unmistakably mystical overtones.

There is an analogy of ineffabilities here: As the mystic is immediately related to the influx of the Divine Life, so am I immediately related to my own life.

THE PHILOSOPHICAL FOUNDATIONS OF MEDIEVAL
MYSTICISM (AUGUST 1919)

If Heidegger had held the course projected for WS 1919–20 under this title, one might well suspect that its central themes would have been defined by his four years of reflection on the Phenomenology of Religious Consciousness and Life. This proves to be only partly the case, at least insofar as this can be determined from the very preliminary notes which he drafted for this announced two-hour course before abandoning it entirely. The notes betray instead an overwhelming concern for the phenomenological methodology required to develop an atheoretical dimension like religious life. They thus continue the deliberations of the previous two semesters on phenomenology as a pretheoretical primal science. It is perhaps not by chance, therefore, that the methodological course, "Basic Problems of Phenomenology," initially announced for one hour a week in WS 1919–20, is now expanded into a two-hour course, and will also incorporate some of the religious content planned for its canceled companion course. And even though Heidegger will be fond of reiterating that the "intuitions" of phenomenology are not to be equated with "mysticism," he will also note that such an intuitive "going along" with life to allow its meaning to give itself requires, like religious experience, a *humilitas animi*. We shall have occasion to note other such parallels between the phenomenological life and the religious life. Had the course been held, for example, Heidegger would have overtly continued his polemics, begun in 1916, against the purported "irrationalism" of the supposedly "amorphous" mystical experience, in kinship with his refusal to regard the "facticity" of lived experience as such as irrational, ineffable, and so inaccessible. Through the "primal understanding" that phenomenology aims at, mystical experience, like lived experience as such, is brought into the "sphere of absolute understandability," that is, into a sphere of pure meaning. The "concepts" which such a pretheoretical primal understanding explicates are not "rationalizations" which destroy the immediacy of the original experience by dissolving it into its "logical components." Rather, such an understanding seeks to determine the "form of expression"[49] indigenous to the experience itself in order to understand it in its "primal (absolute) history." Beyond the problem of mysticism understood as a form of expression and the forms of expression (e.g., prayer) belonging to different phases of the religious experience, the course would have raised the problem of expression as such and its role in the fulfillment of any experience. The replacement course on "Basic Problems of Phenomenology" will in fact publicly deal with this methodological issue for the very first time.

The course on medieval mysticism therefore would have constituted a convergence and fusion of hermeneutic phenomenology of life and the phenomenology of religious experience, the two main lines of Heidegger's development at this time. Moreover, the growing sense of the hermeneutic rationality of all experience is still coupled with Husserl's centering of eidetic-transcendental phenomenology in the pure consciousness.

The first phenomenological step is the renunciation of all "constructive" philosophy of religion. In Heidegger's day, this meant the neo-Kantian approach to the religious apriori (Troeltsch), the neo-Friesian philosophy of the holy (Otto) and Hegelian constructivism (no figures named). The latter comes closest to starting from the historical fullness, but it leaves the historical itself unclarified. For the structures of experience are to be drawn from the concrete fullness of their possible situations, and not by way of isolated genera, into their essence as this is motivated and constituted in the "pure consciousness." Both genetic and eidetic phenomenology play a role in comprehending the aspects of religious experience: its preliminary forms and their pregivens, the basic stages and movements, the emerging motivations of "time," the types of experiential fulfillment. Analogies with the theoretical and the way it constitutes its cognitive object must be diligently avoided in determining the constitution of the "religious object." Is God somehow already pregiven in faith? Or is it in love? Is He constituted in prayer, or does prayer already presuppose faith and love for the constitution of its Object? How is this manifest historicity of the religious experience related to the historically fulfilling experiences of religion, those of revelation, tradition, and community? What is the experiential action of the "power," "grace," or "anger" of God? Such questions must be examined within the religious world of faith itself. The more fundamental problem is the regional distinction of the lifeworlds of science, morals, art, and religion and their historical position in the "pure consciousness." Are they all equally "primal-historical"? Is the genesis of the basic level also in the religious dimension? What precisely are the founding-founded relations or motivating connections within this absolute historicity of the "pure consciousness"?

Once one has seen the problem of the origin of the different lifeworlds—here especially the distinction between the religious and the scientific—the "problem of faith and knowing" will no longer be viewed as genuine, since it will be exposed in its one-sided orientation toward the cognitive sphere of the scientific lifeworld. Once we have clearly

distinguished religiosity from theology, then the further phenomenological problem of theology as the "science of faith," its relationship to
the other sciences, emerges. It is especially to be noted how dependent
theology is on philosophy and the overall status of the theoretical consciousness as such. Theology has not yet found its originary theoretical
orientation corresponding to the originality of its object.

Heidegger begins the course by distinguishing two types of "philosophical foundations," the historical and the systematic, which then tend
to interweave themselves in the specific themes he proposes to examine.
Foundations derived from the history of philosophy can be divided into
the inherited metaphysical and epistemological presuppositions, ethical
and scientific doctrines. The latter for the mystics meant especially the
"scientific" psychology in which they apprehended their experience. The
foundations of medieval mysticism thus take us back to figures like
Augustine, Neoplatonism, the Stoics, Plato, and Aristotle.

The "systematic" foundations are those of the "primal-scientific" (i.e.,
phenomenological) approach to mystical experience in its intentional
structure and especially its dynamics. Here, one must be careful to sort
out any theory of experiencing (psychology) and the experienced (mystical theology), along with any metaphysically "mystical worldview" thus
developed, from the experience itself. One objection that could be raised
here: Only a religious person can understand religious life; all others
do not have access to what is truly given in such a life. This is not an
insuperable obstacle for an empathetic phenomenologist. The "religious
person in herself " of course constitutes a kind of norm for those who
are becoming religious and seek entry into the religious world, so that
the modes of coming to religion are to be understood from that norm.
Heidegger underscores the importance of the dynamics of the intentional experience especially in the religious world, which "is centered on
the movement of conative experience which is detaching itself in the
process of finding God." Whence his interest in the forms and figures
of practical guidance provided by devotional manuals, and the self-con-
scious teleology of strategies like asceticism. He plans to map the entire
gamut of negative and positive movements of the religious life—for
example, the repulsiveness of a corrupt world—around the master concept of "detachment," which is oriented toward not a theoretical but
instead an "emotional nothing." It is therefore important to examine the
ways in which the Middle Ages characterized the emotional life, but
purely, in a way which is not tied to its characterization by the scholastics.

At this point, Heidegger refers to a passage in which Dilthey distinguishes between the Aristotelian-scholastic and the Platonic-mystical anthropology developed in the Middle Ages.[50] The roots of the former
in Aristotle's psychology is not without interest for Heidegger's later

development, in providing the central distinction within the emotional comportment of striving (ὄρεξις, which Heidegger will come to translate as "care") between the "attractive" concupiscible and the "repulsive" irascible appetites. But at this point, Heidegger is attracted to the less classificatory, more dynamic "mystical" anthropology geared to the "journey of the soul toward God" (*itinerarium mentis ad deum*). Here, the stages of affective comportment are directly tied to the Christian drama motivated by its peculiar eros, caught in the conflict between slavery to the sensory and freedom through dedication to the suprasensory, a drama underscoring the affective life of love which underlies the cognitive life of meditation and contemplation.

The admixture of historical with systematic foundations occurs again in the mini-history of faith from primitive Christianity to the Reformation, culminating in the contrast between Catholic *fides* (intellectual belief) and Lutheran *fiducia* (trust). These are phenomena which can only be understood within the larger motivational context of the constitution of the religious world as such, within which one might well understand the difference between "justification" by faith versus the sacraments, the relationships between grace, nature, and freedom, the difference between *gratia operans et cooperans*, and so on. What Luther achieved is not to be found even among the medieval mystics who influenced him. Mystics like Bernard and Tauler kept the monastic-mystic ideal of humility and letting-be (*Gelassenheit*) before Luther and allowed him to see the signal importance of this dimension of detachment for the preparation of the grace of faith and so the reception of the experience of God: "Mysticism gave Luther a world of inner experiences and showed him the methodological way for securing and enhancing that world. This is also why the motivating force of humility could not in the long run operate merely as an impediment to the jubilant and sure development of *fiducia*. Humility, tribulation itself becomes the expression of a personal certainty of salvation."[51]

Here we have perhaps a third reason, in addition to lack of time for preparation in a crowded postwar year, as well as overriding methodological concerns, as to why this course was never given. It might well have been controversial, if not scandalous, had Heidegger taken this Lutheran tack in "Catholic Freiburg" so early in his public career and at such an early stage in his Luther studies. This "Lutheranism" will surface publicly in Freiburg only briefly in SS 1921. Not until Marburg does it emerge in sustained fashion, in Heidegger's collaboration with Rudolf Bultmann and the Marburg theological faculty. But by then, Heidegger is also posing more skeptical, even atheistic, questions to his Lutheran colleagues, which he had developed from his reading of Franz Overbeck, Nietzsche's close friend.

SUMMARY: A RELIGIOUS PHENOMENOLOGY?

Phenomenology is the return to the origins of experience, and so a return to the original experience. Having already found a parallel for this movement in Eckhart's detachment and return of the soul to its vital ground and intimate root in the "primal intentionality," Heidegger now finds modern parallels for such a return in the life-philosophies of Schleiermacher and Dilthey, who underscore the dimension of history in our immediate experience. Schleiermacher bids us to listen to ourselves in the original unity and becoming of consciousness, to return to the "first beginnings of consciousness" in its experiential fullness. Dilthey's hermeneutic sense sees this origin as the initial upsurge of sense in human experience. This immediate sense of the universe which comes from putting ourselves in touch with the fullness of our being, this receptivity and submission to the immediate relationship of our being, is religion. Attuned to this tradition, it is small wonder that Heidegger's own descriptions of the phenomenological return to life in its originality, authenticity, and pretheoretical immediacy betray decidedly religious accents. One need not wait until August 1921 for Heidegger to testify that the very impetus of his thought lies in the "fact" that he is a Christian theo-logian. Let us eavesdrop on his correspondence around 1919 which, in contrast with and, in part, in response to this nadir in Germany's public life, resounds again and again with an enthusiastic panegyric to the "give and take" of life.

> We must again be able to wait and have faith in the grace which is present in every genuine life, with its humility before the inviolability of one's own and the other's experience. Our life must be brought back from the dispersion of multiple concerns to its original wellspring of expansive creativity. Not the fragmentation of life into programs, no aestheticizing glosses or genial posturing, but rather the mighty confidence in union with God and original, pure, and effective action. Only life overcomes life, and not matters and things, not even logicized "values" and "norms."[52]

And to his Schleiermachean correspondent, Elisabeth Blochmann,[53] Heidegger observes that life is genuine only in its "inner adherence to the central I and its God-directed striving toward goals." Attunement to the essence of one's personal stream of life in both its ebb tides and its peaks requires

> inner humility before the mystery and grace of life. We must be able to wait for the high-pitched intensities of meaningful life, and we must remain in continuity with such gifted moments, not so much to enjoy them as to work them into life, to take them with us in the onrush of life and to include them in the rhythms of all oncoming life. And in moments when we immediately feel ourselves and are attuned to the direction in which

we vitally belong, we cannot merely establish and simply record what is clearly had, as if it stood over against us like an object. The understanding self-possession is genuine only when it is lived, when it is at once a Being. I do not mean by this the triviality that one must also follow what one knows. Rather, in a vehement life, becoming aware of one's directedness, which is not theoretical but a total experience, is at once entering into it with gusto (*Schwung*), the propagation of a new momentum through and in every movement of life.

It is but a short step from this personal "ontic" attitude to the phenomenological attitude, which likewise wishes to overtake and keep to our vital, pretheoretical, preobjective origins, the very wellspring of life itself. Is the phenomenological life therefore the religious life? The course of KNS 1919 seeks to set phenomenological philosophy as a pretheoretical primal science outside of any connection with the ultimate human questions, which would turn it into a worldview. To make this step in the present context, a kind of "religious reduction" is called for. For all that Eckhart, Schleiermacher, Dilthey contributed to shaping the phenomenological topic for the young Heidegger, there is a qualification to such assertions as "The stream of consciousness is already religious" which must be kept in mind. The "is" here is not an expression of identity between religion and life but of the identification of the motivating ground of religion. But the very same vital source is also the motivating ground of philosophy, art, morality, science, in short, of all human culture. The conditions that make the soul receptive to religion thus also make it receptive to philosophy. For all their efforts to go beyond the theoretical paradigm of consciousness-over-against-an-object, Schleiermacher and Dilthey still tend to stress the certitudes that reside in immediate experience, while Heidegger will eventually stress the disquieting character that resides at the very heart of life and serves as a motivation to both religion and philosophy. The pretheoretical and preworldly primal something which is the topic of phenomenology, life in and for itself, gives rise to and so lies on this side of the scientific, ethical, aesthetic, and religious lifeworlds.

Nevertheless, it is not always clear that Heidegger at this time consistently carried out such a "religious reduction," and so separated his research orientation from a personal life with an overriding religious motivation or, in Husserl's words, from a personal "religious orientation in which the theoretical-philosophical interest was predominant." Not until 1922 does Heidegger's personal pathos for his Christian facticity clearly yield to the "fundamental atheism of philosophy," the skepsis of radical questioning which he will later characterize as the "piety of thinking."

This turn of thought is nevertheless still linked to the initial reason for Heidegger's project of a phenomenology of religion, namely, insight into the medieval notion of intentionality. The *unio mystica* spontaneously neutralizes the metaphysical hypostasis of the subject-object relation and directs attention instead to the δύναμις of intentionality as a sheer "directedness toward," regarding it now as the veritable wellspring and "giving" element of life, its *élan vital*. The mystical emptying of the "form" of intentionality down to the level of absolute oppositionlessness or indifference free of all determination likewise provides Heidegger with an early model for the formally indicative approach to intentionality, identified in 1919 as the pretheoretical and pretheoretical "primal something." The need to formalize intentionality has the young Heidegger at one point (in the polemic against Schleiermacher) even distinguishing, in Husserlian fashion, the historical ego in all its fulfillment from the "pure ego" of empty potentiality, "the form of the possibility of being affected and fulfilled," where possibility is however not logical but "vocational," that of being-called, understood as the primal motivation of life. In a similar vein, the pure ego is the primal form of "openness" to value and primary meaning, a note of receptivity which will be amplified by the later Heidegger into the motif of "listening to the voice of Being." It is only after the Interregnum that the Augustinian theme of the "restless heart" inaugurates the gradual emergence of "care" as a more "strenuous" characterization of the δύναμις of intentionality. *Bekümmerung* (the concern pursuant to affliction) is first announced in the last hour of SS 1920 and becomes a guiding motif ("formal indicator") in the two subsequent "religion" courses. This qualitative shift from receptive openness to restless concern as the dominant characteristic of intentionality brings forth a different sense of religion from that of the Interregnum. In lieu of the feelings of wonder, dependence, security, trust, and composed "letting be" characteristic of a childlike or settled sense of religion, the more anxious moments of being placed under judgment in a moment of decision, characteristic of a more mature and questing sense of religion, come forth. A year later, the countermovement of "ruinance" or "falling" also inherent in intentionality will first clearly emerge, serving to cast further doubt upon the entire approach of dedicative submission, immersion, and absorption as a way of getting at the subject matter, if not to condemn it as utterly naive and simplistic, and therefore dangerous.

If we restrict our summary to the Interregnum of 1917–1919, we then find that the old Heidegger's passing hint on the central importance for his development of the sense of hermeneutics in Schleiermacher and Dilthey proves to be the major key to this period of conversion. The itinerary of breaking through the theoretical wall of a petrified scholasticism to a more experiential sense of the religious life had begun with the "Catholic" paradigm of Eckhartian detachment, but was ultimately sustained and carried to completion through the "*hermeneutic* insights extending to the theory of historical cognition" that came from Schleier-macher's and Dilthey's like-minded return to the immediacy of lived experience. Only by extension can Heidegger still speak of "epistemolog-ical insights," since the historical cognition under study here is a "knowl-edge" which precedes overt knowledge, a knowledge which is one with life itself, encountered above under various guises: experientially imma-nent knowledge (Reinach), felt intuition (Schleiermacher), "naked intui-tion of the first truth" (Eckhart), the Lutheran truth as trust, the Scotian *modus essendi activus*, the scholastic *intellectus principiorum*, categorial intui-tion (Husserl), dedicative submission (Lask). The notes of letting-be and receptive listening should also be added, to underscore further the at-tempts, halting and difficult, to get beyond the metaphors of traditional *Lichtmetaphysik*. All of these contribute to shaping the later notion of a prereflective understanding of being constitutive of Dasein, which Hei-degger at this stage is still describing in terms of the primal possibilities of a "pure consciousness," albeit one which is historically rooted in life.

The phenomenological structures of intentionality and categorial in-tuition already in place in 1915 were thus guided by the pretheoretical paradigm of religious consciousness beyond the stasis of the subject-object relationship to a dynamic "historical" sense of their "directedness toward" ensconced within a "hermeneutic rationality" of the emergence of sense within human experience. The return to origins, placing oneself at the wellspring of life to catch oneself in the act of "happening," thus becomes a return to the motivational context of the "élan vital" (ZBP 115)[54] yielding an "archeological" sense of history over and above the neo-Kantian teleological sense. The historical I becomes the "situation-I," where situation is already understood dynamically and hermeneuti-cally—it is thus already a "hermeneutic situation" (SS 1922)—as a given coherence of motivating possibilities or "presuppositions." The life of devotion, for example, can be described historically as an "ever-changing coherence of situations, of the possibilities of motivations" (ZBP 208), posing the problem of a law of stages of founding sequences of presuppo-sitions which defines how the movement reaches its fulfillment. One could argue that Heidegger's religious sense prevents him at this time from interpreting this facticity of "happening" nihilistically, if he had not already entertained a kind of "divine irrationality" within the mystical experience as Eckhart describes it. But against this neo-Kantian sense of facticity, he finds another λόγος within experience for his phenomeno-logy and theo-logy, and is busy working out the intricacies of this herme-neutic λόγος as we leave him at the end of this period. The "theological heritage" which put the young Heidegger onto the path of thought is thus as much Lutheran as it is Catholic, or simply Christian in the most "primitive" sense of that heritage. "I am a 'Christian theo*logian*.' "

THREE

The Deconstruction of Life (1919–20)

At last we are on the move, moving away from the wrenching "primal leap" (*Ur-sprung*) that transformed Heidegger from a competent but pedestrian scholar and teacher of the Catholic worldview into a revolutionary teacher who quickly showed promise of bringing something radically new to the postwar, but still staid, world of university philosophy. Time now to "work out" that promising beginning, to see where it would lead. What takes precedence now, among the projects Heidegger had assumed and, as Husserl's assistant, was called upon to assume, is the implementation of that radical phenomenology, both conceptually and methodologically (they are not really distinct), which he now regarded as its highest and deepest possibility. His description of his working life earlier in the year still holds, at least in part, as 1919 draws to a close: "My own work is quite concentrated, fundamental, and concrete: basic problems of phenomenological methodology, disengagement from the residue of acquired standpoints, ever new forays into the true origins . . . constantly learning in my association with Husserl."[1] We shall now survey the results of a year's worth of forays into the domain of radical phenomenology.

WS 1919–20 is not the beginning, as Heidegger mistakenly recalls in BT (SZ 72n), but it is certainly the continuation of his work on an analysis of the environing world and a hermeneutics of facticity. Especially the latter problematic will be considerably advanced in the coming year. And in point of fact, WS 1919–20 focuses its attention more on the originary self-world than on the environing world from which it emerges. To be sure, the phrase "hermeneutics of facticity" is not yet explicitly used to identify the method and matter of phenomenology. But in the closing minutes of SS 1920, "facticity" is for the first time officially adopted from neo-Kantianism to name Heidegger's own "distressing" topic. The year will thus also mark a development in specifying that topic, phenomenology's domain of originary giving, changing in terminological identity from the somewhat amorphous "life in and for itself" (KNS) to "factic life experience" (WS 1919–20) and "concrete actual Dasein" (SS 1920). On the methodological "hermeneutics" side, the year will see the coining and refining of the method of "destruction" (critique, deconstruction) as the way to return to origins through an analysis of preconceptions. Destruction is first regarded as a counter to the pervasive tendency of objectification (WS 1919–20), and then in its more comprehensive role as an antidote to any and every tendency to lapse or "fall" from originality into the "surface existence" of everydayness (SS 1920). The new method is amply illustrated especially in its application to three very different psychologists or students of "psychic *life*," Natorp, Dilthey, and Jaspers, each of whom plays an important role in Heidegger's own development. The result is a multifaceted deconstruction of the life philosophy of his day, "a necessary stage to radical phenomenological philosophy." By this route, Heidegger gradually emerges from his inherited "hermeneutic situation" and haltingly finds his own voice as a self-styled "radical phenomenologist."

WS 1919–20: BASIC PROBLEMS OF PHENOMENOLOGY

The most basic problem of phenomenology is itself, understood as a science of the origin. What does such an idea of philosophy involve? In this continuation of the problematic begun in KNS, Heidegger will push more deeply into the domain of this primal science, thus into the domain of the origin or the originating domain (*Ursprungsgebiet*), than he did in the preceding two semesters. It likewise brings the clarification that the theme of phenomenology is not simply factic life—this is the comprehensive domain divided by all the other sciences—but life as arising from the origin, in its "primal leap" into the factic. Factic life is thus pursued in an entirely new direction. Phenomenology wants to find the origin of factic life. Along the way, it will also have to find the motives which lead us from factic life to the domain of origin. In other words, what motivates the very idea of a science of the origin? And what does origin mean in this context? The various problems of phenomenology thus proliferate around this central problem, that of its very idea as a "science" of the domain of origin. The course meanders its way through various available and proposed options from the sciences and philosophy in search of the method and matter of the primal science, usually by way of contrast. This is done in conjunction with a running description of the basic characters of factic life, from which the domain of origin will receive its motivation. We shall concentrate on the latter theme in this brief overview of the course.

We must enter into the "self-evidences" of life: my life, your life, her life. Factic life has a definite direction, a tendency, which is not always conscious. Life is a sequence of tendencies: it makes a claim on us, "addresses" us, or passes us by. Whether latent or patent, such tendencies tend to stabilize or "crystallize" around us. I always live in some kind of surroundings or environment, a circle of tasks and life conditions, to which others also belong, where I am with others. To this environing world and with-world can also be added a self-world, given to me in the same way as the environing world. The self-world is what occupies me. One has an interest in art, science, and the like, without giving it too much thought. Another stabilizes his direction by choosing a profession, which can even become a totally dominating and dictatorial tendency: a purely scientific or religious life. But whatever the choice or nonchoice, life always lives in a world, it always has a tendency toward a certain content, it does not run its course in the void. "World" does not add anything new to life. Factic life and life in a world go together as a matter of course. One is for the other.

Surrounding world, with-world, self-world: these three relief characters permeate each other in the flux of life so as to give it its unique and "labile circumstantiality," the very rhythm of my life. This of course is only my surface existence, I am not fully there, expressly and consciously, but it is from here that my personal existence is to be grasped. As a flux of relief characters, it is a kind of "unaccentuated accentuation" defining what we call "everydayness." Beyond everydayness, there are the more consciously accentuated tendencies, like that of a profession. All tendencies strive for fulfillment, which in life tends to be provisional and never final. Life is charged with questionability, and the way this interrogative domain is time and again overcome characterizes the "self-sufficiency" of life. Factic life contains the resources to overcome its own questions. Life as such brings its factic tendencies out of itself and then to fulfillment through itself. All fulfillments happen through life itself. Despite its inadequacies, factic life gives answer to its questions in its own language. If this is so, then it should provide the answer even to the problem of its origin. It is not to be sought "somewhere else," beyond life itself.

Another important character: life gives itself in various contexts of manifestation or expression. It can be seen in different aspects. Everything in life is somehow or other, and only in a "somehow." Everything that we encounter in life expresses itself, puts itself forward, appears, in short, is a *phenomenon*. A person in different moods and situations, my high school years then and now—everything appears in a manifold of manifestations. And when they become objects of science, they enter into new modes of expression, for example, the past worlds of historical research. History will turn out to be the most important discipline for phenomenology, even more important than psychology, with which it was first confused. But as important as the scientific mode of expression is for the ideal of phenomenology, it is only one of many expressive contexts; art and religion have other modes of manifestation. All three worlds can be brought into the expressive context of science. Even the self-world can be made the topic of biographical research of various kinds, assisted by sciences like history and psychology.

It turns out that the center of gravity of factic life can come to rest in the self-world, such that the with-world and the around-world become functionally dependent on the self-world. This does not happen intentionally and consciously, but rather occurs implicitly in the factic course of life itself. Factic life is pointed toward self-life. This focusing of factic life in the self-world is already there unaccentuated in the environing world, so that we do not notice that the entire world is pointed through the situation of the one who is living it. Every world occurrence is determined by the situation of the implicit self. The expressive context in which the world gives itself is a function of the particular situational context of the self-world. Lived life is an echo of the rhythm of a living self. The many-splendored and sometimes chaotic mixtures of life experiences find their unity in the situational flow of the life of the self, its rhythm and style. In short, there is always a connection between the manifestation character of the self-world and that of the lived world. And the very possibility of phenomenology as a primal science depends upon this possibility.

Can this self-world as such, which we each experience first in an unaccentuated way, be made the object of a science? Can we perhaps trace the first stirrings of the self-world out of the environing world? A final trait of factic life experience makes this possible. Everything that I experience has for me the character of being real. This really amounts to its being significant, meaningful, even if it be in the most trivial and worthless of ways. Significance is always and alone the character of factically experienced reality. I live in this reality, I am absorbed in it. Every factic life experience has a particular horizon of significances which characterizes and influences its inner context. This meaningful context is centered in situations which are "open," that is, accessible for motivations from the past and future. Existence without significance simply does not have the possibility of motivation. Significance is defined by the context of expectation in which every vital situation stands.

The character of significance indicates that life is not like a stream which flows on dully and mutely (Bergson), but is understandable. It and the other two characters of factic life, self-sufficiency and expression, make a science of the domain of origin possible. They do not provide a conceptual net for generalization, but rather the basis for understanding life in its own expressive formation. We see this especially in the very first moment of taking cognizance (*Kenntnisnahme*) of that factic life in which we first find ourselves absorbed, the very first step toward articulating our factic experience. It is a remarkable act, a phenomenon on the edge: it remains in the style of factic life and stands entirely within its context of significance, does not break its character or unravel what has been experienced. And yet this very first moment of life becoming conscious of itself does retard the experience, slow down the course of life. The experience is slackened, relaxed of the tautness of the life stream while remaining in it. To what extent is the act of taking cognizance a modification of factic life which violates it, infringes upon it? Is what is being noticed the same as what has been factically experienced? In factic experience, I live from one momentary phase to the other, skimming over these in unrestrained fashion, storming ahead without looking back. And yet this sliding from one phase to another, each open only to the present, shapes an experiential context, which is guided by a certain direction of expectation. The act of cognizance is thus directed to the whole, open not just to the present moments but to the overview of the context. It is an all-sided openness to the past and future through the tendency that threads through all the phases. It is the overview that factic life, which normally does not look back and simply focuses on the present, does not achieve. What exactly then is the modification of taking notice? It overtly takes the tendencies of experience as tendencies of sense, which become binding for what is being experienced, so that its elements merge, consolidate, crystallize into contexts, and emerge as constellations of meaning. All this is guided by the tendency of significance intrinsic to factic life.

Of course, taking cognizance can be taken to the other extreme of its tendency to modify factic life to the point of extinguishing the original situation. This is the "unliving" of reification that especially the natural sciences promote in their quest for total objectification. Clearly, the science of the origin wishes to stay close to the original situation of life. In fact, it seeks the givenness of concrete basic situations in which the totality of life is expressed, in which a "total givenness" emerges. This is the givenness of life as it is "pregiven" to us, which can never and in no way be objectified. Life experiences are not things, but expressive formations of the tendencies of concrete life-situations. The science of experience is the originarily giving intuition of experiential contexts, of situations out of which experiences spring. It is the merit of phenomenology to have stressed the fundamental meaning of intuition as an originary return to the phenomena themselves. But there is the danger, in exemplify-

ing intuition through sense perception (Husserl), of equating it with ob-
ject-intuition. The very first step of phenomenological intuition is in the
sheer understanding of the contexts of sense which are developed by
life-situations. For the self-world in factic life is not a thing nor even an
I in the epistemological sense, but rather a significance to be understood.
Its concepts are expressions of sense and not of an order of objects to
which they must be brought into coincidence. Expressive concepts are
not order-concepts, operating according to subsumptive generalizations.
Understanding gives the phenomenological concept of essence another
sense than that of a generic universal.

Dilthey is never mentioned in these terminological decisions regarding
the basic terms of a pretheoretical science of the original domain of the
self-world, but it is hard to suppress noting the operative ("formally
indicative") role played by the triad "lived experience-understanding-
expression" in Heidegger's critique of the theoretical psychology of the
day (cf. chap. 2 above). We are still a long way from BT, but this precursor to *Befindlichkeit-Verstehen-Rede*, the equiprimordial hows of "being in"
in the magnum opus, will even be telegraphed in the occasional allusion
to the issue of "how I originally find myself" in these culminating two
hours of the course (January 23 and 27, 1920). But the same issue is
posed here as "how I have myself." This nonobjective "having" will carry
far into the next several years of development not only in the radicalizing
of psychology, not only in this quasi-Diltheyean, counter-Husserlian shift
from psychology to history as the "true guiding thread of phenomenological investigations," but also in the ontology which underlies these
terminological decisions: Being (οὐσία) as having.

The purportedly "psychological" concept of experience must be defined originally, beyond the alternatives "objects—experiences," out of
a context in which it literally "makes sense" to speak of "experiencing."
It is also not enough to regard all experiences, as "I-related," as if the I
were to be immediately found in them. The "pure I" or "I-point" just
comes along for the ride, accomplishes nothing in the apprehension of
experiences, and is not at all appropriate for the role of the self. Must
the I be present in every experience? Are there not also "excentric"
experiences? The "pure I" accomplishes nothing for the knowledge of
the vital context of experience. I "have myself" much more concretely
in factic life, say, in memory, than when I am oriented toward an empty
artificial I. "I myself" is really a meaningful context in which I live.
"Situation" is in fact the peculiar character in which I have myself. Words
like "life," "lived experience," "I myself" drawn from daily life pose a
danger of objectification in our descriptions; they cannot be taken univo-
cally, but rather must be understood in their *formal* character as *indicative*
of certain phenomena of the concrete domain. How do I myself live in

my most concrete experiences, how am I involved in my worldly attunement, how do I *find myself* in a lifeworld? How does life experience itself? At this rudimentary level, we discover a certain familiarity that life already has with itself in its fullness, a going along with life as it is lived. This experienced experience is called *history*. What we ordinarily call memory is a more a matter of finding oneself already expressed in experiencing itself. It provides the basis for *understanding* as a going along with personal life experience with great vitality and intimacy. Having oneself is thus the expression of life in its originality. Having oneself is not coming to gaze at an I as an object, but the process of winning or losing a certain familiarity that life already has with itself. The I here is more a rhythm of experiencing than an I-point. The ultimate possibilities of such a familiarity with self are expressed historically in phenomena like vocation, destiny, and grace. Having myself is neither an outer or inner beholding, but the learning experience which expresses my most original life: my personal situation, factic history, life in and for itself. The sense(s) of this "having" must now be put in less romanticist and more formal, albeit still nonobjectifying, terms.

Life derives from certain motives and proceeds according to certain tendencies, as we noted at the beginning of the course. This relation of motive to tendency is the relational sense *(Bezugssinn)* of life, in which it lives itself without having itself. Left open is how near to or far from the relational sense the self stands, whether it is lived on the surface or in the depths of the self. But on this basis, it is possible to achieve an ever-increasing concentration of actualization of the relational sense, up to a full spontaneity of the self. This being with oneself is its sense of actualization *(Vollzugssinn)*. Finally, the tendency has a certain content or containment, it comprises a certain lifeworld which itself becomes a motive for the self. This is the content or containment sense *(Gehaltssinn)* of factic life. Relational, actualization, and containment senses yield the primal structure of the situation. These three elements of sense, or better, senses of direction of the life stream itself, circumscribe what is meant by the self-sufficiency of life. These directions of sense allow us access to life in and for itself, life in its origin. They allow us to approximate this origin in its full situationality. Almost. The nonobjective nature of human situations, how they delimit themselves within factic life, how each acquires its dominant character and unity out of the ultimate possibilities and fatalities of the self: such issues refer to the rhythms of time in which situations are bound up. In this regard, Bergson has indicated the importance of distinguishing "concrete duration" from objective "cosmic" time.

How near to or far from the origin we come also calls for an examination of phenomenological concept formation. As already noted, philosophical concepts have another structural form than concepts which order objects. They are instead concepts expressive of sense. Deriving such concepts from the concrete formations of life must first proceed by way of negations. For factic life gives itself in a peculiar deformation, that of objectification, which must be canceled or critically "destroyed" in order to move from ordering concepts to expressive concepts. (Note that the methodological term "destruction" first arises in opposition to the "natural" tendency of objectification.) This is really the idea behind dialectic. In phenomenology as a science deriving from the origin, such a dialectic is not so much a synthetic setting apart of concepts as it is a "diahermeneutics" drawn from factic life itself.

SS 1920: PHENOMENOLOGY OF INTUITION AND EXPRESSION: THEORY OF PHILOSOPHICAL CONCEPT FORMATION

The titles reflect the continuity with the themes of the previous semesters: the pairing of "intuition and expression" derives from the old objections from KNS against the accessibility and expressibility of immediate experience, and the problem of concept formation was the emerging concern of the semester just concluded. Given the catalytic role that this pairing will play into BT itself, it is at the very least odd that the old Heidegger, in his "Dialogue on Language between a Japanese and an Inquirer" (1959), erroneously (or perhaps ironically) entitles this course with the pair "Expression and Appearance" and places it in 1921. Even the report of the Japanese attending the course and taking a transcript of it with them back to Japan appears to be a literary invention (US 91/5, 128ff./34ff.).

Is the concern for concept formation something supplementary to an already extant philosophy, something secondary, a philosophizing about philosophy, a reflection on itself which only slows its progress? Lask's "logic of philosophy," for example, is liable to the objection of being a mere hyperreflection. This may be the case for critical transcendental philosophy, but it will be shown that a theory of philosophical concept formation is not an extraneous reflection for phenomenology, but the concrete way and access to the idea of its fundamental structure. It is thus related to the attempt to derive the very idea of philosophy. It raises the basic question of the position of the concept in philosophy. This will be developed out of the present situation of philosophy, which itself is concerned with the very idea of philosophy.

The present situation is governed by the tension between the idea of "philosophy as strict science" (Husserl's Logos-essay) and the "worldview" philosophies, the demand for a philosophy that founds and orders practical life. It takes into account the basic goals, norms, and values of practical life. But whatever the idea of philosophy, all agree that life is the primal and basic phenomenon, whether from a biological

(James, Bergson) or a historical perspective (Dilthey). Transcendental philosophy (Marburg, Rickert, Windelband, the latest Husserl) does not regard life as such but life in its relation to aims, norms, ultimate values, which are definitive for philosophy as well as for concrete life. Its predominantly epistemological orientation puts it in opposition to "skeptical-relativistic" life philosophy.

Life is thus understood in two basic directions: 1) Life is creative shaping and objectification, expressing itself as "culture." Life is self-*expos*iting (*Aus-sich-heraussetzen:* the terms here are fraught with later consequences on the "ins and outs" of ex-istence). The basic sense of being and existence is creative shaping: the externalizing direction. 2) Life is lived experience and encounter. The life thus shaped is gathered into itself (*in sich hineinholen*) and the form, the contexture, is itself lived, experienced. Being and existence are this experiencing: the internalizing direction.

The first direction leads to the problem of the apriori. Life as objectification takes life under the aspect of historical development into systematic forms of culture, which is a collective concept for the creations of the self-unfolding of spirit in three basic arenas: the logical, ethical, aesthetic; ergo science, morality, art, to which a fourth, religion, is sometimes added. Transcendental philosophy seeks to go beyond the factic historical context to the suprahistorical, absolute norms or "ideas" of science, morality, art, and religion. Life is not considered as such, but instead in relation to ultimate values. From this perspective, the historical appears as relative, particular, and deficient uniqueness. How does this historical facticity stand to the ideal content? This is Plato's problem, magnified by history. The antithesis of the unconditioned validity of values, rational ideas, and principles versus historical uniqueness, facticity, and change, is to be bridged by a dialectic, understood as a logic of the limits of historical dynamics (Troeltsch). The problem of the apriori can be illustrated in the fate of Protestant theology in the nineteenth century, when the development of a sense of historical Christianity challenged its absoluteness. Schleiermacher's distinctive historical sense of Christianity set the problem of founding the absolute validity of Christianity in the face of the development of the history of religions and comparative religions. But is such a line of argument appropriate? Did the primitive Christian community come to its conviction through the history of religions? Is its sense of unconditioned validity to be equated with the absoluteness of science? Has one not allowed the apriori here to be compromised by the theoretical? Is this not an excessive extension of the theoretical into the nontheoretical? Does not each domain of life have its unique apriori?

The second sense of life leads to the problem of the irrational. Here, life is to be experienced in its fullness, in all of its obscurity and intimacy.

Modern man's emotional capacity and open-mindedness is to be expanded by the drive to enter into all possible domains of life. The theoretical attitude is regarded as only one possible attitude, placed in its limits while the other attitudes are cultivated. This cultivation of consciously different life-possibilities raises a basic difficulty for philosophy: Can life in its nontheoretical forms be apprehended in its totality by the theoretical attitude? Could it be that certain forms of spirit are from the start distorted by theoretical considerations of them? Philosophy has posed this critical question against itself in two ways:

A. In connection with Kant's transcendental concept of knowledge, where the understanding spontaneously forms the sense data pregiven through receptivity. Marburg maintains the absoluteness of positing and so does not recognize the independence of receptivity, while Rickert (transcendental empiricism) maintains the independence of sense content which limits understanding's bestowal of structure. The irrational experiences of sense passivity are never formed through and through by spontaneity, without remainder. This is extended to all conscious acts: even theoretical acts are a lived experience and so are not completely transparent to the understanding.

B. In connection with the problem of language, Bergson has emphasized that meaning-laden words are patterned after the real world to provide the understanding with a way of coping with practical life. Thus, all the basic meanings of language have a spatial character; every logic is a logic of space. The mastery of lived experience is accordingly a spatialization of consciousness. Once again, a tension between experiencing and knowing, the irrational and rational, which is to be smoothed over by a dialectic of the opposite.

This renewal of Hegelianism now makes it possible to incorporate philosophy itself into culture (Spengler's philosophy of culture) or into experience (Jaspers's psychology) and so to understand its universal function. Both involve a measure of skepticism.

Rather than trying to smooth over the tension beween the problems of the apriori and the irrational (linked, for example, in the "irrational apriori" of religion), let us rather try to trace the problem situation back to its meaningful origin. Rather than bridging the opposition with a new schema, let us instead ask: Is the opposition of absolute-relative, apriori-history, irrational-rational, really a genuine one? Placing the schema itself in question and perhaps dissolving it is to be realized with the help of critical destruction, a basic aspect of the phenomenological method.

Phenomenology as the basic science of philosophy is problematic as long as we have not come to a radical concept of philosophy along phenomenological lines. Its success in clarifying meanings already indicates that it deals with basic philosophical concepts which refer to broad contexts: objectivity, situation of lived experience, and so on. The search for clarification of meaning contains the danger of stopping at and becoming possessed by individual meanings instead of regarding the entire context of meanings. This danger exists when the phenomenon of situation is itself not phenomenologically clarified. Various directions of meaning refer back to various domains of objects, and the question then becomes how these in turn become accessible. Their clarification presupposes situations in which these domains of meanings and objects can be regarded comprehensively.

When this is done, it becomes clear that phenomenological destruction is not a senseless devastation but a very precisely guided and systematic deconstruction (*Abbau*). Individual meanings must first be regarded as indeterminate and unclear, just as they emerge in factic life, and must be retained in this indeterminacy. This in itself serves to point to contexts whose pursuit leads to the illumination of the meaning of the concept. How is this possible? Every prefiguration of the context of meaning and the motivation for understanding the situational context is a "preconception." This preconception is not ultimate but itself points back to the philosophically basic experience. Every phenomenological-critical destruction is "tied to a preconception" and grows with the prefigured context of sense to which it refers. Phenomenological destruction is therefore not primordial, it refers back to the basic phenomenological experience from which the entire problematic of philosophy originates. But it is also not something secondary which could be omitted. It of itself belongs to philosophy, as a goal of philosophic method, because philosophy does not belong to the domain of definition and universal concepts, the domain of construction, but rather to the fullness of the factic experience of life.

This does not necessarily lead to a positivistic philosophy. For it is not just factic experience which is the object of philosophy, since every factic experience has its original structure given in the character of meaningfulness. But this character can fade in certain contexts, and what is thus experienced falls away (*abfällt*) from its original accessibility, is no longer accessible in its originality. This is not merely a matter of forgetting or loss of interest but something quite peculiar. This fading can also affect the manner of experiencing (the relational sense) and the reactions of life thereto (the sense of actualization), so that what is experienced in it passes over into the character of mere usability, that is, it is taken in an everyday fashion. Experience no longer bears the relation to me which its sense demands. All knowledge and all interest, the entire content of education, likewise fades in this way, calling for an effort to restore functionality to originality. Since factic life nowadays is saturated with the concepts of science and the like, it undergoes an attenuation of its original sense, making it necessary to inquire back to this original sense. This restoration of life experience from its jaded state back to its originality is the goal of critical-phenomenological destruction. Since all of philosophy is burdened by such an experience, it dictates such a destruction if it is to be a genuine philosophy.

This method of conceptual clarification, now more aptly called phenomenological destruction, is to be applied to a concept from each of our two problem-complexes. From the first, we shall single out the concept of history. For it is history which puts the apriori in danger. Here, we can point to the ambiguity and plurivocity of the term in the contemporary historical consciousness, by illustrating six senses of the term at the level of factic life, which appear to be accidentally thrown together:

1. My friend studies history.
2. My friend knows the history of philosophy.
3. There are people (*Volk*) who have no history.
4. History is the magister of life.
5. This man has a sorry history.
6. Today I underwent an unpleasant history.

Ad 1. This refers to the intellectual appropriation of a certain domain, that of historiology, history as a science, which calls for assuming a specific theoretical attitude, directed toward a context of tasks calling for certain methods. But what constitutes the horizon of this theoretical attitude? Here one will also have to specify the domain of objects of historiology.

Ad 2. To this last question, one would once again reply "history," but now in the sense of the past, whatever has happened, what one then did, the field of facts which once was. What this was is the facticity of the past independent of history taken as an attitude. Nevertheless, the historical past becomes an object only in a particular approach. The domain of historical science does not necessarily coincide with the past as a whole, which is always increasing. Everything historical is past, but whether everything past is historical is another question. It is not necessary to be concerned with historical method in order to have access to the past.

Ad 3. Thus the medieval period had no historical science but nevertheless had a history, insofar as it lived in a tradition—a religious one—as no other culture before or after. To have a history in the sense of a tradition seems preferable to being "barbaric"—a term of disparagement applied to a people without history. Not that a folk does not have a history in the objective sense. But this past is not related to its existence as a people, that is, as a subject to which the past is accessible by way of a bent to preserve its past, by placing itself in a living tradition. Such a bent need not be conscious and theoretical. This relation to a people involves a sense that I, as a latecomer, am following something that preceded me. I sense that this past is being preserved for the sake of my own becoming. Only when a people actively cultivates this attitude and continually renews its past do we then have the possibility of a theoretical attitude toward history.

Ad 4. *Historia vitae magistra. Historia* here is not historical science but that part of the objective past which is accentuated by the interests of the present, say, for an active politician. It is a much looser relationship to the past than the third sense, less intimate, since it is not my own but an alien past which serves as a lesson. This latent familiarity with a past not my own comes into play only occasionally in the present, it is not a continual orientation to the past.

Ad 5. "This man has a sorry history." He does not have a history in the way a people has a tradition. That was more a circuitous relation to the past by way of active achievement. Here, it is a deeper and more intimate relation with the past, which is present in its own self-world and the inner tendencies of the self. It is much deeper than just a familiarity with one's past.

Ad 6. History here is something which has happened to me, a particular and significant moment of my life-story which bears upon my present and forces me to take an interest in it in particular.

Every sense context is characterized by the directions of a relational, containing, and actualizing sense. We shall first consider the six meanings of history especially in their genuine relational sense, that is, to the one who requires history in its unique sense. To the one who becomes aware of history, what is the sense in which it is experienced, lived, had? Various shades of this sense of "being had" became clear in meanings 3–6, where history is correlated to my own living Dasein. "Being" and "having" are basic concepts of philosophy yielded by the basic experience, the point of origin to which the phenomenological destruction has brought us. But how is the relational sense shaped in meanings 1 and 2?

The first meaning clearly conveys a richly differentiated and organized theoretical relation to history. There is also a relation to this attitudinal relation which itself need not be theoretical, where the theoretical relation itself is genuinely had in actualization. This actualization sense bears the genuine relation to one's own history, and not the universal, theoretically diluted relation. This dilution is more manifest in the second meaning: history as the objective past is, as a theoretical object, an idea. It is related to an ideal subject which has the entire past as present. This idealization moreover broadens the historical to include all pasts yet to be. We thus are at the opposite extreme from the concrete subject of meanings 3–6. In these, the relational sense is had in full factic actualization, which now becomes the phenomenological norm. It runs counter

to philosophy's tendency toward the apriori ever since Plato. This traditional tendency is oriented toward the ultimate worldview, seeking an
absolute domain which sets the standards for human life, the solution to
the mystery of life. The apriori purportedly provides the supratemporal
norms for the temporal. Thus for Scheler, the human being is the place
for the emergence of a suprahistorical order. History here is that of the
second meaning, where the relational sense is subsumed under an ideal
abstract process, where the human being is simply an "instance" of that
abstract history. The apriori is the supratemporal, historical happenings
are the temporal. Thus, in the theory of judgment, the judicative actualization is temporal and the judicative content supratemporal.

Temporality here is clearly objective temporality. But the supratemporal should be defined not from objective time but from the time of the
self-world, which is the original historical existence in constant relation
to its own past (meaning 5 of "history"). This is history in its full character
of actualization. The six meanings of history must accordingly now be
investigated in terms of their sense of actualization.

First a methodic remark about phenomenological destruction. It
comes into play with the experience of life which has become diluted,
and seeks to place meanings back into their proper contexts. One thus
arrives at the sense of actualization of the experience. In order to establish whether the actualization is original or not, the proximity or distance
of a sense context from the origin must be determined. This decision is
called dijudication. The criterion for this decision lies in the origin itself.
From our present provisional position, characterized in formally indicative fashion, this origin is nothing other than our factic Dasein. An actualization is original when it is the actualization of a genuine relation, which
is at least co-directed by the self-world. Second, this actualization involves
a requirement of renewal which co-constitutes self-worldly Dasein.

Applying these criteria to the six contexts, we find that meaning 5 is
more original than all the others. One's own past is here experienced,
as if for the first time, in its self-worldly significance. But even here,
this significance is ever subject to dilution, to lapsing (*Abfall*) from its
originality into environmental significances, and so must be constantly
renewed, made fresh time and again in its originality.

The actualization of the two theoretical senses (1 and 2) are the farthest removed from originality. Likewise, the tradition is not original, is
to be found only on the second tier of existence, since the past is there
on the level of the environing and the with-world. The same can be said
of meanings 4 and 6, even though all three secondarily maintain some
relations to the self-world and its renewal.

In sum, we have come to two results with regard to the problem of
the apriori: 1) The concept of the apriori is subject to contrary tenden-

cies, first by coming to a head in the human being and his cultural achievements, and then by reducing the human being to an instance in an abstract historical process. 2) More positively, it has yielded the clue that the origin is to be situated in the facticity of the concrete Dasein, in its self-world. It is an initial insight into a new sense of the old contrast between fact and sense.

The latter result brings us to the second problem-group, that of life as irrational experience, which philosophy must somehow rationalize. It must be subjected to an analogous destruction and understood from the origin, which would link it more closely with the first group.

The problem of lived experience can be approached as the problem of self-apprehension. Through the self-reflection of the I on the experiences, they are made objective and thus can be encountered. This gives rise to the danger of reification. How can lived experience be grasped in thought and knowledge? In what way is the experiential context had, what is to be the basic sense of having here? To which three other points can be added to our destructive considerations: What is the structure of unity and multiplicity of such an experiential contexture? How does the I relate to it? How is the I itself had? These four points of view then lead over to phenomenological dijudication: Are the relations of apprehension original or not? Are they originally motivated, which means by a pretheoretical experience, or do they stem from a theoretical deliberation which is then philosophically overextended?

We shall place under destruction several crucial directions in contemporary philosophical psychology, all of which still belong in the Cartesian tradition of the subject: 1) Paul Natorp, 2) William James, 3) Hugo Münsterberg, and 4) Wilhelm Dilthey. (Because of lack of time, only Natorp and Dilthey will eventually be treated.)

Natorp is first for several reasons: his is the most radical and comprehensive treatment of the problem of the subject, coupled with the tendency to concrete life; he likewise speaks of the return to the origin, which will allow us a radical contrast in our respective concepts of "intuition"; he is clearly the propaedeutic to certain tendencies, which now seek to cultivate the connection with Fichte and Hegel; it will allow us to supplement our remarks begun in the previous semester.

(In WS 1919–20, Natorp had been discussed primarily in relation to the problem of givenness, harking back to his two objections against the possibility of its intuition and expression. In Natorp's neo-Kantian scheme, the relation between the apprehension of an object (intuition) and its conceptual determination (expression) is fundamentally reversed. Givenness first arises from the determination and is to be resolved finally in pure determinations of thought. After the mathematical model of the infinite series understood as a Kantian idea, aposteriori content must in the end be derived from the apriori, like a member of a series of integers. The Marburg School naturally concedes that thought always determines "something" which as an ultimate remainder is pregiven, namely, the sensations. But sensations as sensations are only given, obtained, and determined in thought. This is ultimately why Natorp along with the other neo-Kantians, as a consequence of their form-content theory of knowledge, maintain that factic life is wholly inaccessible to the concept.)

Heidegger devotes six class periods (three weeks) to Natorp. We can only summarize some of his most salient points here:

The first question is the manner of the "having" of experiences. The experiential context must be apprehended in its fullest original concretion, in the psychic (the soul, the "subjective"). This ultimate concretion is the unifying dimension, in which all objectivations converge. Psychology is the ultimate discipline of philosophy, its conclusion. And because it has this ultimate place in the unity of the system, the peculiarity of its method must be made clear. The metaphysical apprehension of the subjective must be radically distinguished in opposition to all objectivation. Despite the importance of the apriori norms in guiding the accomplishments of the subject, the question here is not these objective norms but rather the unique subjectivity of the subject. What is the subjective? What is the immediacy of the soul, the totality of lived experience? Subjectivation is exactly the opposite of objectivation, while the two stand in strict correlativity. The subjective is strictly not an objective domain, it is always only "for" the objective. In the progressive objectivation, say, in the natural sciences, the subjective is more and more "put aside," and yet it remains in this progression as the obverse side of the objective, in a reciprocal relationship. It should therefore be possible, on this basis, to devise a method of reconstruction of the subjective without objectifying it. How? By way of the basic concept of potency (Aristotle's δύναμις, philosophy's ultimate concept, its concept of origin), the determinable in contrast with the determined (the actual). The lower limit of consciousness is pure potency, the chaos prior to all determination; the upper limit is pure actuality, the thought of thought, complete determination. Between these ideal limits, there is the real consciousness with the levels of sensation, representation, and thought (with analogues for feeling and willing). Add to these levels the directions of consciousness, the positing of being and of the ought, and we have a complete picture of the natural disposition of consciousness, the "phenomenology" of consciousness. But we do not yet have the concrete individual, we are still mired in the genera and species of consciousness.

The primal concretion, the ultimate individual is the experiential context. How does Natorp approach this problem of lived experience? His basic tendency is to apprehend an experiential context in its all-sided totality though the strictness of method. Concretization is to be found in the unity of all lawlike structures, objective and subjective, in an origin that precedes the distinction of objective and subjective. This takes us back to the primal logic, the primal ground out of which the distinctions of being and ought, theoretical and practical consciousness, first arise. Here, the ultimate individual in its all-sided totality is likewise to receive its full logical determination. Contrary to Windelband and Rickert, the factic individual is not alogical and amorphous but "apeiromorphic," wholly determinable logically. The law of infinite series is the *principium individuationis*. But this is only one moment of the individual; we wish to apprehend it in all of its moments. Only the individual which knows itself as individual is completely determined. This gives us an indication of where its ultimacy is given: the individual exists only when it knows itself in the totality of its determination. Accordingly, the individual is first defined only in the religious consciousness, where the I knows itself over against the ultimate universality: God. In absolute self-consciousness, the I knows itself as much and as certainly as God knows it. The concrete comes to itself in pure self-consciousness. With this self-knowing primal consciousness which thinks itself, where the distinction of subjective and objective is lifted, Natorp arrives at an idealism of the origin or an absolute idealism.

In order to try to understand Natorp's psychology out of its original motives, one must seek to understand the preconception guiding his entire position. His preconception is totally dominated by the idea of constitution as the ultimate idea of philosophy. Constitution means determination in and through consciousness, determination of all relations and their contexts, right down to the primal logical context. The experiential context, its vitality, actuality, originality, receives its determination from constitution. On the basis of the presupposition that all of philosophy consists in demonstrating the constitution in consciousness, Natorp shows that, strictly speaking, the I cannot be an object of thought. It is the condition of thought, the presupposition for all givenness without itself being given. It is the relational point to which all of consciousness relates. Through constitution, Natorp reinterprets intentionality as the relation of contents of consciousness to the relational point of a pure "I." It has a sense of relation and content, but the entire sphere of actualization is denied. There is no such thing as activities of consciousness, the actual hearing of a tone, only the formal relations of ultimate determination. This is already a first step toward the reification of consciousness. From here, it is also understandable why, for Natorp, phenomenological description is abstraction, subsumption under an abstraction, and accordingly a stilling of the stream of experience.

Constitution thus broadens consciousness into a supratemporal context of relations, a context whose universality can only be a logical and theoretical one. The idea of constitution is the expression of a preconception which is motivated from the emancipation of the theoretical as an attitude. It is the dream of the European spirit since Plato, the idea of science as the ultimate goal of human development. (The destruction of Natorp thus ultimately extends back to Plato, a harbinger of things to come.) It is of course conceded that this idea is difficult to carry through. But compared with other domains, the theoretical attitude is really the easiest attitude, for one can always leave it to others to carry through in the future. The individual is spared by ordering himself in a universal progressive development. For "easy" and "difficult" are really categories of the self-world. This already suggests that the idea of constitution does not meet the dijudicative criteria of originality, which are oriented toward the context of actualization of the concrete self-worldly Dasein. This question of the actualization of the philosophical attitude is really alien to Natorp's philosophy, but it must be posed if we wish to grasp the idea of constitution radically. It is motivated by the ideal of philosophy as strict science. But every philosophy claims to be more than a mere science, and this "more" leads back to the very motive for philosophizing. The question of the actualization of philosophizing is not merely a supplementary question, it is a fundamental question in the search for principles which are not simply to be known but are to have ultimate significance for the whole of life. Natorp's philosophy is not original, does not derive from the genuine motive of philosophizing. A comparison with Dilthey will help bring this out.

Regarded externally, it seems as if Dilthey only wanted to found the human sciences, thus placing him in the epistemological tradition from Plato to Natorp. However, despite the quest for cognitive certainty in a comprehensive philosophy of all the sciences and its attempt to give normative support to all human endeavors, much like transcendental philosophy, Dilthey's problem of the human sciences was not a specialist's problem but the expression of a radical philosophical motive: to interpret life originally, from out of itself. Contrary to the empty formality of transcendental philosophy, life philosophy is a necessary stage toward a radical phenomenological philosophy. For philosophy, in its ultimate rationality, still continually experiences its concretion and fulfillment from life, from history. The various objective achievements of cognition and value which define the teleological contexts of humankind, even when they are set off from life, still receive their efficacy from, and thus remain in, life. "Thought is by an inner compunction bound to life, it is itself a formation of life." Even more comprehensive than the normative teleological contexts developed by humankind is the "operative context" (*Wirkungszusammenhang*) of a generation, epoch, or age. This is the basic concept of the human sciences, and their actual reality (*Wirklichkeit*). The core of the operative context, its primary cell or element, is the individual. The typical structures of this vital unity must be detached from its facticity and regarded in their typicality. These structures are not created, they are already given in the vital unity, they are lived in the pre-theoretical. They are accordingly accessible to description and immediate analysis. This is the task of a "descriptive and analytical psychology" or a structural psychology. Its tasks are to provide cross-sections through psychic life, to lay out the longitudinal sections of a universal biography, and to determine the acquired context of psychic life derived from the operative context. Its overall task is to grasp the correlative relationship of self and milieu originally, which means pretheoretically. It is Dilthey's sense of intentionality, in its basic motives and tendencies, its passions, actions, and cognitions.

Dilthey's crucial methodic insight: Psychic life is accessible in an inner perception, which is not a detached reflection. It of itself manifests a rich structure, an inner conceptuality and intellectuality. It articulates itself in itself, it understands itself. Every psychic experience bears within itself a knowledge of its own worth for the whole of the psychic individual. Every living person lives in self-feeling. Inner intuition constantly grows from its experiencing and living of life. Moreover, experience always works itself out in its context: I always experience myself in situations. Psychological research is merely the explication of this original experience of the self-world.

Unfortunately, Dilthey never makes this inner rationality itself into a problem. But his grasp of the problem of lived experience in a truly original fashion provides us with a direction which has not yet been exhausted. We can pursue this direction by proceeding to a destruction of Dilthey's philosophy, which can now be expedited by a running comparison with Natorp's philosophy and its proximity to the origin.

In Dilthey, the concrete self is the primary cell of the operative context, while in Natorp the concrete I assumes a secondary position (for him the pure I is the problem-ground, thus not itself a problem). This juxtaposition is necessarily schematic; consideration of the problem of the self-positing of the consciousness and its stream in James and Münsterberg would have given this return to the origin more concreteness. Nevertheless, we shall see that, while Natorp is absolutely removed from the origin, Dilthey stands close to the origin.

The concept of context is for Dilthey fundamental, it is his preconception. The whole of lived experience is an operative context. Experience thus has the basic trait of reality (*Wirklichkeit*), which Dilthey repeatedly characterizes as "objective," while for Natorp it is psychic and therefore subjective. Dilthey attempts to understand the entire world in terms of life. But his original insights are distorted 1) by vestiges of the moment of constitution which are smuggled in from transcendental philosophy, and 2) by a traditional terminology which is alien to the return to vital origins.

1) Life is a real operative context which is historical and so subject to development, and which possesses an inner articulation and rationality. Life can therefore be interpreted from itself and in terms of itself. The experiential context accordingly finds its functional value in being the "condition of the possibility" for the understanding of the vital unity. The operative context as the condition for understanding permeates all of Dilthey's philosophical and psychological considerations. Lived experience is itself a preliminary form of understanding. Life has in advance the character of understanding.

2) When Dilthey is posed with the task of characterizing the ultimate center of the psychic unity, he says: the human being is, to begin with and originally, a bundle of feelings and drives. Will, needs, and their satisfaction are the elementary psychic forces. Psychic reality is thus reified and reduced to an object, a position which approaches the biologism of the time. Even though Dilthey's original tendency is not biologistic, this double order of constitution and elementary forces serves to distort his sense of the reality of life and the originality of understanding. His view of the inner core of psychic reality is conditioned by external influences from his extensive work in intellectual history and biography, especially of the eighteenth century: Goethe's ideal of humanity developing toward a harmonious Gestalt of the soul. His concept of context as a harmony is thus ultimately aesthetic. By not putting these traditional concepts under radical scrutiny, Dilthey is unclear about the new origin toward which he is groping and from which he is already drawing. This is the peculiar contribution of phenomenology, with its radical orientation toward our actual Dasein, which has thrown its disruptive torch into modern philosophy and its systems.

Both Natorp and Dilthey seek to understand the experiential context as a whole. For Natorp it is the whole of a logical constitution, for Dilthey the whole of the operative context of life. For Natorp this whole cannot be grasped through objectification, but requires the method of reconstruction. Dilthey's method is in its way also a reconstruction, that of a "constitution" in the context of life through an understanding of what has in and out of life been "uttered," *out*ered, expressed, and so objectified. The context of reconstruction for Natorp is purely formal, but for Dilthey it is defined by the triadic interconnection of lived experience, expression, and understanding: experience leads to expression, this to understanding, and then back to lived experience to close the circle. In both, the actual self-world, the historically actualized Dasein of the individual as individual, tends to dissipate. The self, in short, becomes secondary, in Natorp as the x of a universal context of determination, in Dilthey as the absolute Gestalt of a harmonious soul.

These two philosophers illustrated two typical positions to the problem of life and lived experience. Our destruction of the other problem-group, that of the apriori, led to a similar conclusion, that transcendental philosophy pursues its secure, that is, theoretically detached, course by forgetting the *unum necessarium*, the actual Dasein. In neither problem-group does it become a possible philosophical problem. Thus, the destruction seems to have yielded a series of "no-sayings," but it in fact is a positive expression of the original motive of philosophizing, which serves to make our own Dasein insecure (*Unsichermachen*) at its core, counter to the security of the trend to turn philosophy into a wholly theoretical endeavor, a strict science. Philosophy is neither a strict science nor a doctrine of worldviews, though the latter tendency still carries with it some of the restlessness (*Beunruhigung*) of our individual Dasein that prompts the original motive of philosophizing. Carrying out the destruction out of the tendency to get at the original, and to determine it originally, will take us to a radical and original idea of phenomenology, which will revive the original motive of philosophizing to its fullest distress (*Bekümmerung* = the trouble and affliction of "concern").

The questions of intuition and expression are to be understood in this original context of insecurity. Intuition queries the how of philosophical experience, and expression the manner of explicating whatever is given in the how. The problem of philosophical concept formation is thus not a secondary supplementary problem. It is the problem of arriving at the philosophical experience. It is the task of the ways and means of approaching the origin, of securing it so as to bring the motive and tendency of the philosophical experience to expression in genuine philosophical concepts.

Contrary to the neo-Kantians, the "problem of facticity" is not that of the transcendental determination of the individual out of ultimate logical laws. For the original facticity is not an absolute consciousness, the place of the determination of transcendental constitution (Natorp), nor the x of logical determination (Rickert), but rather a primal reality ever to be experienced, the self in the actualization of life-experience. (Here, for the very first time, Heidegger clearly coopts the neo-Kantian term "facticity" for his own unique technical use.) It is to be experienced not by taking cognizance of it, but by vital participation in it, being distressed by it, troubled and put out of ease, so that the troubled self who "minds" or "cares" is continually affected (*betroffen*) by this affliction. Every reality (around-, with-, and self-world) receives its original sense from the distress of the self and its modifications. This affliction of the self is a continual concern over the possibility of falling away from the origin. Facticity as actualization is not to be shunted out and avoided. Philosophy has the task of maintaining and intensifying the facticity of life. Philosophy as factic experience of life needs a motive which maintains the concern and affliction over it. This preservation of the motive is what we designate as the basic philosophical experience. It is not a special illumination, but is possible in any concrete Dasein in which the tribulation has restored us to our actual Dasein. In the reversal of this renewal, factic experience is oriented to the self-world, from which the entire conceptuality of philosophy is to be understood and determined. From it, the original determination of philosophy receives its sense. The strictness of philosophy is more original than any scientific strictness. Its distress, in its constant renewal, raises us into the facticity of Dasein and makes the actual Dasein radically insecure. The only one on the way toward such a philosophy, to be sure without seeing that he is, is Karl Jaspers (*Psychologie der Weltanschauungen*, 1919). The way is possible only on the basis of Dilthey's intuitions.

"CRITICAL COMMENTS ON KARL JASPERS'S *PSYCHOLOGY OF WORLDVIEWS*"

The essay bearing this title was meant to be a review of Jaspers's groundbreaking book, which will inaugurate German *Existenzphilosophie*, for publication in the *Göttingische Gelehrte Anzeigen*. It was not published until 1972, but in June 1921 Heidegger distributed a typescript of it to Jaspers, Husserl, and Rickert. As a "private communication," it was a topic of conversation and correspondence especially between Heidegger and Jaspers, and copies of it were also transcribed by some of Heidegger's students at the time (F. J. Brecht, Walter Bröcker, Herbert Marcuse).

The first editor of the text, Hans Saner, places its composition "in the years 1919–21," but also notes that its first draft could not have been concluded before 1920, in view of a reference to a 1920 book by Rickert criticizing life philosophy. Reading the text in the terminological context of the above lecture courses indicates strongly that the first draft took definitive shape in the weeks following SS 1920. The review utilizes terms like "dijudication" (GA 9:22) and the abstraction "facticity" (22, 32)[2] and refers time and again to the fundamental "distress" (*Bekümmerung*: 22, 30, 32ff.) of factic experience, all of which are first terminologically introduced in SS 1920. Likewise, it utilizes the distinction between life as creative shaping and as vital experiencing, which plays a central role in that course's destruction of life philosophy. Needless to say, the vocabulary first coined in WS 1919–20 (destruction, having-myself, the triads of around-, with-, and self-world, as well as of relational, containment and actualization senses) is also very much in evidence in this review.

The review can be regarded as a continuation of the course of SS 1920, providing a destruction of Jaspers's psychology after the pattern already followed in the critiques of Natorp and Dilthey. From the opening sentence and throughout the review, Heidegger identifies what he is doing as a "critique which reveals the positive" in this remarkable book, precisely in the way in which he first described the phenomenological destruction in SS 1919. We have accordingly translated the somewhat flaccid German title (*Anmerkungen*) as "*critical* comments" on the text. Also in this review, Heidegger maintains a careful distinction between the positive *critique* of a work or a figure and the more comprehensive "historical *destruction* of the tradition, a task which is equivalent to the explication of the original motive-giving situation from which the basic experiences of philosophy originate" (3).

The critique aims at what is fundamental, namely, the "immanent intentions" (1) of this unique groundbreaking book, in order to bring into sharper focus and contour the true tendency and basic motives of Jaspers's problematic and its method. Are the motives and tendencies taken radically enough, in view of the tentative basic direction of the philosophizing toward limits being carried out here? The critique does not seek to provide fixed norms of orientation, especially the methodic ideals of scientific-philosophical rigor which would judge the investigation in terms of its "absolute validity of truth," "relativism," and "skepticism." It aims to be more radical. It seeks to inquire behind such cognitive ideals toward their "sense-genetic motives of origin in our intellectual history" (3), in order to determine whether they are adequate to the fundamental sense of philosophizing or belong rather to the inauthenticity of a decadent tradition. Critique thus joins the larger project of destruction of what has been transmitted by that intellectual history, questioning whether the sense of theory itself merely comes to us tailor-made from its origin in Plato and Aristotle. In putting aside such traditional norms, one can call such a critique phenomenological, that is, "presuppositionless," without denying that every intuitive actualization "lives in a particular orientation and preconception which anticipates its region" (4). For the phenomenological sense of originality is not a suprahistorical idea. It is instead intent upon "pursuing its object of investigation in its immanent prefigurations" (6), where "presuppositionlessness itself can only be won in a self-critique which is factically and historically oriented" (5). "It may well be that even the directions of access to the matters of philosophy lie concealed and require a radical deconstruction and rebuilding, an authentic confrontation with the history which we ourselves 'are' " (5). There is thus at once a negative and a positive edge to the critique; it is a "destructively self-renewing appropriation" (4), a "radically destructive, but always fundamentally oriented 'preliminary labor' " (6). The critique succeeds in its "preliminary labor" when it "calls attention and lays claim to this or that crucial experience of motivation for the explication of the phenomena which come into question" (6).

As extensive as this opening statement already is, Heidegger will feel the need time and again in the course of his review to amplify and supplement his radical method of critique with other aspects of the phenomenological method which he is then busily conceiving. The review is thus as much a "discourse on method" of Heidegger's own devising as it is about the substance of Jaspers's book. Small wonder, then, that Jaspers from the start developed a sense of alienation from this written critique, which spent so much space on esoteric questions of method, a sense which was ameliorated only by the sympathy for the book's contents and perspectives that Heidegger expressed in their personal conversations.[3] Instead of the creative ideal of "loving struggle" which Jaspers had hoped for in their philosophical conversation, the relationship between these two philosophical geniuses gradually lapsed into separate monologues before it broke off completely.

Jaspers himself lays down a double task for his book: 1) the constitution of psychology as a whole and its basic question, what the human being is. This holistic task is to be realized not by the usual generalizing approach (Natorp's "general psychology") but by way of 2) a psychology of worldviews, which seeks to "pace off " the limits of the soul and so to provide a clear and comprehensive *horizon* for the psychic (1). As the Foreword (PW 5f.)[4] notes, such a psychology does not offer a particular view of the world, but rather seeks to understand what ultimate positions the soul can assume and what forces move it to do so. It accordingly provides "elucidations and possibilities as means for self-examination" of such worldviews. The assumption is that the limits of psychic life are crucial in defining worldviews:

> Such an attempt to fix the region of the psychic whole, which by such a route and on such a scale has never before been undertaken, let alone aspired to, from the very onset of the problem works with a certain basic assumption of psychic life. This life has limits, there are "limit situations" to which certain "reactions" are possible, such reactions to the antinomically structured limit situations "play themselves out" in the "vital process" of psychic life as their medium. Spiritual existence arises through antinomy. (7)

Terms like limits, antinomy, reactions which "influence" spiritual existence, already suggest a "traditionally charged preconception" in need of exposition, not necessarily to dismiss it as an "unwarranted presupposition" but rather to determine whether it is true to the guiding tendency of the problem: Is the task of arriving at the whole of psychology thereby

served in its requisite radicality? Jaspers, who claims to have "no dominant method, but sometimes this, sometimes that," all within the basic
attitude of "mere observation and contemplation" (*Betrachtung*: 10), is
in need of a more radical discourse on method in his work. But the
preconception not only brings with it a sense of method but, more importantly, assumes a certain object of study tentatively called "psychic life."
The lack of a "rigorous" sense of this constellation of preconception,
method, and object can more fatally lead to the surreptitious entry of
an "intuitive and conceptual surrogate" (10), which in the end makes
itself out to be the genuine phenomenon under study.

It is therefore important to note from the start what Jaspers's object
of study really is. "The truly objective dimension in question may in
formal indication be fixed as existence (*Existenz*). In such a formally indicated signification, the concept is intended to refer and point to the
phenomenon of the 'I am,' the sense of being which lies in the 'I am' as the
starting point of a fundamental phenomenal context and the problematic
belonging to it" (10). Jaspers himself introduces the term as a Kantian
Idea, "something which counts as the whole, or as existence." He then
traces it back to its sources in Kierkegaard and Nietzsche, for whom
Existenz refers to "the life of the present individuality" and always implies
the question of the genuineness of psychic life and the extreme movement of unrest (*Unruhe*) in psychic Dasein (PW 12f.). Rather than as a
Kantian Idea asymptotic to the ineffable, Heidegger approaches existence as a "formal indication"—a crucial methodic idea, as we know from
previous semesters, which he refuses to explain in this review (10f., 29)
and will do so for the first time only in the following WS 1920–21[5]—precisely to avoid merely lapsing back into the particulars in which Kierkegaard and Nietzsche understood the term (11). Likewise, he does not
explain the uniquely ontological twist he gives to the term, which will
take fruit years later only in the very last draft of BT. But he does accept
Jaspers's approach to a genuine sense of the phenomenon of existence
through limit situations, provided that one takes the precaution of being
alert to the preconceptions operative in Jaspers's account. Jaspers, for
his part, will over the years steadfastly reject such an ontological conceptuality in his own approaches to the question of being human.

Thus, only on one point do they really join forces: the phenomenon
of existence is illuminated in and through limit situations, those decisive
situations "which are tied to what the human being as such is, and are
inevitably given with finite Dasein" (11; PW 229). They all pose ultimate
incompatibilities or antinomies which frustrate our desire to see our finite
situation as a whole, to ascertain the totality of the world and of life.
Thus the limit situation of death contradicts life, chance contradicts necessity and meaning, war contradicts reciprocity, guilt contradicts inno-

cence. We react to these antinomic situations by looking for ways to resolve them and to find stability in relation to them. For the antinomic means destruction,[6] which is always experienced in a co-experience of the whole, of the unity which is somehow being broken. "Contradictions remain as antinomies at the limit of our knowledge *in the face of* infinities" (12, 25; PW 232). The consciousness of limits is the consciousness of the infinite whole of life, the experience of antinomy is at once the experience of its unity. The sense of antinomy and limit is traceable back to a particular aspect of the infinite. From antinomy springs the will to unity as a force of life, which in fact is the life of the spirit (11f., 25f.).

A unity broken, a totality disrupted, an infinity limited: it is clear that the preconception of the "whole" (unity, totality, infinity) is precisely what imparts sense to the talk of "antinomy," "contradiction," and "destruction." Insofar as the human being sees himself situated in the whole of life as an ultimate, experiences his existence as encompassed by this unbroken medium, he stands in antinomies. It is only from the perspective of flowing life as a whole that the antinomies destroy and divide. This is the experience of the limit situation (12).

Jaspers's preconception suggests that he belongs among the life philosophers of that time, and is therefore subject to the usual critique, newly posed by Rickert (1920), of vagueness of concepts, totally devoid of any methodical sense of philosophical concept formation. But on the positive side, it must be said that life philosophy, particularly with the superior level it attains in Dilthey, dares to take a radical direction in philosophy, concealed as it is in traditionally derived rather than the originally drawn means of expression which it demands. It is a matter of seeing that the most highly developed life philosophies tend toward the phenomenon of existence. From the fruitful plurivocity of the word "life" as primal phenomenon, two predominant directions of sense can be drawn, both of which express the tendency toward the phenomenon of existence: 1) Life as objectification in the sense of creative shaping and achievement, setting *out* from itself and thus **"being there"** (*Da sein*) *in* this life and *as* such a life. 2) Life as vital experiencing (*Er-leben*), as the peripatetics (*Er-fahren*) of learning encounter, apprehending, drawing to itself and thus **"being there"** *in* such experiencing (13–15). Thus, some three years before Heidegger will define Dasein as a technical term (in SS 1923), he utilizes its hyphenation, admittedly with some obscurity and ambiguity, to suggest in a single term both the "ins" and the "outs" of life, the complex vectorial relations of "being out toward," in-volved with in-terest "in" the world. It will take as long for Heidegger to let the term "life" go and replace it with "Dasein" as his central topic of investigation, the "primal phenomenon." It will take even longer for him to identify its "outering" formally with an etymologically understood sense of exsistence.

(*Existenz* thus would in some sense hold together, in equiprimordiality, both vectorial directions of "Da sein." To sum this up in Heidegger's later terms, being-in is at once being-out. Heidegger had already analyzed the hermeneutic situation of SS 1920 in terms of this double direction of life according to two modish words, "culture" and "lived experience," from the two philosophies of the day, transcendental value-philosophy and life-philosophy, their respective problems, the apriori and the irrational, and diverging philosophical goals, strict science and worldviews. Thus, *Dasein* and *Existenz* are here being discreetly groomed to find a resolution to this polarity of the rational and the irrational, the ins and outs of life, at that threshold of experience where the implicit initially becomes explicit. Dilthey in his more Hegelian moments liked to say, "Culture is the ex-pression of life." Life, however, was by and large not considered as such, but instead in relation to ultimate norms and values, to the devaluation of life *itself*. Phenomenology's *genealogically* oriented formal indication accordingly seeks to bring us closer to the immediacy of life *itself* than Jaspers's *teleologically* oriented Kantian Idea is capable of doing.)

Jaspers makes an advance over life philosophy by concentrating on the problem of existence, in the context of psychology, by way of hitherto unseen phenomena like the limit situations. He fails to get at the problem philosophically by believing that this pre-grip from the whole of life truly gives him a grip on the phenomenon of existence, and that he can grasp it with the conceptual means of the prevalent scientific milieu (15). The effort betrays an objectifying perspective which sees life as *the* enveloping region, an infinite flowing whole in which the constructive and deconstructive processes of life unfold (18). Even when it is noted that the primal phenomenon of life is the subject-object split, this makes sense only when the "unsplit" is regarded as the basic reality. "Everything split, all movements, actions, and reactions break out of the whole and return to it and, time and again, pass through it" (21). This would make the ultimate striving of life toward the encompassing absolute into a movement toward an ineffable "mystical" unity beyond the subject-object split.

Nevertheless, the basic sense of the relation between subject and object would be the split. But if we move from this theoretically distorted sense of intentionality back to the pretheoretical triple sense of relation, content, and actualization which governs our concrete existence, we find a more determinate basic striving toward a unique future, not toward the mystical. "This authentic dimension . . . is the prestructuration of one's own existence actualized in a selflike appropriation in each particular facticity of life, that is, the opening and holding open of the concrete and trouble-laden horizon of expectation which every context of actualization as such develops" (22).

What basic bearing or experience motivates Jaspers's preconception? Where does it come from? If he were asked, the question might seem trivial and hollow, or he might answer:

> Life as a whole is for me a leading idea, I only have to look around, this life is everywhere simply there. This whole, unified, unbroken, beyond opposition, enveloping every life, alien to fracture and destruction, ultimately harmonious, guides me. In its light I see every detail, it provides true illumination, it prefigures the basic sense in which everything encountered is determined and grasped as forming itself and breaking forth from this life and sinking back into it. This whole provides the essential articulation of the objective dimension which the contemplation has sought to order. (23)

Jaspers's motivational experience is accordingly the holding in view of the whole of life as such, as an idea. It can formally be called an "aesthetic basic experience." This means that the relational sense of the primary experience, which pregives life as an object which is "everywhere simply there," is a looking at, a covetous be-holding (*Be-trachten*) of something as a spectacle (23). It is the bearing that contemplatively holds (*Haltung*) the whole of life in unity and harmony, untroubled by any self-worldly concern (37). (Two years later, Heidegger will comprehend this attitude under the heading of "curiosity.")

Where historically does Jaspers get his absolute of the whole of life? Jaspers's "contemplation" clearly stands in the heritage of Kant's doctrine of antinomies and the concept of infinity which guides it, along with Kierkegaard's concept of the absolute purified of its specifically Lutheran or theological elements. These two components are then inserted into the current concept of life in all of its dilution, which in fact becomes the prevailing element. Assumed in this uncritical fashion, this "accidental" heritage only serves to obscure the genuine insights (via limit situations) into a genuine problem (existence) which Jaspers might have to offer (27).

The three major points of critique of Jaspers are remarkably similar to those developed in the previous semester (SS 1920) against Natorp and Dilthey. The real question is whether Jaspers's preconception, in its objective regionalization, aesthetic attitude, and terminological heritage, can approach the phenomenon of existence at all. How does it stand with existence? How is it to be even approached?

> *Existenz* . . . is a particular way of being, a certain sense of the "is," which "is" essentially the sense of (I) "am." It is a sense that is not genuinely had in theoretical intending, but instead in the actualization of the "am," which

is a way of being of the "I." The being of the self thus understood signifies, when formally indicated, existence. This also provides the indication of where the sense of existence as the particular how of the self (of the I) must be drawn from. What becomes decisive is that I *have myself*; this is the basic experience in which I encounter myself as a self, so that, living in this experience, I can question the sense of the "I am" in a responsive way, appropriate to *its* sense. This having-myself assumes different senses in different regards, so that this manifold of sense must be made comprehensible not in orderly contexts set off for themselves in systematically regional fashion, but in specifically *historical* contexts. (29)

Existence thus gives an ontological spin to the original experience of phenomenology that we have encountered in previous semesters. But it is the same concrete self-worldly Dasein, which is actualized in the way "I have myself." I am in having myself. The concepts of "being" and "having," Heidegger already noted in the previous semester, are to be developed out of the basic experience (5). The truly actualized ground experience of the "am" thus "goes about [*geht um* = concerns] me myself radically and purely" (29). It is not experienced as an I which stands in a region, as an instance of a universal; the I is simply experienced in its full actuality and facticity, as itself. Every attempt to set it in a "stream of consciousness" or "context of lived experiences," and the like, would only congeal the sense of the "am" and turn the "I" into an object. Whence the necessity of a radical suspicion of all objectifying and regionalizing preconceptions. "Followed to its origin and genuine ground experience, the sense of existence is precisely *the* sense of being which cannot be obtained from the 'is' which explicates specifically by taking cognizance and so somehow objectifies, but from the *distressed* having of itself which is actualized *before* a possible supplementary, but for the actualization unimportant, objectifying cognizance of the 'is' " (30). The "I am" of existence, as a sense or how of being, can also be formally addressed as "he is," for example. But it should also be noted that this can assume different nuances of significance, and this variability serves to articulate a manifold of life contexts or regions of objects: 1) "he is" in the sense of being on hand, or "present at hand," an occurrence in objective nature; 2) "he is" as playing a role in the environmental with-world, as in "Why is he in the cafe?" This latter "is" includes a "was" and "will be" which are of decisive significance for the "he" (31).

Aside from their ontologizing tendency, these pages (29–36) will be familiar enough to readers of Heidegger's surrounding lecture courses on the proper topic and method of phenomenology. He takes time off here from his function as a reviewer to present some of his own work on the basic experience of phenomenology. In this basic experience, the facticity of the I is decisive. One's own here-and-now lived factic experience, brought to actualization in this historical situation, also actualizes the original experience that arises from it, remains in it, and returns back to the factic. This factic experience of life is not a region in which I stand; it is essentially a historical phenomenon in accord with the how of its own actualization. "Historical" here does not mean object-historical, which regards my life as playing itself out in the present, as in the historical sciences, but rather is actualization-historical, experienced in the process of actualization. (This distinction within the "historical" will play an important role in the religion courses of the coming two semesters.) It is not the correlate to objective historical observation but to the what and how of the distressed concern (*Bekümmerung*) of the self for itself. Like the later "care," this forerunner is experienced as a peculiar nonobjective union of the self's past, present, and future. Self-having grows out of, maintains itself in, and tends toward this distress. And the troubled self is the self actualizing its conscience, which serves time and again to renew this distress. Having myself is having a conscience. This suggests a connection between conscience and historical experience, when history is understood more fundamentally as the history which we ourselves are and by which we are burdened and borne. This sense of conscience and responsibility carries over into history in the ordinary sense, the "object-historical" sciences, whose roots go more deeply than mere curiosity to the distress that we ourselves are. But the tendency to fall away from these deeper sources must constantly be counteracted by way of the destruction of the tradition which, once again, has as its positive function the revival of these motivating original situations, in this case, the motives for the very return to the originally historical (32–34).

Heidegger finalizes his excursus into the "present position of phenomenology" with a list of urgent tasks toward the self-clarification of its philosophical sense: 1) To what extent does the basic bearing of phenomenology, with its problematic of existence, provide philosophy with its most radical origin of sense and the decisive direction of concern which governs every problematic? 2) To what extent is "history" appropriated here in such a way that it becomes more than a discipline of philosophy? Does it make clear that the historical in its very meaning from the very beginning and originally is already indigenous to the philosophical problematic, so that the problem of connecting history of philosophy to systematic philosophy is at its roots a false problem? 3) To what extent can the phenomenological attitude be misused for any intellectual and literary mischief, providing the apologetic grounds for a made-to-order orthodox dogmatics to which it is currently being perverted? (36)

Heidegger concludes his review with a recapitulation especially of his critique of Jaspers's method, and even his lack of concern over this issue. A recurrent excuse has been the purported "ineffability" of life (19f.,

24), in view of its "infinitely flowing" character, where concepts would only disrupt and "still the stream" (Natorp). This "specifically Bergsonian argument" only leaves the real methodical issue of the relation between concepts and meanings of phenomena begging. Besides, this sort of gesture gives the impression that one has really caught a glimpse of inexpressible dimensions. But if one has really succeeded in exposing new contexts of phenomena, as Jaspers has in fact done, such a perverse theory of expression is superfluous. Then it is more a matter of noting how the terms that mark the ineffability, like "life," function in context. For Jaspers, "life" is the enveloping realm, the basic reality into which all phenomena are inserted. The term therefore performs a definable linguistic and methodical function. Heidegger thus in the end sees a further task in any appeal to ineffability: "Instead of repeating again and again the oft-quoted *individuum est ineffabile*, it is high time we ask what sense the *fari* [speech] should thereby have and what sort of apprehension should come to expression" (39f.). This is in fact Heidegger's problem of "formal indication."

There are also the hidden motives being betrayed in such appeals to ineffability, in Jaspers's case, that of the detached observer who only describes what is "already there" and in the process erects elaborate typologies of human behavior. This is the major point that Heidegger is trying to communicate to Jaspers, namely, that his own interpretative behavior is very much a part of his topic. What Jaspers thus classifies is not just bare and naked "life": it is life that has already been brought to understanding and conceptual expression. And what Jaspers does is to insert all of this into his own context of understanding through his own preconceptions. Jaspers thus should become more attentive to his own historical situation of interpretation, " 'historical' not only in the external sense that the interpretation is valid for a certain time, but rather that it, in its ownmost sense of actualizing its 'contemplation', has something essentially historical for its object" (38). Heidegger accordingly concludes his review by advising that "mere contemplation must go on to the 'infinite process' of a radical questioning which holds itself in the question" (43).

The surprising new development in the Jaspers review is accordingly the overt ontologizing of the topic of the phenomenology of life. The original experience of phenomenology is a (pre)ontological experience. Radical phenomenology is ontology, an ontology of "Da sein," an ontology of the "(I) am." Existence, a term subject to the same incidental and casual uses as "being," is to indicate the "sense of being" (*Seinssinn*) of the "I am." And this sense of being is to find its sense of actualization within the triple sense of intentionality operative in the concrete Dasein. One is reminded of Heidegger's scholastic training as he makes "I am" the prime phenomenon, and thus the prime analogate from which other analogates, like "he is," are to take their bearings. But in the context of the review, the first effort is to shift the locus within the central question of psychology, "What is it to be human?," from the psyche, human life, to the "is," and even more tellingly, from the "I" to the "am." Heidegger already seems to be aware of the dangers of anthropologization of his starting point with this turn. The locus of the "am' is not in the psyche but in history, the history "which we ourselves are," therefore (against Jaspers's metaphysical proclivities) not in life as an infinite medium but in time and as time. One can however doubt whether the titular question of "Being and Time" is yet fully grasped at this point, or even whether Heidegger has yet begun to refine his concept of time to any great extent. Some steps in this direction will be taken in the following semester. But the final refinement of time comes only after a crucial refinement of "existence" of its last vestiges of ousiological dross, which brings it to its full formal potential, just before the final draft of BT.

With Heidegger's reluctance to let go of the term "life" altogether, the shift from "life" to "Dasein" will take several more semesters to complete, and to "existence" not until the final draft of BT. He perhaps senses that the shift to the personal "I am" could irretrievably overpower his initial sense of being as an impersonal "primal something," an It which worlds, properizes, and so "happens" to me (KNS 1919). But this impersonal function is now to be taken over and conveyed by the "facticity" of the "I am." Almost exactly a year after he first sent his review to Jaspers, Heidegger writes to him to reinforce its most telling points, and first of all "the basic sense of the facticity of life":

> It must be made clear what it means to be involved in "making up" human *Dasein*, to have a part in it. But this means that the sense of being of *being*-alive, of *being*-human, must be originally won and categorially defined. The psychic is not something that the human being "has," consciously or unconsciously, but something that he is and *which lives him*. Fundamentally, this means that there are objects which one does not have but "is"; objects whose What rests simply in the "That they are."[7]

Heidegger then goes on to explain that, for this task, the categorial structures of the old ontology of the Greeks—terms like What versus That—must be subjected to a "critique at their roots" and "newly built from the ground up." It is now mid-1922. Clearly, the ontological direction first struck in the Jaspers review two years before is beginning to shape itself into the double-pronged ontological program, at once systematic and historically destructive, which will eventually become BT.

But in 1922, the ontological thrust of the program, its formal indication, focuses first on the full *facticity* of the "I am," and not on the *project* of "existence" understood as a forward-tending "(having-)to-be" (*Zu-sein*: 1925). Significantly, when Heidegger first broaches the formal indication of the "I am" publicly to his students in the last two hours of WS 1921–22 in late February 1922, he never even mentions the term "existence" (GA 61:172–181, 145–155).[8] But in this early attempt to get at the peculiar "objectivity," or sense of being, of factic life, the bridge between the facticity of the "I am" and the later project of "to be" emerges in the question "Am I?" by which the "I am" is concretely actualized in the context of factically "ruinant" life. The question in all of its disquietude and distress does not admit of a ready and simple Yes or No response, becomes more concrete and original the more counterruinant it becomes, and for the philosopher is all the more indeterminate and labile by its focus on the "am" rather than the "I." This counterruinant questionability of factic life is really the new immediacy of life's facticity, exposing it in all of its mobility as the new "object" of philosophy, breaching the "insular sacrosanctity" (152) of the old immediacy of the givenness of the lived world which temporalizes itself in factically ruinant life, from which the factic Dasein itself is in fact absent, is simply not "there" (148, 154f.). The new "object" of philosophy is therefore not an object at all in the traditional sense of an in-itself, but a deliberate countermovement which brings us to a new kind of "ob-ject" (*Gegen-stand* as "counter-stance": cf. WS 1920–21) which is insuperable in its resistivity and opposition when compared to the purported resistance of the object in the traditional sense (177f., 148). This new ob-ject is in fact the moving context of factic life in the full vitality of its facticity, that is, in its specific temporality, which is accessible only in the questioning which reverses life's ruinance and counters the annihilation of its very being. Pursuing this countermovement to its originality opens the possibility of genuinely illuminating the basic experiences in which factic life qua life can encounter (*begegnen*: 176) itself.

This oppositional "immediacy" between life's temporal movement and its countermovement constitutes the nuclear insight which will structure the systematic part of the program first developed later in the year of 1922. It will eventually bear the title "Being *and* Time."

FOUR

The Religion Courses (1920–21)

From a genealogical perspective which has followed the initial, and to some extent secret, development of the various seeds of Docent Heidegger's phenomenology of the religious life (chap. 2 above), it would seem a virtual inevitability that he should teach a course or two on the philosophy of religion. And the year's incubation which followed his cancellation of the course on "The Philosophical Foundations of Medieval Mysticism" would seem sufficient time for such a task for someone who, at least to those close to him, manifested such an intense continuing interest in matters of religion and theology. Given this background, after a year spent in deconstructing life, what could be more natural than a year devoted to the philosophical deconstruction of the religious life in all of its tacit pretheoretical possibilities? And so it turned out, in a year which would prove consistent with the in-depth development of 1) the *Bekümmerung* of life, first introduced at the end of SS 1920 and now traced back to its patristic and biblical roots; and of 2) the dimension of history which, as Schleiermacher and Dilthey had already taught Heidegger, was absolutely central to the religious life. The distinction between the object-historical and actualization-historical, first introduced in this year, will prove to be an indispensable "formal indication" for the later problematic of "Being *and* Time."

And yet the reasons which led to the cancellation of the course on the philosophy of mysticism in 1919 were still valid in 1920 for a course in the philosophy of religion, and in fact to a greater degree, to which new reasons arising from another year of teaching at Freiburg could now be added. The "overwhelming concern" (chap. 2, p. 108) for methodology which entered into the plans for the earlier course now drown out a discussion of religious phenomena in the new course to such a degree

149

that some of the less methodologically inclined students will complain to the dean! This is most unfortunate for posterity, since Heidegger was in the middle of his one and only truly sustained treatment of the "formal indication" at the time; he abruptly dropped this vital but somewhat advanced topic and never really returned to it again. The fact that the autograph for this course is missing may be due to the same troubled circumstances. All that remain in the archives directly from Heidegger's "hand" are some notes on the brilliant but erratic interpretation of the Pauline letters which succeeded the uniquely important treatment of the formal indication. These may well have been the notes from which Heidegger improvised an entirely different conclusion to the course than the one which was undoubtedly carefully worked out in the original lecture manuscript. At any rate, the unusual circumstances surrounding this *cursus interruptus*, prematurely thwarted in its original thrust and then carried to a different climax, should be duly noted in any study of its contents from the extant student transcripts.

In retrospect, we find a remarkably prescient remark by Heidegger, in a letter to Löwith on October 9, 1920, about this course three weeks before it begins (on October 29): "This semester, I want to start a little earlier. Not that I am particularly enthusiastic about my lecture course. I have the feeling that it will come to grief and fall apart in the course of the semester, since I am at the moment making good headway for myself, so that some of the lectures are already a bit obsolete. Trying to patch things up never really works."[1] Other letters to his student Löwith suggest that Heidegger is assuming the role of philosopher of religion in Husserl's school of phenomenology, already assigned to him by the Master in 1918, with great reluctance, and even antipathy. "I myself am no longer even regarded as a 'philosopher' [by Husserl, "der Alte"], I am 'still really a theologian' " (October 20). He complains about the poor theological grounding of his seminar students, who nevertheless want to study Kierkegaard or Descartes with him. "Kierkegaard can be truly exposed *only* theologically (as I understand theology and will develop in the Winter Semester)."[2] And ever since Heidegger's study of Dilthey, Descartes's "Cogito" can only be understood in the context of all of Christian philosophy going back to at least Augustine. "I myself want to learn something in my seminars, through objections and difficulties. Since these are posed with the necessary sharpness and precision only when the participants are equal to the matter at hand, I have for now decided to forgo a seminar in the phenomenology of religion. For, to be frank, all that would come of it is the kind of babble in the philosophy of religion that I want to eliminate from philosophy, this talk about the religious which is familiar to us from reference works" (September 13). "I would like to do away with 'talking' about the religious, but it is perhaps inevitable. It is also a false expectation regarding my lecture course, if anyone thinks that is what I plan to do. It is probably best to say so from the start" (September 19).

WS 1920–21: INTRODUCTION TO THE PHENOMENOLOGY OF RELIGION

On its face, this two-hour lecture course divides "naturally" into two parts, an "introductory" methodological part (10 hours) closely related to the themes of the previous semesters on radical phenomenology, its matter and method, and a second part (16 hours) devoted to the phenomenological explication of concrete religious phenomena. Focused on the interpretation of Paul's more eschatological letters, this second part has become famous in the Heidegger literature[3]—whether justly or not is still to be seen.

But Heidegger himself provides no such advance outline for the course. Perhaps he intended to give equal time to each part, divided by the Christmas break. But because of the academic incident which erupted in class, he makes short shrift of the first part as he plunges abruptly into the second prior to the break. In point of fact, his opening remarks promise quite the opposite to a second part which would examine concrete problems and "construct a worldview." In his opening remarks, he clearly seeks to disenchant those who had signed up for a course on the philosophy of religion looking for something that would "stir the heart" or expecting some "interesting" content. In fact, here he sets the precedent for many of his future titles by noting that the philosophically operative term in the course title is really the incidental stock word "Introduction." Never arriving at answers but always "leading into" questions: that is the essence of philosophy. "I wish to aggravate this need of philosophy to be ever turning upon the preliminary questions so much, and to keep it before your eyes so relentlessly, that it will in fact become a virtue." Hardly an introduction in a pedestrian sense, aimed at attracting nonmajors into a philosophy course. Instead, the word is meant in a profoundly philosophical sense, presaging the main term of this exercise in the self-understanding of philosophy as perpetual intro-duction, which Heidegger had already named the "formal indication."

Accordingly, the phrase "Introduction to Philosophy [= Phenomenology]" is for Heidegger already a pleonasm. Thus much of Part One of the course is laboriously spent in making a pleonasm just as obvious to his students! This tentative, probing character of philosophy into the questionability of life clearly carries over into its conceptuality, which is where Heidegger starts the first part. It should therefore not surprise us that this part comes to a climax in Heidegger's first detailed explanation of the "formally indicative" concept, that crucial element and "probing tool" of his hermeneutic phenomenology which has been begging discussion ever since he first discovered it in the four part schema in KNS 1919 and named it in WS 1919–20. No less important than the discovery of the kairological character of lived time, in the second part glossing the Pauline letters, is this development of the formal indication in the methodological first part of the course. (Kairology and formal indication will together constitute the *most* essential, but largely unspoken, core of BT itself.) From the opening considerations, one who is attuned to the genealogical context senses the growing need to come to terms with the nature, role, and necessity of the formally indicative concept in a hermeneutic philosophy.

Part One: Introductory and Methodological
The first task of the course is to come to a preliminary understanding of the concepts in the course title. But these are all philosophical concepts which, contrary to scientific concepts, are quite peculiar. Scientific concepts assume a fixed form and so are definable by being ordered and classified within a particular, objectively formed material context. The scientific concept assumes better definition and greater precision as its context becomes better known. Philosophical concepts, on the other hand, never assume such definition and fixity. Constant uncertainty belongs to the very sense of a philosophical concept: it is always vacillating, vague, plurivocal, always in flux and subject to variation. Its accession and formation are fundamentally different from that of a scientific concept. Philosopical knowledge thus differs essentially from scientific knowledge, inasmuch as philosophy does not have an objectively formed material context at its disposal. There is a fundamental difference between science and philosophy: this is not a scientific hypothesis but a philosophical "thesis"—insofar as philosophical experience works itself out as a linguistic thesis or proposition—which will be demonstrated in the course of these considerations. Needless to say, this will not be a scientific demonstration.

The course title assumes any of three nuances, depending on which of its three key concepts is emphasized: "Introduction," "Phenomenology" (= Philosophy), or "Religion". Proceeding by way of such word clarifications, we will soon encounter a peculiar core phenomenon that underlies all three meanings, namely, the problem of the historical. It will define the limit of our aspirations in this course, insofar as it makes the connections among the three concepts even more questionable.

What does "Introduction" mean? An introduction to the sciences tends to provide the domain of the subject matter, its method of elaboration and a historical overview of the various attempts that have been made to pose and to resolve the pertinent problems. Such introductory questions never interest the scientist as much as the true, concrete scientific problems. There is a palpable *insecurity* manifest in any introduction, especially a philosophical one. We know a philosopher by how he does an introduction, so much so that it must be taken into account with every step that he takes in his endeavor. For the scientist, it is not such a major matter. And the philosopher never adopts, without further ado, the same sort of introduction as the sciences, which name their subject matter and method, and then provide a genetic history. It is said that the sciences "arise" from philosophy. If that is so, they do so by modifying and transforming a moment which in philosophy remains unmodified, kept in its original form. The sciences do not reside in philosophy. Philosophy and science are essentially different.

What then is philosophy (= "phenomenology")? We have only noted its intrinsically "introductory" character. But how does philosophy arrive at an understanding of itself? Simply by philosophizing itself, just doing it. And it does not do it by scientific means, say, by trying to define itself, which means to order itself within an objectively formed material context. But surely it has an object, vague as it may be, with which it is concerned in a certain way? Putting it in this way, along the way pointing to its deficiencies, is to apply to philosophy the idea of science as the guiding standard. But it is this very idea which here stands in question. Nevertheless, such attempts, such questions of definition and object are also justified for philosophy, but in a purely "formal" way which has yet to be clarified.

Factic Life Experience

If one grasps the problem of the self-understanding of philosophy radically, one finds that philosophy springs from factic life experience . . . and then springs right back into factic life experience! To call philosophy a cognitive or rational activity is to say nothing at all. What is fundamental is the "concept" of factic life experience, from which philosophy takes its point of departure and to which it returns (cf. SZ 38).

What is factic life experience? It means at once the experiencing activity and that which is experienced. Both the active and the passive sense must be maintained. In short, the experiencing and the experienced can never be torn asunder like two things. Experiencing does not merely have the rational and cognitive sense of "taking cognizance of." On the other hand, it is not merely passive encounter, confrontation, a joining which includes being set apart, but also active shaping and self-assertion. In the same [middle-voiced] vein, "factic" (factual) cannot be understood passively according to epistemological ideals to mean naturally real, real like a thing, or causally determined; it can only be made comprehensible in its full amplitude, where it is at once broad and definite, from the concept of the "historical."

Philosophizing is a constant encounter, a constant "face-off" and coming to terms (*Auseinandersetzung*) with factic life experience. Its expansion beyond a mere cognitive activity likewise means that the sciences can no longer be regarded philosophically in the same way as before. The sciences can no longer be regarded as objective formations of sense or ordered constellations of true propositions (cf. SZ 11). They too must now be grasped concretely "in act," realizing themselves practically, developing historically, and actively assuming the above "finished" shapes out of factic life experience. Contemporary philosophy not only overlooks but openly rejects this historical dimension of science-in-process. [Heidegger here not only anticipates by decades, but also spells out, the deep philosophical core of the orientation of the Anglo-American "new philosophers of science," like Polanyi, Toulmin, and Kuhn.]

But the common root of philosophy and the sciences in factic life experience makes it into a danger zone which hinders the emergence from it of philosophy proper. How to liberate philosophy from the danger of "secularization" into science or into a doctrine of worldviews? How to bring it to confront factic life experience, where it finds its true self-understanding, without the aid of readily available scientific concepts, even without declarations of what the "object" of philosophy is? For even the concept of "object" has become questionable vis-à-vis life experience. To arrive at the philosophical level, a mere change of viewpoint is not enough. This is what Natorp has done in simply reversing the objectification involved in knowing objects into a subjectification which is to represent the philosophical (psychological) process. Knowledge here remains in principle the same.

Because factic life experience is more than a cognitive experience, more than even the simple initial experience of taking cognizance, philosophy in the face of it must undergo a total transformation. What is had, lived, experienced in factic life experience is more than a mere object for a subject and its theory-forming activity, it is a world *in* which one can *live*. (One cannot live in an object.) This formal indication of the world can be further articulated formally as our environment or milieu, as that which encounters or confronts us. It includes not only material things but also ideal objectivities, like those of science, art and religion. In this environing world, there also stands the with-world, that is, other humans socially characterized as relatives, superiors, peers, strangers, and not as instances of the scientific genus *homo sapiens*. Finally, in the very same world also stands "I myself," the self-world. Insofar as it is possible to absorb myself in science, art, or religion, so that I live in them totally, these can be called "*genuine* lifeworlds" (cf. chap. 1!), the self-world in which I as scientist, artist or devout person live. But these are also accessible in the manner of a surrounding world, as we have noted.

It would be a violent distortion to try to rank and stratify these worlds, as if they were particular regions and domains, to separate them sharply from one another, to order them into genera and species. Epistemological questions play no role whatsoever here. What matters is that these different lifeworlds become accessible in a specific way in and for factic life experience. We must try to characterize this manner of becoming accessible, of experiencing. This how of experiencing the worlds is the relational sense of factic life experience, relating the how of experiencing to the what of its experienced content. In the factic course of experience, however, the how of experiencing never comes to consciousness. Instead, factic life experience is totally absorbed in the what, the experienced content. In the course of a day, I busy myself with an astonishing variety of things, and yet the variegated how of relating to this variety never comes to consciousness. Factic life experience in this way manifests a remarkable "indifference" with respect to its way of experiencing, its relational sense. This indifference bears witness to the "self-sufficiency" of factic life experience.

If we take heed of this peculiar indifference of factic experiencing to all of factic life, even the highest things, we become aware of a certain sense pervading the environing world, with-world, and self-world, namely, the character of significance which sustains everything that I experience. All that is experienced, all content, bears the character of significance, is defined by it, but not in epistemological terms. I experience or live all my life-situations in this nonepistemological sort of significance.

This becomes clear when I ask how I experience *myself* in factic life experience. Here, philosophers tend to assume some theoretically developed concept of the psychic, like soul, coherence of acts, or transcendental consciousness. But I never experience myself factically as an experiential coherence, a conglomerate of acts and processes, or a detached I-object. I experience myself factically in what I do and suffer, what confronts me and what I accomplish, in my concern and disregard, my states of depression and elevation, and the like, where I am always caught up in the environment, captured and captivated by the surrounding world. This self-experience is not a theoretical reflection or "inner perception" (Dilthey) or even an I-experience, but an experiencing of the self-world. Experience itself has a worldly character, it is accentuated with significance, but in such a way that my experienced self-world is not yet set off from the surrounding world. This sort of self-experience is the only possible point of departure for a philosophical psychology.

This indifference to the "comporting toward" and resulting lapse toward the world, into its given significance, is only aggravated by our cognitive comportments. The factic which is known in factic knowing, the initial acts of simply taking cognizance, still have the character of significance rather than that of an object. But the acts of comparing, relating, and ordering that follow lead to the stabilizing developments of science, a "logic of things" which divides the facticity into objectively formed domains. The initial tendency to lapse (*abfallen*) built into factic life experience thus now conditions a tendency toward the determination of objects and the objective regulation of lived life. Philosophy simply continues this theoretizing tendency with Plato, who adds an objective domain of ideas to that of sensory objects. Modern philosophy, by taking consciousness as its peculiar object, is but a further continuation of this tendency. Nowadays, accordingly, we do not have the slightest idea of how a radical separation of philosophy and [objective] science can possibly come about. It seems as if our deliberations have only magnified the difficulties for philosophy to come to an understanding of itself.

Not so. We now see that factic life experience, which is to be the starting point of philosophizing, is also the starting point of that which hinders philosophizing. Experience itself again and again *conceals* its own emerging philosophical tendency, nips these motives in the bud, as it were, through its indifference and self-sufficiency. In this self-sufficient concern, it continually falls off into significance and its objectification and finally into the "scientific culture." It becomes totally absorbed in the what of the world, and how to control it, and forgets the how. Factic life experience is the "attitudinally adjustable, lapsing, self-sufficient concern for significance which is indifferent to the relational." It is at once the origin and repression of the philosophical impulse [both its motive and countermovement, Heidegger will soon say]. By making, for the very first time, factic life experience itself into a problem, we have the possibility of reversing this decadent tendency, finding in experience itself the motives for this about-face and the transformation it can promote. These are the motives for philosophizing out of factic life itself.

Troeltsch's Philosophy of Religion

In view of such opposing tendencies, to find these motives out of one's own experience is extremely difficult. But there is a way already begun for us, in our acquaintance with past and present philosophies. To be sure, the existence and possession of a history of philosophy is in itself no motive for philosophizing. But it can be used as a factual point of departure for making some such motives clear to us. We can at least take note of them by considering some of the present currents in the philosophy of religion. [This *incidentally* will also provide an answer to the titular question, "What is the philosophy of religion?"]

Ernst Troeltsch [1865–1923] is today rightly recognized as the leading authority in the philosophy of religion. He commands vast erudition in the concrete materials in the history of religion as well as in the problem-history of the philosophy of religion. Originally a theologian, he has an intimate firsthand sense of its problems. For Troeltsch, the goal of a philosophy of religion is the elaboration of a scientifically valid definition of the essence of religion. This he pursues according to the demands of the contemporary scientific consciousness in terms of a fourfold discipline: factual psychology, apriori epistemology, philosophy of history, and metaphysics.

1. To begin with, the facticity of religious phenomena must be made accessible by describing them in themselves, in their naiveté, free from all theories (especially positivism) and attitudes colored by worldviews (e.g., Max Weber). The central phenomenon of all religions is the belief in the experienceability of the presence of God. In short, the primal phenomenon is mysticism, the experience of unity in God. Immediately given in the central phenomenon are certain demands of moral comportment. Peripheral phenomena include the sociological phenomena and the mythos of religion.

For this rudimentary phenomenology, which would include a typology of the historical religions, Troeltsch marshals a potpourri of methods and extant sources: individual and folk psychology, psychopathology, prehistory, ethnology, the "American methods of statistical questionnaires," William James's *Varieties of Religious Experience*, and Dilthey's descriptive psychology. The result is a psychological essence of religion, a kind of typology of psychic processes in terms of genera and species of religious phenomena.

2. Upon this factic ground, one can now develop an epistemology of the moment of validity contained in the psychic processes. The epistemology of religion explores the apriori lawfulness which underlies religious appearances, the rational moment which makes religion possible. But is the religious apriori rational or irrational? It is not rational in the sense of theoretical rationality but rather in the sense of being universally valid or necessary for reason. The epistemological essence of religion is the apriori of religious reason. It leads to the metaphysical problem of how the logical, ethical, and aesthetic apriori come together or are "consolidated" in the religious apriori.

3. The philosophical history of religion considers the realization of the religious apriori in the factual course of human history. To understand the present and to project the future of religion, it would decide whether it will ever come to a universal religion of reason (e.g., the syncretic "evangelical Catholicism" of Söderblom) or whether one of the positive religions will obtain hegemony in the future. Or does the devel-

opment of religion culminate in an ultimate ideal? Troeltsch now says that every period of religious development has its own sense arising not only from rational moments but also from spontaneous forces of life (Bergson, Simmel). These forces then detach themselves from their roots and finally dissipate in their independence. The historical essence of religion is thus the realization of the factic-psychological as well as the rational apriori in history.

4. The metaphysics of religion unifies all other apriori in the religious one. This is philosophy of religion in the strict sense; the other three disciplines are only sciences of religion. Insofar as a single reality asserts itself in religious life, the idea of God, this idea must be considered in relation to the total reality of our experienced world and the entire context of reason. The metaphysical essence of religion is the religious as the principle of every apriori.

Troeltsch thus gives us a series of concepts of essence whose content need not be criticized here. Religion is here ordered into contexts into which we could just as easily have placed science or art. This is possible only because religion is from the beginning regarded as an object. Why precisely these four disciplines? Are they even intrinsically related to each other, let alone to religion? This philosophy of religion does not originate from religion but from a preconceived concept of philosophy dominated by science. It is determined by the four disciplines but not by the essence of religion. These disciplines do not arise from religion qua religion. How are religion and philosophy related, how does religion become an object for philosophy? For Troeltsch in the end, religion is related to philosophy precisely as an object of knowledge, and philosophy is related to religion in an object-cognizing sense. Even if it be the object of objects, religion still stands in an external (scientific) relation to philosophy. Small wonder that Troeltsch finds that religion lends itself "naturally" to scientific elaboration, easily revealing itself to be a psychic phenomenon which has a history and refers to metaphysical contexts. But religion must first be regarded in its full facticity before approaching it in a particular philosophical attitude.

The Historical

An important step toward this phenomenological goal is our opening thesis of the radical difference between philosophy and science, not only with regard to their "objects" but also their manner of relating to the object. But if neither object nor object-cognizing applies, it is no longer possible to foresee how philosophy is supposed to deal with religion. Even the title of the course suggests that religious experiences will eventually become the object of phenomenological observation. Given this impasse, let us therefore now go one step further and approach the task of the clarification of the course title by way of the core phenomenon which permeates the meanings connecting its three key terms. In anticipation of this moment, we have already *indicated* this core phenomenon under the heading of "the historical." In fact, it seems self-evident that all three are historical phenomena, subject to historical development and conditioned by its historically particular context. But does this not fit any phenomenon whatsoever, say, science and art? This is no great bit of knowledge. How does this bring us to the authentic self-understanding of *the authentic sense of philosophy*, which is still *our primary goal in this course*? Philosophy and religion are historical phenomena in the same way as the Feldberg and Kandel are mountains in the Black Forest, or the university, the cathedral, and the train station are buildings in the heart of Freiburg. By such a subsumption into a universal concept, the sense of the historical would still be directed by a preconception fixed upon the object. An object is historical: it has the "property" of being historical, of coming to be and taking its course in time. By now, we know that this is precisely what we do not want. We mean instead the historical as the phenomenon just as it meets us in life and not in the "fact of historical science," which exists only in the minds of neo-Kantians and logicians and, moreover, is the epitome of "unliving." We are raising the question of the possibility of uncovering an entirely different sense of the historical, a sense which cannot be attributed to objects at all. Perhaps the current sense of the historical as object-historical is but a derivative of this original sense.

If so, then it still may be useful to come to terms with this current sense of the historical just as we meet it today, but at a more vital level. It is said that contemporary culture, like no other, is motivated by the "historical consciousness" (Dilthey). This means that the historical attitude "disquiets" us in a double direction, 1) insofar as it excites, stimulates, incites and 2) insofar as it impedes and inhibits. It is at once an enriching fulfillment and a burden. The historical is today a power against which life has to assert and secure itself: 1) The secularization and self-sufficiency of contemporary life, which wishes to secure its proper life by innerworldly means, leads to a voracious understanding of alien ideas, strange worlds and exotic cultures, right up to their belief systems, and so cultivates a widespread tolerance for the strangest manifestations. Through this hegemony of understanding, one then arrives at a new sense of security in one's own life. Whence the mania for the typification of worldviews, where we think we have arrived at the ultimate and can safely rejoice in the multiplicity of life in all its forms. 2) But the reverse side of this is the "burden of historicism," having to choose arbitrarily from among the types of worldviews. Or the fascinating look into the past provided by the historical inhibits by distracting us from the tasks of the present, destroying the naiveté of our creativity. All activism is an attempt to stem the tide of history. It deliberately stands in the way of the "logic of history," which has nothing to do with what really moves us contemporaries.

The phenomenological clarification of the problematic adjective "historical" first needs to make its actual present usage totally clear. It is thus understood as the property of any space-time object, including the human being. But this sort of attribution blurs certain distinctions, a blurring which over the centuries has assumed the character of a fateful obfuscation. An anticipatory excursus into these distinctions will for the moment serve as a cautionary note. For it is so easy to confuse an object (*Objekt*) with a "counterstance" [*Gegenstand*: an etymological translation of what perhaps might be called a circumstance or state of affairs], which we ourselves have tended to use synonymously. Not every counterstance is an object, although every object can be regarded formally as a counterstance. The determinations of a counterstance apply formally to any something. [A counterstance is a "something in general," Lask's most basic reflexive category, but in a more intensely intentional sense, as a "standing toward" rather than an "over against."] Thirdly, a phenomenon is neither an object nor a counterstance. Of course, a phenomenon is formally also a counterstance, but this says nothing essential about the phenomenon and places it in a sphere in which it simply does not belong: the fateful blurring, which makes phenomenological investigations eminently difficult. Objects, counterstances, and phenomena cannot be lined up in a table of categories, as on a chessboard, or in a subsumptive scheme of concepts. Phenomenology works with an entirely different kind of "concept." For the moment, however, let these cautions at least warn us against taking the human being merely in object-historical terms, as an object in time with the historical as one of its properties. Such cautions reflect philosophy's distrust of, and so its struggle against, "sound common sense."

We have already noted that the phenomenon of the historical moves contemporary factic life to a double-edged disquietude. We can question whether that against which factic life then asserts itself is in fact the historical. Because of the historical consciousness, we now have not only the historical sciences (= human or cultural sciences) but also a mania for philosophies of history. Without going along with their views, we might try to understand the motives for these respective views of history and, more basically, how the historical even becomes a problem for them or, as it turns out, a burden or hindrance against which they must do battle. We might in general and very schematically distinguish three ways (current philosophies of history) in which the present seeks to protect or secure itself from history: 1) the Platonic way, a radical renunciation of the historical; 2) the exact opposite, a radical surrender to history (Spengler); 3) a compromise between these two extremes (Dilthey, Simmel, Rickert, Windelband):

1. Plato's radical solution is the most popular, and the most readily available, in view of the continuing influence of Greek philosophy upon contemporary intellectual life. Historical reality is not the only and final reality, it is comprehensible only through its relation to the supratemporal realm of ideas. With this positing of a supratemporal reality, security against the historical is in principle realized. History is from the start a secondary problem. For Plato and all Platonists, the motivation for the discovery of this suprarealm results from the dominating position of theoretical knowledge as it manifests itself in their battle against skepticism. Over against the cognitive processes taking place in time, there is still the cognitive content which is true and valid in itself. Contrary to the purely epistemological founding of the other two ways, the first way, with its suprareal lawfulness, adds a theory of being: Anything is only insofar as it is known. Plato expresses this primacy of the theoretical (over against the ethical, artistic, and practical) in the position he takes against Socrates' "Virtue is knowledge." It is first a matter of securing knowledge as knowledge before the virtuous life is at all possible. The only problem is the precise connection between temporal and supratemporal reality. Three positions are, up to the present day, expressed in Platonic terms: a) The temporal world is an imitation (*mimesis*) of the supratemporal, the supratemporal being the paradigm of which the temporal is the copy or image. b) The temporal takes part or participates in the supratemporal through *methexis*. c) The supratemporal "appears" in the temporal, manifesting its "presence" (*parousia*) in the temporal. Clearly, in every case, historical reality ("the temporal") is secondary.

2 and 3. Both the second and the third ways are purely epistemological, and this epistemological foundation is most clearly expressed by the extreme representative of the third way, Georg Simmel. He asks, "How is the theoretical configuration which we call history developed out of the stuff of immediate reality?" The stuff undergoes a forming process guided by the two categories of reality which we find in the natural and the historical sciences. History itself is the product of the freely forming subjectivity. The human being who knows makes nature and history; only the human being which is known is a product of nature and history. Inasmuch as history is nothing but a theoretical picture dependent on the gratuity of the freely forming subjectivity, history is completely under its control. The human being cannot be subjugated to history, for it depends upon him as to what history is and how it is shaped. But why this particular forming process and this unique constellation, out of which history as reality arises? Any particular historical picture depends

in its orientation and development upon the present which sees history. But what motivates a historical rather than a natural conception of reality? A sum of processes and effects is conceived as effective, by way of an interest which is awakened to feel such effects in the immediately given stuff. This historical interest has two cooperative directions: a) the joy and enjoyment in the interplay of fate and personal energy, in the rhythm of the play between winning and losing, plan and execution, in short, in the excitement that comes from encountering the complexity of human events; b) add to this emotive content a sense of its *brute facticity*, that what is experienced is real, in actuality efficacious, and the historical interest is complete. The decisive point of this epistemological machinery is that history loses its disquieting character, since it is nothing but the product of the freely forming subjectivity.

This epistemological tendency is assumed by Spengler and radicalized by him into the second way. To the human historical interests, he adds the nineteenth-century interest in raising history to a science in its own right, against the monopoly usurped by the natural sciences. For Simmel, historical knowledge is still dependent upon the standpoint of the observer. What is needed, accordingly, is a Copernican revolution to free history from its condition of dependence upon the present. How? By not absolutizing the present which drives and knows history, where, for example, it is made into the highest stage of development, but instead plunging it into the objective process of historical happening. Spengler thus joins a Kantian epistemology to a "wild metaphysics" of becoming in which historical reality is no longer juxtaposed to a suprahistorical one. Instead, the reality and the insecurity of the present is experienced historically within the objective process of historical becoming, which as a whole is nothing but a continual flow and ebb of expressive gestalts "of the life resting in the center."

The third way directs itself against the extreme [Dionysian] fluidity of the second by joining the formative process of history cognitively to the norm of truth. History in its becoming is nothing but the continual realization of supratemporal values and validities. These are of course never fully and purely realized, never absolute, but always given in a particular historical gestalt through which the absolute "shines." It is neither a matter of stripping away the historical reality nor of relegating it to an absolute process of becoming, but of shaping the future from the full treasure of the past in a process which strives to realize the universally human. It is by putting myself into the temporal cognitively, understanding it as the dialectic of a universal history, that I realize the supratemporal.

A closer look would readily show that all three ways are pervaded by the Platonic schema of thought. Even Spengler in his overt anti-Platonism is quite Platonic, not merely in the "realm of ideas" generated by his morphological typologies, like a mathematics of world history. Opposed as he is to the absolute validity of Platonism, the way in which he finds security against the historical is still the same. He does this by acknowledging historical reality as the ultimate, albeit the only, reality. Granting this, I have no recourse except to install myself in this historical reality, to go along with it in a conscious cooperation in the "decline of the West." Here, as in the other two ways, liberation from time and history is achieved by way of a theory of reality. Security is achieved in a cognitive attitude to an object called history.

Oddly, all three ways pay scant attention to the phenomenon of disquietude itself, and this only within the securing scheme, a Platonic scheme. What exactly is disquieting and what is disquieted, thus in need of security? What motivates the disquietude? What is disquieted and so seeks security—human Dasein, life as unique and historically accidental—is not taken in itself but instead treated as an object, and as object set into a historically objective history. The disquietude (*Beunruhigung*) of life and its tendency toward security are not as such addressed, but disposed of by an objective theory *about* history. Life is made to tend toward Ideas in order to secure itself against history (first way), with history (second way), and out of history (third way). This comes from the tendency of factic life to fall away from itself, typically by way of an attitude (*Einstellung*) of "setting itself onto" (*sich stellen ein*) an object. The distressed Dasein then becomes an object-part cut out of a large whole object, the entire objective happening of history. But the sense of history which is already prefigured in "distressed concern" (*Bekümmerung*) cannot be made comprehensible by way of an attitude, or a historical science. These superordinated contexts must be suspended in order to get back to the true disquietude in its original context. What sense of the historical resides in the distressed concern itself, exercising its effect prior to the distortion of theories? We are seeking to go from the externalization of the distressed (concerned) Dasein back to itself, to understand it from its own life experience, in its original distress (concern). This is actually a reversal in approach to the problem of the historical. How does my own living Dasein as already disquieted by history comport to history itself? How does the distressed Dasein simply out of itself stand to the "historical"?

Oddly, our guiding clue in this more original consideration is still the old concept of the "historical," as it was understood in our prior discussions and in the philosophies we considered. At the same time, it is becoming more and more evident that it may perhaps be impossible to conceive the sense of factic life with our present "objective" philosophical means. Could it be that *the categories of factic life are so radically new* that the entire system of categories transmitted to us is exploded? In order to see our way around this apparent conflict between old and new, we must first present a mainstay of the phenomenological method.

Formally Indicating the Historical

Let us review the most salient points concerning the disquieted Dasein protecting itself against change, in order to sharpen our sense of distressed concern: 1) Factic Dasein, which was first grasped as an objective and temporally coursing happening, cannot simply be regarded as a blind, purely processual being; it must have a sense, a tendency toward giving sense. It demands a certain lawfulness for itself. 2) My own present Dasein does not merely want a sense in general, but a concrete sense drawn from its own living present, accordingly a sense different from that of past cultures, a new sense which exceeds that of earlier life, as the present in its historical continuity incorporates itself into the future.

Through this tendency of sense bestowal, factic Dasein receives special emphasis and comes into sharp focus. All our attention and efforts are now drawn to it, as we also note how much it has heretofore been neglected. With this new focus, let us try to put aside the conceptions of history discussed above and ask simply: How does the historical itself stand to factic Dasein, what sense does it have out of factic Dasein itself? But does not the question itself introduce a particular, and perhaps even disturbing, sense of the historical? Do I not already have a particular sense in mind, in terms of which I decide in what sense the historical happens to factic life experience? But the question cannot be broached and approached in any other way, if I want to discover the historical *itself* in factic life. This difficulty is a recurrent disturbing element in all phenomenological analyses. It is not given sufficient attention and has led to some overhasty theories and views within phenomenology.

We shall call the methodic use of a sense which is conducive to phenomenological explication the "formal indication." Its task is to prefigure the direction of this explication. It points the way and guides the deliberation. The phenomena are viewed on the basis of the bearing of the formally indicating sense. But even though it guides the phenomenological deliberation, contentwise it has nothing to say. Methodological considerations must make it clear how the formal indication, even though it guides the deliberation, nevertheless interjects no preconceived opinions into the problems, in no way prejudices the content of the explication. Such a clarity of the sense of the formal indication is necessary to avoid lapsing into attitudinally objective tendencies or into regional domains which are narrow in content and yet conceived as absolute. The problem of the formal indication belongs to the "theory" of the phenomenological method. In a broader sense, the problem of the "formal" belongs to the larger question of the sense of the theoretical, of theoretical acts, and first of all the phenomenological problem of distinguishing as such, of making the "first cut," as it were. This larger problem shall concern us later [it will not, because of the abrupt change in direction of the course]. For the time being, we shall search out the difficulty only in our concrete instance of formally indicating the historical.

In its usual sense, the historical is "the temporally becoming and, as having become, the past." If we apply this formally indicative sense to the explication of factic life experience, if it is viewed in terms of this sense, we would ask: to what extent does something temporal occur in it, a becoming take place in it, a past as past consciously occur in it? Thus the explication is after all, in content as well, determined by this particular sense of the historical. On the other hand, it seems that our sense of the historical is so universal that we can without fear of hazard apply it to factic life. In a phrase, it "makes no difference" when it is thus applied to factic life. It may well be that factic life experience is only a particular sphere of reality, while our definition says nothing at all as to which domain of reality the historical is restricted. Our operative principle is thus the most universal, and can differentiate itself accordingly. Any other sense seems to be only a further determination of it, falling into its domain as an external determination of this universal temporality.

The General Versus the Formal

The matter, however, is not so simple. Two questions arise: 1) In what sense is this concept of the historical itself universal and to what extent can this universality be regarded as philosophically fundamental? 2) If this latter claim does not hold, but the sense is nevertheless universal, to what extent does it still prejudge nothing, when it, as a nonfundamental sense, nevertheless is intended to guide a fundamental deliberation?

For centuries, universality has been regarded as a characteristic of the object of philosophy. It serves there to establish demarcations within the unity of being. It performs a specific labor in dividing this totality into different regions of being which are then allocated to different sciences. In conjunction with Plato, Aristotle constantly reiterated that "being is said in many ways." But Aristotle may well have meant something more than what we normally attribute to this statement: there may be more implied here than just objective ontological considerations. Aristotle's metaphysics may well be further along than we are today.

This division of being is the ontological direction of philosophy. Insofar as beings as being are only for a consciousness: corresponding to the ontological division there is also a conscious one. In this context, one speaks of the modes of consciousness in which beings constitute themselves, that is, become conscious. This direction was first clearly worked out by Kant, but Husserl's phenomenology first brought the means to follow it through concretely, while at the same time radicalizing the entire question. On the ontological side, philosophy has to do with the most universal, and on the side of consciousness with the most fundamental, insofar as it is possible to investigate the object as such in its constitution in consciousness. And consciousness is primordial since everything stands under it. In Husserl's phenomenology, consciousness becomes a region. As regional, consciousness is not only primordial but also universal. Thus, the universal and the original coincide in transcendental phenomenology, just as it does in Hegel and the Marburg school.

The universal becomes accessible through universalization. Prior to Husserl's phenomenology, universalization was never considered seriously. Husserl (*Ideen I*, §13, but first in the final chapter of the *Prolegomena*) distinguishes two types of universalization: formalization and generalization. This distinction, known to mathematics at least since Leibniz, is now for the first time given its logical explication by Husserl. He sees the significance of this distinction above all from the side of pure ontology, that is, the formal ontology of a pure logic of objects (*mathesis universalis*). We shall try to go beyond him and understand the sense of this distinction more deeply, by developing it into a phenomenological explanation of the sense of the formal indication.

Generalization is universalization according to genera and species: red is a color; color is a sense quality. (Or joy is an affect, and affect is a lived experience; a stone is a material thing, which is a thing in general.) One can, it seems, go on: quality in general, thing in general, essence, object (= "counterstance"). But the universalizing transition from "color" to "sense quality" is not the same as that from "quality" to "essence" or from "essence" to "counterstance." It can be asked whether the determination "sense quality" defines "color" in the same sense as "essence" or "counterstance" define "quality." The latter transition is formalization, representing a break in the parade of generalizations. Generalization is in its actualization bound to a particular domain of subject matter. The sequence of levels of generalities, the genera and species, are matter-bound. Taking its measure from the what-content is essential to generalization. In contrast, formalization is matter-free as well as free from any sequence of levels. I do not need to run through the lower universalities in order to arrive at the highest, "counterstance in general." I can say, "It is an object (counterstance)" of anything whatsoever, without having to go through other universalities in order to be absolutely sure that the formalizing predication holds.

But if it is not matter-bound, formal predication must still somehow be motivated. It is motivated not by the what but through the how, for it arises from the *sense* of the attitudinal *relation* itself. I do not draw the determination "counterstance" *out of* the given, but instead *to* it, as it were, by a kind of "at-traction" (*an-ziehen*). I must look away from the given what-content, and instead see *that* the given content is given, grasped attitudinally. The formalized counterstanding does not arise from a what-content "in general," but from the relational sense of the attitudinal relation itself. Starting here, we can now grasp the relational senses themselves as counterstances and further as formal categories: something, other, and, or. On this basis, in short, the relational determinateness of the various attitudes can for the first time be seen. This manifold of relational senses expressed in the formal-objective categories circumscribes the theoretical attitude in its pure relational sense. But this is the inauthentic, and not the authentic, theoretical attitude, under which we understand the theoretical attitude in its original actualization. The pure attitudinal relation must itself be considered in its actualization, in order to understand the origin of the theoretical. As we shall later see [another casualty of the pending course change!], philosophizing must be considered in its original attitudinal actualization in order to illuminate the relationship between phenomenological explication and the conduct of thought. Important for the moment is to see that the origin of the formal lies in the relational sense of the theoretical attitude.

Does the "formal" in "formal indication" mean the formalized, or something else? We shall see [!] that it means something more original. In formal ontology it means the objectively formed, standing over against us. In a wider sense, the "formal region" is also a "domain of matter," and thus bound to the "material content." In contrast with this universal region, however, we shall see [!] that the formal indication has nothing to do with "universality." It falls outside the realm of the attitudinal theoretical.

The last hour on Part One—the tenth of the course, November 30, 1920—continues, innocently enough, toward a more precise determination of the formal indication. After a review of the salient points of the previous hour, as was Heidegger's custom, he raises three further clarifying questions: 1) Is formalization, like generalization, universalization in the strict sense or only externally? 2) Behind this question is the following one: In what sense and under what conditions can the universal be regarded as the ultimate goal and destination of philosophical deliberation? 3) If that is not the case, how can we use "universal concepts" (formal indications) like that of the "historical" in a phenomenological investigation without prejudicing it?

Ad 1. To begin with, in what sense is generalization a universalization? Generalization is a mode of ordering of determinate particulars within an encompassing material context, which in turn can be ordered within a more universal context. It is thus a matter-immanent ordering according to levels of determinations which stand under one another in the relation of reciprocal pertinence, in such a way that the most universal determination refers back to the very lowest. Generalizing determining is thus in its very sense the determination of an object according to its material content by another, such that this determining other, as encompassing, itself belongs to the same material region in which the What to be materially determined stands. In its very essence, accordingly, generalization actualizes itself in a determinate material sphere to such an extent that its direction is from the start prefigured by this materiality.

It is questionable whether formalization is ordering, and so universalization, in the same sense as generalization. When I generalize, I remain in a determinate material region which nevertheless provides various directions of generalization. But once an organizing direction is assumed, it must be maintained to the end; leaping from one direction to another is not possible. Formalization, by contrast, is not bound to the determinate what of the object to be determined. From the start, its determination turns away from the material content of the object, it regards the object only from the side *that* it is given. The object is determined merely *as apprehended*, as that *toward which* the cognitive relation moves. The sense of "object in general" (now really a "counterstance") is simply this "toward which" (*Worauf*) of the theoretical attitudinal relation. This attitudinal relation, for which the material content of the object is indifferent and void, has in itself a manifold of relational senses which can now be explicated and so objectively grasped in formal-ontological categories. Such categories constitute the theory of the formal-ontological. But the coordination of formalization is primarily such that that which is to be determined is not assigned to a region of objects but to the relational sense. And the relational sense is not like a region and so an order, at least not directly. Indirectly, it can be so regarded, insofar as the relational sense is "formed out" [i.e., externalized] into formal-objective categories, which correspond to a "region." By thus being formed out of the relational sense, the formal categories now enable the process of mathematization and so the execution of mathematical operations.

We thus have the following levels of development: a) formalization; b) theory of the formal-ontological (*mathesis universalis*), through which a theoretical region is posited as detached; c) phenomenology of the formal, an originary consideration of the formal by explicating its relational sense within its actualization sense.

Ad 2. If such externalized formal-objective determinations are approached as universal, and such ultimate universal determinations of the counterstance in general are regarded as the fundamental task of philosophy [it is to become, in a *non*objective sense, a *mathesis universalis*!], the question then is whether their very nature as "universal" works preju-dicially against philosophy. Posed on this basis, the question is meaning-less: formal determinations cannot prejudice since they offer no prejudg-ments but only the basic determinations. The question can only be raised when these determinations are prejudicial concerning something which distinguishes itself from formal objectivity. The question does make sense if we recall our background thesis that philosophy is not a science, and so is not an attitude. Against this background, the assumption of the formal-ontological determination of counterstances would then work prejudicially on phenomenological determination.

What is phenomenology? What is a phenomenon? Such matters them-selves can be made clear only by means of a formal indication! Every experience (as experiencing as well as the experienced) can be "taken into the phenomenon," that is, considered according to the original sense of that which is experienced in it: 1) according to the original sense of the content, 2) the original how of being experienced (relational sense), and finally 3) the how in which this relational sense is itself actualized (actualization sense). In this schematic and external order, it seems as if these senses simply stand next to one another externally. This is not the case. It is simply a matter of seeing the "problem-direction" of phenome-nology, its basic task, its simple and single focus. Phenomenology is noth-ing but the understanding explication of the phenomena. It gives the *logos* of the phenomena, *logos* not as logification but in the sense of "inter-nal word" (*verbum internum*), that which gives itself in the phenomenon, so that the manner of explication is determined by the phenomenon itself and not by an ideal theoretical attitude. And as formally indicated, the phenomenon is a sense totality according to three directions of sense, that of content, relation, and actualization. Following this intentional schematism, phenomenology is accordingly the explication of this triadic sense totality.

Does a formal-ontological determinateness prejudice this task of phi-losophy, which means the phenomena which are its counterstance? One could point out, for example, that such a determination says nothing at all about the What of that which it determines. But precisely because the formal determination is completely indifferent to the content, it is all the more fateful for the relational aspects of the phenomenon, inasmuch as it prescribes or at least implies a relational sense which is theoretical. It completely conceals the aspect of actualization, which might even be more fateful, and directs itself onesidedly toward the content. A mere glance at the history of philosophy readily shows how much it is domi-nated by a theoretical and formal objectivity.

The intention of the formal indication is precisely to ward off and avoid this prejudice. It is an essential methodological moment inherent in the phenomenological method. Why is it formal? Because the sense of the formal stems from its emphasis on the relational aspect. The formal indication is intended primarily as an advance indication of the relational sense of the phenomenon, but in a negative sense, as a warning. A phenomenon must be pregiven in such a way that its relational sense is held in suspense, left undecided. One must guard against assuming that its relational sense is theoretical. In contrast with the sciences, phenomenology holds the relational sense at a distance. It avoids the attitudinal action of "placing itself into" a material domain, and of installing its object into a material context. The formal indication is thus a defense, a safeguard, so that what is indicated is kept free from any particular relation. The necessity of such a precaution results from the attitudinally lapsing tendency of factic life experience, forcing us into the theoretical, always threatening to slide down into the objective, from which we must nevertheless draw the phenomena. The formal indication reminds us that every pregiven phenomenon is theoretically predetermined not only in its content but also in its relational sense.

We can now distinguish the formal indication from both formalization and generalization. Both are attitudinally theoretical methods in which things get ordered, directly in generalization, indirectly in formalization. The formal indication, by contrast, is in no way concerned with ordering, which means that it stays clear of all arranging and classifying, leaving everything undecided. It has sense only as an indication of the phenomenon, only in relation to the explication, and is thus nothing theoretical.

Ad 3. One can therefore question whether the proposed task of philosophy as universal determination of the objective and constitutive is fundamental, whether it stems from the original motive of philosophizing and so constitutes the fulfillment of the tendency to philosophize. In order to decide this, we must allow ourselves to be drawn into a new situation and come to understand the way in which phenomenological deliberation is to be approached. This is done by the formal indication. Its sole significance is a methodological one, to find the approach to phenomenological explication. [One senses how Heidegger's new methodology, the very novelty of it, must have been "heavy going" even for advanced students like Becker. He will now pay the pedagogical price for his abstruseness.]

Cursus Interruptus

Let us apply these results to our problem of the historical: If the sense of the historical as the "temporally becoming and as such past" is taken as a formal indication, it is not claimed that this definition is that of the sense of the historical in general. It is questionable whether this formally indicative definition is sufficient to define the objective historical world in its historical structure, indeed to provide the "most universal" definition prefiguring an ultimate sense. We can make this clear by way of the concept "temporal." It is taken here in an extremely vague and indefinite sense. We do not even know what time is being spoken of here. Because it is so indefinite, we can regard it as something which prejudices nothing, which accordingly is the most universal sense of "temporality." We can put it forward as universally formal and find in it the basic schema for every other definition of the concept of time. Finally, it might be thought that, insofar as any objectivity constitutes itself in consciousness, it is temporal, in accord with the basic schema of the temporal.

It thus follows purely deductively that this universal-formal definition of time is not so much a founding as it is a falsifying of the problem of time. It prefigures a framework for all subsequent problems which stems directly from the theoretical.

The problem of time must instead be first apprehended as it is factically experienced, entirely apart from how something like pure time constitutes itself in the pure consciousness. We wish to pursue precisely the opposite path. Access to the problem of time must be obtained from the understanding of factic life experience. Our questions are: how is temporality itself originally experienced in factic life? And what is the meaning of past, present, and future in such an experience? Our way thus starts from factic life, from which the sense of time is to be won.

With this, the problem of the historical is at least to some extent characterized. We thereby take into account whether . . .

Oskar Becker's transcript, in its terse way the most dramatic, concludes with this unfinished sentence. In brackets he adds the following nonphilosophical commentary by way of concluding the First Part of the course: "Broken off on November 30, 1920, owing to the objections of nonmajors (*Einwände Unberufener*)." Whether classroom etiquette was breached by shouts or loud remarks from the gallery, whether Privatdozent Heidegger entertained questions at this point, perhaps at the insistence of the nonmajors, is not clear. What is clear is that the course does break off at this point—this is duly (and uncomfortably) recorded in the transcripts—and Heidegger puts a hasty end to Part One of the course as he makes an abrupt transition to a completely different set of hitherto unannounced topics. Given the content of Part One, we are methodologically more than prepared, one might even say "overprepared," to handle the "phenomenological explications of concrete religious phenomena in conjunction with Pauline letters" which is the announced subject of Part Two of the course. But was this part of Heidegger's original intention for the course? And to what extent?

What exactly provoked this abrupt transition in the pivotal hour of the course? There is an anecdote circulating among Heidegger's students, those who later became the "elder statesmen" of his school (Becker, Bröcker, Gadamer). According to their testimony as well as Heidegger's (he apparently told the story himself), the abrupt change in course content was the direct result of student complaints to the Dean of the Philosopical Faculty over the lack of religious content in a course on the philosophy of religion. This complaint was apparently couched in others, whose tenor we can surmise to some extent from Heidegger's sarcastic concluding statement in that hour, carefully recorded in the transcript of Fritz Neumann:

> I must break off at this point. Philosophy as I see it is in a bind. The auditor in other lecture courses from the start receives assurances by getting something in return: In a course on art history, he gets to look at pictures, in other courses, he covers costs by being coached for his qualifying exam. In philosophy it is different. And I can't change that, since I did not invent philosophy. But I still want to rescue myself from this calamity and break off these highly abstract considerations. So in the next hour I shall lecture to you on history and, without any further consideration of approaches and method, take a concrete and particular phenomenon as my point of departure. This I do under the assumption that you will misunderstand the entire procedure from beginning to end.

With this change, Heidegger now approaches the course from the "Religion" end of its title rather than from "Introduction" in the profoundly philosophical sense we have been following. For it entails the problem of philosophy's self-understanding, which finally gives the very term "introduction" the highly methodological sense of "formal indication." The break thus comes at a very inopportune time, since we never hear Heidegger's always valuable and sometimes creative review of the previous hour, which in this case would have been a synopsis of the ever more esoteric notion of formal indication at its very core. And formal indication itself is perhaps the very heart and soul of the early Heidegger. He will never again return to this subject in the deliberate and systematic way that he had begun here, preferring instead to mention the term in passing, with little or no explanation (the *lectures* of WS 1921–22 are really no exception), as he applies this method of philosophical conceptualization in one context or another in the years to and through BT.[4]

This is perhaps the single most important casualty of the premature interruption of the methodological considerations of this course, which was centered upon the "self-understanding of philosophy." In the three hours remaining before the Christmas break, Heidegger hastily embarks upon an abortive interpretation of Paul's letter to the Galatians, for which he seems, uncharacteristically, unprepared. It was not until after the Christmas holidays that he finds, in the two letters to the Thessalonians, a more appropriate set of "concrete religious phenomena," focused more directly on temporality and historicality, with which to round out the course. But the seemingly unprepared state of the interpretation of Galatians suggests that Heidegger had an entirely different course planned, in which the transition from philosophy to religion, carefully timed to take place with the holidays, would have proceeded with more care, so that the discussion of the ever delicate relation between philosophy and religion would have systematically contributed to a further enhancement of the main theme of the course, namely, "the self-understanding of philosophy," but now in its confrontation of religion. This is the second major casualty of this *cursus interruptus*, with its aborted climax. We are left to surmise what Heidegger wanted to say on this theme as he time and again pauses in his "phenomenological explication" of concrete religious phenomena—"Part Two" of the course—in order to make some reference or connection to what he now calls his "general methodological introduction" (January 11, 1921). But from now on, the course takes on a different tenor, that of a straightforward, albeit insightful, philosophy of religion, rather than a course pursuing its original intent of radicalizing phenomenology, that is, of "introducing" us to the very heart and driving force of the philosophical endeavor and how this is to be approached.

Part Two: Phenomenological Explication of Concrete Religious Phenomena in Conjunction with Paul's Epistles

Through an interpretation of Paul's letter to the Galatians, we shall try to obtain access to the lifeworld of primitive Christianity. Methodologically, this does not aim to be a dogmatic or theological interpretation, nor an interpretation based on the history of religions, nor a religious meditation, but a phenomenological interpretation. The peculiarity of such an interpretation is the attempt to arrive at a preunderstanding as an original way of access to the Christian lifeworld of the New Testament. But the formally indicative approach of phenomenology renounces all claim to an ultimate understanding, which can only be given in genuine religious experience. Such a preunderstanding nevertheless opens the way to providing theology with a new foundation. This would include a critically revised version of the method of the history of religions.

The letter to the Galatians is given a historical stress and weight by Paul himself. It is the original document of his religious development, the history of his conversion against the historical backgrounds of Judaism, Christianity, and the Greek world. It needs only to be supplemented by the Acts of the Apostles for its historical completion. [This is the first indication of why Heidegger, on short notice, selected Galatians as his "concrete religious phenomenon" for explication. Since 1919, he had been under the influence of a text by Dilthey which suggested that the "historical consciousness" began in the West with primitive Christianity. The one example which Dilthey gives clearly points to the text of Galatians: the personality of Paul as the arena of a struggle of conscience where Jewish law, the pagan consciousness of the world, and Christian faith meet, where belief in the law and faith in Christ are held together in the experience of the living God, where a great historical past and a great historical present are present together in the experience of transition between religious foundations.][5]

A general understanding of Galatians can only be attained by entering into the basic phenomena manifested in the original life that it depicts. This means that we must enter into the spirit of New Testament Greek. If a translation is used as an aid, it cannot be Luther's, which all too often is dependent upon Luther's theological standpoint. Luther sees Paul through Augustine. Luther and Paul are religiously at radically opposite poles. Instead, the (German) translations of Weizsäcker or Nestle are recommended.

In the letter to the Galatians, Paul is at war with Judaism and the Jewish-Christian community. This religious struggle, which defines Paul's existence as an apostle, is provisionally waged between the poles of "law" and "faith." These are two distinctly different ways to salvation, which for Paul means toward "life" (ἡ ζωή). It is on this basis that the basic structure of the religious consciousness of the primitive Christian is to be understood, in terms of its senses of content, relation, and actualization. These are to be understood out of the original historical situation, without the interjection of modern positions. Herein lies the value of the methods of the history of religions.

The letter to the Galatians divides into three parts:

1. Demonstration of the autonomy of Paul's apostolic mission and his call by Christ (chaps. 1–2).
2. The argument between law and faith, at first theoretical and then in its application to life (chaps. 3–5).
3. Christian life as a whole, its motives and tendencies (chap. 6).

After this seemingly organized introduction, Heidegger spends the remainder of the three "hours" (one is a very short one) before Christmas by opening with some general remarks and closing the hour with a pedestrian, somewhat directionless and uninspired scholarly tour through the Greek text, selecting terms to discuss almost in glossary fashion. He barely reaches the fifth chapter. Let us see if we can find some order in his almost random remarks, and salvage the more telling points which will resurface and take seed in future hours. For, if we are to believe Heidegger (as he tells us after the holidays), this pre-Christmas interpretation of Galatians is deliberately a straightforward and routine exegesis, a "superficial noting of its contents," in order to illustrate an "object-historical" consideration of the text. It is a propaedeutic phase which must be traversed in order to proceed finally to the authentic "actualization-historical" understanding of the textual situation.

Paul finds himself in a dispute over the "correct" gospel (Gal. 1:8–9). He himself has come to Christianity through an original experience and not through an historical tradition (1:12), thus through a complete break with the past, and so with every non-Christian conception of life (1:10). (Isolating such passages, others have accused Paul of trying to institute a new mystical religion of his own, without having to go through the historical Jesus. Since he had no direct experience of the life of Jesus of Nazareth, this historical lifetime was entirely irrelevant to him.) Original Christianity is to be grounded out of itself, without regard to already given forms of religion, in Paul's case, without the Judaic pharisaical and rabbinical forms. But in asserting the Christian life experience against the Jewish-Christian communities, he uses the available and inadequate means of rabbinic teachings to express himself. The talk of justification by faith (2:16ff.), using Abraham as his paradigmatic example (3:6), thus invests a Jewish legal-theological concept and a Jewish patriarch with Christian meaning. This is climaxed with the allegory of Abraham's sons (4:24), after the fashion of Philo Judaeus, Paul's contemporary, to distinguish the Jewish and Christian covenants. On a less dogmatic note, there is also a continuity in personal comportment: Paul's passionate zealotry (1:14) persists even after his conversion (4:18) as an essential element of the religious life.

Despite the borrowing, however, this is an original explication out of the sense of Christian life itself, which is then developed further out of the basic religious experience. This return to the original experience is crucial for the understanding of the problem of religious explication. There is a tendency to regard the problem of expression (= explication) as secondary. But this seemingly external problem takes us to the heart of the religious phenomenon. It is not a mere technical problem separable from the religious experience. Explication always accompanies religious experience and drives it. The basic religious experience is to be exposed and, in it and with it, the context of all original religious phenomena is to be understood. This is an explicative context and not a theoretical context, even though it may present itself as something like a theoretical context. For example, to know here (4:9) means to love, on the basis of God's love for humans, and so is not primarily theoretical knowledge. The life of faith is not developed by intellectual or logical argumentation, but by a λογίζεσθαι ("reckoning") explicated from faith itself. The connection of faith (πίστις is *not* belief) and hope (5:5) is also important. Happiness is not consummated here and now, but in the higher world. All depends upon the "race toward the goal" (cf. 5:7, 2: 20), which is history. Why "run"? Because Paul is in a hurry, since the end of time has already come. The present time (αἰών) has already reached its culmination and the new "world without end" (αἰὼν τῶν αἰώνων) has begun (1:4, 5). Paul's sense of history, the original historical understanding of his own Dasein, is best expressed in Philippians 3:13f.: "but *this* one thing *I do*, forgetting those things which are behind, and reaching forth unto those things which are ahead, I press toward the mark for the prize." (Here especially, Heidegger's purported "object-historical" summary of Galatians begins to point to the "actualization-historical" elements which he will highlight after the break.)

Harnack dates his "history of dogma," the dogmatizing of Christian religion through Greek philosophy, from the third century. But the actual problem of dogma is the problem of religious explication itself, and so already lies in primitive Christianity. Paul's explication contains not only rabbinic but also Stoic and other Greek elements (4:3), which eventually would somehow have to be "destroyed." The problem culminates in the struggle between the "hearing of faith" and the "works of the law" (3:2), where law is to be understood primarily as the ritual and ceremonial law, the secondary moral law which follows the calendar of the feasts and is governed by the time of the stars (4:10).

Methodology Again!

After the Christmas break, Heidegger first asks how we are now to take this concrete content from Galatians into account. This question can only be understood and decided in relation to the guiding aim of a phenomenology of religion. It is Heidegger's opportunity to put the course back on its original methodological track, which he seizes with alacrity and in great detail.

Religion is to be understood and conceived philosophically (the problem of philosophical concepts!). It is to be placed in a context in terms of which it comes to be understood. This task is accordingly dependent upon the concept of philosophy (which has in fact been the course topic since the opening hour!). The philosophy of religion current today [neo-Kantianism] makes the following presuppositions (about which it is itself unclear) in its approach to the problems: 1) Religion (say, the primitive Christianity of Galatians) is a historical fact which serves as a concrete case or example for a lawful supratemporal order, the consciousness [for neo-Kantianism]. 2) But only the conscious aspect of religion is thus taken into consideration. The total phenomenon of religion is shortchanged of its nonconscious elements. As a purported alternative, the prevailing philosophy of religion [Rudolf Otto] operates with the contrast "rational-irrational," where the "irrational" still remains obscure because the term "rational" itself is left unquestioned and unclarified. This conceptual contrast has nothing to do with the religious phenomenon. Thus, no advance in philosophical conceptuality has really been made with this distinction.

Posing the problem in such extraneous ways thinks away its object, and it accomodates by disappearing. Phenomenology, on the other hand, aims to think "the matters themselves," and even more emphatically, to encounter them in their originality. Does the history of religions provide the matter, like the content of Galatians, which phenomenology can use? Is such an "object-historical" discipline adequate to its subject matter? In drawing its material from such disciplines, phenomenology must always be alert to the guiding preconception by which this material has been gathered, handled, and understood. Its selected subject matter is never mere matter, but is preconceived already in the kind of questions being posed to it, and so in its criteria of selection. The guiding preconception, of which the historian knows nothing, evokes the tendencies which already motivate the problems. Thus, all the concepts and results of the history of religions, which does the essential spadework for a phenomenology of religion, must themselves be subjected to a phenomenological destruction.

This material drawn from various disciplines must then be phenomenologically understood, out of itself and not just historically or whatever, explicated in its own sense. With our surface acquaintance of the contents of Paul's letter to the Galatians in its neat tripartite division and so on, we have not really reached our goal of understanding the religiosity of primitive Christianity. This naive and indifferent acquaintance has simply listed all and sundry points together without any sort of rank or order of priority. We have regarded Paul in the way the Athenian philosophers did (Acts 17:17ff.), with an aloof curiosity tinged with cynicism. Or, more to the point in our present age, our very familiarity with Christianity might prompt us to regard this Pauline communication as something obvious and self-evident, that Paul, called as an apostle, proclaims a doctrine and then adds an admonition to his letter to the Galatians. It is never asked whether this very communication is really so obvious. Nor does one ask whether the connection between biographical profession, religious proclamation, teaching, admonition has a motivated sense which belongs to the very sense of religiosity itself. The bare letter *itself*, the very reportage of apostolic pronouncements related to the Galatian community, may be *the* central religious phenomenon, which has to be analyzed in terms of all of the phenomenological directions of sense (containment, relation, actualization) now familiar to us as a basic schematism of the intentionality of life experience.

Once again, how do we go from an object-historical understanding to a phenomenological understanding? The object-historical understanding is in its origin defined scientifically from the *relation* to the phenomenon in such a way that the beholder is not taken into account. Though it constitutes a mere external beholding, it is an essential prephenomenological phase. 'Phenomenological understanding is defined out of the *actualization* of the beholder and his situation, so that the definition is always subject to the historical situation, which is never completely defined. In order to arrive at a basic definition of the phenomenon to be understood, therefore, it is necessary to make a beginning, and that means to approach it through a preconception. This arises from a familiarity with the phenomenon. One proceeds with methodological surety when the basic definition is approached purely formally, intentionally allowing the concepts to have a certain lability, securing their definition only in the course of the phenomenological explication. And the phenomenon comes to explication in and through its actualization, its how.

As methodological leads guiding us toward the basic definition of the phenomenon under question, Heidegger therefore proposes the following two phenomenological explicata or formal indications:

1) Primitive Christian religiosity is in factic life experience; a radical follow-up to this "proposition": it is actually factic life experience itself.

2) Factic life experience is historical; its radical follow-up: Christian experience "lives" (*verbum transitivum*) temporality as such. That is to say, it is actualization-historical rather than object-historical.

These are not "propositions" or "theses" to be proved but pointers which must stand the test of phenomenological experience (which is not the same as empirical experience). They can be maintained only hypothetically: "If they speak to its basic sense, they then prefigure the phenomenon in this or that way."

The Central Phenomenon

Out of this particular context of life experience, we draw out the phenomenon of "apostolic proclamation" (*Verkündigung*, ʿεὐαγγελίζεσθαι; Gal. 1:8ff.) as central to a religion focused on the "hearing of faith" (Gal. 3:2). The tedium of "preaching" does not do justice to this complex religious phenomenon with variegated evangelical-hermeneutic functions, suggesting how situation-sensitive it is. It includes making known (*annunciatio*) the "good news" of the gospel, explicating and interpreting it according to the occasion, teaching and transmission, personal profession and testimony, interpersonal guidance (exhortation, admonition, reminder), prophecy, and so on. The hermeneutic phenomenon of pronouncement clearly takes us to the heart of Paul's self-world in its vital relation to the environment and with-world of the first congregations. It will serve to place Paul's letters in the context of his situation which motivates the manner and matter of his epistolary communications. It will guard against regarding these letters too externally, in terms of their form or style (as valuable as these considerations might sometimes be), destroying their uniqueness in classifying them within "world literature."

Purely formally, we can ask a number of questions in this context: Who proclaims, to whom, in what context and when? What is proclaimed and how? And so on. Which is the decisive question? In factic life experience (our formal indicator), one's own actualization of life, the how of its actualization, is the decisive sense of direction. Following this indication, we shall dwell, without further justification, upon the how of the proclamation in our investigations.

Within the history of religion, the Pauline proclamation comes to us in a series of letters that span less than a decade. The first was written to the Thessalonians in A.D. 53, twenty years after the Crucifixion. It is the oldest document of the New Testament. Predating even the Gospels, it and the other letters of Paul are the most immediate sources of primitive Christianity available to us. Burdened with less dogmatic content than the letter to the Galatians, the two letters to the Thessalonians will be the focus of our attempts to explicate and understand the Pauline proclamation in the actual situation out of which it emerges. Keeping to our guiding explicata that this basic phenomenon is 1) factic life experience and 2) this in turn is historical, we must first define the factual historical situation by way of the available object-historical reports. This prephenomenological step is naturally already guided by phenomenological motives, by the aim of the phenomenological explication.

First Thessalonians

First the object-historical report of the situation: Paul first wrote to the Thessalonian congregation from Corinth during his first great missionary journey through Greece. After a three-week stay in Thessalonica, he had been prevailed upon to leave, "by night" because of a threat of imprisonment, a congregation of some Jews and many Greeks behind still under siege by the Jewish opposition. He himself did not find safety from mob action until he reached Athens (Acts 17:1–16). Concerned about the situation of his fellow Thessalonians, for whom he had developed a great attachment as much as they themselves felt "fatefully joined" (προσκληροῦσθαι: Acts 17:4) to him, he sent his companion Timothy to aid them in their plight. The letter was written upon hearing from Timothy personally that the bond between himself and the Thessalonians still prospered (1 Thess. 3:6, 2). The good news apparently also prompted Paul to a vigorous proclamation of his Christianity to the Jews in Corinth (Acts 18:5).

The "fateful" bond (Acts 17:4) between Paul and the Thessalonians already suggested in the report of the objective historical situation thus provides at least one clue to the historical situation in its actualization, which must now be explicated.

We now regard the situation in such a way that we write the letter with Paul, actualize with him the writing (dictation) of the letter. In this situation, how does Paul stand to the Thessalonians? How are they experienced by him? How is this with-world given to him and understood by him in the situation which prompts the letter? According to the schematism of factic life experience, the content of Paul's with-world must be considered in conjunction with his relation to it, in order to arrive at the how of this relation, its actualization. Such questions are meant to guide us into the full situationality which Paul actualizes here. But there are at least three methodological difficulties to consider in this transition from the objective historical context of occurrences to the original historical situation of actualization:

1) The problem of empathy into Paul's ancient and so alien environment is falsely posed in epistemological fashion when this world is regarded in an objective way as if it were a thing. It is instead a matter of approaching this world nonrepresentationally in the continuity of the tradition with our situation, out of which we are already motivated to come to understand the sense of Paul's situation.

2) The problem of linguistically representing this unique situation of actualization is more difficult, since the words used to depict it, as words, are the same as the words used in objective historical depictions, and so immediately fall to the same level of reification. One simply must reacclimate oneself to the possibility of an immanent explication in a philosophical conceptuality more original than our customary thinglike objective concepts, out of which context of actualization these everyday words in fact have their origin.

3) The problem of explication itself involves bringing the explicated moment out from the implicit total background of actualization and, it seems, apart from it, in abstraction. But the kind of "universal" involved here differs from the usual objective, theoretical, regional, and so separable universals which order genera and species. In phenomenological explication, when one of the worlds (around-, with-, and self-worlds) or senses of direction (content, relation, actualization) is explicated, the others are not simply pushed aside and left out. Instead, the how of their projection into the sense just explicated is at once co-defined by the explication itself.

Philosophy *is* the return to the original-historical in its absolute unrepeatability, to the historical situation in its unique actualization. Its step-by-step movement, which is called phenomenological explication, working its way through the manifold of phenomena which make up the unity of that situation, brings us ever closer to the true historical facticity. It thus becomes ever more individual, as it were, narrower and closer to home, and not higher and more universal, as the usual image of philosophy has it. The term "situation" applies strictly speaking to this factic context of actualization. The unity of its multiplicity is not formally logical, and can only be formally indicated. This does not mean that a situation is static and fixed, as the popular understanding has it. Nor is it dynamic, as one understands a coherence of phenomena to be a flux or a stream, a conception which moreover suggests the homogeneity that belongs to ordered universals. The temporality of factic life can only be derived from its context of actualization, which in turn then decides on the static or dynamic character of the situation.

Every situation implies the "I-like" (*Ichliches*), which we understand absolutely indeterminately, formally indicatively. It does not mean to say that the I-like is the factor bestowing unity upon the multiplicity of the situation. The non-I-like also belongs necessarily to the situation. And nothing is said about the relation between the two, say, a subject-object relation. The Fichtean sentence, "The I posits the (form of the) non-I," is far too prejudicial of the situation, taking it in a Kantian direction. All we have is the I and the non-I, the two standing together in context. The only distinction that we have, in formal indication, is: The I-like *is* and *has* [the non-I-like as well as itself?]; the non-I-like only *is* and does not have. The problem of the origin of the concepts of being: The predicative "is" of theoretical explication arises out of the original "I am" and not the reverse.

That the I-like *has* something can be taken as a point of departure for the situation. For what is had seems to give itself as objective, and is so characterizable. It offers a beginning for explication. The relation of the people to Paul: what he has and how he has them. We thus begin with that moment which was already indicated in the objective historical report (Acts 17:4), and ask whether this relation is maintained with and in Paul's own situation of actualization, and how. Finally, what does this relation mean to him? Paul finds himself involved in how the people have congregated, insofar as they have "fatefully bound" themselves to him and are "beholden" to him. In them, in their relation to him, he necessarily experiences himself. How does this relation come to expression in the letter he writes?

The bond is such that everything he attributes to the community also says something about himself. The striking repetition of certain key words which abound in the letter suggests that Paul experiences the

Thessalonians in two ways: 1) he experiences their "having become" [followers of Christ]; 2) he experiences that they have a "knowledge" of their having-become. Moreover, their having-become is at once Paul's, he is included in and affected by their having-become and its accompanying know-how. And the act of repeating these words is not a curious external feature of the letter belonging to objective history. It serves rather to recall this tacit knowledge of having-become, thereby reinforcing a motivational tendency which is constantly arising in their factic life experience. Their recall (μνημονεύετε: 1 Thess. 2:9) is the essential extension and sustenance of their know-how. The expressed repetition is thus part and parcel of their history of actualization. It is different from the repetition of a natural event. Thus, Paul's recollection of the "event" of his initial fateful entry into their lives is couched not in "object-historical" but in "actualization-historical" terms—"For you yourselves know . . . that it was not in vain" (1 Thess. 2:1)—so that he himself became, and continues to be, irrevocably linked to their lives. It became a bond which went beyond his "official" relation to them as an apostle of Christ: "Having thus a fond affection for you, we were willing to share not only the gospel of God but also our own lives with you, because you had become very dear to us" (1 Thess. 2:8).

We have said that the hav*ing*-become (= the facticity of *being* a Christian) is accompanied by a certain knowledge. But this way of putting the matter still rips apart what is originally and wholly experienced together. The having-become is not merely occasionally known; knowing makes up its very being, and it makes up the very being of that knowing. This knowing differs radically from any other kind of knowing and remembering, defying the usual scientific psychologies; it emerges directly from the situational context of the Christian life experience. It is the point of origin of theology: the explication of this knowledge is the sense and task of theology. This in turn is a new theology calling for a new kind of concept formation. [After BT, Bultmann will in fact make the facticity of understanding central to theology.] In order better to apprehend this knowing, we must take a closer look at the having-become.

Having become is not just a past and bygone event, but something that is constantly co-experienced by the Thessalonians, so that their having become is their present being. What is the nature of this peculiar (Christian) becoming or "genesis" (γενέσθαι)? Paul's letter takes us to the very core: "And you became followers of us and of the Lord, having received the word in much affliction, with the joy of the Holy Spirit" (1 Thess. 1:6). The becoming is a receptivity to the good news being announced, accepted in great distress and tribulation, which persists insofar as we make this condition our very own (3:3f., 7). The how of the receptivity is characterized by a constant "in trepidation." But the receptivity also awakens a joy which is not self-made or motivated out of our own experience but comes from the Holy Spirit, like a gratuitous destiny, a gift wrapped in dread. The facticity of a Christian, the way she finds herself and habitually comports herself, is a receptivity wrapped in persistent dread and joy.

As if to underscore its importance in defining the becoming, Paul marshals a second Greek word to describe this receiving. There is not only the "receptive appropriating" (δέχεσθαι: 1:6, 2:13) of needy distress as the very condition of our life as Christians, but an even more "receptive receiving" of the "word *of* God" (double genitive), insofar as we acknowledge its operation in us as basically *of* God, *from* God (παρα-λαμβάνειν, "taking-from": 2:13). With this reception, we enter into the operative context of God, in a working relation in His presence. To receive is to change before God. The decisive determination in becoming is accordingly our "turning to" God (1:9); the turn "from idols" is secondary. This turn manifests itself explicitly in two concretely receptive directions: serving and awaiting God (1:9f.).

At this crucial point of Christian intimacy, at the beginning of the next hour (January 28), Heidegger summarizes by sketching—in a horizontal diagram on the board greeting the students upon entering the class—a "formal schema" of Paul's Greek categories prefiguring the actualization of Christian life, which gives us a sense of his total context for becoming a Christian. We present it here in the original Greek and in English, along with a locus of the terms in First Thessalonians (fig. 2).[6]

The "turning to" provides for the first time an operative context for "the living and true God" (1:9). It thus poses the task of how the "objectivity" (counterstance) *of* God is given in this Christian context of actualization. It would be a lapse in true understanding if God in this active context were regarded as an object of speculation. This becomes clear simply from the most superficial explication of the conceptual connections manifest here. But this has never really been done, since Greek philosophy from the start forced its way into Christianity. Luther was the only one who made a beginning in this direction, which explains his hatred of Aristotle. What it means to be "before God" or "in the presence of God" depends, as we shall see, on whether we understand the "waiting for God" in terms of an objective time or in the more persistent living element of hope.

This element is expressed in Paul's participation in the becoming of the Thessalonians. "For now we live, if you stand fast in the Lord" (3:8). Paul's life depends on their steadfastness in faith, which puts them even now "before our Lord Jesus Christ in his coming (παρουσία). For you are our glory and joy" (2:19f.). It is in relation to the Parousia that the Thessalonians are Paul's hope, glory, and joy. Is Paul seeking his

Lecture Course by Privatdocent Heidegger:
WS 1920-21 - Introduction to the Philosophy of Religion
Text being diagrammed: Paul's First Letter to the Thessalonians
Lecture date: January 28, 1921

Oskar Becker's version of the "FORMALES SCHEMA" in the Greek:

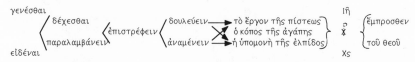

English rendition:

Textual Source	in 1. Thessalonians
'knowing' (13), becoming (12 times)	
receptive receiving, receptive appropriating	2: 13
turning to	1: 9f
waiting, serving	1: 9f
patience of hope, labor of love, working of faith	1: 3
before God	1: 3

Figure 2

own justification from his success with the Thessalonians? A little earlier, he had denied all glory-seeking from humans (2:6), as the wandering preachers of Greece then did. The apparent contradiction is overcome when we note that hope, glory, and joy acquire a special sense in Paul's life-context. The hopeful anticipation of the Parousia is more a matter of enduring the Parousia, holding out, than a calculated waiting for it. If the glory and joy are defined by this steadfast enduring, this in turn is defined by the absolute affliction and need which defines every moment of the life of the Christian. Twice in the letter, Paul admits that he "could endure it no longer" (3:1, 5). And yet it is of the essence of Christian life to do just that. Christian receptivity means to put oneself into this plight. It is the very self-world of Paul, out of which he writes his letter. In another famous passage, Paul asserts the preference to be seen, not in his glory, but in his weakness and affliction, which he describes as "a thorn in the flesh, a messenger of Satan to buffet me" (2

Cor. 12:7). Here, "flesh" is not concupiscence, as Augustine would have it, but the sphere of origin of all affects which do not come from God. Likewise, the reference to Satan is to be taken more in the sense of actualization than of content, as that which thwarts or hinders (1 Thess. 2:18). In the Old Testament Hebrew, "Satan" first referred to the opponent, the enemy in war, and more ethically, "he who does battle against what God wants." In any case, Satan intensifies Paul's affliction, the absolute apostolic distress in his profession in this end-time, which in turn spurs him on to greater efforts to hold out. It is in weakness rather than in ecstasy that he enters into a close relationship with God. It is in need that he truly *has* his life, and so *is*.

Out of this exponentialized plight, Paul now comes to the climax of his proclamation, a clarification of the Parousia in response to the "dogmatic" questions usually asked about it: 1) What is the fate of those who have already died, and so will not experience the Parousia? (4:13–18); 2) When will the Parousia take place, when will the Lord return? (5:1–12). Both questions are based on dogmatic misconceptions which would misguide the practical Christian bent upon actualizing his life. Thus, Paul does not answer especially the second question literally and directly, so that the exegetical tradition has accused him of avoiding the question and not knowing the answer. (This also contributed to challenging the authenticity of the letter.) But for Paul, the question of the when is not an "examination question" with a neatly packaged content. The way he answers will appeal to a different kind of knowledge, the know-how that belongs to the facticity of the Thessalonians in their beleaguered but steadfast faith. It is in view of this different answer that Paul has motivated and prepared the Thessalonians throughout the letter, by his reiterated appeal to the peculiar "knowledge" they possess through having become followers of Christ. It also explains why this letter had to be approached at a deeper, "actualization-historical" level, as compared with the more superficial cognizance of the dogmatic contents given to the less "personal" letter sent to the Galatians.

In Paul's time, "parousia" no longer retained its classical Greek and Septuagint sense of "presence" or "arrival," but referred to the reappearance of Christ, His second coming. This clearly suggested an impending future event (*Ereignis*)[7] to be expected and awaited. And yet the experiential structure of Christian hope, which (as we have seen) is in fact the relational sense associated with the Parousia, runs counter to any expectation which might be defined in terms of objective time. It is out of this experiential context and its cognizance that Paul now replies to the question of the when. He immediately deflects the question of the when away from the question of the "times and seasons" (χρόνοι καὶ καιροί) to the Thessalonians' own awareness "that the day of the Lord so cometh as a thief in the night," which "you yourselves know perfectly well" (5:1f.), a knowledge which moreover is independent of that of the "times and seasons." In short, look not to the actual timing, but instead look to yourselves, for the real decision implied in the question depends on your own life, on your "having become," the status of which only "you yourselves know full well." Paul then juxtaposes two ways of living, two Hows of comporting oneself to the Parousia. First, "they" who say, "Peace and security!," "Nothing to fear!," "Don't let it bother you!," those in short who wish to ignore the travail indigenous to life, are apt to be surprised by "sudden ruin, like the birth pangs which come upon a woman with child" (5:3). "They" are the ones who are absorbed in this world, become attached to it because of the peace and security that it offers and that they come to expect from it. Whatever "they" encounter in their worldly comportment sustains no real motive for dis-ease. "They" have forgotten themselves in favor of the world, they cannot save themselves because they do not have themselves, they do not seek themselves in the clarity of their own knowledge and so live "in the dark."

"But you, my brothers, are not in the dark, for that day to surprise you like a thief" (5:4). Those who are alert to the essential insecurity of life are the "children of the light and the children of the day" (5:5). Instead of "Peace and security!" their hortatory maxim is "Let us be watchful and sober!" (5:6). Light, the opposite of the dark, has two senses here, the light of self-knowledge and the light of the day of the Lord. One may surmise that the first is based on the second, which is operative even before that day dawns in any chronological sense. Actualization involves a peculiar "kairotic" moment of illumination that comes with full alertness to my situation. The sense of the when, of the time in which the Christian lives, now assumes a more fundamental character for the factic life experience that is "historical." The when of the Parousia (being "before God") is now determined by the how of my self-comportment—armed (i.e., battle-ready) as I am with the "breastplate of faith and love" and the "helmet" of hope (5:8)—and this in turn by the actualization of my factic life experience in and through every moment. How the Parousia stands in my life refers back to the full temporal actualization of my life, and not to a passing when. We are beginning to approach the full amplitude of our initial formal indication: "Christian religiosity lives temporality as such." And what temporality is here can only be understood by the careful distinction of the three senses of direction (content, relation, actualization) which structure factic life experience.

Second Thessalonians

It is commonly said that the Second Letter to the Thessalonians contradicts the First, by providing the apocalyptic signs which allow us to predict the when of the Parousia, like the coming of the Antichrist. Heidegger will dispute this claim, and will instead try to demonstrate their continuity. For the Second Letter can be read as an echo or reflection of the effect which the First Letter had on the Thessalonians. There were those in the congregation who had understood Paul, whose sense of need and affliction was intensified to the point of being brought to the threshold of despair. They were genuinely worried over whether, in the goals of true concern, they could hold out and carry out the works of faith and love demanded of them. Paul answers not by comforting them but by further heightening their sense of trial. The persecutions and tribulations that they are enduring are "a clear indication that God's judgment is just, so that you may be deemed worthy of the kingdom of God, for which reason you suffer" (2 Thess. 1:5). This supercharged way of putting matters, this "pleophory" of expression, typically Pauline, will define the mood of this Second Letter. Paul loses no time to emphasize his point of concern repeatedly: "With this in mind, we constantly pray for you, that our God may consider you worthy of this calling" (1:11). For it is not enough to belong to the called, chosen, elect, rather than the rejected and damned; one must still earn one's glory. "It was for this that He called you through our gospel, that you might earn the glory of our Lord Jesus Christ" (3:14).

Over against this first group, there were others who understood the First Letter differently. They are briefly identified as the ones who had disturbed the communal order by refusing to work: "they are not busy; they are busybodies" (3:11). These are the ones, Heidegger presumes, who assumed from Paul's First Letter that the Parousia would come soon. So they spend all their time asking the question of when it will come, whether the Lord will come immediately, and the like. In this context, such chiliastic questions become busybody questions, which stem from the worldly concerned rather than the Christian concerned, a division of two modes of factic life that was already fully developed in the First Letter. But Heidegger here takes note almost in passing—in addition to the fallen everydayness that characterizes the mode of factic life oriented totally toward the worldly—of a kind of _authentic everydayness_ that provides a stable infrastructure to the Christian travail. It appears in both letters: Appealing to his own example as a still active tentmaker, Paul recommends that each should out of "brotherly love" quietly give the daily its due, do his own business, work with his own hands and eat his own bread (1 Thess. 4:9–12; 2 Thess. 3:7–13). It constitutes a kind of model of everydayness for the early Christian community.

As to the famous apocalyptic passages of the Second Letter (2 Thess. 2:2–13), Paul wishes to approach them more in terms of actualization history rather than content. The decisive passage is accordingly verse

10, which speaks of the rejected or damned "because they did not receive the love of the truth." Even though it is negative, "not receiving" as a basic decision is as positive an actualization as the Christian response (cf. the "formal schema" above on receptivity in a Christian actualization). Just as in the First Letter, this passage juxtaposes two distinct ways of factic life and the decision between them. It is only on this basis that the objective signs of the imminence of the Parousia can be recognized. In order to recognize the Antichrist as the Antichrist (e.g., his claim to be God), one must first have entered into the actualization context of the religious situation.

Heidegger, without denying the importance of the objective content of these apocalyptic passages, accordingly does not accept the argument that they serve to soften Paul's stand by taking back the severity of the tone of the First Letter, inasmuch as he no longer proclaims the immediate imminence of the Parousia: "that day shall not come until the apostasy occurs and the man of lawlessness is revealed" (2 Thess. 2:3). On this basis, it is claimed that Paul has become more cautious and wishes to calm his congregation instead of intensifying their insecurity, as he had done in the First Letter. But the very tenor, the "pleophoric" manner, of the supercharged expressions of the Second Letter speaks against this claim. The letter therefore represents not a reduced but rather a heightened tension, reflecting the urgency of Paul's profession as an apostle. He continues to press his followers to the point of despair in order to make them understand their situation of decision, each alone and already "before God."

The eschatological problem, in its deep nondogmatic sense, is the very center of Christian life. The oddity is that the genuine problem of its actualization went into decline and so became concealed in its conceptuality at the same time as the more "object-historical" approaches to the eschatological did, after the turn of the first century. The latter however were repeatedly revived, in medieval chiliasm and modern adventism, for example, and justified on the basis of late Jewish, Babylonian, and Iranian pictures of the demise of the world. Such pictures tend to be fanciful and highly constructive. For the eschatological is not a picture or representation at all. As we have seen, Paul's language has an entirely different expressive function from which a representational content cannot really be assumed. Persisting in hope is not reducible to a representable [calculable] "waiting," in the larger context of actually becoming a Christian. The entire process of enduring is instead a question of "serving God" (1 Thess. 9f.; cf. formal schema above, fig. 2). The intensification of need even to the point of bearing despair is a "proof" of one's calling. This intensified need of the "Apostle" himself, the pressure of his personal calling as a "preacher," is precisely what motivates the exaggerated articulation of the Second Letter to the Thessalonians. His "proofs" never refer to a purely theoretical context, but first to an original context of becoming which is either actively being assumed or not being accepted. The traditional opposition between the saved and the lost (2 Thess. 2:10: ἀπολλυμένοις = those who are perishing) is therefore in the present participle, and not the perfect, to convey this still ongoing actualization. The reiteration of the opposition is actively decisionistic, for it indicates that the Event of the Parousia is directed toward humans who decide for themselves where they now stand. It is the ultimate attitudinal and fateful decision of receiving or not receiving "the love of the truth" (ibid.). This enables the saved to withstand the "test" of the Antichrist, before whose "deluding influence" the others will inevitably succumb (*verfallen*) because they are unprepared and thus defenseless. Against this inevitability understood as a point of no return, we must therefore prepare ourselves "in advance." This is but another example of Paul's rhetoric of intensification of the Christian facticity to the foremost need which it must actualize now: "Therefore, stand firm and persist in the teachings that have been transmitted to you" (2 Thess. 2:15). Against the eschatology of the late Judaism of Paul's time, which put the primacy on a future event which is to be awaited, the temporality of Christian facticity emphasizes the moment of decision between past and future in which the Christian constantly stands, in the present "before the God of old" (ἔμπροσθεν, with connotations of both time and place) from which the future receives its sense. Temporality thus first arises from this context of actualization before God.

Thus, Second Thessalonians, also viewed as a context of actualization, likewise verifies our formal indication, that Christian religiosity lives temporality as such. As the formal schema for First Thessalonians has shown, all the primary connections of becoming a Christian converge upon God and actualize themselves "before" God. The sense of temporality is defined out of the basic relationship to God, so that eternity merely endorses and looks after what temporality in its actualization lives. It is only out of this context of actualization that the sense of the being of God is defined. Traversal of this temporality is a precondition in order to understand how such actualization contexts yield the concepts of dogma. Here above all, it is essential to maintain the initial "good news" in its full vitality, and not just as a verbal memory.

Christian Facticity in the World

But for all its originality and radical shift toward actualization, primal Christian facticity does not achieve any extraordinary or special status with respect to worldly facticity. The accentuation in Christian life first occurs in an actualization "all alone before God." Having become a Christian in turn affects especially the relations to the self-world, relational directions which Paul describes in the then current and easily misunderstood terms of "spirit," "soul," "flesh." But since everything now proceeds toward God and not toward the significances of future content, what sense do the relations of the with- and the environing world, defined precisely in such rejected terms, have for the Christian? Heidegger devotes what is left of the course (three hours) to this final question. In traditional terms, it is the question of the Christian's relation to the "world." Lacking a central textual focus, the course's conclusion dissipates into a potpourri tendering of loose ends, without the usual dramatic flourish of a Heidegger ending, which typically would have exposed a hitherto unsuspected aspect of the themes under discussion. This is but a further indication of the improvisation entering into this portion of the course.

What is changed in the Christian's relation to the world, upon undergoing the radical change involved in becoming a Christian? Nothing . . . and everything. The world retains the same content of significance, and the Christian is not obliged to change that content. "Let each remain in the situation in which he was called" (1 Cor. 7:20). As far as the world is concerned, the becoming is a remaining. The slave remains a slave, while becoming the Lord's freeman, and the freeman free, as he becomes Christ's servant (7:22). It is a matter of indifference in which worldly state and significance the Christian happens to stand, since worldly content in no way defines the facticity of the Christian. And yet that content is maintained and remains the temporal possession of the Christian. He does not seek to flee the world or even to "bear" it. But its content and relations simply do not have the possibility of motivating the archontic sense of primal Christian religiosity, which is all that matters. Nor is it even a matter of "bracketing" the world. To regard worldly relations "as though not" in unconcern is a poor, because objectifying, translation of the Greek in 1 Cor. 7:29–31, Heidegger insists, without offering an alternative translation for ὡς μή. Such worldly relations instead undergo a retardation within the Christian actualization, so that they now arise from and pass through the new origin of the Christian life-context in all its urgency and "fear and trembling" (Phil. 2:12) before God. This "retardation" is the breach in the continuity which is otherwise maintained without infringement in the Christian's relations with the world. The very context of this discussion indicates that it has nothing to do with [what Nietzsche called] a "resentment" of the world.

The life of the Christian is enormously difficult, always actualized in need and affliction (θλῖψις:· *Trübsal, Bedrängnis, Bekümmerung*; to be found *passim* in 1 and 2 Thess., 1 and 2 Cor., etc.). This intensification of need and affliction gives the becoming Christian the consciousness that the actualization of this life exceeds human power, that the *Christian facticity accordingly stems from God* (2 Cor. 4:7f.). (This of course is the Christian phenomenon of the work of grace, which Heidegger will eventually conclude cannot be treated philosophically.) This becoming through serving and waiting is always profoundly imbued by a knowing of a peculiar kind, which includes "proving" and deciding. What is this "knowledge" guiding us through the straits of life, allowing us to hold out in the face of life's distress? This knowing requires "having spirit" (1 Cor. 2:10-3:4), which provides the foundation for serving and persisting. Spirit here, like "flesh," is not a thinglike entity but a context of actualization, a φρόνημα (Rom. 8:6), a way or tendency of life which might be called "Christian-mindedness." Paul never speaks of humans being spirit, but rather having spirit, thereby distinguishing himself from the Greek mystery religions.[8] Not the hermetic and gnostic "knowing all" but rather "examining, searching out all, even the depths of God" (1 Cor. 2:10) is the way of the spiritual, apropos of the Christian's situation in salvation history. The Christian is to remain always "awake and sober," not succumbing to the enticements of the enthusiastic, not becoming caught up in the "en-theos" which transports us out of this world. These hortatory parameters themselves indicate the enormous difficulty of the Christian life, which is to remain very much in this world while taking its bearings "before God."

Heidegger then makes the brief Concluding Remark on why his particular focus had to be Christian religiosity in order to arrive at a genuine relationship to the historical connections of our own facticity (cf. chap. 2, p. 80).

Despite the feeble ending, even scientifically oriented students like Becker were impressed by Heidegger's mastery of the biblical text and command over the theological literature which interprets it. Becker will look back with gratitude at the interruption which precipitated this hermeneutic improvisation, since it for once forced Heidegger to "come out with the presuppositions of his thought, which otherwise would have remained hidden. He thus unveiled the source from which his thought had received its crucial impetus."[9] With the dam broken, in the following semester Heidegger will not be so reluctant to display his unique ability to make the biblical and patristic texts speak in new and unsuspected ways. In fact, one is now surprised in the opposite direction, over how unabashedly religious Heidegger's orientation becomes, free from most of his former inhibitions,[10] as he now looks at the biblical texts through Augustine's eyes.

SS 1921: AUGUSTINE AND NEOPLATONISM

The Object-Historical Augustine[11]

Founder of medieval theology, and through Bernard of Clairvaux and Bonaventure also the founder of medieval mysticism, Augustine became the conduit for certain Platonizing currents coursing through the Middle Ages. Luther came to Paul through Augustine. He thus came to be the most highly regarded of the Church Fathers by Protestantism. Descartes, Malebranche, the Port-Royal School (Jansenism, Pascal) revived Augustine in Catholic France. Nowadays, in conjunction with Bergson and, in Germany, through Scheler, the Catholic movement of Modernism also goes back to Augustine, not the original Augustine but the Augustine of the medieval Church, with several of his main motifs put out of play.

With the recent ascendancy of historical science within the domain of theology, Augustine *himself* has come to be regarded anew. Three prominent recent studies on Augustine's relation to history and the philosophy of history will serve by contrast to delimit further the already delimited course topic reflected in our title:

1. Ernst Troeltsch, *Augustin, die christliche Antik und das Mittelalter,* 1915. Troeltsch views Augustine's *City of God* as a universal history which founds a philosophy of culture. Augustine makes Christendom itself receptive to its culture by resolving, through his unique interpretation of the *summum bonum,* the old problem of the compatibility of Christian values with the goods of the world. The success of a religion, but not its religiosity, stems from its cultural situation. Augustine's cultural role at the waning of antiquity was unique. It cannot be transposed into the Middle Ages, when his role as a founder of dogma was far more important.

2. Adolf von Harnack, *Lehrbuch der Dogmengeschichte,* [2]1893–97, [3]1910, esp. the Third Volume. A truly historical treatment of dogma (= "proposition," statute or doctrine proclaimed especially by an ecclesiastical—and not a theological—authority to a designated community) is a product unique to Protestant theology. Harnack's history of dogma ends strictly with Augustine, but he addresses not only Origen's and Augustine's styles but by extension a third, the Reformation's (Luther's) style of dogma form(ul)ation. Harnack takes his stand against Hegel by regarding the development of dogma not as an immanent process of thought, but in its dependence upon cult and the vital practical needs and tendencies of a church community. The main development was the adaptation of the teachings of the primitive Christian faith to the doctrinal context of antiquity, in a process which Harnack generically—and negatively—identified as the "Hellenization of Christendom."

3. Wilhelm Dilthey, *Einleitung in die Geisteswissenschaften*, 1883. Dilthey here seeks to found the human sciences by tracing the historical development of modern epistemology. He traces knowledge back to descriptive psychology, to "lived experience" understood as self-reflection and inner perception. What role does Christianity in general and Augustine in particular play in the founding of the human sciences? Christianity involves a radical transformation of psychic life. The Kingdom of God is not of this world. The soul turns away from the images of the external world to its own inner models of the will and the "heart" (Dilthey, GS 1:251/229),[12] thus becoming aware of what is given in the person, in self-consciousness. It no longer orients itself externally but finds its model in the living person of Jesus; this unique self-surety in the relationship to God becomes fundamental. The limits of ancient science, which took its models from the external world, are thereby breached and, for the first time, psychic life itself becomes a scientific problem. This includes the fact that the Christian God reveals Himself in historical actuality, that of redemptive history, thereby being extricated from the merely theoretical transcendence portrayed by Plato, and instead entering into the arena of experience. The Christian no longer conceives God in the self-enclosed substance of antiquity but in a historical vitality that fills his own psychic life (253f./230). With Christendom, we therefore have the origin of the "historical consciousness."

Dilthey goes on to show how Christendom, by continuing to explain itself in the language of antiquity, once again becomes a kind of knowledge, a doctrine and a philosophy. What role does Augustine play within this process? On the one hand, Augustine establishes, against ancient skepticism, the absolute reality of inner experience in a manner that prefigures Descartes's "Cogito, ergo sum." But this epistemological insight takes a metaphysical turn when *veritates aeternae* are found in human consciousness, and these are rooted in the absolute consciousness of God. Moreover, the analysis of willing and knowing takes a turn toward the dogmatic concept of substance: since the human soul is changeable, it requires an unchangeable foundation. This is the inner experience of the existence of God (GS 1:258–264/233–237). At this point, Dilthey observes that what Augustine sought was first brought to fruition by Kant and Schleiermacher. With that remark, Dilthey shows that he completely misunderstood Augustine's inner problem.

Instead of regarding these three historical interpretations of Augustine in terms of their content, Heidegger poses two major questions: A. What sort of approach do they take, what is the direction of access taken to Augustine? B. What motives and, in particular, what motivational basis determine that approach?

A. The three interpretations are directed toward different sides of the historical object "Augustine." Troeltsch takes Augustine as an ethicist, Harnack as a religious reformer, and Dilthey as an epistemologist. But the basic sense of the regard is in all cases the same: Augustine is defined as an object in a historically ordered context of development. We characterize these three approaches to an object of history in an ordered chronological sequence called "time" as considerations within the "object-historical" attitude. Essential to this objective order is the establishment of a chronological succession of historical appearances. In a chrono-logy, time functions 1) as the determining framework which enables the order and at once cooperates in defining the objects qualitatively (note that chronological numbers, like dates, are not simply arithmetic numbers); 2) as a period, epoch, or age, time itself becomes an object of historical regard and is thus viewed in its distance from the present. Both meanings of historical time, closely related in the genesis of their senses, must be phenomenologically defined from the sense of the historical itself.

B. It is important to note the motivational basis of the object-historical attitude, operating unconsciously in the background. But when the philosophical significance of a historical interpretation is at issue, its motivational basis is subject to a critique which we call phenomenological destruction. The motivational basis of our three authors, the fundamental convictions in their occupation with the historical, are as follows: 1. Troeltsch is convinced that the perspective of universal history is the sole means of overcoming the current crisis of culture. 2. Harnack believes that a reflection on the history of dogma can purify the contemporary Christian consciousness, raise it to a new plane by liberating it from the aberrations of dogmatics. Dogmas were originally theological formulations and explanations of religious phenomena. But when they are acknowledged ecclesiastically as doctrine, they become directives for future religiosity and theology. The Church is convinced that dogmas are revealed truths and not just theological products. 3. Dilthey believes that, in the present cultural situation, a truly vital human life, that is, a rich and fertile life of the mind, can be achieved only by a thoroughgoing and comprehensive historical command of the past. What is needed is not more system building, but a devotion to history free from construction (Hegel) and naturalistic interpretations.

In each case, it is claimed that "the historical has such-and-such a meaning for the present." This in itself already poses a problem.

Such motives, and the lapse into object-historical considerations, will be shunned in this course. We do not wish to depict "Augustine's Life and Works" as an expression of his person and his culture. Nor does this mean that we shall present a "subjective" interpretation of Augustine; that would be but an inferior form of "object history." In such a history, "Augustine and Neoplatonism" is a familiar problem. This object-historical problem of the "Hellenization of Christendom" came to be posed by our three authors through Ritschl's theological influence. While this problem does not affect our phenomenological question, it is for us a necessary point of entry and transition into this question. Yet we cannot take an object-historical point of view and regard Augustine's relationship to Neoplatonism as an "instance" of the Hellenizing of Christendom. To start with, it would be a most inappropriate example of that relationship, since Augustine grew up in and so already took over a Hellenized Christianity. On the other hand, Plotinus already incorporates much that is Oriental as well as Christian. It is also not crucial for us that Augustine (according to Dilthey) leads Hellenistic metaphysics and cosmology back to the consciousness. What is important is not the question of the depiction of psychic life but the underlying problem of theoretization as such.

But then it would also be a mistake to think that Augustine's relationship to Neoplatonism is a typical historical instance of a supratemporal problem, that of theoretization. The historical for us does not fall apart into supratemporal ideas and their "relative" outgrowths. This is a Platonic-Hegelian prejudice which renders the resulting problematic of the relative and the absolute insoluble. Augustine and Plotinus are not mere historical "instances." The truly historical in them is to be magnified and shown to be still very much alive and operative in us today. It is a history which affects us constantly. The tragedy of the present is to think that, by objectively dominating historical reality in its entirety, it has thereby overcome its inhibiting influence. But in this very opinion, we meet history, feeling ourselves compelled by it to create a new "culture." We must accordingly first learn the significance of the effect which history has on our own existence. For these reasons, we can consider the philosophical and the theological together in Augustine. We do not make this distinction since, in the following attempt to understand the motive forces which are operative in the constellation "Augustine and Neoplatonism," we want to pass through this [historical] whole in order to get to its underlying fundamental phenomena. On the other hand, we do not want to do away with the distinction between philosophy and theology.

At this point, Heidegger presents a bibliography of the basic editions of Augustine [A.D. 354–430] and Plotinus [A.D. 204–270], singling out the texts which he is especially interested in having the students read.

The Phenomenological Augustine

The phenomenological interpretation of Augustine seeks to understand him and not to classify him historically. The point of departure of the interpretation, and orientation point throughout, will be book 10 of the

Confessions, the last of its autobiographical books. As the interpretation gets into the details and the philosophical problems become more concrete, it will be necessary to draw not only on other works of Augustine but also on those of Plotinus [Heidegger does not get that far].

Toward the end of his life (426–427), Augustine composed book 2 of his *Retractations*. Here he summarizes all of his earlier writings, stating the aim of each and improving upon whatever now seems objectionable. In his opening remarks, Augustine speaks of his motive for such a resumption and review: "The proverb, 'You will not escape without sin from that which is charged with gossip,' frightens me the most, since many of my declarations now seem to be not so much false as unnecessary. The fear of having written superfluously now forces me to review my life's work with the rigor of a judge." There he also notes the protreptic intentions of the *Confessions*: they are intended to stir the human spirit to action, as they had stirred him. The first ten books were written about himself.

The overview of the tenth book will assume a distinctive methodological character, which will become stricter, more penetrating, and more creative in its means of apprehension as it proceeds. But at first, it assumes the attitude of the naive reader who begins to understand only after he has read all the books. Only then is one in a position to understand the opening chapters! There are other difficulties in understanding the *Confessions*. Augustine uses traditional philosophical terms in a new way, he creates new concepts and designates them with old words. These concepts cannot be defined according to the usual subsumptive schemes of the philosophical systems. And in spite of the reinterpretation, the philosophical terminology available to Augustine is inadequate both in quantity and in type, outstripped by the phenomena to be explained. There is a surplus of psychic phenomena beyond the concept. This will force us to ask how the psychic as such expresses itself. But it is not our intention to go beyond the basic questions present in the phenomenal context which we find in Augustine and wish to understand in its proper sense.

Now to the course of thought in the tenth book of the *Confessions*. Having in previous books recounted the course of his life leading up to his conversion, Augustine now (chaps. 1–4) confesses before God and before humanity what he now is, and describes the nature and diverse purposes of such a public confession. "I will therefore confess what I know and do not know of myself" (chap. 5), a statement that does not sit well with those who claim that Augustine was the discoverer of the absolute evidence of self-consciousness. But first, what do I discover about God in the confessional relationship? "But what do I love, when I love Thee?" (chap. 6). In what experiential contents of my life does He find confirmation? God is not to be found in nature, as a body. And the soul? "Thou art indeed the better, O my soul, for thou giveth life to the body . . . but God is even unto thee Life of thy life" (chap. 6, conclusion). How is this Life of life experienced in psychic life? I must go beyond my animating powers of movement and sensation, which animals also have, in order to find God (chap. 7). In my ascent to God through my soul, the "inner man," I thus come to the "vast court" and "boundless chamber" of my memory (chaps. 8–19).

Here we find already articulated sense objects (chap. 8), nonsensory objects like those of mathematics and other assertions, along with the discerning and other theoretical acts by which we arrived at them and recall them (chaps. 9–13), and the affects of the mind (chap. 14). I experience myself as well in the memory, where, as it were, I "occur" to myself. I even recognize in the memory memory itself as well as the acts of remembering and forgetting (chaps. 15f.). How to analyze the aporetic structure of the act of remembering forgetfulness, the privation of memory? For in forgetting, something has "slipped my mind," something does not "come to mind" which in "bringing to mind" (envisaging, *Vergegenwärtigen*) and "keeping in mind" is there. "When I remember forgetfulness, both memory and forgetfulness are present (*praesto est*): memory *whereby* I remember and forgetfulness *which* I remember" (chap. 16); that is to say, *praesto est* here includes both the *actualizing* of envisaging or bringing to mind and the actualized *content* of memory, here the forgotten, as Heidegger translates Augustine into his "sense of direction" terminology of that period. For memory is the mind, "and this am I myself" (chap. 17), namely, intentionality. How then do forgetfulness (*oblivio*) and the forgotten, the "privation of memory," stand with the sense of relation, intentionality itself? The relatedness in envisaging something, when compared to the relatedness in forgetting, has a plus. Forgetting is thus the *not*-being-there (*Nicht-Dasein*) of memory, where the *non praesto est* (*non adest*) is precisely the sense of relation, the relatedness of intentionality. Augustine is puzzled because he is applying *praesto est* indifferently to the three different senses of direction of the phenomenon of forgetting, its senses of content, relatedness, and actualization. But he eventually does get things straight, as we shall later see.

Great as the memory is, I must somehow go beyond it to find God, for even the beasts and birds have memory (chap. 17). God is outside the memory, the mind. But can I really go beyond consciousness? How can I seek and find Him without the memory? The question of the sense of the real implicit within seeking itself will now lead Augustine to a completely new concept of existence. For we must be able to recognize what we find as that which we have sought, and how can we recognize it unless we had remembered it (chap. 18)? Memory would therefore seem to be indispensable in seeking. What then does it mean to seek God? What concept or memory guides me when I seek Him? Or must

I go beyond the memory to seek God? On what basis do I decide, when I have found God, that He is truly what I have sought?

Answer: "When I seek Thee, my God, I seek a happy life. I will seek Thee so that my soul may live" (chap. 20). What guides us in our search is thus the distress, the concern (*Bekümmerung*) over one's own life, that it be truly living. The leading tendency is to seek life as such. In this chapter, the reflection shifts in a markedly distinctive way, even though Augustine does not arrive at a totally radical formulation of the phenomena which emerge here. Perhaps he could not see them in their full distinctiveness. He wants to define *how* the happy life, and the search for it, is psychically alive, and distinguishes two ways of seeking something: by remembering it or "by desiring to learn (*per appetitum discendi*) it as a thing unknown, either never having known, or so forgotten it, as not even to remember that I had forgotten it" (chap. 20). [The second way of searching threatens to "lift" the classical anamnesis thesis, i.e., that learning is always remembering.] He does not ask whether we once had the happy life and how we lost it (the approach through "original sin"). Rather, *how* the happy life in the search for it is alive in us will expose *what* is thereby intended. And so Augustine does not get around to defining the *vita beata* contentwise, as he had originally intended. Instead, the question abruptly changes and he confronts the problem of *how he can come to* the happy life.

The happy life was already a problem in earlier philosophy, and so arises in Augustine's confrontation of Christianity with Greek philosophy, especially Stoicism, which provided him with the argument for the existence of the happy life, as well as how it now exists: Everyone wants the happy life. But they could not love it if they did not know about it. Therefore, the happy life must already be present in the memory. But how? Not as we remember sense objects, "for a happy life is not seen with the eye" (chap. 21); nor as a number, which the memory contains in itself and seeks no further to attain it, while we know and love the happy life "and yet still desire to attain it, that we may be happy" (chap. 21); nor as the art of eloquence, which I have observed in others and would like to learn from them. But the happy life cannot be taken from another, even if she perchance has it, which is difficult to determine since, as we have said, it cannot really be observed. No, the happy life is to be found in myself, as a tendency or "gravity" of the soul (*pondus animae*: *Tractatus de musica* 6, chap. 11, §29) which draws it and directs it. It is like a joy which I remember even when I am sad. But not every delight brings us to the happy life. Though all human beings want the happy life, they do not will it strongly enough in order to make themselves capable of and equal to its possibility, and so settle for lesser delights now within their power (chap. 23). The happy life must be taken up into the will so intensely that it is capable of putting me in touch with how the *vita beata* "stands toward" me, a "counterstance" (*Gegenständlich-keit*) which I myself first cultivate and shape. The happy life takes shape only in the strong will and intense desire for it. It first "stands toward" me in the pressure of affliction (*Bekümmerung*); otherwise, it is simply not there. Something that is there of itself is not the *vita beata*. The happy life is elsewhere.

With this phenomenon, we come in contact with a "context of consciousness" which does not resemble the usual structure of consciousness, not even on the phenomenological level of observation and reflection. The solution is not to be found even in the structure of intentionality involved here. On the contrary, it is only on this basis that intentionality itself first becomes comprehensible, since it is derived from the simple center and heart of this phenomenon. [Recall the Eckhartian "still point" from 1916, which Heidegger now links to Augustine's *cura*.] From this point on (chap. 23), with the naming of this phenomenon, Augustine's account becomes ever more difficult and ponderous, and he must utilize the full gamut of means in his dialectic in order to make his insights accessible to us.

If the happy life is thus a how of experiencing, then it can never be found even if I were to scour the whole world. It is not an object (*Objekt*) and cannot be appropriated from others. The having of a happy life, its actualization, is formally always an "own," so that the individual who experiences it is always actively involved in it.

The question of how I have the happy life also yields an answer to what it is. It is given in a *delectatio*, a delight. But despite this prefiguring of a specific sense of what the happy life is, it must also be noted that the phenomenon of *delectare* here and perhaps in general is never made clear by Augustine. *Delectatio* assumes different meanings: 1. the rejoicing as relation; 2. that about which I rejoice (content); 3. the rejoicing in its actualization; 4. a phenomenon to which Augustine faintly alludes, which will be discussed later.

Augustine makes clear in what sense the happy life is a delight when he states that it is a "joy in truth" (*gaudium de veritate*: chap. 23). This concept of truth outstrips the entire conceptual context then available to Augustine from the philosophy of his time, especially Neoplatonism. The truth that resides in the happy life has a sense more basic than the truth of a theoretical assertion. It now draws upon Augustine's religious life. It also alludes to the theological sense of Christ as the Truth. And it raises the question of what philosophical truth really implies.

With the concept of the happy life as a "joy in truth," Augustine juxtaposes two points: that all long for the happy life, and that all balk at the thought of being deceived. But if these two points hold, why then is the concern (*Bekümmerung*) for truth not more radical, more deeply rooted in the memory? It is there only "faintly" (*tenuiter*), drowned out by other loves, even though "there is a little light still left in humans" (chap. 23). Each would have the thing he loves to be the truth. And since all resist being deceived, they find it hard to be convinced that they are. They love the comfortable truth, but when she asks disturbing questions, they shut their eyes. "They love truth when she enlightens, they hate her when she reproves" (chap. 23).

The happy life is truth, and Truth is God himself, Who is my delight (chap. 24). But God is nothing physical, nor is He an affection of a living being nor the mind itself. "Thou art the Lord God of the mind; and all these are changed, but Thou remainest immutable over all of them" (chap. 25). Here we abruptly get the Neoplatonic influence: for Augustine and the Greeks, the immutable is the highest good (*summum bonum*). While Augustine gives this Neoplatonic speculation his own meaning (which Dilthey does not see), it nevertheless mars his religious orientation. The highest good, immutable Being and Truth, is experienced as a *frui* (enjoying), everything else is accordingly experienced in *uti* (using).

Schematizing Factic Life as Caring

The next chapters (27–29) of book 10 prompt Heidegger into a detailed excursus into factic life, by way of a wide-ranging reading of various Augustinian texts on *uti* and *frui*, now understood as modes of caring (*curare* = *Bekümmertsein*, being-troubled), and the hierarchy of values which their relationship to the highest good implies. Though the context is Christian, since Augustine discusses factic life specifically as alienation from and striving toward God, the terms still bear a formal sense which is not specifically Christian. Thus, believing is a confident acceptance, hoping an expectant openness, and loving a devoted giving (*Hingabe*) of self. But clearly we are dealing with the Christian factic life here [cf. the formal schema of "before God" in WS 1920–21]. Thus the despair of chapter 28 bears its seed of hope only because it is tempered throughout by the mercy of God. "And all my hope is nowhere but in Thy exceeding great mercy" (chap. 29). A total despair without remission would suffocate and destroy the soul.

But for this gift, God "enjoins continence," the mighty effort of containment or pulling oneself together. "By continency we are gathered and brought back to the One, whence we were dissipated into many" (chap. 29). Unity and multiplicity here are not quantitative terms: the many refers to the multiplicity of meaning in factic life, and the basic tendency toward the One is a basic attitude adopted from Plotinus. "Enjoining" (*jubes* = "Thou orderest/exhortest") here is a directive of the heart and not an ecclesiastical decree oriented in objective belief. The confounding of the two leads to hypocrisy, the inclination to please human beings rather than God. The righteous man must therefore be examined, tested, and "proven" in his "private parts," in his secrets, that

is, in his "heart" (inner reflection) and in his "loins" (Psalms 7:9, where
renes = "kidneys" = the delights, especially of the lower [*malum* =
"dirty"] parts) (Augustine, *Enarrationes in Psalmos* 7:9).
  Finis curae delectatio est (ibid.). "The goal of care is delight; for each
strives in his concerns (*Bekümmerung*) and thoughts to attain his delights."
But God Himself responds in the conscience and sees our concerns and
our goals. "He Who searches out the heart sees our cares. He Who examines the loins likewise sees the goal of those cares, which are delights"
(ibid.). In short, God searches out what we secretly search. Note that
Heidegger still translates *cura* here as *Bekümmerung* (distress, concern,
the trouble of search), in keeping with his prior allusions, and for the
time being resists using the dictionary translation of *Sorge*, his translation
of *cura* in BT. There is a Latin etymological tradition which relates *cura*
to *quaero*, seeking, and its concomitant tribulation or anxiety. But this
text from his *Expositions on the Psalms* (7:9) is one of those rare places in
which Augustine thematizes *curare*, and Heidegger makes this excursus
discovery central to the schematism of the Christian factic life which he
now develops from the *Confessions*.
  "Is not the life of man a trial [*tentatio*: but Jerome's Vulgate of Job 7:
1 reads *militia*, "hard service"]? But who wants troubles (*molestias*) and
military hardships? Thou enjoinest us to endure them, not love them"
(chap. 28). *Molestia* is an appropriate characterization of the facticity of
life, though not a complete definition. Life is hard, but hardship is to
be endured and not enjoyed. Endurance is the way to overcome the trial.
The movement opposing *continentia* is the "dissipation (*deflexus*) into the
many." It is in dissipation, which is led on by delight, that factic life
develops itself out of itself. But the basic characteristic of factic life is
curare, "being troubled," which is a middle-voiced phenomenon and so
also involves the response of troubling oneself to take care of the troubling situation. It therefore implies a good and a bad side; there is a
genuine and not so genuine troubling of oneself. Examples of the latter
can be found in the "hustle and bustle" of everyday life.
  The basic phenomena within *curare* are *uti* (using), which involves
coping with (*gehen "um"*) what life brings to me, and *frui* (enjoying). The
object of *frui* is always enjoyed for its own sake, without reference to
anything else, whereas the object of *uti* is sought for the sake of something
else, as a means to some other end. The eternal unchangeable things
are to be enjoyed, the temporal changeable things are to be used as a
means to that end. It is a perversion to enjoy money and to make use
of God. One should not worship God for the sake of money, which is
the height of hypocrisy, but should spend money for the sake of God,
the highest and unchangeable good, "Beauty of old, yet ever so new"
(chap. 27).
  Frui, more specifically *fruitio Dei*, is therefore the basic characteristic

of Augustine's orientation toward life itself. Since its most proper correlate is Beauty, *frui* incorporates a basic aesthetic moment in its sense of
summum bonum. The Neoplatonic influence is especially noticeable here:
the beautiful belongs to the essence of being (cf. chap. 27). But *fruitio Dei*
is for Augustine not specifically Plotinian enjoyment, which culminates in
intuition, but receives its unique stamp from the Christian conception
of factic life. In the end, *fruitio Dei* stands in opposition to, and stems
from a different root than, even the life of the self; the two have grown
together merely externally. This may be connected with the fact that,
for Augustine, the goal of life is rest, repose, quietude (*quies*). The present life consists of trouble and toil, but in hope it consists of rest. In the
flesh, it consists of decadence, falling away, but in faith it consists of
renewal. Note that "flesh" in Paul is not merely the sensual libido but
factic life as such.

The phenomena of factic life discussed by Augustine are now organized by Heidegger into an "overview schema" of the basic Latin terms
discussed above (fig. 3):[13]

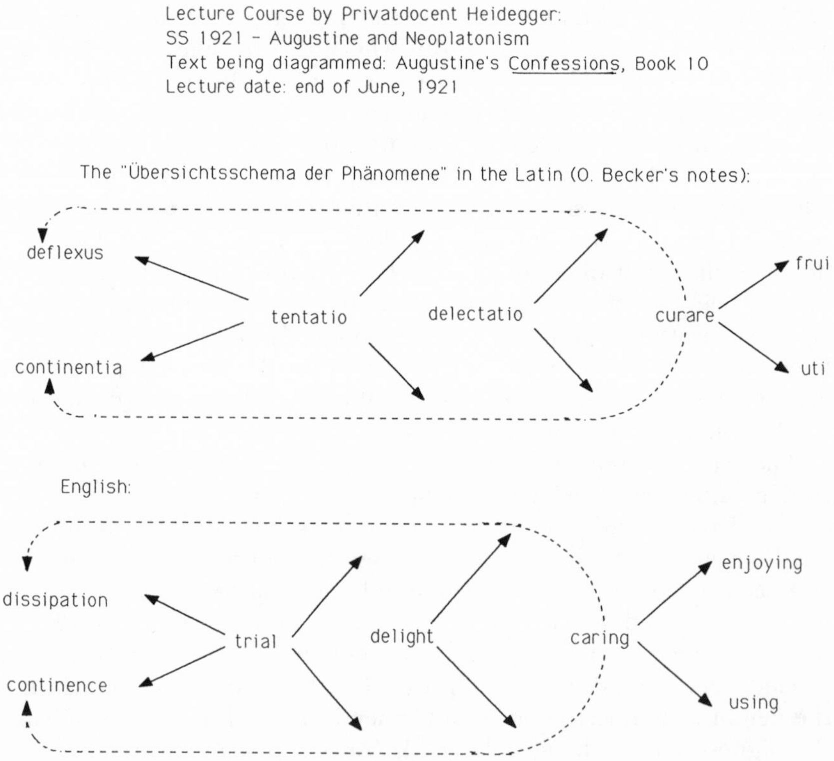

Lecture Course by Privatdocent Heidegger:
SS 1921 – Augustine and Neoplatonism
Text being diagrammed: Augustine's Confessions, Book 10
Lecture date: end of June, 1921

The "Übersichtsschema der Phänomene" in the Latin (O. Becker's notes):

The "Übersichtsschema der Phänomene" in the Latin (O. Becker's notes):

deflexus — tentatio — delectatio — curare — frui
continentia — uti

English:

dissipation — trial — delight — caring — enjoying
continence — using

Figure 3

A few points emphasized by the schema: Using and enjoying are the phenomena which make up caring. The basic direction of life, arising from caring, is delight. The trial lies in the delight itself, which has the possibility of being deflected into either dissipation or containment, the many or the One. [Sharing the spotlight with the end of delight, at the core of the diagram, is the infinitive *curare*, its central formal indication which emphasizes the relational sense, where the infinitive form now functions in the same way as the impersonals of KNS: "It's troubling," "it's of concern," "it issues": *mea res agitur*. The countermovements of *deflexus* and *continentia* have by now become central to Heidegger's approach to Dasein, suspended as it is between the poles of "falling" or "rising" to the occasion of existence.]

Axiology of Fearing/Loving

The dissipation operative in troubling oneself or caring is better understood in its two basic tendencies of fearing and desiring (chap. 28: "In adversity I desire prosperity, in prosperity I fear adversity"), the opposing movements of seeking to avoid something or to draw it to oneself and make it one's own [the irascible and concuscipible appetites!]. The situation is either prosperous or adverse, either conducive to or running counter to the direction of the care. The adverse is not simply confirmed but experienced in the contrary effort of continually seeking to make the beneficial my own. Likewise, in making the beneficial my own, I am fearful of (*habe Angst vor*) what can work against me. Fear and desire thus always belong together. One is not possible without the other.

As if this were not enough, Augustine uncovers a new discordance within the fearing/desiring itself. He asks whether the feared is something lamentable or joyous, good or bad (chap. 28). Thus, the distress of concern is not simply there but is itself experienced in a specific way, as miserable or joyful. *Curare* itself is pervaded by ambiguity and insecurity. This discordance is itself indicative of the trial that belongs intrinsically to being human, not just to something that comes from the outside [not just fear but dread, in Heidegger's later distinction]. *Molestia* is an all too human onus: "I am a burden to myself" (chap. 28). Inasmuch as this burden and insecurity constitute the essence of factic life, "I have become a question to myself" (chap. 33: *quaestio mihi factus sum*). The question belongs to the very being of human life.

There is a trial by deception and a trial by testing. Only the devil resorts to the first, while the second is also used by God, as we have seen. But the true trial is the trial by tribulation, where I myself become a question to myself. It is necessary in order to perfect and to confirm. "A man does not know himself if he has not come to know himself in trial" (*Contra Faustum*, Bk. 22, chap. 20). Such learning and coming to know reflect the historical character of concrete factic self-experience. Trial is a specifically historical concept belonging to the domain of self-experience.

With the introduction of diabolical suggestion, trial (*tentatio, temptatio*) now assumes the connotation of "temptation" (chaps. 30ff.). Its maturation from factic life actualizes itself in various stages, from the carnal to the spiritual. From what basic direction of experience does it get its sense? An examination of the foundation of its actualization will bring out another connection of Augustine with Neoplatonism.

What is decisive in temptation is the preference, love, or delight which predominates. The devil sets before me something which I have not yet personally overcome. When I have mastered greed, the allure of money will be resisted. Everything depends on the predominant direction of delight. This gives preference to something other than money, say, justice, and an inner struggle ensues. In the face of sin, I am divided against myself. "For the flesh lusteth against the spirit, and the spirit against the flesh."

The role of preference and condemnation in trial points to a certain order which underlies this phenomenon. It is now a matter not only of the relation to God but of the how of the order. How the order occurs and gets founded, and the conceptual framework in which the rank order is regarded, are significant questions. It is not self-evident that what is experienced in delight stands in a hierarchy of values. This is rather based on an "axiologization" which ultimately stands on the same level as theoretization. The hierarchy of values stems from Greece, in the end from Plato. This is evident, for example, from the relationship to the immutable. But does this axiologization really correspond to the phenomenon being explicated?

The hierarchy of values is connected with a certain conception of reality. What then does Augustine understand by *res*? The two modes of troubling oneself as they relate to the *res* lead to the following tripartite division: things to be enjoyed, things to be used, things to be enjoyed and used (*De Doctrina Christiana* I, 3). And the human being? "We who enjoy and use things are ourselves things" (I, 22). But the human being, created in God's image, is a noble being, since she is rational. "So the great question is whether humans ought to enjoy themselves or merely to use themselves, or whether they may do both" (ibid.). We are commanded to love one another, but the question is whether man is to be loved by another for his own sake or for the sake of another: if for his own sake, we are enjoying him; if not, we are using him. But it seems that man must be loved for the sake of another. For that which is loved for its own sake constitutes the happy life. But we do not have the happy life in reality (*in re*) but in hope. The human being is thus not meant to be the object of enjoyment. When he loves himself for his own sake, he does not relate himself to God. When he turns to himself, it is not to something immutable (ibid.).

To live "holy" for Augustine, that is, to love truly, one must therefore live out of the sense of the "whole" of things, i.e., one must have an order of preferences. Our question is whether such a hierarchy of values is intrinsically necessary or whether it is simply the untoward interjection of Greek thinking into Augustine's thought.

We are to love for the sake of God. We love those useful things which lead to God and those who in association with us are accountable to God, like other human beings. There are four types of things to be loved: 1) what is above us; 2) ourselves; 3) what is next to us and so equal to us; 4) what is below us. 2) and 4) require no particular rules in order to love them (I, 23). No one naturally hates himself or denigrates his own body (I, 24). This self-love belongs to the facticity of life. But the mode and manner of right self-love does dictate regulation by way of a certain order. This involves a certain phenomenal complex of self-experience which must be explicated.

Consideration of the next chapters (30ff.) of book 10 of the *Confessions* calls therefore for a wide-ranging consideration of the following groups of problems:

1) The problem of trial (*tentatio*), that is, the context in which I actualize my concrete and full experience of the self: how I make my decisions. It is through trial that we come to the basically *historical* sense of self-experience.

2) Trial is connected with the "dissipation into the many" (falling away into the multiplicity of the meanings of factic life). Trouble and hardship (*molestia*) prove to be constitutive of the concept of *facticity*.

3) The problem of the sense of "I have become a question to myself," which finds its sense in the concrete context of self-experience. The self's coming into question is not a matter of objectively being on hand (*Vorhandensein*) but of *authentically existing as a self*.

4) The problem of the basic orientation of preference (*dilectio*) within a particular axiological system. We must investigate to what extent this originates from an inherent experience and to what extent it is determined by Augustine's particular situation in *intellectual history*.

Interlude: Luther on Romans 1:20

The axiological problem of a general theory of values is related to the Neoplatonic doctrine of the highest good, especially with regard to how we gain access to "it." Basic to all of patristic "philosophy," to its orientation in developing Christian doctrine in the context of Greek philosophy, is the Pauline text from his letter to the Romans (1:20). This oft-quoted text provided the Church Fathers with perhaps their primary inducement in their endeavor to underpin Christian dogmatics with a Greek infrastructure, thereby yielding the hybrid of a "Christian philosophy." This infrastructure was already deeply installed in Christian thought by Augustine's time. It would therefore be a misunderstanding to think that one can simply strip away the Platonic elements from Augustine in order to arrive at what is genuinely Christian in him. Primal Christianity cannot be reached through Augustine.

"For the invisible things of God from the creation of the world are clearly seen, being understood through the things that are made" (Romans 1:20). For the early Fathers, this text provided a Pauline confirmation for a graded Platonic ascent in thought from the sensory to the suprasensory world. But this is a basic misunderstanding. The young Luther was the first to see what the text really means in its own context (Romans 1:20–23), and so opened up the possibility for a renewed understanding of primitive Christianity and a return to the original Christian life. The theses of his Heidelberg Disputation (1518) likewise provide crucial insights into the long-standing historical relationship over the centuries between Christianity and culture. The theses numbered 19–22 are the most relevant, but Heidegger does little more than to provide a somewhat idiosyncratic translation of three of them before quickly dropping the subject of Luther in Catholic Freiburg:

19) "To see the invisible things of God through that which is created does not make someone a theologian." One does not arrive at the object of theology by way of a metaphysical contemplation of the world. [As Luther himself notes, Paul clearly identifies such would-be "theologians of glory" as "fools," whose "wisdom," oriented as it is to the things of the world, is but a speculative form of idolatry (*Götzendienst*: cf. Rom. 1: 21–23).][14]

21) "The theologian of glory, who aesthetically gloats (*ergötzt*) over the wonders of the world, calls sensory things God. The theologian of the cross tells us how things really are." [Although Heidegger is quite sparse in his gloss here, later hours will suggest that the "theologian of the cross" is comparable to the philosopher of factic life in their respective descriptions of life as trial, care, and travail.]

22) "The empty wisdom which sees the invisible things of God in works puffs up, blinds, and hardens." [In his proof of this thesis, Luther discusses the unrequitable nature of the desire for this sort of knowledge. He thus clearly relates such a vain and insatiable quest to the second temptation of the "lust of the eyes" (cf. below), curiosity, the craving for signs and wonders in the spectacle of the world (Matt. 4:7).]

Heidegger never mentions the "theology of the cross" again, but it will by implication appear time and again in the remainder of the course. For its deconstruction of the axiological approach to God, as well as its concern for factic life experience in its actualization rather than in its content, provides an essential complement to the other three ground phenomena or problems (trial, dissipation in the face of difficulty, the self thrown into question) which are to guide the exegeses of the remainder of book 10 of the *Confessions*. This confessional character of the search for God is in fact the key to the focus on actualizing the experience of God rather than observing Him aesthetically in terms of objective content. The fourth ground phenomenon, ostensibly a destruction of an intellectual history which has made God into an object, ultimately blossoms in the course into the phenomenon of God's "counterstance" (*Gegenständlichkeit*) in the actuality of religious experiences.

But if we take seriously the historical movement of actualizing God in human experience in something like a *confiteri*, then we at first must move away from God, to the moment of the absence of God. When I "become a question to myself," the distance from God increases. One must first lose God in order to find Him. But this is the most decisive—the performative—sense of sin. He who flees from God loses him. [We are but one step short of what Heidegger in the following year will call the essential "atheism" inherent in philosophical questioning.]

The Three Temptations of Man

The problem of *confiteo* in fact arises from a consciousness of one's own sins. With phenomena like sin and grace, we begin to encounter limits to our possibilities of interpretation, since they call for conditions of understanding which cannot be reached in this philosophical context. Moreover, the consciousness of sin and the way in which God thus becomes present is here further complicated by Augustine's involvement with Neoplatonism. For these reasons, his conception of sin cannot without exception lead us directly to the "true" phenomena in need of phenomenological explication.

Nevertheless, Heidegger now plunges deeply into a detailed exegesis of the Latin text of the chapters (30–39) of book 10 which deal with sin consciousness. We cannot dwell on the details here, but must at least highlight the direction and salient conclusions of this gloss.

"Thou enjoinest continency from the lust of the flesh, the lust of the eyes, and the ambition of this world [pride of life]" (chap. 30: cf. 1 John 2:16 for the bracketed *koine* formulation of the third temptation). These are the three forms of trial, or better here, temptation, which even in its theological form still reflects the insecurity of life. Even the knowledge of one's own insecurity is insecurity: "Perchance I am deceived" (chap. 32). No one can at any moment think that he is in total possession of himself. This once again reflects the fundamentally historical sense of life as a trial. A trial is not just a "psychic process" but an occurrence experienced in factic life itself. Moreover, the trials time and again refer to the onus and potential dissipation of everydayness: "the evil of the day," "the daily ruination of the body," "I struggle daily" (chap. 31); "the multitude of intrusions from all sides of our daily life" (chap. 35); "the daily assault of temptations," "Our daily 'furnace' is the human tongue" (chap. 37). The issue of the "daily battle" is that of losing or gaining one's self, that is, finding one's way to God. And despite all appearances, Augustine's account of the forms of temptation is just such an account of the factic actualization of Christian life. For it is not a classification of the soul's faculties, but this process of actualization which is the basis for the different directions of trial. If we wish to understand the problems of actualization, that is, the facticity of experiencing itself, we must wean ourselves, even if gradually, from such traditional classifications. All this will become clear if we follow the progression from the lust of the flesh and of the eyes to worldly ambition.

Every experience involves a basic attitude of delight in its attractive allure and enticement, of *delectare* in its two modes of using and enjoying, in short, a certain kind of caring. This in turn involves an "appetite," a particular striving after something. The first form of appetite tends toward pure sensual pleasure, a "delighting in the flesh." Sensuality here is not a faculty but a particular way of total experiencing within a particular content. What is seen or heard is not something detached from us, as it is in perception, but rather something totally experienced within the body in sensual enjoyment. This is even more evident in the initial carnal enjoyments of eating, drinking, and "coition" (*concubitus*: chaps. 31f.). When he moves on to the more aesthetic pleasures of the ears and eyes (chaps. 33f.), Augustine is more inclined to envisage their elevation to Absolute Beauty. "Singing is a matter of loving," especially when the New Canticle (New Testament) is being sung. But even though his tract "On Music" with its Neoplatonic numerology is rightly celebrated, it is Augustine's Neoplatonic panegyrics to the "glory" of God as the "light of man" (John 1:4) that are best known. Heidegger will now pursue this path through the last of the senses, the sense of sight, subject to the first type of temptation, the lust of the flesh, to an unusual conclusion.

A Lutheran Excursus

The aesthetic "pleasure of these eyes of my flesh" (*voluptas oculorum*: chap. 34) is not to be confused with the second type of temptation, the lust of the eyes, which will be the topic of the following chapter. There are two types of temptation of the eyes, seeing *in* the flesh ("delighting in the flesh": chap. 34) and seeing *through* the flesh ("experiencing through the flesh": chap. 35). Chapter 34 deals with the first: what "the eyes love" is the light (*lux*) itself, "this queen of colors" which "bathes" all that I behold and glides by me in fair and varied forms in a medley of bright and soft colors and so, "with an enticing and dangerous sweetness," "soothes me when I am engaged in other things and not observing it." This is seeing in its most original sensual sense, still far removed from the cognitive attitude of perceiving, which comes about only by a transformation of the more rudimentary aesthetic sense of seeing into seeing as taking cognizance. Perceiving is by no means primary in the experience of sensuality. So delightful is this noncognitive experience of light, so strongly does it insinuate itself in our aesthetic experience, that its withdrawal evokes our longing for it and its long absence a sadness of the mind.

Instead of this corporeal light (*lux*) whose "enticing and dangerous sweetness" seduces the corporeal eyes, Augustine commends the invisible light (*lumen*) seen by the inner eye ("ill*umin*ed heart"). If this light of luminosity is darkened (Matt. 6:23), then we are blind at heart and incapable of receiving the more objective light of life, the Word in the Beginning which is life which in turn is *lux hominum* (John 1:4). We must become "pure in heart" in order to be able to see God (Matt. 5:8), just as the corporeal eye must rid itself of grime and smoke and rheum in order to be able to see its light (*Tractatus de Joannis Evangelio* 2, 18f.). "Cleansing" of the inner eye (the heart) thus becomes the condition of access to God. And the way this purification is realized, its sense of actualization, is through faith (Acts 15:9). Faith is the context of actualization "which worketh by love" (Gal. 5:6) and hopes for what God promises (cf. the Pauline schema of WS 1920–21, fig. 2 above). It allows us now "to see through a glass, darkly, but then face to face" (1 Cor. 13:12). But because faith still leaves us in the dark for the present, there is no reason to return "to your own face," that is, to your own constructions or cosmological reifications of God. Instead, "put your mind on the face of the heart. Force your heart to think on divine things; urge it; compel it. Cast out from your mind any bodily similarity that rushes into it" (Sermon 53, chap. 12, p. 72).[15] Access to God cannot be constructed. Rather, the self must first carry out the conditions for experiencing God. In that very effort of selfly living, God is there, understood as the "face of the heart" (interiority) efficacious in the authentic life of the human being. You must look to yourself to understand what is "the breadth, and length, and depth, and height" of the "fullness of God" in the "love of Christ" (Eph. 3:18f.). "Do not wander in imagination through the spaces of the world" (Sermon 53, chap. 15, p. 74) in order to fathom God, say, in some gigantic human form (Isaiah 66:1). Breadth, length, depth, and height are accordingly not cosmological dimensions. Breadth is in the good works which reach out to give aid wherever they can, extending even to one's enemies. The length is the long-suffering perseverance to the end. The height is the hope of attaining the eternal life on high to which "we lift up our hearts." The depth, the part buried and hidden, is in the unsearchable judgments of God, the secret of freely given grace in which we are founded and rooted as Christians. These dimensions of the factic Christian life can be located upon the figure of the cross, the breadth of its transverse beam, its upright beam in its height and length and hidden rooting. This crucifixion schematism, Heidegger insists, is not meant to be merely an objectively palpable symbolism, "a vainly fictitious but usefully true" (letter 140, chap. 36, p. 133) interpretation, but an outline [formal indication!] serving to restore factic Christian life back to its full actualization, much like, we might add, his Pauline schema on becoming a Christian in WS 1920–21. Thus, Sermon 53 (chaps. 12–16), letters 140 (chaps. 25f., 36) and 147 (chap. 34), and other texts show how much Augustine's hermeneutic art, despite his Neoplatonic predilections, is oriented toward actualizing the Christian factic life rather than toward an objective specification of its content.

In this stress on the dynamics of the inner life and aversion to any cosmic-metaphysical reification of God, Augustine is assuming the role of what Luther later will call a "theologian of the cross," rather than a "theologian of glory." This theological side to factic life experience is perhaps also what Heidegger had in mind at this time when, a month later, he identified himself as a "Christian theo-logian." Heidegger does not even mention Luther's distinction at this point of the course, but his entire interpretation in this excursus, down to his selection of texts from the Augustinian opus, is clearly being guided by that distinction. Formally, it is the distinction between content sense and actualization sense. Thus Heidegger is now subtly bringing the full possibility of his own methodology of formal indication to bear onto such a theology of the cross, as he extends his two conceptual diagrams prefiguring what it means to be (= become) a Christian (figs. 2 and 3), one Pauline and the other Augustinian, in the direction of a verbalized "crucifixion schematism" of the Christian factic life, which is at least in the spirit of Luther.

The cura of Curiosity[16]

Heidegger eventually picks up the trail of the three temptations again in order to explicate the nature of their progression. The second temptation, the "lust of the eyes," takes us a giant step beyond the lust of the flesh. Although the very same senses are involved, led by vision, this new lust has an appetite not for sensation as such but for the knowledge it brings, not for fleshly enjoyment ("delighting *in* the flesh") but for "the experience it brings *through* the flesh" (chap. 35). The lust to see is now the lust to know, pointless, rudderless, undisciplined knowing, like the Devil's attempt to evoke signs and wonders from God (Matt. 4:6, Luke

11:16, John 4:48) "not for any saving purpose but simply for the sake of the experience or experiment" (chap. 35). To which Jesus replies, "Thou shalt not experiment with the Lord thy God!" (Matt. 4:7), using Him instrumentally to "satisfy" one's curiosity. For its fruits are a "knowledge" without focus or purpose prompted by a hollow and idle concern (*vana cura*: chap. 35) for the "unnecessary" (*supervacanae*: chap. 37). Augustine's text is replete with examples of such experiential and cognitive "sensations" which distract him from his center (his prayer life) and disperse him in a welter of daily intrusions by the strange, alien, and exotic: chance occurrences of the unusual, scenes of horror, the "curiosities" of a circus or carnival sideshow, the theater (like the Gulf War on TV!), magic and astrology, nature lore, necrology, and other "sacrilegious mysteries."

Heidegger's less example-laden and more formal gloss of this Augustinian text in this early context is of special interest because it sets the stage for the interpretation of the very same text in the section entitled "Curiosity" in the last two drafts of BT, which serves to illustrate the movement of "falling" in all of its peculiarly "tempting" quality.[17] The very first gloss is in closer touch with its biblical-patristic context in its concern to distinguish the lust of the eyes from the two temptations that flank it, while tracing the continuity through all three. Thus curiosity arises, not by a liberation of the circumspective concern hitherto totally absorbed with the smooth functioning of the proximate world of production and tool-use (SZ 172), but by a modification of the even more immediate and absorbing life of consumption, enjoying "in the flesh" that which is thus produced. What sort of modification? Curiosity finds a base in the infrastructure of sensuality by transforming it from a noncognitive immersion in the flesh into a cognitive beholding or, more precisely, an objective beholding. For the primary function of the senses is not really the beholding of objects, although seeing, as a faculty of distance, comes closest to that. In curiosity, the other senses by way of imitation then arrogate to themselves (*usurpant*: chap. 35) the business of seeing, of singling out objects for perception. But for all that, having mobilized the entire spectrum of senses to its purpose, bringing them all to bear on the spectacular, curiosity acts as if it were not bound by the specific objective content of its experience. There is a rambling or roaming quality about it which serves to make all and sundry accessible to it, without concern for the value and worth of any particular object. It assumes a peculiar willfulness which dismisses all critique and confirmation. It is therefore not knowledge at all. It merely assumes the cloak of knowledge and science, but in reality it is a pseudo-knowledge, a *perversa scientia* (chap. 35). It is ultimately not related to the content of knowledge, but to the sheer actualizing of cognizance. It is swept along by the sheer dynamics of cognition, but without its substance. If sensuality "goes about" absorbed in enjoyment, curiosity "looks about" absorbed in that very activity of spectacle, but not in the content of the environing world.

Sensuality goes about the world absorbed in sensual enjoyment, curiosity looks about the same world absorbed in the zest of the spectacle. But for all that, flesh and spectacle, the delights of the sensual and of the sensational (the "spectacular") are equally absorbed in the world-about, and so belong together in the loss of the self in their respective encompassing elements. In its absorption, the self not so much lives, but instead is "being lived" by its environment, so that it is only by extension that one can speak of "self"-enjoyment.[18] This changes with the third temptation of worldly ambition, the pride of life, where for the first time the Self as such, albeit still somewhat dissipated, is the "end of the delight."

Worldly Ambition

Augustine's text (chap. 36–39) on the temptations of worldly success, in keeping with Christ's own third temptation (Matt. 4:8), restricts itself to the temptations of power and glory. Wealth is regarded only as a means to satisfy any one, or pair, or all of the three basic lusts (chap. 37).[19] In keeping with the two remaining worldly ambitions, Augustine develops two distinct emotionally laden set of relations. In matters of power and authority, "it is necessary to be loved and feared by men, on account of certain functions in human society" (chap. 36). In matters of glory, fame, and repute, "word of mouth and deeds made known to men bring with them a most dangerous temptation. Its source is the love of praise, which solicits approving opinions as a beggar gathers alms, for the sake of a certain personal importance" (chap. 38). Both clearly hinge on "human society": in Heidegger's terms, we are no longer in the world-around-us, but in the world-with. Moreover, in these with-contexts, the issue is self-importance, self-worth, self-repute (*Selbstgeltung*), being someone who carries "clout" and so "counts," stands out, a person of consequence, a VIP . . . important, that is, in the eyes (!) of the world-with. This concern for prestige, repute, public image suggests a continuity with curiosity's spectacles and world of sensational appearances, the "look" of things. Only now, 1) the self sees itself 2) before others, in its significance for others, how the self "looks" to others in the world of prestige and authority.

As Augustine himself notes, such a self-recognition stemming from being recognized by others is necessary in the social situations of authority, as well as in the life of the self. "Praise usually and properly accompanies a good life and good works" (chap. 37). A deliberately self-imposed total deprivation of praise, for reasons of continency, verges on madness.

And yet, praise and recognition are subject to *fallacia hominum* (chap. 36), human deceit. The opinions of humankind are fickle and uncertain, perhaps even untrue. Better to praise than be praised. Better to rejoice in a natural gift than in the praise for having that gift; for the praise is the gift of humans, whereas the gift itself is from God (*donum dei*: chap. 36). Such a gift does not really belong to either the with- or the round-about-world, but to the self-world. The self-world is the sphere of one's own possibilities and capacity (i.e., one's profession); it is the concrete shape of one's own facticity, one's own past and future. In the face of my own self-world, I naturally regard myself as important. This is rooted in the genuine concern over myself (*Selbstbekümmerung*) and my own life, but this very tendency includes the temptation of the love of praise, and one still more dangerous.

For the self-world poses even more dangerous forms of taking oneself as important in its variegated self-deceits. Dismay over misguided praise may indicate that I wish the other to have the same opinion as my own about me. What pleases me in myself pleases me more when it also pleases another. "I am myself not praised when my judgment of myself is not praised" (chap. 37). Or in reproving the love of praise, and just because it is reproved by me, "it is often the case that a person glories more vainly in his very contempt of vainglory" (chap. 38). "We may be pleased at being loved and feared not for Thy sake, but in Thy stead" (chap. 36). All of these contain the seed of the most dangerous temptation of all in the interior life, more dangerous than the love of praise: simply to be pleased with myself, regardless of how I relate to others, whether I please, displease, or am indifferent to others (chap. 39).

To summarize: each of the three levels of temptation contains a characteristic way for the self to lose itself, and so also to find itself, through the self-examination (*exploratio*: chap. 37) that is involved in the process of curbing and containing these addictions. But the third, in all of its intensity and refinements, provides the greatest possibility for knowledge and clarity about oneself.

This concludes Heidegger's running commentary on book 10 of the *Confessions*. He now announces that the single "methodological" purpose of that interpretation was to lay out the phenomena which are important for the problem of the sense of being which is indigenous to the concept of life [in effect, a phenomenological ontology]. It is essential to see how a particular sense of being spontaneously emerges out of this experiential context. Only in this way can we hope finally to get to the bottom of the problem of levels of being, and so to free ourselves from persisting tendencies like the axiological hierarchization of the Neoplatonic tradition, and the faculty psychology we have inherited from the Greeks.

Love/Fear of God

A recurring topic in this commentary, both overt and latent, has been the topic of love, from the glutton's love of partridges (in order to kill them, consume them into nonbeing) to self-love in relation to the love of others and, finally, to the love of God in his "counterstance" toward us as Light and Delight, Highest Good and Beauty, Unchangeable Substance. At one point, Heidegger had discussed the "noble" love of benevolence, wishing the other well, the will toward the being of the other, helping the other to her existence so that she may come to herself, the pure gift of our love even when we have no other gift to give to the other, which makes it all the purer (cf. "being-for" in SZ 122). For over and above the works of mercy to those less fortunate than we is the nobler love between equals, in which benevolence is sufficient for those who love, where we wish only that the other be, while we stand together under the One which can be given by no human being (*In Epistolam Joannis ad Parthos* 8.5).[20]

As a supplement contributing to the phenomenological aim of the course, Heidegger now ventures into some concluding remarks on the joint theme of the love *and* fear of God, as true love, pure fear. That the two belong together in a single experience was suggested by the worldly ambition "to be loved and feared by men" which, Augustine notes, "is a major reason for not loving Thee and not living in chaste fear of Thee" (chap. 36). In this experiential complex, it turns out that *timor Dei* is a crucial way in which we relate to God and He "stands toward" us. [For Heidegger, this joint theme is clearly a direct descendant of Rudolf Otto's problem of the ambivalent emotions before the Holy as *mysterium tremendum et fascinans*.][21]

For Augustine, the experience of God is not an isolated act. It belongs rather in the full historical facticity of one's own life. For God will eventually be Augustine's answer to his somewhat rhetorical question posed earlier in book 10, "But what is nearer to me than I myself?" (chap. 16: cited in SZ 44). To begin with, love's tendency is concern for self, love of self, which leads directly to a temptation of the greatest affliction. Being oriented purely toward oneself evokes "the trembling of my heart" (chap. 39) which is pure fear (*timor castus*), a phenomenon which is constitutive of self-concern. Augustine's biblical source for the term is Psalms 18:10 (19:9 in the King James version): "The fear of the Lord is pure, enduring forever" (cf. *Enarrationes in Psalmos* 18.10). What then is the difference between genuine *timor castus* and the nongenuine or impure *timor servilis* (servile fear)? This question, which is destined to develop into the famous distinction between dread and fear in BT (SZ 199n), must be framed by two related questions: 1) What is fearing as a whole and its possible motives or motivating affects, its motions of aversion and attraction in both their active and passive modes? 2) What sense does genuine fear have in the context of self-experience (which means, at the same time, in the basic experience of God)? How does God come to stand toward us in genuine fear? How is His absolute counterstance determined from such an experience?

Such large questions naturally cannot really be answered at such a late stage in the course. But Heidegger, in keeping with his previous procedure, wishes merely to develop a few insights into the phenomenon of fearing from a close hermeneutic exegesis of a few key texts in Augustine, hoping to expose at least some of the phenomenological concepts which would address the questions under consideration. He therefore chooses several texts from Augustine's much-neglected tract, *Expositions on the Book of Psalms*, where the psalms of lamentation especially prompt Augustine to comment on the plethora of biblical texts bearing on the fear of God, while the psalms of trusting faith provide some resolution to the relation of fear to love.[22]

In one remarkable text, Augustine gets at the problem by way of the phenomenon of fearlessness and two possible motives which underlie it, from which the two forms of fear may then be developed. One is inured to the fearful admonitions of God because of hardness of the heart ("many proud men by too much pride fear nothing"). Another "shall not fear what flesh can do unto me" (Psalms 55:5 [56:4]) because of the confidence of his hope in secure anticipation of God. Augustine considers three affections of the body, health (*sanitas*), stupor, and immortality, in relation to the twin torment to fear, namely, grief or pain (*dolor*). While health in this life is beset and afflicted by grief and illness, the perfect health and sanity which is immortality is devoid of all grief and the possibility of corruption. But the stupefied body made insensitive by pride also feels no pain. Does that mean that immortality and stupor are equivalent states? By no means. He who feels no pain owing to insensitivity has not put on immortality merely by stripping away sensitivity. "Closer to immortality is the health of grieving rather than the stupor of not feeling" (*Enarrationes in Psalmos* 55.6). Is the proud man in his supreme arrogance, who has stoically conditioned himself to fear nothing, braver than Paul, who found himself beleaguered by "wars without, fears within" (2 Cor. 7:5); or Christ when he cried, "My soul is sorrowful even unto death" (Matt. 26:38)? True courage must endure the possibility of fear, and so cannot hold itself dispassionate to the point of stupor.

Genuine fearlessness is attainable in the constellation of Christian virtues: trust or confidence (*fiducia*: 1 John 4:17), hope, and love. Thus we read: "There is no fear in love: but perfect love casts out fear, because fear has to do with punishment, and the one who fears is not perfected in love" (1 John 4:18). And yet, "the fear of the Lord" which is pure fear "endures forever" (Ps. 18:10 [19:9]). How do we reconcile these two apparently contradictory texts, which Augustine at one point in his homilies (9.5) on John's First Epistle compares to two flutes which must be brought into hermeneutic harmony with each other? The discordance is overcome by the distinction between the two types of fear: *timor servilis seu poenalis* which "has to do with punishment"; and *timor castus*, not as servants fear but as friends (*En. in Ps.* 5.9; cf. John 15:15), lest perchance they be separated or the one leaves the other. Servile fear fears grief and punishment, and tends to be more wary of evil than desirous of the good. It must be "cast out" in order to purify fear to its authentic state. Such "outcast" fears may be divided into two main kinds, with two main objects: temporal ills, the "thousand natural shocks that flesh is heir to" (see e.g., Rom. 8:35) and eternal punishment, whereby one fears "burning" more than sinning. "They contain themselves from sin . . . but still do not love justice" (*En. in Ps.* 127.7). Only when they begin to seek the good for its own sake does their fear become pure. There is accordingly a basic reversal of direction with the purification of fear: it does not so much hold itself back from the body as allow itself to be drawn by higher things. This of course is love, for chaste fear originates from the love of God. But in what way is it still fear? What chaste fear still fears is separation, losing touch with the Good toward which it strives, *timere Deum, ne recedat a te*, "fearing God, lest He recede from you. . . . So when you fear God lest His presence leaves you, you are embracing Him, and longing to enjoy Him" (*In Epistolam Joannis ad Parthos* 9.5). In this fear, the soul, despite (or because of) the security of its trust and confidence in God, senses the majesty of God vis-à-vis the human being. In this way, fear of separation is at once a manifestation of the love of Truth. [Thus, without mentioning Otto, Heidegger implies that the awesome experience of the Holy will persist in not only its fascinating but also its terrifying aspects in the "Beatific Vision," which therefore is not as totally quiescent as Augustine, through his Neoplatonic proclivities, more often than not indicates.]

"Fear is a flight of the spirited soul (*animus*)" (*En. in Ps.* 67.2). The traditional theme of fearing as a "fugitive" e-motion will be made central in Heidegger's later treatments of fear and dread (GA 20:392/283ff., SZ 184ff.), in order to prepare for the potential reversal of the flight of Dasein from itself. This is prefigured in 1921 by a development of an analogous constellation of motions in the fear of God.

If you fear a robber, you hope for help from someone else and not from the one who threatens you the most, the robber. But if you fear God, to whom shall you then turn? " 'Whither shall I flee from Thy face?' (Ps. 138:7 [139:7]). He sought a place to escape from God's judgment, and found none. For where is God not? . . . If you want my advice, flee to God himself if you would flee from Him: flee to Him by confessing, not by hiding" (*In Epistolam Joannis ad Parthos* 6.3). "Whither are you to flee from an angered God, except to Him placated?" (*En. in Ps.* 94.2).[23] The from-which and the to-which of flight are here the same, as it will be later in the dread *of* Dasein itself (GA 20:402/290, SZ 188).

There are thus two basic fears, first, *timor servilis*, "worldly fear," the anxiousness which befalls us from the world-about and the with-world. In contrast, there is *timor castus*, "selfly fear," which is motivated in true hope, in the confidence brought alive purely out of itself. This fear is developed in connection with the concern (*Bekümmerung*) of life for authentic self-experience.

Augustine's "Cogito"

This renewed probing of the life of the self in its depths and its heights, "in the face of God," prompts Heidegger to a concluding comment on the presumed Augustinian "cogito." It recalls some of his earlier studies spurred by Dilthey, where Heidegger now even glosses the same text from the *City of God* (11.26ff.) that Dilthey cites (GS 1:260/234). Augustine's thoughts on the life of the self were in fact drastically diluted by Descartes. Self-certitude and the having of self in Augustine's sense are totally different from the Cartesian evidence for the *cogito*, for one thing because they reach back so much more deeply into the life (*vita*: hardly a mere word or formal concept for Augustine) of the self than just the thinking self. Consider the self regarded in one of Augustine's favorite images of the Trinitarian God: we are, we know that we are, and we love this being in both cases. This highest trinity is devoid of the least "shadow of illusion to disturb us" or objects subject to the stormy, churning play of fantasy. "Without any illusion of image, fancy, or phantasm, I am certain that I am, that I know that I am, and that I love to be and to know" (11.26). It is even certain that I love not only to be and to know that I be, but also the love itself. "Here, our knowledge embraces no error, our love meets no resistance" (11.28).

But in spite of the self-certitude that we have of our being, we are nevertheless uncertain how long we shall live (*quamdiu futurum sit*: 11.28), whether that being will not one day ebb and fail. The self-certitude must accordingly be understood and interpreted from our factic being. It is ultimately possible only by faith. *Crede ut intelligas*. The evidence of the *cogito* is there, but it must be founded in the factic. It must not be taken out of the factic context in piecemeal fashion, as Descartes did. This dissolution of the indivisible "trinity" of self-certitude only resulted in a degeneration in the history of thought.

CONCLUSION: TWO RELIGION COURSES

Heidegger will never again publicly venture so deeply into things religious as he did in these two courses, at first reluctantly and then with gusto, accompanied by pedagogical fireworks. In Marburg, of course, he held joint seminars with Bultmann on Paul and Luther, but by then, he had also developed the measure of reserve toward religion which he had acquired from Nietzsche's friend, Franz Overbeck. This reserve first manifested itself in his pronouncement in October 1922 of the inherent skepticism and "atheism" of philosophy. But this was already latent in the deep philosophical need to make questioning into a virtue that Heidegger began with in WS 1920–21, then explored in its biblical roots in the sense of life as trouble and trial, affliction, care, and restless quest: "I have become a question to myself." The insistence that "life in itself" be regarded in its full disquiet and distress rather than treated as an object is reflected in the difference in emphasis in the *historical* sense of religion which thereby emerges. This contrasts sharply with the earlier *eidetic* sense of religion that the young Heidegger developed during the war years from Eckhart, Schleiermacher, and Reinach. It is the difference between already being religious and becoming a Christ-follower, never really arriving, always under way (a point central to ex-sistence as a formal indication)—no longer feeling composed (*gelassen*) and sheltered (*geborgen*) in one's dependence on God in self-surrender (*Hingabe*), as Reinach did throughout his last year at the front lines, but instead always on the desperate razor's edge of decision in the kairotic Moment, poised in judgment between the opposing tendencies of decadence (*deflexus*) and transcendence (*continentia*). Of course, these two, the childlike and adult senses of religion, are not incompatible, but Heidegger never quite gets around to resolving the Pauline paradox of trust and confidence on the one hand, and the despair of decision on the other, while complaining that Augustine spoils the delicate balance by emphasizing quiescence to the detriment of the dread of God which will "endure forever."

But the real contribution of this academic year to Heidegger's development is not this religious content but rather the abstrusely formal elaboration of his hermeneutic phenomenology which inaugurates the year. It is therefore no accident, not just a matter of bringing the discussion down to the student level, that this methodological treatment of the formal indication is followed by two guiding conceptual schematisms, extracted from the texts of Paul and Augustine, of the dynamics of becoming a Christian. For these schemata governed by Greek and Latin infinitives, which grammatically convey the very indefiniteness of the formal indication, are not just pedagogical aids, but are rather direct descendants of Heidegger's sense of hermeneutic formality. It is a new kind of formality seeking to go beyond the static subject-object schematism governing the traditional *mathesis universalis*. It is a formality seeking to accommodate itself to the intentional dynamics of the phenomena that phenomenology wishes to articulate, which Heidegger here ideally identifies as the *logos* given by the phenomena themselves and not by any sort of ideal-theoretical attitude. Formality always emphasizes the relational aspect of phenomena. And phenomenological formality carries the warning, against the ever-present tendency of lapsing to the level of objects which is built into experience, that all relations, and especially the subject-object relation, be held in suspense. For the forms which phenomenology seeks, as temporal "forms," verge on the contradictory. What it is really after is to develop the relations that are inherent in experience, beginning with the relation of intentionality, in their actualization, to catch experience in the act of experiencing, as it were. In short, formal indications, as phenomenological explicata which prefigure the phenomena in the full panoply of their vectorial tendencies, ultimately seek a nondisruptive access to the very temporality and historicity of the pretheoretical phenomena. Of these, the religious experience is the most pretheoretical, and so in its way an ultimate test of the phenomenological method.

The two conceptual schematisms which in effect "diagram"[24] the movement of becoming a Christian are, as representational diagrams, only advance (*vor-läufige*) indications which must accordingly always be held in suspense. They undoubtedly provided Heidegger's students with a firm guide through the texts and their issues, and much food for thought. Oddly, it is the somewhat more "generic" and so impoverished Augustinian schema which begins to anticipate the structure of BT. The core infinitive (replacing the impersonal of KNS), caring (*curare*), on the one end of the diagram is tried by the opposing tendencies of falling into dispersion in the many or rising toward an integrated and unified self. On the other end, it is ontologically oriented toward things of use versus things to be enjoyed for their own sake. Especially the latter distinction, amplified by *Nicomachean Ethics* 6, points to the two extant Divisions of BT. It thus gets refurbished in the less God-centered and more self-centered ontological framework of human action that Heidegger finds in Aristotle, especially his distinction between the two virtues of practical action: art, whose object is always something external to us, and prudence, which begins and ends in the self, so that living well is its own end, action for its own sake. This transformation will occur in the very next phase of Heidegger's development.

PART TWO

Confronting the Ontological Tradition

The plot now thickens with the claim that the years 1921–24 mark Heidegger's entry into a new phase of development toward BT. What are the marks of this "break" with the old and of the emergence of the new? The initial appearance of Heidegger's lifelong topic in KNS 1919, which places him on the path to BT, and beyond, has already been characterized as "the hermeneutic breakthrough." Can we, following a tradition of commentary, just as glibly identify the new shift in emphasis, marked by a swelling crescendo of "the talk of Being," as "the *ontological* breakthrough"? For had not this "talk of Being" abruptly disappeared in the initial attempts to explicate "life" phenomenologically in the direction of a hermeneutics of facticity, after a habilitation work which talked of nothing but *ens* as objectivity, the transcendentals of being, and the division of the field of being according to its regional categories?[1] This would be a most superficial characterization of the years we have just surveyed. For the ontological predilections that dominated Heidegger's student years are not suddenly turned off and stifled, but rather lie just beneath the surface of his conceptual innovations of 1919–21. In fact, such predilections only grow to new levels of sophistication during this period, as they outstrip his earlier traditional concerns.

To begin with, the talk of "something as such" or "anything whatsoever" (*Etwas überhaupt*) which he retains from his Neo-Kantian days was then merely the modern way of talking about *ens*. More than a thinly disguised ontology, it was in fact the prime category of what was then openly identified as "formal ontology," understood as a subdivision of a *mathesis universalis* (cf., e.g., Husserl, *Ideen I*, §§ 8ff.). Accordingly, the "original something" (*Ur-etwas*) which Heidegger identifies as the condition of worlds and theories is but a modish expression of the prime transcendental of medieval *ens*, with the proviso—and herein lies the revolution—that this be no longer regarded as objectivity but as "life in and for itself," which is never an object. This primal something, as an initially indeterminate something in which I live without knowing what it is, so that it sometimes assumes a threatening, ominous, uncanny character—like the *mysterium tremendum* of the religious world—is therefore not to be confused with the more theoretical indeterminacy of the formal-logical something. Nevertheless, the fundamentally novel approach of "formally indicating" this original something, which is ultimately nothing but "sheer" Being, is a methodology steeped in the lore of traditional ontology, beginning with the famous Aristotelian premise that "being is not a genus." Formal indication is a thoroughly ontological method, it is of the very essence of ontology. If we had kept this firmly in mind from the start, we would not have been so startled by the overtly ontological terms with which Heidegger abruptly identifies the formal indication operative in Jaspers's book, as *Existenz*, which refers to the "sense of being" of the "(I) am." And the process of identifying the central theme of this period, factic life experience in its pure phenomenality, with "concrete actual *Da sein*," a German synonym for "existence" or "being there," had already begun the semester before. Accordingly, ontological clues abound from the start and breach the outer terminological surfaces toward the equation of "life," "facticity," "phenomenon," and "experience," even "hermeneutics," with being itself. The hermeneutic breakthrough of KNS is at once and from the start designed to be an ontological breakthrough. The hermeneutics of facticity is in its gestation already understood not merely as a phenomenology of life but also an ontology of life long before the lecture course of SS 1923 entitled "Ontology: Hermeneutics of Facticity."

And time? Is this the missing term that emerges from the background and takes center stage in this new phase, in such a way that Heidegger for the very first time truly finds his way to the problem of "Being *and* Time"? We have already had occasion to doubt whether this titular question was fully grasped in mid-1921. But a similar flurry of precursors, preceding even KNS, comes to mind to refute the suggestion that "time" is the outstanding missing link. KNS itself climaxes in the kinetics of an It which, in its worlding and properizing, "happens," as a way of describing the "vital impetus" of life in its fundamental intentionality. Is that not already fundamental history, and thus original time? In the first course on religion, two kinds of time emerge in the distinction between the object-historical and the actualization-historical and, in a clear ontological statement, it is formally indicated that Christian factic life *is* itself temporality, which is then found to culminate in the Christian καιρός. Is this not enough to spell out the "substance" of the titular question of Being "and" Time? Yet the old Heidegger, in series of autobiographical statements, scoffs at his "juvenilia" to such a degree that he puts the decision to publish them on hold, since they antedate the most fundamental insights which prompted the very first outlines and sketches of BT around 1923. Let us accordingly, in the doxographical reconstruction which follows, be alert especially to the emerging temporal clues that will shape the basic question of BT.

Three final points regarding the years 1921–24 must first be made:

1. If this period is initially described as the "confrontation of the ontological tradition," a glance at Heidegger's teaching activities immediately makes it clear that the source and focus of that tradition is being sited in the name of Aristotle and not Plato and/or Parmenides, the earlier loci for the origins of the transcendental and ontological tradition. In the early Heidegger's recounting, they are, for all their importance, but mere precursors. Moreover, the Aristotelian texts are stretched well beyond the deconstructive exercise that we would expect from Heidegger's methodology at this stage, so that they are made to yield a plethora of constructive insights as well. A very ambiguous figure of Aristotle thus emerges in Heidegger's story of Greek philosophy, at times typically Greek in his ground concepts, at other times more modern than the moderns, perhaps the first, certainly the best, of its phenomenologists!

2. The threshold "happening" of my own unique I out of an impersonal It which "properizes" it and willy-nilly "worlds" it in a context which belongs to it and to which it belongs (KNS 1919); the self's historical way of "having itself" understandingly in and through its situation (WS 1919–20): These two themes are in fact one, and lie at the core of Heidegger's lifelong topic. They now assume, in this developed Aristotelian context, the ontological proportions of a generalized having or ownership, incorporating objective as well as nonobjective property, and so betray their hitherto suppressed Greek roots in οὐσία, "that which is one's own," being as having and the "had."

3. Since it will at this point suddenly be resumed, we might also recall the aletheic thread spun in the remarkably prescient habilitation work, but muted in the ensuing years by the overriding concern for the kinetic articulation of life. Aside from a fleeting cameo appearance in KNS, ἀλήθεια now suddenly reappears among the "transcendentals" with an emphasis and amplitude that will never allow it to be again overshadowed by the other "convertible" terms for οὐσία, by φύσις (κίνησις) and λόγος. In the habilitation, transcendental *verum*, being as knowable and intelligible and in this sense "true," is located in the realm of simple encounter at the interface of the orders of knowing and being. Prior to the truth of judgment understood as validity is the prejudicative truth of simple apprehension, truth as meaning. The young Heidegger already identifies this "transcendental" realm of pretheoretical meaning flowing through intentional life as the original setting of the human being, in

which we are already absorbed in the "reality" (so in WS 1919–20) of
meaning and so "live in truth" (i.e., intelligibility, meaning), a phrase
from Lask's aletheiology which is repeated in BT. In keeping with this
truth that stems from the simplicity of apprehension, empowered by it,
the phenomenologist, in his desire to describe the pretheoretical immediacy of experience, has but one recourse: "to look, to grasp actually all
there is to grasp, to draw out the pure self of what is offered" by reality,
to "read off" its articulations directly from reality itself. For when it comes
to access to this rudimentary dimension of experience —in Heidegger's
simplest and terminologically most prescient statement of method to be
found in this student work, in that portion of his juvenilia which he did
authorize to be republished—"facticities can only be *pointed out*" (FS 155).

It is now 1921. No real word of truth in five years, and it will not
appear until October 1922. Does Heidegger really need to invoke it even
now, or is it a mere verbal solution to the mighty problem of gaining
access to the immediacy of experience? The problem does not really
lie in "truth" but in the simplicity of the apprehension. Do we really
apprehend, grasp, take—Aristotle's word is "touch," θιγεῖν—the immediacy of experience in its sense? Instead of *Hinsehen*, a *Hingabe*, a receptive submission; heeding and not looking, more a suffering than an action? Or somewhere in the middle, that Greek voice which will continue
to recur as Heidegger moves from Paul's verbs *of* God to Aristotle's
search for a middle between passion and action? The Christian middle
of trust, troth, will begin to infiltrate Heidegger's understanding of the
Aristotelian senses of practical truth. Does it really belong? What actually
"happens" at this first level of experience? Do we know how to be here,
have a know-how of what it means to be, having already experienced,
undergone It, "having become"? Natorp's objections ring like an echo
through Heidegger's reading of the *koine* and the rhetor's Latin as Heidegger searches their understanding of the structures of immediacy, the
"truth" of "simple" touching and being touched. Aristotle will at least
help Heidegger to sharpen his formal indications of these structures.
The direct structure: The world "gets to me" (*geht mich an*), approaches,
meets, solicits, afflicts, or otherwise affects me. The more self-referential
structure: Dasein is a being which in its being "goes about" (*geht um*)
this Being . . . understandingly, heedingly, trustingly, lovingly, caringly?
Certainly intimately.

To be sure, there is an element of naiveté in the doctrine of "simple"
apprehension which is about to be moderated by the implications of the
privative character of the Greek sense of truth. But despite the need to
wrest truth from its hiding places, for all its subterfuges, does Heidegger
ever really give up the Paradise of a simple dwelling placed in the proximity of truth, which for all its oblivion still offers access to itself?

FIVE

What Did Heidegger Find in Aristotle? (1921–23)

As we have seen, Heidegger's growing perception of the poor theological grounding of his students gave him pause, in his curricular decisions for 1920 and 1921, in scheduling a seminar on the phenomenology of religion. "For in all honesty, all that would come of it is the kind of drivel over the philosophy of religion that I want to eliminate from philosophy, this talk about the religious that one picks up from the secondary literature. Perhaps we could risk it next summer. I then thought of Plotinus, but once again the same problems in part. So I decided on Aristotelian metaphysics" (letter to Löwith on September 13, 1920). Thus almost casually and seemingly by way of default, Heidegger in SS 1921 gave the first of a series of seminars and courses on Aristotle's texts which would last without letup every semester until the end of 1924. It was against this academic backdrop that the project of BT first came into being and underwent its initial drafting. The double-pronged program of this project is first clearly and dramatically spelled out in October of 1922 when Heidegger, under academic duress to publish something for promotion to a university chair, described his publication plans by way of an Introduction and Overview to a projected book on Aristotle.

What really prompted this seemingly arbitrary and fortuitous plunge into the Aristotelian opus in SS 1921, from which Heidegger never recovered for the rest of his life? The old Heidegger's repeated recollections in this context of the gift of Brentano's book on Aristotle which he was already reading in his gymnasium years, while providing general background, clearly does not account for this critical decision. But perhaps Heidegger betrays his most immediate philosophical motive for this backtracking to a secular figure who predates Christianity when, in the very next sentence of the letter of September 1920, we find him suddenly responding to a question posed by Löwith regarding the "Bonn edition" of Luther's works. Luther's vitriolic attacks against "that liar" and pagan, Aristotle, who openly consorted with "that whore, reason," have as their constructive goal the restoration of the simple tenets of primitive Christianity, which accordingly must first be purified of the age-old Greek contamination perpetrated upon it by the medieval theologians. Dilthey's and Harnack's thesis on the "Greekification" (GA 61:6) of primitive Christianity was clearly on Heidegger's mind at the time. And young Luther's plaint against the Greek Fathers' spoliation of the Scriptures plays a brief but central role in the Augustine course, whose overriding theme is the corruption of Augustine's insights by Greek Neoplatonism. It was clearly time for Heidegger to take another step back into the tradition in the application of the "destructive" weapons which he had been wielding in regressive order, having begun with his contemporaries in 1919 and gradually proceeding backwards. There was therefore a not so hidden agenda connecting the Augustine course with the concurrent seminar on Aristotle in SS 1921, though Heidegger, with his usual reserve, left it to his students to deduce the obvious. It was not until the opening hours of the following semester's course that he unleashed a volley of particularly derisive expletives against "the pagan" Aristotle (more so in the auditors' transcripts than GA 61:7) drawn from his newly purchased "Erlangen edition" of Luther's opus. But if this destructive motive provided the initial impetus toward Aristotle, clearly something happened along the way. Still to be identified are the more positive discoveries which prompted Heidegger's repeated return in the ensuing semesters, as he became more and more "carried away" by his work on Aristotle, to the detriment and ultimate demise of his work on religious figures like Luther. What did Heidegger find in Aristotle?

None of these "Lutheran" motivations are recalled in the old Heidegger's more "Catholic" reminiscences of this period of breakthrough. Nevertheless, forty years later, Heidegger could still pinpoint some of the surprises contained in this return to Aristotle, impacting so deeply on his thinking that he kept returning for the rest of his life. He first found a remarkable affinity between his own original phenomenological researches and Aristotle's texts, in method as well as content. Bringing his earlier interpretations of the dynamized facticity of life to bear upon these texts, he found in this Greek life-philosopher with a sense of the history of philosophical problems a proto-phenomenologist as well! The most memorable achievement of this innovative textual practice was the insight, in book 6 of the *Nicomachean Ethics*, into ἀληθεύειν as a multifaceted process of revealment. The discovery led to a deeper comprehension of the nature of phenomenology, the λόγος of φαίνεσθαι, which in fact played a governing role throughout this evolution of insights. The insight into ἀλήθεια as unconcealment in turn prompted the recognition of the fundamental trait of οὐσία, the being of beings, as presence. But then the entire endeavor was counter to Husserl's sense of phenomenological "seeing," which also "demanded that one give up interjecting the authority of the great thinkers into the discussion."[1]

Truth as unconcealment, the "logic" of phenomena, being as constant presence, with the nature of phenomenology providing a normative axis of orientation before, during, and after these three Hellenic discoveries: these are the chronological/dialectical "trailmarkers" provided by the old Heidegger, which must now be confirmed or disconfirmed against the extant doxographical record available in the archives. Our own genealogical context makes it clear that Heidegger's two contexts of memory—an epistolary Preface to a book by Wm. Richardson, S.J., which Heidegger in fact retitles "*Through* Phenomenology to Thought," and an essay entitled "My Way to Phenomenology" written to honor a publisher pioneering in the books which brought the Phenomenological Movement into being—are thus being guided and so curtailed by their orientation to phenomenology. This results in the exclusion of other determinants operative in Heidegger's development at the time, especially the religious determinants. Given this common point of recall, we could excuse the old Heidegger when he acts as if two courses on religion did not intervene between his course on phenomenological method in SS 1920 and the first Aristotle course of WS 1921–22.

Therefore, as a supplement to the two reminiscences that we have directly from "Heidegger's hand," let us pause to outline the accounts of the chronology of this period related by Otto Pöggeler, a leading exponent of the "religious element" in Heidegger's thought ever since he first introduced the two religion courses to the world in 1959. For Pöggeler's accounting has the added weight of being in part guided by a series of conversations he had with Heidegger from 1959 to 1963.

1) While studying and teaching Aristotle and Husserl's *Logical Investigations* together [this could be as early as WS 1921–22], Heidegger arrives at the thesis that the character of philosophical knowing since the Greeks has been defined by intuition. Philosophical truth is truth which is "seen." In a critique in part directed at his mentor, Husserl (e.g., inner time made conscious by *perceiving* a melody), Heidegger breaks with this traditional model for theoretical truth and gives primacy instead to phenomena which involve practical and even religious truth, the phenomena of historical encounter rather than psychological experience.

2) In his reading of Aristotle's account of the different kinds of truth in *Nicomachean Ethics* 6, Heidegger thought he also found an original experience of the καιρός paralleling that of primitive Christianity. And yet *Physics* 4, with its understanding of time as a series of nows, betrayed

an ontological option which in its "leveling" character only obscured that original experience. [This would have to be Oct. 1922.]

3) In the years 1922/23, Heidegger had a "flash of genius" (*Geistesblitz:* so in the repeated conversations with Pöggeler) which he came to regard as the real beginning of his life's work: οὐσία for the Greeks means constant presence, and so is oriented toward only one dimension of time, the present, after the model of things "present at hand." Contrary to this tradition, therefore, Heidegger redefines his task toward the understanding of being in terms of time in its fullest and most fulfilled sense.

4) Finally, perhaps Heidegger meant that all three insights occurred in the years 1922/23, or better, that it was the time in which the first two converged upon the climactic third insight, resulting for the first time in that temporal sense of the "question of being" which occupied Heidegger for the rest of his life. "This date must of course be checked against the documents."[2] Let us see to what extent the available archive evidence from this period confirms these accounts of the early Heidegger's confrontation of Aristotle and the series of surprises ensuing from it.

SS 1921: PHENOMENOLOGICAL PRACTICUM "RELATING TO" ARISTOTLE'S DE ANIMA

These exercises (*Übungen*) constitute a kind of zero-point for the period, an hors d'oeuvre before the main meal. Within our present genealogical context, they yield a somewhat plodding exegesis with only a few suggestive moments to be gleaned for what is yet to unfold over the problem of οὐσία, a halting start toward the climax that we have been led to expect. But the genesis of great ideas have their routine moments which might well mask a mighty struggle. Shortly before the beginning of this semester, Heidegger (on April 2, 1921) reports to Löwith that he is now under way in a "self-destruction" toward a "new explication of life." From this seminar context, we can surmise that the phenomenological account of factic life begun in 1919 is now to be taken in an overtly ontological direction, utilizing Aristotle as a kind of norm and sounding board, and so as a source of new insights.

The problem of defining the soul in the first two books of the *De Anima* is raised briefly only at the start and finish of the semester. Most of the semester deals with the more comprehensive problem of defining οὐσία as it is treated in book 7 of Aristotle's *Metaphysics*. Whatever his initial motives for choosing these texts, Heidegger is now clearly interested in the talk about life in the most basic and universal of terms, which for Aristotle are ontological terms. And yet this metaphysical tendency toward the universal ὂν ὡς ὄν, toward the *sense* of being, is always determined from the concrete, for example, from the "biological," the "shaped," and the like. This proximity between psychology (accessibility and expressibility of the soul, life) and ontology (accessing and expressing οὐσία, which is "had" being and not "substance") must be maintained in our formal considerations of philosophical concept formation. ("Formal indication" is mentioned twice in this connection between what will be called the ontic and the ontological.) Heidegger accordingly presses the text toward those points where language and life come closest, where the dynamic λέγειν of assertion finds entry into the λέγειν belonging to the experience of direct acquaintance with life, where I first "have" things and therefore being. Being must be "had" before it can be "given," "intuitively" given. Thus, even the "principle of phenomenology" is placed in question by this prescientific sense of having, whether it be an object or a world, or life itself. It is out of such prior experiences of having that our scientific and philosophical questions arise. The how of questioning is already determined by the sense of having, which is first a "lived having" (not yet called a "pre-having") before it is conscious (cf. 1041a11 on the essence of questioning: Heidegger never quite mentions that the first dictionary definition of οὐσία is *Habe*, belongings, property.) Aristotelian concept formation still manifests this close proximity to the natural attitude of immediate prescientific acquaintance, it lacks sophistication, it is, in a positive sense, theoretically naive. Heidegger therefore defends Aristotle's proto-phenomenological tendencies against Natorp's interpretations of the same texts, which turn the "becoming" individual into a logical individual to be found at the end of an infinite series of form-determinations. For Aristotle attempts to get at the ultimately existing individual (ἕκαστον ["each"], τόδε τι ["this-here"]) both in itself and by way of heterothesis. He tries to get at the "some" (*Et-liches*, "a thing or two, one thing or another [ἄλλο]") of the "some-what" or "it-what" (*Et-was*) of something, from which οὐσία ultimately derives its "is-sense." But this attempt is marked by the tendency to regard the environing world in terms of shaping, ποίησις. By way of shape (μορφή), οὐσία comes to be regarded as form (εἶδος), which becomes the dominant "what" asserted of an "it." This tendency will prove to be decisive and fateful for occidental ontology and logic.

In approaching the difficult question of οὐσία, Aristotle's real starting point and basic phenomenon of his thought turns out to be the statement or assertion, λόγος. The statement, saying something (typically a What) "of" (*von*, also "from") something (this individual), reaches its philosophical climax in the definition, ὁρισμός, which determines that something through (*durch*) something which is nothing other than the original something καθ᾽ αὐτό, a for-itself "in accord with itself."

But "being is said in many ways" (the first line of *Metaphysics* 7). In defining οὐσία, Aristotle quickly narrows his options (chap. 3) to four fundamental concepts transmitted to him by the λέγειν of his tradition and, almost as quickly, eliminates the genus and the universal from serious contention. (As we have seen from KNS on, Heidegger's method of formal indication follows Aristotle in this series of ontological decisions.) This leaves τὸ τί ἦν εἶναι (not "essence" but "is-sense" for Heidegger) and ὑποκείμενον (subject or substrate). Substrate as matter yields the indeterminacy of being, but for Aristotle it must be given form to stand by itself. Only when it is understood as relationship-to-form, potency, can matter be a serious contender for the status of "being." Accordingly, the "is-sense" enfolded in the copula of the assertion becomes the primary locus for the one-in-many senses of οὐσία. The remainder of the seminar is devoted to the complications in the project of "defining" being that arise from the assertions of the phenomena of becoming (γένεσις) and change (κίνησις).

Heidegger, obviously already taken by Aristotle's problem of οὐσία, is in fact just warming up to the related ontological problem of life's kinetics, and will return to the same Aristotelian texts again and again in the coming semesters.

WS 1921–22: PHENOMENOLOGICAL INTERPRETATIONS TO ARISTOTLE: INTRODUCTION TO PHENOMENOLOGICAL RESEARCH: *EINLEITUNG*

The peculiarly prepositioned course title ("to Aristotle") will recur in SS 1922 for a course dealing directly with the Aristotelian opus, in WS 1922–23 for a seminar on the *Nicomachean Ethics*, and becomes the title of a projected book on Aristotle upon which Heidegger worked from 1922 through 1924. The manuscript of this course of WS 1921–22 itself became the basis for the "Introduction" (*Einleitung*)[3] to that book, so that the published "Ausgabe letzter Hand" incorporates addenda and changes, of which the reader is not forewarned, which date to at least as late as 1924, when the last of these Introductions appears to have been written. Terms like "existenziell" and "existenzial," for example, which proliferate in excess in the published version of the course, are not to be found at all in student notes of the same course.

One soon discovers that the topic of the course is not Phenomenological Interpretations *of* Aristotle. That will come in the following semester. Instead, we find the "new explication of life" ensuing from the "self-destruction" which Heidegger is carrying out at this time. But this ontological revision of the categories of life (Third Part) is preceded by an extensive re-view of the question, "What Is Philosophy?" (Second Part), recalling the course title of early 1919 and the contents of subsequent courses. The upshot of this particular review is a change in Heidegger's

"fundamental definition of philosophy" in the direction of a phenomenological ontology.[4] It accordingly manifests an increasing concern for life's
"sense of being," in its way also a return to Aristotle's most basic sense
of οὐσία. But the deeper goal of this Introduction to Phenomenological
Research, further accentuating its counter-Husserlian direction, is to develop the intrinsically historical character of such ontological research,
in keeping with the fundamentally historical movement of life itself. Ultimately, therefore, there is no difference between the ontological and the
historical—this is clearly not Aristotle or Husserl—and philosophy must
bring its methods in accord with this deeper movement of factic life
itself. Here therefore, for the first time, Heidegger develops a full notion
of the presuppositional context of interpretation called the "hermeneutic
situation"—first called the *Verstehenssituation*, the "situation of understanding"[5]—in large part in preparation for the Aristotelian texts: A
year later, the "Introduction" to the Aristotle book will bear the title
"Indication of the Hermeneutic Situation."

It is of course not by chance that the more basic "pre-having" (but
the one use of the term *Vorhabe* in GA 61:19 is a semester too early) will
soon join "pre-grasping" (*Vorgriff*), which had carried this weight by itself
since KNS 1919, in structuring the hermeneutic situation. It is the "prescientific having," mentioned in the previous semester's seminar, which
enters into the question of definition. The issue of having will now be
even more broadly conceived and exploited in several directions in the
task set for Part Two of the course, that of formally indicating a fundamental definition of philosophy. Far from being a mere search for a
universal genus qualified by a specific difference, such an indicating action, which seeks to define limits at the outskirts of the usual run-of-
the-mill universal concepts, from the start forebodes the risky moves of
resolute decision! (GA 61:17). Indeed, in a far cry from the academic
tones which led to its demise in the classes of WS 1920–21, formal indication, which seeks a middle ground between abstractly strict universal
definition (its overestimation) and concrete experience (underestimation
of definition), is now charged with the skepticism of radical questioning;
it is thus situated in a fundamental experience which "is not the saving
coastline but the leap into the tossing boat, where everything hangs upon
getting hold of the sail line and looking to the wind. . . . Solid ground
lies in seizing questionability" (37).[6] "Philosophy is not a matter that you
play with" ("Philosophie ist eine Sache, mit der man nicht spielt": Brecht/
Weiß transcript): this was the message that Heidegger sought to convey
to his students with regard to the "fundamental having" (19) that is philosophy. Hardly the security that one would expect from our guiding
term of "having." Having here is assumption of the conditions that struc-

ture the decision to philosophize: having the situation of understanding and the passion for questioning, to begin with.

Defining philosophy, obtaining access to this "object," thus involves a multifaceted having. "Like any 'object,' philosophy has its way of *genuinely coming to be had*; corresponding to every object is a particular way of access, of holding on to it or *losing* it" (18). Having here involves a claiming, an addressing *of* the object (*Ansprechen des Gegenstandes*). The genitive objective "having" predominates here to the point of the introduction (not in class) of an "out of season" military metaphor of laying siege upon the "object" (ibid.). But the genitive subjective "having," the receptivity to a prior claim of already "being had" (*Vorhabe*), still receives its due ("Life makes its claim upon me," already in WS 1919–20). If any definition is out to stake a claim upon its object by determining or defining it, it must nevertheless do so in a way that "befits," is "meet, proper, becoming, due" to the situation in which the object is had and already grasped (*Vorgriff*). The simple apprehension and determination of an object is not so simple, as Heidegger probes its underlying conditions in their role of illuminating the what and how of an object in a situation of familiarity which precedes knowledge (18). In the radical definition that befits philosophy, the situation itself is in fact the "object" of the definition. As an "object," philosophy is not really a "thing" but the "fundamental having," having the very fundaments of one's being. Philosophy is philosophizing, a how of life, a rhythm of having and holding, gaining and losing, taking and letting go. In short, philosophizing as fundamental having is more particularly specified as a "sich verhalten zu . . ." (52), a comportive holding/relating itself to, but also, to follow through on the middle-voiced ambiguity of the grammatical "reflexive," a being held/related to. From KNS, we know that we are now at the meaning-generating core of being as intentionality, the "primal something," the very first "object" of the formal indication. Heidegger takes this occasion to refine the triple sense of intentionality and to add a fourth sense that comprehends the other three, the temporalizing sense. For example, in the present context of full-fledged having, *Gehaltssinn* is no longer the termination of the holding relation in a content (*Gehalt*), a What. As a middle-voiced formal indication, it is more the countermovement of containment which completes the relation, describing how it contains or holds . . . and is itself held! This holding or containment sense is formally left open, flexible enough to indicate phenomena at both ends of the spectrum of activity and passivity, from the containment of meaningful objects by a world or region to the comporting self "being had," held, fascinated, captivated by the objects it beholds, in attachments that border on addiction (53, 55).

One final point: the tentative, probing "having" of formal-indicative definition, for all its decisiveness, is an insecure and so "inauthentic having" which never fully determines or defines its object. This in fact is its formality, in providing only the "on-set" of determination, seeking promising beginnings and directions of development to articulate its dynamic topic, like maps drawn lightly, in filigree, to prefigure "the" way, only to be recast to point to a new way. Philosophizing is accordingly a never-ending "way." The formal is thus closely tied to its indicative quality, which points the way; the two cannot be separated as form and content (GA 61:33f.). The ever-present insecurity of skeptical questioning must be kept in view especially in order to avoid construing the formally indicative definition of philosophy, as a "cognitive comporting to beings as being" (58ff.), into a "scientific" cognition. The true having of philosophy is not in the cognition but in the comporting, the persistent bearing toward inchoate being. Otherwise put, the authentic having of philosophizing is in the "full stretch" (*Voll-zug*) of the actualizing sense (*Vollzugssinn*) itself, pursuant to the temporalizing sense of always being "under way" (34, 60f., 171). Further light will be thrown on this tenuous having when philosophy is eventually defined not as "cognitive" but as "illuminating comportment" (54) and, in the ensuing months, gradually described in its full aletheic character.

In view of the chronologically compromised character of the published edition, much of the analysis of this verbose, baroque, and turgid course can, for our purposes, be put off until we come to the later, somewhat clearer draft of the *Einleitung* of October 1922. This is a course caught up in the turmoil of transition, complicated even in its actual delivery by frequent interjections from a separate Appendix (GA 61: 157–181), as well as by the above-mentioned emendations pursuant to later drafts of the *Einleitung*. In fact, the period initiated by this course is characterized by a further degeneration of style, a loss of the simplicity of expression in which some of the discoveries of the prior two years had been cast, a kind of scholasticizing of older insights. Heidegger's acute awareness of this problem of style will contribute to his hesitation to put his work into print.

But let us glean enough from the course to prepare for the Aristotle interpretations of the following semester. After the brief opening remarks (Part One) on the need for a fundamental clarification of the relation of philosophizing to its history on the level of factic life itself, on the then fashionable reception of Aristotle as a naive epistemologist, and on the problem of the "Greekification" of the Christian consciousness of life, precious little is said in the next two Parts of the course itself to justify its title connecting the phenomenological interpretations "to" Aristotle. Problems with the formal definition of philosophy and a glance at the grammar of statements about "life" allude to the need to return to the treatment of logic and grammar in Aristotle and the Greeks (21, 83). Regarding the basic categories of life centered especially on the primary ontological category of "caring," which Heidegger introduces here for the first time, along with the very sense of the categorial which is indigenous to life itself and so not just an extraneous "table of categories," Heidegger anticipates a more detailed clarification from his concrete analyses of Aristotle himself (89ff., 79). But caution must be exercised here, since help from Aristotle is ambiguous: On the one hand, οὐσία for him still carries its original practical sense of holdings (*Haben*), property, the goods and "substance" of "house and hold," thus by extension the power of a "man of means" or "substance";[7] it is this sense which Heidegger abundantly exploits throughout this period well beyond its peripatetic usages. On the other hand, Aristotle also contributes to its eventual theoretical constriction to the level of a bare object stripped of all "value," a sense of being that we must hold in abeyance in comprehending the already meaningful things of the world which are the "objects" of caring. Under the promptings of the equally ubiquitous Aristotelian paradigm of ποίησις, Heidegger begins to rethink his environmental analysis more in terms of using and making than in terms of seeing, as it is presented in its first version in KNS (25, 96ff., 129). His extensive discussion of the dominant tendency of "ruination" ("fallenness" a year later) in the movement of life finds support in Aristotle's doctrine of the Golden Mean of virtue, how difficult it is to achieve, how easy to err by excess or defect; ergo the tendency to take the easy way out (108). And we have already alluded to the search for a similar middle ground between hyperbole and ellipsis in Heidegger's attempt to define philosophy.

But once again, the task of interpreting Aristotle had lapsed into the background of the course to such an extent that Heidegger, upon return from the Christmas break, interrupts his prepared course with a special addendum ("Beilage zu S. 29" in Heidegger's autograph) in order to underscore the equiprimordiality of this historical task in unison with the ongoing "systematic" task of the *Einleitung* (GA 61:110–117). The *Einleitung* in fact seeks to develop a situation in which the philosophical distinction of systematic versus historical is no longer viable or necessary. The systematic articulation of the categories of life centers upon demonstrating the inherently historical character of the facticity of life. As fundamental knowing, philosophy itself must find its way to "appropriate" life at this most rudimentary level, such that it is itself already thoroughly and fundamentally historical. "Philosophizing as fundamental knowing is nothing other than the radical actualization of the historical of the facticity of life" (111). But how is this pure achievement of the sheer dynamics of facticity—a purity reminiscent of Husserl's and Bergson's sense of a "life stream"—*in fact* to be related to the concrete historical circumstances in which we are concerned with disciplines like the history of philosophy and activities like interpreting Aristotle's texts?

The entire discussion needs to be made more tangible by recalling the concrete life-context in which such questions arise: the university, with its tradition and its life in and among the sciences, the focus of the very life of science, in which philosophy has from the beginning been measured according to its own ideals of fundamentality and comprehensiveness. While proposing this concrete start, Heidegger gives precious few broad hints, let alone concrete answers, on why this dictates a return to Aristotle: the tradition-bound character of inherited philosophical thought, whose hold presumably must be broken (113); the fundamental insecurity arising from rapid historical change (114), presaging perhaps the "Decline of the West" (76); the widespread crisis among the sciences, whose concrete logic must be developed from their "lifeworld" and not by some abstract logical or methodological approach (115). Thus, most of the issues of the course, both systematic and historical, are yet to be resolved, when our facticity is approached through this concrete context which is the center of the life of science:

> Still to be settled are the following matters: what is to be fundamentally (philosophically) understood under the *fundamental knowing* which originates from such a facticity and returns to it; how this fundamental knowing stands in the facticity of this factic life-context [the university]; how the Aristotle-interpretation develops in it as a genuine and concrete research project; what requirements fundamental knowing itself imposes upon this, its concrete realization. Finally, it must be shown how this philosophical problematic brings the direction of *phenomenological* research back to its intrinsic originality and in what sense the interpretation of Aristotle is to be called phenomenological. (115f.)

But the beginnings of an answer to the question of the specific directions which the forthcoming interpretations *of* Aristotle are to take have already taken shape in the course itself. In a "schematic orientation," Heidegger summarizes three groups of problems which have already emerged (112):

1. The problem of the "principle," the fundamental (ἀρχή—αἴτιον).
2. The problem of defining by apprehending, of conceptual articulation (λόγος).
3. The   problem   of   any   being,   its   sense   of   being (ὄν—οὐσία—κίνησις—φύσις).

Conspicuous by its absence is the problem of ἀλήεια, though the second problem alludes to the "truth of simple apprehension" and the course itself accordingly makes frequent allusion to this achievement of "having" under the heading of "illumination" (*Erhellung*). As we have seen, there is clearly a large problematic waiting to be developed in the different ways of having an object, "of apprehending and defining it by way of familiarization [*Kenntnis* vs. *Erkenntnis*], the specific ways of illuminating each and every experience" (18). Thus (in a remark that postdates the course), if we had taken our starting point from Plato's Allegory of the Cave, philosophy could have been more originally described as "illuminative" rather than "cognitive" comportment (54). Such a comportment more readily comprehends that radical "having" involved in interrogative illumination, which "first discloses the authentic horizon of factic life" (37). The movement of life as well as of philosophy is a movement of illumination (128, 135).

But what dominates at this stage of the orientation *to* Aristotle, in keeping with the repeated concern for the fundamental "problem of the historical," are the ways in which we "have" mobility, the "movedness of life *in* which and *through* which it *is*." The problem of facticity is a "κίνησις-problem" (117). This then becomes the guiding problem for the specific interpretations *of* Aristotle that now follow.

SS 1922: PHENOMENOLOGICAL INTERPRETATIONS TO
ARISTOTLE: ONTOLOGY AND LOGIC

This was a four-hour lecture course, the longest of the early Freiburg period, providing ample time for the extensive and innovative translation paraphrases of texts, selected largely from the *Metaphysics* and *Physics*, which Heidegger developed line by line in class. Heidegger opts for the freer form of translation, backed by meticulous and exhaustive expository supplements, in order to loosen the sedimented expressions of the tradition and draw out the context of meaning out of which the texts speak. This style of exegesis will in later courses become Heidegger's hallmark, recurring in other guises en route to other thoughts. The course is therefore not only substantial but also important. After the turmoil of the previous semester, Heidegger now asserts himself as master of the Aristotelian opus, pressing new and unsuspected dimensions out of its well-worked but rich hold.[8]

With an ever-clearer sense of the intertwined ontological and historical character of philosophy, Heidegger seeks in this course to arrive at a basic understanding of what is called the "ontology" of Aristotle, who represents the classical source of that discipline. In what particular research context did the ontological question of being first arise? What motivated the question and in what research direction was it taken? What role did the question play in Aristotle's philosophy and why did it assume that role? It is therefore not simply a matter of understanding Aristotle's "doctrine" of being and related fundamental concepts. What must first be understood is what Aristotle meant by research, as well as the context, attitude, and style of interrogation in which he approached his ontological research. We can establish this by way of an interpretation of the first two chapters of the first book of the *Metaphysics*, which Aristotle himself regarded as an "Introduction" to his ontology. Its introductory "story" of the "cultural" origins of art, science, and philosophy out of "experience," and the sense or "nature" of the "wisdom" which is philosophy that accrues to this story, addresses a problem which had been on Heidegger's mind ever since his early years of engrossment with neo-Kantians like Lask, namely, the problem of the "genesis of the theoretical" (ZBP 88, 210ff.).

Πάντες ἄνθρωποι τοῦ εἰδέναι ὀρέγονται φύσει. "The urge to live in seeing, the absorption in the visible, is constitutive of how the human being is." Heidegger's departures from the usual translation of the famous opening line ("All men by nature desire to know") quickly put in place two of the leitmotivs for the rest of the translation and the subsequent detailed exegesis: φύσις as "how-being" and εἰδέναι as "seeing." The latter translation has deep roots in pre-Homeric usage, where εἴδω is more properly the digammated Ϝίδω (cf. the Latin *video*). But by Homeric times, the perfect form οἶδα, "I have seen," assumed the function of the present active "I know." Here, Heidegger not only returns to the earlier meaning but also carries this over to its cognate, εἶδος, translating it like its further cognate, ἰδέα, first as the "look" or "appearance" of a thing, from which the usual translation of "form" then follows. "Look" in this way implies the becoming of a making, having been shaped, relating it to the equally mundane origins of οὐσία (goods of the house-and-hold). One immediate consequence of these verbal connections will be the equating of "form" with "regard" (*Hinsicht*). Philosophy will seek to accentuate the look at which one "sees the most": in regard to the object as such, its whys, wherefroms and wherefores. From the text at hand, Heidegger can trace a continuous progression of seeing from the direct cognizance (*Kenntnisnahme*) and initial orientation of αἴσθησις to the pure beholding (θεωρεῖν) of philosophy, including en route the "looking around" of artisan shaping and the seeing of science, which looks straight at a thing in order to highlight its look with emphasis and exactitude.

In actual fact, the starting point of this progression, understood as a human development, is really ἐμπειρία, that "experience" made thick and temporally taut (and taught) by memory (980b28ff.). This fusion of practical knowing and savvy doing includes, in an inchoate unity, the double character of "getting around" (*Umgehen*, also "getting along, about, by"; likewise "going about, around") and "know-how" (*Auskennen*), in short, an adept coping. "Experience" is thus not so much a passive undergoing as an active "go-round" replete with its own kind of "knowledge." All the other stages of human life are to be understood as refinements and developments of this first stage, which is therefore never really left behind. Even philosophy is an *Umgangsweise*, in this case an interpretatively illuminative mode of moving about and making one's way in the business of life.

Life's movement is also the key behind the translation of φύσις as "how-being," clearly seeking to counter the substantifying "what-being" which a long tradition has invested in phrases like "by nature" and "human nature." But for Aristotle and in the Greek experience, the basic trait of φύσις is clearly κίνησις. To describe this Greek fusion of being and becoming, Heidegger employs the German idiom, *es kommt darauf an*, "it comes down to that." Life "depends upon" specific activities and augmentations thereof for its very being. Human life must "come to" see in order to be. In seeing, man is. In seeing more, he is more human. He is most alive and "arrives at" the pinnacle of human excellence (ἀρετή) in seeing the most, which is σοφία, the "original understanding" which is the goal of philosophy. The How of being human is to be found in the movement of coming to understand.

Clearly, concern for the "κίνησις-problem" in the activity of philosophizing and its relation to the dynamics of human life, analyzed in the previous semester in terms of the guiding tendency of "caring," is consciously being made dominant in this semester and almost flagrantly allowed to influence even the translation and interpretation of specific Greek words. This hermeneutic procedure is openly announced immediately upon conclusion of the translation paraphrase; and the *Vorhabe* of "caring" accumulated over the previous years and now being brought to bear upon the text is summarized in some detail in a language largely alien to the immediately preceding content, before Heidegger proceeds with his more exhaustive exegesis. At its conclusion, he admits that his category of "caring" cannot literally be found in the Aristotelian text and has served to push the text to interpretative extremes. This, however, is of the essence of philosophical interpretation which seeks to bring the underlying context of the text into sharp relief. It is not arbitrary but continues to be led by the matter while subjecting it to radical questions, for example: Is that supreme mode of going along with the matter called θεωρία, by leisurely lingering with it, really without care or a peculiar escalation of its movement? Is perhaps βίος θεωρέτικος the authentic βίος πράκτικος? Is not knowing, contrary to the modern epistemological tradition, also a movement of life, a way of going along with the world? For Aristotle, who first regarded the "intellectual virtues" in their cohesive unity, even τέχνη has a share in σοφία, which in turn is always related to the creativity of bringing forth or pro-ducing (ποίησις).

In a subsequent course (GA 20:380/275) and in BT (SZ 171)—in both cases under the heading of "Curiosity"—the opening line of the *Metaphysics* is translated "The care for seeing belongs essentially in man's being." There, "care" operates as the "provisional indication" of the temporality of human Being. This development is first prepared in these earlier Aristotle courses, where caring is developed especially in the intentional direction of its *Zeitigungssinn* (temporalizing sense, but more idiomatically, "fruition sense"), a term used only in these courses to amplify more fully life's "sense of actualization" (*Vollzugssinn*). *Zeitigung*, which suggests the pro-ductive power of time and which translates words as different as ποίησις (981a5) and συμβεβηκός ("chance event," 982b23) in the paraphrase, stands closer to its original vitalistic senses of "ripening," "maturing," "unfolding," in this Aristotelian setting than in later contexts. But none of this is to be taken either biologically or psychologically, but ontologically. Making, doing, seeing, knowing, understanding are ontological modes of temporal movement, ways of getting on with the world, in sum, ways of caring. All are matters of vital concern, and going-about is at once caring: *es geht um mein Leben, mea res agitur*, "my life is at stake."

Heidegger even finds a foothold in the Aristotelian text for his own hermeneutic procedure and his growing sense of the "hermeneutic situation" (so named first in this course) of presuppositions out of which an interpretation operates. For Aristotle also speaks of how τὸ ἔχειν ὑπόληψιν, "having an assumption" (981a8), naturally develops from our going about our business with things. Factic life is "had" in certain "take-ups and receptions." In other words, factic life is always already interpreted and is in fact accessible only in and through such interpretations, from which it receives its meaning and through which it is understood. These interpretations, more often than not implicit, can be explicated and improved upon in the direction, say, of the arts, sciences, and philosophy; or they can be allowed to lapse and become leveled into mere opinions. In the text under study, Aristotle in effect develops his own *Vorhabe* (i.e. his ὑπόληψεις) on the nature of philosophical inquiry by first explicating what "we consider and assume" (981a25ff., 981b20) about "who is wiser," in order then to outline the five "received" assumptions regarding the wise as such (982a7ff.), finally subjecting them to critical examinaton in order to establish something definitive about the nature and goals of philosophy.

One of these received assumptions is worth closer examination in anticipation of coming developments. In previous semesters, Heidegger, speaking out of both biblical and Greek contexts, had already pointed to the difficulty of life at its best, and how easy it is to go astray. The reason given by the Greeks is the difficulty of achieving the Golden Mean of Virtue, where it is so easy to miss the mark by doing too much or too little. The theme now is the commonly accepted difficulty of philosophy, because it seeks the whole, the most universal, and so is most removed from the immediate experience of the senses. But what precisely is the obstacle to the natural tendency to see more until one sees the most καθ' ὅλου, thus to see by way of being, the authentic seeing or excellence which is philosophy? What leads us astray from this seemingly natural progression? Heidegger suggests that it is curiosity, which satisfies our desire to see more by seeking out novelties and a variety of visual opportunities, that is, hitherto unseen particulars, without breaking out of the absorption with the immediately visible. By contrast, the wise man achieves the whole by restraining the desire to see every particular, recognizing it as an impossible task. With this zest for the particular, curiosity errs by excess without ever reaching for the whole, its error by defect. In this same context, Heidegger becomes more wary of formerly favored methodological terms like intuition, simple apprehension, direct cognizance, and even "devout submission" (*Hingabe*). This is due to his increasing sense of the obstacles and tendencies of "ruination," which in fact led to the distinction hard-easy. Built into factic life itself is a certain pull toward making things easy. In BT (SZ 127–128), this "tendency to take things lightly and make things easy" is located in the phenomenon of the Anyone, which serves to "unburden Dasein of its being."

Life and philosophy are hard not only because of the necessity to overcome the resistance of inertia but also because of the obstacles they encounter on their way to fulfillment. The two are not unrelated. This in fact is the way Aristotle relates the difficulties of life to the need for philosophy. His account is concerned more with the dynamics of the birth of philosophy than with the nature of the difficulties that prompt it. He speaks of the impasses that bring our normal goings-on in the world about us to an abrupt halt in the startling mood of astonishment. For one thing, it is the early Heidegger's first real opportunity to discuss how we "find ourselves" in a situation (*Befindlichkeit*), without however making much yet of the obviously passional movement of "wonder" (cf. SS 1924 below). More to the point for Heidegger at this time are the other kinetic terms in which Aristotle describes the emergence of "authentic understanding" (σοφία). The "impasse" (ἀπορία) and the "halt" in the pressing busyness create the temporal space for leisure (ῥᾳστώνη) and provide the opportunity for pure whiling (διαγωγή: 982b24). This whiling of θεωρεῖν, temporary as it may be, imparts a different tempo to life which proves to be of the very essence of life, life at its fullest. It takes us back to the whys, wherefroms, and wherefores of life as a whole. For διαγωγή in the Greek also refers to the entire course of life, how it is "carried through" to its fullness (voll-zogen), fully actualized, and so "takes (its) place." This is really why the "holdup" is at once the opportunity to discover life as such. Release from the constraining necessities of the environing world offers the freedom of movement toward all things. The whole of life is given free rein and full autonomy—at least for a while—and can now be defined simply in terms of itself. Accordingly, θεωρία, the pure beholding of authentic understanding, is the way-to-be in which life has first and last autonomy and, being master of itself, determines its movement from out of itself in terms of itself. In this original movement, we discover the true sense of life as life, in which the ultimate sense of its movement is fulfilled. All the other modes of getting around thus stand in a relation of particularity to the sense-giving of θεωρία. And if Aristotle calls this original movement divine, he nevertheless finds its rhythm in nature, in the circular movement of the heaven of fixed stars which is the self-contained τέλος "desired" by all the other movements. The self-contained movement of θεωρία is therefore not a δύναμις but ἐνεργεία, pure actualization or "temporalization," the stable self-fulfillment of νόησις νοήσεως which is the fulfillment of all the other modes of getting around that led to it.

Having concluded the Aristotelian account of the genesis and dynamics of philosophical research, Heidegger devotes the remainder of the course to the opening chapters of the *Physics*, the book of nature's movements. The choice is not at all surprising, since the above account had already stressed that all the phenomena of life are modes of movement. Hence beings, the topic of ontology, "temporalize themselves" in our experience as the "with which" of our getting around. It is becoming clear that the basic concepts of Aristotle's ontology likewise have their origin in the same active dealings with the world. Heidegger's translation-paraphrases of the first four chapters of the *Physics* follow through on these assumptions.

Chapter 1 poses the task of determining the ἀρχάι ("whences") by starting from immediate experience. But the following chapters do something entirely different: They seek to get at the same topic by way of a critique of the tradition, in particular the Eleatic thesis that Being is One. Being, however, "is said in many ways" (185a22). The critique thus points to the categorial multiplicity of the structures of Being already operative in the articulation of the Eleatic concept of the One, in refutation of its own thesis. The problem of the Λόγος, especially the "logic" of parts and wholes (Husserl's Fourth Logical Investigation is mentioned here), thus assumes central importance in any kind of ontological problematic. Since λόγος itself is a form of κίνησις, the problem can only be resolved by way of an original determination of the basic phenomenon of movement.

But the critique already brings out the close relationship between the "is" and the "what" which finds its manifestation in the Greek concept of οὐσία, and how this "what" is articulated in relation to the "why" and "whence." Is this an accidental relationship or an equiprimordial one? Aristotle will opt for the latter in his categorial scheme. And this is the task of ontology, to come to a categorial unity of the multiplicity of the structures of being.

After three weeks of paraphrasing these four chapters line by line, with very little additional commentary, Heidegger takes the overview and asks: Where, in the present situation of the prevalence of epistemology, is ontology to find its starting point? How is research into being to be motivated? Where does the fundamental sense of being, which would guide philosophical research, come from? Does it find its motivation in the epistemological problem, in the sphere in which being is apprehended theoretically? Or is there an entirely different sphere of being to be revealed, before and outside of this sphere, which would give us the basic sense of being? With this line of questioning, philosophy finds itself drawn to the analysis of life, human life in its facticity and its historical being. But such an approach must itself come from history, which is the very principle of such research. Philosophical research and its domain are not free-floating phenomena, but themselves stand in history. A true approach is possible only by going back to the decisive approaches of philosophy, to the buried tradition in which we stand.

This principle has in fact guided every step of the exposition and translation of Aristotle. Entry into the understanding of Aristotelian ontology was made by way of the theme "scientific research." Beings here become the with-which of getting around (*das Womit des Umgangs*), yielding possibilities of interpretation which differ from the epistemological approach; for knowing is itself but one way of getting around. That mode of research called critique is also a way of getting around, and it is in this context that the phenomena in which critique as such operates and comes to fulfillment must be developed. Aristotle's critique of the Eleatic tradition in which he stands must now be examined so as to bring out these operative phenomena which lead him to his particular domain of investigation and how it is to be articulated, in short, to his particular *Vorhabe* and *Vorgriff*, prepossession and preconception. This extensive examination will finish out the course. Aristotle's Book of Nature is thus transformed by Heidegger into a study of the concrete movements of History as these operate in philosophical research: how traditions are formed, appropriated, preserved, and lost.

Almost parenthetically in this propaedeutic to his concluding exegesis, Heidegger announces a new direction for his own developing project of an ontology of factic life. Where is its most basic movement, and so its most decisive structure, to be found? The being of facticity finds its basic sense in its "that it is" and not in the what-being made central since Aristotle. This peculiar that-character is most concretely accessible to research in its specific "not," which we call death. The crucial question pertains to how death is found and "lived" (!) in that facticity. Jaspers, with his notion of the limit situation, is the first to have seen this question, without however having a sense of its ontological possibilities.[9]

Because the movement of critique constitutes the initial phase of onto-logical research in the *Physics*, it provides us with the possibility of under-standing the very genesis of Greek ontology. The very necessity of cri-tique already implies that the field of ἀρχαί is not simply given and readily accessible, but must with some effort be brought into the posses-sion of research with a view to its articulation. In the end, one looks to the Λόγος, to the categorial as such as the ultimate goal. One begins with transmitted knowledge in the form of sentences and theorems with the expectation of encountering the object in its fundamental "look." The domain aimed at in the Eleatic thesis is characterized as that which is in movement (τὸ κινούμενον), or that which is in the manner of nature (τὰ φύσει ὄντα). There is a double movement in the critique: 1) The prepossessive movement of getting along seeks to prepare and cultivate the domain to be investigated. 2) the preconceiving movement implicated in the same go-round seeks to relate that domain to categorial structures. The two movements are not to be identified as content and form. United as one formal indication, they are mere pointers toward the direction of research without any foregone conclusions on the degree to which their expectations will be met.

In the Eleatic thesis, the object is addressed as τὰ πάντα, τὸ ὄν, and discussed as ἔν. But do these two as-characters succeed in bringing the whences of the field into demonstrative regard and conceptual specifica-tion, so that an investigation of the field of intuition becomes possible? In this case, what is addressed does not find demonstrative fulfillment in the direction taken by the discussion. The critique must bring out the motivational context underlying the disappointed expectation: despite the oneness of being, in fact on the basis of it, the sense of being in addressing and discussing entities is manifold. The brunt of Aristotle's critique therefore seeks to illustrate such manifold senses in the domains of οὐσία (what), πόσον (how much), and ποῖον (how).

But if we return to the Eleatic thesis, we find that it addresses a more original encounter with the being of the world about us: Whatever is encountered *is*. *Dasein* is *the* basic trait of its look. The overriding experi-ence here, which has a way of obtruding upon what a being is, is *that* it is. It is in this sense that any being in its look of be-ing is simply one. Parmenides' thesis is the expression of an original encounter with being itself. The force, simplicity, directness, and so the underivability of this encounter of an entity from itself and for itself correspond to the latent difficulty of illuminating and exposing such a Being, and so reflects the constant danger of completely missing the possibility of bringing it out into the open. The Eleatic thesis is therefore the historical paradigm for the immediacy of the encounter with Being.

This original source of being at the beginning of our history thus merits closer examination to avoid the dangers that come from restricting ourselves to Aristotle's critique. Heidegger accordingly provides his own translations of selected fragments of Parmenides' poem. In acknowledging the fateful importance of Parmenides' interpretation of ἀλήθεια (here already translated as unconcealment), Heidegger stresses Parmenides' persistence in holding fast to the purity and simplicity of the experience contained in the single Greek word Ἐστί ("It is"), by the sharp repulsion of the obtrusive tendency to address being in terms of δόξα, as coming to be and passing away, having been and will (not) be. For the experience of the One that pervades the All, of the ἕν τὰ πάντα, transpires in the factic environment of the δόξα, thus takes place in this very repulsion. The original encounter with being is thus described as allowing oneself to turn with it (Dabei-bewenden-lassen), abiding or holding up (Aufhalten) with it, which at once entails the holding back of abstaining from δόξα.

But in thus keeping with just Being and looking only at It, something else is brought into the persistent saying of Ἐστί, namely the looking intention, the thought itself (νοεῖν, λέγειν). It is, as it were, "said into" Being. The illuminative access and address belongs to Being itself. Being, as it were, looks back upon the encountering and encounters it so that the regard is there in Being itself. Being is therefore the same as its regard, as sojourn with it, and this sameness is explicitly contained in the illumination of the πίστις ἀληθής (true view).

The πίστις ἀληθής, the sojourn in the sameness of the encountered Being and its illuminative access, can now be regarded as a situation. The facticity of this situation contains a vital movement which might be called the overstepping of bounds, involving the twofold character of 1) concealment and 2) going too far. Both refer to a failure in the kinds of access operative here. 1) The concealment resides in the encounter with being which does not allow it to come to expression out of itself in terms of itself. Bounds are overstepped by the lack of concern for the prepossession, what one has in advance. 2) The going too far lies in addressing the very first regard that is discovered. It becomes for Parmenides the discovered pure and simple. It is a case of an overly powerful urge to know on the basis of an overly narrow truth itself incapable of development, which in its dominance repels all other looks and gives up all other means of freely illuminating and addressing a freely given being. The failure here is a blindness to the *preconceptuality* of the situation.

Thus, the overstepping of bounds in Parmenides' illumination of the world shapes and prefigures the basic sense of Being which, like a fate, overshadows all later ontologies. Parmenides' thesis is the very first address of Being, and yet is itself not an ontology. Inasmuch as Being is, it makes no sense to ask about its whence. The illumination simply addresses the "there" as the entire something-which-is. The "it is there" determines the sense of "it is" and so also the sense of what-being. The that-being is decisive, from which the what-being draws all of its determinations. The concept of οὐσία thus contains the moment of that-being, of being accessible and available.

[It is July 21, 1922. Heidegger at this point is but a hair's breadth from equating οὐσία with "constant presence" . . . but he does not. All the elements necessary for this essentially Parmenidean equation are in place: expulsion of having been and will be from the being which is simply there, available for the looking-right-at it. Constant presence is the toward-which of the direct look. Parmenides' overstepping of bounds is a fate overhanging all later ontologies. And yet, there is still hope for Aristotle, that philosopher of the multifarious saying and revealment of οὐσία. Heidegger's own fateful breakthrough must await a detailed tour of the Aristotelian complex.]

This detour away from Aristotle's critique and into Parmenides' poem thus provides a critical precaution regarding the object and method of Aristotle's ontology and any other ontology that presumes to be even more original. The question of the whence and how of origin cannot be simply attached to any already extant investigation. Instead, the situation of interpretation itself takes its point of departure from the objects themselves. This applies to the development of any hermeneutic situation. This development is not carried out by the old formal considerations. It is the basic task of a phenomenological hermeneutics, the method of philosophical research. The "logic of philosophy," like the Greek logic, must be a productive logic and not a logic *post festum* (the fate of Lask's logic, a "second-story" logic).

Aristotle's ontology treats the problem of being with a view to its λέγειν. His critical decisions relate to the possibility and impossibility of Λόγος as such. Such a consideration would have been impossible for Parmenides, even though he too was concerned with the possibility of determination. But this determination disposed only of *Dasein* as such; insofar as it is and only as such. For Aristotle, however, Λόγος disposes of a manifold of determinations, that it is so *and* so, according to the vital development of modes of interpretation of what is encountered and is. The Λόγος is accordingly not φύσει but has its own origin and movement, that of usage and "custom" (*Brauch*). What then is the relationship of λέγειν and εἶναι? Aristotle's critique of the sentence (i.e., λόγος) ἕν τὰ πάντα provides initial insight into this focal question of the Greeks. Such a λόγος is first ἀπό-φανσις, a saying from out of something, which is why λόγος is itself a fundamental part of ἀρχή-research. But λόγος primarily has something *to* say, it is toward something, the taking-as of something, which motivates a multiplicity in the field of being.

One sees this multiplicity finally in the analysis of τὸ ὅπερ ὄν (*Physics* 1. 3; Aristotle coined the phrase), "just being," the "always-somehow-being-something," in relation to the "central concept" of συμβεβηκός (accident). The course concludes with an in-depth discussion of what Aristotle means by ὄν κατὰ συμβεβηκός, being in the mode of happening-along-with. Heidegger makes much of one example in *Metaphysics* 6.2, 1026b6–10: the true being of a house is to be found in the production which gives it existence and form. The multiplicity of the further hows of the extant house do not belong to its true (produced) being: whether it is comfortable or harmful to some, useful to others, and, at its extreme, different from anything else that is. All of these are "incidental" to the house as produced. The oddity of this narrow conception of the "look" of a house equated to its producedness, including the making of a shape but excluding all other environmental significations such as its inhabitability, stems from Aristotle's theoretical concerns. Indeed, Aristotle goes on to observe that such "accidental" attributes are not only not amenable to theory but also border on nonbeing (b22). The incidental is saved from oblivion only by making it the terminus of λέγειν, by having it "fall to" something, hardly an uncommon way of speaking about being.

The λόγος thus proves to be a more original being than the just-being. Its multiplicity points the way to the multiplicity of equiprimordial whences which prove to be irreducible to simplicity.

OCTOBER 1922: THE *EINLEITUNG* TO A BOOK ON ARISTOTLE

In the midst of this linked pair of courses on "Phenomenological Interpretations to Aristotle," in January of 1922, word came from Marburg that Paul Natorp would be retiring shortly, that Nicolai Hartmann would be taking his place, and that as a result the junior position in philosophy would once again be vacant. Natorp had been impressed by Heidegger's book on Duns Scotus and, on the strength of this one publication, had considered Heidegger for this position in both 1917 and 1920. By 1922, Heidegger was renowned in university circles throughout Germany as an outstanding teacher. But he had published nothing since the Scotus book and, moreover, remarks Husserl in a letter to Natorp on February 1, 1922, "does not want to publish yet," adding that this "highly original personality" is still "struggling, searching for himself and laboriously shaping his own unique style." (We have already noted the "turmoil of transition" evident in WS 1921–22.) But apparently in response not only to Natorp's interest in Heidegger for the chair at Marburg but also to a similar query from Georg Misch regarding Husserl's old chair at Göttingen, plans were soon initiated for Heidegger to publish a work on "Phenomenological Interpretations to Aristotle" in a forthcoming issue of Husserl's *Jahrbuch* (vol. 7, 1924/1925). Even so, when Natorp wrote Husserl again in late September for at least a "publishable manuscript" from Heidegger in support of his candidacy for associate professor (*Extraordinarius*) at Marburg, Heidegger was still struggling with the problem of how to introduce such a work. For the next three weeks, into mid-October, Heidegger labored over the manuscripts of his Aristotle courses in order to extract and distill from them an Introduction serving to found and develop the "hermeneutic situation" in which Aristotle's texts were to be interpreted. To this *Einleitung* (28 pages of typescript), he added an Overview (*Übersicht*: 22 pages) of Part One of the projected book. On the strength of this typescript, essentially a "private communication" addressed to his older peers at the two universities, Heidegger was appointed to the post at Marburg in the following year.[10]

Accordingly, on the one hand, this *Einleitung*, entitled "Indication of the Hermeneutic Situation," was a kind of research report summarizing Heidegger's work of the previous three years.[11] On the other hand, and more important for our Genesis Story, it breaks new ground in a number of directions, first of all in its overall structure. For here we find an initial resolution to the problem of WS 1921–22, that of fusing the "historical" with the "systematic" approach in a phenomenological philosophy in accord with the essential relation between philosophizing and a life which is already historical and so "hermeneutical." The upshot is a concentrated methodological statement of the phenomenological hermeneutics of the research situation outlining for the very first time the double-pronged program familiar to us in BT of 1) a fundamental ontology and 2) a destruction of the history of ontology:

1) For the very first time in Heidegger, concepts like the averageness of the public "one" and falling are juxtaposed with the possibility of a more original seizure of my own death in order to define an ontological way of access to the temporality and so to the historicality of human existence. The specific terminological "firsts" in this text include "interpretedness," "averageness," "publicness," the "Anyone" and the replacement of "ruination" (WS 1921–22) with "falling" at the one pole. To specify the direction of the "countermovement against falling," Heidegger designates the opposite pole as *Existenz*, which marks the very first official entry of this fateful term into the authentic Heideggerian corpus.

But *Existenz* here has the narrower meaning of life's most unique and authentic possibility, just one of the possibilities which can be temporalized within life's facticity, and not the more comprehensive sense that it assumes in BT itself, as the formal indication of Dasein's possibility as such. What is important in this *Einleitung* is the introduction of the polar space (here already called the "not" or "against" of the countermovement) of interrelationships within which the various homologous structures discovered through the analysis of Dasein will find accommodation: the "not" of death, the transcending movement of *Angst* (here still called *Bekümmerung*, "distressed concern," that hybrid between *Angst* and care) and the interruptive call of the phronetic conscience.

2) For the very first time in Heidegger, with Aristotle understood as an original fount of the Western tradition, the problem of an original retrieve of our Greek conceptuality rooted in ἀλήθεια, λόγος, and φύσις (especially its κίνησις) is posed. In the Overview of Part One of the book on Aristotle which accompanied the *Einleitung*, Heidegger summarizes his interpretation not only of the opening chapters and books of the *Metaphysics* (the problem of λόγος, especially that of the genesis of the theoretical) and the *Physics* (the λόγος of φύσις), familiar to us from the previous semester, but also of the Sixth Book of the *Nicomachean Ethics*, regarding the different ways in which "the soul trues," ἡ ψυχὴ ἀληθεύει. Thus, with a certain abruptness and comprehensiveness—it had been mentioned several times in passing first in the previous semester— ἀλήθεια already understood as a process of unconcealing disclosure enters into the Heideggerian thematic. In fact, it enters in such a way that this interpretation of *Nicomachean Ethics* Z, which follows hard upon the *Einleitung*, implicitly guides and influences that Introduction from its opening paragraphs, for example, through φρόνησις understood as interpretative insight into a concrete situation of action, coupled with resolute decision, and truth as a countermovement to concealment. This influence lasts into BT, for the φρόνησις into human action constitutes the exemplary paradigm of its Second Division, just as the other nontheoretical "dianoetic virtue," τέχνη, concerned with making and using, is the basic example of the First.

Just as the extraordinary semester of 1919 is the zero-point of Heidegger's entire career of thought, in like fashion, this version of the *Einleitung* is the zero-point of the specific project of BT. Here, we behold with fascination, in a kind of gestalt switch, the very birth of that book, after almost four years of gestation from early 1919, against the background of its double program of a new ontology (the systematic "position of sight") and destruction of the old (the historically directed "line of sight"). Of course, Heidegger himself was then not yet aware of the fact that, in introducing a book on Aristotle, which he never really managed to write, he was laying the ground for another book which would precipitate him to world fame, and then shame. But as early as February 20, 1923, Heidegger reports to Löwith that he is expanding his Introduction to include basic elements of his earlier interpretations of the facticity of life (his "position of sight") to the extent that these are related to the interpretations of Aristotle that are to follow. And when the very first draft of BT does take shape, it is still regarded as an outgrowth of the Aristotle-Introduction, thus as a preliminary work designed to serve as a ground for the destruction of Greek ontology and logic.[12]

The importance of this seminal text thus cannot be overestimated. While this version of the *Einleitung* is a vast improvement over the first version, the course of 1921–22, many of the topics are the same as those outlined in the Table of Contents of that course: what is philosophy?; appropriation of the hermeneutic situation; the basic categories of life; ruination (now called "falling"). But the style is almost as dense and turgid, compounded by the terseness demanded by an Introduction. By now, however, we know what any of Heidegger's "Intro-ductions" is supposed to do, spelled out by the title of this one, "Indication of the Hermeneutical Situation." Like "interpretations to . . . ," it is synonymous with the incipient on-set of the what and how of the investigation which is the function of the "formal indication," even though this hitherto frequently used methodological term appears nowhere in that Introduction and ebbs in usage in coming semesters. Likewise, the triple-sensed formal indication of intentionality now abruptly disappears, even though the verbally "unsensed" terms—relation, actualization, temporalization (content less so)—continue to schematize intentionality in this Intro-duction.

What follows is a streamlined outline and summary of this most cele-brated *Einleitung*, which seek to provide a seamless sequence outlining the major ideas of this opaque but all-important ground-laying text in an idiomatic paraphrase, without its cumbersome formulations and ex-cessive detail, in the order they were meant to hang together. This will be followed by a summary of the attached interpretation of *Nicomachean Ethics* Z, whose implications not only take us into the hidden background of BT but also point beyond toward the "turn" and the later Heidegger's excessive preoccupation with the problem of "truth." But more impor-tant for what follows, especially this gloss of Aristotle already permeates the preceding "indication of the hermeneutic situation" from its opening page: the talk of resolutely "unlocking" and securing the sense of that situation in advance of specific interpretations is thoroughly steeped in the Greek idiom of phronetic disclosure of a situation focused on the "living present" in all its kairological opportunity, which we overtly hear about only in the later pages on Aristotle's senses of truth. But one is forced to write and read linearly . . . and in brief. Other Greek elements likewise permeate the *Einleitung* from its beginning. By later standards, for example, Heidegger is, like the Greeks, excessively and almost obsessively visual in his opening metaphors: the position and line of sight (*Blickstand und Blickrichtung*, in later drafts *Blickhabe und Blickbahn*) of the hermeneutic situation, and the resulting breadth of vision; insight by way of circumspection and inspection (*Umsehen und Hinsehen*) into how a thing looks (*Aussehen*), to the point of finding that the experience of "*having* death" imparts a "peculiar kind of sight" to life!

In its sheer innovative thrust, the typescript of October 1922, like no other of this period, deserves to be called Heidegger's breakthrough to his magnum opus. Is this the aletheic breakthrough that the old Heidegger has us looking for? It is certainly not the ousiological breakthrough, since οὐσία as constant presence still does not put in an appearance. Regardless, the sheer concentration of new insights dictates that we tarry a while over this seminal text.[13]

Phenomenological Interpretations to Aristotle:
Indication of the Hermeneutic Situation

The following interpretations contribute to a history of ontology and logic [that is, of a doctrine of being and of the ways in which being is said and spoken]. Interpretations are subject to certain conditions of understanding. In order to come to a suitable interpretation, in order to have the thematic object speak for itself, the hermeneutic situation relative to that interpretation must be secured in a sufficiently transparent outline. That situation of interpretation includes a certain [1] position of sight and [2] directive line of sight, along with the [3] range of vision resulting from them.

Interpretation is always situated in a "living present" [Husserl, Bergson, James]. History itself, the past appropriated in understanding, is apprehended in direct proportion to the originality of the decisive choice and development of the particular hermeneutic situation. The past opens up only in direct relation to the measure of resoluteness (*Entschlossenheit!*) and disclosive capacity that a present can muster. The originality of a philosophical interpretation is determined by the specific sureness in which philosophical research maintains itself and its tasks. The way philosophy defines itself, in its research of its concrete problematic, in turn already decides its basic attitude toward the history of philosophy. The actual field of objects to be placed under question is determined by the direction or *line of sight* into which the past can be set. Such "interpreting into" an object not only is not contrary to historical knowing but in fact is the basic condition needed to bring the past to speak at all. Interpretations which maintain that they operate without the "constructions" of a history of problems, and so interject nothing into the text, allow themselves to be caught in the act of interpreting into the text without orientation and with conceptual means from the most disparate and uncontrollable sources. The lack of concern for what one "really does" and the accompanying ignorance of the means being applied is lauded as a bracketing of all subjectivity. The insensitivity and carelessness toward one's own hermeneutic situation, when it is taken up in this often confused and casual manner, is interpreted as an attitude free of all bias.[14]

The clarification of the hermeneutic situation for the following interpretations and so the demarcation of its thematic field grow out of the following basic conviction: Philosophical research is of its nature something which a "time" can never borrow from another; nor will it be able to claim to lift the burden and distress of radical questioning from future generations. The possibility of influencing its future can never be located in the results of a past philosophical inquiry, but instead in the originality of the questions which a time attains and concretely develops. As a paradigm for eliciting problems, philosophical research, through the [revolutionary power of] renewal implicit in that interrogative radicality, has the capacity to become the living present [καιρός] ever anew.

This powerful opening statement of the living present's relation to its past, where the philosopher's relation to the history of philosophy is not just a matter of making history but of being history, will persist throughout the text.

[1. Position of sight: what is philosophy? (p. 3)] The "object" of philosophical research is factic life or human Dasein questioned in its being. This basic line of philosophical questioning is not to be understood as something added and attached to its object externally, but as the explicit apprehension of a basic movement of questioning within factic life itself. For factic life is such that it, *in* the concrete temporalizing of its being, is concerned *about* its being, even when it goes out of its way and evades this issue.[15] Factic life has the character of being weighed down by itself, to the point of being difficult to bear. The unmistakable sign of this is the tendency of factic life to "make things easy" for itself. But in fact, in the basic sense of its being, life *is* hard. If it truly is what it is in being heavy and hard, then the genuine and adequate approach to life, the way to preserve it in the truth of its being, can only consist in making it difficult. All the attempts to make things easy, all the seductive sedation of life's demands, all the relief provided by metaphysics of those needs which themselves were acquired for the most part only through reading, simply fail to bring the object of philosophy into our line of sight and keep it there.

Philosophy makes its own history a relevant object in the present not in order to add to its knowledge, but by an intensification of its questionability. This distressed appropriation of history calls for the radical understanding of what placed a past philosophical inquiry in *its* situation and *for* this situation in its basic distress, where understanding is not just acknowledgment but also the *original repetition* of what is thus understood for one's own situation. Factic Dasein is what it is always only as fully its own and not as a Dasein in general of some sort of universal humanity. Critique of history is always but a *critique of the present* [cf. SZ 397], and not a matter of imagining what might have been, if . . . The critique must instead keep the present in its line of sight, with a view to the originality attainable by it. History is not denied because it is "false," but because it is still operative in the present without actually being able to be it. [From Heidegger's marginal note: The past is encountered in existence not as something to be viewed but to be borne. . . . It is not a matter of "doing" history but of "being" it.]

This specification of the basic historical attitude toward interpretation grows out of the foregoing exposition of the sense of philosophical research. Its object was defined *indicatively* as the factic human Dasein as such. The concrete specification of the philosophical problematic is to be ascertained in terms of factic Dasein not only because it is the object, but also because philosophical research itself is a particular "how" of factic life. In its very actualization and not just in its supplementary "application," therefore, philosophical research co-temporalizes, brings to fruition, the concretely particular and temporal being of life in itself. The very possibility of such a co-temporalizing is based in the fact that philosophical research is the explicit actualization of a basic movement of factic life and so receives its constant sustenance within that movement.

[1a. Constitutive elements of life's facticity (p. 5)] But in this "indication of the hermeneutic situation"[16] we do not want to work out the basic structure of facticity in its entirety but simply, by way of an enumeration, to bring its most important constitutive elements into our prepossession.

The confusing plurivocity of the word "life" cannot be the occasion for replacing the word. One thus forgoes the possibility of pursuing the directions of meaning which inhere in it, which would enable us to get at what its object means in its multifaceted particularity. The term ζωή, *vita*, signifies a basic phenomenon constituting the center of the Greek, Old-Testament, New-Testament Christian and Greek-Christian interpretations of human Dasein. The plurivocity of the term has its roots in the signified object itself. Philosophy can either put this uncertainty of meaning aside or, if it is to be a necessary uncertainty grounded in its object, make it into an explicitly appropriated and transparent uncertainty. Such an attitude to plurivocity (Aristotle's πολλαχῶς λεγόμενον, "it is said in many ways") is not just a matter of poking around isolated word meanings, but the expression of a radical tendency to make the signified objectivity accessible together with the motive source of the different ways of signifying it.

The basic sense of the factic movement of life is caring (curare),[17] being out toward something (Aussein auf etwas: first use of this crucial vector), and that "something" is the temporally particular world. The dynamics of caring has the character of getting along and coping with (Umgang) its world. The toward-which (das Worauf) of care is the with-which of getting along. The reality and existence of the world receives its sense and definition from its character as the with-which of caring and coping, getting around. The world is there as always already some-how taken into custody. In terms of the possible directions of care, the world is articulated into an around-world, a with-world and a self-world. Care is correspondingly the concerns of livelihood, profession, enjoy-ment, not being disturbed, not being killed, being familiar with, knowing about, being cognizant of, securing life in its ultimate aims.

The movement of concern thus manifests many ways of actualization and of relatedness to the with-which of getting around: tinkering with, providing for, production of, safeguarding by, putting to use of, employ-ing for, thus ranging from holding in troth to neglect, allowing some-thing to get lost. What is dealt with in each case always stands in a certain habituality and familiarity. In going about its business, caring always has its with-which in a certain sight. Helping to temporalize and guide the getting around is a looking around, a circumspection. In fact, care as circumspect looks not only to secure but to increase its familiarity with the object of its coping. In circumspection, what is dealt with is in advance apprehended as . . ., oriented toward . . ., interpreted as . . . ["herme-neutic as" in WS 1925–26]. The object is there as meaning such and such, the world is encountered in the character of meaningfulness. Concerned coping has not only the possibility but also, on the basis of an original tendency of factic life, the inclination to forgo the concern to get things done. Obstruction of the tendency of concerned coping results in merely looking around without looking to performance and accomplishment. Looking around assumes the character of merely looking at, circumspec-tion (Umsicht) becomes inspection (Hinsicht).

In just looking at something, in curiosity, the world is there not as the with-which of the coping which gets things done, but rather in the regard which only regards how it looks (Aussehen, p. 7). Inspection is actualized as a regard which defines and outlines looks, which can accordingly be organized into a science. Science is thus a way of coping with the world by just looking at it, a way temporalized from factic life and for it. The content of such inspection then coalesces with circumspection. Circum-spection is now actualized by speaking-to and -about the objects of coping. The world is encountered [and so "had"] by being addressed (*ange-sprochen*), making claims about it and so staking claim (*Anspruch*) to it.

By halting its proclivity to get things done, coping takes pause. Inspection itself becomes an independent way of getting around, by staying with and holding to the object while holding back from doing. By such tarrying, by way of a particularly directed and step-by-step theoretization, there arises, out of our factic encounter with the world (the meaningful), "the objective" understood as mere things.

Factic life always operates in a specific *interpretedness* which has been transmitted to it in reworked or newly worked form. Circumspection lays out a world interpreted in regards, in regard to which the world as object of preoccupation is encountered and expected, posed in tasks and sought as a refuge. These by and large implicit regards, into which factic life lapses out of habit more than making them its own by design, already designate the paths of actualization to be taken by the movement of caring. The way the world has already been interpreted is factically the interpretation in which life stands. It provides tacit directions on how life takes itself into custody, a certain sense of life, the "as what" [hermeneutic "as"] and "how" in which humans maintain themselves in their own prepossession, in what they already have.

The movement of caring is not an independent process taking its course over against an existing world. The world is there in and for life, though not in the sense of a bare intention and observation. This latter mode of existence of the world temporalizes only when the movement of concerned coping takes pause. It is what it is only in and out of this pause-taking, which itself is in and for that movement of concern (*Besorgen*). This mode of existence of the world, taken as "reality" or even in the objectivity of a nature impoverished of human significance, by and large becomes the point of departure for the epistemological and ontological problematic.

For its part, concern is not merely an indifferent actualization and straightforward fulfillment of an original intentionality toward its world. Alive in its movement is also a propensity (*Hang*) to become totally absorbed in its world. This proneness is the expression of a basic tendency of life to turn away from itself and gravitate toward the world, an inclination of decadence or "fallenness" (*Verfallen*). This propensity is the innermost "pendency" [*Verhängnis*: an im-pending condition, "hanging" like a menacing doom; but also the tendency to become addicted or "hung up"] by which life is factically weighted. Weighing down is the way in which pendency "is." It is not an objective event which "happens" to occur in life, but must be understood as an intentional "how" and approached as a constitutive element of facticity, a basic character of the movement of caring.

The pendency of falling expresses itself in the three dynamical characters of temptation, tranquilization, and self-alienation [SZ 177f.].[18] It is a temptation for life to draw from the world the possibilities which allow it to take things easy, thereby rendering it prone to miss itself. As tempting, it is at once tranquilizing by holding factic life in the locations (*Lagen*) of its fallenness, so that life considers these locations as its quasi-situation. (A location is not the situation of factic life, which is found by deliberately taking one's unique place in life in a movement which counters falling, and chooses one's particular distress by rendering itself transparent to its taking-place.) As tranquilizing, the tendency to fall which cultivates temptation is at once alienating. In its absorption in the world of concern, factic life becomes more and more strange to itself and more and more removed from the possibility of taking itself in its distressed concern (*Bekümmerung*)[19] as a goal of appropriative return. These three characters of falling apply not only to manipulative coping but also to circumspection and its possible autonomy, to inspection and to the cognitive determinings of address and interpretation. Factic life also speaks the language of the world whenever it speaks with itself.

[Now, in a remarkably terse and concentrated burst of novelty, Heidegger suddenly introduces a series of new terms and organizes them in such a way that, for the very first time, we have before us the nuclear structure of the book BT, or more precisely, of the *Daseinsanalytik* which is to serve as a fundamental ontology. But here, it is understood as an ontology of facticity and not of existence: pp. 11–16 of the typescript.]

As a result of falling, factic life, which in fact is in each case the life of an individual, is for the most part not lived as such, but instead in a certain *averageness* of the *public*. It is *the "one"* who in fact lives the life of the individual, who in the end is "no one." In the world in which it is absorbed, in the averageness in which it makes its rounds, life conceals itself from itself. The tendency of falling is the way life evades itself. The most incisive demonstration of this movement is given in the way life stands to death.

Death is something which lies in store for life and awaits it, before which it stands as before something inevitable and impending. Life is such that its death is always somehow there for it, as a prospect, standing in sight of it, even if this be such that the "thought of it" is denied and repressed. Death gives itself as the object of care precisely in the persistence of its prospect, and is thus encountered as a how of life. The forced lack of concern of life for its death takes place in the flight into worldly concerns. But avoiding the sight of death is hardly a seizing of life in itself [as it is sometimes thought: *carpe diem*], but rather life's evasion of itself in its true character of being. One stands before death in the flight of concern as well as in the voluntary seizure of its distress. This double

standing is constitutive of the character of being of facticity. In the deliberate seizure of my certain death, life in itself becomes visible. "Having"
death thus provides a peculiar sight to life which constantly puts it before
its ownmost present and past, relentlessly growing within and behind
life.

This purely constitutive ontological problematic of death has nothing
to do with a metaphysics of immortality and the "what then?" The impending prospect of death standing before me has its own way of making
life's present and past visible. It is a constitutive element of facticity, and
so is likewise the phenomenon out of which the specific temporality of
human Dasein is to be explicated. It is from *this sense of temporality*[20] that
the basic sense of the *historical* is to be defined, never by a formal analysis
of the kind of concept formation involved in writing about history.

The being of life is thus accessible only by way of the detour of a
countermovement against falling. "Becoming absorbed in," like every
movement of factic temporality, has within itself a more or less explicit
and avowed look back toward that from which it flees. That from which
it flees is however life itself, as the factic possibility which is to be explicitly
chosen, as the object of distressed concern. The countermovement, as
distress over the prospect of misspending life, is the way in which the
authentic being of life, as a possible choice, temporalizes itself. This being
of life, which is accessible in life and for life, may be designated as *existence*. The individually possible existence of factic life, as something that
can be missed or misspent, is in principle a worthy topic for life's questions. *Existence* is always the possibility of a concrete facticity, it is *one
way of temporalizing* this facticity, that is, of bringing it to fruition in its
temporality. What existence shows can never be inquired into directly
and in general. It becomes evident in itself only in the actual enactment
of making facticity questionable, in the concrete *destruction* of facticity
in its temporally particular movements and motives, propensities and
tendencies, and what it makes overtly available [that is, in the way it has
already been interpreted].

The countermovement to falling cannot be interpreted as flight from
the world. Flight involves not intending life in its *existentiell* character or
choosing it in its inherent questionability, but instead re-imagining it into
a new and tranquilizing world. Distress over existence does not change
the factic situation of the temporally particular life. What changes is the
how of life's movement, which as such can never be a public affair of
just "anyone." The concern over getting by is one of distress over the
self, over its existence. It is not a self-brooding in egocentric reflection.
It is what it is only as a countermovement to the tendency to lapse in
life, and so is itself a movement of the individually concrete concern
over getting by. The "not" of this "against" thus manifests an original

accomplishment constitutive of being. In this constitutive sense, negation has primacy over position precisely because the human being is in fact defined by a falling, a worldly propensity. The sense of this primal fact and its factuality as such can be interpreted, if at all, only as a chosen facticity and relative to this. The actualization of the insight of addressing life with regard to its existentiell possibility has the character of a distressed interpretation of life in its sense of being. Facticity and existence are not the same, the factic character of the being of life is not defined by existence, which is but one possibility temporalizing itself *in the* being of life called factic. But this means that the potentially radical problematic of the being of life is centered in facticity.

[1b. Facticity of philosophy (p. 15)] Accordingly, philosophy is not a pure invention, a casual trafficking in some generalities and arbitrarily posited principles. It is itself radical interrogation and research. As such, it is 1) the explicit actualization of the interpretative tendency already operative in the basic movements of the life which "goes about its self and its being." Philosophy must 2) seek to bring factic life in its decisive possibilities into our sight and grasp in clear and radical fashion, without tangential concerns for worldviews; in short, philosophy must be *fundamentally atheistic*. It will then have decisively chosen, having made factic life in its facticity its object. Its investigative "how" is the interpretation of life's sense of being in terms of its fundamental categorial structures, that is, the ways in which factic life temporalizes itself and so speaks with itself (κατηγορεῖν [as ἀληθεύειν]). Philosophy does not need to don a worldview or other such superficial concerns for relevance in the present, if it has understood that its chosen object has entrusted it with the *original ontological conditions of possibility* of any worldview, as something to be interrogated and made manifest only in strict research. These conditions, understood categorially, are not "logical forms" but rather the genuinely accessible possibilities drawn from the actual temporalization of existence.

Inasmuch as philosophy is concerned with the very being of factic life, it is *fundamental ontology*. It is from this *ontology of facticity* that the worldlike regional ontologies receive the ground and meaning of their problems. In its concern for categorial interpretation, that is, for the ways in which the being of life is addressed and articulated, philosophy is *logic*. Ontology and logic are to be taken back to their original unity in facticity and understood as outcomes of fundamental research. We call it *phenomenological hermeneutics of facticity*. Such research has the task of taking the concrete interpretations already operative in factic life in their temporalized unity, from the circumspective insight of caring to the more extreme insight of distressed concern, and making them categorially transparent in their prepossession (What is the basic sense of being in which life places itself?) and in their preconception (In what ways of address and articulation does life speak to itself?).

This hermeneutics is phenomenological. This means that the field of its objects, factic life in the how of its being and speaking, is in its theme and research method regarded as a *phenomenon*. Its structure is to be characterized in its *full* intentionality (relatedness to, that to which it is related, the actualization of self-relating, the temporalization of the actualization, holding the temporalization in troth). Intentionality, regarded simply as relatedness to, is the most immediately distinguishable phenomenal character in the basic movement of life, namely, that of caring. Phenomenology is what it already was in the initial breakthrough made by Husserl's *Logical Investigations*, namely, radical philosophical research. It is not just a propaedeutic science serving merely to provide descriptive clarification of the concepts of philosophy . . . as if this could be done without a central and fundamental orientation, time and again renewed and reappropriated, to the very object of philosophy.

[2. The historically directed line of sight (p. 18)] Recapitulating our opening words, we have now indicated the *position of sight* that the following interpretations take as phenomenological interpretations and as investigations in the history of ontology and logic. The very idea of a phenomenological hermeneutics of facticity includes the tasks of formal and material logic and a theory of their objects, a theory of science, the "logic of philosophy," the "logic of the heart," the "logic of fate," and a logic of "pretheoretical and practical" thinking [in short, any and every form of "categorizing"]. But it is not yet clear what historical investigations belong to such a hermeneutics, why Aristotle is the focus of that investigation, and how it is to be carried out. The motivations involved in certain *lines of sight* come from the concrete conception of the position of sight. The very idea of facticity implies that only one's own facticity—the facticity of one's own time and generation—is [in a "critique of the living present"] the *authentic* and proper object of research. Owing to fallenness, however, factic life lives for the most part in the inauthentic, in what is transmitted to it and appropriated in an average sort of way. Even what is originally cultivated as an authentic possession soon lapses into the averageness of publicity, loses touch with its provenance from its original situation and so comes down to us uprooted, couched in the customary forms of the "one." The inclination of falling affects factic life in all its forms of getting around and looking around, including its interpretative actualization fulfilled in prepossession and preconception. Since philosophy itself is but the explicit interpretation of factic life, its way of questioning and finding answers is likewise affected by this movement of facticity. The phenomenological hermeneutics of facticity also begins in a factic situation in which factic life has already been interpreted for it, assumed in an undiscussed "self-evident" matter "of course" which, without explicit appropriation from its origins, is a mighty force inauthentically influencing the posing of problems and the direction of questioning.

The way in which factic life addresses and interprets itself lets its ways of seeing and speaking be given by worldly objects. Thus, human life, Dasein, is "already had" in a prepossession as something occurring in the world, as "nature," in analogous categories such as soul and spirit. Even when objects can no longer be regarded as "substances" in the crude sense—from which Aristotle was further removed than is commonly thought—the interpretation still operates with fundamental concepts and ways of questioning and explaining which spring from experiences to which we today no longer have access. In short, philosophy today for the most part operates inauthentically in its Greek conceptuality, which itself is pervaded by a historical chain of variegated interpretations. But with all its analogues and formalizations, it nevertheless retains within itself a portion of the genuine tradition transmitting its original sense. Philosophy today operates with an ideal of man, his life-ideals and his senses of being, which flow from basic experiences that have been brought to fruition by Greek ethics and especially by the Christian conception of the human being. Even anti-Greek and anti-Christian tendencies are sustained fundamentally in the same *lines of sight* and ways of interpretation.

Phenomenological hermeneutics of facticity must therefore loosen the hold of the dominant typical interpretation, uncover its hidden motives and unexpressed tendencies, and, by way of a deconstructive regress, find its way back to the original motivating sources of explication. Hermeneutics realizes its task only by way of a *destruction*. Once it has understood the kind of being and object which is implied in its fundamental theme, the facticity of life, philosophical research becomes "historical" knowledge of a radical kind. Its destructive confrontation with its history is not a secondary afterthought for the sake of illustrating how things once were, curiosity over what others have done, projecting entertaining world-historical perspectives. The destruction is rather the way in which the present in its basic movements has to be confronted. The ensuing *critique of the present* [SZ 397] bears not upon the fact *that* we stand in the tradition, but upon the *how*. To what extent is the present troubled by appropriations of its history? Whatever is not primordially interpreted and so expressed is not truly preserved. Neglecting the primordiality of interpretation is at once the renunciation of the possibility to assume custody of oneself in one's roots, in short, the possibility to *be*.

[2a. Theological anthropology (p. 21)] The complex of crucial forces of influence constituting the present situation can, with an eye to the problem of its facticity, in brief be designated as the Greek-Christian interpretation of life. This also covers the relatively anti-Greek and anti-Christian tendencies. The idea of man and of human existence in such an interpretation defines the philosophical anthropology of Kant and of German idealism. Fichte, Schelling, and Hegel come from the theology of the Reformation and derive the driving force of their speculation from it. But this theology succeeded only in small measure in coming to a genuine explication of the new religious attitude of Luther and its immanent possibilities. Luther's attitude in turn comes from his original *appropriation of Paul and Augustine* [WS 1920–21, SS 1921] coupled with his concurrent argument with the late scholastic theology of Duns Scotus, Occam, Gabriel Biel, and Gregory of Rimini. Late scholasticism elaborated theological doctrines like God, Trinity, original sin, and grace with the conceptual tools provided by Aquinas and Bonaventure, which in turn derived from the idea of man and human existence developed through the selective use of Aristotelian physics, psychology, ethics, and ontology. *Augustine and Neoplatonism* [SS 1921] were also crucially influential.

These general connections drawn from the history of the literature are fairly well known. But a real interpretation of them, founded and focused in the basic philosophical problematic of facticity, is completely lacking. The Middle Ages are explored according to the leading insights involved in the schematism of a neoscholastic theology and a neoscholastically developed Aristotelianism. To begin with, the scientific structure of medieval theology, along with its style of exegesis and commentary, must be understood as mediated interpretations of life. Theological anthropology must be traced back to its basic philosophical experiences and motives. In relation to these, we may then come to understand the influence and kind of transformation stemming from the religious and dogmatic attitude of the time.

The hymnology and music of the Middle Ages, its architecture and plastic arts, in short, what "gothic" implies, are historically accessible only on the basis of an original phenomenological interpretation of the philosophic-theological anthropology of this time, which was imparted in that world through the sermon and the school. As long as this anthropology is not overtly disclosed, "gothic man" will remain a cliché. The hermeneutic structure of the tradition of commentary on the Sentences of Peter Lombard, which sustained the development of theology until Luther's time, as such lacks even the possibility of being questioned and developed. Already what the Sentences themselves chose from Augustine, Jerome, John Damascene, and others, their very variety, is of significance for medieval anthropology. In order to obtain a measure for this transformation, an interpretation of Augustinian anthropology must be provided which does not merely excerpt his works for sentences on psychology in accord with a textbook of psychology or moral theology. The focus for an interpretation of Augustine in terms of the basic ontological and logical structure of his life's teaching is to be drawn from his writings against Pelagianism and his teachings on the Church.[21] The idea of man and of human existence operative here points to Greek philosophy and the patristic theology founded upon it, as well as to the anthropology of Paul and of John's Gospel.

[2b. The destructive line of sight (p. 23)] In the context of the phenomenological destruction, the important thing is not simply to depict the various currents and influences, but to bring out the central ontological and logical structures at the decisive turning points in the history of occidental anthropology, by leading them back to their original sources. This task can only be realized by providing a concrete interpretation of *Aristotelian philosophy aimed at the problem of facticity*, thus moving toward a *radical phenomenological anthropology*.

In the light of our problem of facticity, Aristotle is but the completion, the concrete outcome of previous philosophy. At the same time, in his *Physics*, Aristotle comes to a fundamentally new approach, out of which his ontology and logic grow, which in turn pervade the history of philosophical anthropology, which we have just sketched in reverse. The central phenomenon, the explication of which constitutes the theme of the *Physics*, thus becomes the entity in the how of its being-moved.

The literary form in which Aristotelian research is transmitted (expository and investigative treatises on specific themes) offers the single appropriate basis for the methodological aims of the following interpretations. Going back to Aristotle allows us to define Parmenides' doctrine of being and understand it as the crucial step which decided the fate and direction of occidental ontology and logic [cf. SS 1922].

To complete this task of phenomenological destruction, these investigations will focus on late scholasticism and the theological period of the young Luther [allusion to the journal article promised to Rothacker]. Even so, this framework includes tasks whose difficulty is not easy to overestimate. Thus, out of our position of sight (exposition of the problematic of facticity), we have determined our basic bearing toward history and our line of sight aimed at Aristotle.

[3. The range of vision (p. 24)] By way of the position and line of sight, every interpretation must overilluminate its thematic object. It can be adequately defined only when we come to see it too sharply, not arbitrarily but out of the accessible definitional content of its how. By dampening the excessive illumination, we may then restore the proper outlines of the object. An object always seen only in twilight can be apprehended in *its* semidark givenness only by a passage through excessive illumination. As overly lit, however, the interpretation must not go too far in its questioning and claim for itself a phantasmal objectivity in the spirit of historical knowledge in general, and presume that it is dealing with an "in itself." To question "in general" about it means to mistake the character of the object of the *historical*. To end up in relativism or skeptical historicism, upon not finding such an in-itself, is only the reverse side of the same mistake. My translation of the interpreted texts and above all the translation of the basic ontological concepts have grown out of the concrete interpretation and contain it, as it were, *in nuce*. The coinages arise not from a desire for novelty, but from the subject matter contained in the texts.

[3a. Outline of Part I (p. 25)] Our approach to interpreting Aristotle which is determined by our position of sight must now be made comprehensible and the first part of the investigation selectively outlined.

The guiding question of the interpretation must be: In terms of what sort of object, what character of being, is being-human—"being in life"—experienced and interpreted? What is the sense of Dasein in which the "object," the live human being, is set and interpreted? In what prepossession of being does this kind of object stand? How is this being of man conceptually explicated, what is the phenomenal basis of the explication and what categories of being emerge as explicata of what is thus seen?

Is the sense of being which ultimately characterizes the being of human life genuinely drawn from a pure basic experience of precisely this object and its sense of being? Or is human life taken as an entity within a more encompassing field of being, or made subject to a sense of being which is regarded as archontic for it? What exactly is being for Aristotle, how is it accessible, apprehensible, definable?

The field of objects which yields the original sense of being is that of the *produced* object accessible in the course of usage. Accordingly, it is not the field of things in their theoretical reification but rather the world encountered in going about our producing, making, and using which is the basis, the according-to-which and toward-which of the original experience of being. In the movement of getting about and producing (ποίησις), the finished product, having arrived at the status of being on hand (*Vorhandensein*) and so available for usage, is the measure of what *is*. Being means *being produced*, and as produced, being accessible for use and disposable, meaningful in regard to one particular way of getting around. To the extent that it becomes the object of circumspection or even of the autonomous apprehension that looks directly at it, the entity is considered in terms of its *look* (εἶδος). Direct apprehension articulates itself in addressing and discussing (λέγειν). The object, what is addressed (λόγος), and its look (εἶδος) are in a way the same. But this implies that what is addressed in the λόγος as such is the actual entity. In its object of address, the λέγειν brings the entity in its look-like being (οὐσία) into our preserve, in "troth" (trust, truth). But οὐσία has the original meaning, still operative in Aristotle as well as later, of house-and-hold, stable possessions available for use in our environ. It means *property* and *possessions*. What comes into our purview and "troth" as the being of the entities of our go-round, what we regard as our *belongings*, is their having-been-produced. In the production, the object arrives at its look or "form." The field of being of the objects with which we get about (ποιούμενον, πρᾶγμα, ἔργον κινήσεως) and how they are addressed, a very particular type of λόγος, specifies the prepossession from which the ways of defining and addressing the object "human life" are drawn.

How do these ontological structures originate and develop? By way of a form of research based on a fundamental experience of objects in their motion. The actual source motivating Aristotelian ontology in regard to its choice of objects is therefore to be found in Aristotle's *Physics*. But a phenomenological interpretation also dictates a consideration of how Aristotle researched his objects as well as what he meant by research to begin with. Research is a non-circumspective form of getting around the world; it inspects, looks directly at its objects; it is an ἐπιστήμη. It arises out of the prior circumspective go-around by way of the questions of "in what way?" (αἴτιον) and "whence?" (ἀρχή). Insight into the genesis of inquiry is to be found in the opening chapters of *Metaphysics* A.

But the understanding that inspects and defines (ἐπιστήμη) is but one way in which entities come into purview and are taken in "troth," especially those entities which necessarily and for the most part *are what they are*. But one way of getting about with those entities which *can also be other than they are* is through producing, treating, handling them. This form of holding being in troth (*Seinsverwahrung*) is τέχνη. In accord with these two distinct regions of being, Aristotle interpreted the different ways of illuminating (circumspection, phronetic insight, inspection) our coping with things as different ways of realizing the pure intuition which gives sight to all and so allows us to appropriate being and hold it in troth. By way of the interpretation of *Nic. Ethics* Z, we shall obtain a phenomenal horizon in which research and theoretical cognition may be situated as ways "in which the soul 'trues,' " οἷς ἀληθεύει ἡ ψυχή (1139b15). Part I of our investigations thus comprises the interpretation of *Nic. Ethics* Z, *Metaphysics* A 1–2 and *Physics* A, B, Γ 1–3.

Nicomachean Ethics Z [pp. 29–39]

Provisionally disregarding the specifically ethical context, the interpretation of this treatise will elucidate the "dianoetic virtues" as different ways in which being is brought and held in troth [in the double sense of "trust" and "truth"]. The two authentic ways in which νοῦς, pure beholding (*Vernehmen*) as such, are fulfilled are σοφία (authentic inspective understanding) and φρόνησις (*fürsorgende Umsicht*, "solicitous circumspection," implying a "concern for" the well-being of others as well as my own). These two phenomenal modes therefore provide access to the entities each holds in troth in direct beholding; they thus yield the possibility of defining and delimiting these entities with respect to their genuine character of being. There is therefore a direct connection between this interpretation of the "virtues" and our ontological problematic. The structural difference between these two modes of beholding at once brings out the difference between their respective regions of being.

In addition to these three "virtues," chapter 3 of book 6 lists two remaining ways in which the human soul takes entities as unveiled or unconcealed in troth: τέχνη, productive working procedure, and ἐπιστήμη, inspectional demonstrative determination. To understand each of these concrete ways of fulfilling the most basic vital activity of pure beholding, the correct interpretation of ἀληθές-ἀλήθεια is of fundamental significance. Contrary to the current epistemological interpretation, there is no trace in Aristotle of a "correspondence" theory of truth which finds its seat in the "validating" judgment, and least of all a "copy theory" of knowledge. The true as the unconcealed and intended in itself is by no means explicatively drawn from the judgment and thus also not originally located there. ᾿Αληθεύειν does not mean "seizing possession of the truth" but [a more careful having], taking the intended entity as unveiled in troth and on trust.

Αἴσθησις, beholding in the sensory mode, is not merely by extension from the λόγος also called "true." Rather, in its very intentional character, it gives its intentional toward-which "originarily" in itself. In view of this directness, the word "false" never applies to it, but rather only when there is a "synthesis" (*De Anima* Γ 3 and 6). Falsity presupposes the intentional structure of taking together or with, taking "as," in which the object can give itself out as something which it is not. Thus ἀπόφανσις, even though it draws from (ἀπό) the object under discussion, addresses and discusses it as something, and so must risk the detour of falsity in its passage to truth. [In SS 1922, in the context of Aristotle's need to say being "in many ways" against the Parmenidean ONE, Heidegger notes that the "from" is one but the "toward," the apophantic taking-as of the original something, is many, and it is the passage through this field of multiplicity and dispersion that is the source of ψεῦδος.] The "as" structures of truth must be wrested from the hiddenness of deception and guarded from possible loss. Truth becomes a continual task which requires the stability of ἕξεις, habits. The highest are σοφία and φρόνησις, which guard the ἀρχαί in their respective field of being and hold them in troth.

The addressing and explicating "as," λέγειν, is accordingly the way in which νοεῖν is fulfilled. The virtues are dia-noetic, a beholding apart, διαίρεσις." Their objects are addressed only in ex-plication. But νοῦς itself, that unique feature of the human being which, like light, gives sight to all his concrete getting around in the world, is itself ἄνευ λόγου and so itself not articulable. What it gives can only be approached in an ἐπαγωγή, which is not so much induction as a simple direct leading-up-to. What we thus catch sight of are the ἀρχαί; for σοφία, it is the region of being that always and necessarily is what it is; for φρόνησις, that which also can be otherwise.

The latter brings us into the realm of πρᾶξις, human action, the get-ting about of human life with itself. The entity which constitutes itself in φρόνησις, which makes the *situation* of the human agent accessible, is the καιρός, the moment. More completely, it makes the human situation accessible in establishing its οὗ ἕνεκα, its why, in providing a particular what-for, in apprehending the now and in prefiguring the how. It leads us to the ἔσχατον, the utmost extremity at which the concrete situation comes to a crisis. The φρόνησις is possible only because it is primarily an αἴσθησις, an ultimately simple "overview" of the fulfilled moment (*Augenblick*). Circumspecting culminates in over-viewing, something akin to νοῦς in its simplicity free of an as-structure, in taking the full moment into troth. The πρακτόν that it reveals is an entity which is at once a "not yet" and an "already" in unity and poised in a specific movement. The ἀλήθεια πρακτική is nothing other than the specific unveiled full mo-ment of factic life in the how of its decisive readiness to get on with itself in the factic context of its concerns with its specific world. Φρόνησις is "epitactic" (prescriptive rather than apophantic), it gives its entity in the form of to-be-cared-for, it contains every determination of the moment: the temporally particular how, what for, to what extent and why. It is a seeing "in accord with the means to the end" (1142b 32). As an epitactic illumination, it brings our getting about into the basic attitude of readi-ness for . . ., breaking away toward . . ., [resolute decision]. The moment is regarded in the fullness of its possibility, as meaningful for . . ., what must *now* be settled and consummated, an object of total concern.

Aristotle's method clearly brings out the intentional structures of the phenomenon of φρόνησις: the epitactic relatedness to the moment of decision and how this striving is concretely fulfilled through εὐβουλία, deliberating well, by contrasting it with the other ἕξεις. The interpreta-tion thus also comes to an initial understanding of the being of φρόνησις in itself as well as of its entity. It is an ἕξις and so a "having" that the soul has become, bringing life into a certain state. It thus manifests a doubling of the regard in which the being of life as possibility comes to stand in the facticity of the human being. This becomes decisive for the historical destiny of the categorial explication of the sense of facticity in its being. In φρόνησις life itself comes into play directly as the with-which of the getting about.

But life here is not ontologically characterized positively but merely formally, as that which also can be otherwise and not that which always necessarily is. Its ontological characterization is performed by negating another being, authentic being, the "always necessarily is." This in turn is not explicated from the being of human life. Instead, its categorial structure is derived from a particular ontological radicalization of the idea of entities in motion which makes the movement of production exemplary. Being becomes the *finished product*, the being in which the movement has come to its end. The being of life is seen as a movement which takes its course within itself, in particular, when the human life has come to its end in its most distinctive possibility of movement, that of pure beholding. This movement is to be found in the ἕξις of σοφία. Such a pure understanding does not bring human life, whose being can also be otherwise, in the how of its factic being into troth. On the contrary, this being must now be regarded within the pure temporalization of σοφία in its orientation toward νοῦς, pure beholding. And νοῦς finds its genuine movement when it has foregone all outgoing orientations and simply beholds; it is the movement which, when it has come to its end, not only does not cease but precisely then is movement.

As an underway toward, every movement is in its very sense something which has not yet reached its toward-which: learning, going, building. By contrast, having seen is contemporaneous with seeing. Something is beholden precisely in the beholding. Only the νόησις as pure θεωρεῖν is therefore adequate to the highest idea of pure movement. The authentic being of the human being is temporalized in the pure fulfillment of σοφία as the undisturbed leisurely lingering of pure beholding with the pure ἀρχαί of eternal entities. The being of ἕξις and ἀρετή, that is to say, the ontological structure of being human, thus becomes understood in terms of a particular movement and the ontological radicalization of this movement.

The overview accompanying the *Einleitung* concludes with a renewed gloss of the texts familiar to us from SS 1922: the opening chapters of the *Metaphysics*, with emphasis on the genesis of the theoretical from factic life; the opening books of the *Physics* on the manifold ways of expressing being in its motion. In book 2, for example (chaps. 4–6), Aristotle faces the problem of the "*historical*" movement of factic life under the headings of τύχη (chance, fortune) and αὐτόματον (a "self-moved" happening, thus "without cause," by chance), which Heidegger finds to be untranslatable terms in their Aristotelian usage. On the basis of the issues raised by these texts, especially the conflicting "archontic" ontological paradigms for motion between ongoing factic life and finished production, Heidegger sketches plans for a second part of the book which would concentrate on *Metaphysics* 7–9, *De Motu Animalium*, and *De Anima*.[22]

The year or so that followed the composition of the *Einleitung* which was dispatched to Marburg and Göttingen included a massive effort to prepare the Aristotle book for publication. In WS 1922–23, Heidegger dropped plans for an announced course on "Skepticism in Ancient Philosophy," the first semester in which he did not lecture since coming from the war, and restricted himself to the seminar exercises on Aristotle for advanced students as well as one for beginners. In a card to Löwith in February 1923, Heidegger reports that the Aristotle Introduction is now being expanded to include basic elements of his earlier interpretations of the facticity of life (in the courses of 1919–21), to the extent that these are related to the Aristotle interpretations that follow. But soon after, letters to Löwith indicate that Heidegger is encountering great difficulty in the composition of his *Einleitung*, to the point of considering withdrawing the work entirely from publication. Thus, he is not particularly saddened when, in September, Niemeyer suspends publication of the *Jahrbuch* (apparently because of the worsening inflation in late 1923). But in the meantime, Heidegger was trying to tailor his teaching program to the time demands of book-writing. Thus the course of SS 1923, "Ontology: Hermeneutics of Facticity," had been reduced to one hour, designed to present only what he needed conceptually for his seminars of that semester on the *Nicomachean Ethics*. By the end of the summer of 1923, he was planning a course on Augustine for the following summer, but this was later changed to a course on Aristotle, focusing on his *Rhetoric*, for SS 1924, in a final effort "to get the book out." Even when, in July 1924, his priority shifts to essays on "The Concept of Time," Heidegger spends the first half of his course of WS 1924–25, entitled "Platonic Dialogues," mainly on Aristotle's *Nicomachean Ethics*! At the end of this period, in early December 1924, he gives a talk in several cities in the Ruhr valley and in Cologne for the local Kant Societies on *Nicomachean Ethics* Z under the title "Dasein und Wahrsein."

We shall have occasion later to compare these interpretations of *Nicomachean Ethics* and the emergent problem of truth in Heidegger with the very first one which we have just glossed. But already in October 1922, we have noted the peculiar backflow of the Aristotle interpretations into the more systematic account of philosophy and life in the *Einleitung* proper: a sharpening of the sense of the hermeneutic situation of philosophy compared with WS 1921–22, so that the "phronetic" elements of this situationally oriented philosophy are brought out: taking sight of the unique situation, its distinction from a mere location (*Lage*), the decisional elements of resoluteness accruing to the insight. Reading Aristotle against Aristotle, Heidegger thus continues his endeavor (since 1919) to replace the theoretical sense of philosophy with something else. Here, it might be called a "phronetic" sense of philosophy, since its object is no longer the eternal and necessary ἀρχαί, but that which also can be otherwise, the situation of factic life itself. Likewise, in the talk of the "peculiar sight that death gives to life," Heidegger begins to pinpoint the elements of phronetic illumination in the situation of life itself. Using the above summary of the text of the *Einleitung* as a starting point of comparison, we shall also have occasion to follow Heidegger's growing development of the phronetic character of death in the ensuing years, and especially its parallelism with the phenomenon of conscience, and how this likewise finds its roots in the Aristotelian texts.

Even the tardy introduction of this phenomenon does not radically alter the polar structure of factic life, already in place in this *Einleitung*, which underlies the systematic analysis of Dasein in BT. What will change significantly with BT are some of the historical high points in the program of the destruction of the history of ontology. The oddity of the *Einleitung* is its focus on the theological anthropology of the Christian Middle Ages—an apparent throwback to Heidegger's "religion" courses of the year before—coupled with the pronouncement—for the very first time in Heidegger—of the inherent atheism of philosophy in view of the thoroughly provisional and interrogative character of its object, factic life. Of course, the one does not contradict the other: among other worldviews, the Christian worldview must also be dismantled of its ontological presuppositions in order to get at its fundamental philosophical experience. Upon concluding his *Einleitung*, Heidegger promises Erich Rothacker (in a letter dated October 20, 1922) a journal article with the title, "The Ontological Foundations of Late Medieval Anthropology and the Theology of the Young Luther," a promise which he reiterates in late 1924, but never fulfills. The interest in the influence of this period on Kant and German idealism—which, in Nietzsche's words, were thoroughly "corrupted by theologians' blood"—dates back to as early as 1917 and is overtly announced in the opening hour of WS 1921–22 (GA 61: 7). Likewise, Heidegger's reading of Descartes in the historical context of Christian theology (Augustine) dates back to 1919. Thus the final form of the project of destruction in BT—Aristotle, Descartes, and Kant—can still be regarded as a mere secularization of Heidegger's old theological interests.

The highlighting of this interest in the *Einleitung* proved telling in Protestant Marburg. Paul Natorp marveled (in a card to Husserl dated November 9, 1922) over finding so many of his own ideas there on the development of the "German spirit" out of the "theologia teusch" from Eckhart to Luther and into German idealism.[23] (Moreover, Natorp had been lecturing on ἀλήθεια as "unconcealment" since 1917, whereas

Misch's copy of the *Einleitung* is spotted with question marks precisely on this point of translation.) This interest in theological anthropology receives a thorough airing in SS 1923 (GA 63:21–29) in the form of a history of the sense of the human being as "person" from the Old Testament to Zwingli and Calvin, in which "dismantled" form it is absorbed into the interstices of BT (SZ 49). And it is also in SS 1923 that the systematic structures of the *Einleitung* generally begin to take hold and develop in the direction of BT.

WS 1922–23: SEMINAR: "PHENOMENOLOGICAL INTERPRETATIONS TO ARISTOTLE" (NICHOMACHEAN ETHICS VI; METAPHYSICS VII; DE ANIMA)

The latter two texts are already familiar to us from as early as the seminar of SS 1921. They are brought into play here to supply the ontological underpinning for Heidegger's new focal interest, book 6 of the *Nicomachean Ethics*. This new interest will intensify over the next two years and play a crucial role in the composition of BT. Perhaps because it is a new interest, the seminar exercises are somewhat introductory and exploratory, and so somewhat loosely organized. We shall restrict ourselves to the high points and new developments in the interpretation of the three texts.

The opening day of the seminar alludes to the problem of the hermeneutic situation as posed in the *Einleitung*: the position and line of sight of the interpretation, and the breadth of vision ensuing from these. The central problem is to understand Aristotle's "ontology" and "logic," that is, his doctrine of ὄν ᾗ ὄν and of the ways in which being is spoken. The exposition of ontological categories is connected with the λόγος, which always plays a role in ἐπιστήμη (σοφία). To understand Aristotelian ontology and logic, one must begin with its research basis in the ἐπιστήμη of the *Physics*. But this in turn calls for an explanation of the phenomenon of scientific research and knowledge. Is knowing a "primal" phenomenon for Aristotle, as it is in today's "epistemology"? Or are there other motives for knowing? What is the basic sphere in which knowing is encountered and in which it remains, insofar as it is philosophically defined? Ever since Aristotle, these problems have been covered over, for reasons which are already present in Greek philosophy. Thus we do not approach Aristotle without presuppositions, but with these historically inherited questions. Radical philosophy itself is historical and must interrogate its own history. It is the sort of philosophical research which phenomenology does.

If one must approach the *Metaphysics* through the *Physics*, ontological research is characterized by the "Dasein" of a particular field of objects which is approached as "being." To ask about the basic sense of being is to identify the archontic region of being. Which then is the exemplary entity and how is its character of being made visible? What is the basic experience of being which renders it accessible? What are the ontological categories of its conceptual field?

Heidegger's answers to these questions clearly reflect his past work on factic *life* and his present concern over its *being*, that is, the ontologizing of the categories of life.

The original being *is* life and, of the two powers of the soul, κινεῖν καί; κρίνειν, movement is the more basic phenomenon. The *De Anima* (here 3. 9) can only be understood by way of the *Physics*. Life's movement is a κίνησις κατὰ τόπον, a "movement in space" or a going-about in the particular world of the living being. Ζῆν is *Da-sein*, it is somewhere, at a particular place, there, from the start *in* its world. Life encounters itself in a worldly way. Life moves itself in its world, it has its "abode" or "pause" there. The pausing (*Aufenthalt*) of earth's sojourn is itself a mode of κίνησις, a way of relating itself to its world.

De Anima 3. 10: Of the two "movers" of life, ὄρεξις is the original one given with life itself, while νοεῖν is the separable moment. And yet the pure toward-which of the striving, the ὀρεκτόν, already implies the νοητόν. The motivation to give priority to the latter over the former already resides in Aristotle. He already works with the separation, he is not radical enough to see their unity in an original way, even though he is constantly concerned with that unity (433a22).

The world is there to the extent that the living being "lifts" it "out" (*abheben* = κρίνειν) in its contrasts of lights and shadows. To that extent the world is "unveiled" (ἀληθές). To the extent that the living being lives in a particular environing world, only that immediate sphere is lifted out. The rest is left in the dark. There is a way-of-being of life whereby it illumines its goings: by going further, it makes the hitherto veiled visible, it unveils (ἀληθεύειν). This is the original basis for the Greek ἀλήθεια.

The go-around of life involves one or another form of ἀληθεύειν, which is thus a way of ψυχή. What then are the basic structures of ψυχή? Aristotle derives ἀληθεύειν originally from αἴσθησις, out of which νοῦς is in turn established by analogy (*De Anima* 3. 4). The general character of αἰσθάνεσθαι is πάσχειν, the influencing of one body by another. But plants are thus affected and nevertheless have no sensation. For they have no δέχεσθαι, no reception, since they have no middle (μεσότης: *De Anima* 3.12. 424b2). And *intentionality is a* δέχεσθαι, the "take-up" of perception. "Something happens with me." *This is the real problematic of facticity*, a primal phenomenon of ontology which defines the human Being, how it is there, in the world, as well as how the world is there. Facticity actually concerns neither life nor the world, but rather the relation between them. The relation is what is original.

The aim of philosophy is to make facticity transparent, to learn to see the world. In order for philosophy to understand such a task again, to see that something like it was once already given, calls for a historical orientation. We have such an investigation in Aristotle. Today it is often said, by Dilthey and others, that the later Christian psychology is much broader than the Greek psychology. It may be true that Paul's and Augustine's "anthropology" manifest much richer life-contexts than that of Aristotle. But these are rendered accessible not so much in a philosophical interrogation as in faith, that is, from a completely different fundamental orientation toward Dasein. But from a philosophical perspective, all later psychology remains far behind the Greek. The original explication found in Aristotle has never again been attained.

Nicomachean Ethics 6: It is precisely in the five ways of ἀληθεύειν that the world is "held in possession" (*im Besitz gehalten*). This is to be understood in close association with οὐσία as the belongings of house-and-hold, being as possession. The take-up of perception is a taking into possession and safeguarding against error, the all too human condition rooted in its λόγον ἔχον, being there in the mode of διὰ νοεῖν. Insofar as the living being "has" a world, it can deceive itself. According to a dubious German etymology, therefore, ἀληθεύειν is a preserving (*verwahren*), a holding in "troth." This holding of the world is also expressed in the favorite Aristotelian word in this context, ἕξις, the way of getting about with the world which courses through all five modes of "trueing." One "has on" the habit of ἕξις as a garment, so that habit and habitat, life and world, are the same, as in other instances of identity of knowledge and object (*De Anima* 3. 5. 430a19). This concrete concept is to be incorporated into the formal concept of ἕξις as δύναμις. That is why the being of man as meaningful, εὖ ζῆν, "living well," is not a "lived experience" but a concrete being in the world, a how of our going about in the world.

The problem of facticity is accordingly the problem of ἀληθεύειν. But in its different ways of going about and apprehending (κινεῖν καὶ κρίνειν), a fundamental ontological division emerges on the side of the world, within what is apprehended or "had." The modes of νοῦς, σοφία, and ἐπιστήμη, apprehend that which "always is" (ἀεί), while τέχνη and φρόνησις deal with that which "can be otherwise" (ἐνδεχόμενα ἄλλως ἔχειν). The central question therefore is: Where does Aristotle get this distinction? This question leads Heidegger into a long but inconclusive study of *Metaphysics* 7. 1–4. Some results: The ἀεί, as that which always and already is, does not need to be produced. The prime example of such a finished perfection for Aristotle are the heavenly movements. And yet, Aristotle's generic name for "object" is πρᾶγμα, that which somehow is pro-duced, in the German *her-gestellt*, that which is brought to stand and so comes into its being . . . like the world encountered by the human being! Indeed, the Greek etymology for "knowledge" (ἐπι-στήμη) also suggests a standing before, and one of the formulae for οὐσία, τὸ τί ἦν εἶναι, refers to that which is as that from which it comes. And knowledge originates from a prior getting-about which already has its distinctive illumination and kind of sight.

Heidegger's treatment of the five modes of ἀληθεύειν is still somewhat tentative, but his concluding gloss already betrays a special interest in φρόνησις. For it is the mode which reaches its culmination in "deliberative excellence" (εὐβουλία: Nic. Ethics 6. 9), which appropriates the total situation of action in a thoroughly concrete fashion. Φρόνησις is the "eye" of πρᾶξις, apprehending at once its τέλος and ἀρχή (1143b14f.). Its concern is with the particular ultimate, namely what is to be done here and now. It scrutinizes the situation as a whole to the very limit (πέρας) of experience (ἐμ-πειρία). The particular (ἕκαστον, which comes from ἑκάς, "far"; ergo the farthest) here necessarily implies ἔσχατον, the ultimate, which is where the matter is decided. Deliberating καθ᾽ ἕκαστα is thus not simply seeing the particular in a totality. That could just as well be the "each" of pure theory. The concern is rather with *das Je-weilige* (the temporally particular, but literally the each-while-like), that is, the special "each" in which I while, which only I have. (In his course of SS 1923, Heidegger for the first time formally introduces Dasein as a *terminus technicus* precisely in terms of the "particular while" which each of us has. The above Aristotelian background to eachness developed toward the end of this seminar therefore occurs roughly concurrently with the course, since Oskar Becker's notes, which we have been following, includes the continuation of this advanced seminar into SS 1923, without any internal dating.)

SS 1923: ONTOLOGY: HERMENEUTICS OF FACTICITY

This one-hour lecture course in the proximity of the *Einleitung* (which was essentially a "private communication" between scholars) will continue publicly in the development of some of the structures which it first put in place in the direction of BT. For the very first time here, Heidegger formally names his topic "Dasein" rather than "factic life," precisely in view of the "particular while" (*Jeweiligkeit*: GA 63:7) which each of us has. It is an alternate term for "facticity," which continues to define the *being* of *our own* Dasein. Nevertheless, in order to keep the term Dasein ontologically neutral, so that it may also refer to the impersonal side to the human situation, all references to the "human" Dasein are to be avoided and the traditional concepts of the human being as "rational animal" and as "person" are to be deconstructed (GA 63:21). In the same vein, the term *Existenz* maintains its narrow sense of reference to the ownness of Dasein. It is merely Dasein's ownmost and most intense possibility, the ability to hold itself awake and be alert to itself in its fullest (GA 63:16). When we interpret our facticity, understood as our prepossession (in BT, "existence" is the *Vorhabe*!), upon its *Existenz*, we then develop those special categories called the *Existenzialien* (ibid.). Thus, temporality is "not a category but an existential" (GA 63:31). But beyond these two occasions early in the course—contrary to the published edition (GA 63:35, 44, 66)—Heidegger thereafter diligently avoids this newly found existential vocabulary and continues to speak publicly of "categories" or else of "ways of being," "characters of being," or "basic characters" of Dasein where he should have said—and is sometimes purported to have said in the lecture (GA 63:35, 66)—"existentials." He thus establishes a pattern, which lasts until the very last draft of BT, of diligently avoiding existentialist terminology in public. Even though he here first publicly acknowledges his debt to Kierkegaard, in particular in his descriptions of the "public" (GA 63:30)—Heidegger adds "everydayness" (GA 63:85; it was first used in WS 1919–20) and "chatter" (GA 63:31), for the first time in this course, to his descriptions of the averageness of the Anyone—he is apparently still wary of the modishness of "Kierkegaardism" at this time.

In order to characterize the everyday world and to develop the formal indication of Dasein as being in a world, Heidegger establishes here (GA 63:85) for the very first time a basic trio of questions which will persist through all the drafts of BT: What does "world" mean here? What does "in" a world imply? "How does 'being' in a world appear?" (The last later becomes simply the question of "Who is in a world?"). Only the first question is dealt with in this course. Out of the characterization of world as meaningful context comes its characterization as disclosedness (*Erschlossenheit*). On the other hand, the habitual absorption in averageness involved here, the ἕξις of this particular ἀλήθεια of disclosedness (GA 63:99), is at once a concealedness (*Verdecktheit*) of the ownness and potential authenticity of Dasein (GA 63:85), that is, its potential discoveredness (*Entdecktheit*). This terminology of the "truth" of Dasein and its world will persist through the penultimate draft of BT. Only with BT itself will Heidegger reverse his terms and speak instead of the disclosedness of Dasein and the discoveredness (usually) of entities within the world. But following hard upon the Aristotle *Einleitung*, this course is the first installment of the truth problematic into the basic terms of the discussion, in BT and beyond.

Setting the stage as it does for the drafts of BT, SS 1923 will be analyzed in greater detail in the context of the first explicit draft of BT (chap. 7 below).

SIX

Aristotle Again: From Unconcealment to Presence (1923–24)

WS 1923–24: INTRODUCTION TO PHENOMENOLOGICAL RESEARCH

This first of the long lecture courses (all four hours) held in Marburg begins with an outline of the First Part of the course, which will be "repeated," that is, re-viewed and re-vised, and so amplified in far greater depth and detail in SS 1925:

1. Clarification of the expression phenomeno-logy.
2. Initial breakthrough to phenomenological research in Husserl's *Logical Investigations.*
3. The ensuing course of phenomenological research: To what extent the original tendencies were diverted under the influence of modern philosophy.

Only the etymological first point is developed in any great detail in WS 1923–24. The last point traces a shift in the professed phenomenological concern for the "matter itself" to a concern for "known knowledge" traceable back to Descartes, by way of Husserl's obsession for the absolute scientificity of phenomenology. This perhaps accounts for the erroneous title sometimes given for this course: "The Beginning of Modern Philosophy (Interpretation of Descartes)." The exegesis of Cartesian texts in fact dominates the Second Part of the course. And yet the opening hour announced a more "thematic" plan for this Main Part of the course: a "systematic" tour through the fundamental matters to allow them to speak for themselves, in the following order: "Dasein, world, getting around in the world, temporality, language, expository interpretation of Dasein, possibilities of interpretation, science, research, phenomenology," thus circling back to the above opener of the course. Heidegger

276

nevertheless manages to touch on most of these themes in his detour into the first full-scale, and self-consciously phenemenological, destruction of the history of ontology and its logic focused on the key intermediatory between Aristotle and Husserl, Descartes. This change in the course outline was first announced just before the Christmas break, giving the students ample time to acquire their unexpectedly requisite Descartes texts. Heidegger thus supplies tangible proof for his repeated insistence on the inseparability of the systematic and the historical in phenomenology.

But of interest to us in our present genealogical context is the development of the first point above, which represents the very first of several attempts to develop the meaning of phenomeno-logy from its two Greek roots. It is indicative especially of the incorporation of Aristotelian insights, sometimes against Aristotle, into Heidegger's own conception of phenomenology. Aristotle is pitted against Aristotle, for example, in Heidegger's opening remarks urging his students to adopt a more "phronetic" attitude toward their chosen science, contrary to the traditional equation of scientific comportment with θεωρεῖν, intuitive comportment, which in fact places us more at the finished end of science rather than at its interrogative beginnings. Instead, he recommends the restless passion for the genuine questions of a particular science ensconced in its situational presuppositions, and acceptance of those presuppositions as one's very own, contrary to the "utopia" of presuppositionlessness, which is the most dangerous presupposition of all. Only when each of us, in his particular place and chosen science with its particular questions, has learned that here he is encountering himself, does he come to understand what science is. It is not a matter of speculation within a system but of becoming a "native" in an ongoing science by confronting its particular matters and resolutely seizing the particular opportunities which it transmits to us.

As the old Heidegger has led us to expect (in the Niemeyer Festgabe), the etymological approach to the term "phenomeno-logy" restores its field of research, modernized by Husserl into the domain of consciousness, its acts and its objects, back to the more originary Greek "Dasein of the world and the being of life." However, it is not so much the aletheic lead (so in the letter to Richardson) but more this sheer "phenomenal" route which first leads us to the issue of pure presence. It does not "dawn" on us, as the old Heidegger appears to suggest, in the guise of the lowly Anwesen (οὐσία) of real estate and household goods, but rather as that dominating presence of the Greek world, the overwhelming Anwesenheit (παρουσία: De Anima 418b17) of the sky.

First employed in the school of Wolff in the eighteenth century, the term "phenomenology" referred to the theory of appearances, that is, to the means by which knowing could avoid appearance as sham. How is it that φαινόμενον came to mean sham? The history is complex: the eighteenth century gave special attention to appearance as sensory, distinguished its primary and secondary qualities, accordingly felt it necessary to "save the appearances" from deception by the secure positioning that science provided, and so on. But regarded purely externally, phenomeno-logy does not refer to sham, but simply means "speaking about phenomena": φαίνω = to bring something to the light of day; the middle-voiced φαίνεσθαι = to show itself. Thus, φαινόμενον refers to that which shows itself in the light of day. The stem is φῶς, the transparency of light, which prompts Heidegger into an exegesis of Aristotle's *De Anima* B 7, the chapter on seeing and visibility.

De Anima, "On the Soul," treats on the modes of the Dasein of the living being in the world, in which this world is itself immediately present (*präsent*) to it, there to be-hold (*ver-nehmen*). Perception, seeing, is in this vein a direct access to the world. As long as I see, I am not deceived (418a11). It gives access to the visible, color, "which overlies what is in itself visible. . . that which has in itself the cause of its visibility . . . which is actually transparent" (418a28ff). For color is visible only "in light, in the bright, in the transparent" (418b3). As the "without which not" (visible), the bright light is the condition of possibility of seeing things in their true look, the letting see and be seen (*das Sehenlassende*). Everything therefore depends on what we mean by the light and the bright, the trans-parent (δια-φανές) through which something can be seen. We are accordingly concerned mainly with the diaphanous condition of light, itself colorless and so invisible "or barely visible" (418b28) in its transparency. What then is light? What is this "something" which through itself lets something else (*anders*) be seen? It is not a thing nor any sort of body, not something that travels or moves, nor even fire, say the fire of the sun, but rather "the *presence* of fire or something resembling fire in the transparent" (418b17). Light is the presence of the sun, what we normally call day. In the broadest terms, light is the presence of the sky. For it is there that the sun moves, the bright light is there (*da*). Light is the being-there of the sky, its presence. It is not a What—light is not a body—but a How, a way of being. The day, its light, is a way of being of the world, how it is *there*, as condition of possibility. But *how* is it there? we may yet ask. Another tack may "throw some more light" on the topic, "Light is the way of the world."

Put otherwise, "light is the act (ἐνέργεια) of the transparent as transparent" (418b9). *Es tagt*, "it dawns, it days," is a fundamental expression of the "energy" of being. Not potency but act, and so for Aristotle ἐντελέχεια ὄν, that which is in its being finished and thus constantly is. Putting the two strands together—Heidegger does not do this here—we thus arrive at the "constant presence" of the sky. If fundamental φαινεῖν is διαφαινεῖν, if fundamental showing is showing-through, then for Aristotle, phenomenon is a determination of being designating that entity of the world which is always already there. What is truly seen is color in the bright of day. Color is the "proper object" (ἴδιον) of sight. But a phenomenon is first κατὰ συμβεβηκός, improper, common, appearing in a mixed context, and not ἴδιον. Color "in itself" turns out to be an isolated and even artificial visual experience (for we first see chairs and tables, etc.). For this proper object is normally accompanied by a context of other visual experiences κατὰ συμβεβηκός, which already introduces the "as"-structure of perception and so the "germ" of deception. Another complication which Aristotle himself notes (419a4): Certain luminous phenomena and the like require as their condition of appearance not light but darkness. And darkness is not normally regarded as a positive condition but as a privation (στέρησις). This category problem persists to the present: our categories as well as those of the Greeks tend to be "categories of the day."

Turning to the other component part of the word "phenomeno-logy," λόγος (speech), Heidegger is in search of an "inner connection" between it and φαινόμενον as self-showing. This he readily finds in the doctrine of λόγος ἀποφαντικός in *Peri Hermeneia*. But there is more to λόγος than the declarative sentence that "shows" or "points out." There are questions, requests, and commands, for example. Even the apophantic "as," in pointing out, implies a critical "as" in its concomitant action of distinguishing and contrasting, although the apophantic "as" (so named here for the first time) is more basic. It is there even when I apprehend an object "as" itself. And critical distinguishing can be traced into the heart of perception itself, since the focus on its proper object involves its selection and extraction from the common "accidents." In putting a judging sense in the common sense (426b25), Aristotle thus comes close to equating even purportedly "error-free" perception to a λόγος, which "is said in many ways" and so places us in the realm of multiplicity with its potential for error. It is because of this deep penetration of language into perception that humans "spend the greatest part of their time in error" (427b1). Language guides our beholding, we see through language, which therefore begins to compete with light in its function as a diaphanous medium of perception!

Speech is in fact that characteristically human trait by which we strive for the highest possible human existence, εὖζῆν. What we have μετὰ λόγου includes φρόνησις and τέχνη as well as ἐπιστήμη and σοφία. This larger context will have to be clarified before we can truly arrive at a sense of the degree to which sham and deceit belong to being human. The goal here is to determine this only at the points of contact between φαινόμενον and λόγος.

This nevertheless dictates the examination of the larger context of a human life which is a ζωὴ πρακτική τις τοῦ λόγον ἔχοντος, a practical life concerned with getting along with a world which is sayable. For all the other possibilities of human life are somehow sublated under this more original possibility of λέγειν. Thus the possibility of perception in the human being is from the start already grounded in the fact that he speaks and cares. On this basis, therefore, Aristotle can maintain that αἴσθησις is a λόγος. Human perception operates not only in a milieu of light but also in a milieu of speech through which the human being sees things. It is the element in which the human being lives . . . but also by which he is lived. For speech both covers and uncovers. Speech contains within itself the seed of its possible perversion. With speech, we thus come to the major source of deception in human existence. Undercutting the three senses of ψευδής discussed in *Metaphysics* 5. 29—false thing, false speech, false human (the liar)—Heidegger finds their unifying source of deception in the "facticity" of speech itself, simply in the way speech is, the fact that it is spoken, repeated and habitually passed along in the circle of human beings in the "with-world." Speech as such constitutes the manifold complex of possibilities of deception. Some examples in speech itself: "I mean (want to say) something" implies the further possibility of also hiding this very same thing by speaking. Or there is the possibility of irresponsible chatter about nothing whatsoever, "more dangerous than a Big Lie," notes the Heidegger of the 1920s. Add to this the possibilities of deception in speaking that derive from the world itself: its "circumstantiality" of manifold aspects κατὰ συμβεβηκός, always allowing the world to "give itself out" to be something other than it is; its "recessibility" or elusiveness, as a kind of reverse side to the accessibility of the world through language. For fleetingness or transitoriness belongs to the world as much as light and dark, day and night.

With this conclusion to the Aristotelian portion of this course, it is small wonder that next semester's course, devoted entirely to Aristotle, spends an inordinate amount of time on the *Rhetoric*, that art of moving human passions through speech. In fact, the present course itself concludes with the first detailed development of the passion that will interest Heidegger the most, *Angst*. In between, the ongoing destruction of Descartes (i.e., Husserl: a critique which must be omitted here, for reasons of space) returns again and again to the category problem, obviously in response to the deficiencies of the "categories of the day," but without a sustained follow-up. Passing mention is made of the "existentials" needed to elaborate Dasein in its being. For the existentials are the preconception, Dasein the prepossession and being the pre-view (*Vorsicht*, used here for the first time) of the present hermeneutic situation. And in conjunction with the basic Aristotelian distinction between that which always is and that which can be otherwise, Heidegger lists the fourfold determination of being which he learned from the much touted dissertation of Brentano (1862), but which he never really employs directly even here. The last one is ὂν ὡς ἀληθές, which is now coming into central prominence in the early Heidegger's reflections.

"BEING-HERE AND BEING-TRUE" (1923–24; DECEMBER 1924)

There is some question on the dates of the composition and delivery of this talk. The question is not unimportant for our conceptual genealogy, inasmuch as the text includes perhaps the very first clearcut identification of οὐσία with presence, which the old Heidegger came to regard as the major caesura in his thought. Heidegger himself dates the composition of this text in "1923–24" which, as broad as it is, does not really conflict with any of the evidence of the conceptual genealogy being developed here. Later, however, the old Heidegger, his quivering hand still quite visible in the scribble, notes that the talk, first drafted under the title "Wahrsein und Dasein (Aristoteles Ethica Nicomachea Z)," was delivered under the title "Dasein und Wahrsein" in "WS 1923–24 at the Kant Society in Cologne." Yet there is ample evidence to indicate that a talk announced under the title "Dasein und Wahrsein nach Aristoteles (Interpretation von Buch VI der Nikomach. Ethik)" was given to the local Kant Societies in at least three of six cities in the Ruhr-Rhine region, including Cologne, on December 1–8, 1924.[1] One possibility is that the talk was indeed first scheduled for delivery in WS 1923–24, and Heidegger began to work on such a talk. But then it was postponed because of the Inflation rampant in Germany in the last months of 1923; after it was rescheduled, he outlined an updated and streamlined version of it for delivery at the end of 1924.

On January 10–11, 1924, in his lecture course, Heidegger in fact refers to the questions suggested by the talk's title, itself mentioned once in passing and even translated into Latin, "vita et veritas," in the context of alluding to some of the themes to be treated in his forthcoming course on Augustine: How is truth "rooted" (*eingebettet*) or located in Dasein? "What is (*heißt*) the truth of life, the truth of Dasein?" It is a question for which the present, with its concern for "known knowledge" and its emphasis on theoretical truth, is not prepared. Heidegger had prepared his students for it by redefining the traditional definition of man so that ζωή, life, means to be in a world, to be there, and ἀληθεύειν is a way to be there in the world in such a way that we have (ἔχον!) the world unconcealed, as it is. Having the world in turn refers to the habits, ἔξεις, which range from the everyday to the authentic, ἀρετή, excellence or virtue. The latter forms of having the world or "having reason" (ζῷον λόγον ἔχον) would then be the ways "to be true" to/for the There. This of course would dictate a gloss of the account of the "intellectual virtues" in *Nicomachean Ethics* Z. Ergo the subtitle of the talk.

But the same course context suggests an entirely different approach to the question of "in vita veritas," as Heidegger, by now deeply involved in the collateral activities of his new Marburg setting with Bultmann and the Theological Faculty, telegraphs the direction, both constructive and destructive, that his course on Augustine in SS 1924 will take. For the dominance of theoretical knowledge has been so strong in Western thought that even the phenomenon of faith came to be regarded in those terms. But it is impossible to interpret something like the truth of a life in this way, beginning, say, with the Greek orientation to the truth of λόγος as assertion and the primacy thereby given to theoretical truth. Yet an attempt to give truth a new sense took place in the New Testament and later in Augustine, where the original sense of truth was not explicated theoretically, since this was not the task of the Evangelists. It would have been a meaningful task for theology to explicate this original sense of truth contained in faith, "theoretically," so to speak, but without losing its intrinsic nontheoretical character. But theology failed to do so by becoming ensnared in the concept of theoretical truth acquired from philosophy. This basic neglect persists to the present day in Kierkegaard's talk of the "paradox" of faith.

The course on Augustine was not held and, in accordance with a decision made in March 1924, was replaced by a course on Aristotle in which his *Rhetoric* plays a prominent role.[2] The talk in December concludes with a vague reference to the possibilities of Christian theology, but is otherwise thoroughly Greek in its orientation, like the earlier text of the talk, even when it refers to the *Augen-blick*, the moment of phronetic insight. The inordinate amount of space devoted in the text to the kind of everyday speech discussed in the *Rhetoric*, especially the three forms of public address and their impact on their hearers by way of their "moods," may therefore be datable to March 1924; but without further evidence, this can only be a tentative conjecture.

The talk, with its reference to the truth (more the untruth) of rhetoric, is itself composed with an eye to rhetorical effects. It must have been a challenge to Heidegger at this time to effectively focus his rapidly developing ideas on the concept of truth in the compass of a brief talk. In its starting point in the "fundamental concept" of truth and the "expression 'true,' " in its movement from the truth of sentences to the truth of life, the talk is distantly reminiscent of the later, more celebrated talk "On the Essence of Truth," and might well be regarded as its older distant cousin. There is of course one major difference: From its starting point in the aletheic cliché of conformity of judgment, through the everyday sense of speech found in *Peri Hermeneia* and the *Rhetoric*, to the five ways of "trueing" in *Nicomachean Ethics* 6, the early talk is through and through Greek, or more precisely, Aristotelian in its orientation.

Opening remarks define the problem in a metaphorology both pastoral and militant: Does truth really find its ground in judgment, or has it been "uprooted" from a more native soil (*Bodenständigkeit*)? If so, we must find the original ground for the "stock of deeds" (*Tatbestand*) that is brought to concept in "truth," and then appropriate, step by step, the field in which we encounter truth and being-true. This will be the battlefield (*Kampfplatz*), chosen by us in historical self-responsibility, for a radical confrontation of Greek philosophy in its greatness, which itself did battle on this same inherited ground with the concealing chatter of the rhetoric and sophistry of its day. This is the real ground which tacitly determines the manner of seeing out of which Aristotle's text has grown, which we must take into account in our interpretation, though one might object that it is "not really there" in the text. The "armaments" (*Zurüstung*) needed for such an interpretative struggle will become apparent by allowing these "richly stocked" texts to speak for themselves. (All this on the "inherited ground" of the then French-occupied Rhine-Ruhr valley!)

From this introduction, Heidegger then divides the talk into three main parts, leaving room for a concluding "fundamental deliberation":

1. Speech and "Judgment" (λόγος).
2. Being-true and Being-here.
3. The Ways of Being-true and Its Outstanding Possibilities.
    (4. Being-true—Being-here—Being and the Tasks of an Ontology.)

In our necessarily brief tour of each main part, our focus will be on the genealogical high point of this text, the unique collision which occurs here, for the very first time in Heidegger, between truth as unconcealment and being as presence, *Unverborgenheit und Anwesenheit*. On their titular surface, the two courses that follow this text of early 1924 are dedicated respectively to the two great manifestations of concealment in the Greek world, rhetoric (SS 1924) and sophistry (WS 1924–25). But looking below this surface, we find that SS 1924 is aimed directly and through and through at Greek being understood as presence, and we must wait until WS 1924–25 for the full-scale confrontation of truth as unconcealing concealment. It is in this way that the text of early 1924, out of which the talk of December 1924 is derived, provides the introductory framework for two of Heidegger's greatest courses, breaking ground not merely in Greek philosophy but also for his entire path of thought.

1. Speaking as "demonstrative letting-be-seen," spoken out of its nuclear apophantic "as" and thus raising the possibility of the falsity of the

cognitive judgment through non-conformity with being, is as usual the first place to look for such a convergence between truth and being. Falsity of judgment is thus one form of concealment, and to be true is to be uncovered, which is soon identified as an "outstanding mode of the *presence* of beings." But for Aristotle, this demonstrative uncovering through judgment (λόγος) is not the original way to be true, in view of the passage through error involved in the "logical" road to truth. Moreover, if we look at the *locus classicus* on λόγος, *Peri Hermeneia* 4, we discover that it does not mean judgment but discourse, and that not every discourse (e.g., requests, wishes) is subject to the judgment "true" or "false." Demonstrative discourse aiming at apophantic knowledge is but one form of speaking, and by no means the most immediate. The basic aim of discourse is not knowledge but understanding, ἑρμηνεία, beginning with the everyday circuit of speaking with and to one another and, accordingly, listening to one another. The nature of this everyday discourse can be found in its full scope in the investigations made by the loquacious Greeks, who thus arrived at the first "logic," the first fundamental doctrine of λόγος, and called it "rhetoric." This hermeneutics of everyday life (= speaking) thus classifies peak moments of discourse into the festive and political speech and the judge-jury plea, and analyzes these further into the three "confidences": the ethos of the speaker, the pathos of the hearer, and the argument that speaks to the "heart" of the matter, and so of the listener. Talking here is "talking into" (*Über-reden*), convincing, and its "truth" more a matter of the attunement (*Abstimmung*) of mood than judicative correspondence (*Übereinstimmung*). It is not in "reason" but on this everyday level that we find the full measure of the Aristotelian definition of man as the speaking animal.

2. But in appropriating a fuller range of human speech, are we not moving precisely into the realm of concealment from which demonstrative discourse attempts to free us? What is to be gained by this return to the concealment of mere opinion and idle talk within which everyday life moves? To begin with, it takes us back precisely to the level at which Greek philosophy embarked on its struggle for truth against the concealment of appearance. The oddity that the Greek word for truth is negative suggests that it must be "wrung" from beings by a process of un-concealment. Everyday discourse thus serves to expose three forms of concealment of the world as well as of human life: a) the concealment of opinion, doxic concealment: "it seems, it looks that way, as far as I can tell, there is something to be said for that," and so on; b) concealment pure and simple, complete ignorance of something which is not at all disclosed, an area with which we are not yet familiar; c) concealment of something which was once out in the open, but which becomes disguised and lapses back into hiding through the prevalence of clichés and worn-out con-

cepts. The original creation thereby becomes deracinated and loses touch with the ground from which it draws its creative substance. This last is the most dangerous concealment, since it becomes equated with self-evidence, thereby becoming refractory to the need to be interrogated once again. (Cf. SZ 36 for a variant trio of concealments.)

If truth is a disclosive letting-see-and-be-seen, we then have a three-fold sense of truth here: a) disclosure of a being by way of prevalent views of it, which include something already seen in them; b) disclosive entry into hitherto unknown domains of being; c) constant struggle with the chatter which gives itself out to be disclosive and knowing. In all three cases, disclosure is a human affair, a basic comportment of Dasein. As Aristotle puts it, being-true is a "habit" of the soul, which for Dasein always means "having" a world, being in the world. To say that the living being is disclosive in its very being means that it is not merely on hand, but rather present for the world in such a way that it encounters (*begegnet – gegenwärtig*) its world. This being present for the world is what Aristotle means by entelechy.

3. This leads to the five ways of being-true which Dasein as being-in-the-world has at its disposal, both theoretical and practical, familiar to us from *Nicomachean Ethics* 6. To get at the Greek problem of truth most expeditiously, it is advisable to start at the top of this articulation of the "trueing" virtues. There is a way of uncovering which is "without λόγος," namely, νοῦς itself, from which we must always start (i.e., not from λόγος, as we have just done) in our path to original truth. Truth is ultimately not διαλέγειν but instead διανοεῖν. Thus, among the five ways of uncovering and "being true" available to Dasein, the living being "having λόγος," we find that one is beyond λόγος [is in effect "transcendence"]. This is accordingly the highest uncovering. It asserts itself among the remaining four "dia-noetic virtues" in the ever increasing desire simply to see, and to see more of the world. What specifically? Beings: not just those which can also be otherwise, the changeable, but especially those which are always already there, purely and simply "on hand," the ἀρχαί. In production, there is always that out of which we produce—wood, stone, water, in short, the world, and above all the sky under which the world is—which is always simply there, in no need to be produced. This also provides the criterion of priority among the ways of uncovering, where priority is now given to those which uncover the ἀρχή. For it is the ἀρχή which makes beings visible in their being.

From this, it becomes clear what being means for the Greeks. On the one hand, there are the beings of the environing world, in their being-finished, -produced, -available, and accordingly, being-present. These are the things nearest to us in the environment: house and ground, real estate (*Anwesen*), οὐσία, a meaning still retained by Aristotle in his *Ethics* and *Politics*. On the other hand, the beings of the world, already there before any production, in no need of it, being-finished pure and simple, being-present pure and simple, Presence (*Anwesenheit*), οὐσία as παρουσία. Presence is decisive, the always present is the authentically present, in short, Being, what always already is from before and from which everything else is there, the ἀρχὴ καὶ τέλος, ὑποκείμενον, ὑπάρχειν, being on hand, at the ready. (The passage approaches panegyric heights in its celebration of Heidegger's discovery of οὐσία as Presence.)

The pure beholding of these principles, νοῦς, is possible for humans only in a certain manner, in relation to the other four modes of uncovering. These are actualized with speech and reasoning (λόγος), in addressing something as something, while the First and the Last can no longer be addressed as something other than it is. The uncovering of principles must be without speech. Here, it is simply a matter of "bringing ourselves before the matter itself," traversing the way that leads directly to it (ἐπαγωγή, which is not "induction"). Thus, the resolute choice of my concrete situation of action, which takes into account the various circumstances entering into the situation, abruptly terminates such an accounting (συλλογισμός) and culminates in a simple "oversight" which takes charge of, and acts on, the situation in the "blink of an eye" (*Augen-blick*), in the instant of insight. The principle that guides and orients my action and makes it authentic, the ἀγαθόν, is thus approached, although it never really shows itself. (To be true here is accordingly to be under way, to be dis-covering.)

Having devoting a great deal of attention to describing the craft of master builders and apprentice shoemakers—even an ironmonger puts in an appearance, in preparation for the Ruhr region!—Heidegger does not really get very far into the other three dianoetic virtues. The text breaks off in mid-thought, and remains a fragment. But he has made his main points, at least in identifying the major loci of the Greek sense of truth.

SS 1924: GROUND CONCEPTS OF ARISTOTELIAN PHILOSOPHY

Of the thirty concepts outlined in Aristotle's philosophical lexicon in *Metaphysics* 5, apparently for a course among the Peripatetics, this course will seek to treat only several of them. For we no longer possess the same presuppositions that Aristotle's students had, we are not in a position to understand Aristotle as they did, and must proceed by a more "fundamental" route. We must get at the ground (*Boden*) out of which these ground concepts (*Grundbegriffe*) grew and see how they grew. In short, the very conceptuality of these concepts must be considered: how the matters they intend are seen, to what end they are addressed, in what way they are determined. Considering concepts in this way in fact gives us insight into the basic requirements for any kind of scientific research. Such a fundamental consideration is not philosophy nor its history, still less is it a "history of problems." If philology is the passion for what is articulated, then that is what we are doing. He who has chosen a science must also assume responsibility for its concepts and their presuppositions.

It is in this context on the opening day of the course (May 1, 1924) that the much-bandied quotation on Aristotle's life—which has become an ideological shibboleth against biography in philosophy, especially Heidegger's—occurs. In discussing the writings by and on Aristotle, Heidegger concludes: "In the personality of a philosopher, there is only *this* interest: he was born at such and such a time, he worked, and he died. The figure of the philosopher or the like will not be provided here" (1).[3] Yet the remarks that precede and follow belie the rejection of all but this most superficial of biographies. The use and abuse of this quotation over the years, to the point of becoming a staple ideological shield for orthodox "Heideggerians," deserve to be regarded as one of the most notorious examples of quotation out of context. For it occurs at a point when Heidegger is beginning to draw the conclusions regarding the nature of a philosophy drawn from the hermeneutics of facticity. The interdependence between beings and their being, the interplay of the ontic and the ontological (a distinction in terminology clearly drawn for the first time in this course), is underscored in the very first of the ground concepts (only number 8 in Aristotle's lexicon) developed in great detail by Heidegger, namely, οὐσία. The equiprimordiality of the historical with the systematic in a situated or "grounded" philosophy is asserted almost in the same breath as the above quotation, in the form of the course presupposition that "history and the historical past has the possibility of giving impetus to a present or a better future" (2). The central thrust of the course, that philosophical concepts are homegrown in and out of their native ground, early on falls back upon a biographical facticity which at first sight might seem trivial. But in this context, this biographical statement proves to be no less significant and "deep-structured" than the philosophically relevant confession from Heidegger's letter to Löwith, "I am a 'Christian theo*logian*.'" The opening hours of the course thus draw on at least the following biographical facts, now regarded as basic premises pertaining to the autochthony of concepts: "Aristotle was a Greek," "Heidegger was a German," and "Both are intimately conjoined in the facticity of the Occident."

In his first application (in the third hour) of such a deeply rooted and autochthonous biography at once revelatory of his autobiography,

Heidegger is speaking of those multivocal and yet extreme concepts that we call "terms." Terms are sometimes shaped from the newly discovered matter by a new word. But they are also formed from a word already in common usage, so that a moment of meaning implicit in its current usage now becomes thematic in its terminological usage. This common currency of meaning operates in the averageness of "self-evident" understanding, of expressions which are the "common good" of the language into which each new human being grows and gets acclimated. In Aristotle's naming of being itself, accordingly, the coined term οὐσία is still accompanied (especially in his *Ethics* and *Politics*) by its everyday sense of property, house-and-hold, real estate. Even in ordinary usage, the reference is to an entity which is "there" in a distinctive way, namely, that entity which is there "to begin with and for the most part" in life. Thus, even common usage has words which refer both to the being and (implicitly) to the how of its being, property and its being had or ownedness, household goods in their everyday familiarity, real estate in its underlying "substantiality." "We likewise have, in our German expressions, particular meanings which refer not only to a being but also mean it in the how of its being: *Hab und Gut, Vermögen, Anwesen*" (8); translated *seriatim* into English: possessions as had and "good," wealth as capacity and power, real estate as present (*anwesend*). In short, in both common and scientific usage, "Being for the Greeks from the start means *Da-sein*, being-there. The further clarification of being in its being must move in the direction of the question, What does *there* mean?" (8). The whole course is therefore designed to view οὐσία, *Da-sein*, the How of being, through the bifocals of Greek and German.

Logic tells us that a concept receives its determination by means of a definition. A real definition thus determines what a *res* is in itself. For Kant, a concept, in contrast with an intuition, comes into its own in a definition, where it is understood in its inner possibility and becomes universally valid. But for Aristotle, ὁρισμός (definition, but ultimately "horizon," already a favorite word of Heidegger's in the previous semester) is not yet so sharply contoured and logically complete: it is rather a λόγος which determines an entity in its being as limited and measured by its πέρας, its "perimeter." Being means being finished. Aristotle can therefore take us back to the origin of the process of decay of this term of terms, in the course of which "definition" becomes a mere technique of thinking, and thus strays from being a "ground" possibility of human speech.

In definition, the concept becomes explicit. And yet, it is not thereby clear what the concept itself actually is in its conceptuality. [In order to come to this, we must turn from its logical completeness to its phenomenological origins, at the interface of the concept and its matter, ground, rooting.] Coming to the conceptuality of a concept is not really a matter of becoming acquainted with its content, but of asking 1) how the matter intended by the concept is concretely and fundamentally experienced, not on the level of theory but on the level of life's go-around; 2) how what is originally seen is primarily addressed, that is, what "leading claim" is made upon the matter, whether this regard lies in the phenomenon itself or is taken over from extant concepts and theories; 3) how the phenomenon is then further unraveled, into what sort of conceptuality it is placed and in what direction it is understood; that is, does the explication continue to be original and proper to the phenomenon, or is it just something imposed upon it? These three moments—fundamental experience, leading claim, direction of understanding and intelligibility—in fact are intimately interwoven with one another and with the place where they belong. Together, therefore, they constitute the "autochthony (*Bodenständigkeit*) of the conceptuality," and accordingly not of just any conceptuality but, in this case, of that which is indigenous to Greek soil.

It is along these three lines that Aristotle's ground concepts are to be interrogated. By thus bringing his incipient moment of conceptuality into movement, by animating the actualization of questioning and definition that constituted his scientific research (and in fact constitutes any concrete scientific inquiry), by following this actualization to its conceptual fulfillment, we are in turn provided with an opportunity to establish a genuine and true and serious relationship with the matters of our own respective sciences. We can then do in our situation what Aristotle did in his time and place and the compass of his research, namely, to see and determine our own "thing" with the same originality and authenticity.

Returning to the problem of definition not only takes us back to its original sense as well as to that which we now call a concept, but also provides a "natural" (i.e., phenomenological) entry into the conceptual autochthony of the Greeks. A course which upon first announcement seemed to promise only a random selection of fundamental concepts from the Aristotelian opus now spontaneously takes us into the central core of the conceptual web governing Aristotle's research. Even the famous Aristotelian definition of the human being which quickly surfaces is no random example for the sake of mere illustration but is, from Heidegger's perspective, the most crucial feature in Aristotle's core concern for being.

For Aristotle, ὁρισμός addresses the matter in terms of what it is; it is therefore a λόγος οὐσίας, a formula which also succinctly locates the autochthony of the concept, since it identifies Aristotle's fundamental experience. And λόγος is the fundamental determination of human-being, the ζῷον λόγον ἔχον. Even the ousiological connective ἔχειν (having, *Habe*) must be understood in a thoroughgoing fundamental fashion. *Metaphysics* 5. 23 gives us a start: Speech is had by man like an all-governing drive (ἄγειν), like a tyrannic ruler and consuming fever. This passional character of "having" will become a central motif of the course.

The basic function of λόγος is to bring the entity to show itself in its being, its οὐσία. Οὐσία is *the* fundamental concept of Aristotelian philosophy, from which we not only learn what ὁρισμός is, but also gain the ground upon which all the other basic concepts are to be understood. It is the ground of ground concepts, and so the first which has to be examined. Three early hours which orient the remainder of the course therefore give us the most intensive treatment of οὐσία that we are likely to get from Heidegger, who then "repeats" it throughout the course. It is thus clear that, by the beginning of May 1924, not only οὐσία as presence but also its multifarious ramifications are firmly in place in Heidegger's framework of thought.

The fact that οὐσία is multivocal (it is "said in many ways") need not be regarded as a state of dangerous confusion due to ignorance or to the undeveloped articulation of the conceptual field. Instead, it may be an indication of a genuine relationship and familiarity with the matter, which itself may demand an articulated and ever-limpid multiplicity of distinct meanings. So it is in fact with many of the concepts listed in *Metaphysics* 5. Multiplicity becomes a mark of proximity to the matters themselves.

At least since Parmenides, being for the Greeks meant being-there, *Dasein*. With Aristotle, the age-old question, τί τὸ ὄν, is transposed into τίς ἡ οὐσία (*Metaphysics* 7.1.1028b4), an ontological foundation of which Plato had not even the faintest idea. [Curiously, in such ontological contexts, Heidegger never mentions the staple in Greek etymology, that οὐσία comes from οὖσα, the feminine nominative present participle of "being."] In short, what specifically is this "there" of being, what is its "how"? And since being is always the being of a being, from what particular entity can this character of being be read off? *Metaphysics* 7.2 begins by noting that οὐσία shows itself "most obviously in bodies." The character of being highlighted here is not the corporeality of the entity but the obtrusiveness of the showing, so that the entity in its brute "there" is at my immediate disposal. It includes all the things which are there first of all and most of all in the everydayness of living. Σῶμα, body, later came to mean slave, prisoner, thus what belongs to me, what I have, there for me in its specific obtrusiveness and obviousness. Even the sky stands at my immediate disposal, for telling time, for example. Thus, in the next chapter, Aristotle notes that whatever is accessible through perception is οὐσία.

Hence, the first sense of being-there listed for οὐσία in *Metaphysics* 5. 8

is ὑποκείμενον, what already lies there beforehand and is therefore "on hand," *vorhanden*, available. Then Aristotle lists the more subtle senses regarding beings which are "present in" (ἐνυπάρχοντα) the more everyday things: 2) the soul "in" the living body, 3) the parts defining the individual body, for example, its surface, "whose destruction bring about the destruction of the whole" (1017b19). The soul is not obviously there, but it must be there in order for something to be alive and in the world; likewise for the "essential" parts of a whole. The first comprehensive character of the "there" of οὐσία is now clear: the word itself suggests that it is but an abbreviation of παρουσία, presentness (*Gegenwärtigkeit*), the present. But a second dominant—one is tempted to say "equiprimordial"—character is already manifesting itself in and through this first: being finished, complete (thus ready and available). Aristotle's example of the surfaces which bound bodies, giving them their shape and form, is not a casual one: bodies assume de-finition, manifest their "finish" through the "look" of their surfaces. Aristotle's onto-logic of essential presences and co-presences is clearly the forerunner of those extreme thought-experiments out to test limits that are associated with Husserl's eidetic variation, in order to establish "that without which a thing cannot be what it is." Such a sense of reality is traceable back to the famous Greek respect for limits, bounds, perimeters, horizons, de-finition, that now manifests itself as a fundamental character of the There of beings.

The allusion to limiting presences which define individuality points to the second character of οὐσία: being finished, complete. Thus, the fourth sense of οὐσία listed in 5.8 is the true λόγος ὁρισμός, which is τὸ τί ἦν εἶναι ("essence" is the usual translation, but Heidegger insists on the literal "what it was," something understood out of its origin), which is the οὐσία ἑκάστου, the being ("substance") of each thing in its particularity (1017b23) . . . or so is each term usually translated. These defining limits, however, are not immediately evident in the everyday things, and so call for an "event of an unusual kind" to make them present. Temporal particularity (*Jeweiligkeit* = ἕκαστος) is neither "each" nor individual and certainly not "general," and yet, as γένος (genus), it is that in which and out of which I "while," circumscribed in its outermost here and now. It is not immediately and directly given—in fact, it disappears in the usualness of the everyday—but rather demands a certain distance (ἕκας) in order to become present. In this presence by distance, we are given an opportunity to see what is there in terms of where it comes from (τὸ τί ἦν εἶναι), in its provenance or "history," and how it has come to its limit (πέρας). Authentic presentness is to be found in the extremity (ἔσχατον: *Metaphysics* 5. 17) of a particular being, in its "finish," what it "was to be." Such ultimate aspects of being in the εἶδος (the silhouetted outlines of a "look," ergo a "form") and τέλος (end) receive their accounting in the character of πέρας. Whence the Greek abhorrence for ἄπειρον: with the *regressus ad infinitum*, one is no longer among beings. Their sense of being comes from a very concrete experience, of a world overarched by the sky, self-enclosed and in itself complete. It is in the world of limits that the true autochthony of the concept is to be found, when one resolves to *speak radically* with this world, to question it and investigate it with resoluteness. The language of definition is such a speaking, in addressing being in its finish and regarding that completeness as present. But it is not the "surface," slurred speech of the everyday, of the child who calls all men "father," clearly an inarticulate speech which knows no ὁρίζειν.

There is accordingly far more to ὁρισμός than just the technical affair of logical definition with which we began (cf. likewise WS 1921–22 on defining philosophy). It is an affair of human Dasein which bears directly upon the very limits of its being in the world, its being there. For the limits defining this very human "there," endowed with the capacity of λέγειν, also define the native soil out of which it develops its conceptuality. The remainder of the course is therefore devoted, not so much to the Parmenidean Dasein infecting the double sense of Aristotle's οὐσία as presentness and completeness, but more to Aristotle's understanding of the human Dasein in its πέρας, which in its first approximation is called ἀγαθόν. Heidegger joins this Aristotelian gloss with his own developing insights into the limits (and so the scope) of human Dasein, pursuing a conversation, as it were, between his own "hermeneutics of facticity" and the Aristotelian texts in a mutual impregnation and fructification designed to get at the "things themselves."

We thus find a very constructive Heidegger, who joins his issue with Aristotle's, in this last-ditch effort "to get the Aristotle book out once and for all." We are at the parting of the ways between two Daseins, where the Aristotle book is about to ripen into the first drafts of BT. As such, SS 1924 provides us with perhaps our best glimpse into how that book on Aristotle might have looked. All signs indicate that it would have been a remarkable book. From all indications, it would have been even more difficult than BT, in view of the staggering depth, detail, and density of this Greek-German dialogue with the original texts of Aristotelian opus, in a frenetic intensity that must have overwhelmed the students of this course. Heidegger provides no advance outline for the course, but wends his way selectively through the Aristotelian corpus, working with strategically chosen texts as foci for his plunge into the specifics of an analysis of Greek-German Dasein. Fortunately for the students (and us), however, he pauses at certain critical junctures to clarify the overall movement of the course from each new vantage. In hindsight, we thus recognize the circular and so "repetitious" movement between being and human being familiar to us from BT. And yet, how remarkably different, in view of the heavily Greek ground which the course traverses, starting with its overall aim to come to terms constructively with the meaning of οὐσία and ὄν on the one hand, and, on the other, to do this by way of the Greek definition of the human being as the "speaking animal," in the full range of its gregariousness as covered by Aristotle. Hence, many themes that were given short shrift in BT, according to critical readers, are dealt with in great detail in SS 1924: animality, corporeality, the life of pleasure, Dasein both as consumer and as producer; speech in its full amplitude of possibilities, authentic as well as inauthentic, practical as well as theoretical; being-with as speaking to one another toward communal ends, with special attention to the problem of political rhetoric.

And let us not forget Heidegger's starting point in the problem of concept formation, which is the proximate and most specific motive of the course. The opening lectures already suggest how radically Heidegger wishes to pose this problem, to understand conceptuality from the ground up, "making Dasein itself visible and understandable as the possible soil of ground concepts," as he puts it later. "And if conceptuality is thus autochthonous, that is, rooted in the soil of Dasein itself, then in a certain sense Dasein itself must *be* conceptuality; which does not necessarily mean that this has already emerged as such in its moment of conceptuality, [for] it can be there implicitly" (109f.). What this may mean is suggested by another unique feature of this course on some of the "ground concepts of Aristotelian philosophy," a feature especially significant for our genealogical context. Of the thirty ground concepts listed by Aristotle in his lexicon in *Metaphysics* 5, four of them recur again and again in an ever-rising crescendo in Heidegger's development of Dasein as being-in-the-world, until their fundamental correlation cannot be ignored. The central one is διάθεσις, disposition, which "must be a kind of position, as the word itself suggests" (5.19.1022b2). Heidegger translates it as *Befindlichkeit*, which refers not only to a situation but also to *how* one "finds oneself" situated, positioned, disposed. It is destined to become the very first mode of "being-in," which lies at the heart of BT. Closely related to this central category are ἕξις, habit (5.20), and πάθος, passion or affection (5.21), both of which are in turn to be understood in terms of ἔχειν, having and being had (e.g., being "possessed" by fever: 5.23), a crucial word in Aristotle's ousio-logic.

Furthermore, in a comment that Heidegger will have occasion to exploit in his continuing use of the ousiologic of having, Aristotle already notes the close relation between "having" and "being in" (a world, for example: 1023a25). This constellation of ousiological categories now plays a crucial role in Heidegger's de-finition of the human situation, of Dasein in its ἕκαστος, its particular while.

Of the four-hour courses of Heidegger's Marburg period, this virtually unknown course in particular confronts us with an embarrassment of riches which we can hardly begin to communicate here. It is the same situation in which Heidegger finds himself, in the sixth hour (of forty-three) of the course, as he reconnoiters the massive Aristotelian opus in search of an initial guiding thread to follow the articulations of οὐσία through its roots in the human οὐσία. The specific problem of the course had already been set in the previous hour: definition, the resolve to speak radically with the world, finds the ground concepts it requires in the soil of human Dasein, when it is itself driven to its limits. Is the traditional definition of human being adequate to the task of laying bare this ground? Two more limiting formal characteristics of Dasein as life should first be made clear, its situatedness and its self-referential movement: Life in its way of being is being in a world; life is a being which in its being is concerned about its being, finds what matters to be in this very being. Moving from this formal structure to its various concrete possibilities, Aristotle finds among them a final possibility of being in the world, in a sheer whiling out of which that radical speaking with the world called definition is motivated. The theoretical life is a life of tarrying in pure beholding.

But another consideration of the extremities of the life of the speaking animal seems to take us in the opposite direction. Learning to move (κινεῖν) with the world in accord with the basic activity of discriminating (κρίνειν) suggests that the most fundamental way of be-holding (Vernehmen) and the truest possibility of perception reside in hearing, which corresponds (ent-spricht) to speaking as its most essential response or counter-word (Ant-wort). This way of being with others in ἑρμηνεύειν residing at the very core of speech clearly runs counter to the possibility of theorizing, with its emphasis on seeing.

To remove this contradiction, the entire context of speaking and hearing, the context of being with one another in the πόλις, is in need of clarification. Heidegger therefore launches the detailed exegetical work of his circular course with a central text early in the Politics (A. 2.1253a9–18) which explains why "man is by nature a political animal," more so than the other gregarious animals, like bees. For all these merely have "voice" (φωνή) to sound and indicate their pleasure or pain (being well- or ill-disposed to their environment), whereas the power of speech (λόγος) proper to humans is far more discriminating, in making manifest the useful and the inexpedient, the fitting and the improper, the just and the unjust. In short, human beings alone have any real sense of good and evil. "And such a being-with-one-another (κοινωνία = association, communion) cultivates a household and city" (1253a18). Being-with-one-another is therefore speaking with one another in our common concern with being-in-the-world.

Animals, too, in a certain sense, through voice, are "political." But whether human or animal, the world is always (constantly) there to be encountered, not necessarily as "objective reality," but for the most part in being enhancing or repressing, advancing or obstructing, attracting or repelling, and so on. As Heidegger puts it in a recurring "formal" statement spelling out one of his own major supplements guiding this exegesis of Aristotle, the world in which I find myself "gets to me" (*geht mich an*), approaches and solicits me and thus concerns me. It meets (*betrifft*) me and so afflicts or otherwise affects me. This is so even when many of the encounters in daily life do not get to me, are without import to me, as when I say, "That doesn't concern me." Unimportance or irrelevance is itself the everyday way in which the world approaches me. All this in the milieu of speech and being-with-one-another.

Rather than following this enormous course step by step, let us foreshorten our approach by tracing several of its most significant recurrent leitmotivs.

Pleasure

The animal encounters its environing world in terms of pleasure and pain. It gives voice to this in a kind of "animal rhetoric" which entices or warns. Luring and alluring signs seek to bring the other animal into the same disposition, threats and warnings would deflect it from a certain disposition.

Even though pleasure, on the level of the speaking human being, will undergo the modification from ζωή to βίος, thereby adding a sense of the temporal How to "life," it will continue to be the basic disposition (διάθεσις, *Befindlichkeit*) of human life. What then is pleasure? Verbally, it is good health, the state of well-being, "finding oneself well-disposed" (*sich Wohlbefinden*). Ontologically, it is the most natural and normal way of being-in-the-world. One might almost call it the state of nature. Aristotle describes it as "a movement of the soul, of the being of the living being in its world, a movement by which the soul as a whole is all at once set and settled into its natural and normal state, and this settlement of catastasis is perceived as such" (*Rhetoric* A.11). Heidegger describes this abrupt easing of tensions as an experience of "suddenly being elevated, that very distinctive lightness of being (*Leichtigkeit des Seins!*) in the world which belongs to joy" (17). Underlying this turning movement toward pleasure is the flight from its opposite, pain.

On the other hand, pleasure is not a movement at all but, much like seeing, is already complete in itself, and so does not need to become complete in the course of time (*Nic. Ethics* 10.3). And since all living beings are out to be complete, pleasure is already there in all. Though they claim to be "out for" different pleasures, they are in reality pursuing the same pleasure, namely, to live, to be. Aristotle calls it the "divine" in all (*Nic. Ethics* 7.13), which is not religious but ontological, meaning simply "to be always." Pleasure is accordingly an inescapable pathos "ingrained in the fabric of our lives" (*Nic. Ethics* 2.3.1105a3). It is not a "lust" but simply a determination of being as life. It is there even in the highest activity of human life, theoretical contemplation, as an inescapable companion. Even the sensual pleasures sought by the mass of humanity in common with plants and animals, like the "merely physiological functions" of nutrition and reproduction, are expressions of this "divine" tendency "to always be" (*De Anima* 2.4.415b1). Heidegger concludes, "This has nothing at all to do with religion, but instead is a circumscription of the concept of being in terms of being always. Being for the Greeks means to be present, to be always present" (43). Pleasure accordingly is the mood captured in the Parmenidean insight into being as constant presence.

Despite this Greek infection, however, Heidegger still seems to accept pleasure as the background disposition of being-in-the-world, at least in the environing world of the living. Moreover, pleasure as a self-finding is the most primitive way in which Dasein "has itself," and thereby has a disclosure about its being-in-the-world. "Having" is a pallid expression for knowledge about it. But "reflection" is an exaggeration which errs too far in the opposite direction in describing the character of this self-affection. "The ἡδονή reaches into the being of Dasein so originally that it can be identified with the ζῆν" (100).

Hearing and Fearing

In Aristotle's scale of temporal, human life-styles, between the life of enjoyment and the life of theoretical contemplation is the life of the political. He who resolves upon this life finds his end, it seems, not strictly in pleasure but in honor, a disposition which is notoriously dependent upon the other. Even if this may not be the ultimate goal, the rhetor, to achieve his end, must master a number of virtues which bear upon the very heart of being-with-one-another in the world. He must speak *of* the expedient and the inexpedient to be found *in* a temporally particular situation (καιρός) of a common There *to* those who would hear. Rhetoric is thus concerned with the convergence of at least three different human powers: being able to speak, to see what speaks for the matter under discussion, and to hear. Almost perversely, Heidegger's interest in rhetoric gravitates toward the latter power, in which speaking has its end. For speaking finds its completion in the communication, in being received or accepted by the auditor who undergoes or "suffers" the speech. A seemingly marginal topic, the "suffering" and resulting "passion" (πάθος) of the listener, is made central to the problem of finding the ground for concept formation in the ζῷον ἔχον λόγον. Waiting in the wings for us is the inversion of this definitional having into a "being had" by speech, or better, by a λόγος deeper than the one to which the loquacious Greek rhetors were accustomed. Or as Heidegger himself restates his course aim at this point, "The λόγος [is regarded] as a ground phenomenon of Dasein in such a way that, through it, a more original kind of human life becomes visible" (45).

Heidegger's gloss on Aristotle's *Rhetoric* is therefore introduced by an hour (the fourteenth of the course, May 30) which includes a "precursory" or advance indication of the "place" of hearing in speaking. Is it within or outside of speech? Is it itself a form of speech, and perhaps the highest? The most authentic possibility of being with one another is in fact listening, the perception and reception of speech. The human being moreover is not merely a speaker and listener but also a being who listens to himself and so speaks to himself. This gives him the possibility to respond to himself, to "obey" himself as well as others, to "heed" his own λόγος. To hear is to obey. Such a correspondence is moreover in keeping with the self-referential character of Dasein which was "formally indicated" in the opening lectures: Dasein is a being which in its being "goes about" (*geht um*) heeding this being.

But for Aristotle, even rhetorically central phenomena like advising, reproving, and exhorting already place us on the margins of the λόγος, properly speaking, next to the other-than-λόγος, the ἄλογον or "irrational." The will or the "desiring element" in the soul, when it "*listens* to reason*," can "in a sense be said to share in the λόγος" (*Nic. Ethics* 1. 13.1102b30ff.), improperly speaking, but the emotions may well be entirely out of bounds. These same bounds underlie Aristotle's distinction between the intellectual and moral virtues. The point need not be pushed too hard: being able to listen, listening to oneself, heeding the directives dictated by our practical life, or in Heidegger's phrase here, "letting something be said to oneself," whether by oneself or others, phenomenologically speaking all seem to be clearly within "reason."

The *Rhetoric* clearly places the listener and listening (hearkening, obeying) on the side of pathos and suggests that without it λέγειν simply could not be. Could it be that the play of passions is the very ground of λόγος? For passions are prone to affect and change our judgment, κρίσις, and in precisely definable ways according to the passion. For all their change of mood according to the circumstances, they have their own fluid order or λόγος. On the one hand, there remains something tumultuous, chaotic, and uncontrollable about the passions, which by definition "come to pass," happen (παθεῖν = to befall) to me willy-nilly as passive receiver,

affect and change me, making me ever other as I am "got to" and swept
along by them, gripped, overpowered. On the other, this sheer happening character is not only disclosive but also orienting with respect to my
situation as being in the world. "Through the πάθη, the possibilities of
orienting oneself to the world are essentially determined" (97).

One needs only to read Aristotle's lexical definition of πάθος (*Metaph.*
5.21) to recognize how powerful, revolutionary, and thoroughly "upsetting" the passions were understood to be. Emotions are intrinsically
"peace-disturbing." Heidegger's strategy of shifting the origin of the rhetorical situation to the passions therefore has the effect of transforming
it and the rhetorical process blandly described as "opinion formation,"
κρίσις, into an acute crisis situation of life and death[4] in which a more
radical kind of concept formation might well find its locus (*Rhetoric*
2. 1.1378a26). And although I am not responsible for my emotions as
such, since they "just happen" to me, I am responsible for how I cope
with my anger, fear, sorrow, and so on (*Nic. Ethics* 2.5.1106a1).

Thus, Aristotle's discussion of the emotions, those "dispositions characterized by shock" (67), is balanced by a discussion of the more steady,
practiced predispositions (ἕξεις = habits) which at their best (ἀρετή)
allow us to recompose ourselves in ways appropriate to the critical situation. The practiced prudent judgments made in resolute decision are
hardly the routine repetition of stereotypical judgments regarding stereotypical situations, like the imposition of a preexisting fixed grammatical paradigm (2.3.1105a22). Our temporally particular situation, surcharged with its sheer happening character, admits of no absolute and
once-and-for-all norm. As each situation is new, we must think anew and
act anew, περὶ ἕκαστον, in a φρόνησις and προαίρεσις which Heidegger
still calls "repetition," though its sense of time is no longer ousiological.
Aristotle himself seems to admit this breach in his ontology when he
notes that the "middle" (μέσον) of passion and action in any particular
situation is hard to find and easy to miss. "That is why it is so hard to
be good" (2.9.1109a25). "For the end of action varies according to the
καιρός" (3.1.1110a14).[5] For Heidegger, accordingly, the mean sought
for in action, its end, is the καιρός, feeling and acting "at the right time,
on the right occasion, toward the right people, for the right purpose
and in the right manner" (2.6.1106b21). Time is its own norm. And this
is never the same, even though we always seek to hold, and so to "repeat,"
that middle of our temporally particular situation against the ever-threat-
ening dispersion of multiplicity from both excess and defect. Or do we?
Is it not more the rhythm of loss and restoration, lapse and return? The
violent vacillations of the passions suggest as much, the swings away from
the mean toward the extremes of excess and defect contribute to this
straying temporality. What we repeat then is not the mean but the resolve

(προαίρεσις) to anticipate "the possibility of seizing the moment as a whole. This is why action out of and in the μεσότης (hold of the middle) is rare" (75). Excellence for Aristotle therefore resides in the "predisposition of resolute anticipation of our particular mean (μεσότης πρὸς ἡμᾶς, "for us") as defined by the λόγος found in that human situation through phronetic circumspection" (2.6.1107a1). And when Aristotle here cannot say ἀεί (always) but instead says, "Act oftener," he means, "Repeat oftener," "Resolve to seize your particular moment oftener." Since the possibilities that dispose us to human existence are, through lapse and loss, not always there, the usual determinations of constant time fail, so we must, in the "oftener" of repetition, espy entirely different temporal connections, connections which are kairological rather than ousiological in character (75).

Heidegger thus establishes, to his own satisfaction, the connection between πάθος (historical happening) and λόγος (speech) and how this λόγος comes to fruition in κρίνειν, the definitional decision resolutely open for its moment. Without a crisis, there would be no language. 'Hδονή understood as the background disposition of constant stasis, which underlies the Parmenidean insight into being as permanent presence, cannot account for the articulation of language and of time. If pleasure is a stasis, it is not an emotion in all its troubling upsets. No pain, no history.

[Of the three forms of human life that Aristotle examines, accordingly, only the political life manifests a sense of the full temporality of the particular human situation in its momentous decision. Only the political, accordingly, takes a hard look at the full rawness of life, at the prior pause of indecision, hesitation, doubt and the like. The constancy of presence achieved by the life of theoretical contemplation, portrayed primarily in its telos by Aristotle rather than in the aporetic shock that startles its interrogation, simply reflects, on a higher level, the life of pleasure of a hedonist intellectual. With this overriding ousiological emphasis, the long history of the Western "metaphysics of presence" since Parmenides is but an extended hedonism, its vaunted skepticism only the reverse side of the same coinage, at its best an insignificant underground subculture, at its worst a closet hedonism indulging itself in the luxus of fictional puzzles, the glee of idle games. "When I am, death is not. . . ." Did ancient skepticism ever truly confront the full pain of time? It would have been instructive if Heidegger, already infected by the Nietzschean skepticism of Franz Overbeck, had taught his course on ancient skepticism planned for WS 1922–23. But the deadline for his book on Aristotle was pressing, and there was more than enough in these ancient texts, read in their margins and so pressed to their limits, to find the same cycles of confrontation and evasion of the kairology of being in Aristotle.]

To illustrate this point, Heidegger concludes with a detailed exegesis of the structures of fear as expounded by Aristotle in his *Rhetoric*. The danger signals of an impending threat that comes to meet us now out of the near future, there and not there at the same time; the reaction of flight which signals the hope to be spared, ἐλπὶς σωτηρίας ("hope of salvation"):[6] these two poles together signal the critical juxtaposition of a to-be and to-not-be, which makes us a receptive audience to counsel, whether in the rhetorical or the personal situation. "Fear is the kind of disposition which brings us to speech" (106). Heidegger takes the occasion to point to its much more original fundament in angst, and suggests that Aristotle had a glimmer of its ontological scope. "Fear as angst for the Greeks is co-constitutive for the way of addressing that which both is and is not. Aristotle viewed this phenomenon so broadly that he too became aware that there is also a fear when nothing is there as the immediate occasion for fearing. The fear of nothing: from this it becomes understandable how the Greeks see being in the present, being as presentness" (75f). Contrary to the Greek horror of the infinite, however, the Christian *timor castus*, the pure fear that comes from the presence of God, could entertain such a radical fear in its full magnitude, and in fact saw in it "the beginning of wisdom." Such passions are the "ground out of which speech grows . . . the ground possibilities in which Dasein primarily orients itself concerning itself, finds itself. This primary orientation, the illumination of its being in the world, is not a *knowing*, but a *finding oneself*, which can be defined differently according to the manner of Dasein of a being. Only within this finding oneself and being in the world is the possibility given to speak about things, to the degree that they are stripped of the look which they have in the immediate go-around of life" (105).

Having reached the climax of his course two weeks before semester's end, Heidegger spends the remainder of the semester in an apparently unrelated gloss of the opening books of the *Physics*, Aristotle's book on Nature's motion. And yet, his central themes continue to erupt on the margins of the Greek sense of being that Aristotle is seeking to solidify. In a notable passage, Aristotle remarks that "the sun and stars and entire sky are always active, and there is no fear that they will ever stop, as the natural philosophers feared they might" (*Metaph.* 9.8.1050b22). Thus the possibilities posed by time, that these finished beings once were not and likewise will not be, are excluded, in a way betraying that very fear and its coupling "hope of salvation." "The fear guiding the analysis of being here lives out of the hope or conviction that beings nevertheless ought to be and have to be always there. . . . This interpretation of being tends to extirpate the fear of Dasein itself by transposing the puzzling into the familiar" (117), like the child who out of its narrow familiarity calls all men "father." It is the old Parmenidean pleasure of the constant presence of being, beheld in pure theoretical contemplation, the true pleasure of Greek science, which in fact receives its enjoyment from contemplating a world in which nothing more can ever really *happen*.

But when the concluding hour touches on Aristotle's distinction between an active and a passive νοῦς, we see that even "νοεῖν is in a certain sense a πάθος, solicited and encroached upon by the world" (133). Here, the middle-voiced ambiguity of action and passion reaches into the very center of the Greek contemplation of the world and life. Thus, Aristotle suddenly discovers that he has a new definition for motion, the actualization and bringing to an end of indivisibly united active and passive capacities (*Physics* 3.3.202b27). The example given by him for such passionate action is the indivisibility of teaching and learning. Teaching means to speak to an other, to *get to* (*angehen*) the other by way of communicating, so that the other in hearing *goes with* (*mitgehen*) the teaching. The νοεῖν in the human soul is always a δια-νοεῖν, involving the capacity of δέχεσ-θαι, being able to receive. And on this point in a nevertheless remarkable finishing flourish, Heidegger could have added that perhaps the Christian tradition had a more developed insight into the nature of such a "receiving" (cf. WS 1920–21 and SS 1921). After all, this massive course on Aristotle was supposed to have been a course on Augustine.

WS 1924–25: INTERPRETATION OF PLATONIC DIALOGUES
(Σοφιστής, Φίληβος)[7]

After the Pentecost break in SS 1924 (June 17), in a review and overview of that course, Heidegger already enunciates the "self-evident" hermeneutic principle by which he intends to come to terms in the following semester with these two admittedly difficult later dialogues of Plato on the topic of δόξα. It is the old principle of always proceeding from the clear to the obscure. Heidegger accordingly presumes that a philosopher of the stature of Aristotle understood his teacher better than Plato understood himself, that therefore what Aristotle said is but the more radical and scientific development of what Plato meant. From this working premise, he then proposes to approach these dialogues on being and nonbeing, truth and appearance, on the sham philosopher who calls himself a sophist, first by way of the most thoroughgoing exegesis of *Nicomachean Ethics* 6 we can ever expect from Heidegger, since it is virtually exhaustive. This exegesis of about seven weeks (total eighteen hours), with a week off to give the talk on the same content in the Rhine-Ruhr region, lasts until the Christmas break. As in the previous semester, its general intent is to make clear just what being the Greeks really had in mind when they raised the question of being.

Heidegger wastes no time in getting to the central problem of the course, namely, concealment. Why did the Greeks name falsity, ψεῦδος, positively and truth privatively, ἀ-λήθεια, as if something were lacking or missing in a phenomenon which nevertheless rightfully belongs to it? It is at least an indication that the Greeks understood the fact that un-concealment of the world from the beginning had to be fought for and won. The world is first disclosed only to the extent that natural needs demand it. And what is disclosed in the natural consciousness is at once covered up by speech. What is perhaps originally seen in an initial domain becomes a set of opinions fixed in sentences which through repetition only serve to cast that insight into oblivion. Philosophy (phenomenology) therefore has a double task of unconcealment, not only to overcome the initial ignorance in order to get "to the things themselves," but at the same time to do battle with the concealing chatter and rote repetition of language. This is evident in the struggle of the Greek philosophers against rhetoric and sophistry. The price of getting to the matters is no less cheap today, since we are burdened with an ever richer tradition. The more tradition, the more chatter.

Unconcealment is a determination of beings insofar as they are encountered. Truth does not belong to beings as if they could be without it. Nature is there even before it is discovered. Unconcealment is a peculiar character in beings insofar as they stand in a relationship of being looked at. This viewing which discloses the beings of the world, this knowing, is itself a Being, namely a way of being of that being which we call human. [Now the transition from Parmenides to Aristotle:] This way of being first shows itself in speaking. Human being expresses itself, to begin with, about the world. Λόγος is the mode of knowing in which the world is first disclosed, its basic function being ἀπόφανσις or δηλοῦν, either as affirmation or as denial. Even the negative assertion is a making manifest. Speaking in all these ways is the human way of life, its very being. Speaking is not mere noise, but a sound that indicates and means something, an ἑρμηνεία, the understandable semantic noise apropos of a human being (De Anima 2.8.420b5). Moreover, as living, every praxis of the human being, every νοεῖν, is at once movement, μεταβολή, a changeover from one thing to another, here un-concealment. All such enunciatory movements of the human soul, which intrinsically involve an ἑρμηνεία, taken together are understood by Aristotle as the movement of ἀληθεύειν.

Nicomachean Ethics 6

We thus come back to Aristotle's main investigation of the five movements in which the human being, by affirming or denying (accepting or rejecting), discloses beings. Contrary to certain misunderstandings, Heidegger reaffirms that all five, including the two more "practical" virtues concerned with doing and making in the realm of beings which "can be otherwise than they are," are in fact forms of "knowing": τέχνη is knowing one's way about a certain craft, and φρόνησις is circumspective insight into one's own situation of action. But more importantly for this course context, Heidegger now emphasizes that Aristotle supplements his list of five by adding two additional modes of "ἀληθεύειν" which are particularly "susceptible to deception and error" (*Nic. Ethics* 6.3.1139b17): ὑπόληψις (supposition, holding something for something) and δόξα (view, opinion). But for that matter, four of the first five, excepting νοῦς, are μετὰ λόγου and so are likewise subject to the falsity of the "as" structure of λόγος. The upshot: every effort of Dasein to know must prevail against the forces of concealment, that is, against 1) ignorance, 2) prevalent opinion, and 3) error. This pervasive encounter shows what is involved in the Aristotelian statement that truth is a character of the human being, that ἀληθεύειν is a determination of life (the soul), that human Dasein is as such true, it is "in the truth."

By extension from the entelechy (its being) of the human soul, "being true" is said in several other senses, so that we can also say that a thing is true (ἀληθές), the act of saying is true (ἀληθεύεν) and, by a final extension, what is said is true (ἀληθές).[8] It is from the last sense that the tradition of truth as correctness of assertion has sprung, and detached itself from its underlying senses. Truth thus gradually came to be regarded as an independent "value."

The four ways of "trueing" by actualizing νοῦς, the process of διανοεῖν μετὰ λόγου, may further be distinguished according to what is taken out of concealment. For the mode of psychic comportment or disclosive capacity differs accordingly as the kind of being which is revealed differs, according to Aristotle's well-known principle of distinction. Thus, science and wisdom, oriented to always-being, belong to the scientific faculty, ἐπιστημονικόν, while skillful know-how and phronetic insight, "contemplating" (θεωρεῖν) things which can be other than they are, are classified under the estimative faculty, λογιστικόν, of that portion of the soul possessing λόγος (*Nic. Ethics* 6.1.1139a5–13). Which of the four can be said to have the greatest possibility to reveal beings, which is the most true, which is the best habit or disposition (1139a16)? For "trueing" is subject to gradation, beings are not equally disclosed in each of these habits [suggesting another dimension to concealment].

The highest estimative faculty is of course phronetic insight, and the highest scientific one is "authentic understanding," wisdom. But which of these two is the "best habit"? We already know how this Greek story will end: σοφία with its "exalted" eternal object will win the field from φρόνησις. But in his detailed gloss, Heidegger will time and again look for ways, both in and out of the Aristotelian opus, in which phronetic insight asserts its potential superiority over contemplative wisdom. For

does not the human being find its own being to be the most important
being, so that its discovery would be the highest and most crucial? And
Plato himself made no distinction between these two highest virtues. On
the other hand, the turmoil of search of the unique self, which can always
"be otherwise than it is," is no comparison to the sheer hedonic pleasure
of beholding the "always is," which by definition is without trouble, turmoil, interruption, and confusion. In the presence of constant presence,
mood itself is constant. Moreover, only that which always *is* as it is can
really be known. That which can be otherwise is strictly speaking not
known. The historical cannot actually be known; I must come back to it
"time and again" to make it actual again in its temporal particularity.
Since that which always is does not change, I do not need to alter my
opinion of it.

Heidegger's reflections on φρόνησις reach their high point in his gloss
of *Nicomachean Ethics* 6.5, in a conclusion which has since become legendary.[9] Chapter 5 begins by appealing to our natural understanding:
Whom do we call a prudent person? He who knows how to deliberate
well about what is good and beneficial to himself. The truth of φρόνησις
applies to the person himself and not to an external thing, as it does in
the other practical virtue, skilled know-how. Contrary to this external
outcome, the deliberation of φρόνησις ends where it starts, in the action
of the person. Such a deliberation is not about some particular aspect
of the person, his health or his strength, but instead concerns the very
being of the human being, the εὖ ζῆν, "living well," the good life in
general (1140a28). Being here is not merely life, but the active life,
human action itself at its best, εὐπραξία. "Doing well is itself the end"
(1140b6), for its own sake, οὖ ἕνεκα, the *Um-willen* which is the very
character of Dasein (SZ 84). The praxis of being human (*Da-sein*) is at
once the ἀρχή and τέλος of φρόνησις. And Dasein *is* its praxis.

We have already encountered, in the very first of Heidegger's interpretations of Aristotle, the formula for this ontological circle of Dasein
which is destined to be frequently repeated in BT: "Dasein is a being
which in its being goes about this being" (SZ 12). But unlike the circle
of σοφία and νοῦς, φρόνησις is not an autonomous ἀληθεύειν, since its
object is the πρακτόν and its goal the εὖ πράττειν, authentic action. Its
function is to give "sight" to action, to clarify it, to make the action transparent to itself. This occurs within Dasein itself, so that this making-true
is affected by the "internal" disposition of the passions, which however
can prevent the discernment of the action's ἀρχή. But here we glimpse
the reason for φρόνησις and how precisely it "trues." It is possible for
a human being to be "beside" himself and not with himself. Through
the passions, the human being becomes concealed, does not see itself, and
so requires a certain ἀληθεύειν to become transparent to itself. Phronetic

insight must thus be won and maintained against the danger of "perversion and self-destruction" (1140b13). "Vice tends to destroy the sense of principle, ἀρχή" (1140b20). Put in terms of a suspect etymology, σωφρο-σύνη, temperance, means σῴζειν τὴν φρόνησιν (1140b12), saving insightfulness. And since pleasure belongs to the basic disposition of Dasein, human beings are always in danger of being concealed to themselves. There is accordingly a resistance to φρόνησις, it stands in constant conflict with the tendency of Dasein to conceal itself. Φρόνησις is thus a task which must be carried out in and through the pre-choice (προ-αίρεσις) of resolve.

How intimate φρόνησις is to the human being is suggested by a contrast with the more externalizing movement of skilled know-how. Both practical virtues are directed to a being which can be otherwise. Since τέχνη does not keep its own ἔργον, one might think that phronetic insight is its perfection and consummation. "But while know-how is subject to perfection, phronetic insight is not" (1140b22). Know-how is subject to experimentation and proceeds all the more certainly by risking erroneous experiments, in this way finding its way to the right possibilities. Intentional error is an advantage for τέχνη but not for φρόνησις (1140b23). Where the subject is one's own Dasein, self-violation is not a consummation but a degeneration. Φρόνησις is an either-or and not a both-and or more-or-less; it is στοχαστική, thereby involving a fixed orientation aimed at the "middle" as its fixed target. Φρόνησις is in itself already an excellence, and so not subject to perfection. Its mode of fulfillment is thus different from that of know-how.

As a sight or kind of knowledge, is φρόνησις perhaps related to ἐπιστήμη, at least in its preliminary deliberations? Within scientific knowing, there is a way of revealing which, like phronetic insight, bears upon beings which can be otherwise, namely, δόξα, which itself is not actually an ἀληθεύειν. But in a cryptic passage at the end of chapter 5 (1140b28–30), Aristotle rejects this connection. "Phronetic insight is not merely a 'logical' habit (ἕξις μετὰ λόγου μόνον). This is shown by the fact that a purely logical disposition can be forgotten (λήθη), whereas a failure of phronetic insight is no mere lapse of memory." We have already seen that there is a moment of phronetic insight which transcends λόγος toward νοῦς (chap. 5). But what is in question in this passage is a contrast between the concealment of forgetting characteristic of the dimension of theory and the mode of degeneration peculiar to φρόνησις. Heidegger interprets the contrast as follows (on November 11, 1924):

> Aristotle's explanation is quite curt and nevertheless clear from the context of book 6 as a whole. We are not straying too far in our interpretation when we observe that Aristotle here has happened upon the phenomenon

of conscience. Φρόνησις is nothing but the conscience already set in motion in order to make action transparent. What conscience yields cannot be forgotten. But what it says can be disguised, distorted, and distracted by the passions, rendered ineffective by pleasure and pain. It nevertheless announces itself time and again, and cannot be forgotten. Φρόνησις is not an ἀληθεύειν which we can regard as theoretical knowledge; it is not the ἀρετή of ἐπιστήμη and τέχνη, which is σοφία, philosophical reflection, the epitome of existence for Aristotle. (Cf. now GA 19:56)

Heidegger makes his final summary at the beginning of the next hour: φρόνησις as an ἕξις πρακτική is not μετὰ λόγου μόνον, cannot be forgotten, and lies outside the context of mere seeing [ergo in a context of "listening" to a different "speech"?]. It is not a speculation about ἀρχή as such, which is σοφία. It does not aim at a science (ἐπιστήμη) nor even an ethics. Instead, its ἕξις is what it is by its being embedded in πρᾶξις [the irrevocable facticity of conscience, as a "voice" beyond λόγος, as a deep structure identical to Dasein itself, which is praxis]. It is what it ought to be when it is the "sight" [site?] of a concrete action and concrete decision in the temporal particularity of Dasein.

For the remainder of the course, we hear nothing more from Heidegger about this startling equation of φρόνησις with conscience, on how this insightful entering into the very movement of praxis involves the movement of conscience, although there are perhaps some hints in the sporadic allusions to the phenomenon of listening. We must in fact wait until BT for more on the conflictual character of conscience which divides (κρίνειν) as an either-or and articulates the call of care. But some of the elements have been taking shape since the first exegesis of Aristotle in 1922: disclosure of the situation of action in the καιρός, resolve as the proper response to it, the self-referential character of its structure, the seeds of which Heidegger had in fact already found in the structure of flight in the fear of God in SS 1921, in which the from-which and the toward-which are the same.

The Question of the Eleatic Stranger

In the first week of December of 1924, Heidegger takes time off from his course in Marburg for a trip to the Rhine-Ruhr region, where he delivers his speech on Aristotle's concept of truth. It concludes with a "fundamental deliberation" on the future task of ontology, on the "great task" of phenomenology to develop an "ontology of Dasein" to supplement the ontology of the world which the Greeks have transmitted to us. Without such a phenomenological ontology, we shall continue to misuse the Greek categories of the world by applying them, for example, in Christian theology to the being of God, in short, "to a being whose manner of existence is presumably different from that of the sun and the eternally cycling sky" (perhaps a veiled critique of Max Scheler, who was present at the Cologne talk). Likewise, in the conclusion to his article on time completed the month before, Heidegger complains of the neglect of the question of the being of this being, that is, of Dasein, of the being of the person in the Christian interpretation of Dasein, of the being of the conscious ego in Descartes's interpretation.

But in all these complaints of ontological neglect, there is one final question lurking in the background which Heidegger does not yet explicitly raise, and so himself neglects. This will be corrected with his reading of the *Sophist*. Decades of exegesis of the opening pages of BT tell us where to expect the question and how it will be raised. And we are not disappointed as we follow Heidegger's meticulous exegesis of the Greek text of this dialogue, as he approaches the passage (*Sophist* 244A) to be made famous by his use of it in the first lines of BT. The paradigm question which the Eleatic Stranger asks in frustration, in a mock conversation with the dualists and pluralists, is first rendered by Heidegger as follows: "Since we find ourselves at an impasse from what you say, you will have to explain to us what you mean when you use the word 'being.' " What does the word "being" mean? What is its sense? This for Heidegger is not only the upshot of this passage but also the central concern of the entire dialogue (GA 19:446f.).

It is now early 1925 (February 10, to be precise). Heidegger is for the first time rehearsing the elusive basic ideas which a year later will structure the opening sections of BT. In the "battle of the Titans over οὐσία" (246A) historically fought by the early Greek philosophers for the middle ground between matter and idea, the one and the many, being and non-being, he sees the conquest of "the milieu in which ontological research as such can operate." Plato himself deserves the credit for following the inclination to go beyond the ontic toward the ontological, and so for the "unprecedented discovery of seeing the difference between being and beings, toward which Parmenides, albeit unclearly, took the first step with his proposition, 'being is.' " This apparent tautology, for all its self-evidence, is (!), precisely as self-evident, to be made the topic and clear concept of the most fundamental of sciences, for which "the nature of being is quite as difficult to comprehend as that of not-being" (246A). In addition to its self-evidence, a second objection against the concept of being, likewise symptomatic of the oblivion of this central question, is that it as the "highest" concept is undefinable. Heidegger answers: It is not at all clear what sort of "logic" is needed in order to conceptually elaborate the initially indeterminate concept of being, except that it will not be a logic of beings. Nevertheless, it is not enough simply to raise the question of the sense of being formally (GA 19:447f.). The milieu for ontological research, this middle ground between being and beings, must be prepared by the concrete elaboration of the very placing [and place] of the question. This will entail its analysis into 1) what is asked for (the sense of being), 2) what is asked about (being), but to begin with, 3) what is interrogated, the entity whose structure is to guide us toward what is asked for, the sense of being itself. The question then becomes: What being is truly adequate to/for the sense of being? What characters does such a being yield? From this perspective, it can be said that the Greeks themselves left the question of the sense of being unasked. For they took it to be self-evident that being means presence, but never really asked what being must be present in order to justify such an assumption, and why precisely this being. For only from a being which always is can the sense of being as presence receive its justification. Moreover, this sense of being depends on the possibility of encountering such a being in its presence. What then makes this encounter possible? What are the conditions of access to such a being? This line of questioning was not pursued by the Greeks, though there were hints of it in the presence of the phronetic soul in the *Sophist* (247A), and earlier in Parmenides' dictum that "thinking and being are the same." In noting such Greek clues, Heidegger is clearly paving the way for his own approach to the question of being through the phenomenological structures of intentionality embodied in Dasein. This will be the central theme of his course of the following semester, somewhat inaptly entitled, "History of the Concept of Time," reflecting the lag in the academic calendar in which the title announced in advance is surpassed and outstripped by rapidly developing new insights.

These passages from the *Sophist* add a kind of esoteric ontological purity to the ensuing drafts of BT in 1925 and 1926, and give us the palpable verbal quality of the question of the sense of being as such, a concern for its concept. Yet Heidegger regards this last step as continuous with his earlier concerns for the underlying assumptions entering into the Greek sense of being. Heidegger says as much in March of 1925 when he reports to Löwith that he is now expanding his "Time" essay of 1924 in order to situate it "in the context in which it was first elaborated, as the ground for the destruction of Greek ontology and logic." And in a letter to Rudolf Bultmann at the end of 1927 which spells out the complex of motives which entered into BT, first and foremost is the Greek motif: "My opus seeks to radicalize ancient ontology and at once tries to build [into it] the relation to the region of history."

PART THREE

Three Drafts of *Being and Time*

Another book is born. One could conclude, from the old Heidegger's account of it, that it simply occurred to him sometime in SS 1923 to start jotting down notes for a book which would bear the title "Being and Time" (US 95/9). But the Story we have been telling uncovers a far more complex context which places this matter-of-fact anecdotal simplification in a far richer trajectory of precedents and tendencies. BT as an overall program had its birth in the Introduction to an Aristotle book drafted in October 1922. The work on Aristotle dominated Heidegger's publication plans well into 1924. The following two years, through 1926, were dominated by the publication project which first bore the titles "The Concept of Time" (1924) and "History of the Concept of Time" (1925) before it eventually was entitled "Being and Time" (1926). But this overlapping of publication projects is already an indication of their interdependence. Of course, in 1922, Heidegger was not yet aware of the fact that, in introducing a book on Aristotle, which he never managed to publish, he was laying the ground for another book which would precipitate him to world fame. But in 1922, he was already acutely aware of the close relationship between the historical and the systematic dimensions of his overall program. Thus, as early as February 20, 1923, he reports to Löwith that he is expanding that Introduction to include basic elements of earlier interpretations of the facticity of life—the systematic part—to the extent that these are related to the interpretations of Aristotle that are to follow. And when the very first draft of BT does take shape, it is then redrafted in 1925 to relate it back to the historical purpose from which it sprang, "as a basis for the destruction of Greek ontology and logic"[1]—literally the same goal which was operative in the book on Aristotle. The same backflow undoubtedly took place with the treatise on

Aristotle. It existed in manuscript form into 1926, when Heidegger first drafted the historical Second Part of BT with its final Division bent on "destroying" Aristotle's texts "with the problematic of Temporality as our clue" (SZ 39f.). Since that portion of BT was never published, how previously thoroughly glossed texts like *Nicomachean Ethics* Z would have looked when examined from this newfound ontological perspective can only be the tantalizing subject of reconstructive and "deductive" speculation.

Thus, on August 5, 1925, the Marburg Philosophical Faculty could announce to the Berlin Ministry of Education that their candidate Heidegger now has two books "in the works": In addition to the old Aristotle book, which "will soon appear," "there is now also a systematic work of recent origin entitled *Time and Being*—now being printed—which shows Heidegger from another side, namely, as an autonomously developing philosophical thinker."[2]

The drafts prefigured. When this nominating petition was dispatched to Berlin, Heidegger had indeed already drafted two semblances of BT in accord with the circumstances of a very busy academic life. He would not really draft the third and finally published version until the petition for his promotion was rejected by Berlin late in January 1926 (see Appendix C). That he would do this draft in the "space" of a month once again relates to the same academic necessities. The surprise is more in the number of conceptual innovations that still occur at that late stage in such a short period of time. This is the "inside story" that we wish to recount. What goes into the making of a Great Book?

Our focus is primarily the published "systematic" portion of BT, which nevertheless was written in a kind of envelope of promissory notes addressed to the never-published historical Part. BT as a text finds its start in the Introduction to the Aristotle book of October 1922, which in large part contains the only known preview of BT as a program, already distinguishing a systematic part from the historical part that Heidegger was then busily composing. With this outline in mind, Heidegger, perhaps by mid-1923, begins to think of composing at least a systematic *essay* to supplement his more historically oriented treatise on Aristotle. The course of SS 1923 concludes with a triad of questions that sets the pattern for the analysis of the environment which becomes a substructure in all of the drafts of BT. By the end of 1923, Heidegger has found the occasion and context, with the publication of the Dilthey-Yorck correspondence, to plan such a systematic essay in the form of a brief journal article. The actual drafting of texts which will eventually develop into the book of 1927 is thereby begun. Our book about a book now becomes the inside story of the movement of drafts and redrafts, the shuffling of texts which include not only articles and talks but also portions of course transcripts being modified for their new purposes, incorporated into settings still bearing signs of incomplete integration, with the gaps sometimes still showing (e.g., SZ §82). On the conceptual level which is our main focus here, it is the Story of a core idea (movement—countermovement) being amplified to its fullest, then nuanced in a different direction by another guiding idea (the kairological), of a swelling framework which still remains intact for all its modifications, of substructures contextualized in new ways, of largely latent ideas remaining latent and kept suppressed, overdue for development or developed prematurely in unfruitful directions (like *Verstehen*), of hesitations followed by quite precise terminological decisions (existence), of old terms used tentatively in a broad way and then revamped for a more specific purpose (*Bewandtnis*), of obscurities left unclarified, deliberately or not.

I shall pursue this genealogical story wherever it leads, dead ends (*Holzwege*) and all, in accord with the BCD trail that points it out (see Appendix C for the factual documentary). The reader will not find a systematic section-by-section genealogical analysis of BT at its conclusion to tie the loose ends of the Story together. We will end where we are now, still under way toward BT, but by then into its unpublished Part, with Heidegger himself still under way. But by way of an initial overview of the road still to be traversed, as a kind of advance announcement or "formal indication" to guide the reader through the maze of drafts, an outline of the major threads, interwining their way through the three drafts, may prove useful.

Such threads of dominant progression are necessarily large and coarse, but perhaps they will mitigate some of the complexity of conceptual movement of the more subtly converging and diverging strands, hopefully without overpowering them with labels. As we progress from one draft to another, as we move from 1924 to 1925 to 1926, the dominant question becomes in turn "What is history?," "What is being?," "What is time?," with the other two however always lurking in the background. We might therefore speak of a hermeneutic draft, an ontoeroteric draft (focused on the question of being *as such*), and a kairological draft. Each has its dominant figure who becomes its focus of deconstruction: whence the Dilthey draft, the Husserl draft, and the Kantian draft. Behind both Husserl and Dilthey is the deconstruction of Descartes, to which we were first introduced in WS 1923–24. In a way, the same deconstruction is behind Kant as well, for the very same reason: the ocular issues of immanent perception, intuition, reflection contaminating the core of immediate experience. But Kant suddenly assumes a powerful positive role on the verge of BT itself, and so throughout its pages. Most important of all, the core of the drafts, the formal indication used in guiding their respective analyses of the human situation, nuanced differently in each of the drafts in its attempt to indicate the immediacy of experience—under way rather than finished, undergoing understanding instead of the stilling reflection of intuition—although they are *almost* the same: being in a world, to-be, ex-sistence. Especially the last indicator involves a secret incubation period, held in abeyance, before it is overtly adopted and quickly develops its surprising new consequences, only to be gradually displaced by a fourth indication especially geared to the historical Part of BT: transcendence. But that in turn takes us to another story, a sequel, the Demise of BT.

SEVEN

The Dilthey Draft:
"The Concept of Time" (1924)

"THE CONCEPT OF TIME" (JULY 1924)

The core idea of BT as we know it receives its first "oral publication" in the public address entitled "The Concept of Time" presented to the Marburg Theologians' Society on July 25, 1924. Gadamer aptly calls it the "Urform" of BT. Not yet a draft of BT, it is nevertheless the first major and quite public step toward the extant book BT, by elaborating its core structure, which in retrospect finds its seminal roots in the 1922 Introduction. For in that *Einleitung* (cf. chap. 5), Heidegger for the very first time juxtaposes the deliberate seizure of my certain death, through which the very being of life becomes visible, with the countermovement of falling through absorption in the averageness of the public "one." Death's peculiar sight into the very being of life therefore provides a unique ontological access to the temporality properly belonging to human being, and so also to its historicality. This polar space of interrelationships between life's movement and its countermovement first unveiled in the *Einleitung* receives its first full-fledged development in July 1924 in terms of two basically different ways of "being temporal" (*Zeitlichsein*).

But something peculiar has happened terminologically between 1922 and 1924. For precisely at this point of staking out the polar space of countervailing movements in his *Einleitung*, Heidegger for the very first time also formally introduces the term "existence" to define the authentic way of temporalizing one's facticity. For this authenticating is always an "existentiell" (i.e., individual) possibility and choice by which to counteract the tendency to lapse in life. And in SS 1923 (GA 63:16), interpreting one's facticity in terms of this ownmost possibility of "existence" generates those conceptual explicata or categories which may be called "existentialia." But in his public address of 1924 (*and* in the ensuing drafts of BT save the very last), Heidegger diligently avoids this "existentialist" vocabulary, even though the main thrust of the lecture is to show that "Dasein is authentically with itself, it is truly existent" (BZ 18),[1] by persistently forerunning the certain possibility of its "being gone" (*das Vorbei*). Why this diligent evasion of a vocabulary which Heidegger began to develop in his early Freiburg period and which will eventually inundate BT itself? The reasons are obscure, but one reason that can be gleaned from Heidegger's correspondence at this time is a strong aversion, which he apparently developed upon first arriving in Lutheran Marburg, to the "Kierkegaardism" then in vogue in theological circles.[2] Given this burgeoning antipathy, the Marburg Theologians' Society was the last place for him to wax "existential"!

Of course, two other key terms central to this old polar constellation are also not explicitly used. 1) But the countermovement of "falling" does appear implicitly in the lecture in the "flight from goneness" (BZ 20) opposing the "run forward" which anticipates this uttermost possibility of being gone; and the addictive "pendency" (*Verhängnis*: cf. chap. 5, p. 256) of falling is suggested when Heidegger writes, "Dasein flees before the How and attaches itself to (*hängt sich an*) whatever What is present at the time" (BZ 21). 2) The old standby, "facticity," also never appears, but instead is replaced by its more temporally charged counterpart, the *Jeweiligkeit* (eachness, temporal particularity) of the "I am." It was first introduced as the "more precise expression" of facticity in SS 1923 (GA 63:7), and plays perhaps the central role in this public lecture as a backdrop for distinguishing two ways of *being* temporal, "there," particular and individual, "in each case mine." Moreover, Heidegger in SS 1924 had discovered a new way of talking about facticity through his gloss of Aristotle's *Rhetoric* and loses no time in applying it. Augustine had already seen that the self experiences time immediately in an "affective disposition" (*Befindlichkeit*: BZ 11), and this immediate self-experience is the way in which "Dasein has itself" and "*finds* itself with itself" (BZ 14) without reflection. "The primary relation to Dasein is not contemplation or observation, but the '*being* it.' Experiencing or encountering oneself, like speaking about oneself, or self-interpretation, is only one particular and distinctive way in which Dasein in each case *has itself*" (BZ 14).

Fresh from his course on Aristotle's *Rhetoric*, Heidegger is here taking the first, albeit quite imperfect steps toward articulating the immediacy of human experience in terms of three equiprimordial ways of "being in." As Aristotle already knew, "the being-in-the-world of human being takes place primarily in speaking. . . . How Dasein in its world speaks about its way of getting along with its world equally yields a self-interpretation of Dasein. It asserts how Dasein in each such case understands itself, as what it takes itself" (BZ 13). This still quite nascent phase in the discussion of *In-Sein*, the equiprimordial constellation of involvement with the world and self through affective disposition, understanding, and discourse, is here still being articulated without the aletheic vocabulary of "truth" also developing out of Aristotle, or the kinetics of "thrown project" unique to BT itself. This constellation will be a major topic of concern in the forthcoming drafts. It will also be one of the very last chapters to find its "true" voice in BT as we have come to know it.

Especially the prereflective immediacy of "finding oneself with oneself" so that one finds oneself "disposed," this "primary relation" to one's situation (Dasein) such that "I am it" (BZ 14: "It" is the old KNS experience), provides a latent key to the recurring leitmotiv of the lecture: Dasein is its time, I am my time. The secret dimension of disposition—the "uncanniness" of angst surfaces but once (BZ 18)—gives concrete substance to the fulcrum statement, "Time is the how" (BZ 27), which allows Heidegger to transform the opening question of the lecture, "*What* is time?," into a concluding litany of new questions: "Who is time? More precisely: Are we ourselves time? Or still more precisely: Am I my time?" (BZ 27). Thus, after arriving at the "answer" that "Dasein *is* time" and not merely "in time," experienced as a how rather than a what, Heidegger in the end questions even this, his one seemingly central point reinforced through reiteration, suggesting that there is more to come. What is waiting in the wings, beyond the concept of time which is the one topic of the lecture, is precisely the concept of being itself, and therefrom a more radical sense of time "itself."

How close does Heidegger come in this lecture to confronting his newly won concept of time with the classical concept of being, let alone the need to "repeat" (and so to review and revise) it in view of this new concept of time? The armature of the lecture, from its proper starting point in the temporal particularity of the "I am" (BZ 11) to its thus virtually tautological conclusion of "I am my time" ("time is in each case mine": BZ 26), operates strictly on the level of the question of the being of Dasein, which is in each case mine. And yet the very last question in the series seeking "to repeat temporally" the what-question, "Am I my time?" (BZ 27), invites us to question even this conclusion, and to question Dasein itself. But is it clear that Heidegger is thus inviting us to question Dasein at the more fundamental level of being itself? To make this step beyond Dasein to being itself in the concluding context outlined here by Heidegger, I see only one possible direction of questioning: How am I *my* time? Is my time ultimately really mine, if I first and always necessarily "*find* myself with myself" (BZ 14)? The concluding summary of the lecture thus begins to restore the notes of receptive acceptance of the one-and-only factic conditions of life out of which the more active forerunning springs, which are at once the conditions toward which it aims. Attainment of the time proper to me is governed by a *principium individuationis* "from out of which Dasein in its temporal particularity *is*. . . . In forerunning, Dasein becomes visible in its unique here-and-now and the once-and-for-all of its unique destiny in the possibility of its one-and-only goneness" (BZ 26f.). This individuating encounter with death, the ultimate facticity, "makes all equal."

And yet Heidegger had just finished saying that at this level of encounter "the Being of temporality means unequal reality" (BZ 26). Through this rather abrupt juxtaposition of sameness and difference, he is thus raising the problem of a reality which belongs at once to each and to all, a problem common to the temporal particularity (*Je-weiligkeit*) of Dasein *and* to the distributive universality of being itself. And even earlier, he raises another paradox: "Dasein is time, time is temporal. Dasein is not time but rather temporality. The basic statement, *Time is temporal*, is accordingly the most proper determination" (BZ 26). I both am and am not my time, because time itself is temporal: it is the same relationship that he discovered in KNS 1919, at the interface of factic immediacy, between me and my life, a life which is given to me before I assume it as mine. And this "before" of not-mine provides the space of transcendence, beyond the phenomenological ontology of Dasein which dominates the lecture, to a more fundamental ontology of being, which comprehends Dasein.

But even though the lecture abounds with the ontological concerns evident since 1921 for the "being of Dasein" and the "being of time" (BZ 10), and closes by raising the issue of the "being of temporality" (BZ 26), Heidegger does not make the reverse move to the genitive subjective "temporality *of* being" which would have completed the ontological destructuring, and so never overtly poses the question of being as such. For this we must wait for WS 1924–25, which will examine the question of being as such more overtly by way of Plato's *Sophist*. But the unspoken possibility of this question was already present from the beginning in the phenomenological goal "to understand time out of time" (BZ 6) *itself* and not from the theological starting point of eternity. This *solus ipse* looms large in the end in the ultimately centering statement of the lecture, "time is temporal" (BZ 26), the seemingly tautological fruit of such a phenomenological return to the matter *itself*, a "reflexive" return which inevitably raises the question of being within phenomenology. "Time is temporal" takes a step closer to but is not quite identical with "It temporalizes" (*Es zeitigt*, "It times"), the ontological strategy of the impersonal sentence already in use as early as KNS 1919 as a way to get to the level of being itself. Thus, the public lecture of 1924 only intimates the turn from Dasein to being, to the "being *of* [T]emporality" (BZ 26) of the famous Third Division of BT. Muted and thoroughly undeveloped as it is, such intimations feed Gadamer's declaration that this deceptively simple lecture, teeming with "ordinary language" statements more than the formal language of ontology, is the "Urform" of BT, if we understand this in the sense of a nascent and incipient "primitive form." It thus marks the zero-point for the coming development of the concept of being out of the filigree of the concept of time, and vice versa. But it is a task which the lecture itself, as an occasional piece, a single evening lecture on "The Concept of Time," from the start overtly states it will not do, namely "to question back behind time into its connection with other categories" (BZ 6). The lecture is a deliberately truncated treatment of the concept of time which is not even supposed to be philosophical. It would thus have been improper to interject the one concept proper to philosophy, being, into this context. The lecture is therefore not really a draft of BT, even though it contains virtually, albeit in very unequal proportions, all the major elements of the Second Division of BT on "Dasein and Temporality," as Heidegger himself notes at one point in BT (SZ 268n). We have already suggested above how incomplete, diffuse, and even chaotic the treatment of the themes of the First Division is in this talk.

As an initial rendering of the Second Division of BT, the lecture concentrates especially on the contrast between the everyday "now" time of clocks and the futural time which anticipates my unique goneness, and concludes by applying this contrast to history and historicality (BZ 22–26). This serves, among other things, to complete the circuit of ordinary language identifying Dasein with its time, so that Dasein not only *is* its present in everydayness and *is* its future in forerunning but also *is* its past in historicality. "We are history," according to Count Yorck, whose correspondence with Dilthey Heidegger is then studying in preparation for a review article which will turn out to be the first substantive draft of BT.[3] "But Dasein is historical in itself insofar as it is its possiblility. In being futural, Dasein is its past, coming back to it in its How. The way of coming back is, among others, conscience" (BZ 25). The possibility of "repeating" the past in the future, in the How of possibility, by way of a critique of the present is "the first principle of hermeneutics. It says something about the Being of Dasein, which is itself historicality" (BZ 26).

Historicality is the linchpin in BT between the systematic First Part and the historical Second Part calling for the hermeneutic critique or "Phenomenological Destruction of the History of Ontology" (SZ 39). To what extent is such a project already operative in the lecture? The possibility of such a project dates back to Heidegger's return to Aristotle's texts since 1921. The major question almost immediately becomes whether the ontological paradigm in Aristotle's *Physics*, "being" taken as a finished product, focusing on the what (εἶδος) of an "it," is adequate for the ontological interpretation of human life. In the first weeks of SS 1924, Heidegger notes in great detail that the how of a produced what, which lies at our disposal, is presence, *Gegenwärtigkeit*, παρουσία. Heidegger puts this temporal clue toward historical destruction to work for the very first time in the lecture through the references to Aristotle's *Physics* (BZ 7f.) which raise the issue of the paradigm of "in time" operative in the time of everydayness and science. It is also at work in the bracketing of the theological approach to time through eternity, "the empty being-forever of ἀεί" (BZ 5), which "turns out to be a mere derivative of being-temporal" (BZ 6). But these are only the halting beginnings of a historical destruction of ontology by way of fundamental insights into time. At this seminal phase, there is hardly a full-fledged program in place for destroying the history of ontology along these newfound lines, aside from the ongoing confrontation of the towering figure of Aristotle. We must wait a while for a full slate of candidates for such a destruction to be named, as various figures are accused of neglecting not only the question of the being of the human being but also of being as such.

In the lecture, it is not so much historical figures as the "parade of sciences," from theology to relativity physics to history to philosophy itself, that is placed under "police" scrutiny, to determine whether their concepts of time are really getting at the matter under investigation or simply "feeding off of traditional and worn-out verbal knowledge of the matter at hand" (BZ 7). In the case of philosophy, this propaedeutic "policing science" would "on occasion carry out a house search of the ancient thinkers, just as they themselves have done" (BZ 7). The same "destruction" is then applied to the concepts of ordinary talk and experience. But with this step into the pretheoretical and even the preontological, we actually come to the potentially revolutionary power of this "pre-science" (*Vorwissenschaft*: BZ 6), the "science" that precedes science and assumes the "subordinate but sometimes urgent task" of conceptual scrutiny or "policing" of the sciences, in this sense deserving to be called the very "logic" of ontology and the sciences. A year later, Heidegger will describe these seemingly stringent policing duties more creatively as a "productive logic" (GA 20:3; also SZ 10), which leaps over the sciences into the domains of reality they investigate, sometimes exposing dimensions of their being which articulate new directions of research, if not new sciences. Such is the case in this lecture, which "breaks" through the traditional conception of time in order to "enter" a new domain of possibility. The method of "destruction" is the radical formality of the formal indication: dissolution of the structured what into the unstructured how of the indeterminate extreme of my certain goneness, which is to be kept free of all what, when, how long, and how much. We leave this necessarily brief lecture with a growing sense of the richness of its direct and simple insights, waiting to be mined on their own terms and not just as passing phases to be displaced by "improved" drafts: the contrasts between what and how, how and how long, losing and having time (how one gives oneself time: BZ 19), two different ways of individuation, death as the only true "past and gone" as opposed to the already experienced past which only seems irrevocably past (BZ 24f.). Nascently crude but pregnantly suggestive, a brilliant rhetorical *tour de force* of ordinary language in a period of so much turgid writing, nevertheless without lapsing into cheap popularization, structured by a sophisticated method, therefore charged with latent insights and unspoken possibilities: small wonder that this lecture enjoyed a certain notoriety in intellectual circles until it was displaced by the more "notorious" text of BT itself. It quickly circulated in transcripts stemming from several sources. One of the two near-verbatim transcripts used to compose the published edition comes to us from the papers of Theodor Haecker, the Catholic publicist and Kierkegaard translator with whom Heidegger had a running "love-hate" relation for decades. Another more deviant transcript was used by Heidegger's student and colleague, Oskar Becker, to develop some of his own thoughts on natural versus historical temporality in the context of "mathematical existence," their differing ways of "repeating" themselves, and even a formal schematization of the "chain" of generations which structures the interpersonal dimension of history![4]

"THE CONCEPT OF TIME" (NOVEMBER 1924)

The Story[5]

This would-be journal article and very first draft of BT originates from Heidegger's involvement and interest in the beginnings of an interdisciplinary journal of the then burgeoning "Dilthey School," and so out of the context of Dilthey's own broad interdisciplinary interests and achievements beyond philosophy in the whole spectrum of human sciences. The initiative in fact came from Erich Rothacker, a follower of Dilthey and coeditor of the newly founded *Deutsche Vierteljahrsschrift für Literaturwissenschaft und Geistesgeschichte* and, as philosopher, in charge especially of the latter domain of "intellectual history." In October of 1922, he writes to Heidegger and explains that though the primary purpose of the new journal would be the history of literature, considerable attention would be devoted to its interrelations with the history of philosophy, religion, and art, with special reference to the Middle Ages. In this regard, he invites Heidegger to submit a title which could be included in the prospectus of the new journal. Heidegger responds with a title excerpted from work on the historical destruction of Aristotle and of his influence upon Christian anthropology into the Middle Ages, and the subsequent Lutheran critique of that influence as it is carried over into German Idealism. It is the historical outline he had just sketched out in his *Einleitung*. The proposed title, "The Ontological Foundations of Late Medieval Anthropology and the Theology of the Young Luther," remains a viable publication project into late 1924, when Heidegger reiterates his promise to Rothacker to write such an article. But it is never written, in part because Heidegger's project of historical destruction assumes a less religious orientation by 1925. Deepening its "guiding clue" (SZ 39) from facticity to Temporality, the destruction becomes more purely ontological and less anthropological, replete with historical figures other than Paul, Augustine, and Luther. Focus on these latter reflects the influence of Dilthey's "Christian" reading of the history of philosophy, which had fascinated Heidegger since 1919 (cf. chap. 2 above).

But toward the end of 1923, Heidegger proposes a second article to Rothacker which he actually does bring to completion in the following year. In requesting the journal's review copy of the Dilthey-Yorck correspondence,[6] Heidegger adds that he wishes, in conjunction with such a review, to make a fundamental statement about Dilthey's work in general. In the ensuing months, this "review" article grows to more than double its originally estimated length and becomes instead a seventy-five-page fundamental statement about Heidegger's own work. Perhaps not only because of the length of the essay but also because of its tortured language and ponderous style, the senior coeditor, the Germanist Paul Kluckhohn, expressed reservations about publishing the article in the *Deutsche Vierteljahrsschrift*. As a result, it was transferred to Husserl's *Jahrbuch*, where it appeared well over two years later, after growing into the full-length book that we know as *Being and Time*.

The Article

The advance title of the article was "The Concept of Time (Comments on the Dilthey-Yorck Correspondence)," but the subtitle was dropped in the final manuscript, which was hand-copied by Heidegger's wife, Elfride, and then sent to Rothacker. A portion of this handwritten manuscript, the five-page review of the Dilthey-Yorck correspondence, finds its way bodily into the final clean copy of BT sent to the printer in late 1926, and appears in §77 (SZ 399/5–403/13) virtually in the form it was written in 1924 (see Appendix C). This passage, along with the sentence acknowledging Husserl's "incisive personal guidance" (SZ 38n), thus turn out to be the very first passages written for the famous book of 1927. More than these verbatim passages, however, it is the structure of the article that warrants calling it the very first draft of BT. Thematically and structurally, the two middle sections of the article coincide roughly with the two published Divisions of BT, and the two outer sections introduce and develop Dilthey's problem of historicality in the ontological context thus projected and developed. In addition, the final section includes an initial historical subdividing of the task of a destruction of the history of ontology along the lines projected in BT. Let us examine the article section by section with an eye especially to its distinctive features as a step in the development toward BT.

I. Dilthey's Line of Questioning and Yorck's Basic Intention[7]
The "occasion" for this "provisional communication" of Heidegger's ongoing investigations on time is the publication of the Dilthey-Yorck correspondence. The aim is to make the understanding of this correspondence "more compelling." In this vein, Heidegger places his entire article under the auspice of a single phrase underscored in one of Yorck's letters, which identifies the central intention of that correspondence: "our common interest in understanding historicality" (see SZ 398). The article accordingly wishes to clarify the line of questioning inherent in this interest. Historicality is not "world history" but rather *being*-historical.

Such an interest precedes the question of a philosophy of science regarding the object of the historical and how it is an object of historiology. The more radical question of what it means *to be* historical calls for the ontological exposition of the structure of a being which *is* history. It considers this entity in its being and conceptualizes the characters of being thus exposed into categories, fundamental concepts.

Accordingly, this entity itself must be brought into the purview of an investigative regard, the entity itself must show itself, it must become a phenomenon and so addressed just as it shows itself. Phenomenology is therefore the only way to carry out such an ontological investigation. Historicality is an ontological character of the human being, Dasein. The basic constitution of Dasein, from which historicality can be read off ontologically, is temporality. The endeavor to understand historicality thus leads to the task of a *phenomenological explication of time*. [A marginal note puts it more in the language of the July lecture: "Here we have the question, which entity *is* actually as history? This is to be answered from the sense of historicality, from that which is primarily inherent in it, temporality. What entity 'is' actually temporal, so that it is time itself? This entity is in actuality then also historical."]

This clarification of the line of questioning which is implicit in the interest "to understand historicality" seeks to allow the heritage of Dilthey and Yorck to take effect in and through productive confrontation. In their common interest, each friend shared a different portion of the labor, which must be taken into account in what follows. From Yorck, who published less extensively, we have only a few largely fundamental reflections and theses, which nevertheless show him to be ahead of Dilthey at a forward post in their common struggle. The way to appropriate his ideas is to place them into Dilthey's work and so to make them fruitful for it. Only in this way do we understand Yorck's letters as those of a friend whose only concern is to help a fellow philosopher in a communication vital to his existence, and in the process to help himself.

Thus, characteristic passages from the letters will serve to bring out Yorck's philosophical intention and direction in regard to Dilthey's line of questioning, which will be described briefly. It is within this horizon that we shall situate our investigation of time. The analysis of Dasein into its characters of being (Section II) provides the basis for the explication of time (Section III). The phenomenal field opened by these two Sections provides the context which determines the basic lines of historicality as a character of the being of Dasein; it also defines the mode of research in which the "understanding" [*sic!* The usage is significant, since *Verstehen* will be used so rarely in this "Dilthey-draft."] of historicality and of Dasein is to be actualized (Section IV). The entire investigation is thus directed back to its starting point and likewise bears witness to its intention "to foster the spirit of Count Yorck in the present in the service of Dilthey's work" (cf. SZ 404: the repetition of this statement in BT itself amounts to a "dedication" of the entire work to Dilthey and Yorck, and not just to Husserl!).

Ia. Heidegger begins Section I with the promised summary of "Dilthey's line of questioning," basing it in part on Georg Misch's comprehensive account of Dilthey's development, which had appeared only months before.[8]

All of Dilthey's works find their impulse in the effort to bring the mental and sociohistorical reality of the human being, "life," to a scientific understanding and to provide solid foundations for the scientificity of this understanding. This scientific striving to disclose life understandingly takes two paths: philosophy, which for Dilthey and Yorck in the end has a moral and pedagogical aim; and historical human science, which depicts life in its "objectivations." The scientificity of human science is based on having that which in the end is the constant theme in and through these objectivations—life itself elaborated in its structure. But as *sciences* of the mental and spiritual, these disciplines need grounding in universal propositions, which provide methodic regulation of their cognitive comportment. Such propositions and rules are to be drawn from that "knowledge" which itself has the "psychic context" (life) as its "underground." The endeavor to raise historical human science to the level of true scientificity is thus pursued from two sides, that of the thematic object and that of the knowledge which discloses it. Both sides lead to *one* and the same task, that of studying the "psychic context" itself in its structures.

But philosophy, to the extent that it seeks to elaborate a theory of the human being according to the basic possibilities of its life, is likewise placed before the same task of an analysis of the "psychic context." Such an analysis must reveal "the whole fact of man," this thinking, willing, feeling being, in terms of the "structural context" of his lived experiences. This structural continuity does not run its course on top of life, as it were, does not happen with it, but is itself "lived, experienced," so that the whole of life is already there in every one of its actions and motivations.

As lived, the structural coherence of the psychic is at once a "developmental coherence." Since life is development, so that it is always concrete and historical, its own history must become an organon of understanding for it. And this history speaks all the more originally and profoundly, the more the human sciences (the historical disciplines) move on their own methodically secured and conceptually elaborated courses. The theory of the *human being*, the concrete *history* of its spirit, and the theory of the *sciences* of man and his history make up the threefold yet unified goal toward which every investigation and every ever-so-isolated inquiry by Dilthey moves. The foundation of all three researches is a "psychology" of life, of the psychic context as such. Because life is to be understood as an original and proper reality, the manner of its scientific elaboration can only be defined from out of itself. This means the exclusion of all attempts to disclose the psychic "scientifically" as a natural object. The psychic cannot be constructed from hypothetically posited elements, it is given primarily as a unity, a context. This whole must always be kept in view, all of its particular structures are to be understood in reference to it. But the description of the psychic context must also have the character of a secure and universally valid knowledge, if it is to be equal to the foundational task spelled out above.

So much for Dilthey's line of questioning in its methodic ground. "It was exclusively in inner experience, in the facts of consciousness that I found the solid anchor for my thought."[9] The "whole man," the full and "real process of life," is to become manifest in these facts of consciousness. With this aim, to be sure, Dilthey takes care to place himself in opposition to all "intellectualistic" psychology. *Nevertheless, the methodic ground of his foundational work still amounts to gaining access to the cogitationes (res cogitans) in order to thematize them, along the lines that Descartes had established and developed in the Meditations.*

Here is where Yorck's critique is to be brought to bear (see SZ 399ff. for the "review" of Yorck, lifted virtually verbatim from the body of this 1924 article). He calls for a critical "breakdown" of the assumptions—ergo a destruction!—of constructive psychology and a more thoroughgoing analysis of Dilthey's analytic psychology, in order to arrive at a ground from which the method itself can be disclosed. What Yorck is asking for in effect is a "logic" which leaps ahead of the sciences in order to guide them, like Plato's and Aristotle's logic. It must work out the differing categorial structures of the being which is nature and the being (Dasein) which *is* history. Dilthey "put too little stress on the generic difference between the ontic and the historical." With historians like Ranke, such an inadequate differentiation has introduced ocular determinations, aestheticism, and antiquarianism into historiology. And it has contributed to the separation of systematic philosophy from its historical investigation. Because of philosophy's special character, its ways of research and its linguistic expression are of a special kind. Yorck himself was already on the way toward a categorial apprehension of the historical as opposed to that of the ontical (ocular).

What in effect is required is an ontology of the historical. Yorck's understanding of the historical makes it clear that such an ontology cannot be found by way of historiology and its object. Its phenomenal ground is rather given in human Dasein. Whether the ontological position of the two friends is equal to the task of understanding historicality can be decided only after the being of Dasein has been brought out by a positive exposition of the phenomenon of time.

II. The Original Characteristics of the Being of Dasein
This section is the very first systematic elaboration of what will become the First Division of BT. Contrary to the disjointed list of eight "basic structures" of Dasein that he presented in July 1924, Heidegger returns to the tripartite outline of questions regarding Dasein precisely as Being-in-the-world, which he first introduced in the closing hours of SS 1923 (GA 63:85). This trio of questions in lecture notes that amount to the very first written notes to BT (US 95/9) will organize this and all future elaborations of the "characters of being" of Dasein in what became the First Division of BT: 1. What is this "wherein" called *world*? 2. *Who* is the *being* that is in the world? 3. What does it mean to be *in*? The last is in the journal article terminologically identified as the question of "in-being as such," and soon "disclosed in-being," and receives its very first detailed treatment in this 1924 context. The treatment of this pivotal dimension will however undergo drastic development until the final draft of BT itself (chap. I. 5). But one hears the echoes of Dilthey's "holistic apriori" of life when Heidegger stresses that all three dimensions are really a single basic phenomenon; they are not three parts to be pieced together into a whole but three different emphases which always imply one another as well as the whole (GA 63:85).

The prefatory remarks stress that this ontological interpretation is not intended to be *the* (definitive) interpretation of Dasein. It aims only to bring out those structures which manifest the phenomenon of time. Why this precautionary remark? An alternative opening paragraph which was crossed out suggests that Heidegger already wished to raise the question of being as such in this context, but decided against it. The section would then have been entitled "Dasein as Being" and the key sentence would have read: "But if the being of time is to be made comprehensible from human Dasein, what we need is a provisional [orientation toward being and the potential] characterization of the being of that entity which is addressed as human Dasein." The phrase in square brackets is itself crossed out.

Instead, the orientation is restricted to that of time itself ("the being of time") with the full knowledge that the manifestation of time is directly proportional to the degree of originality of the manifestation of Dasein in its being. In fact, the term "Dasein" was selected precisely because of this ontological primacy.

Heidegger thus opens with the question, why go to Dasein in order to explicate time? He gives a clear-cut double answer, stemming from his July lecture: a. Human life at its most daily level is oriented toward time, its actions and omissions "count" on time, take it into account. Time occurs in human life, human life occurs in time. The events in our environing world and the processes of nature are "in time." b. Any study of time inevitably comes across the classical texts of Aristotle (*Physics* 4) and Augustine (*Confessions*, book 11), which raise the question whether the "soul" or "spirit" itself in the end *is* time.

The first of these clues points to the task of analyzing Dasein in its everydayness, what it means to *be in* the *world* to begin with, "first of all" (*zunächst*). The only problem is that this everyday dimension is so immediately familiar (*nächstbekannt*) and self-evident that it is usually passed over for more overtly "theoretical" concerns. The necessary reversal of the natural tendency to invoke the isolated perception of a thing as our most immediate experience takes us back to the prior possibility of "encountering" that which is most immediately present (*nächstanwesend*), our environing world. This encounter, itself immediate, is the starting point for the ontological elaboration of everyday being-in-the-world as a first step toward exploring the temporality of this profound but implicit presence.

1. World as Wherein

The world as the in-which of the being of Dasein is at once that "out of which" it lives (GA 63:86). How does the researcher find access to this deep structure of our being? By way of life, in the same way that life does. We get to (*zugehen*) the world by way of getting around and about (*umgehen*) it (GA 63:80, 94, 96), dealing and coping with it, getting by, making do, getting along with it. The everyday world is the world-we-get-about (*Umgangswelt*). The world is the with-which of everyday concern and occupation. We occupy it because it occupies us. Our access to the world is therefore through this normal concern and preoccupation *with* it, and not our objectifying perception *of* it. It is therefore in the familiar go-around of daily preoccupations, in the common actions of using, making, keeping, and losing something that we encounter the world, clearly already a temporal encounter. But then we have a complex of encounters here, which includes not only the world but things, ourselves, and others in our actions toward the things within the world. We clearly encounter all of these, but the encompassing world in which and out of which and through which these all occur? Do we actually encounter (meet, come upon) the global reality of the world in our daily intercourse? Does the world encounter (befall, happen to) us? How? This is the basic question of this subsection (II. 1) of the journal article seeking to expose especially the character of the presentness (*Gegenwärtigkeit*) of the world. The subsection is accordingly devoted to uncovering the characters of "encounterivity" (*Begegnis*) of the world itself. We have caught Heidegger in a transition phase, quietly experimenting with the German language in order to bring the elusive presence of the world into words. In SS 1925, he performs a similar experiment with Husserl's coined word, "appresentation." In the terms of BT, however, the world as such is not encountered, but simply provides the nexus which lets entities be encountered, and this is precisely what the present is, *Gegenwart*, when it is understood as an empowering possibility of time itself. Moreover, by 1923, Heidegger's Aristotelian studies on the nature of aletheic truth had come to the point of experimenting with the possibility that the world itself is a context of disclosedness ("truth"). This subsection of 1924 thus also already bears witness to Heidegger's ongoing struggle to find the right words to articulate the tacit relations of presence and disclosure (*ergo* of truth as time, and time as truth) operative between the surrounding world and its things. Accordingly, a better understanding of this subsection can be gained by a brief glance backward in order to sort out the threads of development coursing into and through it, especially with respect to the receding term "encounter" and the emerging term, "disclosedness."

1a. Retrospective Excursus

The elements of the analysis of the environing world have been gathering for five years in Heidegger's work, ever since KNS 1919. The conclusion of the first environmental analysis, where world is already understood

as an orienting context which gives things meaning, provides the leitmotiv for all of the following analyses through BT: "the meaningful is the
primary, [for] it gives itself immediately to me, without any detour of
thought across the apprehension of a thing. Everywhere and always, it
signifies for me, living in an environing world; it is wholly worldlike, '*it
worlds*' " (ZBP 73). The dynamics (and so the temporality) of this signifying milieu will tend to be obscured by an abstractive categorizing when
it is reiterated over the years that meaningfulness, significance, is the
central and primary character-of-being of the world. "Meaningfulness
is a how of being, and the categorial of the Da-sein of world is centered
in it" (GA 63:86). And because the world is "there" in, through, and as
meaningfulness, it can also be called the primary character of encounter.
Begegnis, like the ultimate event of meaning, *Ereignis*, is a "happening"
word—it really means "occurrence"—and so retains some of the old
dynamism of "worlding" while also conveying a sense of brute facticity
in its happenstance of just coming across something, happening to meet
it. Such an encounter is sometimes called an "experience," understood
as a "jolt" which we endure or undergo (*er-fahren*, the peripatetic *ex-
perire*). This was its sense in late 1921, when *Begegnis* is first used to
characterize "the basic way of Da-sein of worldly objects" (GA 61:91)
within the intentional context of caring in its correlation with meaningfulness. "Meaningfulness as such is not experienced, explicitly; but it can
be experienced" (GA 61:93).

Aside from an allusion here to a transitional experience, oddly
enough, from explicitness to implicitness, this possible experiential transition from worldly objects to the world itself is not undertaken until SS
1923, precisely in the closing hours (July 11, 18, 25 = GA 63:76–104)
which present "the very first written notes toward BT" (US 95/9). But
in contrast with the formal indication of existence which guides BT, the
prepossession guiding this earlier hermeneutics of facticity is drawn from
facticity itself, from the temporal particularity of "everydayness": "Dasein (factic life) is Being in a world" (GA 63:80). The "indeterminate
indicative content" or formal indication of this presupposition aims to
be just as destructuring of traditional distinctions like subject-object (GA
63:80f.) and form-matter as the very first of Heidegger's formal indications, "it worlds," to which it still bears a close relationship, as we shall
now see.

"Welt ist was begegnet" (GA 63:85). With this terse sentence, Heidegger takes the first step toward understanding the first of the three "parts"
of his formal indication, concerning world as the in-which of being. The
oddity of the sentence lies in the undecidability of "begegnet," which can
be both active and passive, like the Greek middle voice of φαίνεσθαι, to
which it is in fact phenomenologically related. Heidegger wants it both

ways: "World is what encounters . . . and is encountered." Moreover, he immediately moves to deemphasize the "what" in the sentence. For the world is primarily a how, the how of all worldly encounters:

> As what and how is it encountering? . . . In the character of references (*Verweisungen*, an ontological term); the references give the world as the cared-for; it is "there" in the how of being cared for. . . . The as-what and how of encountering is settled in what is called meaningfulness, significance. . . . Significance is a how of being, in which the categorial of the Dasein of world is centered. . . . This world encounters, is encountered as the cared-for. (GA 63:85f.)

Encounter is at least a two-way street, a relation or chain of relations. For the first time in this lecture course, Heidegger describes the world of significance as a referential context and continuity of "for" and "to," and with it the worldlily encountered object as something to-hand, handy (*zu-handen*; GA 63:93, 97ff.), a giant leap forward in the road from KNS to BT. The handy thing is "there-to," it comes to the fore and so is encountered out of this vectorial nexus of relations of "to" and "for." Encounter is thus the very happening of articulation and differentiation, uniting and dividing: it worlds, it contextualizes. Thus, uniting and dividing, the functions that Aristotle ascribes to propositional truth, already take place at this more basic prelinguistic level.

Accordingly, to describe this occurrence of *Begegnis* further, Heidegger for the first time invokes the language of truth as disclosure: "Meaningfulness is understandable only out of the disclosedness already found in it, out of which the *encountered* signifies itself upon being encountered, points to itself and so forces itself into the 'there' " (GA 63:96). Meaning and the encounters it enables thus become visible in and with disclosedness.[10]

But meaningfulness likewise becomes visible with two correlative phenomena, familiarity and its disturbance (GA 63:97, 99f.). With the latter, we come to encounter in the more contravening sense of an "accentuated 'there' " (GA 63:100). But such an overt encounter is founded upon the self-evident familiarity of a more habitual there which stands in an "implicit pre-encounter" (GA 63:98). In the care-less absorption in the world through preoccupation with it, world is encountered as self-evidence (GA 63:103), meaningfulness uninterrupted. One does not need a "striking" object—a broken hammer, a missing pocket knife—for encounter to "take place." World is encountered (encounters) not after the fashion of a subject-object relation but in the character of the being of Dasein, *in* and *for* caring (GA 63:102).

1b. November 1924

The subsection written in 1924 follows up the development of SS 1923 with a list of the "characters of encounter" of world itself—meaningfulness, familiarity, disclosedness, fore-appearing and fore-presence—with an eye especially to their temporal implications (encounters). In familiarity, for example, "concern meets with the 'always already so-and-so there.'" The strange is but an extension of the familiar: it is simply "other than we expected" (gegen-wärtigen!). In fact, SS 1923 (Germany is approaching the peak of its runaway inflation) comes close to putting this perennial "perversity of inanimate objects" in the form of a kind of Murphy's Law. Familiarity is essentially and eminently disturbable:[11]

> This lack of familiarity is not something occasional, but rather belongs to the temporality of encountering the world as such. . . . Through the disturbability of our most implicit familiarity [like that of our currency], what is encountered is there in its incalculability. The encountered there assumes the peculiar hardening of the obtrusive and accidental [τύχη]. The "mostly always somehow other" dominates the encounter of the world. (GA 63:100)

But in late 1924, Heidegger draws a more methodological parallel of immediate relevance to his own phenomenological-ontological investigation from this "peculiar hardening," to which our usually limpid intercourse with the world seems to be prone. For it is likewise the source of the reification by philosophers of the smooth "matter of course" of the self-evident world in which we are so immediately and deeply preoccupied. Even Husserl, who identified the methodological necessity to "bracket" this reifying "natural attitude," ultimately misses this originally experienced encompassing world and instead replaces it with the derivative paradigm of an object correlated with isolated acts of perception. A stricter abstinence from this natural tendency is essential for the phenomenological encounter of the immediately encompassing "preperceptual" world whose ontological elaboration is to provide the basis for the explication of time.

Similar problems of reification are to be found in the concept of "nature" understood as something already there in advance. Heidegger treats this issue in the context of two additional "characters of encounter" articulated from disclosedness (GA 63:96): Vorschein (fore-appearing) and Vorhandenheit (fore-presence). First to be encountered in the world of concern, precisely in and through their "useful for" and "conducive to," are tools. But tools come to the fore and fore-appear against the background of that to which they refer in their serviceability. This background of upon-which and toward-which is present in the form of the "already there in advance," the fore-present: field and forest, mountain and stream, earth and sky. The encounter with nature in this environmental context is an extension of the world of concern and has virtually the same referential "character of encounter," for example, in reckoning *with* day and night, protecting ourselves *from* the weather, making things *out of* its stuff. Environmentally encountered nature is in its "always already there" in fact distinctive in not needing immediate attention, not having to be produced. It is on hand, prepresent, first in its immediate availability rather than as an object of the natural sciences. Its on-handness (*Vorhandenheit*) in the form of immediate availability is tacit and referential, and so more comparable to the character of the to-handness of handy tools than to that of a mere object standing before a theoretical observer. The distinction between the two "handnesses" here is not as sharp as it will be in the next two drafts of BT.

This more subtle and richer presence-at-hand is lost in BT itself, when Heidegger restricts *Vorhandenheit* to the presence which has been denuded of a world, like obtrusively "striking" things, scientific objects, and what is traditionally known as "substance." But it still occurs on occasion in SS 1925 (GA 20:270), where Heidegger will moreover, by means of the Husserlian borrowing, "appresentation," try anew to bring out the rich and complex, albeit immediate, presence of the world in relation to its things . . . and to Dasein itself.

2. Who is in the World?

The second question is directed toward *Being*-in-the-world: "how does '*Being*' in a world appear?" (GA 63:85). In 1924, it is put more ontically as the question of "the entity that is in the world" and in SS 1925 more precisely and elaborately as the question of "the entity as defined by the '*who*' of this Being-in-the-world and the *how* of this being, how the entity itself is in its being" (GA 20:211). Just as the first question took us to the most immediate presence of the world, so will the second to the most immediate presence of the "self" which is in-volved with such a world.

As being-in-the-world, Dasein is at once, "at the same time" (*zugleich*), being-with-one-another. And in the very first developed use of this term, Heidegger observes that these two characters of the being of Dasein, being-in-the-world and being-with-one-another, are "equiprimordial" (*gleichursprünglich*). The term will proliferate in BT, appearing there first in precisely the same context of the Self and Other (SZ 114). But in 1924 we have one of the rare contexts which also suggests the ultimate contemporaneity of all such primary characters. Heidegger used the term first in the habilitation of 1916 in precisely the same context of Identity and Difference as in 1924–27: that a One cannot even be thought without the Other, that being identical with itself and being different from something else are equally primordial (the heterothesis thesis: FS 172; cf. chap. 1 above). This is then developed into a contextual thesis: that an object cannot be thought without its state of affairs or "intentional nexus" (*Bewandtnis*: FS 323; cf. chap. 1 above) involving at least One and the Other. The fact that the very first introduction of equiprimordiality in later contexts repeatedly occurs *first* in connection with Self-to-Other relations is too striking to be accidental (cf. also GA 20:328/238, GA 21: 236).[12] As a result, the self and the other are not encapsulated subjects isolated from each other; each arises out of a context of equally primordial relations, any one of which implies the whole which precedes all of them (cf. GA 21:226). With his notion of equiprimordiality, Heidegger is clearly laying the groundwork for a temporal sense of the unity of the self as well as of being itself.

The destructuring of the subject-object relation also suggests that the appeal to equiprimordiality is associated with the reduction to global immediacy that comes with a formally indicative approach, in this case reflected in the moment of indifference between self and other through absorption in the environment. In a letter to Löwith at the time, Heidegger notes that the brief span of an article did not permit him to broach this important methodological point.[13] And even though "formal indication" has become even more of a recessive topic in BT itself, it is first explicitly mentioned there—three times!—precisely in the treatment of the self and the other (SZ 114, 116, 117).

In this 1924 context, formal indication operates from the start with equiprimordiality to articulate the field of relations, and so to differentiate the self and other out of the global immediacy of the environing world. If being-with-one-another is equiprimordial with being-in-the-world, then the immediate "there" of the others with whom one is in the world must be read off from the kind of encounter we have with the environment. The others are already there in the references of the world around us, but by way of a "with" rather than an "around." The table also refers to those with whom one breaks bread daily, and so on. With them, one at once likewise encounters oneself, in what one pursues and accomplishes and how one thus looks and gets placed, out there in the environment itself and not by way of a reflection on inner experiences and the like. It is first out of the environmental encounters that the others are there as a with-world, and oneself as a self-world, the two worlds being co-originally articulated out of the meaningful whole of the world-about-us (cf. GA 63:98f.: "coming forward" [*Vorschein*] in SS 1923 is replaced by "encounter" of the other in late 1924, but much of the wording is similar in the two texts). The modes of encounter are manifold, but one gets-about-with primarily in relation to the comings and goings of just getting about. In all this hustle and bustle, who then is in the world? The "One," just anyone. Like everybody else, "one is what one does," every day and for the most part, which is nothing special and unique to me, nothing that I can call my own. In the immediacy of everydayness, each is with the other *equally* not-own, disowned, inauthentic. This constellation of terms, along with "falling," has been waiting in the wings since October 1922 to describe this domination of the Anyone who is no one, like the averageness which realizes the leveling of publicity, where one "takes things lightly and makes things easy." "Each is the other and no one is himself." Many of the formulations cast in the article will persist through SS 1925 into BT itself.

But fresh from a course on Aristotle's *Rhetoric* in SS 1924, Heidegger focuses the article at this point on the speech of the Anyone, how it listens, communicates, and "chatters." With this detailed discussion on how "talk" (*Gerede*) idles in everydayness, Heidegger takes another step toward the hermeneutic climax he is preparing for this Dilthey-draft of BT. For the inertial phenomenon of idle talk, which deracinates talk from its original subject matter, will also account for the degeneration of language in the history of philosophy. Since it represents the "interpretedness of the generation of a particular age" (GA 20:372, GA 63: 40), idle talk also explains why deconstruction in philosophy is always a "critique of the present age" (first in October 1922), a critique of one's own hermeneutic situation. One can even pinpoint the proximate genesis of the *Daseinsanalytik* of BT out of the preceding publication project, basically oriented toward "destroying" the hermeneutic situation of the twenties in which Aristotle was to be read. For in the course of SS 1923, the ontological characteristics of the "interpretedness of the today" also prove to be the categories of Dasein as such (GA 63:66). Kierkegaard's critique of the "present age" provided many of the essential characteristics of everydayness. But his ultimately religious and theological orientation did not move sufficiently in the direction of exposing the "characters of being" sought by Heidegger (GA 63:30f.), especially that of "in-being." The term first emerges in the closing minutes of SS 1923 (GA 63:102, 100) and, in retrospect, Heidegger looks to it to sharpen his preceding discussion of the "interpretedness of the today," especially by reducing its overly psychological tenor (GA 63:36n, 51n).

3. In-Being as Such

Following hard upon the discussion of idle talk, this "hermeneutic" draft of BT, as the very first elaboration of in-being (*In-Sein*), never mentions understanding, the pivotal term in the more basic treatment of in-being in BT, but focuses on its natural derivative, interpretation (*Auslegung*). For idle talk is one way in which interpretation is preserved, kept in "troth." It is in this sense a positive phenomenon (GA 20:371/269; SZ 167). But idle talk also hardens interpretation into the habit of "*having been* interpreted," in one word, into the "interpretedness" (*Ausgelegtheit*) of "what they say." It is clearly a far-reaching temporal phenomenon which Heidegger in October 1922 and SS 1923 had already applied to the tradition of the historical sciences and philosophy, and will continue to do so in this Dilthey-draft of BT.

Heidegger begins by underscoring the centrality of this character of in-being, since it will take us to the original constitution of Dasein, care. Hitherto, care had been discussed only in its immediate mode, the "in" of the interest of concern in its intimate involvement with the world. It is the mode of intimate familiarity in which Dasein feels "at home" and unthreatened in its dwelling (Grimm's *innan* is cited here for the first time: cf. GA 20:213n/158n, SZ 54n). The know-how of knowing one's way about the world translates correlatively into coming to trust and rely upon the world in its usefulness and availability. But dependability leads to dependence and perhaps even addiction. Counting on the world implies being dependent on the world and submitting to it. "Being dependent (*Angewiesensein*), Dasein follows the references of the environing world as one follows orders, takes its orders (*Anweisungen*) from them in carrying out its reckoning and routine." The seductively comfortable give-and-take clearly has two sides to it. Being dependent upon the world at once means being affected, "put upon," approached (*angegangen*) by the world. That is to say, the "self" is affected, one finds oneself disposed, and this self-finding lets in-being be "there" for itself. How it is its own there varies with the disposition of the world, but more generally, of the situation of in-being as such. Disposedness makes explicit the there in which Dasein finds itself. Dasein *finds itself* there, Dasein *is* this there, and these two aspects are laid bare in disposedness. The two aspects that in-being brings out, that it is its there, that it lets the world be encountered as disclosed, constitute its discoveredness (in BT, Heidegger will call it disclosedness). The analysis may seem obtuse unless we recall that Heidegger is being guided here by Aristotle's insight that there are two distinct dimensions of truth in regard to things temporal, τέχνη and φρόνησις, and that the latter is intrinsically self-referential. Thus it is not surprising that this subsection also invokes the formal indication, for the first time roughly in the formula of ontological commerce with itself which will recur time and again through BT, that Dasein is an entity "which in its in-being goes about (*geht um*) this very being" (see October 1922, p. 3, for the first version: also chap 5, n. 15). More basic than going about the world, and founding it, is Dasein's going about its own being. The referential series of "in order to" ultimately refers back to the "for the sake of itself" (not yet mentioned in this article).

Strikingly missing in this first account of disposedness is the more dramatic vocabulary of "thrownness"—the fact that Dasein is delivered over to its there—which will first play a major role only in BT itself. But one can sense it in the wings in Heidegger's choice of words here: that Dasein is relegated and "beholden" to the world, which "gets to" Dasein:

this point will eventually be comprehended by the more basic relegation of throwness. And in the German, it is but a short step from trust (*Verlässlichkeit*) to forsakenness (*Verlassenheit*), from "leaving it to" the world to "being left," abandoned to the world. And the mood of security changes to reflect the fragility of dwelling toward the end of the subsection with the analysis of angst (first in WS 1923–24), with due acknowledgment to Kierkegaard . . . along with Luther. It had been mentioned in passing, first in the guise of affliction (*Bekümmerung*, by way of the Old Testament and Augustine's "restless heart"), ever since SS 1920. Angst is finding oneself before nothing, which gives no quarter for absorption in the world, which thus refers ["throws"] Dasein back to itself. In this self-reference, Dasein discovers "that it is and that it is not not and that it is itself the there in which a world can encounter and be encountered." This being on hand (*Vorhandensein*: so in 1924!) in which a Dasein is in each case its own, and so is not the naked on-hand of the world, is called facticity . . . and not yet existence or throwness. Significantly, the full formula for the facticity of throwness, "that it is and has to be" (SZ 134f.), is not yet employed. "Having to be" (*Zu-sein*) will become the forerunner to "existence" and its placeholder in the second draft in SS 1925. And at the very end of the semester, the dimension of "throwness" is overtly identified for the very first time, significantly in the context of the angst in the face of my own death. In angst, Dasein is no longer dependent (*angewiesen*, which can also be translated as "thrown"!) upon the world, the world is reduced to the "sheer in-which of just being . . . as merely being on hand as the in-which that I am abandoning." "This implies that the outermost possibility of death is the way of being of Dasein in which it *is purely and simply thrown back upon itself*" (GA 20:439/318).

The terminology of existence itself occurs only in the final draft of BT. In retrospect, however, one can already discern in 1924 the points at which "existence" could find entry in the developing conceptual scheme. For already at the end of this section II, it is said that Dasein is always out toward . . ., on its way to . . ., there. But the special placeholder for existence at this point in the analysis of the "there" of Da-sein is the fact that I am most my own in my "can-be" (*Seinkönnen*), whether this be authentically or inauthentically. This recitation of traits, along with the allusion to an "original choice" under which all my worldly concerns are to be placed, prompt Heidegger merely to posit "care" as the very being of Dasein. But he does so without any attempt to elaborate its complex structure, at the very end of this section. He simply concludes by citing Burdach's article on "Faust und die Sorge" (cf. also GA 20: 419n/303n, SZ 197n), which had appeared in the inaugural issue of Rothacker's *Deutsche Vierteljahrsschrift*.

We cannot leave this subsection on in-being in the "Dilthey draft," which was to have been published in this new "German Quarterly for Literary Criticism and Intellectual History," without noting how much of its analysis is being geared specifically to that context. There is no talk of the equiprimordiality of disposedness and understanding, as in BT, for understanding (central also to Dilthey) is never even mentioned, let alone *Seinsverständnis*. Instead, the subsection again and again goes back to Heidegger's old problem of the "genesis of the theoretical," which at this stage is rapidly developing into a full-fledged philosophy of the sciences. It thus begins not with understanding but with its stand-in, with the know-how (*sich auskennen*) of getting about the world of "in order to," in order to establish that interpretative exposition of its "as what" is the primary form of knowing. Detaching the "as-what" from its "in order to," the *leisurely inspection* of curiosity becomes absorbed and even loses itself in the fascinating "look" of the world, strays from the familiar context of utility in search of the new and exotic. The more serious *investigative inspection* gives us research. If scientific research is to maintain its authenticity, it must through critique always counter the inertial tendency of concealment prompted by the domination of the customary interpretedness, in order to appropriate the genuine possibilities of original experience. For public interpretedness and its curiosity also tyrannize the history of the sciences. Confidence in the possession of universally valid sentences replaces the repeated questioning back to the original ground-giving contexts of being which constitute the respective subject matters of the sciences. This applies especially to the research whose task is to interpretatively expose the self-referential dimension of Dasein itself, in particular "intellectual history" (*Geistesgeschichte* = history *of* the mind or spirit) and philosophy. A time can claim the "historical consciousness" as its own unique possibility for self-interpretation. It works itself out by taking a look at the full range of the most remote and exotic cultures of world history. It controls this wandering look by way of classification and the systematic recording of types. And since the way a time views the past is the criterion by which it interprets and evaluates itself, the present itself is subjected to a comparative typology. (Spengler's physiognomic morphology thus naturally prompts him to predict a "decline of the West," Heidegger observes in his more extended discussion of these points in SS 1923 [GA 63:56, 39].)

Systematic and dialectic philosophy provide the foundations for such ordering schemes. Subsumption under a type becomes the goal of knowledge, that is, of a knowledge whose basic preoccupation is really a concealed curiosity. And although these research endeavors seek ultimately to interpret "humanity," the question of Dasein in its being is seldom raised, or it is explored in terms of an already-finished system or an

unquestioned definition of man as a "rational animal." Even a "philosophy of life" by and large strays into the study of the manifold forms of
cultural expressions of life or its worldviews. To the degree that life itself
in its being and as "being" is thematized, it is interpreted in terms of the
being of the world or of nature. But the sense of being thereby remains
in the indifference of a self-evident and unquestioned verbal concept.
(This is the very first clear-cut allusion in the early Heidegger to the
importance of raising the question of the sense of being itself and of
starting from our self-evident understanding of being, which will loom
large only with the subsequent draft of BT in SS 1925.) The explication
of the being experienced by Dasein *as* Dasein and the development of the
ontology suitable for this entity is suppressed by the latent domination of
Greek ontology in the externalized form in which it has come to us by
way of traditional interpretations.

III. Dasein and Temporality

The title of this new section matches that of the Second Division of BT.
If we give and take a bit in regard to its overall content, thematic development, and emphasis, this section of the article may be regarded as a
rough first draft of the themes of the Second Division, from death to
authentic and inauthentic temporality. Historicality is intentionally postponed until the following concluding section. All of these themes—not
just "several," as Heidegger states in a note opening this section—had
already been "communicated" for the very first time in the lecture of
July 1924. The article of November 1924 seeks to develop this conceptual
trajectory further in the light of a tighter and more detailed preceding
analysis of being-in-the-world. That the July lecture constitutes the baseline for the Second Division is underscored by a note in the middle of
the Second Division of BT itself (SZ 268n), which once again recalls this
public lecture as the occasion on which "the foregoing and following
reflections were communicated in thesis form." The fact that Heidegger
in November 1924 begins this section by simply citing the opening paragraphs from July 1924 (cf. BZ 29) has no direct bearing on the Second
Division as such. Instead, this opening discussion of the differing approaches to time by theology and philosophy simply adds another point
to the philosophy of the sciences which Heidegger is also developing,
and clearly wishes to highlight in this "Dilthey draft" intended for a
journal of the Dilthey School.[14]

The section begins by questioning the adequacy of the interpretation
of the preceding section and whether such inadequacy is indigenous to
the character of Dasein itself. The prolific central abstraction of the July
lecture, the "temporal particularity" of "for the time being" (*jeweilig*) is
only now introduced—as a "formal concept," Heidegger adds later in

a note to himself. In that particularity, Dasein as caring is constantly underway to . . ., its very being is that of being-[out]-toward something which it is not yet but can be. But only when it *is* that which it can be is it apprehensible as a whole, which would provide the requisite guide adequate for the analysis of Dasein. But in thus arriving at its end and being fully there, Dasein is, as it were, "terminated," and so no longer really there.

This embarrassment will call for a clarification of the "formal indication" operative in the analysis, which we find in a handwritten marginal note appended later to this paragraph. Heidegger notes that wholeness taken in this way is not to be regarded as facticity but as existence, not as a being-so (which Heidegger in 1924 draws into his recurrent equation of on-handness with facticity), not as a that, but as a how of being [*the key here is really in the* **out**, *ἐκ, ex of ex-sistence: see chap. 8*]. Such an "existential" of wholeness is at once the phenomenological prepossession of the analysis. Being whole in this way is no longer the wholeness of death but of the character that characterizes Dasein. The note clearly postdates SS 1925, which also remains a nonexistentialized draft. This very first note on the terminology of existence is followed by a series of marginal notes which further existentialize the draft of 1924 in the direction of BT.

Back to 1924: The subsequent discussion of the Dasein of others who have come to their end serves to make the basic term of Dasein more precise, that is, what it means to be my own Dasein, that it cannot be taken as something worldly and on hand, an occurrent process which is still outstanding. This applies equally to the death that stands "before" Dasein, which by formal definition is always my own death. In the realm of possibility which is Dasein, "death" as such does not exist [an apparent rebuttal of Epicurus's famous line on death]. Death is always (*jeweilig*) and particularly mine. Dasein is in its temporal particularity always and in each instance its own death, as its most extreme ("outermost") possibility. In this context, Heidegger acknowledges the importance of Jaspers's "limit situation" for an ontology of Dasein, and expresses solidarity with the basic philosophical attitude expressed in the Foreword of Jaspers's *Psychology of Worldviews*, with its "center of gravity" in this "category" of limit situation (cf. chap. 3 above).

One major difference between the treatments of July and November 1924 is the deeper resolution that comes from the application in the latter of the foregoing categories of everydayness and the lapse of falling (never even mentioned in July) to the analysis of death. Take, for example, the important formally indicative character of the indeterminacy of death's coming. Everyone says, "Everyone dies someday, but in the meantime not yet." And so one falls back into absorption with the world and forgets the possibility of death. Death's coming is completely certain, but also completely indefinite, and everyday concern covers up this indeterminacy with all the intentions that it still has *before it*. The indefiniteness becomes definite and defined (and even located) in worldly terms precisely in the "in the meantime not yet." Its potential disturbance of the peace of daily existence is thereby suppressed.

Another major difference is the development, at this stage somewhat halting, of facticity as extreme possibility in the direction of the original choice of "willing to have conscience," a term which was mentioned only in passing in July. The interpretation that goes into forerunning this extreme possibility reveals the goneness of being-in-the-world as the possible "no longer there," no longer in the world of preoccupied gettingabout. The world thus loses the possibility of defining in-being, of giving it its being. The world withdraws from its meaningful encountering into "something" which is merely on hand. It can no longer "matter" and "get to" me. This ownmost Dasein is no longer "there," in the world. Instead, in its outermost possibility, Dasein is delivered over to itself, it becomes manifest as the being which must be from out of itself and actually wants to be what it properly is. Forerunning, in revealing one's being gone, in placing it before nothing, brings Dasein before the choice which constitutes its proper being, between the two extreme "to-bes" (two "hows") of either willing to be absolutely responsible for its proper being or letting itself be lived by its daily concerns. This willing to be thus responsible for itself is willing to have conscience. This is the pure how of possibility in its indeterminate certainty as opposed to the lapsing how, the how of habit and routine always looking to the what of concern.

The formal indication, never mentioned in the article, is nevertheless by now so deeply ingrained in his approach that Heidegger here virtually spontaneously presents a purely formal choice without content. He calls it a "horizon" of choice which comprehends each and all of Dasein's situations. This does not mean that the how pure and simple is a how "in general." The horizon of choice manifests the how in its determinateness, in this case in the certainty of my own death. Being gone is in its extremity a certain possibility, which however has nothing to do with the indubitability of being on hand versus no longer being on hand in a worldly way. As the July talk emphasized, being gone is not a what but a how. For Dasein to be certain is to *find itself* in this certitude, in a disposition which is at once "at every moment gripped [*ergriffen*: moved, affected]" by indefiniteness.

Given this extreme tension between certitude and indeterminacy, forerunning my being gone is not merely a matter of simply choosing this revealing "how" in which I find myself, but also of sustaining that choice and the revelation. Forerunning is accordingly having chosen, that is, being resolute in its choice. The openness (*Ent-schlossenheit*) of resoluteness is Dasein's discoveredness in the most proper sense. Resoluteness holds itself in the disposition of the sobering angst that corresponds to it, and so holds out against the uncanniness of one's ownmost being as possible being. It holds me out to the certain possibility of my death at any moment in all moments. In going about its being in the persistence of resoluteness, the temporally particular Dasein is not merely in time: in each particular instantiation, Dasein *is* time itself. And this is what it means *to be* temporal. To be *in* time is not to be in-being, and in-being is not in time.

One recognizes the terms and turns of phrase of the July lecture, but now interspersed with the halting emergence of the problematic of conscience-guilt-resolve, which "authenticates" my forerunning (SZ, chap. II. 2). It is being drawn immediately and directly out of the problem of forerunning my death (SZ, chap. II. 1), and not as two separate problematics as in BT. The brunt of this very first analysis of the authentication of temporality is carried by the "being futural" of resoluteness. The other two terms of the triad are still used quite sketchily. Conscience is at this point no more than a stand-in for the ownmost self in its being, with virtually no hint of its "call" to absolute responsibility. The choice is described as between being "conscienceful" and conscienceless. To be conscienceless is to forget oneself by absorption in the world. One lets oneself be chosen, so to speak, by that in which one absorbs oneself. One becomes guilty in not having chosen, and resolve has the revelatory power to unmask such a Dasein in not having properly chosen. But it also lets this Dasein of and from itself become guilty and remain guilty in not having chosen. In being guilty (existentially in debt) in this way, the forerunning Dasein *is* its past. We begin to see what Heidegger meant a few months earlier when he mentioned in passing, in a remark intended to shed some light on historicality, that conscience is one way of authentically coming back to one's past and repeating it in its how (BZ 25). Some further light is shed on this conceptual constellation later in April 1925 and again in SS 1925, where Heidegger centers his brief reflections around a quotation from Goethe, "He who acts is without conscience (conscienceless)." Jaspers had used the same leitmotiv in his reflections on the limit situation of guilt, of the unavoidable guilt that accompanies every act. Every act has its unwanted consequences. He who acts must therefore be ready to assume even this unchosen guilt, the guilt that comes with being one's past.[15]

Clearly, Heidegger still has a long path to travel in this problematic, and we must wait until BT itself for anything like a thorough treatment of this constellation of concepts. The same applies to the remaining pages of this section, which give us the first extensive treatment of "inauthentic" or, better, "improper" (*uneigentliche*) temporality, the time we *have* in common with others in our everyday concerns. The more popularized public talk had already begun the task and sounded the keynote, which tends to get lost in the more complex terminology in the article: Even in everydayness, I am my time. But it is no longer my proper time, but rather the time that "we" are with *one* another in the world, the public time of Everyone, "Everyone's time" (*"Man"-Zeit*: BZ 22). It turns out to be the time that clocks are made of, who make all time into the present. Clocks are made for Everyone, who lives only from, by, and for the present. Everyday care, absorbed in the present, gives us a Dasein which *is* its present.

Improper Temporality

The section concludes its treatment of the authentic temporality proper to my life with an explication of the "peculiar *sight* that death gives to life" (so already in October 1922, p. 12). The very being of Dasein is now defined as temporality, which is really the source of this sight. Out of the most proper and extreme possibility of its voided future and the return passage through its freighted past, Dasein is now uncovered and "sighted" in the full temporal particularity of the "seized moment," where it can take action in terms of the very how of its being. The sight that comes with this full sense of temporality is not the circumspection (*Umsicht*) of everyday concern, and certainly not the direct inspection (*Hinsicht*) that comes with the meandering perspectives of leisurely curiosity, but rather the thoroughgoing perspicuity or total transparency (*Durchsichtigkeit*) of the Dasein which, purely and simply, is its time. For its forerunning has "passed through" the full course of its being from future to past to present, in that order, and seen the whole how of it "at once" (*zugleich*), in a single "per-spection" or thoroughgoing insight. (The allusion to the "holistic glance" of the seized *Augen-blick* does not surface, however, until SZ 328.) "Out of the indeterminate certainty of its own being gone from . . . which makes life transparent, the illumination of forerunning has its unmistakable ~~situation~~ direction" (so in the manuscript). The correction graphically recalls the "dynamic" Aristotelian sense being given to the practical situation of action, which Heidegger has been cultivating at least since October 1922, if not SS 1919. The kairotic situation, which φρόνησις reveals ultimately in a single "glance of the eye," is "an entity which is a 'not yet' and an 'already' in unity and poised in a specific movement" (cf. chap. 5 above, p. 267).

What then is the movement and direction of the less than radical situations of everyday life, which Aristotle himself studied in his treatment of practical truth? The question would naturally come up for Heidegger in 1924, who is still deeply involved in his Aristotle studies. More-

over, he is still translating φρόνησις as "circumspective insight," which
accordingly relates it more to the prudence (*Umsicht*) or practical wisdom
of the life of everydayness. For daily life has its own wisdom or "sight,"
"inauthentic" temporality has its own καιροί, opportune moments, insignificant as they may be when compared to the limit situation of our
mortality and the sobering lucidity that it brings. As the conscience, which
Heidegger equates with φρόνησις (the habit of right insight into human
action), reveals the radical "there" of Dasein and so bestows transparency
upon the most basic action of human existence, so circumspection gives
sight to the action of everyday concern by illuminating the circumstances
in which it is to be carried out. It is the sight granted by the direction
of time, by its movement of disclosure, by the "truth" that time is. Daily
life comes to its resolutions and decisions likewise in phronetic and kairotic terms. Moreover, here as in Heidegger's account of authentic temporality, this is done not by the "natural light of reason (νοῦς)" and its eternal
verities, as Aristotle and the tradition would have it, but by the light of
time! Thus *Lichtung*, the "lighting of the clearing" of being which is time
itself, replaces νοῦς within the otherwise Aristotelian fabric of "dianoetic"
virtues in BT.

Following Aristotle, Heidegger in 1924 takes this last cue literally
when he discusses the insights and decisions of daily life. One decides
daily quite naturally in the "light of day". . . and night. "Time is the sky,"
Plato had already said in the *Timaeus*. As discoveredness and disclosedness, Dasein is dependent on the world for sight. As falling upon
the world and so immersed in it, it takes care of itself in terms of the
most proximate and present possibilities of the environing world, which
is present not as a thing on hand but rather in the character of meaningfulness. Sight is available in virtue of the sun's presence in the sky. Much
like handy things, the sky and the sun in their alternating availability are
encountered in terms of their significance, here as beneficial or conducive to sight. As forerunning seizes its opportune moment of total vision
of its one and only lifetime, so concerned circumspection must literally
seize the day (*carpe diem*), that is, interpret or "lay out" (*auslegen*) the
course of the day in terms of its environmental significance. Its concern
to make the best use of the day's light finds its definition and expression
in terms of its temporally particular circumstances. But once it is determined, from then on, first light means "time to take out the cows," and
the last "time to rest." The everyday talk of time thus finds its origin in
the appropriate now, the right time appropriate for . . . , not quite a
particular while (*Jeweiligkeit*) like Dasein, but clearly a particular when.
In the dialect of a certain village, therefore, "morning" may simply mean
"then, when the cows are taken out." The days yield to the seasons, which
are likewise interpreted according to the urgencies of concern (sowing,

harvest) and their proper occasions (weather). Concern must give each thing the time that is due to it, it seeks the appropriate now, it asks about its optimal when. These disposably appropriate "nows" make up the time that gets taken into account, and that ultimately get counted. Moreover, Heidegger later notes, this always includes an appropriate "where," the place where one is "at home." Time here is always local time. "There's a time and place for everything."

The examples are from the peasant φρόνησις (*schlauer Bauer!*) of daily life in the Black Forest—the "peasant's clock" (reckoning by shadows: cf. SZ 416) and Bilfinger's book on ancient and medieval time-reckoning (cf. SZ 419n.) are already invoked—but the implications are universal. Circumspection looks around, that is, it looks over the "lay of the land" (*Lage*: not as comprehensive as *Situation*), it looks to the circumstances, care-fully looking ahead in search of the right time and place, favorable opportunity, appropriate material; in short, it plans ahead to make provision so that the task at hand may be brought to a successful conclusion. In Aristotelian terms, it seeks "actuality," ἐντελέχεια, in which a being maintains itself in the finished state of readiness and presence. For Aristotle, this dynamic stasis is the actualization of movement itself, the presence of a being in its can-be as such. To the extent that this can-be is present, as when this wood is "at work" in becoming a table, there is movement. Dasein itself, in its concern for worldly affairs and its things, actually cares for itself, that is, for getting finished at the right time and having everything in a state of readiness. The concern for things is ultimately being anxious for oneself as a sojourning with things, anxious especially about the future, that one may succeed, get finished at the right time, that nothing go wrong that would "queer" one's plans, that one can then depend on things to do their thing (ἐντελέχεια) in due course; especially clocks, so that one can likewise rely on others to make their appointed rounds in due course, promptly. But having been finished, these things tend to be forgotten, all the more so as they remain at one's disposal without a hitch, so that one need "pay them no heed."

Anxious about the future, forgetful of the past, worldly concern is nevertheless especially "attached to" (cf. BZ 21) the present, in fallenness (e.g., curiosity) to the point of addiction (*Nachhängen*). It culminates in the obsessively repetitive "now"-saying which is the very definition of the clock, which "tells" the time. And it is the person who is totally absorbed in the world of daily concerns ("now this, then that, and only then that") and lives by his watch who constantly says, "I have no time," and is anxious about "losing no time" (cf. BZ 20f.). Time becomes "precious" when it is regarded as an available commodity, subject to presence and absence. And the more precious time becomes, the finer and handier become the clocks. Not even determining the "right time" should take "time" (cf. SZ 418 for a variant of this).

But every person has time, counters Heidegger in the vein of ordinary language: I have time, because I am it. But this time that I have, I have from the start already given away, only to receive it from the time which is regulated by our being-with-one-another. The time *proper* to me; the time *common* to Everyone: two different times. The time which makes up the whole of my being, and defines my own being at every moment, lives out of the future and the past so that the present takes care of itself. Heidegger even suggests (in April 1925) that the present disappears when we act out of our future past. Common time, by contrast, has a fetish for the present. It is an incessant making-present which forgets its past. And the future? Everyday Dasein does not run "before" its future but is absorbed with (*bei*) a near future which will be, that is, will become present. The future awaits its present (*Gegen-wart*), and so is intrinsically oriented to the present.[16]

Not that the two times are absolutely separate. Proper being is such that it is the improper properly, that is, it "lifts" (*aufhebt*) the improper properly into itself. The "how" seized in the proper resolve of forerunning is proper only as the determination of an action taken in the now of the improper time of being-with-one-another. But he who is resolute has his own time and does not fall into the time of the one who is merely concerned with worldly affairs. Heidegger here cites a maxim of prudence from the apocryphal Ecclesiasticus (20:7): "A wise man is silent until he sees his time, but a garrulous fool cannot abide time." Resolve does not speak of itself and announce itself publicly through programs. Its mode of communication is silent exemplary action with the others and for them. Thus, even though its concernful presentifications are now properly authentic, it is publicly indistinguishable from decadent temporality.[17]

This last point, made near the conclusion of the section, once again exemplifies the phronetic emphasis that characterizes this very first drafting of the theme of "inauthentic temporality." It amplifies, and so complexifies, the more straightforward phenomenology of the ordinary language of time begun in the July talk. It is precisely this emphasis, which brings out some of the more creative moments of everyday concern, which will be lost in BT. There, for example, the appropriate now is mentioned only once (SZ 414), and so very little attention is given to how it comes to be "sighted." As we have noted, many of the details of this one and only prior draft of "Temporality and Everydayness" (= Div. II, chap. 4 of BT) reappear in BT, especially in the very last chapter (II. 6; esp. § 80) of the book, which itself was the only chapter in BT drafted without a prior working manuscript. The basic ontological terms buried in this very last (and so neglected) chapter, like "within-time-ness" and "world-time," are coined veritably at the last minute, on the verge of the composition of the never published Third Division. Moreover, in the interim, much has changed in the preceding terminological context (e.g., thrownness, understanding, but most pertinent here, *Bewandtnis*, the circumstantial nexus which is the being of handy things) which therefore gets "repeated" in chapter II. 4 of BT in ways that differ from the early article (e.g., "forgetting"). For all these reasons, these early pages on immediate (daily) time, its contrast with the extreme (original) time of the self, stand apart and alone as an especially unique "waymark" in Heidegger's development toward BT. To the reader of BT, they are familiar, and yet, so strange and unfamiliar. These matchless pages, unpolished and disjointed as they are, contain points and nuances—I have brought out the suggestive possibilities of only a few of them—to be found nowhere else on this stretch of Heidegger's Way. It is unfortunate for us that Heidegger tendered many of his points without developing them, no doubt because of the restrictions on length. But as a result, the text is more difficult and obscure than it might have been, and suggestive only with the application of effort by the reader versed in the chronological and doxographical context in which it was penned. One can therefore empathize with the puzzlement of its first two unsuspecting—not to say "unwashed"—readers, Rothacker and Kluckhohn, especially here but also in other sections. One can only wonder what reception the article would have encountered if it had in fact been published in early 1925. Clearly, Heidegger had a book-length idea on his hands.

The section concludes with a rehearsal of clearly ontological problems raised by the time of being-with-things: the nonrecurrability of the stream of time despite the recurrence of the heavens, the relation of time and place, time as principle of individuation. Aristotle's treatment of the relation of time to movement evokes the leitmotiv that will introduce the second, more overtly ontological draft of BT (GA 20:8/6): The history of the concept of time can be settled ultimately only if it is a history of ontology. Earlier, Heidegger had encountered an apparently linguistic but ultimately ontological problem which will plague him into the unpublished Third Division of BT, and beyond: the word "present" (*Gegenwart*) has in its meaning "a peculiar indifference" which conflates two different senses: "*Anwesenheit in der Umwelt* (die Präsenz), und dann das 'Jetzt' (*das Präsens*)." Thus, in the English, we have "present" as presence at a place or in a context ("Here!") and "present" as the temporal tense of the "now." The point is crucial for understanding *Da*-sein (*here*-being) as in-being, as Heidegger himself remarks in the margin. He then observes how "presentish" especially the primitive languages are, and looks to his own investigations on time to get to the bottom of the traditional grammar and its doctrine of tenses. He could also have added the task, begun in July 1924 and continued sporadically through BT, of making the ordinary talk of time, beginning with its superabundance of idioms, transparent in its sense and sources. This evidence of the complex and pervasive presence of time in common parlance is still left largely untapped by readers of Heidegger.

IV. Temporality and Historicality

This final section, which in its way anticipates an "ontological exposition of historicality out of temporality" (SZ 377), can be construed as an early version of that penultimate chapter of BT (II. 5) with the same title and the same aim, but only in a few very rudimentary points. It makes the first halting steps toward making three distinctions which underlie that chapter, between proper and improper historicality, between *Geschichte* (the experience of history) and *Historie* (recorded history, historiography and historiology), and between what has been and so still is (*das Gewesene*) and what is past and gone (*das Vergangene*). In fact, less than half of the section is devoted specifically to the way in which Dasein "grooms" (*pflegt*: cultivates and conserves, holds it in troth) its past and so "has" tradition, which takes us to the heart of the historizing action. And this exposition of historicality is accomplished upon a somewhat different basis than the more developed prestructuration that underlies the chapter in BT. Thus, contrary to the previous section of the article, this last section cannot even be called an early draft of the like-titled chapter in BT, but at most an early announcement of some of its themes and issues stemming from a like-minded approach. This only serves to highlight all the more the unique accomplishment of each of these versions. In particular, there is much to learn from the earlier attempt to elaborate historicality out of temporality, which itself has not yet been elaborated into the full and complex structure that it acquires in BT. The terse, almost skeletal treatment itself serves to lay bare all the more transparently the most basic structures constituting the *sine qua non* to Heidegger's approach.

This transparency carries over into the second half of this final section, which makes the transition from historicality proper to how it operates in the historical disciplines, and from them to the history of philosophy. In view of the terse treatment, the need for a "phenomenological destruction of the history of ontology *and logic*" can be traced back more readily to the very character of the historicality of the human being. Accordingly, the two halves of this short section closely confine and clearly focus the not entirely transparent transition between the systematic and historical Parts of the projected program of BT. We also see the historical program of "destroying" ontology, still very much in flux at this stage of Heidegger's development, taking shape before our very eyes. Selecting Descartes as the chief target of destruction is by no means arbitrary in this "Dilthey draft" of BT. For Heidegger had already suggested in the opening section of the article that Dilthey's achievement in the history of philosophy is still marred by the vestiges of Cartesianism operative in his "hermeneutic situation." Without saying so—undoubtedly owing to lack of space—the article thus comes full circle to its starting point.

IV.A. Historicality

The section begins with an apparent review of the manifold of the phenomena of Dasein already traversed: in-being, being-with-one-another, speaking, falling, discoveredness, being-possible (its can-be, later also called "existence"). But then we are told that they are all equiprimordial, and that their structural coherence together with Dasein's being-temporal only now yields the full sense of the being of what had already been called "care." It is out of this "structure of facticity," now exposed, that historicality as a "character of the being of Dasein" can become visible within the phenomenon of temporality, just as temporality was brought into relief out of the prior characters of being. Hence, just as Dasein *is* time, so Dasein *is* history, to paraphrase a maxim which Yorck liked to reiterate.

We thus begin to surmise the logic behind Heidegger's recurrent use of the ordinary statements of identity of being for a whole series of traits prefaced by "being-," and how such seemingly exaggerated one-liners are to be taken. It is the *"logic" of equiprimordiality* of the traits of being drawn from the irreducibly ultimate and ultimately ineffable starting "point," the facticity of Dasein, which ever since KNS 1919 refers to how we first find ourselves in being and as being. These Da-sein statements which underscore the *is* therefore seek to express the irreducible moments of our inescapable facticity. One can even add one's own at this "point," like "Dasein *is* its tradition." Already in July 1924, this culminated in the equiprimordiality of the *articulated* tenses of time (cf. SZ 381): Dasein *is* its future, past, present, and "thus" *is* its time. The return to the original experience of Da-sein involves a peculiar convergence of traits upon the "there" of being: one is reminded of the convertibility of the transcendentals of being in medieval philosophy. But we have already seen that equiprimordiality is undergirded by the "heterothesis thesis." This means that "equal primordiality" must be given to both unity and multiplicity, identification and differentiation, convergence and articulation. In BT, accordingly, Heidegger observes that the *primordial* totality of care, as an *articulated* totality, in fact demands an equiprimordial multiplicity of phenomena. "The primordiality of the constitution of being does not coincide with the simplicity and singularity of a last structural element" (SZ 334). Our ontological return to the origin of our being does not come to a point, as common sense would have it, and now the Derridean reading of the purported "phallocentric" thrust of Heidegger's thought takes it to do. Already in SS 1925, Heidegger describes it as a return to the "*field* in which the phenomenon of time becomes visible" (GA 20: title of the First Division). What is thus made visible will become a "temporal playing field" (*Zeit-Spiel-Raum*) in the later Heidegger. What is behind this development? We have already seen how Heidegger's return to facticity in KNS 1919, as the one subject matter of phenomenology, gave his thought a strong *material* (and therefore mater-nal) thrust from the start, and this hyletic return to the "principle of material differentiation and individuation" is now manifesting all the multiplicity or scatter that matter, in its unity, implies. We are only now beginning to reap the "material" implications which undergird Heidegger's thought.[18]

But even though co-original phenomena by that very character cannot be derived one from the other (GA 20:332/241, GA 21:226), there is a phenomenologically meaningful sense in which it can be said that one has its origin in the other (GA 21:221f.). In the present context, it is said that historicality "shows up" in the phenomenon of temporality, is "brought out of" temporality and so "set off against" it. Let us see if we can gather how (whether) Heidegger demonstrates this nonderivative exposition in his exposition of the phenomenological proposition, "Dasein *is* history. In-*being* itself as *being*-temporal *is* historical."

What is history? After dismissing the thoroughly objectified sense of a series of brute worldly occurrences, either occurring or cognized, Heidegger makes a few formally indicative attempts to give linguistic flesh to his topic. History is past life, to be historical is to be dependent on what earlier has been. To have become history is to be a matter of the past, to belong to the past. "Historical" is an entity's being temporal in the sense of being defined by the past and belonging to the present as this past, implicitly or explicitly.

The last indication allows Heidegger to couple the already established sense of being-temporal as expectant presentifying with that dimension of being-with-one-another already identified as "interpretedness." We have in fact grown up in this already fixed way of having things interpreted, which guides our expectations, preferences, needs, demands, ventures, conceptions, rumors. But not just "things"; we also have already been interpreted. Even at the very core of our being, none of us begins anew. But it is now our interpretedness, that of our time and generation, the present of our being-with-one-another, which in this way is itself articulated temporally in terms of old, up and coming, and middle generations. (Heidegger gives credit to Dilthey here for the "historical category" of generation.) As temporally particular, Dasein *is* at once always its generation, identifying with its particular interpretedness. What is preserved in it reaches back into the past, to an earlier interpretation, to a past concern or confrontation. But it still remains in force today. In its prevalence, it is self-evident, in its having become, forgotten. Since Dasein lives out of its interpretedness, it lives out of this forgotten past, it *is* this very past.

1) This prevalent interpretedness has already decided *what* among the possible concerns is to be especially tended and treated (what the topics of poetry, the themes of fine art, the working domains of scientific disciplines are). Interpretative concerns thus already have their prior topic, their prepossession.

2) Likewise determined is the regard in which whatever is being held in prepossession is to be viewed. The possibilities of sight are held within prescribed limits. Interpretation thus has its preview.

3) In-being and its world are at once interpreted within the compass of a particular comprehensibility. One tends to question the world and life in it "up to a certain point." To this end, interpretation comes equipped with a transmitted conceptuality, it has its preconceptuality.

These structural moments and their ever-changing gestalt strictly regulate the interpretedness of a time. Their implicit character—we are not aware of them—invests public interpretation with the aura of self-evidence, self-comprehensibility. It is understood as a matter "of course!" The "pre"-structure of interpretation nevertheless shows that the past takes precedence, as it were, over the present so pervaded by an interpretedness. Expectant concern, guided as it is by interpretedness, lives its past. Dasein *is* its hav*ing*-been, which must be understood as a motion, the very happening of this being. It now is what it already was. This way of being temporal must at the same time be understood as oblivious *presentifying* absorption in the present; it is this actively immersed oblivion which manifests itself as an implicit and elementary historicality. And if presentifying constitutes an improper temporality, then this way of being historical in the Everyone itself may be called improper historicality.

Since the past, what has been, is already there implicit in our present interpretedness, it can in various degrees become explicit. Since expectant presentifying includes the tendency to forget, one becomes concerned about "unforgetting" what has been. (Heidegger diligently avoids the German *Erinnern*, remembering, resorts instead to the Greekified form, *Nichtvergessen*, from ἀν-άμνησις.) Dasein tends its past, and so *has* a tradition. Having a tradition is first of all a presentifying of the past, making the past present, where the past is first understood as a present gone by, lost, put behind us—"Thank God it's past!" In tradition, the "irretrievable" past is preserved for the present. Maintaining the tradition can become a task in its own right. This task of interpretation is first viewed in the horizon available to us in the present, that is, in the world of concern. Past Dasein is interrogated in terms of its world, what one then did and what happened in the environs of past life. The past becomes the theme of world history. Dasein, historical in itself, can pursue the possibility of being historiological. In its distinction from historicality, historiology means, in accord with the original sense of ἱστορεῖν (to explore, inquire, gain information), the explicit un-covering of the past for a present.

Historiological knowing can therefore provide a new opportunity for losing oneself in the world through curiosity. The variety of cultures of world history can become the subject of endless comparison, for which the present becomes only one of many other, albeit past, times. World history becomes available in encyclopedic typologies (Spengler! Cf. SS 1923), and thereby claims to have achieved an objectivity comparable to the natural sciences. It asks backwards in anticipation of the when of past events. The when is assigned a number, and this historical date establishes the historical time, which tells us what the various concerns of that time were. Likewise here, the date, the historical enumeration, has the function of making present, of making a time available in its comparison with others by containing them within the total presence of a wholly transparent and determinable order. (Heidegger here notes that he himself, in his early student lecture on "The Concept of Time in Historical Science" [1915], had not yet understood this function of chronological enumeration.)

Not only the interpretation which cultivates and preserves the circumspection of daily Dasein, but every interpreting, also that of explicit historical knowledge, is determined by the aforementioned "before"-structure that includes pre-having, pre-viewing, and pre-conceiving. They constitute the "hermeneutic situation" in which every interpretation has its possibility of being. Whether this situation is seized originally or simply assumed by the historical researcher, it provides him with 1) that as which past Dasein is to be apprehended in advance (as the expression of a culture, as a person, as a thing in a causal context), 2) the regard in which the Dasein thus apprehended is to be interrogated, 3) the conceptuality which stands ready for this appropriative understanding. The past is interpreted out of the interpretedness and average comprehensibility—what everyone understands by art, religion, life, death, fate, freedom, guilt—of the particular present of the historian. Thus, interpretations in the history of philosophy and the other historical disciplines maintaining, in opposition to the constructions of the history of problems, that they "interpret nothing into" the texts, are affected by the most remarkable "substructions." What they interpret into the texts is precisely the self-evidence of public opinion, the tired old commonplaces of an averaged understanding. This lack of concern for what has already been decided in advance in the hermeneutic situation necessary for every interpretation is described as the bracketing of all subjective standpoints. (The strong similarity in wording as well as thought at this point to the opening pages of the Aristotle-Introduction of Oct. 1922 (p. 2) is of course no accident, since Heidegger is obviously "repeating" portions of his "Indication of the Hermeneutic Situation" throughout this section for the new purpose of detailing the character of historicality as such, before he applies it to the old purpose of "destroying" the history of ontology and logic.)

So much for improper historicality, grounded in improper or common temporality. In like fashion, proper historicality and authentic historical knowledge receive their possibility of being in proper temporality. In the futurity of forerunning, the past is no longer a present passed by, but rather becomes free in its having been. It manifests itself as the *certain* having-been *of* a being-future, which has resolved itself in the confrontation with the past for that past. To be properly historical is not to make present but to be futural, which, with regard to the past to be disclosed, has brought itself into a readiness to take the initiative, to take exception, even to give and take offense. The futurity of historical knowing thus becomes a critique of the present. But its futurity does not reach so far as to take care of coming generations. Since the proper character of Dasein lies in the originality of resolve, this cannot be taken away from the coming generation nor mitigated for it. Every time, if it has truly understood itself in the proper character of its being, must begin from the beginning. The more originally it can do this, the more historical it is.

Historical knowing is the self-interpretation of Dasein. As such, it must become transparent to itself as to how it disputes its past. Accordingly, working out the hermeneutic situation is part and parcel of the proper actualization of interpretation. It decides the scale and originality of the disclosure of the past. And since the cultivation of the hermeneutic situation is based on how far the researching Dasein itself has become transparent to itself in resolve, it cannot be prescribed in a general way. The historicality of the researcher even varies according to the different senses of being of Dasein's possibilities (art, religion, science), which are to be understood historically in the corresponding historiological disciplines. The history of Christianity differs from a history of poetry not only in its matter and mode of treatment. The very existence of the temporally particular historian in relation to the past is also different. (For a fundamental treatment of these issues, Heidegger refers to the works of the Dilthey scholar, Rudolf Unger, on "history of literature as a history of problems" [cf. also SZ 249n]. Unger also contributed to the justly famous inaugural issue of the "German Quarterly for Literary Criticism and Intellectual History." Clearly, Heidegger's philosophical asides are aimed at some of the interdisciplinary issues raised by this journal, for which Heidegger was writing his article.)

Because Dasein in its being bears a past within itself, i.e. is historical, it can be historiological. Properly understood, Dasein stands to its being-historical as it does to its being-temporal. It is left to the person and to the researcher as a possibility of free choice and of the originality of questioning thus attained.

IV.B. Destruction of Ontology

An ontology of Dasein is faced with the task of interpreting this entity in terms of its being. The task calls for a genuine development of the hermeneutic situation, drawn from the theme itself. Bringing out and interpreting the characters of being of Dasein must place Dasein as such into prepossession, then interrogate it in view of its being, and articulate the characters of being thus sighted in a suitable conceptuality. Is the traditional interpretation of human being, which is ultimately the basic theme of philosophy, adequate to such a fundamental task? Are the basic requirements of such a research understood or even grasped? Is it understood that the historicality of Dasein belongs to the hermeneutic conditions of fundamental philosophical analysis?

If we disregard some minor modifications, modern anthropology can be resolved into three components:

1. The old definition of man as *animal rationale*, a living being endowed with reason, is still operative in it.

2. This definition, which once had its origins in a genuine phenomenal condition, becomes the foundation and fixed principle for Christianity's self-interpretation of Dasein. This interpretation gives us the idea of the person, which from that time exercises its influence across Kant up to the present day. The guiding thread of theological anthropology becomes *Genesis* 1:26: "Let us make man in Our own image and likeness." The interpretation of human being is dependent upon this idea of God (as Producer). But at the same time, according to faith, man in his present "state" is fallen. But being fallen means that there is a kind of being which is not from God. On the one hand created "good" by God, the human being has from out of itself the possibility to fall. The *status corruptionis* is based on the more or less original experience of being sinful, which in turn is rooted in the originality or nonoriginality of the God-relation. This relation is neutralized to a consciousness of norms and values in the secularized philosophical idea of being a person.

3. If this whole of the human being, which "consists" of body, soul, and spirit, is to be made subject to its own reflection, such a reflection

is based on an analysis of the "facts of consciousness" (*cogitationes*), from which one can then proceed to corporeality as well as to personal acts and experiences. Whether in such an analysis of inner experiences the priority of the evidence of inner perception over against the outer is maintained or surrendered, whether cognitive comportments or emotional experiences are the predominant theme of the analysis, whether the theory of consciousness is interpreted as an idealism or understood after the manner of a realistic personalism—all these are secondary questions. What is decisive is whether the question of the being of this being is fundamentally raised or simply neglected. If the latter, then what are the roots of this neglect?

The basic *methodological* attitude of modern anthropology goes back to Descartes. Why is the question of being neglected here and thus in all subsequent analyses of consciousness? One would think that with a fundamental proposition like "cogito, sum," the being of the ego would have to be interpreted. But the sense of being in the statement "sum" is in no way examined or questioned. The question of being is completely neglected. Why? Because this question cannot be raised in the approach that Descartes takes to the *res cogitans*. This becomes evident from the way "consciousness" comes to the fore. Descartes is in search of a *cognitio certa et evidens* to make philosophy into a basic science. Since his ideal for such a science is mathematics, Descartes wants a *fundamentum absolutum et simplex* for *prima philosophia*. This must be given in an *intuitus* (*experientia*) to lay the basis for all further *deductio*. All of Descartes's efforts to found knowledge are guided by the concern for certainty and universal binding force. To know is to judge. But judgment itself is an act of will and will means *propensio in bonum*. The good of judgment is the true. The true is whatever meets the *regula generalis* of being apprehended in a *clara et distincta perceptio*. The true in such a perception is thus an *ens certum et inconcussum*. Along his path of doubt, Descartes comes to a point where there is nothing left which satisfies the predesignated rule. But he persists in his search for the predetermined *certum* and thus encounters the *dubitare* itself. And it implies *me dubitare*, which is *aliquid*, something: the *res cogitans* is: *sum*. A *certum* has been found. But it is not the doubting nor the being of the *me*, but rather " 'me dubitare' est me 'esse' "—" 'To doubt myself' is 'to be' myself"—a proposition! The *certum* is to be found in propositional validity. This shows that Descartes does not want to disclose a particular being, the consciousness, with regard to its being and to define that categorially. He merely wants a foundation for certainty. The ego does not lie within the horizon of an ontological interrogation. On the contrary: the being of the *res cogitans* is understood in terms of medieval ontology. The sense of *ens* is explicitly or implicitly that of an *ens creatum*. Being here is producedness, having been produced, which in turn defines the being of God as the Unproduced. But this is really the concept of being in Greek ontology; only now it has become uprooted and free-floating, and so "self-evident."

For the Greeks, being means availability, presence (*Anwesenheit*). The technical term οὐσία for Aristotle at once still retains its ordinary sense of the present holdings (*Anwesen*) or real estate of a "man of substance." Only by elaborating this sense of being can we understand the distinctions of being in Aristotle, who put the ontology prefigured by Parmenides on solid foundations. Inasmuch as Aristotle drew his concepts out of the matters themselves, it is also essential to expose the hermeneutic situation of his interpretation. Moreover, since interpreting itself constitutes a way in which Dasein is, the hermeneutic situation is determined by being-in-the-world. Dasein is first of all absorbed in the everyday concern of the environing world. Addressing itself to this concern interpretatively, Dasein already operates with a more or less explicit sense of the being of the world. This concerned absorption was already characterized as expectant presentifying. In concern, the in-being of Dasein lets the world be encountered in the present. The world in which we get about is interpreted as presence. What is always present and constantly encountered is the sky, the true presence, the entity pure and simple.

Insofar as Dasein interprets its own being out of that which is of concern, with which it dwells, this also becomes the source of the guiding sense of being which is used to interpret Dasein itself. Consequently, the highest way of being of human Dasein is that which lets the entity proper be encountered in its uncoveredness (ἀ-λήθεια). The ἀληθεύειν which lets the entity itself be present purely out of itself is θεωρεῖν. The being-in-the-world of the βίος θεωρητικός is accordingly defined as pure presentifying tarrying with, διαγωγή. The sense of being is thus read off from the entity, in terms of the environment of immediate concern, out of time. But since time itself *is*, it gets read off in accord with the reigning concept of being. But being for Aristotle, who was the first to interpret time, is presence, the present. In the light of this concept of being, the future is the not-yet-being, the past is the no-longer-being. Time thus serves as the discriminating factor which betrays the sense of being of any particular ontology.

Every interpretation, as a way in which Dasein is, is also characterized by falling. What was once drawn and appropriated from an origin lapses into an averaged understanding. It becomes a result which survives in fixed propositions and hardened concepts. This spontaneous degeneration of our historicality is demonstrated in our own history of interpretation. The Greek concept of being has become self-evident. This is manifest in the ontological foundations of Descartes's fundamental reflection. The being of *res cogitans* means being on hand. The meaning of being in the statement "sum" refers to the being of the world. And to the extent that the methodological bearing of anthropology and psychology lets itself be guided by the Cartesian analysis of consciousness or by medieval ontology, inquiry into the being of human Dasein basically continues to neglect drawing the leading sense of being from the "matter itself," from Dasein. (In the coming months, both Dilthey and Husserl will be accused of this fundamental neglect.) When it is a matter of investigating Dasein ontologically, one cannot let the hermeneutic situation for such an interpretation be defined by the concept of being which is read off from the world. Instead, the being of Dasein must be brought into prepossession in such a way that this immediate way of being we have called presentifying, which reveals the world's character of being, becomes comprehensible as one possibility of Dasein's being. This can only happen when Dasein is interpreted in its full constitution of being as temporality.

But the ontological access to Dasein as such is covered over by the domination of Greek ontology within our own history of Dasein and of its interpretation (e.g., Hegel's Logic). Making it accessible therefore calls for a removal of this layer of Greek ontology which has become self-evident and, as such, is all the less visible in its domination, in order to then make its proper fundaments visible. By way of such a phenomenological destruction, the ontology of Dasein must bring itself before the possibility of deciding about the particular provenance and suitability of the categories which have been transmitted to it. The positive explication of the phenomena thus acquire surety and continuity. The phenomenological destruction of ontology and logic is a critique of the present (Oct. 1922 again!), not a critique of Greek ontology. On the contrary, its positive tendencies are thereby brought out and truly appropriated as an ontology of the world in which every Dasein is. As past, it is freed in its historical potency for a present which has mindfully resolved to understand itself, that is, resolved to be futural. The ontology of Dasein is historical knowledge because Dasein has the basic constitution of historicality, thus serving to define it in its particular possibility of interpretation.

One senses the whirl of haste in which these last paragraphs of the would-be journal article race to a conclusion. Technical terms like "phenomenological destruction," already deeply embedded in Heidegger's way of thinking, are abruptly introduced with little or no explanation. A parting look at Dilthey's and Yorck's "common interest in understanding historicality," let alone the bearing of the deconstruction of Cartesian "inner perception" upon Dilthey's psychology, is left to the reader's imagination. We know from Heidegger's correspondence that he worked to keep this final section short, leaving out essential elements not only in his interpretation of Descartes but also in the explanation of his methodology, like an account of the formal indication, "which is indispensable for an ultimate understanding of the matter."[19]

And as soon as it became clear that it would not be published in its originally intended form, Heidegger's first thought for an expanded rendition was to "treat Dilthey more concretely, add what was previously left out of the Descartes interpretation, and relate all this to Yorck."[20] Several months later, when the work of expansion was in full swing, Heidegger is working to set the original article back into the original context "in which it was first elaborated, as the ground for the destruction of Greek ontology and logic."[21]

The effort of reworking leads to BT itself. But one already sees, from this series of expressed intentions, the close relationship in Heidegger's mind between the systematic and historical aspects of his project. It is therefore all the more unfortunate that Heidegger never found the occasion at this time to spell out the details of the methodology which achieved this union of aspects, especially the connections between the phenomenological destruction and the formal indication. All the other intentions will come to fruition in the coming months, beginning with one final statement dedicated almost exclusively to Dilthey.

THE KASSEL LECTURES (APRIL 1925)

This semipopular series of ten lectures given in Kassel in pairs in five evenings (April 16–21, 1925) bears the general title, "Wilhelm Dilthey's Research Work and the Present Struggle for a Historical Worldview." The decision to undertake them was made just prior to the lecture on time in July 1924, under the provisional title, "Historical Dasein and Historical Knowledge (Introduction to Wilhelm Dilthey's Research)."[22] A scant two weeks away from the opening day of SS 1925 in nearby Marburg, Heidegger will here first rehearse some of his developing ideas on "Being and Time" to be presented in that forthcoming course on the "History of the Concept of Time." But he will also take care of some unfinished business left over from his "Dilthey year" of 1924, by going more deeply into the life, work, and influence of Dilthey than he could in the compass of the article of November 1924. It is this latter aspect which we wish to evaluate in brief in this transition piece between the first two drafts of BT. For, despite the critique of Dilthey's entrapment in the ways and means of modern philosophy, Heidegger is clearly paying homage to perhaps the one thinker whose radical way of asking about life in fact first put him on the path to BT.

Heidegger first tries to clarify his overall title by relating it to a fundamental problem of all of Western philosophy, the problem of the sense of human life. Heidegger of course understands this as an ontological and not an "existential" question. What sort of a reality is life? The most immediate reality available for such a question is that of the world, nature, which in its way implicates the reality of human being. Of late, the question itself begs to be raised and explored scientifically. It is in this form that it finds a central place in Dilthey's work, and is tied to a revolutionary upheaval in philosophical inquiry, a crisis of philosophy as a science. But in the current situation, philosophy is not alone in this predicament. All the sciences are undergoing crises in their foundations and revolutions of the most productive sort: physics, mathematics, biology, historiology, even theology. The crisis sprang from the very continuity of the science, which only underscores the seriousness and surety of its upheavals. (This very first discussion of the fundamental sense of scientific revolution will recur in more detail in BT (cf. §3) and in at least four further contexts, beginning with the opening day of SS 1925.)

The present crisis of philosophy is related to the struggle for a historical worldview, in which knowledge about history determines our conception of the world and of human existence. The awakening of the historical consciousness in the eighteenth century sets the stage. Keeping it awake in the present situation calls for a transformation of the question of history from that of a historical "world picture" or historical knowledge to that of the very sense of historical being. Which reality is properly historical, and what does it mean to be historical? It was Dilthey and Yorck who, ever since the 1860s, had a radical sense of this problem. But did they really solve it, and could they solve it with the philosophical means at their disposal? Heidegger observes, in this opening lecture, that he will have to go beyond them and place the discussion upon the ground of phenomenology. This observation signals the transition from the first to the second draft of BT, from the "Dilthey draft" to the "Husserl draft," but also beyond Husserl. "We shall see that the reality which is properly historical is human Dasein itself, what sort of structures it has, and that its basic determination is nothing other than time." This first hour ends on a political note: it will be seen that the relation to the matters thus established concerns human beings, seeks to awaken their consciousness, and is not an occasion for resignation. "It will be elaborated without splash and noise, showing that science is exemplary for the existence of our entire nation."

The very next hour provides the kind of example that Heidegger has in mind, defined not so much by the externals of Dilthey's life as by what Dilthey himself called the "spiritual world," the forces defining his intellectual life, what Heidegger himself has already called the hermeneutic situation out of which a philosopher's works stem. Dilthey's own efforts at biography (Schleiermacher, the young Hegel, Hölderlin, etc.) were attempts to understand concrete historical individuals from their "spiritual core," their "center" (*Mitte*). The point is important in the currently vexing question of the relation between life and thought, biography and philosophy, when applied to Heidegger himself and his later involvement with Nazism.[23] What he finds in Dilthey's life in fact strikes surprisingly prophetic parallels with his own, suggesting that Dilthey himself represented one of his exemplary models. For Dilthey's theological background proved to be decisive, from which he drew "essential impulses for the understanding of human life and its history." But Dilthey's plan to write a history of Christianity collapsed with his study of the Middle Ages. In the battle between believing and knowing, he chose knowing, "this side," gave up ever coming to a conclusion and instead resolved "to die on the trail, wandering" ("auf der Wanderschaft zu sterben"). This is reflected in the essays he produced: Contributions to . . . , Ideas for . . . , Attempts at . . . , all provisional, incomplete, under way.

Heidegger attempts to distill the tentative "ways" Dilthey takes to his central question, that of the sense of history and of human being, down to three: by way of the history of the sciences, the epistemological, and the psychological way. And like the trio of directions laid out in November 1924, the first two ways always culminate in the third, concerned with the "psychic context" of life, and so traditionally called "psychology." But the problem is more elemental than the compass of an inherited discipline: the question of the concept of life is first a question of "conceiving life." It is therefore first necessary to make life originally accessible, so that it may then be grasped conceptually. Dilthey called his psychology analytic to distinguish it from the psychology that seeks to "construct" its phenomena from ultimate elements like sensations. For him, what is primary is the whole of life. The psychic context is always already there, from which its "members" are to be disengaged. And these are not elements but rather primarily given structures to be read off from the original context, like its basic traits of being self-developing, free, and acquired (i.e., historical). But most basic is its personal selfness which is nevertheless always being "worked upon" by the external world. In fact, there is a reciprocal working connection between self and world, which however is not causal but motivational. The original working context of life is a purposive context.

It is to this subject matter that Heidegger wishes to establish an even more intimate relationship by means of phenomenology. For the true substance of a science is not the demand of concept formation, as his old teacher, Rickert, would have it, but the relationship to the subject matter. Whence the importance of phenomenology's motto," To the matters themselves!" The alteration of this relationship is also what is primary in any revolution of a science. This is to be achieved in philosophy by repeating Dilthey's basic question upon the ground of that research which calls itself phenomenological. The revolutionary potential is contained in the inherently ontological thrust of phenomenology. It is a matter of bringing historical reality to givenness in such a way that the sense of its being can be read off from it.

Taking one's concepts from the matters themselves: this seems to be obvious and self-evident. It only seems so. Both research and life have the peculiar tendency to skip over the simple, original, and genuine in favor of the complicated, derivative, and nongenuine. Today's philosophy is more interested in renewing an already given philosophy than in a new interrogation of the matters themselves. Such a traditional philosophy first has opinions about the matters, concepts which are not questioned with respect to their original suitability when they were first formed.

This of course does not mean that phenomenology, in its drive to get back to the matters themselves, stands outside of history and remains undisturbed by it. This is not possible, for every discovery stands in a historical continuity and context, and so is likewise determined by history. In phenomenology itself, there are historical motives operative which are in part conditioned by traditional approaches that conceal a genuine access to the matters. Phenomenology must itself repeatedly detach itself from the tradition in order to free the philosophy of the past for itself and truly appropriate it. The very nature of phenomenological research necessarily yields a variety of directions that must be made subject to reciprocal critique. There is no such thing as a phenomenological school.

Husserl is not named here, but one senses that some of the most cherished prejudices of the basically ahistorical Husserl are being subject to a discreet critique here. Both Dilthey and Husserl, and before them Descartes, are overtly criticized for their fundamental neglect of the question of the being of the entity which they make central. Whether the human being is defined as a psychic context, a coherence of experience, a center of acts unified in an ego, and so on, none of the phenomenologists ever raised the question of the sense of being of this, our own Dasein. Instead, they fell back on traditional definitions dividing man into reason and sense, soul and body, inner and outer, without a sense of what holds these realities together as a whole.

Heidegger therefore introduces his own contribution to the life of the self—the already discussed tension between the everyday and the proper self—which dominates the middle lectures, by way of a parody of the Cartesian self: how the self-contained subject must go out of itself in order to know the objects out there in the world. But life is always already in a world, its environing world is not something on hand alongside it. Rather, the environment *is* life's very space of disclosure, a lived and not a geometric space. Its things are first not objects of theoretical knowledge but matters with which I have to do and deal. Others do not first stand before me but with me in this disclosedness, and I thus first encounter myself "out there" with them also in this, our environing world. One senses the importance of Dilthey's holistic orientation to immediate experience as a first step in breaking the Cartesian stranglehold of presuppositions that bar access to the immediacy of the world experience.

The lecture series concludes by pronouncing, for the very first time, the question which had been lurking in the background of Heidegger's work for several years without however ever being explicitly raised, namely, the question of the being as such. The question of the being of a particular being is not yet radical, if I do not know what I am to understand really by "being." This central question was first posed by Plato in the *Sophist*. (Heidegger had concluded his course on this dialogue a bare two months before.) The question becomes all the more acute when it is recalled that being for the Greeks means presence and the present, and one then attempts to apply this traditional sense of being so temporally conditioned to realities like history and being human, which carry temporal conditions that seem to work at cross purposes with the Greek notion.

Heidegger is clearly announcing his first thoroughly ontological draft of BT, which he will launch two weeks later in his course of SS 1925.

EIGHT

The Ontoeroteric Draft: History of the Concept of Time (1925)

This intermediate draft of BT can as such easily get lost in the shuffle of drafts. Jaded by decades of familiarity with the final draft, the experienced reader can at certain points easily construe this penultimate draft to be a mere rehearsal of BT to the point of viewing it as a raw and boring duplicate. Our Genesis Story is meant to subvert this tendency by singling out the novelty of its entry, by catching in this draft the emergence of hitherto unsuspected new impulses which are nevertheless consistent with prior developments. It emphasizes the look back to beginnings as much as the vision of the goal.

Moreover, something remarkable now occurs. On the brink of preparing his magnum opus for publication in Husserl's *Jahrbuch*, in a work which will distill years of teaching and unpublished research, Heidegger develops a course context which prompts him to review and retrieve his earliest roots, as much overtly as subtly. Perhaps no other course displays its genetic credentials more than SS 1925, from its misleading start through its conceptual genealogy of phenomenology to its concluding allusions to the classical and Christian tradition. It therefore provides us with the first full-blown occasion to understand BT genealogically, even better than BT itself does, insofar as this final draft will itself be impelled and overlaid, even overpowered, by other surprises.

There is in fact a double radicality involved in this recall of roots, contrary to the old Heidegger's self-interpretation. In placing overriding emphasis on the radicality of Greek ontology, he appeals to the four years of labor prior to SS 1925. But this must be coupled by the equally primordial radicality of phenomenology which Heidegger, two years earlier in his first breakthrough of KNS 1919, already understood as the "pretheoretical primal science of origins." The ultimate radicality that

362

ensues from the fusion of these two radicalities first finds its most pointed expression in SS 1925. The point of fusion between phenomenology and ontology is accordingly the phenomenon par excellence, the ontopheno-menon of "being." In more phenomenological terms, it is our most origi-nal experience, the primal experience of our beginnings in experience itself, which once again is simply "being," at first bland, then exclamatory, and finally interrogative. The primacy that Heidegger now gives to the interrogative phenomenon of being thus yields, not just the phenomeno-logical-ontological draft of BT, as a result of this fusion, but more point-edly the "onto-eroteric"[1] draft, focused on the "question of being as such." In this question of appropriately titling the different drafts, it should be noted that the guiding focus of this draft is not a concept, be it being or time, but "the full force of the interrogative experience" first clearly posed in its "initial vitality" and "full vigor" by Plato in the *Sophist*, 244A (GA 20:179/129). The true thrust of "dia-lectic" in Plato, for all its verbosity, suggests that we are in this interrogation at the very thresh-old of language (201/149).

Having now displayed its genealogical context in its full glory, we can easily pinpoint the direct and immediate connection of this course with the previous semester's themes, and then go on to trace its multifarious roots all the way back to its beginnings in KNS, and earlier.

SS 1925: HISTORY OF THE CONCEPT OF TIME

On its face, this is a course of misnomers, false starts, and false promises, beginning with the irrelevance of its announced title and followed by an inertially faulty introduction, which concludes with a course outline far beyond the scope of a single semester. For neither "history" nor "con-cept" nor "time," nor any combination of these terms, truly gets at the basic impulse of the course which Heidegger actually gives. Even the editor of the German edition, despite the adoption the year before (in 1978) of the principle of an *Ausgabe letzter Hand* for Heidegger's Collected Works, had to do violence to that hand in the very first strokes it put to paper, modifying the publication's title to "Prolegomena to the History of the Concept of Time." The modified title obviously still evades the question: What precisely, among these "prolegomena," is the guiding motif of the course? When he first had to announce, months in advance, the title of this course for the coming Summer Semester, Heidegger had just drafted his more systematic essay entitled "The Concept of Time" (November 1924) and obviously wanted to reinforce it with a sequel performing a historical destruction of the concept. But the initial motiva-tion for such a historical destruction, spelled out in the opening lecture, would still reflect the Diltheyan inspiration of the systematic essay, in its concern for founding the division of the field of the sciences into the natural and the historical (human, cultural) sciences (Dilthey's forte), as well as the mathematical and metaphysical sciences. Such a distinction seems to find its principle of articulation in time (GA 20:7/5). But since what time distinguishes here is not so much the sciences as their domains of being, time likewise provides insight into the being of these regions. Thus, the concept of time is also "the guiding clue for the question of the being of beings"; its history is accordingly the "history of the question of the being of beings" and in the end the "history of the decline and distortion" of this basic question, "the history of the incapacity to pose the question of being in a radically new way and to work out its fundaments anew" (8/6). How so? A student who had skipped the previous semester on the *Sophist* would have had trouble in following all these tersely made connections, presented in staccato fashion, since they have their basis in part in that semester's reflections on Greek philosophy. Even those who were there probably did not recognize that Heidegger, in the last allusion to the question of being "as such," had for the first time also alluded to the purpose that would drive the entire course of SS 1925, in continuity with the basic question raised in the *Sophist* (244A: cf. GA 20:179/129), to wit: "to pose the question of being in a radically new way and to work out its fundaments anew." Heidegger in fact makes clear only in the fourth week (May 28, 1925) what "the real theme of this course" (124/91) actually is, as he burrows ever more deeply into an excessively detailed Preliminary Part on the history and nature of phenomenology, a Part that one could almost overleap to get to the point of the course. Its "real theme" is likewise the driving purpose operative in what proves to be the extant second draft of BT, which at this rather late point in the course is itself still being introduced and has not yet really begun. It will begin only when "the question of being is posed in a radically new way," in the lecture which inaugurates the Main Part of the course (183/135ff.: June 15). Significantly, the course outline from the opening day is now repeated verbatim, before the more radical and novel aspects of the interrogation of being are fully developed (191f./ 140–142).

Ontoerotericism

What then is the "real theme of this course"? It is a "phenomenology grounded in the question of being" (183/135), it is the question of the sense of being taken as the basic question of phenomenology, serving to radicalize it and the understanding of its motto, "Back to the matters themselves!" (124/91). Not just the question of the being of beings, which had been the overt theme of Heidegger's phenomenology since at least 1921, but the more ethereal question of being "as such," of being "in general," or, more phenomenologically put, of being *itself*. Accordingly, going beyond his first draft of BT, Heidegger can now complain of a double neglect of both of these questions by Dilthey, and includes his phenomenological cohorts, Husserl and Scheler, in this double indictment of negligence, that is, not only of the being of intentionality but also of being itself. And with regard to the second question, Heidegger himself is at least guilty of a temporary neglect which he is only now overcoming with his belated recovery of the question of being as such. Recovery, not discovery: for this "higher" (deeper) question was on occasion alluded to whenever Heidegger discussed the dominant traits of being, for example, Greek being as producedness (see Oct. 1922, p. 26). It is therefore not enough to call this new draft of BT the ontological-phenomenological draft, complete with the most detailed exegesis of Husserl's phenomenology we shall ever get from Heidegger. He had an ontological phenomenology clearly in mind since 1921, designed to regard any being in its being or "being-sense" (*Seinssinn*: GA 61:60). And in 1922, he called it a "fundamental ontology" concerned with the being of that entity which "in its being goes about this being" (Oct. 1922, p. 15f.). What we have here is more precisely an "ontoeroteric" phenomenology, a phenomenology which articulates the question of being as such, regarded as the ultimate radicalization of "to the matters themselves!"

This point of "ontological difference" (not so named until SS 1927) in phenomenologies is easily lost even in this course purporting to highlight that difference. To begin with, Heidegger actually thematizes that difference only on three separate occasions, and the last two are relatively brief. In the interim, we are exposed to the myriad traits of the everydayness of Dasein lost in the world and itself neglecting the question of being (the basis for its philosophical neglect, even by phenomenologists). And yet this same "phenomenology of Dasein" is the privileged access permitting us to "place and formulate the question" (*Frage-stellung*), since this entity "has within itself an outstanding relationship of being." This intentional relationship of access to the being-question was in fact already seen as early as Parmenides, when he observed that "Being and thinking are the *same*" (GA 20:200/148).

1. The first occasion (183/135–202/150), the only detailed elaboration of ontoeroteric phenomenology, is prefaced with that ringing indictment of an extra ontological negligence beyond the being of intentionality (Dasein) by the first phenomenologists. And so we are cajoled and seduced to keep an *eye out* for that something "extra" through the very insistence of maintaining the excess superfluity of the "question of being as such," and not just for the being of even the most privileged being. Not only is all of the later Heidegger predicated upon that superfluousness, which sometimes seems like a mere overlay rather than a radical

completion, more a textual refinement than the upsetting insight revolutionizing the entire framework, which Heidegger intends. The "question of being itself" is clearly meant to be the leading edge of BT itself, that thin cutting edge that would bare the immediate and thus radical reality of "being" first described in its fullness in KNS.

Heidegger had already shown that phenomenology's backtracking to the "matter" is capable of turning verbal problems, like the one in the Eleatic Stranger's question, "What does 'being' mean?," into material or "substantive" problems (e.g., "history" in SS 1920). This is clearly his intent here, and by the same strategies of "formal indication" (cf. the KNS-schema): "The question of being as such, however, when it is put in a sufficiently *formal* manner, is the *most universal* and *emptiest*, but perhaps also the *most concrete* question which a scientific inquiry can ever raise. . . . But we come to the question of being as such only if our inquiry is guided by the drive *to question to the very end*, which means *to inquire into the very beginning*; that is, if it is determined by the sense of the phenomenological principle radically understood—by the matter itself—*to allow beings to be seen as beings in their being*" (186/137). Concreteness by way of the passage through beings, but ontological purity, broad and empty, in the goal of being as such: are these two poles not working at odds?

The being which permits the rite of passage is questioning itself, *Dasein*, the entity which is both the questioning activity and the place of the questioning, and more, a happening. "The questioning is here itself co-affected by (*von . . . her*) what it asks for, because the question is after being and questioning itself is a being. This affectedness (*Betroffenheit*) of the questioning being by what is asked for belongs to the ownmost sense of the question of being itself" (200/148). Being befalls me, I am *betroffen*, afflicted, stricken, visited by its sense . . . or nonsense: Greek astonishment, postmodern angst. These middle-voiced vectors of questioning and questioned are about as far as Heidegger gets in this course in pressing to the limit and so testing the language first evoked in KNS to describe the historical I's involvement in an impersonal "original something," the It which worlds and properizes me, so that I am very much in It and of It even before I raise the question. A peculiarly pre-interrogative and prepersonal relationship to being where "I am It. It is a matter of a being which to us is the nearest" (202/149), so immediate to us that It is at once the furthest from our minds. It is the experience of already finding oneself caught up in life and under way, the irrevocable facticity of the "I am," the sheer experience of being *itself*.

This most tacit of our experiences is overtly rediscovered when I "find myself" disposed to dread, the sheer experience of Dasein in its naked factuality, "the fact that I am . . . in the sense of naked being-in-the-world . . . the pure and simple experience of being in the sense of being-in-the-world" (403/291). Here, Dasein is no longer an entity, but more: "Dasein is its very facticity . . . which means: it is in a manner of its being this very being (*Sein*), *that it is* . . . It is its very 'there' and 'in' " (ibid.).

2. The "primary finding" of I-am-already-in-a-world is also invoked against the Cartesian attempt to prove the existence of the "external world" (296/216). Dismantling pseudo-questions by pitting a prior basic experience over against them has been made possible by ontoeroteric phenomenology, "by the interpretation of Dasein with regard to the question of being as such" (293/214). In this second instance in the course in which this issue is raised, we even learn that the interpretation of Dasein toward its being "is" the exposition of the question of being as such. At this basic level we are in the realm of tautologies: Dasein is the question of being. But despite the privative being that comes with interrogation, its being (facticity) is sufficiently intact to render absurd any attempt to prove this being, since it founds even the most skeptical of questions in its very being. The passage also makes clear that the experience of the world as meaningfulness within this "primary finding" is radically different in ontological structure from the "unworlded" world of theoretical physics and its subject-object structures. For the first time since KNS, accordingly, Heidegger now applies the vocabulary of "unworlding" which he used then to describe the genesis of the theoretical from the pretheoretical. The latter is now described as the *sum cogito*: "I-am-in-a-world and therefore I am capable of thinking it" (296/216). What really has to be questioned within this primary finding is the nature and structure of encounter of the world, inasmuch as "the being of entities is found only in encounter" (298/217). The very recognition of such questions can take place only by way of a radical interpretation of Dasein in regard to the question which defines that Dasein, the question of being as such.

3. The final occasion in which our "cutting" question occurs yields a straightforwardly ontological definition of phenomenology which seems like a throwback to less enlightened days: "Phenomenological research is the interpretation of beings toward their being" (423/306). The context, of course, then suggests that the first such entity to be interpreted must be Dasein, in its activity of placing the question of being as such, which is the condition of the possibility of any other research into being. "This *phenomenon* 'being,' which takes the lead and so decides the way for all research into being, must be elaborated. As we have shown earlier, this calls for the interpretation of the very questioning. . . . Placing the question can as such be clearly realized only when it has become clear what questioning, understanding, and taking a view is, what an experi-

ence of an entity is, what the being of an entity in general means, in short, when all that we mean by Dasein has been elaborated" (423/307).

Neo-Graeco Phenomenology

The trajectory of the course which terminates in the above ontological definition of phenomenology can also be briefly followed and deciphered by returning to the original "formally indicative" definition of classical eidetic phenomenology, which in the early hours of the course is derived from a discussion of the three breakthrough discoveries in its early history: "Phenomenology is the analytic description of intentionality in its apriori" (108/79). More precisely, the descriptive approach to the structures of intentionality is based on the discovery of categorial intuition (eidetic intuition, ultimately the free variation of ideation). But even before arriving at this definition, Heidegger is already busy weighting the classical terms in the direction of the hermeneutic phenomenology he developed in 1919–20. The "equiprimordial" constellation of the three early breakthroughs, intentionality–categorial intuition–apriori, is thus transformed into care (420/303)–interpretative understanding (190/140)–time (99/72, 190/140). By the time the course draws to a conclusion, accordingly, we see this hermeneutically modified definition, in terms familiar to us from BT, clearly emerging: phenomenology is the interpretative exposition of care in its temporality.[2] Explicative uncovering rather than descriptive seeing is now the basic form of all knowing (359/260). The ontoeroteric definition thus follows suit: radical ontological phenomenology is the unconcealment of Da-sein in its temporally situated being-quest.

From the start, the traversal of early phenomenology is shadowed by its Greek roots. The start Heidegger had made in WS 1923–24 in tracing the name phenomeno-logy back to its Greek roots, whose "repetition" in terms of the three concealments (first uncovered in SS 1924) will now climax (110ff./80ff.) this genealogical account of early phenomenology, is first supplemented and extended by tracing the Greek lineage of its three breakthrough discoveries. In emphasizing the Aristotelian roots of the notion of intentionality taken over by the scholastics and Husserl's teacher, Franz Brentano, Heidegger moreover rehearses Brentano's philosophical career in a way which remarkably parallels his own, and so can almost be construed as a personal declaration:[3]

> The crucial point is that Brentano himself, through his preoccupation with Greek philosophy, arrived at more original horizons for philosophical inquiry itself. Inner turmoil over the System of the Catholic faith, in particular the mystery of the Trinity and, in the seventies, the pronouncement of papal infallibility, forced him to leave this *intellectual world*. But he took with him some well-defined horizons and a reverence for Aristotle, and

now moved into the current of a free and unrestricted philosophical science (23/20).

But of course, Heidegger the teacher does not have the luxury in this course context to wax autobiographical over his Aristotelian-scholastic years, still not quite unrestricted, which brought him to this particular point in his development. He never cites, for example, his student works on the concept of time and on the "logic of philosophy" (Lask's phrase: 94/69) oriented toward categories and language. These are nevertheless being "repeated" throughout this course from the opening hour, now intertwined with the two major phases of development begun in 1917–19, all of which are fused into his present effort toward a neo-Hellenic phenomenology. Thus, from the start, the students are being prepared for the following semester's course on a phenomenological logic akin to the original logic of concept formation put forward by Plato and Aristotle. This productive logic of anticipatory disclosure and conceptual penetration of potential domains of reality serves not only the several sciences in their moments of revolution and foundational crisis. It first of all serves philosophy in its present crisis, which must now find its way to new fundamental concepts, beginning with a new sense of being, time, and truth (2ff./2ff.). Such a revolutionizing philosophical logic is needed especially to radicalize the broadening of truth and being begun by Husserl in the *Logical Investigations* (LU VI, §39) in his analysis of intentionality. There is a prejudicative truth of perceptual identity between empty signification and intuitive fulfillment, such that I live in that state of identity before I thematize it into overt judicative identification (the standard truth-relation). In Lask's phrase, I "live in the truth" before I know it (69ff./52ff.). This backtracking to a prereflexive truth is already to be found in the habilitation's reception of both Lask and Aristotle (cf. chap. 1 above). But Aristotle has provided other paradigms of pretheoretical truth over and above the perceptual model favored by Husserl, a model which especially lends itself to theoretization. Thus, our logic would include the situations of everyday rhetoric (cf. SS 1924) in what in reality has become its basic task, the elaboration of the apriori structure of discourse (*Rede*, λόγος) in Dasein (364/264). This once again is a theme of the habilitation, following the idea of an apriori logical grammar put forward in the *Logical Investigations* (IV, §13f.). This multi-faceted comprehensive logic is the neo-Hellenic phenomenology of λόγος corresponding to the ontological phenomenology focused on the πάθος of the question of being as such.

In recovering it from the Greeks, we already find that intentionality constitutes the very structure of "life." What this means is no easy matter, apprehensible in a single stroke without further ado. Its apprehension dictates a long and involved process which begins by removing concealing prejudices (37/29). There is moreover a close relationship between the now-central topic of intentionality and its unconcealment. One might even venture to say that the way in which intentionality is gradually disclosed in its being, the laborious process first called "categorial intuition" which strives to apprehend it simply as "bodily given" (64/47), is as a possibility "equally primordial" with it. For categorial intuition is "just a concretion of the basic constitution of intentionality" (98f./72). But in this genealogical context, categorial intuition is to be regarded as second in the series of discoveries that begins with intentionality and ends with the apriori. Thus, even though "a priori" literally means "from before" and so by definition is the "earlier," it is understandable only on the basis of the two prior discoveries; it is their ultimate "concretion." It is the culmination of the sequence which step by step brings out the full and fundamental significance of intentionality. The most obviously Greek of Husserl's breakthrough discoveries—Plato's πρότερον (99/73)—the apriori raises for the first time in this framework, with its suggestion of a before and an after, the central problem of time, and its conceptual relation to being. For the apriori is characterized as the "always already there" on the basis of the Greek concept of being (190/140). Formally defined, "the apriori to something is that which always already is the earlier" (99/73).

Its underlying understanding of intentionality has articulated the field of the apriori into subjective, objective, and relational. Is this articulation the real "concretion" of the structure called intentionality? What is the "self-directedness-toward" of intentionality the structure of? Traditional phenomenology has called It psychic life, consciousness, acts, person, spirit, reason, without questioning what these really are in regard to intentionality. If intentionality is really our guiding clue, these "traditionally defined realities" must be put aside so that we may "see, in intentionality and through it directly into the heart of the matter, that of which it is the structure and how it is that structure" (63/47). What for example does the "*belonging*" of the *intentum* to the *intentio*" really mean (and vice versa, both crucial points already in the I-It relation of KNS)? A more radical internal development in the determination of intentionality would lead to a more radical conception of being as such, which in turn would modify the concept of the apriori, how it is to be articulated and divided, how it is to be apprehended (e.g., ideation versus expository interpretation: 190/140), whether it is a logic of generalization or another approach (e.g., formal indication).

The Categorial Dimension As World

Its apprehension takes us to the concretion of intentionality in categorial intuition. Heidegger is quick to point to its Greek roots in the problem of the objectivity of ideal objects, the being of universals: "there is a simple apprehension of the *categorial*, persisting constituents (*Bestände*) in entities which in traditional fashion are designated as *categories*" (64/ 48 and translator's note). Lived absorption in categorial apprehension but not yet in categories, which are the fruit of categorial explication, by drawing them from the initial engrossment. The ontological thrust must be underscored: a categorial component or modification is operative tacitly, say, in our simple perception of entities, before it is conceptually grasped as a category. This prejudicative apriori structure is the enabling background to any and every experience. Explicating these implicit "objective" structures of experience becomes the task of ontological phenomenology. In fact, that is all that phenomenology is: "There is no ontology *next to* phenomenology. Rather, scientific ontology is *nothing but* phenomenology" (98/72).

We first live in categories as in contexts from which we experience the things included within them. Out of this hermeneutics of lived contexts, Heidegger is developing his ontology of worlds (cf. chap. 1), and their unworlding through theoretization. Earlier in the course (48ff./37ff.), he had shown how the same entity (a chair) perceived in different categorial contexts yielded different realities: environmental thing (in the environing world), natural thing (in nature), sheer thinghood (in full theoretization): A chair can be said in many ways. Later, he will develop, for the first time in thoroughgoing fashion (it was begun in SS 1923), the prepositional nexus of praxis (with, for, in order to, for the sake of) preceding the predications of perception, which environmentally give meaning to those things normally called tools, *Zuhandene* (the Greek word for "things" is πράγματα, "the with-which of having to do": 250/185). Beings thus receive their meaning and so their being from the operative structuration of contextualization, from the "world." They are thereby articulated or "expressed." The active locus of such contexturing "expression"—and this is why ontology is hermeneutic phenomenology—is already in life itself, its comportments, its experiences:

> [L]ived experiences in the broadest sense are through and through *expressed* experiences; even if they are not uttered in words, they are nonetheless expressed in a definite articulation by an *understanding* I have of them as I simply live in them without regarding them thematically. (65/48)

The categories or contextures *of* life are first out of life itself, genitive "subjective." Life spontaneously contextualizes or articulates itself and so discloses beings in their being. Being itself "worlds," "speaks," "trues" them, making beings uniquely as they are. In his gloss of the chapter in the *Logical Investigations* (VI, chap. 6) on "Sensuous and Categorial Intuitions," Heidegger is from the start rehearsing his KNS transformation of Husserlian structures into an ontological phenomenology out of the "primal something," "life in and for itself."

The connection between sensory and categorial intuitional acts is constructional in structuring the particular directedness toward the objects appropriate to each type. The categorial act is accordingly an *expressive* or articulative act which "*discloses* the simply given objects *anew*, so that these objects come to explicit apprehension precisely in what they are" (84/62). The formally indicative "magnet word" in the entire gloss, and beyond, is in fact "structure": the structurations of being itself, in multiplying beings into manifold senses, in providing the apriori structures in and by which beings appear, in articulating different regions, sciences, and logics; in turn, the articulation itself is obviously a structuration calling for examination; the structure of comportment, perception, the perceptual assertion, consciousness, encounter, aroundness, worldhood, in-being, and so on.[4] If intentionality is not the structure of reason (Husserl) or of the spirit or person (Scheler), then what is its structural locus? How is it that structure and what is the "sense of structure itself"? (63/47). The same would have to be asked of its concretion in apriori categorial structures, and finally of the apriori itself as a temporal structure, after it has been rendered "indifferent" to the structural distinction of subject and object (102/74). This overriding concern for the structurations of being, its λόγος, will reach a dramatic climax in the coming semester in Heidegger's burst of enthusiasm for Kant's schematism, and precisely as a key to the temporal structuration of the apriori of human experience at the nexus of conception and sensation. Heidegger's "retake" of his own genealogy here is thus as much exploratory for new insights as it is reminiscing over roots.

Decades later, the reminiscing old Heidegger on two separate occasions still recalls Husserl's chapter (LU VI, chap. 6) on categorial intuition as a particularly "captivating" theme, 1) because of its bearing on the old Aristotelian theme of the "manifold meaning of beings"; 2) because it broadens the notion of givenness far beyond that of sense givenness; 3) because Husserl here "brushes" the question of being in particularly allusive passages that prefigure both the scope of the truth of being (e.g., the disclosedness of context) and the issue of the ontological difference. For Heidegger, accordingly, categorial intuition is "the focal point of Husserlian thought."[5] We have already alluded to some of these ontological possibilities, which receive their first full-length treatment as "basic problems of phenomenology" in SS 1927. But an oddly detached phrase announcing the gloss of that chapter stands out boldly from the text of SS 1925, like an echo from the past, serving to recall where we are in our genealogical tracking: "*Intuition and Expression*" (GA 20:65/48). From Natorp's double objection in KNS 1919 to the very title, and so thematic, of the course of SS 1920, this recurrent phrase was used as Heidegger's focal cutting edge for both the historical critique and the systematic transformation of phenomenology into the hermeneutics of life's facticity. Already in WS 1919–20, Heidegger warns of the danger of objectification or "reification," and so of "unliving," that comes from exemplifying intuition through sense perception, as Husserl does. He suggests instead that the very first level of phenomenological intuition is in the sheer understanding of the meaningful contexts developed by life-situations, since these "pregivens" in which the totality of life tends to be expressed can never in any way be objectified (chap. 3 above, p. 121). By SS 1925, both 1) the critique of the primacy of perception and 2) the displacement of intuition by a more fundamental understanding are virtually complete, although the fairly loyal gloss of Husserlian terminology in the early stages of the course disguises this. The final draft of BT can thus proclaim that intuition and seeing of all forms, as ways of "access to entities and to being . . . are derivatives of understanding, and already rather remote ones. Even the phenomenological 'intuition of essences' is grounded in existential understanding" (SZ 147).

1. Questioning the Primacy of Perception

The critique of Husserlian primacy of perception is nowhere so loud and clear and direct as in SS 1925. Husserl makes perception a superlative case of intentional fulfillment because of the kind of givenness which occurs within it, bodily givenness. Not just the self-givenness that fulfills any empty intending, which also occurs, say, in re-presenting and in imaginative envisaging (*Ver-gegenwärtigung*), but a more emphatic givenness and presence. Formally, the heart of perceptual intentionality on the side of its *intentum* is its perceivedness, which is not the perceived as an entity, but the entity in the *how* of its being-perceived (GA 20:59f./ 44f.), *as* it shows itself in concrete perception: the how of ontological difference, a way to be. This way and manner, this structure in which the entity is perceived and "presents itself" has the feature of 1) bodily presence (*Leibhaftigkeit*, bodiliness), and 2) always being presumed in its thing-totality. The two are not unrelated. In the circumambulation of a thing in its totality, the perceived thing itself in its bodily selfsameness persists in and through all of its adumbrations (57/43).

In such fulfillments, there is always a surplus of intentions which allow perceptions to be expressed in assertions. The how of such givenness is accordingly expressedness. The origin of these expressive moments does not lie in inner perception, in the reflection upon consciousness, but in the fulfillments themselves (78–84/58–62).

As perspicuous as these intentional analyses are, Heidegger will on the occasion of his analysis of worldliness drastically qualify their sense of primacy as well as their sense of presence, givenness, and immediacy. To begin with, in this new context of worldhood, perceptual bodi*liness*, "which Husserl claims to be the authentic presence of the world" (264/ 195), is a presence founded on the more immediate presence of the "handy within reach and grasp." But in turn, "this presence of the environmental, *this presence* that we call hand*iness*, is itself a founded presence. It is not something original but is itself grounded in the presence of [what can be called 'concern*edness*']" (264/195). "It is the *presence of concernedness (Besorgtheitpräsenz)* which first and foremost brings to light what we in our orientation to theoretical apprehension designated as the immediately given" (264/194). There are more layers of "give" to the presumed opaqueness of the "immediately given" than meet the blindered theoretical eye. What then is concernedness, which is even more immediate than the handiness of the nearest available things, handy instrumentalities? What has "priority of presence" over these nearest available things? When they break down and become conspicuous and obtrusive in their presence, we first get a glimpse of the familiar order of references, now interrupted, which *has all along been operative* as a "pale and inconspicuous presence . . . the background of a primary familiarity . . . present in this unprominent way . . . namely the world" (255/189). Absence of reference thus allows us to encounter the world that is always already present, a has-been which still is. "The very nearest thing which is at-hand is there in its 'there' only from an 'already there' which precedes and accompanies it" (258/190). (As the categorial accompanies sense intuition, the ideal there with the real? A priori, "always" already there like the Greek world of constant presence? The apriori of the practical "work-world" clearly suggests something less ideal and eternal, something more historical.)

In this context of layers of presence which are nevertheless linked, Heidegger for the first time, albeit still with occasional lapses, lays down a clear set of terminological distinctions central to his later ontology (258/ 190). For the tacit presence of the world concerned with work, in its how of worldliness, lets us encounter the nearest available things in handiness (*Zuhandenheit*) with the presence of "ready to hand." Then, after a series of transitions in which we first thematize the handy through circumspection and proceed further to sheer inspection (265/195), it lets us encounter the "present at hand" in its on-handness (*Vorhandenheit*), in what Husserl calls the perceivedness of bodily presence. Three different presences in their how of being intended: worldliness, handiness, extantness; in the how of their access: understandable, circumspectional, inspectional (= perceivedness). Even the direct inspection which "unworlds" things is a "concerned coping (*besorgter Umgang*)" seeking in remotion to get along with the world (cf. SS 1922 on *Metaphysics* A). Isolated perception in its directedness-toward is still an intentionality derivative from the more encompassing "already involved with" of the structure of care (420/304).

The world in some sense makes possible the worldly thing. Seeking to underscore the relation of co-presence involved in this empowering, Heidegger adapts a term which Husserl first coined in *Ideen II*, "appresent, appresentation." Husserl, it seems, sent the unpublished manuscript to Heidegger precisely in response to the announced themes of this course (168/121), which was first meant to provide "prolegomena to a phenomenology of history and nature" (its subtitle). But Husserl's usage of "appresentation" begins with the overtly phenomenal: the primary presence of the front side points to the additional presence of the hidden back sides of a perceived thing, and so "appresents" them; the directly perceived human body "appresents" the person. Generally, the sense intuition appresents, evokes the additional (in this sense secondary) presence of categorial intuition. Thus, when Heidegger states that the world "appresents" world-things, lets them become present, encountered, disclosed (258/190), he has inverted the term from a phenomenal to a phenomeno-logical one, from an ontic to an ontological starting point; as it were, a retrieval of the ontological difference from its oblivion. Over and over, he asserts that the "primary given" (265/195) is the world and not things, that the "primary presence" (311/226, 318/232) is meaning and not objects. In short, because it empowers, lets things be, the "pale and inconspicuous" nonobjective presence of worldliness and concernedness takes *primacy* over the overt bodily presence of perceivedness. Not the surface presence of the world of perception, but the deeper presence of the world of concern *comes first*. For the presence of concernedness, "that for the sake of which concern is concerned" (264/194), the how of the "intentionality" involved here, takes us to the heart of the matter, where the world of work joins with Dasein in its concerned absorption in that world. The most immediate given here is Dasein in its inconspicuous presence. For Dasein itself *is* time (267/197), here the time of appresenting, making present. At its deepest, what is of concern is time itself. Only a temporal ontology can answer the questions generated by this "intentional analysis," such as: "To what extent is there actually a world present in concern and why does reality mean nonobjectivity?" (263/193f.). What and how is this world that "presents itself" by indirection, "in the character of references" (252/186), as a totality of references rather than a totality of things?

2. Understanding at Last!

Heidegger now proposes, with some embarrassment, to designate this complex of referential correlations formally, in its how, as meaning*fulness* (Bedeut*samkeit*):

And I frankly admit that this expression is not the best, but for years I have found nothing better, in particular nothing which gives voice to an essential connection of the phenomenon with what we designate as meaning in the sense of the meaning of words, inasmuch as the phenomenon possesses just such an intrinsic connection with word meanings, discourse. This connection between *discourse and world* will now perhaps still be totally obscure. (275/202)

The remarkable feature of this embarrassment is that the primacy and immediacy of meaning in the sense of empowering contextualizing, as the most immediate experience of the being of historical life—"The meaningful is the *primary*, it gives itself to me immediately . . . It signifies for me everywhere and always . . . It worlds, It contextualizes" (ZBP 73)—has been a constant of Heidegger's *Denkweg* since KNS 1919. And it will persist with little permutation until the end (e.g., in 1962 in the contextualizing reach of time: *Es reicht*, "it realms"). We are at the core of Heidegger's own "question of being" in its full, personally felt mystery.

This expression of embarrassment is perhaps not unrelated to a peculiar lag in our ongoing saga of conceptual genesis. When we move from the level of life to that of philosophy, we come to phenomenology's problem of the accessibility and expressibility of immediate experience. In response to Natorp's double objection against phenomenological "intuition and expression," Heidegger already in 1919 discovers an *understanding* which follows life in familiar accompaniment without reflective intrusion. This understanding access that life has to itself presents the possibility of nonobjectifying foreconceptions which, in a precursory indication, at once retrieve and forerun life's course without intrusion. Replacing objectifying intuition with nonobjectifying understanding thus resolves both objections against phenomenology. Yet over the intervening years, this clearly central feature of hermeneutic phenomenology is never really thematized by Heidegger. The desultory early attempts to explain the formal indication never even mention understanding. In 1921–22, *Verstehenssituation* briefly appears, only to be replaced by the "hermeneutical situation," where the foreconceptions find their place with barely a passing mention of the operative word "preunderstanding."

Conspicuous by its absence over the years, *Verstehen* finally finds its conceptual home and receives its first systematic treatment in SS 1925. 1) With the introduction into this ontoeroteric draft of an "unoriented and vague preunderstanding"(GA 20:194/144) of the "is" as the indispensable basis necessary even to give rise to the question of being; 2) with the entire realm of "self-evidence" (*Selbstverständlichkeit*), in which we understand "being" as a matter "of course!," begging investigation, Heidegger can no longer procrastinate. In addition, this somewhat disjointed first attempt plays directly to our purposes. For it thereby betrays its genealogical roots more readily than the developed thematization in BT, where understanding is neatly and tightly interlocked, almost in scholastic fashion, in temporal equiprimordiality with disposedness and discursiveness. This equiprimordiality of in-being is the veritable "formal" deep structure of BT, which will be plumbed ever more deeply in later years in order to enter into the core and center of our immediacy, the "clearing of being" itself.

In German, *Verstehen* is a *"Heimat"* word: to be so intimately familiar with something that one "is at home" with it and in it, like a native to a land or to a language, that "second nature." It is the intimacy and familiarity of things become self-evident that comes from living, from "experience," from be-ing. *Seinsverständnis ist Selbstverstandlichkeit.* Simply from living, one knows what it means to be among (*bei*) things with (*bei*) others in (*innan*) the world, one knows how to get along with others, get by with things, get around the world; in short, one knows how to live, to "cope" with life. But the prepositions of intimacy, the talk of "second nature" and "native," combine to suggest that the "know how" of a person "experienced" in life is not just knowledge. Being familiar or familial, being at home, being versed in life, outstrip the diremption of mere knowledge (e.g., reflection) and point instead to a union of being. To get along, not only with others but especially with oneself, *Sichverstehen*, suggests a oneness that borders on the mystical, taking us to the very "heart" of the intentional relation (cf. chap. 2 above), where "being is the nearest."

Nevertheless, *Verstehen* remains a relationship, one that belongs essentially to in-being, "the primary being-relationship of Dasein *to* the world and *to* itself" (GA 20:286/209) in the same sphere of immediacy we have just found in the environing world. More basic than knowledge, even the "knowing one's way about" (*Sichauskennen*) central to Aristotle's sense of experience (chap. 5), understanding is always a "self-understanding in understanding its world"; but first of all it is the relation of "being toward . . . the being of Dasein" (286/209), the "basic movement of Dasein itself" (354/256). "Dasein is the being which in its being comports itself *understandingly to* this being" (SZ 52f.). This circle of ontological self-appropriation, this coincidence of being with being in the self-comportment of understanding, is in fact its ultimate orientation, the orientation of the understanding *of* being. Phenomenology's structure of intentionality situates the coincidence traditionally called "truth" first in the tacit identification resulting from intuitive fulfillment (GA 20:66/49). In like terms, understanding as the "primary being-relationship of Dasein" is the more basic "fulfillment on the level of being (*Seinsvollzug*) of discoveredness" (355/257), that is, of the truth of being. In this aletheic vein, one might say that understanding is the movement of re-covering the initial discovery (*Ent-deckung*) of self-finding, where the alienating effects of initial encounter spontaneously evoke the movement of re-closing in order to restore dis-closedness back to the temporal whole that life is, back to the fulfilled completion of the "circle in understanding" (357/ 258).

Heidegger here is simply ontologizing one of the most basic insights of his early life-philosophy. The formal schematism of intentionality in early 1920 terminates in the *Vollzugssinn*, the sense of fulfillment (enactment, actualization), the familiarity that life already has with itself that comes from a spontaneous "going along" with life as it is lived (chap. 3). This familiarizing movement of return now called understanding is distinctive of that self-referential being which "in its very being goes about (*geht um*) this being" (chap. 5). The *Umgang* of life with itself is just as immediate as its *Umgang* with the world; they are "equiprimordial." I have myself "as" I have the world: the equiprimordiality stemming from the "as" (= at the same time) in fact also sets the trap of equating them, the trap of decadence or "falling." I discover myself as I discover the world at this primordial level of simply "getting around" and "making do," in short, of living:

> The co-discoveredness of in-being itself, that I am to my Dasein itself first in a worldly way, that is, that *I have myself in a self-worldly way* as an accompaniment in my concerned absorption in the world: this is not a consequence of the disclosedness of the world, but is equiprimordial with it.

This passage from SS 1925 (GA 20: 350/254, my emphasis),[6] which introduces Heidegger's first full-scale treatment of Dasein's self-finding and understanding as being-in-the-world, clearly echoes his language of early 1920. Such language will disappear completely in BT itself. Nevertheless, the echo repeats much of BT in the simpler schematism of a phenomenology of life. The situated I instead of modern philosophy's "pure ego," the "I myself" as a meaningful context instead of a pointilistic ego, is the way I "find myself" in and by way of a lifeworld. That I already *have myself in a self-worldly way*: that is precisely what understanding is. This "being with myself" is my own sense of actualization and fulfillment as well as that of the world. This initial self-having is my situation, my forehaving or prepossession, the preunderstanding on the basis of which I can intensify or, by ignoring or misinterpreting it, diminish my sense of the hermeneutic situation that I am (chap. 3).

To be sure, as a *self*-finding, disposition is also a way of self-having, "the way to have itself as discovered, the manner in which Dasein itself *is* its there" (354/257). Disposition uncovers not only *how* Dasein is its there, in its various moods and attunements, but also *that* it is its there, its *own* there (352/255). Finding itself there is finding itself already uncovered. In disposition, however, Dasein does *not* discover itself (*sich entdecken*): once again the passive/active threshold, the ambiguity of the middle voice. This active "reflexive" is reserved for the function of understanding, of its essence in close proximity to disposedness. Understanding is the "disposed being-intimate-with of disclosed concernability [with the world] which always discovers itself as well" (356/258). To repeat, understanding is the completion of discoveredness, which as a How of "the being whose essence it *is to be*" (354f./257) gives itself as a *possibility* for Da-sein to be, specifically to be its temporally particular There. Understanding simply amplifies the discovery of the possibilities of self-finding. Its function is simply to uncover and disclose, and so to cover the scope, and to close off the reach of Dasein's possibilities to be. The fulfillment of being that belongs to understanding "always extends to its *full* understandability, which means to world, co-existence with others, and one's own Dasein" (356/258: cf. SZ 146). When understanding thematically focuses upon the world, for example, the phenomena which constitute the full understandability of Dasein itself are always co-understood, found within the implicit background of the experienced immediacy of being. "The possibility that there is something which cannot be understood is first given with the orbit of understandability prefigured [schematized!] and marked out by discoveredness. . . . It is only on the basis of understandability that there is a potential *access* to something which is in principle incomprehensible, that is, to nature" (356/258). (Recall from 1920 that the experience of experience, the movement of turning back upon itself by which life becomes familiar with itself and so understands, is precisely history. Thus the distinction history/nature is that of the comprehensible/incomprehensible.)

In ordinary discourse, "understanding" is normally used in two senses (366/265). The first of these is plain from the above: understanding is gaining access to something, "taking it over," covering discovery, making it present. Understanding in this productive sense can assume the magnitude of the groundbreaking disclosures of those who thereby become great leaders for having understood something for the very first time. For all its revolutionary potential, this first sense is not unrelated to the second, more receptive sense, understanding as apprehending, that is, hearing and having heard. And to heed is to obey, to hearken is to comply, to respond to the demand exacted by discovery. Correlative to the seemingly independent initiative and leadership of the great discoverer, the second understanding "stands under," follows the lead of another. To listen to (*hören auf*) the other is to be in bondage (*hörig*) to the other, and so to belong (*zugehören*) to her (366/266). Belonging in turn points to the fundamental harmony of togetherness, the identification of agreement which is called truth and in turn calls upon us "to be true." But this belonging is the sphere of immediacy from which the above

"intentional" analysis of understanding took its start. Much of this ontological analysis, which is in fact a direct description of the preunderstanding of the background of being that comes with the global immediacy
of experience, is, despite its relevance, not carried over into BT itself,
at least not into the published fragment. We come into the familiar territory of BT only toward the end of the course when Heidegger, in situating the phenomenon of understanding in the full context of care, notes
that understanding, hitherto taken formally as a primary "being toward,"
has referred to the "already discovered" of preunderstanding, and to
the discovering process as making present. But it has by and large neglected an element which also clearly belongs to understanding "know
how," namely, the "can do," the "I can" (413/299). It is this futuristic
element which will in fact overwhelm the account of *Verstehen* in BT
itself.

But before moving on to this revamping retrieve, let us first recall
how understanding, much like intuition which it is "now" designed to
replace, can be the "*primary* appresenting" (347/252). This odd Husserlian way of emphasizing the present, which disappears after an ample
usage only in SS 1925, first and foremost refers to the function of the
world, as tacit and nevertheless primary presence, to appresent things.
But the world itself is appresented as meaningfulness by understanding
concern (289/211, 379/274). This is appresenting in the order of being.
The order of knowing reverses the direction of appresenting, regarding
environmental things as signs which appresent the meaningfulness of the
world from which they arise. This is expository appresentation, generally
called interpretation, the "basic form of all knowing" (359/260). But expository interpretation is itself simply the cultivation of an already operative understanding. The two converse senses of appresenting thus stem
from the primary appresenting, understanding concern itself. And this
is purely and simply a "*letting-become-present*—a remarkable kind of being
which is understood only when it is seen that this *making present and
appresenting is nothing other than time itself*" (292/214).

In the last week of the course, Heidegger first performs a Greek-
scholastic retake on understanding as possibility of discovery. The understanding intimacy with something is now at once anticipatory, an
"ahead," forward-looking. Taken together, this means that such relations
are "sighted," not in the sense of being seeable but more as a "can see."
To paraphrase Aristotle's famous opening line of his *Metaphysics*, Dasein
by nature has a light. A *lumen naturale* is intrinsic to it, constitutes its
essential definition. Understanding is always sighted, lighted, clarified,
cleared (*gelichtet*). Understanding empowers Dasein to discover. Its very
being is a power. "I am" is essentially "I can" (412/298). This is the basic
sense of the fore-structure of understanding which articulates my herme-

neutic situation into a prepossession, pre-view, preconception. Fore-sight thereby prefigures the incipient conceptuality which is already taking shape in our ongoing interpretative discourse.

The evening fare of SS 1925 is still sparse on possibility. Foreconception has been around ever since the formal indication was discovered in KNS. And around that, the notion of the hermeneutic situation has been taking shape since the Aristotle courses began. What is still missing in understanding, but already prefigured in 1919 in the talk of life as motivated tendency, is the movement of thrown project (*geworfener Entwurf*), where "projection" carries the dynamically "graphic" nuance of prefiguration, advance outline, schematization of sense. In the closing hours of SS 1925, there is at least a hint of this dynamic element in two seemingly random remarks: Being-ahead-of-itself means that in care Dasein "has *thrust* its own being *ahead*" (408/295), to which Heidegger later pens in, "as existential facticity." In a final context: "The utmost possibility of death is the way of being of Dasein in which it is purely and simply *thrown back upon itself*" (439/318). The term "thrownness" thus may have its origin in the thrownness unto death, which opposes mere thrownness into the world, of being relegated to the world and thus made subject to it, dependent upon it (the "pendency" of fallenness).

By way of sometimes publicly confessed hesitations, embarrassments, indecisions, and reversals of decisions, but (as we shall see) also by some backdoor entries and reentries, Heidegger is gradually working toward the thoroughly revised sense of understanding that he will pen for BT. In the context of SS 1925, the tentative, halting entry of two new conceptual loci, two "firsts" centered a) first on the Other and b) then on the thing, which in turn then bear on the self and its world, gives us another glimpse into the refinements of this transformation of understanding:

a. Being-With, and Caring-For the With-World. The work-world also appresents the "public world" of the Anyone indifferently absorbed in its functions of user, wearer, consumer, owner, producer, and the like. The world thus appresents not only environmental things but also Dasein, that of others as well as my own (330/240). Moreover, this worldly encounter of the others who are not environmental things nevertheless first occurs not merely with, but in the encounter of those things: the farmer in the poorly cultivated field, the wearer in the gown on the bed, the guest in the extra chair at the table, his absentmindedness in the umbrella he (Nietzsche!) left behind.[7] Now bodily absent, the others are nevertheless "appresent" in the thing. By way of the world, things appresent the "person" (so Husserl in *Ideen II*), not however from the specific referential context of "for" and "in order to" appropriate to things, but rather from another (albeit related) context "with a different structure of appresentation." Others are encountered in that "with which they have to do" (ibid.), in the with-which of their getting around or getting along, the with-which of their particular occupation or preoccupation (field, gown). (Note that "for the sake of" e.g. the guest does not yet play a major role in this draft. And yet it belongs to the same initially indifferent immediacy of experience being unraveled here.) Before and after the fact, as it were, and even during the fact, what I really encounter is the others' comport*ing* to the world, in a particular how of that comportment. One is what one does, even during the fact of encounter. Even when I encounter the other as bodily present, "in the flesh," she is in fact first appresented "out of her world or out of our common environment . . . always in a concern or nonconcern depending on her in-being" (331/240), in the field, going to work, strolling along leisurely, according to her particular intimacy with that world, doing her thing *as* I do my thing. What the world thereby appresents is how the other "functions" in the world (a functional how taken broadly enough to include e.g. Nietzsche's absentmind*edness*), his concern or lack of concern, in sum, his "*Sein* bei ihr" (330/240),[8] the particular relational comport*ment* of being-intimately-involved-with the environing world that springs from the very core of the other's being-in-the-world, his Dasein. *Not* mine, *but* the other's: equiprimordial in their heterologic: distant echoes from the habilitation's reflection on the transcendental *unum*. As in the two drafts flanking this one, the habilitation's term "equiprimordial" has its first use precisely in this context of the Self and the Other emerging from the indifferent Anyone (328/238: cf. chap. 7 and 1). In and through a mutual comporting, I am there in the world, others are there in the world. Others are there with me, I am with them, we are with one another. Being-with-one-another combines the being-structure of my *being-with* others and the others *being-there-with* (*mit da sein*) me, their co-Dasein (*Mitdasein*). The others are appresent to me not as things but as Daseins, and that relation of initially inconspicuous appresence differs from the inconspicuousness (*bei*) of the "to hand" or "on hand" of things precisely by way of the co-comportive With (*mit*). Dasein with Dasein, I *with* the others *in* the inconspicuous world. So now, the remarkable thing about this world is that it appresents not only world-things but also "the co-Dasein of others and my own self . . . it lets us encounter Dasein, alien Dasein as well as my own Dasein" (333f./242). I discover others as well as myself by way of the world. "This environmentally appresented being-with-one-another . . . is an environmental and worldly concern with one another, having to do with one another in the one world, being dependent on one another, *thrust (angewiesen) upon one another*" (331/240), counting on others, having nothing to do with one another, and so on. The With already present in our concerned being-in-the-world thus has the further possibilities of "*being-for* and *-against* and *-without-one-another* down to an indifferent tandem *next-to-one-another*" (331f./241). There is far more to ponder in this phenomenological grammatology of prepositions—genealogical shades of the habilitation and Deißmann's "in"—than we can manage here. Out of its ever more refined prepositional complex, it has just distinguished and made central, for the very first time in the sequence of drafts, the matched pair "being-with" and "being-there-with" or co-Dasein. More such prepositional refinements will soon follow. Heidegger is breaking new ground. But at this point, he interrupts his conceptual innovation in order to look back across the years and admit to a long-standing confusion in his earlier terminology. The interregnum is therefore significant not only for its attempt to clarify terms but also for the authorial stamp it gives to our Genesis Story.

The flashback: Just as the world-things give us the "around-world," so the others, also encountered in a worldly way but as distinct from environmental things, can be demarcated into the "with-world." "And my own Dasein, insofar as it is encountered environmentally, can be taken as the 'self-world' " (333/242). This triad of worlds had become a staple of Heidegger's courses since WS 1919–20. As late as the article of November 1924, Heidegger expresses the relationship between Self and Other in the strongest of ways precisely in those terms:

> Inasmuch as our encounters are first and foremost by way of the world, the others are there as a with-world and oneself as a self-world. In the immediacy of Dasein, one is the world of the others, and in this world is one's own world. This equiprimordial with-worldly and self-worldly articulation must become understandable as worldly out of the primary character of world-encounter, that is, out of meaningfulness. This must be done in such wise that, on the basis of meaningfulness, the "with" character is set off from the "around" character [of the world].

But now Heidegger declares this entire scheme of worlds developed repeatedly in his earlier courses to be null and void, perverse and false:

> Whenever the qualification "with" is added to the phenomenon "world" and we speak of a "with-world," the matter gets falsified. That is why I now used the term "being-with" [instead] from the very beginning. For the world itself is never there *with*, but instead is that *in* which Dasein as concern is in each instance. (GA 20:333f./242)

The very sense of being-with subverts that of the with-world. But nothing is said here about the self-world. Would not the abandonment of "with-world" at least modify the sense of the "self-world," if not disqualify it as well? Is it, under the changed circumstances, still a viable notion? And what of the public world, the public environment of the indifferent Anyone, where "everyone is the other and no one is himself"? Does the insistence on the clear division between *Mitsein* and *Insein*, which are nevertheless equiprimordial (328/238), also affect its worldly character? Is Anyone *in* the public world? (Where else? Are the two not elaborated correlatively?) In spite of Heidegger's disclaimer, both of these worlds are thematized in the very next hour. The self-world, however, as we have seen, occurs in a one-time-only flashback (350/254, with the correction noted above), never to appear again in the Heideggerian opus.

The "public world" or "public environment" persists into BT and in fact undergoes an implicit further development, in the running contrast between a public "we-world" and one's own immediate private (domestic, familial) world (SZ 65). (But the public-private distinction is never really explored.) The work is ready-to-hand not only in the domestic world of the workshop but also the public world, "the world in which wearers and users live, which is at once our world" (SZ 71). Any particular tool-world has its pertinent public environment (SZ 359). In fact, that is precisely where the public environment, along with environing Nature, is "co-discovered" (*mitentdeckt*, one surrogate in BT for "appresented": SZ 413). Temporal matters on this front have not really changed from SS 1925: "Making present . . . is constitutive of the familiarity according to which Dasein as being-with-one-another 'knows how to get about' the public environment" (SZ 354).

And finally, the with-world itself, both public and private, reappears in BT, more forcefully than ever! Heidegger's own objection proves to be contrived: "the world is never there with, since it is but the in-which" (SS 1925). Only Daseins are-with, and Daseins "have" their world. But Daseins can share what they have with others, their worlds as well as their concerns. To share with others is to *have with* others. "On the basis of this *with-laden* being-in-the-world, the world is always and in each case the world which I *share with others*. The world of Dasein is a *with-world*. In-being *is with-being* with others" (SZ 118). "One's own Dasein as well as the co-Dasein of others is encountered first and foremost out of the with-world in which we are environmentally concerned" (SZ 125). This "first and foremost" world is the public world. "Factic Dasein is first in the with-world which is discovered in an average manner" (SZ 129). The how of the "with," the how of the being-in the with-world, is average*ness*. The how defines the who: the Anyone. From the start, Heidegger cannot shake off the with-world. The real task is to outstrip the initial indifference of the with-world in which "everyone is the other and no one is himself." How do I *really* find myself? By finding my world? Not so. Unlike the with-world, the self-world is not restored in BT, although it could claim an equiprimordial legitimacy "to be," inasmuch as the self also "has" its world, and must have it in order to be able to share it with others, in order for there to be a with-world. Instead, the "self-world" is outstripped by a more radical movement of the "transcendence" of self, in BT and beyond. We shall soon see how, and so why.

In the semester following his disclaimer, Heidegger replaces the triad of worlds with a triad of cares. The context is at once formal and concrete. In keeping with a course on the problems of a phenomenological logic, Heidegger at one point in WS 1925–26 presents a somewhat foi mal, that is, structural summary of his increasingly more articulated Dasein-analysis. These purely structural considerations, focused on the "structural concepts" of care and concern, are developed from the immediately "concrete example" of the dynamic classroom situation, of communicating by my lecturing and "understanding on your part" (GA 21:217). The classroom environment is self-evident, which makes it "no less puzzling" and in need of examination. In my (here Heidegger the teacher) efforts to communicate, "I live totally in my lecture" and, without thinking, tear the paper cover from the chalk in order to sketch a diagram [say, the KNS-Schema] by hand[9] on the board in order to emphasize my points, to facilitate retention, to provide the opportunity for more precise note-taking and reliable transcriptions [for posterity, for now, in the year 2001], all for the sake of communicating my formal analysis of care and concern, to bring the matter of thought before you, to have you understand "Logic: The Essence of Truth" (218). A series of comportments, a series of "in order tos," from the initial "concerned getting-by" with the chalk to the understanding of the essence of truth. Not only concern and care but also getting-about (Umgang), as phenomenological terms, are to be understood in a fundamental breadth and emptiness which nevertheless have their definiteness. As a structural concept, "concern" for the environment cannot be restricted to concrete comportments like producing, providing, and "making do," but must also comprehend "modes of the not" like letting something alone or go to waste, putting aside or mislaying, surrendering or losing. Neglect is comprehensible only when there is something like care or concern (225). The series also suggests that, although care and concern are equiprimordial, concern in some sense has its origin in care, since the care for one's being in its being is more original than concern for the world. But even care is not the final focus of this formal analysis, "but rather the interpretation of this phenomenon in the direction of a primary understanding of being" (220).

But the above analysis, necessarily focused as it is on the being of Dasein, my own Dasein, has accordingly neglected and left one vital and essential context out of its consideration. Since the goal of the series of comportments is the communication of understanding, the series also "revolves around" (geht um) or "goes about" the particular Dasein of the listener, the one who understands, albeit in another way than what the communicator is "about." (Note the point made in SS 1925, already rife with implication for the impending "Heidegger Affair" of 1933: there are both leaders and followers in understanding and discovery.) Here we encounter—for the first time in Heidegger's opus—a third form of care:

> Care as communication and guidance toward seeing the matters is never a concern, inasmuch as the seeing of these matters by you can never really be produced, like a product, but only awakened, evoked, elicited. What is placed under care in communication cannot, at its most authentic, be a matter of concern, but rather is in each case an affair of care by the other Dasein as care. Correspondingly, the manner of being of the communicating Dasein to his listener is not a being-involved-in, a concern, but instead a being-with, with-care, or more precisely: care-for, solicitude (*Fürsorge*). This expression must also be understood as a phenomenological concept. (222f.)

What follows is Heidegger's very first description of the two extreme forms of "being-for" long familiar to readers of BT (SZ 122). But here, the context clearly identifies them as formally indicative relations pointing to the limits of the possibility of this prepositional experience of the other. Noteworthy as well is the concrete example out of which this formality is drawn, reflecting Heidegger's situation as a university teacher and, later, rector. Here we also catch a glimpse of his philosophy (in its way betraying his *Weltanschauung*) of teaching and learning, of leading and following in the matter of understanding being. 1) The inauthentic extreme of "leaping in for the other and dominating her" serves to take over her rightful tasks and make the other dependent on him. He cares for the other in her stead and takes care to make a possession ("knowledge") available to her. He understands the other only in terms of the needs he should take care of by way of worldly concern. Such a solicitude removes the other from her situation in order to take care of what needs to be done, then placing her back into her now secured possession. Such a solicitude treats the other (Let us call her "Johanna A.": it was her last semester in Marburg) as a nothing vis-à-vis her Dasein. In such a solicitude, she is not there as her own Dasein, but as an inauthentic one, as something on hand in the world which cannot manage its own affairs. 2) The authentic extreme of "leaping ahead and liberating" gives the other her care so that she can come to herself, perhaps for the first time. In such a solicitude, the other is not at all understood primarily out of the world she is concerned with, but out of herself. The solidarity in such a being-with the other is not out of the matter in which and for which one has been employed, but primarily out of the owned Dasein who is with the other. Only out of this solidarity with the other can a true concern for the same matter arise. Only out of this comes what we are here calling communication, and, in general, being-with-one-another in our concern for the same world (GA 20:224).

Care in its fullness is accordingly concerned and solicitous care, comprehending a multiplicity of equiprimordial possibilities in a peculiar unity which the history of philosophy has called the I or the self. Here, the term "care," and the phenomena it includes, is basically a formal or structural phenomenon which has nothing really to do with its everyday sense, that "life is trouble and toil" (227), a sense that might also be drawn from the Judaeo-Christian (WS 1920–21, SS 1921) and Greek (WS 1921–22) worldviews. On the formal level, to say that care is self-care is to express a tautology (SZ 193, 318), since we are dealing here with the being "which in its very own and temporally particular being goes about this very being."

But this same, and now, full structure of care also begins to place the notion of the self-world in question. In the argument against the tradition of the theoretical I in the early courses, the self was drawn out of the world and so was very much in and of the world, in drawing its contextual sustenance from that world. The context is the self-world, and the contextual self is the worldly self of everydayness immersed in that world, and so in need of gaining a greater measure of familiarity with itself. But then the extreme possibility of death places us at the very limits of our being-in-the-world, and thus places this everyday There also in question. The condensed analysis of November 1924, which conflates the thereafter tandem accounts of death and conscience, is particularly telling. SS 1925 still betrays some of its roots in that abbreviated draft. In the utmost possibility of death, Dasein is delivered over to itself in forerunning the possibility of the goneness (*Vorbei*) of being-in-the-world, of being no longer there, that is, in the world of concerned getting-about. The world thus withdraws from its meaningful encountering into "something" which is merely on hand "as the wherein which I am leaving" (GA 20:440/318). Stripped of its meaningful ties to the world, Dasein "is wholly by and of itself." "Only in dying can I to some extent say absolutely, 'I am!,'" which I utter in the face of my nothing. *I by myself of myself*, a measure which differs from the self which measures itself from the world. It is the measure of *conscience*, which brings me before the choice which constitutes my proper being, places me between two extreme "to bes," between two Hows: either of willing to be absolutely responsible for my proper being or of letting myself be lived by my daily concerns.

Yet despite this possibility of the self being separated from its world, dying (so in SS 1925) is still a way of being-in-the-world. But it is a world upon which Dasein is no longer dependent, no longer subject to its measures. The world is now the bare wherein of still living on, as Dasein withdraws to commune with its conscience, like Jerome in the desert and Heidegger at Beuron. The quiet abandonment of the "self-world" is no accidental slip or minor refinement. It is at the core of the transcendence of the world to original temporality, and at the threshold of the turn from Dasein to Being itself, that Being which, like conscience, calls, evokes, summons, invites us to think.

b. Bewandtnis

"Meaningfulness is the specific structure of the *whole* of understandability" (287/210). This does not necessarily mean that the holistic ability of understandability, which first expresses itself in knowing how to cope with the world, a "can-do" and "can-be-in-the-world," is empowered wholly by the apriori of meaningfulness. Understand-ability can be regarded as the peculiar how of the *intentio* to meaning-fulness, which as *intentum* is in turn the way the world is present, its world-liness. Oddly, in his own copy of the course transcript, precisely at the point where he first announces it as the structure of worldliness (cf. 251/186 with 274/200, title), Heidegger strikes out "meaningfulness" and replaces it with the "deployment (stanced) totality" (*Bewandtnisganzheit*) of orienting bearings (it replaces "orientation" on p. 349/253). We are catching him again in the act of reshaping his basic concepts after the course itself. Recall his long-standing embarrassment over the very term "meaningfulness" (*Bedeutsamkeit*: 275/202). Moreover, he now seeks to replace it with one of the most formidable terms facing the translator of Heidegger into any language: *Bewandtnis*.[10]

The "*whole* of understandability," the orienting totality, first refers to the environment, which nevertheless includes the self-world and the with-world. It is therefore from the environment that I first draw my understanding not only of myself but also of others. The common understanding and self-evidence of the world "understandable to all" (335/243) is at once a mutual understanding. There is no need for theories of empathy to account for how we come to know the other. There is always some understanding of the other even in the strangest of worlds. Not especially prone to science fiction (as Descartes already was, with his HAL-like demon), Heidegger once again transplants his savage from KNS to indicate the kind of understanding that is still possible for an alien visitor of strange worlds populated by extraordinary beings (334/242). Another favorite example of an abrupt shift at the interface of familiar/strange is the possibility of understanding the alien worlds of the historical past, mediated to us by ruins, monuments, artifacts, and written sources (335/243).

When he, according to Moser's stenographic typescript, in actual fact first orally interjects the term *Bewandtnis* within the course itself (July 17, 1925), Heidegger observes how deeply ensconced it is in the idiomatic structure of the German language (357/259). The translator will in like fashion have to search out the idiomatic resources of his own language to express this orienting How of the with-world or of the thing within it.

In BT, *Bewandtnis* applies specifically to the being of handy things (SZ 84). It, its *-nis*, is thereby meant to formalize the ontological sense of their intentional *state* or quality of handi*ness*, readi*ness* to hand: the hammer prepared to hammer, the knife (well or ill) equipped to cut, the room furnished to sleep, the soldier in battle array trained and (well or poorly) armed to fight, the planes geared and tuned to fly, the pump primed, the boat trimmed to sail. All hopefully in good *shape* and condition (= *Bewandtnis*), in a state of repair and provision to do their thing. "Wie ist die Straße bewandt, beschaffen?" "How is the road, its condition? In good shape or in disrepair, in a state (Illinois!) of neglect? Is it at all drivable? And in these weather conditions?" What broader and emptier, but still precise how of quality, subject to the further qualification of well or ill, is the phenomenological concept *Bewandtnis* meant to express about these working relations? The state of readiness, availability, and accessibility, or the function*ality* of the handy, "its service*ability*, us*ability*, detriment*ality*" (SZ 144)? For understanding not only discloses the world as possible meaningfulness, "but also that which is within the world is itself freed, which *makes* such a being *free* for *its own* possibilities [*freigeben* instead of "appresent"]. . . . The functional totality is unveiled as the categorial whole of a *possibility* of handy interconnection" (ibid.). For it is of the character of understanding, "whatever the essential dimensions of that which can be disclosed in it [the disposition of the self, the standing of the other, the deployment of the handy], to always press forward into possibilities" (SZ 145). Understanding thus discloses the dynamic status of the There and the In, the situation of others and things, but first of all of the self. "Dasein is such that in each instance it has understood, or not understood, that it is to be so and so, thus or thus. As such an understanding, it 'knows' its *whereat* (*Woran*) with itself [*how* it stands with itself, what to make of itself], that is, with its can-be" (SZ 144). Accordingly, "to be thus or thus" for Dasein is really to be its possibilities, its for-the-sake-of-which, project, leeway (*Spielraum*: SZ 145), clearing.

It is precisely in this same context of idiomatizing "states of possibility" that we find the very first usage of *Bewandtnis*, tentatively put forward for the first time late in SS 1925, but in a more generalized sense than its usage in BT. The translation of *Bewandtnis* as "standing" in this earlier context is in keeping with the fact that Heidegger has not yet clearly spelled out the connection of the whereat with the can-be in the nature of understanding:

> The primary sense of the term "understanding" as we use it here becomes clear in certain idioms which we often find in language. When I say to another, "you have understood me," I mean by that, "You know where you're at with me as well as with yourself." Understanding in this sense gives us its authentic original sense, namely, that *understanding is the discoveredness of the whereat-being (Woran-seins) with something*, how matters stand with it, the discoveredness of the standing (*Bewandtnis*) which It [the matter of being, its facticity] has with the environing world, my own being-there and the being of others. Discoveredness of the standing, in such a way that one has become It in one's in-being, means having understood. Having understood means nothing other than being this temporally particular standing. (357/259)

The German *Be-wenden* would suggest more of a dynamic stasis, a kind of "turning in place" or verve potentializing the situation, the way the world turns, not so much its chance drift or unusual twists, but more its orderly bent, leaning, slant, bearing, tendency. The situatedness implied here is thus better conveyed by the question "How are things going?" (*Wie geht Es?*) or even "What's up?" (*Was ist los?*) than by "How do things stand?" (with me, between us, in the task at hand, e.g., traveling), although the responses to the latter would still give what is called for here, namely contextual orientation and direction. The more personal question in BT which specifies the matter of understanding is still the paradigm for the other two worlds, the interpersonal and impersonal: "Wie befinden Sie sich?" (How do you find yourself, how do you feel, how are you?), best translated in Aristotelian fashion as "How are you disposed?" The term can readily be applied not only to the disposition of the self to itself and the world, but also to the nexus of any position or situation, to the disposition (deployment, bearing) of things to us and the world and to the disposition (standing, stance) of the other vis-à-vis the self. The reference, in any case, always comes back to the self in the dynamic stasis of its situation—"You're on! It's your turn!" (Du bist dar*an*!)—on the verge between "where I'm at" (facticity) and "what I'm into and up to" (possibility). As the cited passage indicates, the very "discoveredness of the standing" which is the fulfillment of understanding is at once *having become* that potency-laden standing, in such a way that one *is It* in its full temporal particularity. "Become what you are *to be*" is accordingly what is at issue in a temporally particular self-understanding. The account in BT at one point somewhat obtusely suggests this revolutionary shift in Pindar's classical line: "Only because the being of the There receives its constitution through understanding and through its character of projection, only because it *is* what it becomes, or does not become, can it understandingly say to itself, 'Become what you are'" (SZ 145).

Hard upon this generalized—not generic—first use of *Bewandtnis* in SS 1925, Heidegger applies it to the particular context which it will come to dominate in BT. The starting point is once again the context of ordinary language: the child's question, "What is this thing?," answered in terms of what it is used for, "It's for painting, scribbling, popping corn, and so on." which "brings out 'as what' the encountered thing can be taken, 'as what' or how it is to be understood" (GA 20:359f./261). With the answer to its question, "this thing only now actually comes into the environing world [of the child] as something present and understandable, albeit only provisionally, for it is truly understood only when we ourselves have entered into the standing [circumstanced relevance, pertinent in-order-to] which the environmental thing has" (359/261). It is on the more primary level of appresenting, of lived understanding, whereby I simply live in my comportment of using the tool in context, that we find the "temporally particular standing [bearing, relevance, deployment] in which the thing as thing is present" (GA 21:150). The tool is then understood in its "hermeneutic 'as,'" at the more basic level of tacit appresentation which precedes the verbalized "apophantic 'as.'"

What are we to make of such "intentional" concepts seeking to articulate how the environmental thing is present to us? It is not perceived directly, and so is not bodily present. It is rather indirectly looked-over in the direction of its in-order-to, allowed to be present in and through a working context which itself terminates in a final for-the-sake-of, which the thing in its function plays a part in achieving. How to categorize this indirect passive-active presence, how to characterize its way-to-be? How does an environmental thing "find itself," how is it found and so given?

Does the genealogical clue help to clarify this sort of category? *Bewandtnis* is Lask's alternative word for form adopted by Heidegger in the habilitation. In relation to matter, it is a "how" word, the way in which matter is taken, viewed, regarded, faced, namely, "as" such-and-such. *Bewandtnis* thus specifies the "with regard to which" (*hinsichtlich*), the "in view of" (*gegenüber*), for example, matter "as to" its quantity, the regional category generating and ordering the domain of mathematics (FS 177). Or in a sentence like *ens est*, the verb-form "declines" the noun-matter in a certain direction. The turn of phrase has a particular intention, intent upon bringing out a certain aspect or face(t), giving its object a certain "spin." The *Bewandtnis* here is the slant, tilt, *inclinatio* (FS 329), angle, perspective of an *intentio*, and at once a certain "twist" or bent imparted to the *intentum*.

But now we are not dealing with the classical "noun-substance" and its qualities but with the determinations of a "pragmatic" thing, the "with-which of having to do" and the sense of direction it thereby acquires. Nevertheless, form here is still the "shape" of a comportment invested in a thing. But how to talk about the shape of the comport*ment* itself which precedes both the comport*ing* and comport*ed*? What is the *state* or condition of their prior belongingness? It is these apriori contextual states which "initiate" human comportment that Heidegger is really trying to "categorize" here. As intentional states of unity and continuity at the very interface of passion and action, they incorporate, as we shall soon see, both the continuity of time and the union of truth. Heidegger's first model for such a comportment in BT is taken from Aristotelian entelechy, with a dash of Eckhart: the experienced craftsman who "sub-mits" (SZ 87) to his world, who "knows how" to let his tool serve its purpose by having it yield to its tasks and comply with the material it works, to let it take its course (*Bewendenlassen*) along the paths prescribed by his world, to let it "do its thing"; in Heidegger's words, "to let some-thing handy *be* so-and-so *as* it already is and *in order that* it be such" (SZ 84).

The *Be-deutsamkeit* (a meaning-fulness that points, refers, signifies) of the environment, the *Bewandtnis* (compliant bent) of the handy things within it, the *Befindlichkeit* (disposed self-finding) of the self, an equally disposed finding of the self with the other (*Mitbefindlichkeit*: SZ 142).[11] These are the four equiprimordial but interlocking contextual immedi-acies orienting understanding, interrelated linguistically by way of the transitive *Be-* and, despite one variation, also suffixed together; each in its own way a finding of facticity out of the contextual immediacy of experience. The repetition of "perfect" suffixes already surveyed has by now assumed the crescendo of a litany: compliant-ness (*Bewandt-nis*), handiness, readiness, bodiliness, worldliness, meaningfulness; public-ness, averageness, interpretedness, everydayness; perceivedness, con-cernedness, disposedness, discoveredness, disclosedness. Being dis-closed, having been disclosed, thus the state of disclos*edness* that persists and still stands. The "-edness" is not just a state of truth, it carries a specific temporal thrust. Having been, *it still* is. Already having under-stood where one stands, *one still* understands as a matter "of course!" in a state of self-evidence, *Selbstverständlichkeit*, in an understanding that still stands. Heidegger at one point identifies this entire domain of the "already," of a hav**ing**-been that continues *to be*, as the "*present perfect apriori*" (SZ 85). *It* is a plural, as we have seen: various levels of persistent states that stand in mutual presence and appresence to each other, the deeper layer standing as background and hermeneutic context for accessing and understanding the next. And yet we have an It, singular, unique, *the* state, since it is my temporally particular standing in understanding being, the state of *Seinsverständnis*, a present perfect apriori with a future, a καιρός opening in both temporal directions, the temporal opening and "clearing" with access to the whole; not quite the same as the Greeks understood the apriori, as the persistent presence of habitual truth, the truth of in-habitation. Or is it? And what of the Kantian sense of *state* or "condition of possibility"?

Having been true, still "being-true." It is the way Husserl understood the union of truth in its completion as evidence within the intentional relation, from which Heidegger is now drawing. To live *in* the truth is to live in the state of identity and continuity between the signified and the intuited, a stasis which we continually experience but do not grasp. "Being-true is experienced as a distinctive relation, a comportmental relation (*Verhalt*) holding between intended and intuited specifically in the sense of identity" (GA 20:70/52). This state allows us to be true (be disclosed), be in the hold of truth, where being as truth-relation is the "persistence and standing of the state of affairs (*Sachverhalt*) in the relation 'true'" (72/54). Husserl also called such states "static unions," long-standing habitual fulfillments which are the lasting result of the step by step "dynamic fulfillments," where I say and then see and finally recognize tacitly that they are the same (LU VI, §8).[12] Perception intentionally understood thus becomes the precursory indication for Heidegger, a kind of entry into the understanding of being in the stasis of truth, which also serves as a passageway to interpreting as well as dismantling the traditional approaches to being and truth. Perceivedness and bodiliness: the core correlativity of *intentio* and *intentum*. Each suffixed abstraction is actually the correlation itself in its how, the completed and repeatable state of truth. The "-ness" is meant to suggest something of that unifying state, and the stem the condition (so and so), quality, the how (truth) of the correlation. In any case, we are to be drawn toward the simple central thrust of the intentional movement, sometimes more toward the *intentio*, or the *intentum*, ever more undecidable as we near the center, but in each temporal emphasis a specification of truth.

This common core of intentionality is still the cutting edge for the destructuration and restructuration of the traditional theses of being understood as "basic problems of phenomenology" in SS 1927 (GA 24: 446f./314). But even in SS 1925, Heidegger is deep in the throes of shaping formally indicative concepts to the shape of the intentional movement by way of properly qualifying suffixes available to him from the German language. These aim to express the dynamis of the movement as well as the stasis of its completion: the "pendency" (*Verhängnis*) of fallenness (GA 20:390/282); fallenness itself as a basic "movedness" (*Bewegtheit*: 348/252), soon to be joined by thrownness and projection. We ourselves are confronted with a category problem, of sifting through and sorting out these different ontological states, and the ones to come—ranging from *Seinsverständnis* to *Ereignis*—according to their guiding principle, the simplifying assumption around which they all revolve and from which they in fact have devolved. We must now turn to the guiding clue in SS 1925, the specific formal indication which also owes its ancestry to intentionality, which has been guiding Heidegger's formation of concepts all along.

Formally Indicating To-Be

We have thus saved perhaps the most important aspect of SS 1925 for last, partly with an eye to what will happen to it with the onslaught of BT itself. For the ontoeroteric draft, as we might expect, formally indicates the essence of Dasein, the entity who questions being, in a purely ontological manner. The formal indication of "existence" which literally inundates BT itself is totally absent from the penultimate draft. The scattered allusions to terms like "Existenz," "existenziell," "existenzial" which have infiltrated the "Ausgabe letzter Hand" of SS 1925 *all* stem from Heidegger's marginal jottings in his personal copy of Simon Moser's stenographic typescript of the course, and so postdate the lecture course itself. SS 1925 is a purely ontological draft at its very core and through and through. In fact, only BT itself can with some warrant be called the existentialistic draft.[13]

Moreover, Heidegger overtly shapes and tacitly announces his formal indication, hours before it will officially emerge, precisely out of the schematism of intentionality which he had developed years before. He himself therefore rehearses for us, in the peculiar context of this course, at once historical and ontophenomenological, his own genealogy of the formal indication out of the very nature of intentionality. The problem context is the double neglect by the first phenomenologists of both the being of the intentional and being as such. A thoroughly systematic destruction of Husserl's central assumption of a pure consciousness—the Husserl of *Ideas I* and not *Logical Investigations*—is in full swing. In order to arrive at this sphere of pure consciousness, Husserl himself has made a purely ontological "formal indication" of sorts, on the basis of his Cartesian predilections and his own ambition for phenomenological philosophy to achieve the supreme status of absolutely rigorous and pure science. To this end, Husserl overtly insists on beginning with the "most radical distinction in being that can and must be made within the science of categories [= ontology]" (GA 20:141/102), namely, the distinction between "being as consciousness and being as 'transcendent' being 'manifesting' itself in consciousness" (157/114, citing *Ideas* I, §76). This transcendental-phenomenological reduction thus removes us from the "contingency of the world of things" into the purely immanent self-perception (acts reflecting on acts) of a consciousness. In this sense, consciousness is absolutely given to itself and independent, since its self-constitution means that "it needs no thing (*res*) in order to be" (141ff./103ff.). Thus, in his famous thought experiment, Husserl points out, in dramatic Cartesian fashion, that this self-constituting sphere that constitutes everything else is absolute being, inasmuch as it is "unaffected in its own existence by an annihilation of the world of things."[14] The eidetic reduction, ideation, completes the purification by removing consciousness from its individuated setting in reality to the level of the purely ideal essential content and structure of the stream of lived experience (146/106).

It is precisely in this ideative regard of generic "what-contents," to the disregard of the That of acts or intentional comportments, that Heidegger finds the opening to introduce his old schematism of intentionality and thereby to announce, for the first time in this course, the kind of "category" that will express the core, the "vital impetus" of the intentional movement of lived experience. The ideative reduction "regards the what, the structure of the acts, but as a result does not thematize their *way to be* [*Weise zu sein*], their being an act in act and in being. It is solely concerned with the what-contents of those structures. . . the essence of the what of comportments . . . but not the essence of their being" (151/109). And we know from the old schematism that the "content sense" only bounds the periphery of the intentional act. For the initiating core of the act resides in its "relational sense" and its completion or fulfillment in the concrete enactment of that relation, its "actualizing sense." But Husserl's double reduction has even removed us from that concrete setting in which the intentional movement finds both its start and its end. Moreover, the same passage portends something of the "existentialism" waiting in the wings of Heidegger's creative categorizing, and this, surprisingly, in conjunction with the traditional *essentia-existentia* distinction, the what-that distinction! For what the reductions do not ask, and in fact overtly obfuscate, is the question of the "being of the acts in the sense of their existence. . . . From the what I never experience anything about the sense and the way of the that—in any case, only that a being of this what-content can have a certain way to be" (152/110). This loose trafficking with traditional categories is soon followed by the very first full statement of Heidegger's own formal indication, albeit in conditional form: "But if there were a being *whose what is precisely to be and nothing but to be* [?]" (ibid.). An entity that is first of all identified not by its what, but by the fact "that it is" (relational sense) and "has to be" (actualization sense). What if intentionality itself is the very act of being, the be-all and end-all of being?[15]

Against Husserl, therefore, back to the matters themselves means going back to the concrete entity in and through its dependence on the world, back to the prereflective realm of experience, back to the "natural attitude." But not in the way Husserl understands this, which turns out to be quite unnatural. For to regard the human being as something on hand composed of body, soul, and spirit is already a theoretical attitude. "In the natural form of experience, does the human being experience itself, to put it curtly, zoologically? Is this attitude a natural attitude or not? . . . Man's natural manner of experience cannot even be called an attitude" (155f./113). Nevertheless, there is still the question of whether the "reality" of the human being and its acts is the way to experience the being of acts, the intentional in its being, or whether it is not actually obliterated "and the being of acts is defined merely in terms of their having occurred" (156/113). In defending a more "natural" phenomenology, in returning to the facticity and individuality of intentional comportment, Heidegger still finds warrant in the reversal that Husserl called bracketing or suspension. A modification of our objectifying tendency is necessary in order to make the act itself the theme, in order that "the perceived is not directly intended as such, but in the how of its being" (136/99). For the natural way of beholding, Heidegger later says, as he tentatively broaches the subject once again, "tends to live away from itself" (210/156).

Hours later, we come to Heidegger's overt declaration of the "formal indication" or, more tellingly, "precursory indication," although these terms are sparingly used here, as in BT. But here for the very first time, what was already tacitly operative in the first draft of November 1924—in questions like "What does it mean *to be* historical?"—is officially "put up front" and made the core of all forthcoming concept formation and category creation. For what we wish to secure here is not just the initial determination, "it is also the end determination, that determination to which every analysis of being again and again returns" (206/154). The many structures of being which will thus be exhibited are at all times to be regarded "in the light of this fundamental character" (ibid.). And it is a surprisingly simple and direct and pure ontological formulation, albeit a bit awkward, which formally indicates this *essence*, this "fundamental character" of Dasein, of the being which questions being. The formal indication is moreover said in several ways, to bring out its various nuances. Let us take them roughly in the order in which they are first presented in §18 (205f./ 152f.). The self-referential indication: "Dasein is the entity which I *myself am in each instance.*" Nuanced lightly by the modals of obligation (having-to-be) and possibility (can-be): "an entity which *is to be* it in my way, in my instance, as my affair." In the impersonal relation which takes us back to KNS: "to be It itself"; "I am It in the 'to be It in each instance.' " This impersonal dimension spills over into the very coinage of the name selected for this entity, Da-sein, "to be there," to be its situation. The ambivalent unity of the equiprimordial personal and impersonal to-be: "in each case mine (*je meines*), mine for a while" (*je-weils*). The distributive universal: "each according to its time, *je nach dem.*" Not the bland leveled "is" of *ens commune*, but the muscular "to-be" (*Zu-sein*) of tending and directedness-toward.

This ontic-ontological core gradually unfolds into its many categories, the ways-to-be and not whats, *Zu-sein* and its many ways. The prepositional ways to be, reflecting the vectors of being: to-be in, to-be out for, to-be toward, to-be with (*mit*) and intimately with (*bei*), and so on. The (de facto) adverbial ways, conveying the states of being: to-be there, to-be possible, to-be authentic, to-be true, to-be uncovered, to-be concerned, to-be historical, and so on, the "qualities" of the aforementioned dynamic relations. Thus the peculiar shift in ordinary language, where the real "nouns" are prepositional phrases (being-in-the-world, being-ahead-of-itself) and their "adjectives" are really adverbial, since they modify and modalize "to-be" (genuinely, disclosedly, possibly): why *Sein und Zeit* continues to be a strange lexical experience even for native Germans.

Why did Heidegger replace this strictly ontological sense of intentionality with the terminology of existentialism? For it would seem that he had all that he needed in the language of "to-be" to achieve his ontological aims. The ways-to-be as characters of being seem also to be straightforward expressions ("categories") less prone to the jargonizing that the existentials have become, which is why Heidegger himself for a time tried to distance himself from the wave of enthusiasm over Kierkegaard current in the early twenties. What did "ex-sistence" give him that "to-be" did not? The answers begin to emerge only in the very last hour of the following semester (February 26, 1926), when, after its public absence of over two years (since January 8, 1924), Heidegger revives the terminology of *Existenz*. Here for the first time, he identifies *Existenz* as his new focal point for all the structural concepts—the "existentials"—which are to express the being of Dasein. Time itself is identified as the "ground existential" of Dasein (GA 21:402f.). By this time, Heidegger, in an all-out effort to "publish or perish," is feverishly at work on the final draft of BT.[16]

WS 1925–26: LOGIC (ARISTOTLE) [THE QUESTION OF TRUTH][17]

Why did Heidegger choose the topic of "Logic" precisely at this critical juncture in his development, on the verge of the massive effort to get his first major work into print? It is in fact one of Heidegger's favorite course topics, reaching back into his student years with its two logically oriented dissertation topics and extending forward to several courses in the next two decades, up to one of his very last as an Ordinarius, which simply bear the major title "Logic."[18] One could easily write a whole book characterizing Heidegger's entire career as that of a "logician." But ever since the student Heidegger wrote his review of Lask's *Logik der Philosophie* in 1912, logic for him was always a philosophical logic, "a logic of logic" in the Scotus dissertation (FS 230), thus a "transcendental" (phenomenological, hermeneutical, ontological) logic. Beginning in SS 1925 (GA 20:2f./2), it is portrayed as an "original logic" (ergo a "logic of origins") whose first function is to "produce" the fundamental concepts which articulate the incipient ground of all of reality as well as of its particular domains, as the starting basis for further scientific research in those domains. In SS 1923, Heidegger, outranked by a colleague who also announced a course in Logic, changed his title to "Ontology" without any particular strain, since for him Ontology and Logic belong together essentially as "science of being" and "science of the ways in which being is addressed and articulated." As we know from the semesters that precede this course, its very subtitle, "Hermeneutics *of* Facticity," is meant to convey the same connection, and even a virtual identity, between being and language. Contrary to traditional "ontic" and mechanically rote "school logic" (GA 21: §3), this hermeneutically ontological logic, operating at the very interface of being and language, is confronted with as yet unexplored, inchoate pretheoretical realms which demand and "evoke" hitherto unspoken languages apropos of their particular matter. It should come as no surprise that SS 1923 accordingly provides the context in which Heidegger for the very first time mentions, albeit in passing, those innovative and tradition-breaking categories of being called "existentials," meant there to articulate the most unique and highest possibility latent in the facticity of being human.

This course on Logic in WS 1925–26 likewise repeatedly moves, in manifold fashion, toward this same interface at which language is born. Before Heidegger broaches the problem of the existentials again, at the very conclusion of the course, he rehearses his own earliest steps toward the conception of a philosophical logic ultimately designed to discover such existential concepts and their "hermeneutically indicative sentences" (410): the first dissertation through Husserl's critique of psychol-ogism (43–53), the second through his own critique of the neo-Kantian sense of judicative truth as validity (53–88) and Aristotle's prejudicative truth of simple apprehension (180–190). Both senses played a central role in his own conception of the transcendental *verum* in the habilitation, such that his critique of them now amounts to a self-destruction of that second dissertation, as he himself points out with regard to his "earlier investigation into the ontology of the Middle Ages" (64).

"It 'is' not, but instead holds (*gilt*)": We know how fascinated the young Heidegger was with this very first, neo-Kantian version of the ontological difference expressed in the German impersonal (chap. 1). It dominated even Lask, who (so in Heidegger's review) spoke of a "third Reich" of validity and *verum* beyond both physical and metaphysical entities, on the basis of which a "logic of philosophy" would formulate its comprehensive doctrine of categories. We also know that the young (phenomenologist) Heidegger was taking steps to bring this "panarchy of the Logos" of ideally formal validity back toward the matter of meaning which articulates and differentiates it. When this holding and staying power of validity in neo-Kantianism is traced back to the constancy and persistence of the ideal which our judgments necessarily affirm and posit, this firming "position" of "affirmativeness," of compelling Yesness (*Bejahtheit*: 68) and the peculiar optimism of Idealism which it exacts, we know exactly where we are in Heidegger's developing reading of philosophy's history: the Parmenidean-Platonic hedonism (so in SS 1924) of constant presence, of οὐσία (71, 78) now reasserts itself in the optimism of the late nineteenth century in "cultural values" (83). Since even religion must be housed in this cultural system, it has also "invented the value of the Holy," and fortunately so, since "the world after the war has become very religious" (ibid.).

Philosophy's chronology, read quite consciously from a German perspective in this semester, thus brings us to Husserl. To put it in terms of a "comic juxtaposition of Greek and German" (110), we must now proceed from "λόγος-Wahrheit," the truth of discourse, to the more basic "νοῦς-Wahrheit," the truth of intuition. For the sentence is the "seat" of truth only because it gives expression to intuition. And the achievement of Husserl, in giving voice for the first time to a "radical grasp of the concept of intuition"—his intentional sense of intuition, at once broad and fundamental—is to "have thought the great tradition of occidental philosophy to its end" (114).

Husserl's "principle of all principles" for all knowledge and research is intuition. Knowledge *is* intuition. And intuition, broadly conceived, is "the giving and having of a being in its bodily presence" (113). It is an apprehending having, the immediate having of the bodily given. Intuition itself gives the subject matter, the thing itself; it "gives originarily."

And it is up to us to let the "thing" give itself thus, "but also only within the limits in which it gives itself there" (*Ideen I*, §24). Having and giving thus also involve receiving and being had. The issue of receiving has surfaced repeatedly in the genealogical record since at least WS 1920–21, first in the Christian context of grace, but never sufficiently explored. Will Heidegger now finally probe more deeply into it? Can we get on the inside of intuition itself and develop its preintuitional substructure?

As a matter of fact, this process was in full swing in the previous semester, and will now be reviewed and deepened. The language of appresence is gone, but the move is the same: to get at a deeper structure of presence, immediacy, and givenness than the structure of immediacy offered by intuition. The movement is slower than usual, since it is now being done more historically than by way of the systematic approach of last semester. In joining with the issues of last semester, we also pick up the genealogical thread of continuity of this course which will enable us to decipher its telic continuity into BT itself, and beyond.

Intuiting does not lose itself in the matter's content. Instead, this content becomes explicitly bodily present as fulfilling in the self-identification which is experienced but not overtly known:

> The identification fulfills itself and thereby has a clarification of itself without reflection. If this moment of unreflected self-understanding of itself in the intentional enactment (*Vollzug*) of identification is grasped, it is to be regarded as what we call [self-]evidence. Evidence is the act of identification understanding itself as such; self-understanding is given with the act itself, since the intentional sense of the act intends something selfsame as selfsame and thus illuminates itself along with its intending. . . . Evidence is not an act that merely accompanies the demonstrative fulfillment; it is its very enactment, a distinctive mode of it. (107f.)

This is a lucid intentional statement of the upshot of the previous semester: underlying intuition, there is a more fundamental understanding of the truth of that intuition which at once understands itself. Understanding is more fundamental than intuition: a statement which undercuts the entire tradition of occidental philosophy.

Shortly before, Heidegger had suggested that "*having* to do with things," even though this does not give the things strictly bodily as in intuition, is itself clearly a form of having. "The blackboard is in a genuine sense bodily there, in the most proper reality which it can ever have, insofar as it is used in that which it is. In this way, it is in a genuine sense disclosed. But to a primitive native [*wildfremden Menschen*, the savage from KNS!] who happens in and sees it, it is not there in what it is" (104). Once again the understanding familiarity with things that precedes perception, thus a deeper form of having than intuitive having.

With the invocation of the historical radicality of Husserl's sense of intuition as the "immediate having of the bodily given," Heidegger embarks on a brief history of the sense of intuition. By first going back to Kant, who in a way is more radical in invoking the divine intuition, which first produces the objects which it presents bodily (115), Heidegger quietly announces the surprise he will soon spring in the historical dimension of the course. This historical dimension, the first version of the forthcoming "Kant-book," provides an unexpected "marginal" dimension, in the strongest sense, to the final draft of BT. So strong, in fact, that it can be called the Kantian draft of BT, just as the two previous drafts respectively spotlighted Dilthey and Husserl in their destructive movements.

Out of this critical juncture in the course, therefore, we can trace its two major and distinct innovations to the problematic of "Being and Time," in particular to its problem of "Presence and the Present" (*Anwesenheit und Gegenwart*), one systematic and the other historical, the first overt and the other marginal, one speaking directly to its content and the other more to its implicit frame.

1. Having

The first pursues the old ousiological guiding clue from the "having" of intuition or simple "apprehension" (the had held, the held had) back to its more basic pragmatic version of "having to do with something" in understanding know-how. The distinction parallels that of the apophantic and the hermeneutic "as," which is first thematized in this course on Logic and finds its way into the section on hermeneutic logic in BT, bearing the inscription "Assertion as a Derivative Mode of Interpretation" (SZ 153–160, §33). These matchless pages in the course (GA 21: 133–161) are singularly important not only in their anticipation of BT, not only because they bare their genetic roots in Heidegger's continuing reflection on Being and Having, but also in themselves. For here also, Heidegger takes a fresh look at the hermeneutic language of indication he has been seeking for philosophy by contrasting its logic of heterothesis with that of the apophantic assertion, with its deep roots in the traditional predicative grammar geared to the clear-cut yes-no binary logic of synthesis and diairesis. Small wonder that he, in a seminar concurrent with this course, spends the entire semester reflecting simply on the opening triad of Hegel's *Logic*![19]

Just a few salient points on the ousiological feature (*Habe*) in this passage, on how we "have" the environing world, by and large left undiscussed in BT (SZ 57f.), in short, on defining a having within the understanding know-how of environmental concern. Having to do with something in our everyday rounds of usage is a "having" of something as something, used and so "taken" as a chair, blackboard, chalk, and so on, "given" first in its what-for (GA 21:143–5). This "as-like experiencing and comportive holding" (*Ver-halten*) is the primary form of "*simple apprehension* of things," more primary than direct intuition, which the tradition in precisely those terms regarded as the "first act of the mind." "The peculiar and self-understood 'in-itself' of the most immediate 'things' is [first] encountered in the concern of inchoate usage, which can [then] bump into them as unusable" (SZ 74). Things are first be-held (*ver-nom-men*) in those networks of referral by which understanding know-how points (*deutet*) them to their meaning (*Bedeutung*), not directly but by plying them to their "fors" and "in order tos" within the whole of meaning. *Bewandtnis*, pliedness, implication in the environment, is the very presence, meaning, truth, being of such things (GA 21:150). Taken under the wraps of its world, given as an environed thing and not out of its context: the thing is not intuited as white chalk, but understood as to-write in the continuity of what-fors and in-order-tos in which I live. A more subtle give-and-take, this having in the cycles of usufruct (cf. SS 1921), this having of belonging there. It is a having and taking which is one with living as dwelling, abiding, sojourning, "holding up" in a stay which holds to a locale in order to maintain itself (*Sichaufhalten*: 148), a certain firmness of having simpler than "simple apprehension" because it is inexplicit (145). In its way still prehensile, this nonthematic simple apprehension of the environed thing, as it is "most naturally given" (147), is a constant coming back to its already encountered state, as my forehaving in the present perfect tense, from my always-already-ahead. It is the having of my having-been still to be maintained, of my tradition which I conserve by letting the thing be, take its course, allowing its re-course (*bewenden lassen*). It is the old idea (Oct. 1922) of truth as taking into troth (*verwahren*: 150), holding in safekeeping, conserving the environment of what has been and still is. This conservative sense of truth will reassert itself in the later Heidegger's reflections on "Building and Dwelling" in an environment disrupted by the war years.

The "as" of primary understanding is the original articulation of my comportment. I live in the as-what, I live in the understanding of writing, lighting, entering and exiting, and so on. All this is what I already have in advance, albeit unthematically. "I am—qua Dasein—understanding getting-around. My being in the world *is* nothing but this already understanding self-movement" (146). Thus, simply by living, or living thus simply, simply by having to do with it and making do with it, I acquire these peculiar possessions, the habits of my habitat, that constitute my most immediate having, the having of having been, the present perfect apriori, my prepossessions. But life, understanding, goes on. How? On the basis of the habit of having been, on the basis of what is already understood, the "deposit" of tradition. The "as" of primary understanding (*primär verstehendes "als"*: 153) is in this ongoing function now the "hermeneutic 'as' " (not until p. 158), the already understood which serves to further understanding, to explicate the yet-to-be-understood. The hermeneutic "as" accordingly has the very structure of the entity we have come to know as Dasein; it is its very being, and its time (150n).

We speak. We try thus to explicate the very structure of our being. The with-which of having to do, of understanding getting-on and getting-by, now becomes the about-which of an assertion. Sooner or later (Heidegger opts for the latter), we discover that the assertion is designed more to give voice to intuition than to understanding, that is, to understanding in the full scope of the temporality upon which it itself is based. The assertion is a demonstrative letting-see, *apo-phansis*, "showing up," uncovering . . . what? Upon closer examination, we discover that it is only a narrowly "indicative" letting something be seen, in the grammatical sense of the indicative mood, which means not the optative or imperative moods. The apophantic language of direct showing and seeing, the unpunctuated, unadulterated subject-predicate language without the distorting twists given to it by question and exclamation marks, is a highly restrictive language. Apophantic language is the language of direct showing and sharp definition for the sake of clear and explicit communication (133f.; cf. SZ 154f.), with little left to do for the hesitation of the question, the tentativeness of the request, even the presumptuousness of the command (it need not be obeyed). Apophansis is a garrulous language in which the punctuations of silence ultimately play no role. For the explication of the full scope of understanding, thoroughly engaged in the voyage of discovery called life, this language of direct demonstration clearly will not do. Instead of limiting ourselves to this language of traditional logic and science, Heidegger therefore suggests that we include the languages of traditional rhetoric and poetics (130) in our hermeneutical logic, whose first task is to explore the full scope of the hermeneutic "as" that life is all about. Here, more subtle "indications" are needed which let their elusive subject matter be, rather than the direct onslaughts of the apophantic indication, which always begins by a direct address (*Ansprechen*) that amounts to staking a claim (*Anspruch*) upon its topic, laying siege to it. Himself at one time prone to such martial metaphors (cf. WS 1921–22), Heidegger now couches his sought-for language of "provisional" or anticipatory indication in more yielding conservative metaphors.

Not that the apophantic "as" always levels the nuances of a life *in via* down to right (on-)handed presence. Kept close to the understanding familiarity from which it also originates, apophantic language can have its telling moments. For an assertion is in the broadest sense also a having-to-do-with, but now concerning a thematic with-which, say, the chalk. To be sure, apophantic determinations like "The chalk is white" are thoroughly leveling in character, placing the chalk on the level of a mere thing no different from any other thing, a lamp, car, sponge, rock, or whatever. But if I say, in the course of writing, "The chalk is too hard" or simply "Too gritty!," then this assertion made in the course of going about my teaching stands in close proximity to my more vital concerns. It is in fact not a definition of a thing as such-and-such but an interpretation of my comporting, better, of my not being able to relate to my immediate environment. The statement itself is tied to my writing, the chalk surfaces momentarily out of my absorption in my environment as that which keeps me from writing (157). The broken hammer or missing watch uncovers the way things *have been* interwound in the world, as aprioris of human comportment.

At the end of the course, Heidegger distinguishes between a "worldly assertion about something on hand" and a "categorial assertion," in particular "a specifically phenomenological categorial positing" (410). Though the latter has the structure of a worldly assertion, its primary sense is not to show forth something on hand but to indicate the being of Dasein, to point to its structures of time, to index their potential conceivability accessible to the understanding. Such hermeneutically indicating sentences, for example, "Time temporalizes (*zeitigt*: comes to maturity, brings to fruition)," are meant first to break old habits of viewing the tenses of time in objective terms, thus to reorient habitual apophantic ways of understanding toward a non-reifiable index of reference which prefigures our sheer being-there (ibid.).

The categories of such indicative sentences, the broad and empty structural concepts (GA 21:218, 225) which make up such specifically phenomenological assertions, such "ways to be" (209, 229, 414), "characters of being" and not of beings, are first called *Temporalien* or "tensors" (243: *Tempus, Tempora* = [grammatical] tense) before they are finally called *Existenzialien* (402). But in order to arrive at the labile sense of time meant to be conveyed by such categories, in order to break with everyday "now-time" and come to this more "original time" (243), our ousiological guiding clue must now be suspended. The world with which we have to do in the end can be too much with us. Having to do may well be the busywork which obscures our sheer "having to be." And this turns out not to be something we have, a firm possession, but instead something we are. "Having" now is the obligatory "ought" of being itself.

Dasein in its absorption in its concerns persists in these. What concerns it and that for which it is concerned is that in which it abides and holds to, the having (*Habe*) that has become a habit and habitat, about which ever more possessions become the concern. All acquisition and provision, understood in a sense broad enough to include the acquisition of knowledge and know-how, all of this already presupposes a certain possession to begin with. And the one who already has is the one who is in a position to augment his possessions. (232)

The inertia of having which continues to escalate of itself, this having which promotes its own habit, is the pendency of fallenness, de-pendency on the world to which Dasein is relegated. To escape this inertial cycle, Dasein must find its way to the possibility "of giving up all worldly acquisitions and possessions" (ibid.).

It is the leitmotiv of Christianity, which is not merely a staple of medieval philosophy. "All of modern philosophy in its problematic is incomprehensible and would be absolutely impossible without the doctrinal content of Christianity" (233). In Heidegger's formal structure, this new possibility is found by transcending concern toward care, which formally refers to that structure of Dasein according to which it in its being "goes about" (the *geht um* of an *Umgang*) this very being. The "formal logic" drawing out the consequences of that structure is now cited in full below, not only because of the crucial "inside story" it gives of Heidegger's concept formation, but also to suggest something of the formal purity of the gramma-ontology of prepositions and verbs which Heidegger has erected for himself:

> Implicit in this "it goes about" is the consequence that that about which it goes is *not a fixed possession* [*feste Habe*]; and as long as this "it goes about" belongs to Dasein, that means insofar as it is, and that means as long as it is, this says: that "about which it goes" is *never* firmly had, and nevertheless this "it goes about" is precisely a *being-toward* [*Sein-zu*] the "about which." And this being-toward is not a being intimate with something on hand, but purely and simply a being-toward, which indeed is not yet a firm possession and in the end can never become one, according to its most proper sense. This toward-which of the being-toward, which is care, is however nothing other than the being of Dasein, namely, in each instance the being which is not yet but can be; implicit in the "it goes about" there is accordingly a *being-out-for* (*Aussein-auf*) its own being qua can-be. (234f.)

Being-*out*-for its own can-be: the ultimate intentional core of Being-toward within the structure of care itself. All this is now being highlighted with an eye to the ultimate temporality (*Temporalität*: 234) of care.

And now the Moment: We are on the verge of Heidegger's critical terminological re-vision of his formal indication of "to-be." Note the context of influence: Greek ousiology finally severed by transworldly Christian elements operative in the philosophical tradition, which Heidegger has also formalized in the structure of care. Significantly, we have already encountered the upshot of this passage, being-*out*-for, in the first two drafts of BT precisely in their meditation on death as *out*ermost possibility (chap. 7, pp. 336–339). Circling his way from the ontic back to the ontological, Heidegger now repeats these mortal intimations—"insofar as it is and as long as it is," "and in the end can never become a fixed possession"—before moving to his final formalization. Being-*out*-for: another one of those many ways of expressing anxiety in the German idiom—*Aussein-auf*: being anxious to, bent on, eager for—now to be taken literally. The key word is "out," ἐκ, *ex*, that simple adverb in the middle modifying in both directions, also the preposition in the phrase, *auf*, for, to, sometimes *zu*, toward: every nuance "counts" in this precise grammatological game. Always out, never finished, constantly under way toward, never at an end, never in its entelechy: both meditations on death, in their razor's-edge distinction between an unfinished Dasein and a thing which only comes into its own precisely when it is finished (GA 20:430), clearly sound the knell of the ousio-logic of constant presence. The leading indicator, the determining indicator, is now the future, which at once retains its indeterminacy. The present perfect indicator of already-being-in-the-world, the realm of in-habituative *Habe*, is outstripped by the self confronting itself stripped of this being-in, being out of this in, being beyond the world itself.

Genealogical Excursus: The Ins and Outs of Ex-sistence and Trans-cendence
Looking forward, we find that the meditation on death in BT itself is introduced by the same farewell to *Habe* (SZ 233), to ousiology, while it of course also betrays its new departures. The very nature of Dasein puts in question not only any attempt to "have" it ontically, but also conceptually, by way of a conceptual analysis. "Being-out-for" becomes a recessive term in BT, withdrawing almost entirely into the filigree of the text (SZ 195, 210, 261f.). After all, it is no longer really needed. The formal indication into which it has been translated, by way of the Latin, is now front and center, dominating every page of BT: ex-sistence, out-standingness. Heidegger does not admit to his etymological legerdemain until SS 1927 (GA 24:242/170, 377/267), but he slyly plays with it precisely in these pages on death in BT. "So long as it is, there is always something in Dasein that stands out, something which it can be and will be. To this standout belongs its very "end," which for being-in-the-world is death" (SZ 233f.). He then must demystify the ontic pitfalls of the term *Ausstand* (outstanding debts: SZ 242ff.) in the German, but this only serves to bring out the purity of his own formal indication of existence.

Having developed his ek-static temporality out of that same indication, he then once again gradually reverts ex-sistence back to the in-sistence of being-in-the-world (GA 24: ibid.), disguising its Christian upbringing. But that is the beauty of the flexibility of formal concepts! How being-out-to became ex-sistence to begin with, how existence could become the formal indication and preempt that role from facticity, is itself an example of that. At first, existence was but the most unique possibility of Dasein to be found within its facticity (Oct. 1922). But if *ex*-sistence is itself being-*out*-for its own can-be, and this is something that can never find its end and will always remain unfinished, if this end cannot be had, then this never-ending "out" is not only possibility but at once facticity in the very extremity of a very incomplete finitude, to wit, being caught up, "being had" willy-nilly in a precipitous movement beyond its control; one might say, "thrust" into existence as a fact, in its sheer sense of "bare" existence, now understood as sheer dynamism. Existence thus can be turned inside out into its facticity, and made to order for the full scope of care, now taut from the tension of the haves and have-nots, comprehending the addictive pendency of having, which acts inertially as a pull-back on the dynamic forward thrust of existence. Its ousiological roots naturally lead to characterizing "falling" as the drag of substantive fixity characterizing possession, the reifying tendency wanting to maintain the constancy of presence. "Existence" specifically designed as a formal indication of temporality, formally thought through the full "from-to" of always being "under way," becomes amenable to the double sense it plays in BT: narrowed to the future within the structure of care (the role it had in Oct. 1922) and broadened into a formal indication of Dasein in its full vectorial field of relations. One can finally ask whether this broadened version has been sufficiently formalized, detheologized of its initial roots. Heidegger clearly wants an active experiential sense of finitude which is not simply dogmatically equated with creatureliness and createdness. "Thrownness" (Sartre translates it as "dereliction") does that in a brutally dramatic fashion. But the question of finitude will arise primarily with regard to the even more theological twin to the formal indication of existence, to which we now turn.

The "out" added to the intentionality of being-toward in fact yields a second formal surrogate for intentionality, one that has deeper roots in the Judaeo-Christian tradition than Kierkegaardian existence. Stemming from the same deep source both etymologically and traditionally, it shadows "existence" and subliminally assists in sustaining its verbal potency. With a slightly retarded incubation but a more overt doxographic trace in the Heideggerian corpus, it will soon break out and overpower "existence" as a surrogate for intentionality in the coming years of development. Because of its more overt history relating back to the Greeks, it will serve an especially important role in the destruction of that history.

It first surfaces in SS 1923, mediated by that "Catholic phenomenologist" (but cf. GA 24:28/20), Max Scheler, who, in a powerful statement worthy of quotation, was the first to identify it with intentionality. The context is similar to that of the genesis of ex-sistence, namely, that of distinguishing the Greek ousiological definition of the human being from the "theological concept":

> "What is man?"... He is "the intention and gesture of *transcendence* itself, a God-seeker, " a "between," a "limit,".... "an eternal *Out* and *Beyond* [*Hinaus*]," a "door of sudden opportunity" for grace ... "the only meaningful idea of the human being is a *theo-morphism* through and through, the idea of an X which is the finite and living image of God." (GA 63:25)

This laudation of trans-cendence, of the human being as an "eternal out-toward (*Hinaus-zu*)" (GA 20: 181/130) by way of quotation of the Christian tradition (especially Calvin and Zwingli), recurs into BT itself (SZ 49). Heidegger's attraction to this formulation of intentionality is in fact already recorded in his habilitation, where he identifies intentionality concretely with the "transcendent primal relationship of the soul to God" (FS 351). To what extent will its "mystical" sense for the young Heidegger (cf. chap. 2) be carried over to the later development? Transcendence becomes a technical term only after "ex-sistence" launched the trajectory taken by BT itself. But it is important to identify it now, as a twin of ex-sistence, and root it in the same vectorial field of conceptual relations, of care ripening into temporality. Its Christian roots are clearly still manifest when we identify transcendence as the countermovement to "decadence" or fallenness, which itself loudly proclaims its religious flavor. But transcendence formalized will allow Heidegger to develop a peculiar reciprocity of the immanence of transcendence, and the transcendence of immanence, in the same vectorial field (cf. SS 1920). In terms of transcendence, the destruction of the history of ontology naturally becomes that of transcendental philosophy, from Plato to Kant to Husserl. The categories of the being of Dasein can now be called not only temporals and existentials but also transcendentals, to be sure in a transformed sense, but nevertheless circling back to the habilitation and earlier, to the native soil of Catholic Messkirch which the old Heidegger, awaiting "the grave stillness of God's little acre," became fond of evoking.

2. Back to Kant

When was Heidegger not a Kantian? It is almost like asking "When was Heidegger not a German?," in his case, imbibing the very air (*Geist*) of the German university which he attended as a student of the "Southwest

German School of Neo-Kantianism." In his very first semester as a university teacher, the young Heidegger gave a seminar on Kant's *Prolegomena*, and this was shortly followed by a course on "German Idealism." Yet his teaching program after the war betrays a phenomenological provincialism with a proclivity for seminars on Descartes (tied to his religious interests) and Aristotle (cf. Appendix B), but not the German "classics." WS 1925–26 changes all of that. The seminar experience of reading Kant's first critique and Hegel's *Logik* thus came as a precipitous creative shock to Heidegger. It had an immediate impact on the final draft of BT, now shaped by this belated shock of discovery, as well as on his work in the years following. Heidegger's reflection on Hegel's opening triad of Being–Nothing–Becoming triggered his own thoughts on the shaping of the concept of being through formal indication. His fascination with Kant similarly came from his own problem of formally indicating the phenomenological structures of immediacy. It was thus Kant's way of getting on the inside of intuition, of sensing the infrastructure of temporality operating at the interface of receptivity and spontaneity, that ambivalent middle voice at the heart of experience which now speaks imaginatively and schematically, in short, Kant's doctrine of the schematism of the productive imagination, that first caught Heidegger's critical fancy.

We have Heidegger's direct testimony out of that immediate context even of the emotions of discovery (contrary to his discovery of οὐσία as constant presence two years before). From his two letters to Karl Jaspers in December 1925: "My Kant and Hegel seminars are giving me an unusually great deal of pleasure, and I'm glad that I am only now coming around to these things, when it is at least to some small degree possible to understand something of them. . . . The most beautiful part of it is that I am beginning *actually to love Kant*." "I am grateful that fate has kept me from spoiling Kant and Hegel with any one of those pairs of glasses available on the market today. I think I can sense the world spirit in the presence of both."[20] More than three years after the fact, in remarks that conclude his second intensive exegesis of the doctrine of the schematism in the closing minute of WS 1927–28, Heidegger makes the following confession to his class: "Several years ago, as I began anew to study the *Critique of Pure Reason* and read it against the background of Husserl's phenomenology, it was as if scales fell from my eyes, and Kant became for me an essential confirmation of the rightness of the path that I sought" (GA 25:431).

The impact of this sudden revelation on the lecture course of WS 1925–26 was the announcement, on the last class before the Christmas holidays (as in WS 1923–24 regarding Descartes), of the abandonment of the course outline presented in the opening week (GA 21:26), which was oriented toward Aristotle's question of the truth and falsity of assertions, and shifting direction to the more basic question of the temporal basis of such assertoric syntheses. It is now Kant's question which will govern the second half of the course, the question of the temporal articulations (schematism) which join the receptivity of sensory intuition with the spontaneity of the intellect (*Verstand*), at that incipient threshold of linguistic articulation and concept formation which is the main concern of Heidegger's hermeneutic logic. Through the eyes of Kant, it now becomes a productive logic guided by the productive imagination, that capacity of finite human beings which puts them in touch with the dynamic core of their existence, with a "logos of time" (200) different from any known logos, in particular the known quantities of now-time. As he says on both sides of the Christmas break (194, 200f.) and will repeat only a few weeks later (cf. Appendix C below on the writing of BT) in the programmatic opening pages of BT (SZ 23f.), Kant was the only one in the entire history of philosophy even to suspect this rudimentary connection of our most incipient understanding of being with time, and perhaps even to glimpse the different sense of time offered here. But "here Kant shrinks back" (ibid.) before this fusion of Being and Time which is the task of his own book, as Heidegger suggests Kant's terror before the abyss of inconstant presence which opens up at the limits of human existence (the It-experience of KNS).

At about the same time that he is first composing these opening pages of BT, Heidegger is relating the same inner drama to his class to begin the last week of the course (February 22–26, 1926; GA 21:378), and will retell the tale of Kant's "shrinking back" in conceptual context on a number of occasions in the next three years, notably in the two versions of the "Kant-book" that follow this first version.[21] We have our own conceptual drama to relate, and this fresh discovery so late in our own Story presents an embarrassment of new riches that must be forgone as much as possible, if we are to bring our own long tale to a speedy end, with the appearance of BT in the spring of 1927 (cf. Appendix C). We will now construe our task quite narrowly, even too narrowly, namely, the Genesis of the book *Sein und Zeit*, that published fragment wrapped in a mantle of publication promises that were never realized as such, but spin off into other publications. The "Kant-book" (1929), for example, is a clear offshoot of our Story, but in the strictest (i.e., chronological) sense does not yet belong to it. Even the promises that we find scattered in the footnotes of the published portion will be given attention only insofar as they bear on our Story. Assigned a major role in the never-published historical part within the overall plan of BT (SZ 40, Division II. 1 in the outline), "Kant's doctrine of the schematism and time, as a preliminary stage in a problematic of Temporality" is fated to remain in the footnotes of unfulfilled promises that sprinkle the margins of BT (SZ 319n on "transcendental apperception" and SZ 427n. 4 on a "more radical understanding of time than Hegel") as the "First Division of the Second Part." Kant literally "frames" BT, and its first readers were forced to read its margins to divine his role in the ultimate scheme. The two most telling sections in the genealogical development of BT, for example, are preceded by sections which first outline the problem according to Kant (SZ §64, §69b).

But he frames BT more firmly than Hegel, who suffers a different liminigraphical fate. The "history of the concept of time," which WS 1925–26 in the end became, followed the plan laid out in the previous semester (GA 20:11f./8f.) to trace that concept backwards from Bergson to Kant and Newton, finally to their common source in Aristotle's landmark treatise on time in *Physics* 4 (GA 21:249ff.). This was to parallel the history of the concept of intuition, which Heidegger had earlier (114ff.) likewise pursued in reverse, from Husserl to Aristotle, since intuition is intrinsically related to the "now-time" thus being traced historically. Accordingly, Heidegger treats Hegel's concept of time (251–262) before he embarks upon Kant's. The point is worth noting only because this treatment of the "most radical conception" (SZ 428) of now-time is later touched up for transposition into BT, along with the matter of a much-discussed footnote (SZ 432n = GA 21:266f.), and sits awkwardly as an ill-fitting section (§82) which abruptly and inconsequentially introduces the very last section of BT. So much for Hegel. But it does indicate that WS 1925–26 was intended to play an important role in Heidegger's plan for BT, and most of it ended in the unpublished periphery, or in inconsequentially obtrusive roles.

WS 1925–26 thus shows Heidegger hard at work on this larger opus when an absolute deadline, like an ultimatum, was delivered to him as the end of the semester approached. With a delivery to the printer only weeks away, the outline and the central ideas of BT now had to be fixed and maintained with some consistency. That is why the trail laid down especially into the last hour of WS 1925–26 is so important. It is February 26, 1926. All of March will be spent in an isolated farmhouse in Todtnauberg, cut off from human contact, unshaven (the only time in Heidegger's life), not only in finalizing the working manuscript but in penning a legible copy (for Heidegger an effort) for the printer by April 1 (up to the title of §38, SZ 175, as it turned out: cf. Appendix C). Since the first half of the working manuscript is missing, there is a critical gap in the doxographical record that must be filled from other sources. The innuendos of WS 1925–26 thus become crucial for our Story.

Given the timing, it is understandable why BT from the start receives such a Kantian overlay and impetus. In fact, the Latinate *Temporalität,*

first introduced in WS 1925–26 (GA 21:199) to point to a time different
from ordinary conceptions of time like "in time" or "now-time," is more
sharply refined in BT. Introduced by a call to reopen the classical question of being as such (SZ 1), the "Temporality of Being" (SZ 19) as such
is projected as the guiding clue for the historical task of the Second Part
of BT, the "phenomenological destruction of the history of ontology"
(SZ 39), in which Kant now becomes the lead figure. But the term is
used only in the programmatic opening pages, its distinction from the
Zeitlichkeit of Dasein plays no role in BT. It comes into play only in the
course of SS 1927, which continues the destructive task set by BT. In
this new historical approach now aimed at the sense of the "concept of
being," Descartes is re-instituted (from the first draft of November 1924)
as the backup figure to Kant, whose genuine insights were marred by
repeated "dogmatic" lapses into Descartes's "ontological position" (SZ
24).

   In this history which looks to the convergence of the concepts of being,
time, and the immediacy of human intuition (the "question of truth" in
the *Logik* course), Kant's more traditional "faculty" approach to intuition,
thinking, and the "genesis of the theoretical" now overshadows that of
Husserl's intentional approach, which was Heidegger's critical point of
departure in the "Husserl draft" of SS 1925. But both are at times still
invoked in tandem on these issues in BT. Heidegger bows in both directions in noting how understanding concern has deprived pure intuiting
of its priority, "which corresponds noetically to the traditional ontological
priority of the present-at-hand. 'Intuition' and 'thinking' [in Kant's sense]
both derive from that understanding, already rather remotely. Even the
phenomenological 'intuition of essences' is grounded in the existential
understanding" (SZ 147). In the very Kantian section on the "ontological
genesis of the theoretical attitude" (SZ 357, §69b) culminating in mathematical physics, Husserl still manages to get a footnote, and an important
one at that (SZ 363n). There Heidegger points to the thesis common to
Husserl and Kant, traceable back to Parmenides, that "all knowledge has
'intuition' as its goal," which temporally means that "all knowing is a making present (*Gegenwärtigen*), a presentifying." This is a also a Husserlian
coinage, like "appresenting," which it has now replaced. "The intentional
analysis of perception and intuition necessarily suggested this 'temporal'
characterization of the phenomenon. That and how the intentionality
of 'consciousness' is grounded in the ecstatic temporality will be shown
in the following [never published] Division" (ibid.). In short, the issue is
so central to an ontological phenomenology that it will have to be re-
hearsed again on the level of the Temporality of being, the time of being
itself. For with the questioning of making-present, we are toying with

the very phenomenality of the phenomenon, the nature and possibility of access to being in its truth, letting see and letting be, and Kant is now explicitly invoked in BT in the section on 'phenomenon' (§7a). Already in BT, it is clear what the ontological upshot of this destruction of *intuitus, vernehmen* (ergo *Vernunft* = "reason"!) will be: The light of eternal νοεῖν is to be replaced by the more understanding "lighting" of a temporal "clearing." It is no idle speculation, therefore, when Heidegger entertains an entirely new thought in the aforesaid footnote (SZ 363n): "Whether every science, or even philosophical knowledge, aims at a making present, may be left open here." But perhaps the thought is not entirely new. Commenting in WS 1925–26 on Hegel's rigidly consistent exclusion from his now-time of the phenomenon of memory on the one hand, hope and fear on the other, Heidegger is reminded of his work on Aristotle's *Rhetoric* (SS 1924). Turning to the latter's minor work "on remembering and forgetting," he finds the following remark: "There also ought to be something like a science related to hope [and so fear], which some call mantic, prophecy" (GA 21:262).

But we get no real hint of the past and future until the concluding hour of WS 1925–26, with the first mention of ex-sistence as a way of getting at care's "already" and "ahead." In fact, the overriding problem going back to SS 1925, first systematically and now historically approached, has been the present perfect apriori, appresentation, making present, the empowering relation of the present tense to presence, Being and Time still in the old ousiological mold. What Kant saw in intuition was a deeper, more productive sense of the present tense of time than anyone hitherto had surmised. Already in the given of appearances, there is a primary order, a certain articulation, called the "manifold," a prescientific order which appears chaotic to scientific determination (281: Kant does not explore the more immediate order of the environing world). This manifold is the "form" of the intuition of time, the "toward which" (*Woraufhin*: 304) of its orderly regard. The "milling throng" of sensations, externally a primary apartheid, asunder, "*Out* from one another" (*Aus-einander*), in encounter is already a here and there, now and then plurality, however indeterminate and variable: next to or after one another, the "forms" of outer and inner sense, the toward-which of the regards of space and time (287). [It will soon seem as if Heidegger is phenomeno-logically re-viewing Lask's reflexive categories here, culminating in the "toward which" of the "regard," *Bewandtnis*: cf. chap. 1.] Letting the encounter *take place* involves both "forms" as an unthematic toward-which in which I live and take as immediately given and self-evident, the "in-which" of any overt order (288). Are these "subjective"? Lacking a sense of intentionality, Kant in his Cartesian dogmatism simplistically leaned in that direction. But his surrogate question, what are the conditions of possibility for the connection between time and the "I think," between pure manifold and pure unity, transcendental aesthetic and its logic, helps to restore the balance (309f.). Time, the toward-which according-to-which, is the condition of possibility that anything giving can give itself in the articulation of after-one-another.

> The toward-which: a pure self-giving whole of after-one-another. In this prior outlook-taking, the mind or self thus gives itself of itself the basic possibility of being able to encounter something on hand. The outlook-taking toward, this prior albeit unthematic having of the toward-which is the apriori letting itself be encountered; the basic kind of being of the self, in which it lets itself encounter, from out of itself, an other—the toward-which—lets itself be approached by it, in Kantian terms, lets itself be affected. (338f.)

Time is the original self-affection of the mind: I think myself thinking something, unthematically. Self-affecting spontaneity and receptivity are equiprimordial (340).

This unthematic unity generates the schematism, the sensory aspects of our categories, a self-showing "category," a kind of prefiguring "concept," the prefiguration itself, the figuring synthesis of time, time as a pure image (*Bild*) giving shape and articulation, the pure *Es gibt*. "There it is, It gives it. And who (*wer*) gives, who this It is, which gives, is the now" (385). [Cf. KNS: "It worlds, it contextualizes."] What is this Now? Not the crude caricature of a between a not-yet and no-longer. "The Now as now-this—this Now, as it were, speaks away from itself and points out toward: now; here this; there that; now here" (398). Every now has unthematically the character that we notice in the signal for the start of a race: now-here-this . . . and Go! Every now has the pointing character of direction, of "on to" and "toward," the toward-which, not at all on hand. The temporal synthesis is a self-relating, it follows the "on to" and "towards," more concretely, the toward-which as this and that. Take the category of substance, whose character is perdurance. Its schematism, the pure image of time, the temporal synthesis which it accentuates is "This at any time, all the time." Its very nature makes it the basic category. "The schema of substance is thus the most original and purest look to time as a whole with respect to its pure character of reference to the This as the same at all times, i.e., the whole time" (399f.).

And time itself? It gives itself unthematically as the constant precursory letting-encounter. It is not something on hand, simply apprehended. It affects in such a way that, in constantly stepping back and disappearing in its constant referential directing, it lets something be seen. It is "a constant stepping aside and freely giving letting be seen" (401). Accordingly, this now in its pointing to, a direction by which it lets something be seen, "waits to" (*entgegenwartet*), appresents something. It is not the fragment of an incised now-point on hand. As pointing to, it is the "basic structure of the comportment called knowing in the Kantian context" (ibid.). The now in this sense is Dasein in a basic way of its being toward the world, namely, in making present (402). In the making, the present is a comportment of Dasein. For Dasein is time itself (205, 407). As a basic possibility of the very being of Dasein, that is its *Existenz*, the present as making present is an existential, a structural concept of Dasein (403).

The Problem Hour

It is now the last hour of the semester (402–415). Heidegger is concluding his long analysis of Kant by a summary which at once recalls the motive that initiated this historical interlude, namely, to find a sense of time other than the traditional chosistic, substantifying now-time. Specifically, he wants a new "concept" of time which would be capable of expressing the Temporality of the relational structure of care, capable in particular of expressing its "already" and "ahead of" without substantifying them. The point is to express the Temporality of the being of the entity which we ourselves are. Not the entity, in entitative fashion, chosistically, but the being of that entity, relationally or comportmentally (*verhältnismäßig*). In the terms of the traditional substantifying concepts which pervade the innumerable expressions of our everyday discourse on time, these relations of "already" and "ahead of" are "at first obscure characters of time" (245) in need of a more telling language, a language of being rather than of entities.

In his halting way, in the narrow sphere of his particular problem of assertoric synthesis, Kant faced the same problem and the same obscurity. "Within the very narrow chronological sphere within which he moves, Kant already also sees the obscurity of the phenomena which press upon him here" (200f.). It is the obscurity of that "art hidden deep within the human soul" which Kant calls the "schematism of our understanding" (201), which we now perceive as the articulation of time itself expressing itself in and as our comportment of forming concepts and making assertions. Assertion, addressing something as something, now assumes its fundamental temporal sense (402) in the comportment of making something present, letting it be seen as something, letting a being be present. Assertive making-present is the discovery of the presence of something on hand, which can only be in a present. This is precisely what the apophantic "is" of the assertion is meant to express.

The "is" does not have the function of the copula, but is the index of the basic function of the assertion, its making present as pure, pure making present, letting us purely see the presence of the being, of the being in its presence. The expressed assertion preserves in itself the uncoveredness of the being, takes it into troth. But to preserve an uncoveredness means nothing other than being able to presentify at any time, all the time. (414f.)

But this last hour is meant not merely to summarize the results of the analysis of Kant's schematism of the present tense. It clearly points ahead to Heidegger's own task of taking this very relational and tensal sense of time, operating unthematically in an equally unthematic "I think," and extending it to the whole of human comportment, to Dasein in its being. It is a matter of expanding the sphere of analysis from the assertion to the whole of Dasein. That was Heidegger's explicit intention from the very beginning, when he changed the orientation of this course to the question (205), "Was besagt Zeit?," What is time? What is its sense? This is not a question of definition, but of seeing the phenomenon *itself* originally (ibid.). It is a phenomenological question, where the "itself" indicates that it is one of those emphatic questions that can only belong to an ontological phenomenology (ibid.):

It calls for its own ways and preparations, preliminary investigations, it is not to be reached in one fell swoop. And when we say: Time is not only and not primarily a schema for the orderly determinations of changes [Kant's time of Nature and natural science], but is actually Dasein itself, that is at first only a catchphrase, a cliché, just as the initial thesis is [always] an arbitrary one. We know nothing about it and want it to say [something] to us about itself.

"Dasein itself *is* time." That had been an ear-catching statement, a favorite rhetorical device of Heidegger's, ever since his speech of July 1924, often repeated in the first two drafts of BT. It will never be repeated again after the concluding hour of WS 1925–26: "The transition in being from pretheoretical comportment toward the world to pure making-present is a mode of temporality itself—and would be absolutely impossible if Dasein itself were not time" (407). Kant's sense of time as an "on to" and "toward" that steps back into the background as it articulatedly brings forward and reveals things in their categorial structures: this very intentional sense of time is to be equated with Dasein itself. This should not surprise us, from all the past indications we have followed up to this point, especially the last formal indication of Dasein as a very tendentially understood "to-be." And Heidegger does not neglect his old insights. "To-be" thus makes a cameo appearance in this last hour, conceptually in a very strategic way, leading to a hitherto unexpressed dimension of care. Heidegger also reviews for us what he really intended to express in this old formal indication, about to be displaced.

He is discussing the aspect of "already" in the structure of care. "The already is the indication of the apriori of facticity" (GA 21:414). He first warns against taking this in the sense of a brute fact as something on hand. "The structures of Dasein, temporality itself . . . are in their most proper sense possibilities of Dasein *to be*, and only that." But this can-be includes already having decided, either authentically from itself, or by renouncing such a possibility, or by not yet being equal (*gewachsen* = "grown") to such a decision. Accordingly, "Dasein is delivered over [*über-antwortet*] to itself in its to-be. Being delivered over [being charged to, having to answer for]—that means: *already-in*, already ahead of itself, already by the world; never on hand, but always already a possibility decided so or so" (ibid.). In addition to being the very first instance in which Heidegger has distinguished a separate third dimension (the tense of the simple past, not the more complex present perfect), the "already-in," in the structure of care, the passage underscores how the dimension of possibility, the conative future so strongly implied in the muscular "to-be," reaches into the past. Possibility is to be found at once in all three dimensions of care. This flexibility is a trait which the new replacement for to-be, ex-sistence, is meant to have in common with it, and will assume in BT. Which of the two is better suited to perform this conceptual function? Not an idle question, since, by now, we know that every nuance counts when it comes to formally indicating the immediacy of being, which is now to be indicated in its full temporal immediacy. "Being itself is time." Heidegger never actually says this. But, besides the problematic "is" in any statement about being, is he himself "shrinking back" before the horror of horrors, the sheer flux of being, as Kant did before him? For he does make some other rather strange statements in this last hour, at least from the vantage of BT itself. And if time is something like a schematism, if the goal is the "logos of time," a "chronologic" (200), what's to worry? Everything is tending toward the issue of the "Temporality of Being itself," despite the careless use of this term after it was introduced in the middle of WS 1925–26.

"Care itself is time" (409). This appears to be a corollary of "Dasein itself is time," since the being of Dasein is care. But let us try to follow Heidegger's logic here. This is after all still a course in logic, and Heidegger is here busy trying to straighten out his language in reference to phenomena, their categories, and the resulting assertions, hermeneutically indicative versus world assertions (410). He is in effect outlining in his mind the final draft of BT, which is yet to be written. He is wondering about its basic "language game."

Concern and care are structures of the being of Dasein. They articulate its being toward the world. We now wish to situate these structures with respect to time. The problem stems from a traditional concept of time which turns beings into on-hand realities "in" time. But the "ahead" and "already" in the structure of care would be thoroughly misunderstood in terms of such a time. Yet they are obviously characters of time. "In what sense is care, the structure of the being of Dasein, characterized by time? These structures are moreover what they are neither in time nor in some kind of relation to time. Care is instead defined 'by' time so that it is itself time, the facticity of time itself" (409). But later, we read: "Care is only possible in what it is insofar as its being is time itself" (413). The being of care is time itself: a bit less direct and less thought-provoking, a bit more careful, ontological, and obtuse. Perhaps a verbosity without telling power. Heidegger's self-criticism sometimes took this direction, a devastating critique for a phenomenologist. This no doubt was also at least the symptom that led finally to the demise of BT, the withholding of the unpublished Division from the press. It would seem to be an intrinsic hazard of the ontological "language game," where it is so easy to forget that "being" is not a bland abstraction, but the very stuff of our most immediate and most comprehensive experience of "being here," in Kant's impersonal litany of occasional indexicals, "now, here, this." How to maintain this sense of concrete immediacy in questions like "What is time itself?" and now, by way of the master structural concept of care, "What is the structure of time?" or "How does time structure itself?"

Heidegger's answer, the language of existentialism, may have been in part an answer to such problems of misunderstanding and disorders in ontological communication. Recall how important the theme of communication became in WS 1925–26, resulting in the introduction of the question of what it means to be "for others" (225), for Johanna A.

Instead of to-be, the leading formal indicator is now, rather abruptly, *Existenz*. Instead of "temporals" or "tensors" (243), which had only a passing moment of glory, all "specifically structural concepts, which express the being of Dasein and its modes, shall be designated as existentials" (402). *Existenz* is suddenly there, after a two-year hiatus, without explanation for either its absence or its new presence, or how it is the key to the structure of the being of Dasein, say, because it ex-presses the universal ec-static character of Dasein, as the already formalized clue of being-*out*-for earlier in the course (235) tended to suggest. Instead of explanation, we get some more strange statements following hard upon this crucial conceptual decision. "The present (in this activist transitive sense of presenting), as a structural concept of Dasein, is an existential" (402). According to the peculiar logic that Heidegger has designed for himself, this statement then leads to a comprehensive conclusion, and expressed as such. "Accordingly (But this implies): if the present is [*aus-macht*] a mode of time and as such defines the sense of the being of Dasein (inasmuch as Dasein is being-by-the-world), then time itself must be understood as the basic existential of Dasein" (403).

The present is an existential; therefore time itself is the basic existential of Dasein. That is all we hear here about this new ontological language that Heidegger is clearly devising for the last draft of BT. Moreover, *Existenz* is being designed to take over essentially the same conceptual functions that *Zu-sein* performed in the penultimate draft. "We designate the temporally particular and authentic being-possibility of a factic Dasein, regardless of how it may be chosen or determined, as *Existenz*" (402). Being-there is being-possible. The primacy of the possible now becomes the central theme.

From the vantage of BT, this seminal conceptual decision is clearly still in a crude state of nascency, suggesting its recent vintage. In BT, Heidegger never calls time an existential, let alone its tenses. Rather, time itself is ec-static, and its modes are its ecstases. It is not temporality and its modal tenses which, as those categories hitherto called characters of being and ways-to-be, now get renamed as existentials. In BT, the existentials will proliferate, both the relational and the dynamic ones: being-in-the-world, being-with others, being-by things; disposedness, understanding, discursiveness, falling. Even truth and meaning (*Sinn*) are called existentials . . . but not time. Care will become the master existential. And the meaning of care is temporality, original temporality, that original time which is "essentially ecstatic" (SZ 331).

It is February 26, 1926: the last day of class. Heidegger is on the verge of gathering all of his manuscripts and notes, his annotated copy of the Moser typescript of SS 1925, his handwritten article on the "Concept of Time" for the day's train ride from Marburg to Freiburg, then on to Todtnauberg. There he will sequester himself in the Brender-Stube, the room rented from his taciturn old farmer friend for that purpose, to refurbish his manuscripts into a final publishable form. (It is the only time he did not shave, according to Gadamer.) In a matter of a single month, the particular conceptual decisions that are to follow from this central concept of *Existenz* are made, superficially transforming BT into a book inaugurating *Existenzphilosophie*. But that is but a remote by-product of the effort and, over the years, an increasingly obfuscating one, from Heidegger's perspective. For Heidegger's real question now is time itself, just as being itself was the focus of the previous draft. And once again, contrary to the usual characterizations, what Heidegger is after here is not so much a phenomenological ontology as something more basic, what he himself tentatively designated, appropriately in his first Logic course, as a "phenomenological chronology" (199), a "chronologic"

(200). More than an ontology, since it will transcend being itself. For time, χρόνος, "is the condition of possibility for the fact that something like being (not beings) be given, the condition of possibility that in fact gives being" (410). Time "is" the It that gives being: "Es gibt so etwas wie Sein." Already in WS 1925–26, Heidegger has planted a seed that will flourish in the filigree of *Sein und Zeit* "itself," and well beyond.

NINE

The Final Draft:
Toward a Kairology of Being

Despite the overtly "indicative" titles of the first two drafts, Heidegger had not yet, surprisingly, really "worked out" his concept of time. The titles prove to be mere promissory notes. He still has a basic point or two to develop here. He still has a book to write. All that had gone before has been merely leading up to the question of time itself, to its "structure," its logos, to a "chronologic." He now has to deliver on that promise. This concluding chapter of our tale of "The Genesis of Heidegger's *Being and Time*" is accordingly devoted solely to pursuing this limited central task. For it defines the specific purpose of the published portion of that "astonishing torso," the book entitled "Being *and* Time," the volume which first appeared in late April 1927 (cf. Appendix C) and precipitated Heidegger to instant fame.

But to spell out the basic thrust of the finalized draft, the guiding term "chronology" from WS 1925–26 simply will not do. Even as Heidegger had just transposed the sphere of assertoric synthesis into that of human integration, *Wahrsein* into *Dasein*, the truth of sentences into the truth of life, so we must transpose our orientation from the surface time suggested by "chronology," the ordinary (*vulgär*!) conception of time of everyday life, to a more central structure of time. We need a word here to describe this profound temporal particularity of the human situation which Heidegger is about to describe. There is in fact a term that Heidegger used for a brief spell in 1922–23 which we can now revive to characterize what he is truly after in BT. Not a chronology but a *kairology*. Indeed, given the formal indication of an existence which "is in each case mine," a phenomenological chronology simply must be a kairology. The fact that Heidegger himself did not invoke it at this most appropriate point from his burgeoning arsenal of terms suggests another difference between this final draft, this "kairological draft," and the penultimate "ontoeroteric" draft. For whatever reasons, some perhaps unconscious or simply inadvertent, Heidegger in his final draft, contrary to the previous draft, is subtly downplaying, disguising, or otherwise distorting some of the deepest roots of his thought. But it also suggests how conscious he was of the radical novelty of this new "concept" of time which he sought, leading to a greater emphasis on the distance he found between himself and his original sources than ever before. The references to Kierkegaard, for example, testify to that (SZ 190n, 235n, 338n). The final draft "repeats" the penultimate draft, as far as it goes, sometimes section by section.[1] But Heidegger's repetitions are never mere copywork. His very sense of repetition always involves innovation, a re-view at a more profound, new level. The new level of repetition is what we wish now to characterize as kairology. And now he has much to "repeat." But despite all the genealogical tracking that is now behind us, this final chapter of our Story has hardly been rendered anticlimactic. We are not confronted merely with the task of tying up some genealogical loose ends. There is still the great moment of the kairological climax to confront, and the glimpse beyond that it will afford.

All of the available conceptual forces are refurbished and mobilized for this central task. Sense (*Sinn*) is underscored as the "toward which" (*Woraufhin*) of the human project, and its possibility is universalized into the veritable power of time. Even a few lesser tasks of clarification are geared ultimately to distinguish the different levels of time. Thus, what were confusedly called "world things" in the previous draft is now named "innerworldly" beings, and these will eventually be made subject to "in-nertime*ness*" (*Innerzeitigkeit*: SZ 235, 333, 412) for their discoveredness. All of the conceptual innovations are likewise meant to accommodate the emerging new dynamics of time. This final draft accordingly introduces for the first time "thrown projection" to characterize the "movedness" of Da-sein itself, and the dynamics of "clear*ing*" (*Lichtung*) to characterize the unifying temporal dynamics of the being of being-there. The close connection between time and truth, which the "lighting" of the clearing implies, is reinforced by a realignment of the terms for truth. Disclosedness (*Erschlossenheit*) is for the first time specifically attributed to the truth of Dasein to bring it into terminological proximity with the kairotic resoluteness (*Ent-schlossenheit*, etymologically an "unlocking") sustaining the moment of decision, a term all-important also for its "ontic" bearing. After a desultory and disjointed treatment in the previous two drafts, the complex of self-authorship, conscience-guilt-resoluteness, receives its very first thoroughgoing analysis for the first time under the guidance of the interruptive "call" (*Ruf*) of conscience. The content of the call, "Guilty!," is ontologized into a debit of existence by way of the radical facticity implicit in the "thrust" (*Wurf*) of time, to which the *Ruf* is more than anagrammatically related. The basis for the entire arena of conscience is prepared by the formally indicative corollary to *Existenz*, distributive mineness (*je meines*), while the old corollary, distributive whileness (*jeweilig*), begins to withdraw into the background. It never completely recedes into the filigree of the text, however, in view of its tellingly pregnant temporal connotations. Even though the word καιρός is never used, the idea overtly dominates the entire Second Division of BT, not only in the authenticating moment of response to the call of conscience but in its parallel, the holistic move of forerunning my own death. Small wonder that the old kairological term "situation," betraying Heidegger's Christohellenic origins, can no longer be deferred, and slowly, albeit sporadically, and without real explanation, asserts itself in the closing pages of the book. In fact, the best English translation of Dasein itself is the "human situation," provided that one at once retains the full temporally distributed particularity of the indexicals, "here, now, mine," that it is meant to convey.

Now that we have also exposed a similar lineage of "ex-sistence" back to Christian transworldliness (chap. 8), we are in a better position to confront the reading of BT by Heidegger's first habilitation student, Karl Löwith, who saw in it nothing but a "disguised theology." Heidegger would in the end, however, insist on the formality of his assumptions, no matter what the source, since his one goal here is to develop the formal schematism of time which is most appropriate to the wholeness of being itself. Löwith, the existentialist anthropologist, it seems, never really understood the formal indication, in sharp contrast with his more scientifically oriented classmate, Oskar Becker. Becker, on the other hand, was irritated by the pedantic scholasticism of the reiterated outlines and advance announcements of paragraph divisions replete in BT. But Heidegger, sensitive to years of critique of the incomprehensible opaqueness of his style, wanted to make himself clearly understood. He wanted to communicate, and the obsessive architectonic of the book was one way of subverting the anticipated misunderstanding of his intentions. Besides, the hurried deadline under which BT was drafted and printed dictated the stability of a fixed advance outline. The need to communicate the new insight of ecstatic temporality, without tangential plunges into the genealogical roots of his conceptual framework, may have been the more internal reason for such pedanticism. Was BT in the end "framed" by its outline? For despite all this didactic orientation, BT was never an easy book to read. Even now it is not, despite our genealogical tracking, for reasons which however have more to do with where this ontoeroteric kairological endeavor may be heading than with where it is coming from.

It is not our purpose to do a section-by-section genealogy of BT, although we are now in a position to do so. This can be ventured on another occasion. We are still telling a story. Even though the book BT has hitherto been the goal of this Story, the story itself, as Heidegger himself tells it, now dictates that BT be regarded not as a halt in the journey but as one more station along the way. According to Heidegger's own formally indicative "terms," every station is a transition, every work is a way. The Here and Now of Heidegger's "human situation" incorporated in the publication of 1927 is itself ever an "out toward," still under way toward a can-be, ever unfinished. In what follows, we can only venture to pick up a few of the more salient new points at the genealogical cutting edge of this developing conceptual drama, those that are specifically aimed at a kairology of being.

ONTIC ONTOLOGY

As we already noted in the gloss of the course on Plato's *Sophist*, the book begins by invoking the old Greek gigantomachy over being in ways that already point formally through, and so beyond, the classical sense of the concept of being, regarded as a self-evident concrete universal which is indefinable. Genealogically regarded, Heidegger is from the start creatively copying himself section by section to accommodate the ontoeroteric draft to the new driving purpose of a kairology. The new formal indication of ex-sistence, designed for that purpose, is already clearly nuancing the formulations of §2 of BT, even though it will be first announced only in the all-important but dense §4 on the "*ontic* precedence of the *question* of being." The operative formally indicating ex-sistential word here, nondescript, usually unnoticed, often lost in translation, is *ausgezeichnet*, out-standing, ex-cellent: a question that stands out, excels, related to a questioning activity in a "remarkable 'back and forth relatedness'" (SZ 5, 8) in which the questing question is affected, struck, and so motivated by what is questioned! Dasein, "this entity which each of us is ourselves and which includes quest(ion)ing as one of its possibilities of being" is thus found to have a relation to the being-question, "perhaps even one which stands out" (SZ 8). This very relationship belongs to the "most proper *sense* of the question of being" (ibid.). An entity caught in the act of quest(ion)ing, surely a basic temporal phenomenon which will have to be fully elaborated in the course of the book. Alluded to only in the back-and-forth spiraling movement of an outstanding relation, temporality is there in the very sense (*Sinn*) of this relation of questioning, its relational sense, its sense of direction, directed "out toward" what it asks for (*Erfragtes*), the sense of being, which in turn governs and directs the quest from the start.[2] Accordingly, the full sense of the human situation, already caught up in being in such a way that it is already questioned in its being and so put in quest of the sense of its being, will have to be worked out in order to prepare the basis for understanding the temporality already implicit in the question of the sense of being. The very sense of sense will have to be worked out to define at least the temporality of my being, and hopefully of being itself.

In these early pages, Heidegger, from years of similar attempts, is acutely aware of how careful he must be in singling out, and spelling out, his question and the full situational complex involved in the terms of that question. A small error, an oversight in the beginning of this indicative process could spell disaster in the end. One could easily dwell at length on this carefully crafted introduction, culminating in §4, in its phenomenologically formal regress to the experiential origins of the question outstanding, in order to trace the implications of every nuance and innuendo and shade of its indications, as these will then be carried out in the full span of the book. One can easily follow the rich refinements that Heidegger is now interjecting simply by comparing §§ 2 and 4 with their parallel §§ 16 and 17 in the more strictly ontoeroteric draft. Let us at least trace the central new thrust.

The overriding modification is contained in the title of §4 (SZ 11–15), "The *Ontical* Preeminence of the Question of Being." This constitutes a new emphasis based on the old formal indication of particular whileness (now mineness). For onticity received only marginal and incidental attention in the ontoeroteric draft.[3] It is important to note that the entire task of a "fundamental ontology," which is never even mentioned in the previous draft, is spelled out first of all with an ontic fundament in mind (SZ 13). To be sure, the "ex-cellence" of the ontic being who questions being is at once an ontological excellence, in view of its privileged access to something like being, its pre-ontological understanding of being which allows it to raise the question to begin with. But it is an "ontico-ontological preeminence" (SZ 14). It is first as an entity, here, now and mine, that Dasein stands out from other entities (SZ 11). This commonly remarked excellence of the human being over against things, say, by way of the classical definition of "rational animal," is now pressed to the limits of individualization, as one implication related to others within the double formal indication of situated existence, of a "Da-sein" which is not only the tendential "to-be" but also the occasional "here (now, mine)." Unlike particular mineness, Heidegger remarks to himself,[4] particular whileness is not existential, but still formal-ontological. Nevertheless, in BT, the occasionally particular "while" continues to operate in its grammatically natural habitat as an adverb (*je, jeweils, jeweilig*) as an indispensable formal assumption about the temporality within mineness—my while, my birth, my death—to define the finite limits of the individual, which at once highlights the scope of its ever-unfinished striving of to-be, ever under way . . . up to a point. Indexically particular mineness moreover means that the exemplary entity, Dasein, is not merely an example or instance of a genus of things on hand. Fundamental ontology is not to be developed from generic universals which indifferently subsume their instances, but rather from the distributive universals of "in each case mine" (*je meines*) according to the circumstances (*je nach dem*). It requires universals which maintain an essential reference to their differentiation into ontic instances (SZ 42). In opposition to the traditional categories, the existentials are ontological in character because they "are founded and motivated in Dasein's own ontical structure, which comprises within itself the determinateness of a pre-ontological understanding of being" (SZ 13). This implicitly operative pre-ontological "ontology" begging for thematization in fact is not only the concrete ontic fundament for the fundamental ontology of Dasein but also, in turn, for all the regional ontologies which the latter founds, and which hitherto had been based only on an abstract ontological fundament (SZ, §3). This point of temporal particularity has great significance not only for Heidegger's historical sense of philosophy but also for a similar sense of the history of science, and its philosophy.

The need for such characters of being which transcend the common generic universals was in fact already identified in the Aristotelian-scholastic doctrine of the transcendental properties of a nongeneric sense of being. That same tradition even invoked the preeminence of Dasein, the human soul, as that entity (*ens*) which in its manner of being is suited to "come together with all entities" (Aquinas), an entity which "in a way is all things" (Aristotle) (SZ 14). But this ontic precedence of Dasein over all other entities, and the peculiar categorial contexts of analogy and equivocity to which it gives rise, were never really clarified in their fundaments and so remain in the dark (SZ 3). As we have already seen in large part, Heidegger, having refurbished Scotian *haecceitas* by way of a heterothetical logic of equiprimordiality and the guiding indications of phenomenology, claims to have found the "philosopher's stone" for this transforming clarification in an ontically founded approach to ontologic. By extrapolating the insights of a tradition of thought on the concept of being begun by Aristotle, he now claims to have brought this search for the transcendental characters of being to its phenomeno-logical resolution. The metaphors seem a bit mixed, given the downward spiral toward the now ontic "matter" of phenomenology, but the claim of completing this classical tradition by way of a phenomenology of Dasein, understood as the "ontologico-ontically excelling entity" (SZ 37), is unmistakable:

As the basic theme of philosophy, being is not a genus of beings. And yet it relates to each and every being. Its "universality" is to be sought higher up. Being and the structure of being lie beyond every being and every possible entitative determination of a being. *Being is the* **transcendens** *pure and simple.* The transcendence of Dasein's being is an outstanding transcendence because it implies the possibility and necessity of the most radical *individuation.* Every disclosure of being as the **transcendens** is *transcendental* knowledge. *Phenomenological truth (disclosedness of being) is* **veritas transcendentalis.** (SZ 38)

And in the outline of the treatise BT which soon follows, Heidegger once again has occasion to "prefigure" the ontic thrust of his transcendence against the contrary double superlative of the traditional concept of being. "The question of the sense of being is the most universal and emptiest of questions; but the very same question at once implies the possibility of assuming the most acute individualization, when it is focused upon the temporally particular (*jeweiliges*) Dasein" (SZ 38).

In point of fact, this very same tradition ultimately gave precedence not to the human but to the divine being, which as the prime analogate in turn defines the traditional sense of temporality as constant presence. "The divine is the sky," according to Plato and Aristotle, which could be the leitmotiv of one of the first chapters of a long onto-theo-logical history of philosophy. It is in this sense of the indispensability of an ontic fundament for ontology that we are to understand "Aristotle's dictum that the first science, the science of being, is theology":

This indicates that ontology itself cannot be grounded purely ontologically. Its enabling possibility is referred back to a being, that is, to something ontic: the Dasein. Ontology has an ontic fundament. Such a fundament shows through time and again in the history of philosophy up to the present day. (GA 24:26/19f.)

This sense of the indispensability of an ontic fundament is also behind Heidegger's oft-repeated statement that "There is being, 'It gives' being, being is given, only if the understanding of being, the Dasein, exists" (ibid.; cf. SZ 212). The sheer existence of Dasein is thus the ontic possibility of the understanding of being, thus the "give" of being, and thus the possibility of any ontology whatsoever. The same impersonal language of ontic possibility applies to the truth of being, its disclosedness. "Truth is given, 'It gives' truth, only insofar and so long as Dasein *is*" (SZ 226). This ontic possibility has nothing to do with "vicious subjectivizing of the totality of entities" (SZ 14). As it will turn out, the human situation that Dasein is, this It which gives, is a "primal something" which proves to be far more basic than what the distinction of subject versus object conveys. Nevertheless, the old KNS experience of already finding oneself implicated in being, in an It which worlds and properizes me, this "outstanding relationship of being" (GA 20:201/149) which Dasein already is immediately, prepredicatively and pre-interrogatively, is now reiterated in ways in which the "It" could be misconstrued in subjective terms: "Ontically, to be sure, Dasein is not only close or even the closest: we *are* It, each of us, we ourselves. In spite of this, or rather for just this reason, It is ontologically the farthest" (SZ 15).

One sees the full radical thrust of Heidegger's phenomenological backtracking into the ontic fundament that we are, when he then asks about the possibility of this very ontic possibility which enables the question of being at all, and so makes any and every ontology possible. "What is It that makes this understanding of being at all possible? Whence—that is, from which already given horizon—do we understand the like of being?" (GA 24:21/16). From the start, Heidegger regards this ultimate enabling of being itself in its sense and comprehensibility to be a Temporal "horizon," time itself. This is precisely the question that literally bounds the book, "Being *and* Time." Despite its cloak of abstractions, BT begins and ends with the question of ontic fundament issuing from the compunction of having to repeat the venerable old question of being because of its double superlative quality, doubly outstanding in being equiprimordially "the *most fundamental* and *most concrete* of all questions" (SZ 9): "The interpretation of *time* as the possible horizon for any understanding of being whatsoever is the provisional aim of the following treatise" (SZ 1). The treatise BT concludes with the question, "Does *time* itself manifest itself as the horizon of *being*?" (SZ 437).

The inevitable ontical founding of ontology in temporality is the final upshot of Heidegger's efforts since the habilitation "to go all out after the factic in order to make facticity into a problem at all." Although the tradition at least since Aristotle had some sense of this need to found ontology ontically, Heidegger notes, in his letter to Löwith in August 1927, that "no one before me had seen that explicitly and said so. But ontic founding does not mean referring and going back to something ontical *arbitrarily*. The ground *for ontology* is found only in such a way that one knows what ontology itself is and then allows it, as ontology, to wreck (*zugrunderichten*) itself and go under."[5] Ontic founding, it seems, is at once ontology's foundering. At the very least, its vaunted purity as ontology is compromised by an ontic inevitability.

The ontico-ontological relation finds its specificity in Dasein itself by way of the existentiell-existential relation. But now it is an affair of Dasein's understanding of its own existence in two quite distinct ways, constituting two levels of questioning:

1) The question of existence, whether to be itself or to not be itself, is ultimately settled simply by existing. The self-understanding that takes

this path, whether by choice, lapse, or development of one or the other extreme possibility, is an *existentiell* understanding. The question of existence here is an ontic concern of Dasein, how it comports itself understandingly about its very own being, which is precisely its existence. This ontic concern "does not require that the ontological structure of existence be theoretically transparent" (SZ 12).

2) The question of explicating the ontological structure of existence calls for an *existential* understanding, which is a theoretically clarified understanding of existence. It develops the existential analytic of Dasein through which fundamental ontology, the first goal of BT, is achieved. Such a task is in fact "prefigured in its possibility and necessity in Dasein's ontical constitution" (SZ 13). In fact, "the existential analytic is in the end *existentielly*, that is, *ontically* rooted." It can truly perform its analyses "only when the questioning proper to philosophical research, as a possibility of being of each existing Dasein, is itself seized upon in an existentiell manner" (ibid.) But the converse does not hold, as we have seen. Existentiell understanding does not require existential understanding to be itself, or to not be itself. There is no waiting for this, and no escape: Dasein in its very essence implies that "in each case it has to be its being as its own being" (SZ 12). The ontic preeminence and precedence of the question of being, here the being of Dasein which is existence, is thus underscored in a new way, stemming directly from its formal indication understood as a compulsion, an obligation of "having to be in each instance."

Authentic Existentiell Understanding: Resoluteness
The demand to ontically found the ontological possibilities of an existential analytic finds its most noteworthy concrete application at that point in BT at which the purely ontological possibility of being-a-whole by forerunning my own death is "attested in an existentiell manner" by the existentiell possibility of authenticity achieved through resoluteness. "Authentic 'thinking about death' is a willing-to-have-a-conscience which has become transparent to itself in an existentiell manner" (SZ 309). For existential analysis is groundless without an existentiell understanding (SZ 312), here provided by what the conscience "gives us to understand" (SZ 269f.). At this methodological turning point in his book (§63) just before its climactic section, that is, just before Heidegger roots the "ontological sense of care" (§65) in original temporality, he reiterates his early point in §4: Although existentiell understanding does not necessarily need existential analysis, the latter is necessarily developed upon the ground of the former (SZ 316, 312). In one sense, this is simply a reassertion of the phenomenological order of founding between the prethematic and the thematic, between a preontological understanding of being

and the fundamental ontology to be based upon it. But it is also the reassertion of the "self-sufficiency" (so in 1919–20) of an ontical realm which is already "ontological," of the factual which is facticity, of an ontological disclosure which is already under way before ontology proper begins its thematic disclosures. It is finally a reminder to the phenomenologist to become absolutely clear about the presuppositions of the hermeneutic situation from which he inescapably, that is, ontically, starts. How is ontology to reach its goal except by being responsive to the disclosive process already underway in the ontico-ontological realm of Dasein? For this ontic preunderstanding of being is a kind of preontological "ontology," an unthematized fundamental ontology which is the native ground for any and every thematization of the question of being. Being receptive and open to this ontico-ontological dimension of disclosure yields the analysis of Dasein which at once makes up fundamental ontology in the thematic sense. In fact, openness to the prethematic ontic "matters themselves" is the only path to a "more original" understanding of both the ontic fundament and the fundamental ontology seeking to draw itself in accord with that fundament. The goal (or as Husserl will soon put it, "the dream") of phenomenology first spelled out in KNS, to be the "pretheoretical primal science of the 'primal leap' [*Ur-sprung*] of being, of the primal something in its origin," has now become more articulate, thematized, thus perhaps more theoretical ("scientific") than Heidegger would eventually wish. One might however also speak of a double origin seeking to become one, where theoretical transparency is to become one with its concrete evidence; or of an ontological backtrack to its ontic origin in a peculiar "back and forth" interchange seeking to make both transparent. "The existentially more original interpretation also discloses *possibilities* for a more original existentiell understanding, as long as ontological conceptualization does not allow itself to be cut off from ontic experience" (SZ 295).

For all that, Heidegger's admission at this point that there is indeed "a particular ontical way of conceiving authentic existence, a factical ideal of Dasein, underlying the ontological interpretation of Dasein's existence" (SZ 310) has always been disconcerting to commentators. For one thing, it opens up the old Pandora's box of worldviews which can contaminate the very roots of a philosophy claiming to outstrip all worldviews (so in KNS). The methodological §63 which follows this admission, bent on exposing all of the presuppositions, ontic and ontological, of the hermeneutic situation at that climactic point in the development of his book, does not allay that particular fear. For there we are told that this ontical way of taking existence authentically need not be binding for everyone, and that existential interpretation will never seek to make it existentielly binding by way of authoritarian imposition. But must it not then justify those existentiell possibilities which gives ontological interpretation its ontic "ground, soil, and roots" (*ontischer Boden*: SZ 312)? Here, Heidegger appeals to the freedom of Dasein for its ownmost possibilities in choosing those "ontico-existentiell possibilities" which it would project onto their ontological possibility. But this "free discretion" (SZ 313) only intensifies our fear of arbitrariness, especially in view of the admitted "violence" of an interpretation which flies in the face of a long tradition of substance metaphysics by taking the "opposite course" (SZ 311), and claiming that the "substance" of Dasein is in fact its existence, ever unfinished in its can-be, ever out to be its being. This fundamental distinction between traditional reality and this novel sense of existence follows from the formal indication of the idea of existence which has guided the entire analytic of Dasein up to this point. The very formality of this idea, which "prefigures the formal structure of Dasein's understanding" (SZ 313), makes it existentielly nonbinding. But one can still ask, "Where does this idea get its justification?" The answer: "The formal indication of the idea of existence was guided by the understanding of being residing in Dasein itself" (ibid.).[6] This entity which I myself in each instance am and can be, Dasein, "is not merely on hand but has in each instance already understood itself, however mythical or magical [or Nazi!] the interpretation which it gives to this understanding may be" (ibid.). Dasein "stands out" from reality by its understanding of its situation: this is one of the realizations which shape Heidegger's formal indication of ex-sistence, distinguishing it from reality in the traditional sense. "Yet even this formal and existentielly nonbinding idea of existence already harbors within itself a particular albeit implicit ontological 'content' which . . . 'presupposes' an idea of being as such" (SZ 314). So we are back in the ontic-ontological bind, the inescapable "circle" from Dasein to being and back in the "to-and-fro relatedness" of questioning being. And no matter how productive this spiraling questioning may be, allowing us to formally indicate the ineffable individual which thus "puts itself into words for the very first time" (SZ 315), we cannot escape the lurking possibility of extraneous influence by inappropriate ontic worldviews, as my deliberately malicious insertion into the above citation was meant to suggest. By way of the formal idea of existence, Heidegger has clearly refined his sense of being of the coarse dross of solid substance and the primitive conceptions of being that the tradition has yielded, made it "fluent" for a more intensively temporal sense of life. But his first admission still stands as a caution and a warning, as well as a "positive necessity" (SZ 310). It is on this precautionary note that Heidegger himself concludes the book BT, where, in keeping with the very assumptions contained in his formal indication of existence, he sees his entire investigation of Dasein's being as "but *one* way we can take," itself still "on the way" and very much in question: "Can ontology be *ontologically* grounded or does it also require an *ontic* fundament? And *which* being must take over the function of providing this fundament?" (SZ 436).

Accordingly, the outstanding question raised by the problematic climax of BT (§§ 62–65) could be put as follows: Does the existentiell attestation of the authentic can-be which the call of conscience is to provide—more specifically, the resolute and resolving response that this call evokes—give rise to a worldview of worldviews, or instead, as it by way of formality intends, merely the obligatory condition of possibility for any and every worldview? Worldviews are understood in Jaspers's sense as "factical existentiell possibilities" which define the human situation of existence at any particular time with sufficient scope to comprehend the limit situations of death, suffering, guilt, chance, indeed situationality itself (SZ 301n). It would seem that forerunning my death as my outermost possibility, with its potentiality for being-a-whole, gives me such a concrete attitude toward life as a whole. But this is a mere ontological possibility, an empty and extraneous ideal of existence, without ontic fundament. Does Dasein ever actually demand of itself such tragic heroics? Does Dasein ever bear witness to such a demand, actually own up to it and make it its own as its real, live "existentiell" possibility? Does Dasein ever rise to the occasion of its existence and make it its own, in its full individuality and totality? Or better, does it have occasion to rise to the level of existence at its fullest from the leveling of the everyday, thereby taking the "opposite course" and so doing violence to the interpretations of common sense (SZ 312)? How does the ontological can-be turn into an ontic have-to-be? How does existential possibility become existentiell compulsion?

The compulsion to take the "opposite course" receives its ontic justification in the phenomenon of the "call" of conscience, whose sole formal function is to interrupt the initially everyday, then traditionally philosophical, absorption with things by the indifferent "self" immersed in the Anyone, and thus to single out Dasein to own up to its own existence, more specifically, to the "demand" (SZ 266f.) dictated by the unique situation defined by its lifetime. Something like a "call" is thus needed to turn Dasein around from its state of indifference, and so to bring it face to face with the full "reality" of its existence. This awakening to the "facts of life," to a full and honest confrontation of its scope and limits, at once broaches the conditions of its freedom to decide about its being.

Awakening from a dogmatic slumber, turning Dasein around: shades of the μετάωνοια from Plato's Cave and the Christian conversion to which the newly individualized Dasein "attests," confesses, bears witness; moving from an aesthetic can-be to an ethical ought-to-be; conscience calling "Guilty!": the shoals of worldviews everywhere we turn. Does the formalizing schematization of the idea of existence succeed in neutralizing the content of all of these worldviews, from which the very idea of ex-sistence itself has in fact been drawn? Does it want to neutralize all content in its quest for an ontic fundament for ontology? Empty possibility stands in need of ontic attestation: to be sure, not the testimony given at a legal proceeding (Kant), even more removed from the presentation of the evidence needed for scientific verification (Husserl). And yet a confession must be exacted from Dasein, he must be made to acknowledge his obligation to be, express his own "conviction" of shortfall in this arena of dialogue of self with self called "conscience." An ontological "conscience" and not the evangelical call of the Lutheran conscience, although Heidegger could have easily invoked Luther's admirable "Here I stand! I can no other!" to illustrate the kairotic moment of radically individualized resolution that he now wishes to make central for his pending temporal ontology. Our genealogical record of Heidegger's development since the war years literally swarms with the case studies that Heidegger now wishes to formalize into a central ontological paradigm, the paradigm of the καιρός so steeped in religious lore, beginning with Eckhart's *Abgeschiedenheit*, Schleiermacher's "feeling of absolute dependence," and Otto's "creaturely feeling."

At every moment of his account, we sense how constraining the vocabulary of conscience is for what Heidegger wants to say, how this metaphorical vehicle ultimately hampers him. It is not a person who calls, not even myself. Dasein, the human situation, is not a person. Rather, "It" calls (SZ 275), It gives, It gives to understand, which means that It of itself discloses. The gist of the later Heidegger's question is already here: What evokes thinking? What calls for (invites, urges, exacts, demands, provokes) thought? A condition of possibility backed by necessity, a harsh reality that "obliges" thought, a brute facticity that "voices" its demands louder than words. As in an evolutionary niché, there is an ineluctable challenge-response "logic" built into the human situation, into the "way things are." Behind the initially immediate facades of complacency, some harsher "givens" of human immediacy await us individually, to demand our attention, action, and thought. "What is essentially *given* to understand in the call at this time, in each particular while?" (SZ 280): ontically given to the existentiell understanding as "to-be understood," thus as tasks. The language of *jeweilig* is nowhere more evident and emphatic than in this chapter of BT: not ideal and universal tasks (*Seinkönnen*), but "das jeweilig vereinzelte des jeweiligen Daseins: the currently pressing individualized task of the temporally particular human situation" (ibid.). Not the inescapable challenges to a species, but to I myself, existing here and now. All the indexicals of life are now pointed at me, singling me out in my unique moment of decision, fraught with opportunity and shipwreck. The facts of my life here and now, the "original *truth* of existence" (SZ 307) that belongs to an entity, the bare and naked "that it is . . . how it is and can be, has to be" (SZ 276), calling simply for acknowledgment: *Es gibt's!* "There It is!" "So be It!" Clearly an existentielly binding commitment, here however only to be understood formally.

That these irrevocable facts of being here and now are associated with a "guilt" of being, which Dasein must now acknowledge, poses no less formidable metaphorical obstacles to ontological comprehension. But "the idea of 'Guilty!' must be sufficiently *formalized* so that the ordinary phenomena of guilt and debt, related to what we owe to others, will *drop out*" (SZ 283). The shortfall to be discussed here is simply between me and my situation, revealing what is "due" to that situation. For "based upon," "because of," or "owing to" my situation, I am and can be what I am, and in fact "have" (non-ousiological "ought") to be what I am as well as "have" (ousiological) what I am to be. What is in question is still the immediacy of the KNS-experience, now being elaborated as a transition experience in a decisional context, in order eventually to bring out its temporal character: I already find myself willy-nilly caught up in life, already under way in existence. The fact "that it is" means that Dasein "has in each case already been delivered over to existence, and it constantly so remains" (SZ 276). It has been "thrown" into existence "*not* of its own accord," "*not through* itself but *to* itself" (SZ 284f.), in order to exist, in order to be. To begin with, I am not the author (*Ursache*) of my existence, but now have to be that author (*Urheber*: SZ 282), to authenticate my being by making it my own; not being the ground of my existence, and yet having to be that ground. "Dasein is not itself the ground of its being . . . but in being-its-self it is the being of this ground. This ground is always only the ground of a being which in its being has to take over being its ground" (SZ 285). My life *in fact* is not my own from the ground up, and yet it is solely my own as a *can-be*, my own *raison d'être*, mine to own up to and make my own, and that is what I ought to do. I thus owe it to myself to own up to my existence in its entirety, paying due to its can-be which is not yet, at once "taking into account" and paying heed to that and what I already am and am not, or no longer am. In short, at any given time, I owe a debt to existence, which it itself exacts from me, to which I ought to own up, and not disown. There is an obligatory side to the given which is ex-sistence, since, by formal assumption, its givenness (*Gegebenheit*) is at once an unfinished task (*aufgegebene Aufgabe*), its "gift" (*Gabe*) is the "to-be" of a can-be.[7] The moment of obligation, the "ought," thus somehow arises from the basic "not" at the heart of existence, which is accordingly not a privative "not" or a lack (SZ 285f.). To acknowledge an "am not" (the gap, shortfall, or "debit" of being) in existence at once means to acknowledge a "have to be," an "ought" which somehow already bridges and fills the breach of not-being. By way of the formal indication of existence as distinguished from "reality," Heidegger believes he has found the basis for a new "modal logic" in the temporal relations between my being and nonbeing, having-to-be and can-be. This debit (*Schuld*) of ex-sistence is very much in keeping with its temporally driven, ongoing, unfinished character, its non-ousiological character: always finding oneself short in existence, always playing catch-up in a life which unrelentingly makes its claim on us, owning up to an existence which is never our own, even at its best to some extent disowned. Owned existence, authentic existence, thus assumes the status of an asymptotic ideal, since I am called upon to become the author of an existence over which I never have absolute authority. Charged by life to take charge of It, yet never discharging that debt, always remaining in deficit to It, an impersonal taskmaster ever exacting its due, over which I can never achieve mastery.

Thus Dasein is always first on the receiving end of existence, ever in need to be receptive and responsive to its demands. Would not the response to life called "resoluteness" maintain the same formal purity, free of ontic contamination, thus far maintained in this ontologic of the "debit!"-response structure of the human situation? Being alert to the problem, Heidegger will not be trapped into any of the particular versions of his earlier studies of listening and learning, the receptive acceptance of Christian grace, the obediential potency of the "passive" intellect, the receptivity/spontaneity interface, and so on. And yet, it is precisely the completing moment of resolving response that provides the "existentiell attestation" of hitherto empty existential possibility, and so the ontic founding of ontology. Resoluteness is the existentiell attestation of owned can-be (SZ 302), the *Vollzugssinn* of existence.

> Resoluteness, by its ontological essence, is the particular resoluteness of a particular factical Dasein at a particular time. . . . The receptive openness of resoluteness [*Ent-schlossenheit*] "exists" only as a closing resolution [*Entschluß (als End-schluß)*)] which understandingly projects itself. But in what direction does Dasein dis-close [*erschließt*] itself in resoluteness? On what is it to resolve itself? *Only* the resolution itself can give the answer. (SZ 298)

It is in this context of the thoroughgoing particularity of the "closing resolution" that the all-important kairological term "situation" makes its tardy but essential debut, as "an existential phenomenon which we have hitherto passed over" (SZ 299). Of its essence temporally particular, the situation is the particularized correlate of resoluteness. "The situation is the 'here' which is in each case disclosed in resoluteness. . . . The situation *is* only through and in resoluteness" (SZ 299f.). It is of its essence a "concrete situation of human action" given its rise by a "concrete under-standing" (SZ 302, 300), which is precisely what resoluteness is. Accord-ingly, "when the call of conscience summons us to our can-be, it does not hold before us some empty ideal of existence, but *calls us forth into the situation*" (SZ 300). The concrete situation itself gives rise to, shapes, and in fact *is* the "particular ontic way of taking authentic existence, a factical ideal of Dasein" (SZ 310), the existentiell understanding which underlies any and every ontological interpretation of Dasein's existence.

"Resoluteness *gives* itself the temporally particular factic situation and *brings* itself into it" (SZ 307). Through this disclosure, Dasein "owns up to" the original truth of its own existence. Is this owned existence at once the whole of its existence, which comes from forerunning the possibility of my death? Can situational resolve, on the verge of articulating worldviews and so very much this-worldly, give itself and bring itself into that outermost situation of worldly impossibility at the outskirts of being-in-the-world? To complete his ontico-ontological meditation, Heidegger finally seeks to show that situating resolve, which owns up to its tempo-rally particular situation of possibility, at once not only includes and makes possible, but already is forerunning resolve, which comprehends the whole of life by comprehending the limit-situation of possible impos-sibility at the outer extremity of life.

At first, they seem to be poles part. "What can death and the 'concrete situation' of taking action have in common?" (SZ 302). But can the ten-dency of resoluteness be made to undergo an "existentiell modalization" (SZ 305) in the direction of being-toward-death? At least to his own satisfaction, Heidegger succeeds in showing that the situationality of res-oluteness, thought to its end, can assume all those aspects which he had already found in being-toward-death, and so can attest existentielly to that outstandingly outermost possibility which is radically my own in its individuality, not to be outstripped, certain and yet indefinite: death. Accordingly, forerunning resoluteness, which brings itself into that ex-treme situation of life which is at once radically my own and the whole of my life, provides an especially radical and now transparent ontological paradigm. Forerunning my death is no longer merely an empty ideal. It is now a concrete ideal of authentic existence duly attested and justified as an ontic possibility of Dasein, susceptible of existentiell authorship (SZ 309f.). Forerunning resoluteness accordingly becomes the ontico-ontological prefiguration for tracing out the structure of the original temporality of Dasein in BT, or, more simply put, of tracing out my lifetime owned and whole as I live it "from the inside out." A time issuing from the situation of existence itself, and not one imposed on it from without, in which that situation would "take place." This kairological paradigm governs the remainder of the book, even though Heidegger continues to express doubts about the radical comprehensiveness even of this ontically founded ideal: "Does being-in-the-world have a higher jurisdiction for its can-be than its death?" (SZ 313). Death remains the limit situation which defines the ontic ideal of the hermeneutic situation of the book BT, and perhaps even of the unique factic situation of its author.[8]

And Now The Moment

Καιρός. For Aristotle, the comprehending moment of insight, φρόνησις (= resoluteness), into the whole of the situation; for Paul, the fullness of time and the moment of personal commitment to its full significance. Heidegger acknowledges Kierkegaard, by way of Jaspers's book, as "probably the one who has seen the *existentiell* phenomenon of the *Augenblick* with the most penetration. But this does not mean that he was correspondingly successful in interpreting it existentially. . . . If, however, such a moment is experienced existentielly, then a more original temporality [than now-time] is presupposed, although it may not be made existentially explicit" (SZ 338n).[9] In his first usage in BT of this clinching moment of original temporality, in fact shortly before the climactic paragraph first announcing the "ecstases" of time in the climactic §65, Heidegger gives it the Aristotelian emphasis of a "moment of vision": "It is with resolute openness that Dasein has brought itself back from falling, precisely in order to be more authentically 'there' in the 'moment *of insight*' [*Augen*blick] into the situation thus disclosed" (SZ 328). It is not by eternal νοῦς but in the "light" of time, the "clearing" opened by the authenticating holistic movement of original temporality, "by" which being now comes to be understood. Kairological time is the empowering milieu by which resolution, the ultimate ontic thrust of resoluteness, can find the way to its temporally particular situation. More precisely, the present tense of the Moment is that "according to which a resolution discloses the situation" (SZ 338).

There is a metaphorical transgression at play here which persists into the later Heidegger, as resolute openness enters into the light of original time, where it not only gets its sight but takes its bearings vis-à-vis its possibilities. The metaphors of vision and motion maintain an uncertain truce in the *Lichtung* of time. Resolute openness moves toward its closing resolution upon the whole of the particular situation, as in an opening "space" of closure, in arriving at the moment of comprehension: the clearing of being here, now; a temporal "leeway" (*Spielraum*: SZ 145, 368). A present thoroughly saturated with the uncertain possibility of the future, contrary to the ousiological present in old Pindar's ode: Instead, "Become what you are *to be*." The self finds its identity in the direction to be faced in the self-constancy of steady, steadfast resolve (SZ 322).

The self now becomes its time, a project taut between birth and death. It is not a goal to be achieved, since it is never finished, even when it is finished: the peculiar stasis of ecstasis.

> The term *Augenblick*, as an ecstasis, must be understood in the active sense. It refers to the resolute remotion with which Dasein is carried away to whatever possibilities and circumstances are encountered, in the situation of concern, as a matter of concern. This very motion of transport which carries us off is *held* in resoluteness. The Moment is a phenomenon which *in principle* cannot be clarified out of the Now. It . . . is not that "in which" something comes to be, passes away, or is on hand. Nothing can happen "in the moment." But as authentic waiting-toward [*Gegen-wart*], the moment *first lets us encounter* what "in a time" can be as handy or on hand. (SZ 338)

A new and different sense of time concentrated on the moment which is at once my unique lifetime. How? By "at once" (equiprimodially) forerunning the possibility of my death and repeating the possibility of my birth (heredity, inheritance, heritage). The "forerunning-repeating moment" (SZ 391) is sheer possibility, Dasein's own "superpower, the power of its finite freedom," the "impotent superpower" of its fate (SZ 384f.). Resolution is a moment of containment and continence (cf. SS 1921, Augustine diagram), of focus and concentration versus the dissipation of the everyday. It is that by which Dasein "takes place" and is truly "there" in its particular situation, owned and whole, not everywhere and nowhere as in the distracted curiosity which flits from one "moment" of novelty to the next (SZ 347). Curiosity "kills time," emasculates it of its power. Or time itself contains a moment of inertia and dispersal that renders it impotent, thereby calling upon Dasein to "pull itself together."

> The self's resoluteness against the inconstancy of distraction is in itself a stretched steadiness—the steadiness in which Dasein as fate holds birth and death and their "between" "in relation" [*einbezogen* = *Bezugssinn*], draws them thus related into its existence, so that in such constancy Dasein is in fact, by way of the moment, for the world-historical operative in its temporally particular situation. . . . Resoluteness itself implies the existentiell constancy which, by its very essence, has already anticipated every possible moment of vision arising from it. As fate, resoluteness is the freedom to *give up* a particular resolution, in accord with the demands of any possible situation. (SZ 390f.)

Freedom for death, freedom for fate, freedom for the world-historical, freedom to dissolve and resolve resolution according to the "momentous" demands of the temporally particular situation: One begins to see why Heidegger could later point to these pages[10] to justify his own "world-historical" decision to speak fatefully and "*momentously* for his time"; and one could wonder what ontic-existentiell attitude is lurking in the talk of "letting oneself be free for one's death by shattering against it, so that one can at once let oneself be thrown back upon its factical 'there' . . . in handing down its inherited possibility to itself" (SZ 385). Such ontically suggestive attitudes can easily be taken to be entirely consistent with the formal self-constancy of the project of his thought. "Momentous existence temporalizes itself as a stretchedness which is fatefully whole, according to the authentic historical *constancy* of the self. This kind of temporal existence has its time "constantly" *for* what the situation demands of it" (SZ 410). But what ontically possible "world-historical" decision is not consistent with this formally held self-constancy? Even decadent worldviews, as the ever-possible countermovement of falling, find their place in this formal approach. By definition, however, they are not ontic ideals of *authentic* existence.

THE PRIMACY OF POSSIBILITY

Just as "structure" dominates the very interstices of the penultimate draft in its orientation toward being, so this kairological draft oriented toward time comes to be dominated by a new incidental word, as such and in central variants like "can-be" (*Seinkönnen*): "possibility." This development was in fact already beginning to take shape toward the end of SS 1925, as Heidegger struggles for the first time to articulate the nature of understanding.[11] But it first takes center stage only in the very last hour of SS 1925–26, when Heidegger finds, through his new formal indication of "ex-sistence" as being-out-for a can-be, that all three dimensions of time are permeated by possibility. The facticity of the past, for example, is not a brute fact, but rather the possibility of the Already. "We designate the temporally particular and authentic possibility-of-being (*Seinsmöglichkeit*) of a factic Dasein, however this possibility may be chosen and determined, as *Existenz*" (GA 21:402).

Not surprisingly, therefore, this new emphasis in his formal indication is announced precisely in the section in BT (§9) in which Heidegger gives the first full elaboration of what "existence" provisionally indicates: "Dasein comports to its being as to its ownmost possibility." The new provisional ontological assertion is no longer "Dasein itself is its time" but rather "Dasein is in each case its possibility" (SZ 42), which it does not merely "have" as a modifying property. My possibility is "mine" more in the sense of an ex-sistential identification rather than an ousiological relation. The former way of talking about "properties" of Dasein, "ways to be," has all along really meant "possibilities to be" in their reference to the How of the verbal Dasein. "Dasein is primarily being-possible. Dasein is in each case what it can be and how it is its possibility" (SZ 143).

"Dasein is its possibility": the point is reiterated at every opportunity throughout the book (SZ 181, 188, 191, 193, 259, 264, 336, etc.).

Contrary to the tentative account of the previous draft (see chap. 8), understanding now becomes the veritable locus of possibility. "Dasein defines itself as a being always in the light of a possibility which it itself *is* and somehow *understands* in its being" (SZ 43). The identification is a consequence of the thoroughgoing existentializing both of Dasein and of the understanding which it is, where possibility is now the very core of the formal indication of existence. "The mode of being of Dasein as can-be resides existentially in the understanding. Put otherwise, the activity of understanding existentially implies Dasein's kind of being as can-be" (SZ 143). This existential possibility which Dasein itself is is to be sharply distinguished from empty logical possibility, the merely possible which, as not yet actual and never at any time necessary, is regarded as ontologically inferior to actuality and necessity. "Possibility as an existential is the most original, ultimate, and positive determination of Dasein" (SZ 143f.). In Dasein and with Dasein regarded in its being as existence, we come upon a hitherto unknown and especially pregnant notion of lived possibility lapsing and thrown, where to-be, can-be, and having-to-be (traditionally the modals of actuality, possibility, and necessity) are "equiprimordial" in a sense which will only be fully grasped by way of the ultimate condition of possibility, by way of the unity of the temporality of Dasein. "Higher than actuality stands possibility" (SZ 38).

Understanding, first regarded as a disclosedness, a kind of "know-how," is on the level of being a disclosive can-be, disclosing the can-be for the sake of which Dasein itself is (SZ 86, 144). Understanding as existence, accordingly thrown forward into and toward possibilities, always has the structure of a project. "As long as Dasein is, it is projecting" (SZ 145). This very projecting is the leeway (*Spielraum*) allowing Dasein to be "free for its ownmost can-be" (SZ 144, 145), the very possibility and freedom that Dasein is. As disclosive, this leeway is the free play and field of play of a cleared*ness* (*Gelichtetheit*: SZ 147) that provides transparency to the whole of existence. The conflation of free leeway of possibility and disclosedness yielded by the project of understanding thus leads to the halting and ambivalent emergence of Da-sein as the "lighting/clearing" (*Lichtung*: SZ 133) of being, a favorite term of the later Heidegger already playing a central albeit unelaborated role in BT. Already meant to displace the "pure intuitive be-holding" of the Greeks' eternal νοῦς (SZ 171), the clearing provided by prereflexive understanding will soon find its "condition of possibility" in the ecstatic unity of temporality, which "originally clears the There" (SZ 351) of Da-sein. "That by which this entity is cleared, that which makes it both 'open' for itself and 'bright' for itself, was, in advance of any 'temporal' interpretation, defined as care" (SZ 350). Both the truth of the discovery of things, practical as well as theoretical, and the truth of the disclosure of the self in its concrete situation of action, is, contrary to Aristotle, governed by a temporal clearing rather than an eternal Mind in which we partake. "We understand the light of this clearedness only if we do not look to some extant power implanted in us, but rather interrogate the whole constitution of Dasein's being, its "care," in the unitary ground of its existential possibility" (SZ 351). This is the ultimate reorientation of possibility dictated by the extrovertive thrust of ex-sistence which turns human being "inside out," as it were: facultative powers, once possessed by the rational animal, become empowering contexts (later, the clearing of Being itself) in which and by which the human being is "out for" its being, in order to be.

"As long as it is, Dasein already has understood itself and always will understand itself from possibilities. The projective character of the very act of understanding means moreover that the understanding does not thematically grasp that toward which [*woraufhin*] it projects, the possibilities" (SZ 145). The very character of possibility means that it is not grasped thematically, reflectively. "Projecting throws the possibility before itself as possibility and lets it *be* as possibility" (ibid.). This unthematized state of being the possibility demarcates the primacy of possibility contained in the existential assertion that "Dasein *is* its possibility." It is a further specification of the formally indicative statement that "Dasein is the being which in its being goes about (is concerned with) this being."

The explication of these implicit possibilities, expository interpretation (*Aus-legung*), develops these already projected possibilities which constitute the fore-structure of understanding into an explicit as-structure, whereby we overtly understand something as something. To explicate something as something is to understand its sense (*Sinn*) or meaning. "Sense is the forestructured toward-which of the project *out* of which something as something becomes understandable" (SZ 151). I have temporarily left out a portion of this already rich sentence, underscored in BT, and so pivotal to its movement both in its content and its method of concept formation. It would even take us too far afield at this late stage of our Story to retrace its genesis back to the KNS response to Natorp's objections and the ensuing threefold sense of intentionality in 1920. But note the "outering" movement of the "laying out" or ex-position of meaning "out of" a prior whole of implicit understandability which makes interpretation, and that means not only human knowing but also human acting, at all possible. The ex-sistential movement which is the central presupposition of BT is now characterized as a hermeneutic movement of explicating the implicit, the exposition of meaning investing human being with the manifold sense of direction which carries it forward in all that it does, both toward the world and toward itself. The backtrack to the veritable source of that movement of meaning (*Sinnge-bung, Sinngenesis*) defines the phenomenological ambition of the book, in a question already stirring in the habilitation: Whence sense? How does it arise? What are the defining conditions which make it possible to emerge?

We are at the moment catching sense in its movement outward, but are really more interested in the "pre" structure of this toward-which: "Sense is the toward-which already structured by a prepossession, preview, and preconception . . ." (ibid.). The temporal stretch from past into future of these lived pre-suppositions, now clearly identified as lived projects of human possibility rather than explicit propositions, which through the spiraling movement of interpretation are brought to language for the first time (SZ 314f.), has been manifest almost from the start in Heidegger's sense of the "hermeneutic situation" (since SS 1922): The human being is already had and so holds forth, is already sighted in sighting forward, already grasped in its continuing conceiving. The spiraling movement of making sense out of existence in its being is the natural outcome of its precedented character. The question of the sense of being is to be traced back to the pre-understanding of being which prompts and directs the interrogative situation of the question itself. The process of understanding interpretation itself must therefore be accounted for in terms of the temporal conditions of an irretrievably situated existence, situated in the sense already latent in its underlying possibility. This primary possibility, the pre-understanding of being itself, receives its ultimate possibility from the most basic project, time itself. In this final step back into the source of the giving of meaning, as we approach the source of the immediacy of experience, we find ourselves resorting to the double-talk of tautology. The possibility of possibility, the sense of sense, the project of projects, is time itself. Original temporality is the "sense of Dasein" (SZ 331), "the ontological sense of care" (SZ 323), "the original condition for the possibility of care" (SZ 372), "the sense of the being of Dasein's totality" (SZ 373). As the very sense of care, temporality "enables the totality of its articulated structural whole in the unity of its unfolded articulation" (SZ 324). Temporality "is" the very basis (*Boden*: SZ 373; 328) of possibility for the sense, unity and wholeness of existence in its being, its λόγος.

The "outering" upshot of this backtracking to the experiential source of the understanding of being, by way of the guiding idea of ex-sistence, comes with the closer examination of the tendential senses of the tenses of time. "The phenomena of the 'toward . . .', 'back to . . .' and 'among . . .' make temporality manifest as the ἐκστατικόων pure and simple. Temporality is the original 'out-of-itself' in and for itself" (SZ 329). Like an explosive event, time opens the ecstatic expanse that defines the thrust and vectorial context of existence. But rather than foisting a Big Bang theory of ex-sistence upon Heidegger, let us watch him grope for his own terms to describe the dynamo of meaning and possibility that he finds at the experiential source of existence:

> Temporality "is" not an entity at all. *It is not, instead it temporalizes itself.* . . . Temporality temporalizes, and indeed it temporalizes possible ways of itself. These enable the manifold of Dasein's modes of being, and especially the basic possibility of authentic and inauthentic existence. . . . Temporality is not, before all this, an entity which first steps out of *itself*, its essence is rather a temporalizing in the unity of the ecstases. . . . The future has a precedence in the unity of original and authentic temporality. Even so, temporality does not first arise through a cumulative sequence of the ecstases, but in each instance temporalizes itself in their equiprimordiality. But within this equiprimordiality, the modes of temporalizing are different. The difference lies in the fact that the temporalizing can determine itself primarily out of the different ecstases. (SZ 328f.)

A unity and manifold of articulation at the source of meaning: shades of the habilitation's "doctrine of categories and meaning." Even the sentence intentionally underlined resonates with the neo-Kantian theory of meaning that Heidegger entertained then. "It 'is' not, rather it holds, it carries weight (*es gilt*)." But what a far cry this theory of validity, with its ponderous emphasis on necessity, is from Heidegger's new theory of meaning, with its emphasis on possibility: "It clears, It holds forth, It empowers, enables, makes possible." The full statement of this existential-ontological "thesis" serves to accentuate this note of possibility: "Temporality temporalizes itself originally out of the future" (SZ 331). As a verbal tautology, it is clearly a source statement, more intensively focused on the heart of the "matter itself," on the genesis of sense out of the immediacy of life, than its earlier version at the conclusion of SS 1925: "Not: 'Time is'; rather: 'Dasein temporalizes its being *qua* time'" (GA 20:442/319).

As a *solus ipse* or *singulare tantum*, time is a many-splendored power. As the ground of unity and wholeness, it is a cohesive and binding force, an organizational and gathering power according to which "things hang together, fall into place, and so make sense," providing a "work*ing* context" like the world, and a completion to life's sense of direction. Not the repressive holding power of "validity," but the freeing release of an enabling context which lets things be what they are meant to be in their full scope, giving them their sense of place as well as sense of direction to become what they are to be. Thus a directive power as it contextualizes: by the same token, it is the power of articulation of the manifold of meaning. Thus a revelatory power: as a phenomenological sense of time, how the implicit becomes explicit, pro-ducing evidence. But then a productive power, yielding new possibility, the power of opening and un-folding, ripening, maturing and bringing to fruition. "The truth will out . . . when the time is ripe." In the same vein, a drawing power as it withdraws into concealment, inviting further exploration as an arena of disclosure "calling for thought." "Being loves to hide," says Heraclitus. The later Heidegger will find many an occasion to ponder how time itself "with equal primordiality" assumes and so modifies all of the powers invested by the philosophical tradition in its most central terms for being, and especially in λόγος, ἀλήθεια, and φθύσις.

It is perhaps a cliché to say that time is a power to contend with. On the one hand, the ground debit of existence means never to have power over the ground of one's being from the ground up (SZ 284). On the other, it is precisely time's power of sense and direction that forerunning resoluteness seeks to take over "to acquire *power* over Dasein's *existence* and so to disperse all fugitive self-concealments in their ground" (SZ 310): the powers of concentrated integrity, openness, and transparency, in short, the power of existentiell understanding that resoluteness in fact is. Or in another context, by letting death become powerful in itself, the forerunning Dasein "understands itself in the unique *superior power* of its finite freedom . . . which allows it to take over the *impotence* of being abandoned to that very death and so to come to a clear vision of the accidents of the disclosed situation" (SZ 384). Dasein thus becomes its fate as "that impotent superior power which puts itself in readiness for adversities" (SZ 385), just as resoluteness is readiness for dread. In re-peating its death and its fate, the "silent power of the possible" (SZ 394f.) enters deeply into Dasein's own existence, and it comes toward that exis-tence in all its futurity.

HORIZONAL SCHEMATIZING: THE STORY GOES ON

Having reached its climax in original temporality, much of the remainder of BT is spent in showing how this unique time of my lifetime "gets leveled" to the ordinary conception of on-hand now-time transmitted to us by the tradition of philosophy, as well as from the intermediate level of the handy time of daily concerns; how in fact original time "temporalizes itself" into these levels. This discussion of derivative time flowing from its source in a uniquely experienced time was in fact begun in the first draft of BT in 1924 and will spill over into the course of SS 1927, as the book BT first becomes available to the reading public (see Appendix C). This course on the "Basic Problems of Phenomenology," later billed by the old Heidegger as a reworking of the never published Third Division of the First Part of BT, will moreover press more deeply into the original temporality of Dasein in order to work out the Temporality of Being itself. This would indeed complete the reversal of movement from "Being and Time" to "Time and Being" suggested by the announced title of the Third Division in the larger Outline of BT. This program which would have completed the systematic First Part of BT is never really carried out. The content of that First Part is, in the Outline, described as the movement of first interpreting "Dasein on the basis of Temporality" and then explicating "Time as the Transcendental Horizon of the Question of Being" (SZ 39). All we have are two visible shards of the attempts to complete that systematic outline, proceeding from the very odd §69c of BT to the conclusion of SS 1927. They seem to contain at least part of the secret to the eventual demise of the project of BT. That failure, as the later Heidegger will reiterate more than once, was a failure of language to express the insight contained in the very title "Being and Time." Perhaps even the terms of the questions at this point in Heidegger's development failed to point the way adequately.

"The Demise of Heidegger's *Being and Time*": we stand at the threshold of an entirely new story, the *sequel* to "The Genesis of Heidegger's *Being and Time*." It can be told in the same way, by following the doxographical trail of documents in its BCD intertwining, by listening to Heidegger tell it (just as partially as he told his Genesis Story) at different points in his career, by piecing together the fragments of other bits of evidence, ending with a story which will confirm Heidegger's version only in part.

The telling of this new story must be left for another occasion. But as a sequel, it will have its roots in notable portions of the first Story, like the running critique of intuition and immanent perception in Husserl, Descartes, and now Kant, like the never-published opus on Aristotle. Both of these would have played significant roles in the historical Part Two of BT which, along with the Third Division of the First Part, never saw the light of print in any intact version. The Genesis Story is thus the indispensable basis for the story of the collapse of BT.

This is clearly true of probably the very last new conceptual development in the extant book BT, the cutting conceptual edge which then becomes the sticking point in SS 1927 and so blocks at least one of the paths toward completion of the project of BT. The oddity of this new concept is that it appears only in §69c in BT, and nowhere else in the book. Despite its obvious connection to the central thrust of the climactic section (§65) of BT, namely, the temporalizing of temporality, it appears almost as an afterthought in an obscure corner of BT. It is not even mentioned in the last flurry of questions of the book, where it easily could have and even should have been. For it will eventually be invoked to answer precisely those questions that course back from Time to Being: "The ecstatical projection of being must be made possible by a primordial way in which ecstatical temporality temporalizes. How is this mode of the temporalizing of temporality to be interpreted? Is there a way that leads from primordial *Time* to the sense of *Being*? Does *Time* itself manifest itself as the Horizon of *Being?*" (SZ 437).

This concept, put in place already in BT and then made into the way to broach the turn to the question of "Time and Being," is the "horizonal schema" (SZ 365). The questions it will be recruited to answer already acquire a certain clarity in BT: "The question of whether and how Time has any "Being," and of why and in what sense we designate it as actually "being," cannot be answered until we have shown to what extent temporality itself, in the totality of its temporalizing, makes possible something like an understanding of being and an addressing of beings" (SZ 406).

Our new concept for delineating temporality, "horizonal schema," is based on the premise that temporality regarded in its entirety, "as an ecstatic unity, has *something like* a horizon" (SZ 365). "Horizon" is one of those incidental words which sneaks up on us in the Heideggerian opus. Its occasional use since WS 1919–20 is in retrospect, however, not surprising, in view of its multifaceted usage in the early phenomenological tradition. It bounds both life and inquiry, almost in alternation: first a horizon of significances (WS 1919–20), then the horizon of historiology (SS 1920), then the leap back into the "driving boat" "which first discloses the authentic horizon onto factic life" (GA 61:37). "Horizons" for research and inquiry begin to proliferate perceptibly in Heidegger's courses in his Marburg years. The new crop of students who came to his first Marburg semester probably did not even notice the change. At any rate, in the first week of WS 1923–24, in discussing the phenomenon of the Greek sky, Heidegger notes in passing that the phenomenal connections he is making between the light and the bright and the like "give us a horizon for our later investigations" (November 5). His long concern for Greek "definition," especially that of the human being (SS 1923), finally develops, in SS 1924, into a rather extensive thematization of the nature of ὁρίζειν, that radical "determining" that occurs at the interface between language and being (see chap. 6). In the penultimate draft of BT, in SS 1925, "horizon" receives an even more extensive incidental usage. That proliferation escalates in BT where moreover, in its opening and closing scene, the term "horizon" begins to step out of the wings and claim prominence on center stage. Its talent for expressing and projecting the "matter itself" however remains an unknown magnitude throughout the first act of BT. It is not even clear what role it is meant to play. But now that it is vying for more of the limelight, we suddenly recall its years as an "understudy" and wonder, not only about its preparation for its new claim to fame, but also whether its old place in the underlying plot clarifies and justifies its new role.

We are not disappointed by its résumé, outlined in the Index of Lesser

Terms on the occasion of its previous appearance.[12] When we follow the indexical trail laid down by the term "horizon" in SS 1925, we soon discover a remarkable pattern. There is a pregiven question-horizon, problem-horizon, research-horizon which orients and guides philosophical inquiry, providing it first with its field of matters as well as with the directives on how to approach and so interrogate them. The history of philosophy is like a playing field whose horizons vary and so repeatedly offer a different field of opportunity as well as new constraints in perspectives. New horizons must constantly be won, against which, for example, concepts like "history" and "nature" may properly be contrasted and made to stand out in relief. Phenomenology in particular has laid open an especially novel horizon unifying and defining a distinctive subject matter by way of its three breakthrough discoveries, first of all "prefigured by the phenomenon, the fundamental determination, of intentionality. . . . Consider therefore the increasing elaboration of the thematic field, its determination, and the prefiguration (*Vorzeichnung*) of the working horizons ensuing from this determination of the field" (GA 20:123/ 90). At first, phenomenology allowed its unique discovery of a new apriori to be clouded by the traditional horizon of the concept of "being" understood as constant presence (102/75). The question of being must accordingly be articulated anew, in order to "obtain the secure horizon of questioning the being of beings and with it the prefiguration of the steps and the way to seek to find the answer. This prefiguration is that from which the answer is drawn and in which it is confirmed" (193/ 143). A horizon that provides internal prefiguration and direction to the project of questioning, a prefiguration that outlines its outer horizon: a horizonal schematizing already operative not only in the history of phenomenology but also, in Heidegger's own accounting of it, what is going on in his own spiraling progress/regress back to the matter itself of phenomenology! Kant only confirmed what he had been doing all along in his method, based on a hermeneutics *of* facticity, of phenomenological definition by way of formal indication, in order to trace (schematize) the matter as it articulates (schematizes) itself from its phenomenal origins. The prefiguration of horizons is but an alternative way of describing a foreshadowed structure of the hermeneutic situation. The two show their common stripes in the movement of the understanding project which explicates the possibility latent in the situation at the time, where method merely follows matter in its own self-disclosure. In metaphorical English, this is the way understanding already "takes place." You already implicitly "know where you're at and how things stand" (358/259), and the one who wishes to explicate must first develop a sense of that prior context of implicated preunderstanding in order to stand a chance of "working" it out into the open. Defining the situation and movement of research depends first on the situation and movement of the matter of research. It is simply a matter of following the lead of the advance project of the matter, the project which "It advances." It clears, It temporalizes.

And now, It schematizes, It schematizes horizonally. Is this new language game meant to account for the move from one horizon to another? What are the different horizons accessible to us? How do they modulate or modify one another, and so articulate another field of beings? And the horizon of horizons comprehending them as a unified horizon? In what way does it receive its determination, or perhaps determine itself? This new language game is clearly Heidegger's intended translation of his old habilitation problem, the classical problem of the unity and multiplication of the regions of being. This traditional "thesis of being" will naturally appear among the "basic problems of phenomenology" in the sequel to BT.

§69c has always conceptually stood out, like a strange outgrowth, from the textual corpus of BT. Its reincorporation into Heidegger's development was made possible only in part by the publication in 1975 of the course of SS 1927, which provided the further elaboration not only of its notion of "horizonal schema" but also of its correlate, the notion of "transcendence," Heidegger's final formal indication of intentionality. The larger genealogical context of BT, the period of 1916–26 now rapidly being brought out into the open, more fully shows how this project-horizon structure is but the final outcome of Heidegger's prefigurative, formally indicative approach to human immediacy. Our concluding task, venturing beyond the book BT only slightly, is restricted to this natural genealogical issue, and only "schematically" at that.

The term "horizonal schema" does not even sneak up on us in BT (but see SZ 360 for its initial traces). It is suddenly there in its full glory in §69c, and only there, in conjunction with "the temporal problem of the transcendence of the world," as if a world-horizon were more intuitive than a time-horizon (it is), as if a world-horizon should also be regarded as a temporal horizon (a more interesting suggestion, in view of its eventual connection with the "transcendence" of the self, broached in the previous subsection). Intuitively, one thinks of horizons as confining—they are at least defining, which is the real intention here—but from the start, the stress falls on its possibility, on its providing an opening in which and by which things can become what they are. The "ecstatico-horizonally founded transcendence of the world" (SZ 366) *lets* things be encountered within the world, even lets them be eventually objectified scientifically (the previous subsection, §69b). Horizonal schematizing thus provides the specific directive ways *to be* for the various entities that are. The horizonal schema is the "whither" of the ecstasy. At least each temporal tense has its own. And yet the dynamism of the Whither lends itself to modulation, according to the rapport among the tenses, and an ultimate "horizonal unity" of temporality as a whole, which is the ultimate determinant defining the "toward which" (the sense) of disclosure (SZ 365). Thus, the schema of the present "in order to" is modulated by the schema of the future "for the sake of" to define the temporal horizon of the transcendence which specifically belongs to the world and the entities within it (SZ 365). The horizonal schema of the precedented hav*ing*-been, which would of course be the central modulation to the project of historizing, is oddly double, including both the "before which" of confrontation with one's facticity and the "on the basis of which" of irretrievable consignment to that facticity. Why are not the others doubly schematized, say, one constraining and the other enabling? §69c is hardly more than a laying out of the terms of a new language game, raising a host of questions which can only be answered when this horizonal schematism has been fully worked out and concretely applied to its specific immediacies in human experience. In the dossier of his autograph of the lecture course of WS 1925–26, Heidegger has left a thick accumulation of loose notes focused repeatedly on "§69," archivally suggesting what a sticking point this new development was for the conceptual formation taking us beyond BT.

The partial and now ontologically pointed elaboration of horizonal schematism toward the end of SS 1927 breaks off as a fragment, does little to satisfy our specific questions from BT. As the locus of the demise of BT, it in fact raises more new questions which are never really answered by Heidegger. But the later Heidegger at one point does specify what is probably the heart of the problem here: the concept of horizon itself, introduced under the spell of his enthusiasm for Kant's problematic and some of its conceptual formulations.[13] Even the tracing of this specific fault line to its conclusion must be postponed at this late stage. To parody Heidegger, we find ourselves looking outward toward a horizon which opens up a vast expanse of possibilities for exploration. To circumvent this new embarrassment of riches, let us limit ourselves to a few critical remarks drawn from the genealogical framework from which we have just come.

The very interjection of the word "horizon" into the question defining the project of both BT and SS 1927, the project of deriving Being from Time, is questionable. "*Von wo aus*, out of where, whence is something like being at all to be understood? How is an understanding of being at all possible?" (GA 24:19/15). ". . . that *out* of which Dasein tacitly understands and *ex*plicates something like being at all is *time*. Time must be brought to light, and genuinely conceived, as the horizon of all understanding and explication of being" (SZ 17). The fatal conceptual leap is baldly stated a bit later: "What is it that makes this understanding of being possible at all? Whence—that is, from what already given horizon—do we understand the like of being?" (GA 24:21/16). But why does an enabling source, a Whence that empowers, have to be described as a horizon? As we have seen, the pivotal §65 of BT amply describes original temporality as a source, "dynamo" ("wellspring" is the term favored by the poetically inclined later Heidegger) of sense-giving without resorting to the language of "horizon" at all. But in SS 1927, this same source, the *Zeitlichkeit* (small t) of existence, is regarded as a kind of inner horizon whose outer face at once projects the *Temporalität* (Big T) of Being, in a reversal that amounts to a tautological equation of tenses distinguished only by a translation of the Teutonic tenses into their Latin equivalents. The etymologically telling *Gegen-wart* thus becomes *Praesenz*. The fact that Heidegger never even gets around to translating the other two tenses into the Latinates of *Praeteritum* and *Futurum* tells us how far this language game was carried before it foundered. The fault lies not in the tautology—identity philosophy from Parmenides to phenomenology after all always comes down to a *solus ipse* like "Being is"—but in the metaphorology.

In SS 1927, Heidegger depicts the extrapolation of ecstases toward horizons as the (one?) formal, "logical" conclusion following from the assumption of ex-sistence, which, as an ever unfinished out-for its can-be, came to define the project of the last draft of BT. Ex-sistence belongs in the chain of formal indications that stretch from the triple-sensed schematism of intentionality in 1920 to transcendence in 1927–29. All three formal indications are repeatedly invoked together in SS 1927, in a renewed open display by Heidegger, contrary to BT itself, of at least the formal roots of his terminology, as he tackles the traditional theses of being phenomenologically. Ecstasis and existence "hang together" (GA 24:377/267; 170/241) etymologically as a "guiding clue" connecting time with human being in their corresponding "outering" character from the immediate unity of human experience. When the formal need for horizon is first invoked, the stress on its possibility is quite clear, in keeping with existence as being-out-for a can-be. But it leads to a somewhat nonintuitive sense of horizon, whose only sense of limit is in its being de-fined by the ecstasis into a specific "schematic prefiguration" (435/ 306). This is presumably further delimited in being inescapably related to, and so modifiable by, the other two "equiprimordial" ecstases. The horizonal unity is then presumably the result of the presumably compatible interlocking of the three patterns of possibility. The assurance of unity can actually only come from the prior ecstatic unity, which is itself achieved ontically, in the authenticating holistic move of existence. Formally, there is no unity at all in an "outering" movement which is never finished, always on the way to possibility. This formal aspect emerged from the recurrent suggestion that the outermost possibility of death in some sense takes us beyond the secure confines of the world as our possession and throws us back upon ourselves in the sole movement of "going about" our being. But now, the new formal indication of "transcendence of the world" seems to take all that back. For "transcendence means: to understand oneself from a world" (425/300). Thus, a temporal horizon is derived by trading off "something like" a world horizon. Thinking too spatially about time is one of Heidegger's critiques of philosophers like Bergson. And yet he himself seems to lapse into it here, precisely in the early going of his development. Why does a "condition of possibility" have to be regarded as a horizon? This Kantian phase of Heidegger's development, fairly well publicized for decades through Heidegger's own "publication blitz" of 1929, can now be examined in relation to the hitherto unpublished genealogical sources which prompted it. Closer to his sources, fresh from his discovery of a philosophical Promised Land, the young Heidegger had a cruder, rawer, but perhaps still fruitful way of putting his questions.

Erotetic Epilogue

My work is directed toward a radicalization of ancient ontology and at the same time toward a universal structuring of this ontology in relation to the region of history. The fundament of this problematic is developed by starting from the "subject," properly understood as the human Dasein, so that with the radicalizing of this approach the true motives of German idealism may likewise come into their own. Augustine, Luther, Kierkegaard are *philosophically* essential for the cultivation of a more radical understanding-of-Dasein, Dilthey for a radical interpretation of the "historical world," Aristotle and scholasticism for the strict formulation of certain ontological *problems*. All this in a methodology guided by the idea of a scientific philosophy as it has been grounded by Husserl, not without the influence of the logical investigations and philosophy of science of H. Rickert and E. Lask. My work has no ambitions toward a worldview or a theology, but it may well contain approaches and intentions in the direction of an ontological founding of Christian theology as a science. This should suffice to give you an idea of what I am after.

So writes one German academic to another, as Heidegger, on the last day of the Year of Our Lord 1927, responds to Rudolf Bultmann's query on how he himself would, at this stage in his development, write a brief encyclopedia article entitled "Heidegger."[1] Bultmann himself loads the cards somewhat by initially suggesting to his friend that he should not just cite the dates of his vita, "but also your relationship to Husserl and the motives of your philosophy which stem from Luther, Kierkegaard, and Dilthey as well as from Aristotle, Augustine, and scholasticism. As to the relationship to theology, you might perhaps want to say no more than, say, that the motives of the theological tradition are taken up by you because of your relationship to medieval philosophy" (December 29, 1927). Bultmann then took Heidegger's fuller epistolary statement and published it almost verbatim under his own name in the lexicon, *Die Religion in Geschichte und Gegenwart* ([2]1928). The article concludes with a bibliography of just two books, the habilitation of 1916 and "Sein und Zeit I, 1927," serving to demarcate the open decade without publication as the temporal space in which these listed tendencies worked themselves out into BT. Heidegger for his part found the whole thing somewhat ludicrous, to have himself taken apart and put together again in a list of motives, and objectionable, since each would construe a "mere list of names and directions" differently.

The *seriatim* enumeration nevertheless provides a relatively accurate albeit condensed portrayal, direct from Heidegger himself, of the Genesis Story which we have just traversed, though perhaps a bit out of chronological order and certainly reduced to a single unemphatic level of influences: Husserl, Rickert, Lask, German idealism, Aristotle, scholasticism, Dilthey, Augustine, Luther, Kierkegaard, Aristotle again ("ancient ontology"). Conspicuously absent in this particular letter exchange are Eckhart, Paul, and Schleiermacher. But Heidegger, contrary to Bultmann's suggestion, does realign his religious influences by making Augustine first, in the same staccato mentioning "Luther, Kierkegaard," while underscoring *their philosophical* contribution toward radicalizing the understanding-of-Dasein. Significantly, Heidegger's other friend, Jaspers, is not mentioned at all. After all, "Existenzphilosophie" is not yet in circulation as a concept, let alone as a "movement," and so does not even become a topic of the 1928 edition of this encyclopedia.[2]

Bultmann is clearly impressed by the achievement of the book *Sein und Zeit, Erste Hälfte,* and is now seeking to find himself, his own theological impulses and direction, in that book. It is not only being discussed in some early press reviews and in the classroom (Scheler's, Hartmann's), but has also become a heated topic of conversation on campus. Their correspondence, in the scant eight months since the book had appeared, thus revolves around the initial reactions to it by colleagues and mutual acquaintances, by the first reviewers in the German press as well as the reviews anticipated from the theology and philosophy journals. Not only is Bultmann intensely interested in finding his way through that difficult book with some degree of comprehension. He is also eager to know when its sequel, *die Zweite Hälfte,* will appear. But Heidegger is now in no hurry to publish, for one thing feeling that what he had already written was not really being read, "in part out of annoyance over the fact that it does not tread the beaten paths, in part because the topics dealt with are uncomfortable in their content." He then adds, "I have at the very least proven that I can get something into print" (October 6, 1927). He also plans to improve upon his manuscript of the Second Half (up to four hundred book pages: see Appendix C) "by rewriting the whole thing once more, since some important points are not at all worked out yet" (ibid.). No signs of unease yet, still flush with the old creativity, full of confidence that he will achieve his goal of a scientific philosophy, having now seen the way, through Kant (his course at the time), to project Being itself onto the horizon of Time. The unease will surface only toward the end of the following semester, as Heidegger was preparing to leave Marburg to assume the chair in Freiburg being vacated by the retiring Husserl.

The details of this conceptual development will be the substance of another story, the downfall of BT. But at this stage, at the end of 1927, BT is still clearly in its ascendancy for Heidegger and his peers, and for us as well, as we ourselves proceed into the Year of the Force 2001.

Wilhelm Dilthey's son-in-law, Georg Misch, who had played a direct part in the story of Heidegger's rise in 1922, is busy late in 1928 writing the first of the installments of his profound assessment of BT from the perspective of the then equally prevalent "life philosophy" of the Dilthey school. He introduces his problem with the following opening lines:

> Long awaited, Heidegger's book *Sein und Zeit*, which appeared more than a year ago in a volume of the Yearbook put out by Husserl's circle of phenomenologists, has generated an unusual amount of philosophical excitement. One reads this rigorous, difficult, systematic work and is almost palpably drawn into its contents. It took perhaps a decade for Husserl's *Logische Untersuchungen* to become generally recognized in its significance, at which point it then quickly became a classic work; the wide influence that Dilthey now enjoys, beyond the circle of his closest students, came only after his death, and this only slowly with any kind of depth. This single book, however, *struck like lightning*.
>   ... To be sure, Heidegger's work also clearly shows in its filigree the lines that connect it with the entire development of philosophy in the last thirty years. ... So now, out of the older circle of phenomenologists comes a review of the book which refutes its claim to be "revolutionary" and declares: "It is in truth but the synthesis of all of the vital tendencies of philosophy which are current today" (M. Beck, *Philos. Hefte* 1, 1928). And one could easily multiply, if so inclined, all the references that this review gives to the "presuppositions" in Husserl and Dilthey, Aristotle and Augustine, Nietzsche and Kierkegaard. But one will in this way never really get at the *nerve of that undertaking*. ... "I believe I have found the road upon which philosophy can ascend to the rank of an evident science": this line from Fichte can easily be Heidegger's. But he is more cautious. Corresponding to the probing research character of the undertaking, which Husserl has in common with Dilthey, Heidegger declares in the end (SZ 437) that the "present investigation is still only *under way*."[3]

This *Mischreaktion* to the book will also have to be taken into account in our sequel, including that of Misch himself. Misch was in a better position than most to judge "where Heidegger was coming from." For he happens to have copies of Heidegger's still unpublished texts, the "Jaspers Review" (1920) and the "Aristotle *Einleitung*" (Oct. 1922), which he had received as part of the effort to get Heidegger appointed to Husserl's old chair in Göttingen in 1922. But for all that, in his lengthy and penetrating study of Heidegger's work in 1928–29, he himself never gets at the "nerve of the undertaking" of BT, its "probing research character," namely the assessment of the power of "formal indication" in accessing and expressing the full immediacy of human experience. In all fairness to Misch, Heidegger never openly or fully explained, beyond his classroom (but even there, we have the infamous *cursus interruptus* of WS 1920–21), this most crucial aspect of his undertaking: its motivation in a most peculiar "object," thus its character, strategies, ontological intent, and especially its genealogy from a problem situation at once venerable and modern. Even Heidegger's own "name-dropping" of figures in a litany of historical "influences" in the letter to Bultmann gives us only a sketchy sense of the concepts, and certainly not the precise "hermeneutic situation" from which these had "first sprung" (*Ur-sprung*), which led to the book BT. Bultmann's lexicon article would therefore only add to the reductionistic manner and leveling tendency of the initial reception of BT.[4]

In that letter to Bultmann, the first real locus that catches the attention of a genealogical eye is in the variants of the word "radical" (used three times), especially in the cultivation "of a more radical understanding-of-Dasein" (*eines radikaleren Daseinsverständnisses*). Everything tends to fall into place around that core: Dilthey's "radical interpretation of the historical world" goes beyond the meaningful context of the world, essential as it is, to the very movement of historicality as the most radical movement of understanding itself, this nonreflexive return upon itself in simple immediacy which is at once possibility. Thus the "radicalization of ancient ontology," for all its talk of being as persistent presence, is to be made compatible with the "universal structuring of it in relation to the region of history," where the past finds its project in the future in a sense of time which is not at all in keeping with traditional ontology. Clearly, a different sense of time is developing in conjunction, or better, in identity with this deepening sense of "understanding." Perhaps it would have been superfluous for Heidegger to mention "Paul" to Bultmann (they had done a seminar together on "Paul's Ethics") as a fourth on his list of theologians, but it would have been a genealogically truer list.

If we look further, we see that Heidegger's somewhat methodological list, on how to get at this rudimentary historical dimension of the understanding of being, has its more conceptual translations: Rickert's heterothesis thesis and its underlying sense of the equiprimordiality of the characters of being already speaks to the convertibility of the medieval transcendentals (Natorp would have appreciated these connections far more intuitively); Lask's many insights, from categorial immersion to a sense of the ontological difference translated into this concrete realm of being; the scholastic analogy of being and its gramma(on)tology mediated into the KNS-Schema with the help of Lask's (i.e., not just Husserl's) distinction between reflexive and constitutive categories. In the conflation, the many-sided richness of Aristotle's contributions tends to get lost in the imitators who follow. But all in all, despite the superficial wraps of a "history of influence," the letter lies close to the genealogical record as we know it. Undoubtedly the reference to "Luther" meant far more to the two scholars than we have been able to uncover. On this point, eavesdropping on their conversations might open new vistas.

Of course, we have only the systematic portion of BT, and for that matter, only a portion of that. Does this still superficial "history of influences," in which BT was first received and even explained by Heidegger himself, translate into the deep structures of a history of being and bare the needs and precise loci for its destruction? Kant, for example, is never explicitly mentioned by Heidegger and so located within the topic of the "subject" inherited from German idealism. But of the several notes that point beyond to the never-published Second Half (SZ 319n, 363n, 427n), the most tantalizing by far is not historical at all, but rather the reference to a specific chapter (II) in the missing Third Division which would have discussed the temporality of discourse, the origin of its "tenses" (*Tempora*: why Heidegger first looked for "categories" called *Temporalien* rather than *Existenzialien*), the ontological sense of the "is," so that "we might clarify how 'meaning arises' and make the possibility of concept formation ontologically comprehensible" (SZ 349n; these footnotes were dropped or replaced in the later reprinting). This clearly takes us to the heart of the matter of Heidegger's formally indicative hermeneutics of the immediacies of human experience, the ultimate need to spell out the gramma-onto-logy that thereby ensues. The book BT itself testifies to this shift in language game, where prepositional phrases become nouns and the adjectives are really thinly disguised adverbials of the verb of being.

But first a more propaedeutic language game: could Heidegger not explain, could he not give an "indication of the hermeneutic situation" from which he had sprung into the limelight, "flashed like lightning," could he not expeditiously communicate the most radical impulses of BT to peers like Misch and Bultmann? Or was he still too much "underway" to properly pause and look back over the hitherto untrodden path which he had just trodden? After all, when his old student, Karl Löwith, complained about losing the more ontic hermeneutics of facticity in ontological formalization in BT, Heidegger's reply was both systematic and historical, as well as precise and focused. The process of going all out after the factic in order to make facticity into a radical problem was abetted more specifically, within the Aristotelian-scholastic framework, by Duns Scotus and what he stood for, namely, subtle formality applied to the most concrete immediacy.[5] But the habilitation therefore also took a closer look at the "speculative" grammar that might articulate these concretions of "I – here – now – this," which Husserl called "occasional expressions" (LU I, §26) and included among them the impersonals! Heidegger, circa 1921–23, accordingly devoted more than one seminar precisely to these Husserlian texts (see Appendix B), and undoubtedly elaborated on the indicative power of such impersonals, and their ability to point out the sheer happening of concretely lived wholes. This refers especially to the verbal particularity of simply "being here," but applies just as well to a book like BT, which "struck like lightning": *Es blitzt!* (an example from 1914: FS 114).

The closing of the publication gap of 1916–26 thus opens a panorama of new genealogically retrospective questions not especially raised before in the "Heidegger literature." BT can now be understood genealogically. One is not in the same dilemma as its first reviewers. How now to "review" a book like BT? How shall we repeat all that has gone before, which, according to the rules of the game of repetition established by Heidegger himself, means to review it at another ("deeper"?) level. Our Story has come to an abrupt halt, and a section-by-section genealogy of BT is out of the question at this point. The Sequel recounting the "publication blitz" of 1929 will raise a host of new questions, both retrospective and prospective. A quick look at this new story will illustrate how both directions now belong inescapably together.

We find Heidegger at the end of 1927 thoroughly convinced of being within the reach of the goal of a scientific philosophy. The bold claims induced by the spell of the Kantian transcendental philosophy apparently lead Heidegger to believe that something like a Kantian schematism of human existence is capable of definitively articulating the evasive immediacy of the human situation, that is, of "saying the unsayable." This confidence first becomes fully transparent in the extreme statements made in the course of SS 1927, which coincides with the appearance of BT. After vacillating since KNS 1919 over whether the *pre*theoretical venture of phenomenology is anything at all like a "strict science," Heidegger in SS 1927 unequivocally responds in the affirmative. For, just as the particular sciences must objectify their entities against the horizon of their Being, so philosophy, if it too is to become a science, must "objectify Being itself" (!) against the horizon of time (GA 24: §22b).

It is only with the "turn" two years later that Heidegger will undo this very un-Heideggerian way of speaking! Ever since KNS, when Heidegger first discovered and named the unique subject matter of his thought, he had frequent occasion to observe the almost contradictory nature of philosophy: As the primal science seeking to articulate the pretheoretical subject matter of all the sciences, philosophy is like no other science, for it is a nontheoretical science, forcing us to the very limits of science. In view of its ambition to overtake and keep to our vital origins, this original science is not really a science in the usual sense of the word, but "more." Thus, in early 1929, when Heidegger definitively abandons the project of making philosophy into a strict science, he observes that philosophy is not a science not out of lack but instead out of excess, since it springs from the ever superabundant and ebullient "happening of Dasein" itself.

With the "turn," the exaggerated claims for the scientific character of philosophy give way to the judgment that the book BT was an aberrant way from the one topic of philosophy and thought. And when Heidegger first realizes that BT was a failed project, he then re-turns to earlier insights left unpursued in order to begin again. This re-turn is the real meaning of his self-professed and much discussed "turn." In 1928–29, the impersonal "Es weltet" resounds again, after a decade's respite. In the thirties, "Es ereignet sich" reappears with an ever-increasing insistence. In fact, as early as SS 1928, in his seminar on Aristotle's *Physics*, Heidegger finds the very *Eignung* of *Ereignis*, the appropriative capacity of the E-vent, in Aristotle's δύναμις, understood as the very locus of a movement in movement, unfinished, and "underway," like human existence in 1927 and the "primal something" of KNS.[6]

Our story must therefore conclude by following the same trajectory, going beyond BT by going back to its most incipient beginning in KNS 1919. Could it be that the hermeneutic breakthrough of 1919 already contains *in ovo* everything essential that came to light in the later Heidegger's thought? Could it be that there is nothing essentially new in the later Heidegger after the turn, for all is to be found at least incipiently in that initial breakthrough of the early Heidegger? Could it be that not only BT but all of Heidegger can be reduced to this First Genesis, the hermeneutic breakthrough to the topic in KNS 1919? Heidegger seems to suggest as much by using Hölderlin's line, "For as you began, so will you remain" (US 93/7) to place his entire career of thought under a single "guiding star." Such questions call for the closer examination of the very first genesis of BT which has been begun here, of how Heidegger first found his lifetime topic and the initial terms in which it was evoked.

APPENDIXES

To underscore the BCD methodology of fact-gathering that forms the basis of this Genesis Story, there is deliberately no Appendix A, only Appendixes B, C, and D. See the Introduction above for further explanation.

APPENDIX B

Heideggers Lehrveranstaltungen, 1915–30[1]
(German and English)

27. Juli 1915		Philosophische Fakultät erteilt Heidegger die venia legendi für Philosophie.[2]
WS 1915–16	Vorlesung	Die Grundlinien der antiken und scholastischen Philosophie (zweistündig).[3]
	Seminar	Über Kant, Prolegomena.
SS 1916	Vorlesung	Der deutsche Idealismus (zweistündig).[4]
	Seminar	Übungen über Texte aus den logischen Schriften des Aristoteles (mit Engelbert Krebs).
WS 1916–17	Vorlesung	Grundfragen der Logik (zweistündig).[5]

1917–19　　Aus formellen Gründen waren vom Privatdozenten Dr. Heidegger als "Kriegsteilnehmer" die folgenden zweistündigen Veranstaltungen im Vorlesungsverzeichnis angekündigt: SS 1917, Hegel; WS 1917–18, Plato; SS 1918 und WS 1918–19, Lotze und die Entwicklung der modernen Logik. Aber sie wurden nicht abgehalten, weil 1) zum SS 1917 Josef Geyser den Philosophischen Lehrstuhl II übernahm, weil 2) vom Januar bis Mai 1918 der Landsturmmann Heidegger zur militärischen Ausbildung am Truppenübungsplatz Heuberg kaserniert, vom

		Juli bis August in Berlin-Charlottenburg als Luftschiffer in den meteorologischen Grundkenntnissen weiter ausgebildet, vom Ende August bis Mitte November bei der Frontwetterwarte vor Verdun stationiert wurde.[6]
KNS 1919	Vorlesung	Die Idee der Philosophie und das Weltanschauungsproblem (zweistündig). [GA 56/57][7]
SS 1919	Vorlesung	Phänomenologie und transzendentale Wertphilosophie (einstündig). [GA 56/57]
	Vorlesung	Über das Wesen der Universität und des akademischen Studiums (einstündig). [GA 56/57]
	Seminar	Einführung in die Phänomenologie im Anschluß an Descartes, Meditationes.
WS 1919–20	Vorlesung	Grundprobleme der Phänomenologie (zweistündig). [GA 58][8]
	Seminar	Übungen im Anschluß an Natorp, Allgemeine Psychologie.
Mitte April 1920	Vorträge	Zwei Stunden über Oswald Spengler bei einer "wissenschaftlichen Woche" in Wiesbaden.[9]
SS 1920	Vorlesung	Phänomenologie der Anschauung und des Ausdrucks. Theorie der philosophischen Begriffsbildung (zweistündig). [GA 59/60]
	Seminar	Kolloquium im Anschluß an die Vorlesung.
WS 1920–21	Vorlesung	Einleitung in die Phänomenologie der Religion (zweistündig).
	Seminar	Phänomenologische Übungen für Anfänger im Anschluß an Descartes, Meditationes.[10]
SS 1921	Vorlesung	Augustinus und der Neuplatonismus (dreistündig). [GA 59/60]
	Seminar	Phänomenologische Übungen für Anfänger im Anschluß an Aristoteles, de anima.[11]

WS 1921–22	Vorlesung	Phänomenologische Interpretationen zu Aristoteles. Einführung in die phänomenologische Forschung. *Einleitung*. (zweistündig). [GA 61][12]
	Seminar	Phänomenologische Übungen für Anfänger im Anschluß an Husserl, Logische Untersuchungen II.[13]
SS 1922	Vorlesung	Phänomenologische Interpretationen zu Aristoteles. Ontologie und Logik (vierstündig). [GA 62][14]
	Seminar	Phänomenologische Übungen für Anfänger im Anschluß an Husserl, Logische Untersuchungen II, 2. Untersuchung.
WS 1922–23	Seminar	Übungen über: Phänomenologische Interpretationen zu Aristoteles (Nikomachische Ethik VI; De anima; Metaphysik VII) (privatissime, zweistündig).[15]
	Seminar	Phänomenologische Übungen für Anfänger im Anschluß an Husserl, Ideen I.
SS 1923	Vorlesung	Ontologie. Hermeneutik der Faktizität (einstündig). [GA 63]
	Seminar	Phänomenologische Übungen für Anfänger im Anschluß an Aristoteles, Ethica Nicomachea.
	Seminar	Kolloquium über die theologischen Grundlagen von Kant, Religion innerhalb der Grenzen der bloßen Vernunft, nach ausgewählte Texten, für Fortgeschrittene (mit Ebbinghaus).[16]
	Seminar	[Übungen über: Phänomenologische Interpretationen zu Aristoteles {Fortsetzung}]

PHILIPPS-UNIVERSITÄT ZU MARBURG

WS 1923–24	Vorlesung	Einführung in die phänomenologische Forschung (vierstündig). [GA 17][17]
	Seminar	Phänomenologische Übung für Anfänger: Husserl, Logische Untersuchungen II.1.
	Seminar	Phänomenologische Übung für Fortgeschrittene: Aristoteles, Physik B.
7. Dez. 1923	Vortrag	Aufgaben und Wege der phänomenologischen Forschung. (Vortrag in der Hamburgischen Ortsgruppe der Kantgesellschaft).[18]
SS 1924	Vorlesung	Grundbegriffe der aristotelischen Philosophie (vierstündig). [GA 18][19]
	Seminar	Fortgeschrittene: Die Hochscholastik und Aristoteles (Thomas, de ente et essentia; Cajetan, de nominum analogia).
25. Juli 1924	Vortrag	Der Begriff der Zeit (Vortrag vor der Marburger Theologenschaft).[20]
WS 1924–25	Vorlesung	Interpretation Platonischer Dialoge (Σοφίστης, Φίληβος) (vierstündig). [GA 19]
	Seminar	Übungen zur Ontologie des Mittelalters (Thomas, de ente et essentia, summa contra gentiles).
1.-8. Dez. 1924	Vortrag	Dasein und Wahrsein nach Aristoteles. (Interpretation von Buch VI der Nikomach. Ethik.) (Vortrag vor den Ortsgruppen Elberfeld-Barmen, Köln und Dortmund in der Landesgruppe "Westdeutsches Industriegebiet" der Kant-Gesellschaft).[21]

16.-21. April 1925	Vorträge	Wilhelm Diltheys Forschungsarbeit und der gegenwärtige Kampf um eine historische Weltanschauung (eine Reihe von 10 Vorträgen für das Publikum in Kassel im Rahmen der "Kurhessischen Gesellschaft für Kunst und Wissenschaft": Die "Kasseler Vorträge.")[22]
SS 1925	Vorlesung	Geschichte des Zeitbegriffs. Prolegomena zur Phänomenologie von Geschichte und Natur (vierstündig). [GA 20]
	Seminar	Anfangsübungen im Anschluß an Descartes, Meditationes.
WS 1925–26	Vorlesung	Logik (vierstündig). [GA 21][23]
	Seminar	Anfänger: Phänomenologische Übungen (Kant, Kritik der reinen Vernunft).
	Seminar	Fortgeschrittene: Phänomenologische Übungen (Hegel, Logik, I. Buch).[24]
SS 1926	Vorlesung	Grundbegriffe der antiken Philosophie[25] (vierstündig). [GA 22]
	Seminar	Übungen über Geschichte und historische Erkenntnis im Anschluß an J. B. Droysen, Grundriß der Historik.
24. Mai 1926	Vortrag	Vom Wesen der Wahrheit (in der Akademischen Vereinigung Marburg)[26]
WS 1926–27	Vorlesung	Geschichte der Philosophie von Thomas v. Aquin bis Kant (vierstündig). [GA 23]
	Seminar	Übungen im Anschluß an die Vorlesung.
4. Dez. 1926	Vortrag	Begriff und Entwicklung der phänomenologischen Forschung (im Marburger kulturwissenschaftlichen Kränzchen).

SS 1927	Vorlesung	Die Grundprobleme der Phäno-menologie (vierstündig). [GA 24]
	Seminar	Fortgeschrittene: Die Ontolo-gie des Aristoteles und Hegels Logik.
8. Juli 1927	Vortrag	Phänomenologie und Theolo-gie (vor der evangelischen Theologenschaft in Tü-bingen).[27]
WS 1927–28	Vorlesung	Phänomenologische Interpreta-tion von Kants Kritik der rei-nen Vernunft (vierstündig). [GA25]
	Seminar	Phänomenologische Übungen für Anfänger über Begriff und Begriffsbildung.
	Seminar	Phänomenologische Übungen für Fortgeschritttene (Schel-ling, Über das Wesen der menschlichen Freiheit).
14. Feb. 1928	Vortrag	Theologie und Philosophie (in Marburg).[28]
SS 1928	Vorlesung	Logik (vierstündig). [GA 26]
	Seminar	Phänomenologische Übungen zu Aristoteles, Physik III.
Mitte Sept. 1928	Vorträge	Zum Thema Kant und die Me-taphysik, an dem Ferienhoch-schulkurse der Herdergesell-schaft zu Riga.[29]

ALBERT-LUDWIGS-UNIVERSITÄT ZU FREIBURG

WS 1928–29	Vorlesung	Einleitung in die Philosophie (vierstündig). [GA 27]
	Seminar	Phänomenologische Übungen für Anfänger: Kant, Grundle-gung zur Metaphysik der Sitten.
	Seminar	Phänomenologische Übungen für Fortgeschrittene: Die onto-logischen Grundsätze und das Kategorienproblem.[30]

24. Januar 1929	Vortrag	Philosophische Anthropologie und Metaphysik des Daseins (in der Kant-Gesellschaft Frankfurt).
17.-27. März 1929	Vorträge	Kants Kritik der reinen Vernunft und die Aufgabe einer Grundlegung der Metaphysik. Dazu: Disputation in einer Arbeitsgemeinschaft zwischen Cassirer und Heidegger (II. Davoser Hochschulkurse).[31]
8. April 1929	Festrede	Edmund Husserl zum siebzigsten Geburtstag. (mit der Überreichung der Festschrift in der Aula der Universität Freiburg).[32]
SS 1929	Vorlesung	Der Deutsche Idealismus und die philosophische Problemlage der Gegenwart (vierstündig). [GA 28]
	Vorlesung	Einführung in das akademische Studium (einstündig).[33]
	Seminar	Anfänger: Über Idealismus und Realismus im Anschluß an die Hauptvorlesungen (Hegels "Vorrede" zur Phänomenologie des Geistes).
	Seminar	Fortgeschrittene: Vom Wesen des Lebens mit besonderer Berücksichtigung von Aristoteles, de anima, de animalium motione und de animalium incessu.
24. Juli 1929	Vortrag	Was ist Metaphysik? (Antrittsvorlesung in der Aula der Universität Freiburg).[34]
WS 1929–30	Vorlesung	Die Grundbegriffe der Metaphysik. Welt- Endlichkeit—Vereinzelung (vierstündig). [GA 29/30][35]
	Seminar	Für mittlere und höhere Semester: Über Gewißheit und Wahrheit im Anschluß an Descartes und Leibniz.

21.-22. März 1930	Vorträge	1. Die heutige Problemlage der Philosophie. 2. Hegel und das Problem der Metaphysik. (zwei Vorträge in der wissenschaftlichen Vereinigung zu Amsterdam).[36]
SS 1930	Vorlesung	Vom Wesen der menschlichen Freiheit. Einleitung in die Philosophie (vierstündig). [GA 31]
	Seminar	Anfänger: Ausgewählte Kapitel aus Kants Kritik der Urteilskraft.
14. Juli 1930	Vortrag	Vom Wesen der Wahrheit (am "Kongress der führenden Badener in Wissenschaft, Kunst und Wirtschaft" in Karlsruhe).[37]
8. Oktober 1930	Vortrag	Vom Wesen der Wahrheit (in der Philosophischen Gesellschaft Bremen).[38]
26. Oktober 1930	Vortrag	Augustinus: Quid est tempus? Confessiones lib. XI (im Kloster Beuron).[39]
WS 1930–31	Vorlesung	Hegels Phänomenologie des Geistes (zweistündig). [GA 32]
	Seminar	Augustinus, Confessiones XI (de tempore).
	Seminar	Fortgeschrittene: Platons Παρμενίδης (mit Wolfgang Schadewaldt).
5. Dezember 1930	Vortrag	Philosophieren und Glauben. Das Wesen der Wahrheit (vor der Evangelisch-theologischen Fachschaft in Marburg).[40]
11. Dezember 1930	Vortrag	Vom Wesen der Wahrheit (in Freiburg).[41]

Heidegger's Teaching Activities, 1915–30[1]

July 27, 1915	graduation	Philosophical Faculty grants Heidegger the license to teach in philosophy.[2]
WS 1915–16	lecture-course	The Basic Trends of Ancient and Scholastic Philosophy (2 hours).[3]
	seminar	On Kant's Prolegomena.
SS 1916	course	German Idealism (2 hours).[4]
	seminar	Practicum on Texts from Aristotle's Logical Writings (with Engelbert Krebs).
WS 1916–17	course	Basic Questions of Logic (2 hours).[5]
1917–19		As a "serviceman," Docent Heidegger is nevertheless formally mandated to announce the following 2-hour courses in the university catalogue: SS 1917, Hegel; WS 1917–18, Plato; SS 1918 and WS 1918–19, Lotze and the Development of Modern Logic. But none of these courses were taught, since 1) Josef Geyser was appointed to Freiburg's Chair of Catholic Philosophy in SS 1917, and since 2) Reservist Heidegger is called up for basic training at Camp Heuberg from January through May 1918, for further training as Airman in meteorology in Berlin-Charlottenburg in July and August, and

		is stationed with the Front Weather Watch in the Verdun sector from the end of August to mid-November.[6]
KNS 1919	course	The Idea of Philosophy and the Problem of Worldviews (2 hours). [GA 56/57][7]
SS 1919	course	Phenomenology and Transcendental Philosophy of Value (1 hour). [GA 56/57]
	course	On the Essence of the University and Academic Studies (1 hour). [GA 56/57]
	seminar	Introduction to Phenomenology in Conjunction with Descartes's Meditations.
WS 1919–20	course	Basic Problems of Phenomenology (2 hours). [GA58][8]
	seminar	Practicum in Conjunction with Natorp's General Psychology.
Mid-April 1920	lectures	Two lectures on Oswald Spengler at a "Scientific Week" in Wiesbaden.[9]
SS 1920	course	Phenomenology of Intuition and Expression: Theory of Philosophical Concept Formation (2 hours). [GA 59/60]
	seminar	Colloquium in Conjunction with the Course.
WS 1920–21	course	Introduction to the Phenomenology of Religion (2 hours).
	seminar	Phenomenological Practicum for Beginners in Conjunction with Descartes's Meditations.[10]
SS 1921	course	Augustine and Neoplatonism (3 hours). [GA 59/60]
	seminar	Phenomenological Practicum for Beginners in Conjunction with Aristotle's De Anima.[11]
WS 1921–22	course	Phenomenological Interpretations to Aristotle: Introduction to Phenomenological Research, *Einleitung* (2 hours). [GA 61][12]

	seminar	Phenomenological Practicum for Beginners in Conjunction with Husserl's Logical Investigations II.[13]
SS 1922	course	Phenomenological Interpretations to Aristotle: Ontology and Logic (4 hours). [GA 62][14]
	seminar	Phenomenological Practicum for Beginners in Conjunction with Husserl's Logical Investigations, Second Investigation.
WS 1922–23	seminar	Practicum: Phenomenological Interpretations to Aristotle (Nicomachean Ethics 6, De Anima, Metaphysics 7) (private, 2 hours).[15]
	seminar	Phenomenological Practicum for Beginners in Conjunction with Husserl's Ideen I.
SS 1923	course	Ontology: Hermeneutics of Facticity (1 hour). [GA 63]
	seminar	Phenomenological Practicum for Beginners in Conjunction with Aristotle's Nicomachean Ethics.
	seminar	Colloquium on the Theological Foundations of Kant's Religion within the Limits of Reason Alone (selected texts; for advanced students; with Ebbinghaus).[16]
	seminar	[Practicum: Phenomenological Interpretations to Aristotle (continued from WS 1922–23)]

UNIVERSITY OF MARBURG

| WS 1923–24 | course | Introduction to Phenomenological Research (4 hours). [GA 17][17] |
| | seminar | Phenomenological Practicum for Beginners: Husserl, Logical Investigations II. 1. |

	seminar	Phenomenological Practicum for Advanced Students: Aristotle, Physics B.
December 7, 1923	lecture	Tasks and Ways of Phenomenological Research (lecture to the Hamburg group of the Kant Society).[18]
SS 1924	course	Basic Concepts of Aristotelian Philosophy (4 hours). [GA 18][19]
	seminar	Advanced Students: The High Scholastics and Aristotle (Thomas, On Being and Essence; Cajetan, On the Analogy of Names).
July 25, 1924	lecture	The Concept of Time (lecture at the Marburg Theologians' Society).[20]
WS 1924–25	course	Interpretation of Platonic Dialogues (Sophist, Philebus) (4 hours). [GA 19]
	seminar	Practicum on the Ontology of the Middle Ages (Thomas, On Being and Essence, Summation against the Gentiles).
December 1–8, 1924	lecture	Being-here and Being-true according to Aristotle: Interpretation of Book 6 of the Nicomachean Ethics (lecture for the local groups of Elberfeld-Barmen, Cologne, and Dortmund in the regional group "West German Industrial Region" of the Kant Society).[21]
April 16–21, 1925	lectures	Wilhelm Dilthey's Research Work and the Present Struggle for a Historical Worldview. A series of ten popular lectures in Kassel at the Society for Art and Science of the Electorate of Hesse: The "Kassel lectures."[22]
	course	History of the Concept of

		Time: Prolegomena toward the Phenomenology of History and Nature (4 hours). [GA 20]
	seminar	Beginners' Practicum in Conjunction with Descartes's Meditations.
WS 1925–26	course	Logic (4 hours). [GA 21][23]
	seminar	Beginners: Phenomenological Practicum (Kant, Critique of Pure Reason).
	seminar	Advanced Students: Phenomenological Practicum (Hegel, Logic, Book 1).[24]
SS 1926	course	Basic Concepts of Ancient Philosophy (4 hours). [GA 22][25]
	seminar	Practicum on History and Historical Knowledge in Conjunction with J. B. Droysen's Basic Outline of Historical Science.
May 24, 1926	lecture	On the Essence of Truth (in the Academic Union at Marburg).[26]
WS 1926–27	course	History of Philosophy from Thomas Aquinas to Kant (4 hours). [GA 23]
	seminar	Practicum in Conjunction with the Course.
December 4, 1926	lecture	Conception and Development of Phenomenological Research (at the Marburg Cultural Science Circle).
SS 1927	course	The Basic Problems of Phenomenology (4 hours). [GA 24]
	seminar	Advanced Students: The Ontology of Aristotle and Hegel's Logic.
July 8, 1927	lecture	Phenomenology and Theology (at the Evangelical Theologians' Society in Tübingen).[27]
WS 1927–28	course	Phenomenological Interpretation of Kant's Critique of Pure Reason (4 hours). [GA 25]

	seminar	Phenomenological Practicum for Beginners on Concept and Concept Formation.
	seminar	Phenomenological Practicum for Advanced Students (Schelling, On the Essence of Human Freedom).
February 14, 1928	lecture	Theology and Philosophy (in Marburg).[28]
SS 1928	course	Logic (4 hours). [GA 26]
	seminar	Phenomenological Practicum to Aristotle, Physics 3.
Mid-Sept. 1928	lectures	On "Kant and Metaphysics," at the Summer University Courses of the Herder Society in Riga.[29]

UNIVERSITY OF FREIBURG

WS 1928–29	course	Introduction to Philosophy (4 hours). [GA 27]
	seminar	Phenomenological Practicum for Beginners: Kant, Foundation of the Metaphysics of Morals.
	seminar	Phenomenological Practicum for Advanced Students: The Ontological Principles and the Problem of Categories.[30]
January 24, 1929	lecture	Philosophical Anthropology and Metaphysics of Dasein (at the Kant Society of Frankfurt).
March 17–27, 1929	lectures	Kant's *Critique of Pure Reason* and the Task of a Foundation of Metaphysics. Also: Disputation in a Working Group between Cassirer and Heidegger (Second Davos University Courses).[31]
April 8, 1929	speech	To Edmund Husserl on his Seventieth Birthday (with the presentation of the Festschrift in the University Auditorium at Freiburg).[32]

SS 1929	course	German Idealism and the Present Problem Situation of Philosophy (4 hours). [GA 28]
	course	Introduction to Academic Studies (1 hour).[33]
	seminar	Beginners: On Idealism and Realism in Conjunction with the Main Courses (Hegel's Preface to the Phenomenology of Spirit).
	seminar	Advanced: On the Essence of Life with Particular Regard to Aristotle's De Anima, De Animalium Motione, and De Animalium Incessu.
July 24, 1929	lecture	What Is Metaphysics? (inaugural lecture in the University Auditorium at Freiburg).[34]
WS 1929–30	course	The Basic Concepts of Metaphysics: World, Finitude, Individualization (4 hours). [GA 29/30][35]
	seminar	For Middle and Upper Semesters: On Certainty and Truth in Conjunction with Descartes and Leibniz.
March 21–22, 1930	lectures	1. The Present Problem Situation of Philosophy. 2. Hegel and the Problem of Metaphysics. (2 lectures at the Scientific Union in Amsterdam).[36]
SS 1930	course	On the Essence of Human Freedom: Introduction to Philosophy (4 hours). [GA 31]
	seminar	Beginners: Selected Chapters from Kant's Critique of Judgment.
July 14, 1930	lecture	On the Essence of Truth (at the "Congress of Leading Baden Citizens in Science, Art, and Commerce" in Karlsruhe).[37]

October 8, 1930	lecture	On the Essence of Truth (at the Philosophical Society of Bremen).[38]
October 26, 1930	lecture	Augustine: What is Time? Confessions, Book 11 (at the monastery of Beuron).[39]
WS 1930–31	course	Hegel's Phenomenology of Spirit (2 hours). [GA 32]
	seminar	Augustine, Confessions 11 (on Time).
	seminar	Advanced: Plato's Parmenides (with Schadewaldt).
December 5, 1930	lecture	Philosophizing and Believing: The Essence of Truth (at the Evangelical-Theological Association in Marburg).[40]
December 11, 1930	lecture	On the Essence of Truth (in Freiburg).[41]

APPENDIX C

A Documentary Chronology of the Path to the Publication of *Being and Time*, 1924–27

"The strange publication of *Being and Time*,"[1] as the old Heidegger himself characterizes his anecdotal account of the events leading to the final publication of his magnum opus, proves to be even stranger when we bring together all of the extant documentary evidence, now emerging from the archives, that pertains to this series of events. This documentary trail of course transcripts, correspondence, university acts, and other archival evidence serves not only to correct Heidegger's memory but to fill in its gaps. It also takes us back to a point in time which provides an indispensable preface to that genetic account, as well as forward to the postscript to which the later Heidegger repeatedly returned, namely, the demise of BT. For there is not only a factual story to be documented here but also a conceptual history, since "perhaps the basic flaw of the book BT is that I ventured forward too far too soon" (US 93/7). In any event, the documentary account, in its very dynamics, serves in its way to address Heidegger's final wish by transforming even this work, frozen in time by decades of exegesis in abstraction from its genealogical context, into a "way."

1924

July 25 – Heidegger delivers his lecture, "Der Begriff der Zeit," to the Marburg Theological Society. For all its brevity and occasional intent, it may be regarded as the "primitive form" of BT.

September 21 – Regarding a promised article for the "German Quarterly for Literary Criticism and Intellectual History," Heidegger writes to its coeditor, Erich Rothacker: "Sie bekommen meine Abhandlung bestimmt bis Ende Oktober. Titel: Der Begriff der Zeit. (Anmerkung zum Dilthey-

Yorck Briefwechsel). Ich habe die zentrale Frage der 'Geschichtlichkeit' aus dem Briefwechsel herausgegriffen und suche diesen durch sachliche Untersuchung verständlich zu machen. Diese kann nur systematisch-historischen Charakter haben. Der Aufsatz ist circa 4 Bogen stark." ("You will be getting my article no later than the end of October. Title: 'The Concept of Time: A Comment on the Dilthey-Yorck Correspondence.' I have taken the central question of 'historicity' from the correspondence and seek to make it comprehensible by way of an in-depth investigation. This can only be done by an investigation that is both systematic and historical in character. The length of the essay is about 4 galleys [= 64 pages of print].") The article, in the end about 75 pages in length, may be regarded as the very first draft of BT.[2]

November 18 – Plans for the publication of the article collapse in a dispute over its length, and perhaps also because of its ponderous style. Heidegger replies to Rothacker: ". . . Wie ich *kürzen* soll, ist mir unklar. Ich habe den letzten Abschnitt schon so gehalten, daß Hauptstücke der schlagenden Interpretation Descartes', alle Belege, weggefallen sind. . . . Ich mache Ihnen folgenden Vorschlag: Sie schicken mir das Manuskript zurück, ich kann dann Dilthey sowohl konkreter behandeln und in der Descartes Analyse das Ausgefallene neufügen, und somit als Bezugnahme auf Yorck—im Januar im *VIII. Bd. des Jahrbuchs* mit Husserl zusammen erscheinen lassen—unter Verweisung auf die Vierteljahrsschrift." (". . . It is not at all clear to me how I am to *shorten* it. I have already curtailed the last section so much that major portions pertinent to the interpretation of Descartes, all footnotes, were left out. . . . I suggest that we proceed as follows: Send the manuscript back to me. I can then treat Dilthey more concretely and restore what was left out of the analysis of Descartes. Referring in this way to Yorck, it can then appear in January in *vol. 8* of Husserl's *Yearbook*, along with a reference to the Quarterly.") *Sein und Zeit* will indeed appear in vol. 8 of Husserl's *Jahrbuch für Philosophie und phänomenologische Forschung*, but not until 1927.

December 17 – Heidegger to his student, Karl Löwith: ". . . Meine 'Zeit' war für Rothacker zu groß (5 Bogen), erscheint um einiges vermehrt im Jahrbuch. Druck beginnt Ende Januar. . . ."[3] (". . . My [article on] 'Time' was too long (5 galleys) for Rothacker, will appear in a somewhat expanded version in the Yearbook. Printing begins end of January. . . .")

1925

February 10 – On this day in his course of WS 1924–25, in which he had been glossing Plato's *Sophist* since mid-January, Heidegger analyzes the question of "being" raised by the Eleatic Stranger (244A) in the terms long familiar to us from the opening pages of BT. The next two drafts of BT will thereupon become overtly ontological drafts, explicitly oriented toward the question of the sense of being *as such*.

March 27 – Heidegger to Löwith: ". . . Die 'Zeit' kommt im nächsten Jahrbuchband und zwar in dem Zusammenhang, wie sie bearbeitet war—als Boden der Destruktion der griechischen Ontologie und Logik. . . ."
(". . . The 'Time' is coming out in the next volume of the Yearbook, and in fact in the context in which it was [first] elaborated—as a ground for the destruction of Greek ontology and logic. . . .")

June 24 – Minutes of the second committee meeting in Marburg on a new appointment to the chair of philosophy, succeeding Nicolai Hartmann: "Wedekind fragt, welche Schriften Heideggers veröffentlicht vorliegt. Hartmann antwortet, dass eine neue ganz hervorragende Arbeit vorliegt, die allerdings ebenso wie seine frühere Arbeit noch nicht gedruckt sei."[4] ("[Rudolf] Wedekind [Geology and Paleontology] asked what writings Heidegger had now published. Hartmann replied that Heidegger has written a new and quite excellent work which, however, just like his earlier work [on Aristotle], was not yet in print.")

July 30 and 31 – Going beyond his prepared manuscript, Heidegger in these last two hours of SS 1925 lectures on the topics of death and conscience. This course, presented under the title "History of the Concept of Time," is in effect the second draft of BT, mainly of its First Division. Heidegger will utilize his copy of Simon Moser's transcript of the course as the basis for the final draft of BT.

August 5 – Marburg Philosophical Faculty to the Berlin Ministry of Science, Art and National Education: "Proposals for New Appointments for the Ordinariat in Philosophy," with Heidegger ranked first: "Daneben liegt ein jüngst entstandenes systematisches Werk über 'Zeit und Sein' vor—in Druck befindlich—, welches uns Heidegger noch von einer anderen Seite, nämlich als selbständig aufbauenden philosophischen Denker, zeigt. Dieses Werk gibt nichts geringeres als eine neue Aufrollung der letzten ontologischen Grundfragen, stellt also eine Synthese phänomenologischer—hier zum ersten Male von allem Subjektivismus abgelöster—Forschungsweise mit der Auswertung des großen traditionellen Gutes der antiken, mittelalterlichen und neuzeitlichen Metaphysik dar."[5] ("In addition [to the earlier work on Aristotle], there is a systematic work of recent origin—now being printed—on 'Time and Being,' which shows us yet another side of Heidegger, as an independent and constructive philosophical thinker. This work is nothing less than a new elaboration of the ultimate ontological questions. It thus represents a synthesis of the phenomenological way of research—here for the first time free from all subjectivism—with an assessment of the great wealth of the tradition of ancient, medieval, and modern metaphysics.")

August 24 – Heidegger responds from his modest mountain hut in Todtnauberg to Löwith's postcard of a Roman mosaic portraying a human corpse with the Greek inscription "Know thyself": "Herzlichen Dank für Ihre Karte. Sie kam mir in dem Moment auf meinen 'Schreibtisch', als ich das den Tod betr. Kapitel meiner 'Zeit' zum 'Abschluss' brachte." ("Thank you for your card. It came across my 'writing desk' just as I was bringing the chapter on death in my 'Time' to 'termination.' ")

December 14 (last hour before the Christmas break in WS 1925–26) – Heidegger announces a change in plans in his course on "Logic" (GA 21:194), departing from his initial outline oriented toward Aristotle's theory of truth, and replacing it instead with an exegesis centered on Kant's doctrine of the schematism of the understanding and what it says about time. The final draft of BT thus becomes a Kantian draft.

1926

January 27 – The Prussian Minister of Science, Art, and National Education, Carl Heinrich Becker, responds to Marburg's proposal of August 5, 1925: "Bei aller Anerkennung der Lehrerfolge des Professors Heidegger erscheint es mir doch nicht angängig, ihm eine etatmässige ordentliche Professur von der historischen Bedeutung des dortigen Lehrstuhls für Philosophie zu übertragen, bevor nicht grosse literarische Leistungen die besondere Anerkennung der Fachgenossen gefunden haben, die eine solche Berufung erheischt."[6]
("For all the recognition of Professor Heidegger's teaching success, it nevertheless seems inadmissible for me to grant him a permanent full professorship of the historical stature of your chair in philosophy, until his not very large literary accomplishments have found the special recognition of his peers that such an appointment demands.")

February 17 – Heidegger to his philosophical friend and ally, Karl Jaspers: "Vor einigen Tagen hat die Regierung die Liste zurückgeschickt mit dem Vermerk, daß ich der Bedeutung des Lehrstuhles nicht entspreche, und daß sie um weitere Vorschläge bitte. Die Fakultät will auf ihrem Vorschlag beharren – praktisch wird sich nichts ändern – mir ist das Ganze gleichgültig."[7]
("A few days ago, the government returned the list with the remark that I fail to meet the requirements of the chair, and that it requests other

recommendations. The faculty wants to stick to its recommendation – practically, it will change nothing – to me the whole thing is a matter of indifference.")

Sometime in February – " 'Herr Kollege Heidegger – jetzt müssen Sie etwas veröffentlichen. Haben Sie ein geeignetes Manuskript?' Mit diesen Worten betrat der Dekan der Marburger Philosophischen Fakultät eines Tages im WS 1925/26 mein Studierzimmer. 'Gewiß', antwortete ich. Worauf der Dekan entgegnete: 'Aber es muß rasch gedruckt werden'. . . . Nun galt es, langgehütete Arbeit der Öffentlichkeit zu übergeben. Der Max Niemeyer Verlag war durch Husserls Vermittlung bereit, sofort die ersten 15 Bogen [1 Bogen = 16 Seiten] der Arbeit zu drucken, die in Husserls 'Jahrbuch' erscheinen sollte."
(" 'Professor Heidegger, you have got to publish something now. Do you have a suitable manuscript?' With these words the dean of the philosophical faculty in Marburg came into my office one day in WS 1925–26. 'Certainly,' I replied. Then the dean said, 'But it must be printed quickly.'. . . I now had to submit my long-guarded work to the public. Through Husserl's mediation, the publishing house of Max Niemeyer was ready to print the first 15 galleys of the work at once for publication in Husserl's Yearbook.")[8]

February 25 – Minutes of a committee meeting in Marburg: "Die Kommission beschliesst einstimmig, Herrn Heidegger nahezulegen, die von ihm in Ms. niedergelegte Schrift über 'Sein und Zeit' in einer gewissen Anzahl von maschinenschriftlichen Exemplaren herstellen zu lassen und dem Dekan zu überreichen. Weiterhin erklärt die Kom. es für dringend wünschenswert, ausserdem die Schrift in Druckfahnen zu erhalten. Die Kommission wird dann die Ex. einer Anzahl noch zu bestimmender Gelehrten zur Begutachtung vorlegen. – [Max] Deutschbein [(Englische Philologie), der damalige Dekan]
    Herr Heidegger erklärt sich bereit, das fragliche Ms. ab 1. April in Druck zu geben, fernerhin den Dekan über den Stand des Druckes zu orientieren. – Deutschbein"[9]
("The Committee decided unanimously to urge Heidegger to have some copies of his handwritten text of "Being and Time" typed and delivered to the Dean. The Committee further declared that it would be most desirable to have the text also in galleys. The Committee would then send the copies to a number of scholars, still to be named, for review. – [Max] Deutschbein [(English Philology), the Dean at the time.]
    Heidegger declares that he is prepared to get the aforesaid manuscript to the printer by April 1, and to keep the Dean posted of the progress of the printing. Deutschbein")

February 26 – The last hour of WS 1925–26: For the first time since January 1924, Heidegger uses the terms "Existenz" and "Existenzial" in a public lecture course (GA 21:402). This signals the "existentialist" draft of BT, composed in the month of March 1926.

April 2 – Heidegger in Todtnauberg writes to the dean in Marburg (cf. February 25): "Euere Spectabilität, teile ich ergebenst mit, daß der Druck meiner Abhandlung "Sein und Zeit" für Bd. VIII des Jahrbuches für Philosophie und phänomenologische Forschung begonnen hat. Bis Anfang Mai werden 10–12 Bogen gedruckt sein."[10]
("Dear Sir, I respectfully wish to inform you that the printing of my treatise "Being and Time" for vol. 8 of the *Yearbook for Philosophy and Phenomenological Research* has begun. By the beginning of May, 10 to 12 galleys will be printed.")

On the day before, Heidegger had in fact sent Niemeyer a clean copy (a handwritten "Reinschrift") of 136 folio pages of the text of BT, up to the title of § 38 ("Falling and Thrownness," page 175 in the final German), along with 4 pages of footnotes numbered 1 to 39 (No. 39 = "Confessiones lib. X, cap. 35" = SZ 171), in sum, the equivalent of 11 galleys (1 galley = 16 printed pages).[11]

April 8 – Husserl's birthday in Todtnauberg: "Heidegger . . . brachte eine mit Blumen geschmückte Rolle, die die Widmung 'Edmund Husserl in dankbarer Verehrung und Freundschaft' seines eben vollendeten Werkes enthielt."[12]
("Heidegger. . . brought a roll decorated with flowers which contained the dedication 'To Edmund Husserl in grateful admiration and friendship' of his just completed work.") Years later, Heidegger recalls that, on this occasion, he showed Husserl "das nahezu fertige Manuskript," the nearly completed manuscript of BT.[13] The still extant working manuscript of the Second Division of BT ends with the title of § 77 and a few notes regarding Dilthey-Yorck. Apparently §§ 77–83 (the last 40 pages of BT) were written later.

April 14 – The "Buchdruckerei des Waisenhauses" (the "Orphanage Printing Shop," presumably in Halle, where Niemeyer was based) sends the first two galleys to Heidegger in Todtnauberg, and finally galley no. 11 on May 8 to Heidegger in Marburg. On May 15, Heidegger sends the corrected galley 11 back to the printer. Various hands, not just Heidegger's, are involved in these corrections: those of Karl Löwith, Wilhelm Szilasi, Helene Weiß, even Husserl.

Around April 20 – Husserl (in Todtnauberg) writes to Fritz Kaufmann: "An Kollegen Heideggers 'Sein und Zeit' korrigieren wir mit, wir sind am 4. Bogen. Es macht mir viele Freude. Ich bin in eifriger Arbeit."[14]

("We are helping with the correcting of Heidegger's *Being and Time*, and are now on the 4th galley. It gives me a great deal of satisfaction. I am working on it with diligence.")

April 24 -Heidegger (in Todtnauberg) writes to Jaspers: "Ich habe am 1. April mit dem Druck meiner Abhandlung 'Sein und Zeit' begonnen. Sie umfasst ca. 34 Bogen. . . . Die Fakultät will mich wieder vorschlagen und die bereits gedruckten Bogen beilegen."[15]
("I began the process of printing my treatise *Being and Time* on April 1. It is about 34 galleys long. . . . The faculty wants to recommend my name again and will submit the already printed galleys.")

May 24 – Heidegger to Jaspers, about his book in progress: "Ich rechne auf Wenige, die es studieren; in den eigentlichen Intentionen werden nur Sie verstehen, was ich will. Im Ganzen ist es für mich ein Übergangsarbeit. Daraus, daß Husserl das Ganze befremdend findet und es in der üblichen Phänomenologie 'nicht mehr unterbringt', schließe ich, daß ich de facto schon weiter weg bin, als ich selbst glaube und sehe."[16]
("I am counting on the few who will study it; only you will understand its true intentions, what I want. On the whole, it is for me a transition work. From the fact that Husserl finds the whole thing strange and can 'no longer find a place' for it in the usual phenomenology, I conclude that I am de facto already further away than I myself believe and see.")

End of May? in June? – Upon receiving the final page proofs of the first 11 galleys, Heidegger sends the clean handwritten copy for galleys 12 to 14 (§§ 38 through 44, up to SZ 230) to the printer.[17]

June 18 – Dean of the Marburg Philosophical Faculty to the Berlin Ministry: "Da die Fakultät die grössten Schwierigkeiten hat, weitere geeignete Persönlichkeiten zu finden, die berufen wären, den Philosophischen Lehrstuhl von Hartmann bez. von Natorp zu übernehmen, bittet sie den Herrn Minister nochmals, den in der Liste vom 5. August. 1925 an erster Stelle genannten Professor Heidegger zu berufen. Die Fakultät glaubt sich zu dieser Bitte berechtigt, da Herr Heidegger in der Zwischenzeit seine Arbeit über 'Sein und Zeit' zum Druck gebracht hat. Die Arbeit ist in Druckbogen in doppelter Ausführung diesem Gesuch beigefügt."[18]
("Since the faculty is having the greatest difficulty in finding other suitable persons who would be qualified to assume the chair in philosophy once occupied by Hartmann and Natorp, it renews its request to the Minister to appoint Professor Heidegger, who was first on its list of August 5, 1925. The faculty believes itself to be justified in this request, since Heidegger has in the interim committed his work on *Being and Time* into print. The printed galleys of this work are submitted in dupli-

cate with this formal request.") In actual fact, only 11–15 galleys of the First Division of SZ were sent to the Berlin Ministry

July 31 (semester's end) – Heidegger to Jaspers: "Mein Druck is bis Ende Juni gut fortgeschritten. Dann wuchs mir die Semesterarbeit über den Kopf, da ich den ganzen Examenskram an mir hängen habe. Anfang Juni hat die Fakultät den I. Teil meiner Arbeit in Reindruck in 2 Exemplaren dem Ministerium eingereicht und noch einmal betont, daß sie an ihrem Vorschlag festhalte. . . . Ich fahre für 8 Tage nach dem Engadin, wohin mich Husserl eingeladen hat. Dann auf die Hütte, wo ich den Druck zu Ende bringe."[19]

("The printing went well until the end of June. Then I got swamped with the work of the semester, since I am stuck with all the exams. At the beginning of June, the faculty sent the clean page proofs of the first part of my work to the ministry, stressing that it is sticking by its nomination. . . . I am going to Engadin for a week, where Husserl has invited me. Then to the cabin to finish the printing.")

October 4 – Heidegger writes from Todtnauberg ("the cabin") to Jaspers: "Ich hatte Mitte des Sommersemesters den Druck sistiert und kam, als ich nach ganz kurzer Erholung wieder an die Arbeit ging, ins Umschreiben. Die Arbeit ist umfangreicher geworden als ich dachte, so daß ich jetzt teilen muss auf je ungefähr 25 Bogen. Den Rest für den ersten Band [Bogen Nr. 16 bis 27] muss ich bis 1. November abliefern. So ist jeder Tag für mich kostbar."[20]

("The printing came to a halt in the middle of the summer semester. When I got back to work again after a very brief break, I began rewriting. The work has grown larger than I originally thought, so that I am now dividing it in two, each about 25 galleys long. The remainder for the first volume [galleys 16 to 27] has to be sent out by November 1. So every day for me is precious.")

October 13 – Heidegger to Bultmann: "Morgen ist Abschied von der Hütte. Wir hatten noch wundervolles Wetter. Mit meiner Arbeit bin ich so gut vorwärts gekommen, daß ich die ganze Arbeit teilen muß auf je ca. 26 Bogen. Die Umarbeitung und Druckpause hat sich gelohnt, wenngleich alles nicht so vollkommen ist, wie es mir vorschwebt."[21]

("Tomorrow I take leave of the cabin. We still had great weather. My work has progressed so well that I had to divide the whole work in two, each about 26 galleys long. The reworking and printing pause have paid off, although everything is not as complete as I have it in mind.")

About November 1 – The clean copy of the Second Division, which, from the dividing pages listing the footnotes, may have been sent to the printer in two separate units (§§ 45–68 and §§ 69–83), already includes the 5 footnotes referring to to the never-to-be-published "Second Half" of BT: to the First Division of the Second Part on Kant (SZ 319 [§ 64], 427 [§ 81], 432f [§ 82a]: this last long footnote extending to the following page 433 also refers to the Third Division on Aristotle's concept of time); two notes to the Third Division of the First Part (SZ 349 [§ 68d] on the tenses of language, SZ 363n [§ 69b] on the grounding of intentionality in ecstatic temporality). It is of course not clear how much of this outline of the never-published second volume was actually written out in draft form at this time. But Heidegger had at least 26 galleys "in mind."

November 25 – Marburg receives a reply from the Berlin Ministry: "Dem Ersuchen des Herrn Ministers für Wissenschaft, Kunst und Volksbildung vom 11. November des Jahres—U I Nr. 7192—entsprechend, teile ich mit, daß der Herr Minister dem Vorschlag, dem Professor Dr. *Heidegger* die planmäßige ordentliche Professur zu übertragen, auf Grund erneuter Prüfung aller nur dargelegten Gesichtspunkte nicht zu folgen vermag."
("In accord with the request of November 11 from the Minister of Science, Art and National Education, I wish to communicate that the Minister, upon reexamination of all the represented points of view, cannot follow the recommendation to grant Professor Dr. *Heidegger* the tenured full professorship.") On December 1, Heidegger receives the page proofs returned from Berlin. On December 2, he informs Jaspers of this second rejection.[22]

December 22 – Heidegger (from Marburg) to Elisabeth Blochmann: "Eigentlich müßte der Brief von der Hütte kommen. . . . Statt dessen sitze ich hier—am Übergangskapitel" [d.h. zwischen dem 2. und 3. Abschnitt des I. Teils von SZ].[23]
("This letter really should have come from the cabin. . . . Instead, here I sit—on the transition chapter" [between the Second and Third Division of the First Part of BT].)

December 26 – Heidegger (from Marburg) to Jaspers: "Ich komme also am 1. Januar. Die genaue Ankunft teile ich noch mit. Mit gleicher Post erhalten Sie Bogen 17 und 18. Das Übrige bis 23 bringe ich mit. Vier Bogen fehlen noch."[24]
("I am coming [to Heidelberg] on January 1. I shall let you know the exact arrival time. With this post, you shall also be getting galleys 17 and 18. The rest, up to galley 23, I'll bring with me. There are still 4 galleys to go.")

1927

January 1–10 – Early on in the conversations with Jaspers (say, by January 4), Heidegger comes to the realization that the composition of the

Third Division of the First Part of BT, bearing the title "Time and Being" (cf. SZ 39), was "inadequate" (*unzureichend*). He accordingly postpones his original plan to publish the second volume of BT immediately after the first. The later Heidegger (in 1941) recalls this decision in the following words: "Der Entschluß zum Abbruch wurde gefaßt in den letzten Dezembertagen 1926 während eines Aufenthaltes in Heidelberg bei K. Jaspers, wo mir aus lebhaften freundschaftlichen Auseinandersetzungen an Hand der Korrekturbogen von 'Sein und Zeit' klar wurde, daß die bis dahin erreichte Ausarbeitung dieses wichtigsten Abschnittes (I, 3) unverständlich bleiben müsse. Der Entschluß zum Abbruch der Veröffentlichung wurde gefaßt an dem Tage, als uns die Nachricht vom Tode R. M. Rilkes traf. – Allerdings war ich damals der Meinung, übers Jahr schon alles deutlicher sagen zu können. Das war eine Täuschung."[25]

("The decision to postpone came to me in the last days of December of 1926 during a visit in Heidelberg with Karl Jaspers. Out of our friendly but lively disputes over the galleys of *Being and Time*, it became clear to me that the elaboration of this all important Division (I, 3) drafted up to that point had to be incomprehensible. The decision to discontinue publication took shape on the day that we got the news of Rilke's death. – Of course, at the time I thought that in the course of the year everything could be said more clearly. That was a delusion.")

March 1 – Heidegger to Jaspers: "Die Druckerei hat wieder reichlich pausiert, so daß heute erst den letzten Bogen [Nr. 27/28] in der ersten Korrektur wegschicken kann." Helene Weiss solle jetzt "noch einmal eine Gesamtrevision der Bogen bezüglich sinnstörender Druckfehler" machen.[26]

("The printing process has once again been substantially delayed. It was only today that I could return the last galley in its first correction." Helene Weiss shall now do "a complete review of the galleys once again in search of meaning-distorting typos.") To that end, Heidegger asks Jaspers to forward the galleys in his possession to her.

March 22 – The final corrections of the galleys are completed by the printer.[27]

April 18 – Heidegger to Jaspers: "Den Verlag habe ich vor einiger Zeit verständigt, Ihnen ein Exemplar von Sein und Zeit zu schicken." ("Some time ago, I arranged with the Press to have a copy of *Being and Time* sent to you.") On May 1, Jaspers confirms that he has received the book. *Sein und Zeit* thus first appears in late April 1927 and not "in February 1927," as the old Heidegger recalls.[28] Confirmations:

about April 25 – From the reminiscences of Fritz Heidegger, brother of Martin: "Am 3. Mai 1927 starb die Mutter, neunundsechzigjährig,

nach qualvollem Leiden; ihr hast Du bei Deinem letzten Besuch, neun Tage vor ihrem Tod, Dein erst kurz vorher erschienenes Werk 'Sein und Zeit' überreicht."[29]
("On May 3, 1927, our mother died, 69 years old, in excruciating suffering. In your last visit, 9 days before her death, you had given her a copy of your work, *Being and Time*, which had appeared shortly before.")

May 8 – Husserl to Heidegger: "Bekommen Sie die Druckbogen der gegen Schluss für Sie besonders interessanten Becker-Schrift?"[30]
(Are you getting the galleys of the Becker-text, which is especially interesting for you toward the end?")

May 11 – Only in the second week (4th double hour) of the course of SS 1927 does Heidegger for the first time mention "the First Half of my treatise, *Being and Time*, which has just appeared" (GA 24:78/56). The formulation is significant: the Second Half is obviously still "in progress."

May 24 – Husserl to Heidegger: "Haben Sie Beckers Arbeit mitgelesen? Direkte Anwendung der Heideggerschen Ontologie."[31]
("Have you also read Becker's work? Direct application of Heideggerian ontology.")

May 26 – Husserl to Heidegger: "Ich vergaß [vor 2 Tagen], Ihnen einiges zu schreiben: 1) Fink war offenbar durch Ihre Zusendung sehr erfreut; er hat mir davon im Sprechzimmer fast strahlend erzählt. 2) Haben Sie an J. Cohn ein Freiexemplar dirigiert? Er wartet darauf und hält es für eine Selbstverständlichkeit, da er Ihnen seine Dialektik gesendet hat. Es ist eine unausweichliche Notwendigkeit, daß Sie ihm ein Exemplar schicken, er wäre sonst tödlich beleidigt . . ."[32]
("I forgot [two days ago] to write you a couple of things: 1) Eugen Fink was obviously very pleased over your sending him a copy. He told me about it in the office almost beaming. 2) Have you dispatched a free copy to Jonas Cohn? He is waiting for it and takes it as a matter of course, since he sent you his *Dialectic*. It is an unavoidable necessity that you send him a copy. Otherwise, he would be deeply insulted.")

May 29 – Heidegger to Blochmann about a belated birthday present: "Mein Buch ist erschienen. Ihnen ist ein Exemplar zum Geburtstage [am 14. April] zugedacht."[33]
("My book has appeared. A copy is meant for you for your birthday.")

June 14 – Hans Reiner (from Marburg) to Husserl: "Professor Heideggers Vorlesung ist von hervorragender Klarheit. Zugleich ermöglicht das nun endlich erschienene Buch, die Dinge in den Gesamtzusammenhang seiner Anschauungen hineinzustellen und sich damit auseinanderzusetzen."[34]

("Professor Heidegger's lecture course is superb in its clarity. At the same time, the book, which has now finally appeared, allows one to situate the things in the total context of his insights and to come to fundamental terms with them.")

May–July = SS 1927 – Upon first publication in 1975, the old Heidegger identifies the entire course on "The Basic Problems of Phenomenology" as a "new elaboration of the Third Division of the First Part of *Being and Time*" (GA 24:1/1).

October 6 – Heidegger to Bultmann, who is diligently studying BT, and inquires about the still unpublished Second Half: "Am II. Teil von S.u.Z. habe ich streckenweise gebessert. Aber ich muß wohl das Ganze noch einmal neu schreiben, da Wichtiges oft gar nicht ausgewertet ist. Ich lasse mir Zeit; denn was ich so beiläufig höre, hat 'man' keine sonderliche Lust, das bisher Veröffentlichte zu studieren. Am wenigsten in den so-genannten 'Fachkreisen'; zum Teil mag es Ärger sein darüber, daß es nicht in den ausgetretenen Geleisen läuft; zum Teil sind die Dinge 'inhaltlich' unangenehm.

Aber ich habe doch zum mindesten bewiesen, daß ich etwas drucken lassen kann."

("I have improved upon portions of the Second Part of BT. But I probably have to rewrite it in its entirety once more, since a number of important elements are not even sized up yet. I'll take my time. For from what I hear, 'one' has no particular inclination to study what has already been published. At least among the so-called 'experts'; in part perhaps because of irritation over the fact that it does not follow the beaten path; in part because the matters are disagreeable 'in substance.'

But I have at least proved that I can get something into print.")

SUMMARY: THE PRINTING OF BT

With the collapse of plans to publish a 75-page article on "The Concept of Time" in one journal, Heidegger initiates plans in November 1924 to publish it instead in volume 8 of Husserl's *Jahrbuch* in a "somewhat expanded" form. The "Time" thus replaces the "Aristotle" treatise (initially intended for volume 7 of the *Jahrbuch*) as Heidegger's top publication priority. But the pattern of hesitation and delay which prevented the Aristotle treatise from ever appearing now reasserts itself in the drafting of the "Time" essay. The "somewhat expanded" form eventually assumes the proportions of a work of at least two volumes. The first major expansion, concentrated upon what would become the First Division of BT, takes place in the course of SS 1925, which, after the ill-fated journal article, may be regarded as the second (the first ontological) draft of BT.

For Heidegger clearly utilized his copy of Simon Moser's typescript of the course in the final drafting of BT. That finalizing of the draft was prompted by an attempt on the part of the Marburg faculty to renew their recommendation to promote Heidegger to a full professorship, which was initially rejected in January 1926 for lack of publications. Heidegger, at this point suddenly enthusiastic over Kant and belatedly resorting to existentialist terminology on a massive scale, composes the final draft in raw manuscript (up to § 77 on Dilthey-Yorck)[35] in a single month, in March 1926, and manages to get a clean handwritten copy (*Reinschrift*) of a portion of it (amounting to 11 galleys of the final 27) to the printer on April 1. It is not clear whether just these 11 or as many as 14–15 galleys (the entire First Division of BT) were finally dispatched to Berlin in mid-June 1926. In either case, the Berlin Ministry of Education rendered its verdict in November 1926, adjudging the printed fragment to be "inadequate" to justify a promotion. But in the meantime, Heidegger continues to write, finalizing the Second Division for a press deadline of November 1, and roughing out the Third Division and Second (historical) Part in a considerably expanded form. The projected length of the manuscript thus increases from 34 to over 50 galleys, leading to the decision to divide the text into two volumes. But discussions with Jaspers about the extant galleys of BT, in the first days of January 1927, prompt Heidegger to delay the publication of the second volume until he can produce a clearer formulation of the Third Division. This sticking point in the text in the end goes beyond temporary postponement. After several attempts to rewrite the Third Division, Heidegger finally decides to abandon the project spelled out in the context of BT as such (in 1929–30?).[36] The version which first appears in late April 1927 thus becomes a permanent fragment, an "astonishing torso," a bold brash but premature "way" precipitated by academic circumstance.

APPENDIX D

Genealogical Glossary of Heidegger's Basic Terms, 1915–27

The translation of the term is typically followed by its chronological span of usage, that is, when it was *first* and (where pertinent) *last* used by Heidegger as a *terminus technicus* during this period concluding with BT. The genealogies are but the briefest of capsule summaries of the more contextual treatments in the foregoing text, though they at times supplement that text with further doxographical detail.

Abfall, abfallen (lapsing) – The first stirrings of a sense of "fallenness" (*Verfallenheit*), in SS 1920, where *abfallen* serves to broaden the need for *Destruktion* beyond the overcoming of theoretical objectification to that of every lapse from the originality of human experience into everyday superficiality. Cf. also WS 1920–21, WS 1921–22, Oct. 1922, SS 1923, etc., where the lapsing is into narrow regional domains taken as absolute, or is described as a falling off into significance and its objectification, as a result of total absorption in the What of the world to the disregard of its How, approximating what Husserl means by the "natural attitude."

Alltäglichkeit (everydayness) – On opening day in WS 1919–20, it is described as the "surface existence of the unaccentuated accent of life." It receives its overtly temporal sense first in the terminological context of SS 1923.

Angst (angst, dread) – Mentioned in passing in SS 1923, it is first analyzed at the end of WS 1923–24. The analysis is deepened and refined in each of the three drafts of BT. Its precursor, *timor castus* (pure fear), receives extensive treatment in the Augustine course of SS 1921, and is mentioned again in SS 1924 in connection with Aristotle's analysis of fear in *Rhetoric* II. The earliest allusion to dread occurs in WS 1919–20, by way of Otto's "experience of the Holy."

Anwesenheit (presence) — In his gloss of Parmenides' "It is" in SS 1922, Heidegger comes within a hair's breadth of equating the Greek sense of being as οὐσία with "constant presence" . . . but he does not. He likewise fails to do so in WS 1923–24 in his discussion of that dominating presence (παρουσία) of the Greek world, the sky. It is probably not until early 1924, in a talk that he was preparing on *Nicomachean Ethics* 6, that Heidegger first overtly identifies οὐσία as *Anwesen* (property, real estate) with constant presence. This central character first receives its full elaboration in the Aristotle course of SS 1924 under the heading of *Gegenwärtigkeit*, presentness. But already in November 1924, Heidegger is pondering the implication involved in the two distinctly different senses of "present" (*Gegenwart*), as presence (*Anwesenheit*) at a place or in a context (*die Präsenz*), and as the temporal dimension of the "now" (*das Praesens*). Nevertheless, in SS 1925, terms like *Gegenwärtigkeit, Anwesenheit,* and *Präsenz* tend to be used synonymously, even though "appresentation," with its tacit "pale and inconspicuous *Anwesenheit* of the world" (GA 20: 256/189), tends to suggest an absent presence. But in WS 1925–26, being as presence is made possible by the empowering presentifying (*Gegenwärtigen*) of the present tense, understood as the discoveredness of truth, such that presence (*Anwesenheit*) and the present (*Gegenwart*) together constitute *Präsenz* (GA 21:193). Such distinctions were to have been the topic of the never-published Second Half of BT, to some extent developed in SS 1927 (cf. "Präsenz" below).

apophantisches "als" (apophantic "as") — First thematized in the gloss of Aristotle's theory of speech in SS 1922, but named as such first in a similar context in WS 1923–24, as the "as" that "shows" as opposed to the "as" that distinguishes, the "critical 'as.' " Its distinction from the hermeneutic "as" occurs first in WS 1925–26.

Appräsentation, appräsentieren (appresentation, appresent) — Taken from Husserl's *Ideen II*, they appear only in SS 1925 to describe 1) the relations of presence between world and things, and 2) the expository interpretation of such tacit presences. Replaced primarily by *Gegenwärtigen* (presenting, making present, presentifying), also of Husserlian coinage, but also synonyms like *mitentdecken* (co-discovering). Notes in his Moser transcript of SS 1925 indicate that Heidegger first experimented with alternatives like *beibringen* (bringing forward) and *freigeben* (opening, clearing, making free), both frequently used in *Sein und Zeit*.

Augenblick (the moment) — First thematized in translating Aristotle's καιρός in Oct. 1922, where phronetic insight is regarded as the way in which the "full moment is held in troth" (p. 36). This translation from the Greek also plays a major role in SS 1924 in depicting rhetorical-political decisions. Its first usage in BT underscores its visual sense of Augen*blick* (SZ 328), moment *of insight*, in fact a last-minute emphasis in the galleys not in the text first sent to the printer in November 1926. In WS 1929–30, Heidegger identifies this term as Kierkegaard's most prescient insight (GA 29/30:225), thereby acknowledging its Christian heritage (cf. WS 1920–21). But the young Heidegger of 1917 already singles out the term in his reading of Schleiermacher's texts on religion.

Ausgelegtheit (interpretedness) —First introduced in Oct. 1922 (p. 9) as the interpretation of the world transmitted to us through the habits of circumspection, it is in SS 1923 associated with the everyday interpretation promoted by the Anyone.

Aussein auf (being out toward) – First mentioned in Oct. 1922 (p. 6) to specify the directedness involved in caring, how it moves and is moved (p. 49). Related to the Aristotelian-scholastic concept of intentionality in SS 1923, the resolution of the "ins" and "outs" of the intentional movement is tentatively explored (GA 63:70, 86, 98f.). The unfinished character that it gives to the wholeness of Dasein, always "out toward what it is not but can be," is juxtaposed with death's finish first in November 1924. This provides the key, in the closing weeks of WS 1925–26, in shaping the formal indication of ex-sistence, central to the final draft of BT (March 1926), transforming its sense in the direction of the pure possibility of ek-static temporality.

Bedeutsamkeit (meaningfulness, significance) – Already in KNS 1919, regarding the environing world, it is said: "The meaningful is the primary . . ." (ZBP 73). Suffixed as a terminological present perfect "-ness" first in WS 1919–20, and identified as the containing sense of the relational sense of caring in WS 1921–22. In SS 1925, doubts are expressed regarding its appropriateness to describe the phenomenon involved, namely, the relation between discursiveness and world (GA 20:275/202); but it remains the defining character of "worldli*ness*" into BT.

Befindlichkeit (disposition, disposedness) – Mentioned in passing since WS 1919–20 to elaborate the situated character of life, how I find myself (*mich befinden*), it receives its precise sense (and optimal translation) from its Aristotelian equivalent, διάθεσις, in SS 1924, in the Greek lexical context which also relates it closely to the passions. It is precedented in the young Heidegger's preference in his phenomenology of religion for "felt intuition" (Schleiermacher) over perceptual intuition: "I find myself dependent . . . I feel myself dependent" (Adolf Reinach).

Begegnis (encounterivity) – First introduced in WS 1921–22 (GA 61:91) as the basic experience and mode of being-there of worldly objects. Its close association with *Besorgnis* (concernedness: GA 61:136) suggests that the encounter is by and large tacit.

Bekümmerung (affliction, distress, concern, ergo "distressed concern") – End of SS 1920 to Oct. 1922. First introduced as the original motive of philosophizing prompted by the very facticity of life. In the last terminological usage, the emphasis abruptly falls on the active side of the *vox media*. But at first, it tends to suggest both "being troubled" and "troubling oneself, worrying." Translates the biblical θλῖψις (*Bedrängnis, Trübsal, Not*) in the religion courses of 1920 and 1921. Gradually displaced by "care(ing)" (*Sorgen*) and to some extent *Angst*: in SS 1921, Augustine's *cura* is still translated as "being distressed" rather than "care."

Besorgen (concern) – First thematized in WS 1921–22 to express the actualization of caring (*Sorgen*) in world-laden cares, in the persistent state of concernedness (*Besorgnis*; GA 61:135). Cf. *Begegnis*.

Bewandtnis (intentional [orienting] nexus, interwoundedness, circumstanding, standing, bearing, relevance, deployment) – Lask's alternative word for form already adopted by Heidegger in the habilitation to indicate how a matter is to be taken or viewed. In SS 1925, it first replaces *Bedeutsamkeit* to specify the orientation to be taken to an Other in accord with the Other's state, stand, condition in the context of the world ("where you stand with me"; GA 20:357/259). In WS 1925–26, the term is restricted to define the *state* of functionality, compliance and readiness of handy things. In BT, accordingly, it becomes the very being of handiness.

Bezugssinn, Gehaltssinn, Vollzugssinn (relating sense, containing [content] sense, actualizing sense: the triple formal schematism of intentionality) – WS 1919–20 to SS 1922. The comprehensive *Zeitigungssinn* joins the three only in WS 1921–22 and SS 1922. In Oct. 1922, the terms are used without the "sense," but are still schematically and formally associated with each other.

Dasein (Dasein, being [t]here) – At first called the historical I of the "primal something" (life in and for itself), the situation I, factic life, factic life experience, human life is first described as "concrete actual Dasein" in SS 1920. The ins and outs of "da sein" are first vectorially distinguished in the Jaspers-review of September 1920. "Dasein" is first adopted as a technical term, i.e., is "formally indicated," in SS 1923, in relation to the temporal particularity (*Jeweiligkeit*, ἕκαστος) of its facticity or its "being," always "there" before and beyond any "having."

Destruktion (de[con]struction) – First called *Kritik* on the opening day of SS 1919 before it emerges as such at the end of WS 1919–20, thus at times called the "critical-phenomenological destruction" (SS 1920) of the effects of objectification and regionalization (structured by genera and species), and conceived as a method of returning presuppositions back to their origins in factic life experience. Already in SS 1920, it is linked to "systematic deconstruction (*Abbau*)."

Durchschnittlichkeit (averageness) – The averageness of the public lived by the Anyone first emerges in Oct. 1922. The interpretedness of chatter (*Gerede*) in the temporality of everydayness joins this terminological constellation in SS 1923, where Kierkegaard's influence is acknowledged (GA 63:30f., 85).

Entdecktheit (discoveredness, uncoveredness) – The term is introduced in the first draft of BT in November 1924 in conjunction with the disposedness of the in-being of Dasein, as a revelatory phenomenon which is broader than the disclosedness of the world, and so comprehending it. Only in BT is this aletheic dimension belonging to Dasein itself instead called disclosedness, while "discoveredness" is now restricted strictly to the revelation of entities which are not Dasein (SZ 85).

Entschlossenheit (resoluteness, resolve, "un-locking")—It first appears in Oct. 1922 (p. 2) in relation to the "ability to unlock," as Heidegger's handwritten marginalia to the text later underscore. Resolute deciding (*sich-entschliessen*) translates Aristotle's προαίρεσις in SS 1924. The brunt of the very first analysis of the authentication of temporality in Nov. 1924 is carried, not by "conscience," but by the "being futural" of resoluteness, understood as discoveredness open to the disposition of angst.

Entweltlichung (unworlding, deprivation of worldhood) – Of the effects of objectification and reification first outlined in KNS 1919, which include unliving, designifying and dehistoricizing, it is "unworlding" that emerges again in SS 1925 (GA 20:227, 249, 266, 298, 301, 308, 313f.) and so finds its way into BT (SZ 65, 75, 112).

Ereignis (properizing event, appropriating event) – Clearly destined from the start to be the central "terminus technicus" of Heidegger's entire *Denkweg* to identify the very source and "primal leap" (*Ur-sprung*) of experience, this etymologically rich term nevertheless goes into dormancy for almost a decade after its initial thematization in KNS 1919 and SS 1919, replaced during that period by the Christian and Greek kairological sense of time as the Moment. *Er-eignis* is first introduced in KNS as the central characterization of the most intense lived experience (*Er-leben*) of the historical I in close conjunction with the meaning-bestowing dynamics of the It which "worlds" (ZBP 69, 74f.). The I is fully there in the "It worlds" of the primal something such that "I myself properize (*er-eigne*) It to myself and It properizes (*er-eignet*) itself according to its essence" (75). This intimate involvement with the primal It of Being thus prompts the distinction between events which "happen" (*passieren*: ZBP 205) to me passionally and move me by situating me, and processes (*Vorgänge*) which pass before me objectively. The KNS-Schema accordingly distinguishes the sheer indifference of the formal-objective "something in general" from the pretheoretical preworldly "primal something" which is the "index of the highest potentiality of life" in and for itself (ZBP 115).

In BT, however, the occasional use of *Ereignis* at least in the two extant Divisions returns to its mundane sense of objectified and reified impersonal historical events past and gone (SZ 250, 253, 257, 284, 290, 378, 382, 389). It is only in SS 1928 that a tendency back to its originally intimate sense begins to assert itself: in a redescription of ecstatic and horizonal temporality, primal time and primal history are understood dynamically as a generative temporalizing which "worlds," as an "es gibt" which yields the "nihil originarium" of a world (GA 26:270/209, 272/210). This is more ontically described as "the *Ereignis* of the world-entry of beings" (274/212), or the *Urereignis* which is essentially generative temporalizing. Some advance is made in articulating this primal event in the concurrent seminar of SS 1928 on Aristotle's *Physics*, where, in order to express the incomplete "underway" character of movement, δύναμις (capability, power) is translated more phronetically as *Eignung* (aptitude, suitability), and the question is then posed how this adaptation to . . . , appropriateness for . . . , determines the *Ereignung* of generative movement, the primal event of human history. Much like the formal indication of ex-sistence in BT, accordingly, the focus on Aristotle's ἐνέργεια ἀτελής (in 1928 still meant for the Third Division of the never-published *Second* Part of BT) reverses the dominant Greek sense of finished being, pointing instead to the generative event which possibilizes actuality in the absence of presence welling up from the concealment of unconcealment (so in the later Heidegger).

Erschlossenheit (disclosedness) – World as meaningful context of references is first characterized as disclosedness in SS 1923. But as the habitual absorption in averageness, this particular ἀλήθεια of disclosedness (GA 63:99) covers up the ownness and potential authenticity of Dasein (63: 85), that is, its potential discoveredness. Only with BT does Heidegger reverse his terms and speak instead of the disclosedness of Dasein and the discoveredness of (usually) entities within the world. But even then, the world itself in its worldliness or its being-there (SZ 85f., 132) is regarded as disclosedness.

Existenz (existence, ex-sistence) – In contrast with Jaspers's *Psychologie der Weltanschauungen*, which takes Kierkegaard's "existence" as a Kantian idea for the whole of human life, Heidegger in his review (1920–21) suggests that *Existenz* be regarded methodologically as a "formal indication" of the sense of being of the "(I) *am.*" But Jaspers was right in looking to limit situations like death and guilt for illumination into the phenomenon of existence. Thus, existence reappears in Oct. 1922 (pp. 13f.) as the authentic being of life accessible in the distressed questioning of its facticity, in a countermovement to life's tendency to lapse. *Existenz* here is but one possibility in the more comprehensive facticity (being) of life. Moving from these two "private communications" to his peers to the first public usage in the lecture course of SS 1923, we find the same restricted sense of *Existenz*, narrowed down to Dasein's ownmost possibility. It is only in WS 1925–26 that *Existenz* assumes a universalized sense of possibility, by way of the formal clue of "being out toward," and becomes the formal indication of ex-sistence in the last draft of BT.

existenzial (existential) – Coined by Heidegger only during the final drafting of BT (March 1926) to distinguish his ontological categorizing of the *Existenzialien* from the ontic-existentiell level of individual life. The purported earlier usages of this term are either later insertions postdating the courses (e.g., GA 21:151, 267) or misinterpretations of Heidegger's abbreviation "ex." (e.g., GA 61:98).

Existenzialien (existentials) – First in SS 1923, it is suggested that the interpretation of facticity in terms of its unique possibility of *Existenz* will yield special categories which accordingly are to be called "existentials." In WS 1923–24, instead of facticity, Dasein is the prepossession which, when pre-viewed in terms of its being, yields those preconceptions called "existentials." It should be noted, however, that both usages are but passing mentions. Only at the very end of WS 1925-26 does Heidegger's search for "existentials" seriously begin.

existenziell (existentiell) – This Kierkegaardian spelling (almost: cf. GA 61:182, where the Diederichs translation is already modified by the Heideggerian "z") is used once in SS 1920, more frequently in Heidegger's letter of August 1921 to his existentialist student Karl Löwith. But the adjective receives terminological sustenance first in Oct. 1922 (pp. 14f.), with the introduction of *Existenz*, understood as the most unique, i.e., "existentiell," possibility of life's facticity, into the core of Heidegger's conceptual framework. It is first linked to the "ontic" side of Dasein in BT itself.

Faktizität (facticity) – The *locus classicus* of the term is in the post-Kantian "irrational hiatus" between aposteriori and apriori, where *Faktizität* is paired with *Logizität* and specifically set off from it first by Fichte. After discussing it in its neo-Kantian sense, Heidegger then makes the term his own at the end of SS 1920 to refer to the primal reality of factic life experience, already charged with its own hermeneutic "logicity," thereby collapsing and conflating the post-Kantian distinction.

formale Anzeige (formal indication) – Not so named until WS 1919-20, this core feature of Heidegger's hermeneutic method is virtually announced two semesters earlier in the KNS-Schema, which diagrammatically singles out the power of formality to gain access to the pretheoretical, preworldly "primal something" of our being. Never fully explained in his "phenomenological decade," especially after the *cursus interruptus* of WS 1920–21, it is last mentioned in WS 1929–30 by Heidegger himself.

Fürsorge (solicitude) – First introduced as a third form of care in WS 1925–26, and illustrated by the two formal extremes of "being-for" the Other (GA 21:222f.).

Gerede (idle talk, chatter) – Introduced first in SS 1923 to describe in more detail the nature of the interpretedness occurring within the averageness and publicity of the Anyone, elements which were already in place in Oct. 1922.

Geschichtlichkeit (historicality, historicity) – In an oral ad-lib in the last hour of KNS 1919 recorded in student notes but not in the published edition, Heidegger first speaks of the "immanent historicity of life in itself" stemming from its "motivated tendency and tending motivation" which therefore lends itself to a "hermeneutic intuition" (ZBP 117). This "robust reality" (ZBP 135) of historicity as "meaning-giving element" (FS 350) is in WS 1919–20 described as a spontaneous experience of experience, a repetition of experience itself. This having of itself in self-accompaniment, this streaming return of experiencing life upon already-experienced life, defines a familiarity of life with itself which at once indicates its self-understanding and, in the formal schematism of intentionality, its sense of actualization or fulfillment (*Vollzugssinn*). Going back to the fifth of six senses of history in SS 1920, the Jaspers review calls it the "history which we ourselves 'are' " (GA 9:5) to distinguish it from the object-historical of typical historiography. In WS 1920–21, the "historical" is formally indicated as "the temporally becoming and, as having become, past." With the introduction of the problematic of death in Oct. 1922 (p. 13), the historical is to receive its basic sense from temporality. This futurizing of the return to the past continues in the two essays on "The Concept of Time" of 1924, but a full account of historicality is first developed only in BT itself.

Gewissen (conscience) – KNS 1919 makes passing mention of Schiller's critique of Kant for "shoving" every experience of the ought into the "blind power" of conscience (ZBP 45), but otherwise the young Heidegger never overtly mentions this neo-Kantian sense of *consciousness divided* between the normative and the naturally necessary, taut between apriori reason and the factually irrational. In the Jaspers review, however, the "actualization of conscience" is related to the middle-voiced phenomenon of being troubled and troubling oneself in a peculiar nonobjective union of the self's past, present, and future (GA 9:32f.). Having myself (in distress) is having a conscience. The emphasis on responsibility for the historical past in this same context is reinforced three years later in a passing mention of the conscience as one way of coming back to one's past and repeating it authentically in its How (BZ 25). But conscience receives scant development in the following treatments (November 1924, April 1925, SS 1925) of authenticating temporality through conscience-guilt-resolve. Only in BT does conscience receive its functional sense of "call" to absolute responsibility in the only thoroughgoing development of this basic triad.

Geworfenheit (thrownness) – First coined in the final draft of BT, prompted by the formal indication of ex-sistence, as a co-original correlate to "projection" (*Entwurf*). A more psychological version of this dynamic pairing, motive-tendency, was a staple in Heidegger's courses from 1919. The pairing passion-action, already evident in the middle-voiced phenomena of the double genitive of receiving the Word *of* God in WS 1920–21, is thematized in SS 1924 in relation to disposedness, *Befindlichkeit*.

gleichursprünglich (equiprimordial, co-original) – First used in the habilitation (1915), typically in the heterothetical context of the co-originality of the same and the other. Usages in the three drafts of BT tend to point toward the same context of Self-Other relations.

Habe (οὐσία as property, possessions of house-and-hold) – The "had" as property possessed is first introduced in WS 1921–22 as the original sense of οὐσία, stemming from its usage in everyday Greek. It becomes a kind of formal indication of the ousiological element in life and thought into BT.

Hermeneutik, -isch—The old Heidegger mistakenly recalls that "I first used these terms (*Titel*) . . . in SS 1923 ["Ontologie: Hermeneutik der Faktizität"], as I began to sketch out the first notes for BT . . . [and thereby] . . . tried to think the essence of phenomenology more originally" (US 95/9). But a more original "hermeneutic" phenomenology was already being worked out in KNS 1919 by way of a hybridized "hermeneutic intuition" (ZBP 117), along with the more historical route of critical destruction to get back to the "essence of all phenomenological hermeneutics" (SS 1919: ZBP 131). In WS 1919–20, he calls this development a "diahermeneutics." In WS 1921–22 and SS 1922, he develops basic aspects of the "hermeneutic situation" and, in his "Indication of the Hermeneutic Situation" for interpreting Aristotle in Oct. 1922, identifies his "fundamental research" project as a "phenomenological hermeneutics of facticity" (p. 16).

hermeneutisches "als" (hermeneutic "as") – The idea is already contained in Oct. 1922 in Heidegger's interpretation of *Nic. Ethics* 6 and his notion of *Ausgelegtheit*, but is first so named explicitly in WS 1925–26, in contrast with the apophantic "as."

hermeneutische Situation (hermeneutic situation) – There is first talk in WS 1921–22 of an *Evidenzsituation* or *Grunderfahrungssituation* that provokes the "primal decision" (GA 61:35) of passionate questioning, before Heidegger speaks of the *Verstehenssituation* (38) which philosophy must appropriate, by interpreting the linguistic usage which the situation entails (42), in order to indicate the direction in which it is heading. In SS 1922, this situation of understanding is first named the "hermeneutic situation" (GA 61:3 is a semester premature) and structured according to its prepossession and preconception.

Hingabe (devotion, dedication, submission, immersion) – Lask's term to describe our immediate experience of forms of life (like values), in which we are already "given over" (*hingegeben*) to them, as a tacit intuition of the categorial dimension, is extended by Heidegger in KNS 1919 to include the more overt working "intuition" sought by the phenomenologist: a nonreflective categorial immersion or absorption (*Hingabe*) rather than an inspection (*Hinsicht*). But with the introduction of the tendency of ruination or falling in 1921–22, even the nonocular and empathetic *Hingabe*, "lost" as it is in absorbed immersion, is viewed with suspicion as a way to access to the "matters themselves."

Horizont (horizon) – One of those occasional words deeply secreted in the young Heidegger's vocabulary, in part from his reading of phenomenology (cf. *Ideen* I, § 27, 44, 47, etc.). Passing mention in WS 1919–20 of the "horizon of significance" of the world, in SS 1920 of the "horizon of historiology," in the Jaspers review (GA 9:22, 1f.) of the "distressful horizon of expectation" of existence and of Jaspers's own frequent usage of the term in "pacing off" the limits of the psychic for psychology. "Horizons" of research and inquiry begin to proliferate perceptibly in the Marburg years, in conjunction with the Greek "horismic" sense of definition. In this role, a horizon provides prefiguration (*Vorzeichnung*) outlining directions in the field of questioning. It first takes center stage on the opening page of BT when time is projected as the "potential horizon for any and every understanding of being."

horizontales Schema (horizonal schema) – The phrase is only employed in § 69c (SZ 365f.) in BT to name the "whither" of the ecstases of time. After SS 1927, where the move to locate the Temporality of being itself upon the horizons of temporality collapses, the term disappears from the Heideggerian corpus.

In-der-Welt-sein (being-in-the-world) – "Life is always life in a world" (WS 1919–20). In SS 1923, "Dasein is being in a world" is identified as the formal indication of the investigation; the hyphenated phrase first occurs near the end of the course (GA 63:80, 102). It becomes the formal indication guiding the first draft of BT in November 1924.

Innerweltliches (innerworldly thing) – First called "world thing" (*Weltding*) in SS 1925 before it is less ambiguously termed "innerworldly being" first in BT itself.

Innerzeitigkeit (innertimeness) – Perhaps the very last technical term to be coined for BT itself, to identify it as the time of "innerworldly beings" (SZ 235, 333, 412). In Heidegger's working manuscript of March 1926, it is first named "the time with which we reckon." The very last chapter of BT was accordingly tentatively entitled (in § 45) "Temporality and Dasein's Reckoning with 'Time' " before it is first drafted in late summer 1926 under its final title, "Temporality and Innertimeness as the Origin of the Common Conception of Time" (cf. Appendix C).

In-Sein (in-being, being-in) – The coining of being-in-the-world in SS 1923 brings with it the question of what it means to be-in . . . , "the how of 'in'-being as life *out* of the world" (GA 63:86). In-being receives its first full-fledged development primarily in terms of disposedness, discoveredness, and interpretedness in the first draft of BT in November 1924, where it is finally but somewhat tenuously identified with "being-possible" (cf. "Seinkönnen" below). In SS 1925, pains are taken to distinguish in-being from being-in (*Sein-in*) to eradicate every vestige of spatial containment from the former notion. Rather than a being "in" something, in-being is a "way to be," that of intimate involvement in habitative dwelling (GA 20:211ff./157f.).

Jeweiligkeit (at-the-time-ness, particular whileness, temporal particularity) – Against the background of his Aristotelian reflections on phronetic insight into the particular ultimate, what is to be done here and now, and the place of the particular, ἕκαστον, in ousiology, Heidegger in SS 1923 formally introduces Da-sein as his technical term precisely because it indicates the "particular while" which each of us is and has. The term is by and large displaced by *Jemeinigkeit* in BT itself.

kairologisch (kairological) – Only in WS 1921–22 and SS 1923, and briefly, to refer to characters of Dasein that pertain to its peculiar nonobjective time, the temporality of its actualization.

Krisis der Wissenschaften (crisis of the sciences) – The then widespread phenomenon of productive revolutions prompting the revision of the basic concepts of the various sciences, and especially philosophy, is first discussed in the opening paragraph of the Kassel lectures of April 1925 and reiterated in SS 1925 (GA 20, § 1), WS 1925–26 (GA 21, § 3), BT (SZ, § 3), and WS 1927–28 (GA 25, § 2b).

Lebenswelt (lifeworld) – 1918 to 1921, perhaps from conversations with Husserl. In the habilitation (1915–16), it is called the *Erlebniswelt* or *Erfahrungswelt*, the world of experience. In keeping with the neo-Kantian division of values, it tends to be used in the plural to refer to the scientific, ethical, aesthetic, and religious lifeworlds.

leicht und schwer, schwierig (easy and difficult) – First introduced in SS 1920 as categories intrinsic to the self-world: in contrast with the impersonal ease and ultimate security of the theoretical domain, the original motive of philosophizing, which in view of its orientation to actual Dasein is more than a science, is to revive the unease stemming from the distressed concern (*Bekümmerung*, later *Sorge*) inherent in life. Various Augustinian themes—I am become a question to myself, life is a trial, etc.—in SS 1921 bring out the biblical roots of the theme that "life is hard." In WS 1921–22, the Aristotelian account of the "endlessness of fallibility" (GA 61:107ff.) through excess and defect, hyperbole and ellipsis, is used to elaborate the same categories. The Introduction of Oct. 1922 (pp. 3f.) identifies the tranquilizing tendency to make things easy for oneself with the inertia (pendency) of falling. Thus, BT will continue to speak of the "tendency to take things lightly and make things easy" in the Anyone, which serves to "unburden Dasein of its being" (SZ 127f.). SS 1924 associates this comforting sedation with a metaphysics of presence which since Parmenides takes its orientation from the moods of hedonism.

Lichtung (lighting, clearing, lighted clearing) – This central term is first introduced in BT itself to name the "disclosedness of being-in" (SZ 170) under the influence of the tradition of *lumen naturale*, according to which the human being is "lighted within itself" (SZ 133, but already in SS 1925; GA 20:412). Its sporadic use in BT leads to the identification of the lighted clearing with the unity of ecstatic temporality (SZ 351). As the condition of sight and its degeneration into curiosity, the temporal clearing that Dasein is accordingly replaces eternal νοῦς in Heidegger's deconstructed ontology (SZ 170f.). But the clear disengagement of this "clearing of being" from the tradition of *Lichtmetaphysik* occurs only with the later Heidegger.

das Man (the Anyone, Everyone, "they") – First introduced in Oct. 1922 (p. 11) to specify the pronominal "subject" of the averageness of the public, it is first substantified into a noun in SS 1923 (GA 63:31).

Mitsein, Mitdasein (with-being, co-Dasein) – Presaged by the introduction of *Miteinandersein* (being-with-one-another) in November 1924, both terms are first introduced in SS 1925 to articulate the initial encounter of the Other in her having to do with the world, her functioning in the world along with me. In this reciprocity of mutual comporting, accordingly, Others "are there with" (*mit da sein*) me, I "am with" (*sein mit*) Others. The terms are introduced to correct a confusion contained in the the the notion of a "with-world": "For the world itself is never there *with*, but instead is that *in* which Dasein as concern is in every case" (GA 20: 333f./242).

Mitwelt (with-world) – WS 1919–20 to BT: Heidegger in SS 1925 attempts to drop this social worldliness from his triad of worlds (cf. "Mitsein" above), but it is reinstated on a more subtle level in BT as the world that I "*share with others*" (SZ 118), beginning with the publicly averaged "with-world *in* which *we* are environmentally concerned" (SZ 125).

Neugier (curiosity) – The phenomenological problem of the "genesis of the theoretical attitude" in KNS 1919, and the critique in subsequent semesters of the "aesthetic" and contemplative attitude, seemingly detached from worldly concerns, of philosophers like Natorp, Dilthey, and Jaspers, pave the way for an account of such attitudes in terms of the "temptation of curiosity." The stage is set by Luther's critique of the Church Fathers for their aesthetic idolatry of the glories of the world as a mistaken (Greek) way to God, supported by Augustine's critique of the *perversa scientia* of curiosity (SS 1921). In the Aristotelian context of SS 1922, curiosity strays from the theoretical drive to see the whole by its excessive zest to see every particular. In the last two drafts of BT, curiosity is presented as a major moment in the tendency of falling.

ontisch-ontologisch (ontic-ontological) – The "ontic" and "archontic" are already part of the young Heidegger's vocabulary. There is thus some hint of this distinction from previous years (e.g., GA 61:53), but it is first clearly drawn in SS 1924 in distinguishing the different senses of Aristotle's οὐσία. Its first clear-cut usage in SS 1925 (GA 20:268/197) articulates a classic phenomenological statement which will be reiterated for decades to come not only about Dasein (SZ 15) but also about Being and *das Ereignis*: our ontically immediate experience of being, for all its nearness, is at once the farthest removed from us ontologically. It is in BT that Heidegger first openly broaches the problem of founding all ontology upon the concrete "ontic fundament" of the ever-present background experience of our being.

ontologische Differenz—The idea first enters the Heideggerian corpus in the 1912 review of Lask's *Logik der Philosophie*, where the "third Reich" of validity is set off from the two "hemispheres" of sensory and suprasensory entities and their "categories of being" ("Es 'ist' nicht, sondern es gilt."), and Plato is blamed for the "hypostasizing of the [transcendental-] logical realm into metaphysical entities" (GA 1:24). But it is first so named only in SS 1927, as the very first of the "basic problems of phenomenology." In the interim, this ontological difference tacitly asserts itself in various ways: in 1915 in the analysis of "ens est" into its subject matter as opposed to its heterological nexus (*Bewandtnis*: FS 323); finally in BT in the distinction of the ontic and the ontological.

Phänomen (phenomenon) – Already in the habilitation, the young Heidegger expresses a strong phenomenological commitment, by later standards bordering on the naive, to the self-showing of the articulations of reality accessible through *simplex apprehensio*, and thus directly readable from the "facticities" themselves (FS 155). But it is only with the introduction of the triple context of surrounding worlds in WS 1919–20, understood as contexts of manifestation (*Bekundung*) or a "somehow" of expression, that "phenomenon" itself is first thematized. "Everything that we encounter in life expresses itself, puts itself forward, appears, in short, is a phenomenon." In his treatment of the formal indication in WS 1920–21, Heidegger first distinguishes phenomenon from the less comprehensive *Objekt* and "counterstance" (*Gegenstand*), and then notes that the "internal word" or *logos* which gives itself in the phenomenon is accessible only through the formal indication of intentionality in its triple-sensed totality, where the senses of relation and actualization supersede that of objective content. The first glimmers of the Greek etymological approach to phenomeno-logy occur in SS 1923 (GA 63:67), where the problem of the inherent self-concealing of self-showing phenomena is also broached (76). The etymological analysis of phenomeno-logy is first fully carried out in the following semester and, shortly thereafter, the three modes of concealing with which phenomenology must contend (cf. "Verborgenheit" below), on the basis of which phenomenology is then fully defined in SS 1925 (GA 20, § 9) and in BT (SZ, §7).

Präsenz (presence) – This Latinization first becomes important in November 1924 in connection with the inherent ambiguity of the term "present" in the Indo-European languages. Heidegger accordingly distinguishes between presence in a context or at a place (*die Präsenz*) and the temporal tense of the present (*das Präsens*). In SS 1925, the term is used indiscriminately with its German synonyms *Anwesenheit* and *Gegenwärtigkeit*, and even *Gegenwart*. But in WS 1925–26, *Präsenz* becomes the cover concept comprehending both being as presence (*Anwesenheit*) and aletheic truth as *Gegenwart*, the latter being understood in the active sense of *Gegenwärtigen* (presenting: cf. GA 21:192f.). In SS 1927, *Praesenz* (*sic* in the German text: GA 24:433ff.) is the only horizonal schema of the Temporality of Being which is treated, in this second and likewise abortive attempt to draft the Third Division of BT. (Note that Hofstadter's translation of the German *Praesenz* by the purer Latin "praesens" interjects a potential translational confusion by orthographically conflating the distinction made by Heidegger in November 1924.) Cf. "Anwesenheit" above.

Schuld (guilt, debit of existence) – The term first appears briefly in November 1924 in the unmasking quality of resoluteness through "becoming guilty in not having chosen" and as the way of becoming (responsible for) one's own past. SS 1925 explicates the phenomenon a bit further, but only in BT is the term first thematized as the "content" of the call of conscience and as the debit already intrinsic to existence.

Seinkönnen (can-be) – The first stirrings of the universalized "can be" of Dasein are to be found in July 1924, in conjunction with the outermost possibility of death (BZ 15ff.). In November 1924, Heidegger concludes that the most immediate being-in is being-possible, the original choice to be or not to be its There, its "that it is." Accordingly, Dasein *always* is what it *can be*. "The very being of Dasein is characterized as being-*out*-toward what it is not but can be." This "underway" character of Dasein is the complex that later gives birth, literally in the margins of this text, to the formal indication of "ex-sistence." The delayed incubation is reflected in the tardy and halting first emergence of the noun-phrase "can-be" in the second, still nonexistentialist, draft of BT (GA 20:401/290).

Selbstwelt (self-world) – WS 1919–20 to SS 1925: The domain of origin of the around-world and with-world is the self-world, in which I first have myself tacitly in and through that world. The term does not appear in BT.

Sinn (sense, meaning) – Despite the prevalence of the triple-sensed schema of intentionality in 1920–22, understood from the start as three "senses of direction," the very sense of sense itself is not thematized until BT itself, where it is formally defined as the "toward-which according-to-which (*Woraufhin*) of the projection," structured by the threefold pre-suppositional structure of Dasein's hermeneutic situation, out of which something becomes understandable as something (SZ 151). Cf. "Woraufhin" below.

Situation (situation) – The term is explicated and exemplified, with the highlighting of the "situation I," in SS 1919, after Heidegger's reading of Jaspers's book, which appeared in early 1919 and made "limit situations" central in illuminating existence. But the young Heidegger may have been cultivating the term already in 1918 from his reading of Schleiermacher and Spranger. In Oct. 1922, Heidegger distinguishes "situation" from "location" (*Lage*), and makes it the focus of phronetic insight. The term appears surprisingly late in the kairological context of BT itself (SZ 299).

Sorge (care) – Precursors are the biblical *Bekümmerung* (1920) and Augustine's *cura* (1921). Caring (*Sorgen*) is in WS 1921–22 identified as the relational sense of life (GA 61:89) and, when this triple-sensed schematism recedes, as the "basic sense of the factic movedness of life" (Oct. 1922, p. 6). In this same context it is also already called, as a sheer formal indication, simply "care." In BT, the very sense of care is found to be temporality pure and simple.

Temporalien (tensors, temporals) – In WS 1925–26, the tensors are to be those characters of phenomena which are characterized *through* time, in contrast with "zeitliche" characters which take place *in* time (GA 21:199, 243). But in the last hour of the semester, such tensed temporals are renamed the existentials, which, curiously, at first turn out to be the tenses themselves.

Temporalität (Temporality) – At first used broadly in WS 1925–26 to refer to the "time-determination" (GA 21:200) of all phenomena, beginning with the "Temporality of Dasein" (409), *Temporalität* in the opening pages of BT is restricted to the Temporality of Being, in contrast with the "temporality" (*Zeitlichkeit*) of Dasein.

Transzendenz (transcendence) – Heidegger's treatise on the transcendentals, the habilitation of 1915–16, already relates transcendence to intentionality, drawn from its medieval context as the "transcendent primal relation of the soul to God" (FS 351). Heidegger thus cites Scheler's similar equation, calling the human being "an eternal beyond" (GA 63:25), in SS 1923, along with texts from Calvin and Zwingli, which are repeated into BT. But it is not until SS 1927 that transcendence becomes Heidegger's "formal indication," thus detheologized and understood as the condition of the possibility of intentionality.

Umgang (getting around, going about, getting along, etc.) – First thematized in WS 1921–22 to develop the How of the "rounds" (*Um*) in the
world roundabout.

Umsicht (circumspection, looking around) – the first description of the
world-around in KNS 1919 is based on looking around more than getting
around, but circumspection is first so named in Oct. 1922 in contrast
with inspection (*Hinsicht*).

Umwelt (environment, surrounding world, world-around) – In 1915, the
surrounding world was sensory and natural, as opposed to the suprasensory world which was medieval man's first interest (FS 141, 155, 197,
206, 222): the worldly versus the spiritual rather than world as context
of significance (GA 63:96). KNS 1919 provides the first description of
the "*environmental* experience" of a chair in a meaningful context that
"worlds." WS 1919–20 juxtaposes the around-world to the with-world
and self-world. The rounds of prepositional reference of this world of
concern are first woven in SS 1923 (cf. "Verweisungszusammenhang"
below). The young Heidegger was clearly aware of Uexküll's then-popu-
lar notion of *Umwelt*.

Unverborgenheit (unconcealment, Heidegger's basic translation of
ἀλήθεια, "truth") – The move back from the truth of judgment (as conformity) to the truth of simple apprehension (as intelligibility and meaning) is already under way in the habilitation of 1915. The hyphenated
Greek term makes a fleeting appearance in KNS 1919 (ZBP 49). The
stand-in for "truth" in WS 1921–22 is *Erhellung* (illumination). But truth
as "unconcealment" is first thematized only in Oct. 1922 in the translation
of the Greek texts of *Nicomachean Ethics* 6. The translation is contained
in the Greek-German dictionaries of the nineteenth century. Cf. "Phänomen" for another latent strand of development of the young Heidegger's
concept of "truth."

Verborgenheit, Verdecktheit (concealment, concealedness) – Concealment
is first mentioned in Oct. 1922 in relation to Aristotle's sense of falsehood,
understood as "self-veiling" (p. 32). A similar discussion in WS 1923–24
points to the nature of speech, its habitual repetition, as the major source
of concealment, but then points to the world that comes to speech, its
multiplicity and elusive fleetingness, as another source. The talk on truth
drafted in early 1924 for the first time explicitly mentions the peculiarity
of the Greek word for truth which suggests that it must be "wrung" from
concealment, and names the three concealments of opinion, ignorance,
and the lapsing of old truths back into concealment. The subsequent
courses then highlight Greek philosophy's struggle against its two great

manifestations of concealment, rhetoric (SS 1924) and sophistry (WS 1924–25). In SS 1925, the three concealments with which phenomenology must contend are expressed in terms which will be carried over into BT: the not yet discovered, relapse back to a buried state, and disguise (GA 20:119/86 = SZ 35).

Verfallen, Verfallenheit (falling, fallenness; or "decadence" when juxtaposed to transcendence) – Used incidentally in conjunction with *Abfallen* since SS 1920, it is first thematized in detail under the heading of *Ruinanz* in WS 1921–22 before it becomes the "pendency" (*Verhängnis*) of falling in Oct. 1922.

Verstehen, Seinsverständnis (understanding, . . . of being) – The young Heidegger explored a number of precedents of this tacit "knowledge" which is one with life, from Scotus's *modus essendi activus* to Reinach's experientially immanent knowledge, but the term is first introduced and at once made central in KNS 1919. In response to Natorp's objections against the accessibility and expressibility of immediate experience by way of the phenomenological method, understanding is first identified in KNS 1919 as a "hermeneutic intuition" (ZBP 117) based on a nonreflective experiencing of experience; this is regarded as a kind of "sympathy" (ZBP 110) that life has of itself, giving access to its origin and yielding articulable phenomenological preconcepts of its incipient dynamics. This streaming return of life back onto itself in understanding familiarity is in WS 1919–20 identified with historicity and, in the formal schematism of intentionality, with its sense of actualization. Contrary to Husserl's sense of intuition drawn from the objectifying paradigm of sense perception, understanding is more an accompanying familiarity that comes with life itself, giving access to its sense and context, which is nothing objective or thinglike. But beyond a continuing formal stress on the sense of actualization (until 1922), without any real hint on how the *Besinnung* of this "self-worldly experience" (GA 61:95, 157) does not entail reflective intrusion, Heidegger more or less shuns the further elaboration of understanding until SS 1925, when he for the first time broaches the topic of a *selbstverständlichen* "understanding of being" (GA 20:194/144) as the indispensable basis for giving rise to the question of being. Various formulae for understanding are developed there—having myself in the self-worldly accompaniment of my absorption in the environing world (350/254: from WS 1919–20), self-discovering disposed involvement (356/258)—but understanding as can-be or possibility surfaces tentatively only near the end of the course (413/299). The emphasis on the projection of possibility emerges only in BT itself, by way of the new formal indication of ex-sistence as being-out-for a can-be.

Verweisungszusammenhang (referential context) – the go-around of life is first analyzed into its world-constituting prepositional series of references (for, in order to, for the sake of, etc.) in the last hour of SS 1923.

Vollzugsgeschichte (actualization history) – Sept. 1920 to SS 1921, first in the Jaspers review and especially in WS 1920–21. Always adjectivally expressed as the "actualization-historical" in contradistinction to the "object-historical." It is the very core of what since KNS has been called "historicity" or "historicality," which at this time is formally identified with the intentional "sense of actualization."

Vorgriff (preconception, fore-conception) – In KNS 1919, fore-cepts are first paired with re-cepts (*Rückgriffe*), which together reach forth and back into the motivated tendency of life without stilling the stream, as con-cepts do. But in the following semesters, fore-conception naturally assumes both directions of "before." When joined by *Vorhabe* (1921) and *Vorsicht* (1924) to constitute the hermeneutic situation, *Vorgriff* assumes the prelinguistic function of articulation, and of putting into words what is already had and sighted.

Vorhabe (prepossession, pre-having) – There is talk of a prescientific "lived having" of the being of things through direct acquaintance in the Aristotle seminar of SS 1921, but the pre-having which structures the hermeneutic situation is not thematized until SS 1922 (the use of the term in GA 61:19 is a semester too early). It thus emerges with the recognition of οὐσία as *Habe*, possessions.

Vorhandenheit (prepresence, on-handness, presence at hand) – First used terminologically to describe the "already there in advance" in which the around-world is disclosed, and so not yet distinguished from the "handy" (GA 63:97; also November 1924). In fact, so unresolved is this term in November 1924 that even the facticity of the "I am," its "that it is," is described in terms of its "being on hand." The more subtle analysis in SS 1925 of the levels of immediate presence first yields the clear distinction in modes of encounter and disclosedness between the handy (*Zuhandenes*) and the on-hand things (*Vorhandenes*) against the background presence of the environing world.

Vorlaufen (forerunning, running ahead) – First in July 1924 (BZ 17ff.) as Dasein's forerunning to its "bygone" (*Vorbei*) before it is becomes a forerunning of "my death" in SS 1925. The limit situation of death itself is first made ontologically central as a facticity in SS 1922 before its "seizure" becomes the countermovement to the "pendency" of falling in Oct. 1922.

Vor-sicht (pre-view, fore-sight) – First mentioned briefly in WS 1923–24 in describing the hermeneutic situation of ontologically pre-viewing Dasein (what is had in advance) in terms of its being in order to preconceive the existentials. Often left hyphenated (e.g., in SS 1925), pre-view is thus the last of the presuppositional structures of the hermeneutic situation to be terminologically identified.

Weltlichkeit (worldliness, worldhood) – Even though the world as meaningful is already in place in KNS 1919, and the formally indicative question of what it means to-be-in-the-world is being detailed in SS 1923, along with the warning that to be "worldly" is not the opposite of to be spiritual (GA 63:96), the ontological characteristic of "worldli*ness*" as a "How of the being of Dasein" is not introduced until SS 1925 (GA 20: 211, 226ff.) to become the basis of the present perfect apriori.

Wiederholung (repetition, retrieve) – Against Rickert's objection in WS 1921–22 that philosophy is creation rather than a mere repetition of life (GA 61:80, 88), Heidegger insists that philosophy as a "basic How of life" repetitively re-takes life out of its lapse by way of radical research. In SS 1924, Heidegger contrasts the rote repetition involved in human making with the more creative repetition of prior resolutions in human action, through a habituated predisposition to sagacious choice of the proper moment for appropriate action. Authentic history as repetition of the possibility of the past is first mentioned in the talk of July 1924. But repetition in its full historical sense as explicit transmission of a tradition (SZ 385), as well as the ever-deepening methodical repetition of the Dasein-analysis and of the questioning of being, are both first explicated and illustrated in BT.

Worauf, Woraufhin (the toward-which according-to-which) – Against Natorp's objections of the inescapable objectification of phenomenological immediacy in KNS 1919, Heidegger is already suggesting that "object" in an intentional context is no longer a "standing over against" but rather the more dynamic toward-which, "the moment of 'on to,' the 'direction toward' " (ZBP 115). *Das Worauf* , the toward-which, is first explicitly mentioned in WS 1920–21 as the formal indication of any "counterstance" (*Gegenstand*). In WS 1921–22 it is identified with the containment sense of intentionality, where Heidegger insists it is not a what of fulfilling content but a how of the holding relation (GA 61: 53). In the context of defining the "direction of sight" motivated by a hermeneutic situation, Oct. 1922 (p. 1) for the first time suggests the more generalized toward-which according-to-which (*woraufhin*) something is interpreted as something. Time itself emerges as the ordering toward-which in the interpretation of Kant's schematism in WS 1925–26.

Only in BT do we get the complex definition of sense (*Sinn*) as the to-ward-which of Dasein's project structured by the triple fore-structure of its hermeneutic situation. Thus, BT for the first time tries to sort out the full vectorial complexity of this unthematic directional according-to-which of the primary project of Dasein into the in-which of the world's meaningfulness, the toward-which of the for-the-sake-of-which, and the through-which of the interpretation, out of which something is under-stood as something (SZ 150f.), and understands this apriori formal frame of the project as the very sense and temporality of Dasein (SZ 324). It is in view of the vectorially complex empowering character of the toward-which that *das Woraufhin* assumes the secondary sense contained in prep-ositions like "kraft" and "gemäß," the "upon-which" and "according-to-which."

Zeitigung (generative temporalization, ripening, bringing to fruition) – The "sense of temporalization" (*Zeitigungssinn*) is a kind of "fourth di-mension" which rounds out the actualization of the triple-sensed inten-tional movement first against the background of Aristotle's 'biological' philosophy only in WS 1921–22 and SS 1922 (cf. "Bezugssinn" above). But temporalization per se continues to convey the productive power of time in its full generative possibility through BT, and beyond. In the later Heidegger, it serves to formally indicate the generative event (*Ereignis*) of sense, truth, and history.

Zeitlichkeit (temporality) – Having invoked the "rhythms" of the living self in having itself in its origin in the self-world and having formalized its movement into a triple-sensed intentionality, Heidegger concludes WS 1919–20 by noting, in passing, that such motivated rhythms must be comprehended in terms of Bergson's distinction between objective cosmic time and concrete duration. The term "temporality" is first used in SS 1920 in contrast with the "supratemporal" apriori, based on the stereotypical distinction, in the then prevalent argument against psychol-ogism by Husserl and the neo-Kantians, between supratemporal judica-tive content and judicative actualization through cognitive processes "in time." But instead of such an "objective" temporality or even the "pure" temporality of Husserl's "original phenomenological time" of the stream of experience, Heidegger calls for an examination of the "time of the self-world" through historical Dasein's continual relation to its own past. Temporality then becomes a formal indication of Christian life in WS 1920–21, in order to determine the "actualization history" of life rather than its "object history." First in Oct. 1922 (p. 13) is the specific temporal-ity of human Dasein to be found by coming to terms with its impending death, which in turn would determine the basic sense of the historical.

The kairological temporality of Dasein in its contrast with the *Temporalität* of being does not clearly emerge until the opening pages of BT.

Zuhandenes (the handy, ready-to-hand) – First identified in SS 1923 but clearly distinguished from things on hand only in SS 1925, where handy things are understood as their underlying presence. Cf. *Vorhandenheit* above.

Zu-sein (to-be) – First mentioned at the end of WS 1924–25, the conative "(having) to-be" is made central in SS 1925 as the formal indication of the characters of being of Dasein, which accordingly are called "ways to be." It becomes a recessive term in BT as it for the most part is replaced by the formal indication of "existence."

NOTES

INTRODUCTION

1. Martin Heidegger, *Unterwegs zur Sprache* (Pfullingen: Neske, 1959), p. 92; English translation by Peter D. Hertz, *On the Way to Language* (New York: Harper and Row, 1971), p. 6. Hereafter US, citing the page number of the original German and then the English translation within the body of the text, in this case, US 92/6.

Martin Heidegger, *Sein und Zeit* (Halle an der Saal, later Tübingen: Niemeyer Verlag, [1]1927, [16]1986); English translation by John Macquarrie and Edward Robinson, *Being and Time* (New York: Harper and Row, 1962). Hereafter referred to as BT in the text itself (see Key to Abbreviations and Notations) but as SZ in citing the page number, since the German pagination is to be found in the margin of the English translation (the "H" numbers). See the Bibliography for a full list of publication years of the sixteen extant editions of SZ, not counting the GA editions of it. The edition of [5]1941 leaves out the dedication to Husserl. It was reset in [7]1953, with a Preliminary Remark added by Heidegger on the dropping of the subtitle "First Half"; but it does not mention dropping the several references, first made in 1926, to the specific projects relegated to the never-published "Second Half." Macquarrie and Robinson, in their customary scholarly thoroughness, have wisely included these suppressed or altered, but genealogically revealing, footnotes in their English translation.

2. Martin Heidegger, *Prolegomena zur Geschichte des Zeitbegriffs*, ed. Petra Jaeger, GA 20 (Frankfurt: Klostermann, 1979). English translation by Theodore Kisiel, *History of the Concept of Time: Prolegomena* (Bloomington: Indiana University Press, 1985). Regrettably, the Translator's Introduction and Index prepared for this translation under the mandates of the NEH grant supporting the work, and essential for its genealogical understanding, did not appear with it because of the antischolarly policies created literally *ad hoc* by Heidegger's literary executors, and put into practice by "legal" intimidation. Cf. n. 6 below.

3. See Key to Abbreviations and Notations for the distinction between the young, early, later, and old Heidegger, as a convenient notation to connect Heidegger to his major periods of development without the constant need to invoke dates. Also note the abbreviations and rough time frame of the typical Summer (SS) and Winter Semester (WS) at the German universities during this period. Finally, see Appendix B for a semester-by-semester overview of the titles of Heidegger's courses and seminars during this period.

4. In medieval law, when the hand of the deceased is still "quick" enough to be made to hold a quill and passed across the parchment, the mark is a legal signature. Is Heidegger's hand still quick enough to allow his name to be used to "authorize" the present questionable editions of "his" Gesamtausgabe? See n. 6 for more on this.

5. Otto Pöggeler, *Heidegger und die hermeneutische Philosophie* (Freiburg and Munich: Alber, 1983), p. 429, n. 15.

6. I have recently analyzed the contradictory authoritarianism implied in the anecdotal "evidence" being used to establish and "justify" the policies and practices of the *Gesamtausgabe*, in a paper delivered at the International Heidegger Symposium sponsored by the Alexander von Humboldt-Stiftung on April 24–28, 1989, in Bonn. See my "Edition und Übersetzung: Unterwegs von Tatsachen zu Gedanken, von Werken zu Wegen," in *Zur philosophischen Aktualität Heideggers*, ed. Dietrich Papenfuss and Otto Pöggeler, vol. 3, *Im Spiegel der Welt: Sprache, Übersetzung, Auseinandersetzung* (Frankfurt: Klostermann, 1992), pp. 89–107.

7. The entire text of this letter of August 19, 1921, is now published in *Zur philosophischen Aktualität Heideggers*, ed. Dietrich Papenfuss and Otto Pöggeler, vol. 2, *Im Gespräch der Zeit* (Frankfurt: Klostermann, 1990), pp. 27–32, esp. p. 29. Before this, it had been cited piecemeal by Löwith himself in a number of his publications, and analyzed in its full context in my "War der frühe Heidegger tatsächlich ein 'christlicher Theologe'?" in *Philosophie und Poesie: Otto Pöggeler zum 60. Geburtstag*, ed. A. Gethmann-Siefert (Stuttgart: Fromann-Holzboog, 1988), 2:59–75. For another analysis of this letter, more in terms of its relevance for a philosophical biography of Heidegger, see also Theodore Kisiel, "Heidegger's Apology: Biography as Philosophy and Ideology," *Graduate Faculty Philosophy Journal* 14/2–15/1 (1991): 363–404, esp. pp. 375–378.

8. *Zur philosophischen Aktualität Heideggers*, 2:37, which contains the entire text of Heidegger's letter to Löwith on August 20, 1927. We shall soon, and often, have occasion to apply this genealogically telling letter, with remarks fresh from the context of the first appearance of BT in print, to our Story.

PART I: THE BREAKTHROUGH TO THE TOPIC

1. Bernhard Casper, "Martin Heidegger und die theologische Fakultät Freiburg 1909–1923," *Freiburger Diözesan-Archiv* 100 (1980): 541.

2. Hannah Arendt, "Martin Heidegger zum achzigsten Geburtstag," *Merkur* 10 (1969): 893; "Martin Heidegger at Eighty," *The New York Review of Books*, October 21, 1971, p. 50. Also in *Heidegger and Modern Philosophy*, ed. Michael Murray (New Haven: Yale University Press, 1978), pp. 293–294.

3. Hans-Georg Gadamer, *Heideggers Wege* (Tübingen: Mohr, 1983), p. 141.

4. Hans-Georg Gadamer, "Wilhelm Dilthey nach 150 Jahren," in *Dilthey und die Philosophie der Gegenwart*, ed. E. W. Orth, Sonderband der *Phänomenologischen Forschungen* (Freiburg and Munich: Alber, 1985), p. 159.

5. This is a citation of Oskar Becker's distillation which contains the essentials of Franz Josef Brecht's transcript, the only extant firsthand student version of this hour. Gerda Walther's transcript, owing to the illness and death of her father, ends in mid-course on March 14, and afterwards copies Brecht. For the German, see my "Das Kriegsnotsemester 1919: Heideggers Durchbruch in die hermeneutische Phänomenologie," *Philosophisches Jahrbuch* 99, no. 1 (1992): 105–122, esp. pp. 106f.

6. Heidegger's letter to Löwith on August 20, 1927, in *Zur philosophischen Aktualität Heideggers* 2:36f.

1: Phenomenological Beginnings: The Hermeneutic Breakthrough (1915–19)

1. Once again, I am following Oskar Becker's transcript for this "KNS-Schema;" Becker added the outline designations, I.A., I.B., II.A., and II.B. to Brecht's firsthand version, thus providing convenient designations for us in following this important schema. Heidegger's German diagram, as he wrote it across the blackboard in a single row, is contained in fig. 1, p. 22, along with my supplement, the series of German impersonals which serves to outline a main thread in the course. It might be observed here that the term *Ur-etwas* is to be found only in the transcripts (several times), while the published edition speaks instead of the "pretheoretical, preworldly something" (ZBP 115–117).

2. Rickert's report is to be found in Thomas Sheehan, "Heidegger's *Lehrjahre*," in *The Collegium Phaenomenologicum: The First Ten Years*, ed. J.C. Sallis, G. Moneta, and J. Taminiaux, Phaenomenologica, vol. 105 (Dordrecht, Boston, London: Kluwer, 1988), p. 118.

3. I have dealt with this relationship in great detail in my "Why Students of Heidegger Will Have to Read Emil Lask," in *Emil Lask and the Search for Concreteness*, ed. Deborah G. Chaffin (Athens: Ohio University Press, 1993).

4. *Fichtes Idealismus und die Geschichte* (1902) is to be found in Lask's *Gesammelte Schriften*, vol. 1 (= GS 1).

5. John D. Caputo, "Phenomenology, Mysticism and the 'Grammatica Speculativa': Heidegger's 'Habilitationsschrift,' " *Journal of the British Society for Phenomenology* 5 (1974): 101–117, esp. p. 107. Failure to note this hidden agenda of a preunderstanding of being in the habilitation work, with the consequent loss of a precious opportunity for insight into the phenomenon of mysticism, is especially detrimental to Caputo's particular interests in Heidegger. Moreover, he perpetuates and even magnifies the mistake in various ways in his later books on the relation of Heidegger to medieval scholasticism and mysticism. Small wonder that, having missed this noetic dimension of *modus essendi*, he goes on to speak of "the realism of the *Habilitationsschrift*," which prevents Heidegger from seeing the "mystical elements" of the "event" of truth until after the "turn" of 1930. (Heidegger was in fact developing such insights and, for that very reason, already making the turn in 1919!) Cf. John D. Caputo, *The Mystical Elements in Heidegger's Thought* (Athens: Ohio University Press, 1978), p. 152. There is more warrant

for asserting that Caputo himself has allowed subliminal vestiges of scholastic realism to get the best of his phenomenological training. A little dose of transcendental idealism à la Lask might have averted the wrong turn, by recalling the aspects of Divine Idealism operative in the scholastic doctrine of ontological truth. In this regard, I missed the works of Albert Dondeyne in Caputo's book, *Heidegger and Aquinas* (New York: Fordham University Press, 1982).

Cf. also Roderick M. Stewart, "Signification and Radical Subjectivity in Heidegger's Habilitationsschrift,' " *Man and World* 12 (1979): 360–386, esp. p. 365, who notes the active *modus essendi* with some astonishment and does not know what to make of it. Important for the future study of Heidegger is the fact that Stewart has appended a complete translation of the habilitation's Conclusion to his article.

6. In scholastic philosophy, simple apprehension is called the first "act of the mind" and judgment the second. My account here of the various phenomenological moves from Lask to Heidegger must be sparse. See n. 3 for a more detailed account.

7. This very Laskian phrase refers to the truth of simple apprehension or categorial intuition. This relationship between living (or "experiencing" = *erleben*) and knowing, crucial for what follows, first takes shape in Husserl's discussion in the Sixth Logical Investigation (§§ 8, 39) of tacitly experiencing truth as identification in knowing the identical object. See my articles on the Husserlian aspects of Heidegger's thought: "Heidegger (1907–1927): The Transformation of the Categorial," in *Continental Philosophy in America*, ed. H. J. Silverman, J. Sallis and T. M. Seebohm (Pittsburgh: Duquesne University Press, 1983), pp. 165-185, esp. p. 178; "On the Way to *Being and Time*: Introduction to the Translation of Heidegger's *Prolegomena zur Geschichte des Zeitbegriffs*," *Research in Phenomenology* 15 (1985): 193–226, esp. p. 201.

The Laskian phrase "to live in truth" thus first appears in Heidegger's gloss of Husserl's Sixth Investigation in SS 1925 (GA 20:70/52). Heidegger introduces the phrase "in truth" in BT (SZ 221) as if it were common parlance. It is, of course. But shortly before (SZ 218n), he had identified Lask as "the only one outside of phenomenology who has positively taken up" these portions of Husserl's Sixth Investigation, from which Lask's *Logik der Philosophie* (1911) was especially influenced by the sections on Sensory and Categorial Intuition and his *Lehre vom Urteil* (1912) by those on Evidence and Truth.

8. Cf. the excellent Index to the English translation of BT by Macquarrie and Robinson on the forty usages of *Indifferenz* and its cousin, *Gleichgültigkeit*. For insight into the importance of such dimensions of undifferentiation for Heidegger's sense of the formal indication, I am indebted to an unpublished paper by R. J. A. van Dijk and Th. C. W. Oudemans, "Heideggers formal anzeigende Philosophie."

9. I have summarized this course in other ways and for other purposes in my work on Lask (see n. 3 above) and in "KNS 1919: Heideggers Durchbruch," but first of all, strictly on the basis of the student transcripts, in "Das Entstehen des Begriffsfeldes 'Faktizität' im Frühwerk Heideggers," *Dilthey-Jahrbuch* 4 (1986–87): 91–120. This groundbreaking course deserves even more study than

can be devoted to it here. See, e.g., George Kovacs, "Philosophy as Primordial Science (*Urwissenschaft*) in the Early Heidegger," *Journal of the British Society for Phenomenology* 21 (1990): 121–135. For its importance to Heidegger's entire path of thought and our present "hermeneutic situation," see my "The Genesis of *Being and Time*," *Man and World* 25 (1992): 21–37.

10. Cf. "Das Entstehen des Begriffsfeldes 'Fäktizität,' " p. 97, n. 23, which pinpoints Paul Natorp's use of the term *es gibt* in his courses at the time, in order to describe the problem of "facticity" facing the neo-Kantians in their ongoing efforts to overcome ninteenth-century naturalism, for which the "irrationality" of facticity is insuperable. Cf. ZBP 122.

11. Jonas Cohn, *Religion und Kulturwerte*, Philosophische Vorträge der Kantgesellschaft (Berlin: Reuther and Reichard, 1914), p. 21. Heidegger refers to this article in ZBP 145n.

12. Lask likewise writes: "What is at issue here is nothing less than the very life and death of philosophy" (GS 2:89). But what is at issue for Lask is the philosophical institution of the search for the categorial *forms of the* nonsensory *forms* already operative in our experience, and for the forms of those forms of the forms, etc. This, from Heidegger's perspective, is clearly a turn away from the already operative categorial intuitions in experience, which are to be explicated in themselves, toward ever-escalating theoretizations of them. *Ergo* Heidegger's final assessment of Lask: he was the first to see the problem of the theoretical *in ovo*, but this very problem is difficult to find in him since he in turn wanted to solve it theoretically (ZBP 88).

Heidegger's thought experiment of the total reification of the world clearly bears close comparison with Husserl's experiment in *Ideen I* (§ 49) of worldannihilation. The detailed comparison, begun below in chap. 8, n. 14, may be especially revealing for the understanding of the different "system of motivations" (ibid., § 47) accruing to a historically situated and contextualized intentional dynamics as opposed to the dynamics of an immanent and absolute consciousness. There is a great deal in § 47 which must have inspired Heidegger's descriptions of the primal something for the coming decade, like the "not yet" of experience which "belongs to the indeterminate but determinable horizon of my temporally particular actuality of experience. . . . Every actual experience refers beyond itself to possible experiences" and so serves as a motivating source of experience.

13. I have added this terminology from BT (SZ 5f.), not only to relate this early discussion of the structure of a question to a later development of it, but also to raise the question of whether, aside from its use here as an illustration, there is really a point to any formalized question like "Is there something?" What does it ask for *(Erfragtes)*? Is the *Erfragtes* collapsed into the *Gefragtes* here? Later, in examining formalization, Heidegger discovers that its product lacks a *Vollzugssinn*, i.e., it does not follow through to some sort of fulfillment. In short, such a question does not seem to be situationally motivated. It is the "trivial" (*kümmerliche*: ZBP 63) question of *ens commune* by a remote I and not the distressed (*bekümmerte*) question of *ens proprium* by a fully engaged I.

14. In a long letter to Heidegger on September 10, 1918 (Heidegger was then "in the field"), Husserl mentions that, after a pause of five years, he had begun to read Natorp's *Allgemeine Psychologie* (1912) once again and was concerned about Natorp's misunderstandings of his phenomenology. And whatever Husserl thus mentioned in this important letter to his future assistant and protégé becomes an explicit task for the early Heidegger, as we shall see in other instances of these early years in the proximity of Husserl.

15. GA 20:75/56, 65/48. Precisely in this Husserlian context in the course of SS 1925, Heidegger underscores the phrase "intuition and expression," which is a dominating leitmotiv of his courses of 1919–20.

16. *Das Worauf* is the conceptual predecessor of "das Woraufhin des primären Entwurfs" (SZ 324), "the toward-which of the primary project" of Dasein which in BT is formally defined as its "sense" (*Sinn*). It already means "meaning" in the transcendental context of early 1919. From this earlier context of its genesis, we also see why the English translation of this crucial term in BT as the "upon-which" is in need of teleological correction.

17. Cf. my "Das Entstehen des Begriffsfeldes," pp. 102, 106f.

18. But see LU II/1, *Einleitung*, § 7 (Eng. trans., pp. 264f.), where Husserl remarks that the "epistemology" he is after is "no theory" since it does not construct deductive theories nor does it try to explain by means of them, but instead only describes, etc. In SS 1919, Heidegger will of course, following Dilthey, do the same, putting phenomenology on the side of the "understanding" sciences rather than the explanatory. I am indebted to Steven Crowell for this reference, who has also written some perceptive things about Lask's aletheiology and its bearing on the young Heidegger.

19. R I Heidegger 10. IX. 18, Husserl Archive in Leuven; Eduard Spranger, "Zur Theorie des Verstehens und zur geisteswissenschaftlichen Psychologie," in *Festschrift Johannes Volkelt zum 70. Geburtstag dargebracht* (Munich: Beck, 1918), pp. 357–403.

It is the SS 1925 version of Husserl's several courses on "Natur und Geist," in which Husserl confronts Dilthey's "theory of understanding," that we have available to us as Husserliana IX. See the English translation by William Scanlon, *Phenomenological Psychology* (The Hague: Nijhoff, 1977).

20. For example, in a letter to Elisabeth Blochmann on May 1, 1919, Heidegger makes note of his "ständiges Lernen in der Gemeinschaft mit Husserl," "continually learning in my association with Husserl." Martin Heidegger and Elisabeth Blochmann, *Briefwechsel 1918–1969*, ed. Joachim W. Storck, Marbacher Schriften (Marbach am Neckar: Deutsche Schillergesellschaft, 1989), p. 16. Heidegger's correspondence in 1920, on the other hand, already reflects a change in attitude toward Husserl.

21. Gerda Walther to Alexander Pfänder, June 20, 1919 (original in Munich: cf. n. 25).

22. All the courses which Heidegger taught in the three semesters of 1915–17 were historically oriented, but Heidegger's manuscripts of them are no longer extant and even student transcripts of them have not yet been located, so that their very titles are still open to question. See Appendix B for their most likely titles.

23. This Kuhnian language is suggested by a remark by Beaufret. In describing the transition from intentionality to ecstasis, he observes that, despite the fact that the first led to the second, the second is in fact incommensurable with the first, so that "to anyone who places himself in intentionality, the experience of ecstasis is inaccessible, just as relativity physics remains unthinkable from the point of view of Newton, even though Newton already espied the principle which Einstein was destined to develop" (Jean Beaufret, *Dialogue avec Heidegger*, vol. 3, *Approche de Heidegger* [Paris: Minuit, 1974] p. 117).

24. Cf. my "Heidegger and the New Images of Science," *Research in Phenomenology* 6 (1977): 162–181; reprinted in *Radical Phenomenology: Essays in Honor of Martin Heidegger*, ed. John Sallis (Atlantic Highlands, N.J.: Humanities, 1978). For an overview of the Anglo-American side, see my "New Philosophies of Science in the USA: A Selective Survey," *Zeitschrift für allgemeine Wissenschaftstheorie* 5 (1974): 201–233.

25. Gerda Walther, "Zur Ontologie der sozialen Gemeinschaften," *Jahrbuch für Philosophie und phänomenologische Forschung* 6 (1923): 1–158. This is her dissertation under Pfänder by which she graduated from Munich in 1921. For access to her transcript of SS 1919, I wish to thank Eberhard Avé-Lallemant of the Bayerische Staatsbibliothek in Munich; the access number there is Ana 317 B V 3 (a). Her transcript is sparsely dated, but by collating it with Becker's (cf. ZBP 217), I am presuming that this one-hour course was held on the following Tuesdays in 1919: May 6, 20; June 3, 17; July 1, 15, 22, 29. Becker ignores the first and last hours, which tend to relate Heidegger's philosophy of science to the inner structure of the university community.

2: *Theo-Logical Beginnings: Toward a Phenomenology of Christianity*

1. Bernhard Casper, "Martin Heidegger und die Theologische Fakultät Freiburg 1909–1923," *Freiburger Diözesan-Archiv* 100 (1980): 541.

2. Cf. n. 11 below.

3. Hermann Köstler, "Heidegger schreibt an Grabmann," *Philosophisches Jahrbuch* 87 (1980): 104.

4. Hugo Ott, *Martin Heidegger: Unterwegs zu seiner Biographie* (Frankfurt and New York: Campus, 1988), p. 108. Moreover, subsequent to the Catholic ceremony in Freiburg's university chapel, the Heideggers were married in a Protestant ceremony in the presence of Elfride's parents in Wiesbaden. Cf. Martin Heidegger and Elisabeth Blochmann, *Briefwechsel 1918–1969*, edited by Joachim W. Storck, Marbacher Schriften (Marbach am Neckar: Deutsche Schillergesellschaft, 1989), p. 148, n. 44.

5. Otto Pöggeler, "Afterword to the Second Edition," *Martin Heidegger's Path of Thinking*, transl. Daniel Magurshak and Sigmund Barber (Atlantic Highlands, N.J.: Humanities, 1987), p. 264.

6. *Das Mass der Verborgenen: Heinrich Ochsner 1891–1970 zum Gedächnis*, ed. Curd Ochwadt and Erwin Tecklenborg (Hannover: Charis, 1981), pp. 92, 266.

7. The letter is dated "in the field, November 7, 1918." Cf. Heidegger and Blochmann, *Briefwechsel*, pp. 10–12. For the specific data on the books on Heidegger's reading list at this time, see the Bibliography following n. 54 below.

8. Ernst Troeltsch, "Die Zukunftsmöglichkeiten des Christentums," *Logos* 1 (1910–11): 165–185.

9. Husserl's letter to Otto is dated March 5, 1919. Cf. the volume on Ochsner, *Das Mass*, pp. 157–160.

10. The letter is dated July 19, 1914. Cf. Hugo Ott, *Heidegger*, p. 83; Thomas Sheehan, "Heidegger's *Lehrjahre*," in *The Collegium Phaenomenologicum: The First Ten Years*, ed. J. C. Sallis, G. Moneta, and J. Taminiaux, Phaenomenologica, vol. 105 (Dordrecht: Kluwer, 1988), p. 113.

11. In view of its dominant neo-Kantian accent, I would place this note in the months following September 1916, that is, in the vicinity of the habilitation's Conclusion. From the available chronological clues, this would be sometime in the first half of 1917. The extant Heidegger papers are of course full of such "loose notes" on diverse subjects, sometimes on the back of old course notes (paper was scarce in those years in Germany). But in view of the paucity of material from this incipient and germinal period of the young Heidegger's development, it is to be hoped that Heidegger's literary executors will see their way someday to publishing this file of "loose notes" on the phenomenology of religious life and consciousness, which provide the backdrop for Heidegger's sketch of a course in WS 1919–20 on medieval mysticism. The disappointment (misplaced, since the material is extant) of a theological researcher applies to these prior notes as well as to the extant but skimpy course notes: "It is a tragic lacuna in Heideggerian research that his lectures of the winter semester 1919–20, 'The Philosophical Foundations of Medieval Mysticism,' have not survived" (Thomas F. O'Meara, O.P., "Heidegger and His Origins: Theological Perspectives," *Theological Studies* 47 [1986]: 213).

For the original German formulation of these notes, see the most recent articles and addresses of Hugo Ott: "Zu den katholischen Wurzeln im Denken Martin Heideggers. Der theologische Philosoph," in *Akten des römischen Heidegger-Symposions* (1992); "Martin Heidegger—Mentalität der Zerrissenheit," *Freiburger Diözesan-Archiv* 110 (1990): 427–448. Also Otto Pöggeler, "Philosophie und hermeneutische Theologie," (Düsseldorfer Akademie-Vortrag, 1989; to be published shortly [Opladen, 1993]).

12. ZBP 134. The "German Movement" is Dilthey's coinage for the inaugural period of abundant creativity which launched modern German letters and philosophy, beginning roughly in 1770 with Goethe, Lessing, and Herder and ending around 1830 with Hegel and Schleiermacher. It is a continuing source of German pride and, in the postwar Germany of the twenties, of German nationalism, especially among German academics. For further details, see Herman Nohl, *Die Deutsche Bewegung: Vorlesungen und Aufsätze zur Geistesgeschichte von 1770–1830*, ed. O. F. Bollnow and F. Rodi (Göttingen: Vandenhoeck and Ruprecht, 1970).

13. R I Natorp 8. X. 17, Husserl Archive, Leuven. Cf. Hugo Ott, *Heidegger*, pp. 97f.; Thomas Sheehan, "Heidegger's 'Introduction to the Phenomenology of Religion,' 1920–21," in *A Companion to Martin Heidegger's "Being and Time"*, ed. J. J. Kockelmans (Washington, D.C.: University Press of America, 1986), p. 42. One senses the distance traveled in a matter of months by comparing this latter remark in Husserl's October letter with a similar remark in the above-cited

January letter to Grabmann, where Heidegger notes that he "is seeking to come to terms with the philosophy of value [i.e., Rickert] and phenomenology *from within.*" Cf. Köstler, "Heidegger schreibt an Grabmann," p. 104. By October 1917, it is phenomenology alone that is Heidegger's most intense concern.

14. R I Natorp 11. II. 20, Husserl Archive, Leuven. Cf. Sheehan, "Heidegger's 'Introduction,' " p. 44.

15. Husserl writes from Freiburg to Adolf Grimme on June 6, 1918: "Together we read a manuscript on the philosophy of religion drafted by Dr. Reinach on the battlefield" (Karl Schuhmann, *Husserl-Chronik: Denk- und Lebensweg Edmund Husserls* [The Hague: Nijhoff, 1977], p. 226). The "we" presumably included Husserl, Jean Hering, and Edith Stein. Cf. Adolf Reinach, *Sämtliche Werke*, ed. Karl Schuhmann (Munich: Philosophia, 1989), 2:795. On June 8, Edith Stein writes to Ingarden: "This evening I went to Husserl in order to discuss your work with him. But on the doorstep I met the little Heidegger, so the three of us took a long walk—very nice—and instead talked about philosophy of religion." (Edith Stein, *Briefe an Roman Ingarden 1917–1938* [Freiburg, Basel, Vienna: Herder, 1991], p. 36; I thank Hugo Ott for calling my attention to this reference). Heidegger was in Freiburg in mid-June in transition from military training at Heuberg to further training in Berlin-Charlottenburg. It is also noteworthy that Husserl's letters to these military addresses already open with the less formal "Lieber Herr Kollege." During Heidegger's Marburg interim, it becomes "Lieber Freund."

16. R I Heidegger 10. X. 18, Husserl Archive, Leuven.

17. Gustav Adolf Deissmann, *Paulus: Eine kultur-und religions geschichtliche Skizze*, (Tübingen: Mohr, 1911), pp. 84ff. Cf. Adolf Deissmann, *Paul: A Study in Social and Religious History*, trans. William E. Wilson (New York: Harper and Row, Torchbooks, 1957), pp. 137ff. This is but one example of a seemingly stray insight out of this period which will bear fruit sometime later in Heidegger's development.

18. Heidegger and Blochmann, *Briefwechsel*, letter of May 1, 1919, p. 16.

19. Sheehan, "Heidegger's *Lehrjahre*," pp. 94f. and n. 81. There may have been more basic reasons, such as Heidegger finding himself in the throes of transition from one conception of religion to another, as we shall soon see.

20. Wilhelm Dilthey, *Einleitung in die Geisteswissenschaften, Gesammelte Schriften*, vol. 1 (Stuttgart: Teubner, 1922, [7]1973), pp. 250–267. The key chapters are entitled "Christianity, Epistemology and Metaphysics" and "Augustine." Cf. the English translation by Ramon J. Betanzos, *Introduction to the Human Sciences* (Detroit: Wayne State University Press, 1988), pp. 228-239. Also my article, "Das Entstehen des Begriffsfeldes 'Faktizität' im Frühwerk Heideggers," *Dilthey-Jahrbuch* 4 (1986-87): 104f., n. 28.

21. This important letter of August 19, 1921, has been cited piecemeal by Löwith in a number of his publications, but a presentation of its full context is to be found in my "War der frühe Heidegger tatsächlich ein 'christlicher Theologe'?" in *Philosophie und Poesie: Otto Pöggeler zum 60. Geburtstag*, ed. A. Gethmann-Siefert (Stuttgart: Fromann-Holzboog, 1988), 2:59–75. The original German text of the letter is now available in *Zur philosophischen Aktualität Heideggers*, ed.

Dietrich Papenfuss and Otto Pöggeler, vol. 2, *Im Gespräch der Zeit* (Frankfurt: Klostermann, 1990), pp. 27–32, esp. p. 29.

22. Heidegger, without ever referring to Nietzsche, well into the twenties especially pressed the thesis of the relationship of Kant and the German idealists to medieval and Reformation theology. Reading the literature that Albert Schweitzer summarized, for example, he was also aware of how the "Problem of Christianity" dominated continental philosophy throughout the nineteenth century. Cf. the concluding chapter of Karl Löwith, *From Hegel to Nietzsche* (Garden City, N.Y.: Anchor, 1964).

23. Heidegger's letter to Löwith, August 19, 1921. Cf. *Zur philosophischen Aktualität Heideggers* 2:29f, 31f.

24. Oskar Becker's is the only one of the five extant transcripts of WS 1920–21 which contains this *Schlussbemerkung* of February 25, 1921.

25. This is the title Heidegger gives to his excerpts from the Pfeiffer edition of Eckhart's works (see Bibliography following n. 54 below): "Diu Zeichen eines wârhaften Grundes," pp. 475–478; "Von der Geburt des êwigen Wortes," pp. 478–483.

26. Wilhelm Windelband, *Präludien: Aufsätze und Reden zur Philosophie und ihrer Geschichte*, (Tübingen: Mohr, [5]1915), 1:37–48; 2:109–111, 119; *Durchbruch* on 1:46, 48; 2:119. My italics.

27. Ibid. 2:305. In all of the following elucidations, I have usually gone more deeply into the readings cited by Heidegger than he does, to draw out the context surrounding his typically sketchy notes on them.

28. Ibid.

29. Ibid. p. 302.

30. See the Bibliography following n. 54 below, also for any unnoted literature cited in what follows.

31. Deissmann, *Paulus*, pp. 84–94; Eng. trans, pp. 135-165.

32. Wilhelm Dilthey, *Die Jugendgeschichte Hegels* (Berlin: Reimer, 1905), p. 25. Dilthey is citing from manuscripts which were edited two years later by his student, Herman Nohl: see *Hegels theologische Jugendschriften* (Tübingen: Mohr, 1907), p. 161; English translation by T. M. Knox, *On Christianity: Early Theological Writings* by Friedrich Hegel (New York: Harper and Row, Harper Torchbooks, 1961), p. 79.

33. Ibid., p. 26. Heidegger cites only from Dilthey, but cf. also Nohl's edition, pp. 153f., Eng. trans., pp. 68f.

34. Heidegger used the 1843 edition of Schleiermacher's *Sämmtliche Werke* (see Bibliography following n. 54 below), which contains the final revised edition of *Über die Religion*—the Second Speech is on pp. 172–283—but on certain passages he also consulted the first edition of 1799. Although the translations are my own, I have included the pagination of John Oman's translation of the third German edition, *On Religion: Speeches to Its Cultured Despisers* (New York: Harper and Row, Harper Torchbooks, 1958): the Second Speech is on pp. 26–118.

35. So in Heidegger's note. The phrase *geheimnisvoller Augenblick* occurs in the first edition of 1799 (p. 73) but was deleted in later editions. Clearly then,

Heidegger consulted the first edition and/or Dilthey's biography, which paraphrases the first edition Speech by Speech and makes much of this rhapsodic passage. Cf. Wilhelm Dilthey, *Leben Schleiermachers* (Berlin: de Gruyter, ²1922), pp. 430f.

36. This note poses a tantalizing problem of dating. On the one hand, it uses the neo-Kantian vocabulary of values and teleology typical of the young Heidegger around 1917 and, on the other, it anticipates the Jasperian vocabulary of SS 1919 (ZBP 205) in speaking of the living consciousness "being steeped in *situations*." The paginations cited are from the following editions: Friedrich Schleiermacher, *Der christliche Glaube* (Berlin: Reimer, ⁶1884); English translation edited by H. R. Mackintosh and J. S. Stewart, *The Christian Faith*, vol. 1 (New York: Harper and Row, Harper Torchbooks, 1963).

37. Cf. n. 15 above. To be exact, the first section of the manuscript which Heidegger studied was entitled "The Absolute," which was followed by two shorter sections entitled "Structure of the Experience" (Heidegger's long quotation is from this section) and "Skeptical Considerations." Cf. Adolf Reinach, *Sämtliche Werke*, ed. Karl Schuhmann (Munich: Philosophia, 1989), 1:605–611. I wish to thank Karl Schuhmann for an advance copy of this text, the story of its composition and distribution, and discussions on its genesis and role in the history of phenomenology. The section on "The Absolute" was first published in Conrad Martius's Introduction to Adolf Reinach, *Gesammelte Schriften* (Halle: Niemeyer, 1921), pp. xxxi-xxxvi. There is an English summary of it in John M. Oesterreicher, *Walls Are Crumbling: Seven Jewish Philosophers Find Christ* (New York: Devin-Adair, 1952), pp. 123–126.

38. Rudolf Otto, *The Idea of the Holy: An Inquiry into the Non-rational Factor in the Idea of the Divine and Its Relation to the Rational*, trans. John W. Harvey (New York: Oxford University Press, Galaxy Books, 1958). At times, the translation is mine.

39. Heidegger here refers to Paul Natorp's memorial speech, *Hermann Cohens philosophische Leistung unter dem Gesichtspunkte des Systems* (Berlin: Reuther and Reichard, 1918). Since this appeared in print no earlier than June 1918, Heidegger probably began this review of Otto's book, perhaps as a result of conversations with Husserl in June in Freiburg, in July-August 1918, when he found time from his military training in Charlottenburg to visit the Royal Library in Berlin. In addition to Husserl's letter of September 10, 1918, discussed above, see Heidegger's letter to E. Blochmann of October 2, 1918, in Heidegger and Blochmann, *Briefwechsel*, p. 9.

A remark made by Heidegger in WS 1920–21 (on January 11) provides a postscript to this line of critique: "Today's philosophy of religion is proud of the discovery of the category of the irrational and holds that the access to religiosity is thereby assured. But this is meaningless until the concept of the rational is defined. I therefore propose to put aside the distinction of rational-irrational. It has nothing to do with the phenomenon of religious experience, and phenomenological understanding lies outside this opposition."

40. The note is dated September 6 and 10, 1918. Heidegger worked with the Latin text. Cf. *Sancti Bernardi Opera*, vol. 1 (Rome: Editiones Cistercienses,

1957), pp. 14–16; Bernard of Clairvaux, *On the Song of Songs*, trans. Kilian Walsh, OCSO (Spencer, Mass.: Cistercian Publications, 1971), pp. 16–20. Derrideans et al. might be interested in the fact that this third sermon is divided according to the three "mystical" kisses "of the Lord's feet, hands, and mouth," and that the young Heidegger completely ignores this erotology, which abounds in the sermon, in his re-marks.

41. Heidegger cites only from the "First Mansions" in a German translation ("Seelenburg") which I have not been able to locate. Cf. *Complete Works of St. Teresa of Jesus*, ed. and trans. E. Allison Peers, vol. 2 (London: Sheed and Ward, 1946), pp. 201-212.

42. Karl Löwith, *Mein Leben in Deutschland vor und nach 1933* (Stuttgart: Metzler, 1986), p. 29.

43. Heidegger to Löwith on September 13, 1920: "I don't have Dilthey's works, only detailed excerpts, in part *hand-copied* by me as a theologian in 1909–10, which are useful only if you know the context. Husserl has a few texts which, I believe, are now at Szilasi's. I had them this summer." The course of SS 1920 had concluded with a "destruction" of Dilthey's philosophy, beginning with an extensive bibliography of Dilthey's then widely scattered works.

44. Cf. n. 20. Heidegger, of course, used the 1883 edition of the *Einleitung* (see Bibliography following n. 54), but I shall be citing from the more readily accessible volume 1 of the *Gesammelte Schriften* and the excellent English translation (with my modifications) by Ramon Betanzos.

45. Cf. Betanzos's Introductory Essay to his translation, pp. 23, 13.

46. Regarding his forthcoming seminar on the *Meditationes* in WS 1920–21, Heidegger writes to Löwith on September 13, 1920: "Für das 'Cogito' kommt für mich die *ganze christliche Philosophie* in Betracht—da ich es *rückwärts* sehen möchte. Wichtig ist nur, daß Sie die anderen metaphysischen Abhandlungen und die Regulae etwas 'kennen'—damit die Verkehrtheit der erkenntnistheoretischen Ablösung studiert werden kann." Cf. Appendix B, n. 10, for the English.

47. Saint Augustine, *The Trinity*, trans. Stephen McKenna, C.SS.R., The Fathers of the Church, vol. 45 (Washington, D.C.: Catholic University of America Press, 1963), 10.14; p. 308.

48. Some of Augustine's texts excerpted by Heidegger and not noted in my summary come from *On the Trinity* 11.6 (on the will); *On the 83 Questions* 9; *Against the Academics* 3.24 (on the senses); *De Ordine* 2.38 (on dialectic); *De Praed. Sanct.* 5.

49. A note on "medieval mysticism as a *form of expression* of religious experience" refers to the Festschrift article by Dilthey's student, Eduard Spranger (see Bibliography following n. 54 below), which Husserl had mentioned in his letter to Heidegger on September 10, 1918. Heidegger refers to it again in BT (SZ 394n). Its psychophysical hermeneutics of expression may be a bit out of fashion now, but the article was influential in its time and still warrants study here and now for its possible impact upon Heidegger's burgeoning hermeneutical terminology. To this end, see Eduard Spranger, "Zur Theorie des Verstehens und zur geisteswissenschaftlichen Psychologie," in *Grundlagen der Geisteswissenschaften*, vol. 6 of *Gesammelte Schriften*, ed. Hans Walter Bähr (Tübingen: Niemeyer, 1980),

pp. 1–42, 314f. For example, Spranger relates the "psychic situation" (21) motivating understanding to Jakob von Uexküll's then popular notion of *Umwelt* in
connection with values like economic utility, where this "encompassing concrete
situation" as a "historical-individual constellation" is not merely a static milieu
but also a dynamic "happening" and, as an "enchaining concatenation independent of the person to be understood, can in general be called a *fate* or destiny"
(29f.). He also reiterates Natorp's antiphenomenological sentiment against a science of immediate experience, since "life in these circumstances is an ungrasp-
able, incommunicable, formless mysticism, which flashes and disappears, like a
fleeting dream" (16). Out of such readings, Heidegger is already adapting the
terminological framework contained in Dilthey's triad, *Erlebnis-Verstehen-Aus-
druck*, to his own insights, so that it assumes a central position in BT as *Befindlichkeit-Verstehen-Rede*. It is therefore no accident that the course notes of 1919 will
also broach, for the very first time in Heidegger's *Denkweg*, the problem of a
theory of emotions. Note also Spranger's usage of the concept of "situation" in
an article which antedates Jaspers's book on "limit situations."

50. Wilhelm Dilthey, *Weltanschauung und Analyse des Menschen seit Renaissance
und Reformation*, vol. 2 of his *Gesammelte Schriften*, (Göttingen: Vandenhoeck und
Ruprecht, 1914, ^{6}1960), pp. 418–422.

51. Heidegger is here citing Johannes Ficker's editorial gloss of his *Luthers
Vorlesung über den Römerbrief 1515/1516* (Leipzig: Dieterich und Weicher, 1908),
p. lxxxiii.

52. "Brief Martin Heideggers an Elisabeth Husserl" (dated 24 April 1919;
here with a note in Italian by its editor, Guy van Kerckhoven), *Aut aut* 223–224
(January-April 1988): 6–14, esp. p. 8.

53. Heidegger and Blochmann, *Briefwechsel.*, pp. 7, 14. The brief excerpt is
from the letter of June 15, 1918, and the longer quote from the letter of May
1, 1919.

54. The French is used in the above letter of May 1, 1919, while the German
"Lebensschwungkraft" occurs near the end of the course of KNS 1919 (ZBP 115).
In neither instance is the French philosopher, Henri Bergson, acknowledged.

Bibliography of Heidegger's Reading List on the Phenomenology of Religion (1917–19)

Augustinus. *Opera Omnia*, vols. 1–12 = Migne, *Patrologia Latina*, vols. 32–46.

Bernhard von Clairvaux. *Sermones super Cantica Canticorum.*

Bousset, Wilhelm. *Kyrios Christos. Geschichte des Christusglaubens vor den Anfängen des Christentums bis Irenaeus.* Göttingen: Vandenhoeck und Ruprecht, 1913.

Deissmann, Gustaf Adolf. *Die neutestamentliche Formel "in Christo Jesu."* Marburg: Elwert, 1892.

———. *Paulus. Eine kultur- und religionsgeschichtliche Skizze.* Tübingen: Mohr,
1911.

Dilthey, Wilhelm. *Einleitung in die Geisteswissenschaften.* Leipzig: Duncker und
Humblot, 1883.

———. *Gesammelte Schriften II: Weltanschauung und Analyse des Menschen seit
Renaissance und Reformation.* Göttingen: Vandenhoeck und Ruprecht, 1914.

————. *Die Jugendgeschichte Hegels*. Berlin: Reimer, 1905.

————. *Leben Schleiermachers*. Berlin: Reimer, 1870.

Ficker, Johannes, ed. *Luthers Vorlesung über den Römerbrief 1515/1516: Die Glosse*. Leipzig: Dieterich, 1908.

Jülicher, Adolf. *Der religiöse Wert der Reformation*. Marburg: Elwert, 1913.

Mulert, Hermann. *Schleiermachers geschichtsphilosophische Ansichten in ihrer Bedeutung für seine Theologie*. Gießen: Töppelmann, 1907.

Natorp, Paul. *Allgemeine Psychologie nach kritischer Methode*. Tübingen: Mohr, 1912.

————. *Deutscher Weltberuf. Geschichtsphilosophische Richtlinien*. Jena: Diederichs, 1918.

————. *Hermann Cohens philosophische Leistung unter dem Gesichtspunkte des Systems*. Berlin: Reuther und Reichard, 1918.

Norden, Eduard. *Agnostos Theos: Untersuchungen zur Formengeschichte religiöser Rede*. Leipzig and Berlin: Teubner, 1913.

Otto, Rudolf. *Das Heilige: Über das Irrationale in der Idee des Göttlichen und sein Verhältnis zum Rationalen*. Stuttgart: Gotha, 1917.

Pfeiffer, Franz. *Deutsche Mystiker des Vierzehnten Jahrhunderts*. Vol. 2., *Meister Eckhart*. 1857. Reprint Göttingen: Vandenhoeck und Ruprecht, 1906.

Pohlenz, Max. *Vom Zorne Gottes: Eine Studie über den Einfluss der griechischen Philosophie auf das alte Christentum*. Göttingen: Vandenhoeck und Ruprecht, 1909.

Realencyklopädie für protestantische Theologie und Kirche 6:674–682, s.v. "Glaube." Leipzig: Hinrichs, [3]1899.

Reinach, Adolf. "Bruchstück einer religionsphilosophischen Ausführung. Das Absolute." Now available in the critical edition of Reinach's *Sämtliche Werke*, edited by Karl Schuhmann. Munich: Philosophia, 1989.

Reitzenstein, Richard. *Die hellenistischen Mysterienreligionen*. Leipzig and Berlin: Teubner, 1910.

Religion in Geschichte und Gegenwart. Vol. 2, edited by F. M. Schiele and L. Zscharnack, cols. 1425–61, s.v. "Glaube." Tübingen: Mohr, 1910.

Schettler, Adolph. *Die paulinische Formel "Durch Christus."* Tübingen: Mohr, 1907.

Schleiermacher, Friedrich. *Aus Schleiermachers Leben, in Briefen*. Edited by L. Jonas and W. Dilthey. 4 vols. Berlin: Reimer, 1858–63.

————. *Der christliche Glaube*. Berlin: Reimer, [6]1884.

————. *Über die Religion: Reden an die Gebildeten unter ihren Verächtern*. In Schleiermacher's *Sämmtliche Werke*, 1. Abt., "Zur Theologie," 1:133–460. Berlin: Reimer, 1843.

Spranger, Eduard. "Zur Theorie des Verstehens und zur geisteswissenschaftlichen Psychologie." In *Festschrift Johannes Volkelt zum 70. Geburtstag dargebracht*, presented by P. Barth, B. Bauch, E. Bergmann, et al., pp. 357–403. Munich: Beck, 1918.

Süskind, Hermann. *Christentum und Geschichte bei Schleiermacher: Die geschichtsphilosophischen Grundlagen der Schleiermacherschen Theologie*. Tübingen: Mohr, 1911.

Teresa von Avila. *Seelenburg*.

Wehrung, Georg. *Der geschichtsphilosophische Standpunkt Schleiermachers zur Zeit seiner Freundschaft mit den Romantikern.* Strassburg: Müh, 1907.

Weinel, Heinrich. *Biblische Theologie des Neuen Testaments: Die Religion Jesu und des Urchristentums.* Tübingen: Mohr, ²1913.

Weiß, Johannes B. *Das Urchristentum.* Göttingen: Vandenhoeck und Ruprecht, 1917.

Windelband, Wilhelm. Das Heilige" (1902). In his *Präludien: Aufsätze und Reden zur Philosophie und ihrer Geschichte*, pp. 295–332. Tübingen: Mohr, ⁵1915.

3: The Deconstruction of Life (1919–20)

1. Heidegger and Blochmann, p. 16, letter of May 1, 1919.

2. Pagination in parentheses refers to the more readily available GA edition of the review in Martin Heidegger, *Wegmarken*, ed. F.-W. von Herrmann, GA 9 (Frankfurt: Klostermann, 1976), pp. 1–44. The review was first edited by Hans Saner in *Karl Jaspers in der Diskussion* (Munich: Piper, 1973), pp. 70–100, cf. esp. p. 100. For over a decade, the review was the only text publicly available from Heidegger's early Freiburg period. Despite the exaggerations which were prompted by this lack of genealogical context, the following analyses of the review are still useful: David Farrell Krell, "Toward *Sein und Zeit*: Heidegger's Early Review of Jaspers' 'Psychologie der Weltanschauungen,' " *Journal of the British Society for Phenomenology* 6 (1975): 147–156; reprinted as "From Existence to Fundamental Ontology" in Krell's book, *Intimations of Mortality* (University Park, Pa., London: Pennsylvania State University Press, 1986), pp. 11–26; finally chap. 2 of Rainer A. Bast, *Der Wissenschaftsbegriff Martin Heideggers im Zusammenhang seiner Philosophie* (Stuttgart–Bad Cannstatt: Frommann-Holzboog, 1986), pp. 43–51.

3. Karl Jaspers, *Philosophische Autobiographie* (Munich and Zurich: Piper, ²1977), p. 95. In addition to the recently published Heidegger-Jaspers correspondence (see nn. 5 and 7 below), further autobiographical remarks on the two-way discussion of this review are to be found in Karl Jaspers, *Notizen zu Martin Heidegger*, ed. Hans Saner (Munich and Zürich: Piper, ²1978).

4. PW 5f. = Karl Jaspers, *Psychologie der Weltanschauungen* (Munich and Zurich: Piper, 1985), p. 5f. This paperback edition duplicates the pagination of the 4th, 5th, and 6th editions. PW 12f. provides the first elaboration of *Existenz* as a Kantian Idea; cf. also pp. 112, 245, 277, 315f., 378ff., 384, 418ff.

5. The omission is glaring, almost obvious, and clearly intentional. Thus, in his initial response to the review, Jaspers in effect singles out these two passages and rightly highlights in *tu quoque* fashion that Heidegger too lacks a "positive method." "Of all the reviews which I have read, yours is, in my opinion, the one which has dug most deeply to the root of my thoughts. It has in fact touched me profoundly. Nevertheless, I still miss—in the discussions of the 'I am' and the 'historical'—the positive method" (letter dated August 1, 1921: Martin Heidegger and Karl Jaspers, *Briefwechsel 1920–1963*, ed. Walter Biemel and Hans Saner [Frankfurt: Klostermann; and Munich and Zürich: Piper, 1990], p. 23).

6. There is good reason why Heidegger is fascinated with the "destructive" character of limit situations, which goes deeper than their tantalizing parallels with methodical destruction. It is more a matter of method "imitating" life. Just

as limit situations provide access to existence, as Jaspers himself notes (11; PW 245), so does phenomenological destruction aim to bring us back to our original philosophical experiences. But Jaspers is too quick to regard destruction as the break of antinomy and contradiction, while Heidegger dwells on its first moment of destructuration to the sheer indeterminacy of sense, which in an about-face is then reinvested with determinability. Already in KNS, this destructuring is related to "empty" formalization, which, like theoretization at its worst, up to the last hour is described as the epitome of unliving, unworlding, designifying, and dehistoricizing. But at the end of the course, these unacceptably negative consequences of extreme formalization suddenly turn positive in their revelatory capacity, and become the channels of access to the extreme concretization of our most comprehensive but usually hidden experiences. The "boundary" situations reveal the concrete whole of existence precisely because they are the extremes of unliving (death), unworlding (accident), designifying (suffering), which thereby reveal individual life, the world, and meaning at their outskirts, and so as they ultimately are (but not as Kantian Ideas).

7. Letter dated June 27, 1922: Heidegger and Jaspers, *Briefwechsel*, pp. 26f. In the same letter, Heidegger goes on to say (p. 29): "I also see ever more clearly that the critique of *Psychology of Worldviews* is inadequate, not positive enough. I have already expanded upon it, deleted a great deal, and rewritten it. I want to publish it in a new form." For a summary concentrating on the philosophical content of this correspondence, see Walter Biemel, "Zum Briefwechsel Jaspers/ Heidegger," in *Zur philosophischen Aktualität Heideggers*, ed. Dietrich Papenfuss and Otto Pöggeler, vol. 2, *Im Gespräch der Zeit* (Frankfurt: Klostermann, 1990), pp. 71–86.

8. The instances of "existentialist" vocabulary here (GA 61:179f., 148), as in most instances in this edition, postdate the lecture course itself. Note that Heidegger here, for the material he actually delivered to his students in the concluding hours (usually the dramatic high point of a Heidegger course), oscillated between his initial course manuscript and an "Appendix I" (so in GA 61). The correlation between objectivity and resistivity or opposition probably derives from the Dilthey/Scheler thesis that facticity is a brute encounter, as Fichte had already suggested when he coined the term, or that "reality is resistance": cf. GA 20:302ff. (220ff.); SZ 209ff.

4: The Religion Courses (1920–21)

1. As usual in regard to this all-important but, unfortunately, still unpublished correspondence, I owe a debt of gratitude to Frau Ada Löwith for access to it and to Klaus Stichweh for help in deciphering it.

2. "Auch Kierkegaard kann man *nur* theologisch (so wie ich es verstehe und im W.S. entwickele) aus den Angeln heben" (card of September 13, 1920). This is another casualty of the *cursus interruptus*: although the extant course contains a few passing remarks on the nature of theology in the context Heidegger was framing for himself, there is no development of this point, let alone a reference to Kierkegaard. But cf. the following semester on the "theology of the cross."

3. Otto Pöggeler, *Der Denkweg Martin Heideggers* (Pfullingen: Neske, 1963, ²1983), pp. 36–38 (and in numerous articles since 1963); English translation

by Daniel Magurshak and Sigmund Barber, *Martin Heidegger's Path of Thinking* (Atlantic Highlands, N.J.: Humanities, 1987), pp. 24–26; Thomas Sheehan, "Heidegger's 'Introduction to the Phenomenology of Religion,' 1920–21," *The Personalist* 55 (1979–80): 312–324. Both tend to highlight the second part on Paul. The more complete gloss by Sheehan makes the "phenomenon of factic life-experience" central to Part One but never mentions its climax in the formal indication. Although Pöggeler is privy to the course interruption from the anec-dotal reports which he repeatedly heard from his teacher (and the most reliable eyewitness to the incident), Oskar Becker, his running account of this course over the years never quite catches up to the full consequences of this interruption (but cf. n. 8 below): cf. Theodore Kisiel, "Das Entstehen des Begriffsfeldes 'Fak-tizität' im Frühwerk Heideggers," *Dilthey-Jahrbuch* 4 (1986-87): 91–120, esp. pp. 108–112. Moreover, as long as the autograph of this important course remains missing, the extant student transcripts of it, two of which are of high quality, can never be published in the so-called "Ausgabe letzter Hand" of Heidegger's GA. Since no publication of the German texts in any of their forms seems to be forthcoming, I have here taken upon myself the task of reconstructing a reason-ably complete, albeit economical, English paraphrase of the detailed flow of thought in this famous course, woven (and so cross-checked) from four of the five extant transcripts of it, those by "Fritz" (Friedrich) Neumann (only of Part One), Oskar Becker, Franz Josef Brecht, and Helene Weiss (it was her first semes-ter in Freiburg, so she copied some lectures from the transcripts of Brecht and August Faust, who was then Rickert's assistant on leave from Heidelberg). The shorthand transcript by Fritz Kaufmann has not yet been deciphered by the Husserl-Archief at Leuven. When the clarifying and interpretative comments I am adding to this paraphrase might possibly be confused with Heidegger's, as recorded in the transcripts, I have set them apart in square brackets.

4. In BT, the passing references to the formal (or "provisional") indication are sometimes so fleeting and obscure that they are, more often than not, lost or muted in the English translation. Macquarrie and Robinson do not even index the term, in an otherwise excellent compilation. See SZ 14, 17, 41, 43, 53, 114, 116f., 231, 313, 315. And yet the formal indication constitutes the very fulcrum of BT, as we shall see.

5. Wilhelm Dilthey, *Einleitung in die Geisteswissenschaften*, vol. 1 of *Gesammelte Schriften* (Stuttgart: Teubner, [7]1973), p. 254. English translation by Ramon J. Betanzos, *Introduction to the Human Sciences* (Detroit: Wayne State University Press, 1988), p. 230. Cf. also chap. 2 above, and my n. 28, p. 105, in the above-cited article in *Dilthey-Jahrbuch* 4.

6. Only in Oskar Becker's transcript is this blackboard diagram (fig. 2) called a "Formal Schema," thereby relating it to the methodological discussion of the formal indication in Part One of the course.

7. Student notes indicate that Heidegger is using both *Ereignis* and καιρός somewhat loosely to apply to both the object-historical When and the actualiza-tion-historical How, in keeping with the ambiguity of the biblical texts. It is only a year later that he distinguishes sharply between the "objective, happening-like emergence" and the "*kairological character*" of an occurrence, "its particular

relation to *its* time, to the time which lies in the sense of facticity's context of actualization" (GA 61:137).

8. Heidegger here refers to Reitzenstein's *Die hellenistischen Mysterienreligionen*, which was on his reading list of studies relating to Pauline mysticism since at least 1918 (see chap. 2 above).

9. Otto Pöggeler, "Oskar Becker als Philosoph," *Kant-Studien* 60 (1969): 298–311, esp. p. 301. Reprinted as "Einspruch gegen Panhermeneutik: Oskar Becker," in Otto Pöggeler, *Heidegger und die hermeneutische Philosophie* (Freiburg and Munich: Alber, 1983), pp. 365-388, esp. pp. 369f.

10. At least the remaining public restraints must have been a topic of conversation between Heidegger and Husserl. In recommending Heidegger to Natorp for a position at Marburg, Husserl writes from Freiburg on February 1, 1922: "There is one major theme of [Heidegger's] studies, which are centered essentially upon the phenomenology of religion, that he, as a former 'Catholic' philosopher, understandably cannot treat here freely, namely, *Luther*. It would probably be of great importance for his development if he could go to Marburg. There he would be an important link between philosophy and Protestant theology (with which he is thoroughly acquainted in all of its forms and which he appreciates fully in its great unique values)" (R I Natorp 1. II. 22, Husserl Archive, Leuven).

11. As usual, I am adding these italicized headings as a kind of outline to expedite the reader's passage through a long transcript of this three-hour course. For SS 1921, only Becker's transcript is available to me, which nevertheless is of high quality in its insightfulness into the course. Jeffrey Andrew Barash has made good use of this transcript (which he obtained from Fritz Heidegger), referring primarily to this opening object-historical section, to situate Heidegger within his intellectual history. Cf. chap. 4 of his *Martin Heidegger and the Problem of Historical Meaning* (Dordrecht, Boston, Lancaster: Nijhoff/Kluwer, 1988); also his essay, "Les sciences de l'histoire et le problème de la théologie à partir du cours inédit de Heidegger sur Saint-Augustin," in *Histoire et politique: Heidegger dans la perspective du vingtième siècle* (Paris: Ed. Aldines, 1991). In view of these texts, and the impending publication of the course, I can be brief with this opening "object-historical" account.

12. Cf. n. 5 above and the section on Dilthey in chap. 2 above.

13. This Augustinian overview schema for "becoming (= being) a Christian" was clearly meant to complement the like-minded Pauline "formales Schema" of the previous semester.

14. I have translated the theses from Heidegger's German, but for a straightforward English translation of them from the original Latin, along with the important supporting proofs provided by Luther to his fellow Augustinians prior to the disputation (held in Heidelberg on April 26, 1518), see "Heidelberg Disputation," *Luther's Works*, ed. H. T. Lehmann, vol. 31, *Career of the Reformer: I*, ed. H. J. Grimm (Philadelphia: Muhlenberg, 1957), pp. 40f., 52ff. A translation of the missing 20th Thesis might read: "But someone who understands the visible and forthcoming things (*posteriora*) of God seen through suffering and the cross [has earned the name of theologian]." Pöggeler has amplified upon the role that these theses play beyond Heidegger's terse enumeration of them in the course,

by interpreting them (through Luther's proofs) in their full power to "destroy" metaphysics in the context of Heidegger's later development. Pöggeler thus also finds the 24th Thesis relevant: cf. his *Denkweg*, pp. 40/27f., 43/30.

15. Augustinus, *Opera Omnia*, vol. 5 (= Migne, *Patrologia Latina*, vol. 38), pp. 369ff. But for this and the succeeding citations, I am also including the pagination of extant English translations: *The Works of Saint Augustine: A Translation for the 21st Century*, vol. 3, pt. 3, *Sermons*, trans. Edmund Hill, ed. John E. Rotelle (Brooklyn: New City Press, 1990), pp. 72ff.; St. Augustine, *Letters*, vol. 3 (131–164), trans. Sister Wilfrid Parsons, S.N.D., vol. 11 of *Writings of St. Augustine* (New York: Fathers of the Church Inc., 1953), pp. 110ff., 133, 201f.

16. The Latin *curiosus*, which underlies *curiositas*, in its etymological connection with *cura* (care) first referred to the quality of diligent and assiduous care before it degenerated into the zealous but superfluous concern of inquisitiveness. In his development toward making care (*cura, Sorge*) into one of his central concepts or "formal indications," in which SS 1921 plays a pivotal role, Heidegger is fascinated enough by this Latin etymology to allude to it at least twice, in 1922 (p. 7 of the typescript of the Aristotle-*Einleitung*) and 1923 (GA 63:103). Now we have Blumenberg's massive work on curiosity, tracing its origins in Greek and Latin antiquity and ending in the restoration of its innocence in the Renaissance rise of modern science. On the etymology of the word "curiosity," see Hans Blumenberg, *The Legitimacy of the Modern Age*, trans. Robert M. Wallace (Cambridge, Mass., and London: MIT Press, 1983), pp. 258, 262.

17. GA 20:378–384/274–277 (§29b); SZ 170–173 (§36). Already in the semester following SS 1921, Heidegger is specifying the "movedness" of falling (ruination) with the "formally indicative character" of being "tentative," seductive, tempting, in Augustine's sense of the self's tendency to dissipate itself, not so much in the "many," however, as in the world. But from the start, he must constantly reiterate that this choice of terms is purely formal, with no ethical or religious connotations, referring to a movement intrinsic to the facticity to which life is ex-posed and not something imposed from without, although he does concede that this "mobile character was of course first made visible by the Christian [experience]" (GA 61:154, 142, 140).

18. Blumenberg is clearly operating with an entirely different, and perhaps commonsensical and "secular," ontology of the self, its world, and its elementals, when he interprets the same progression from the first to the second "lust" as a movement from enjoying pleasant and beautiful objects to a *self*-enjoyment of one's cognitive capability. See *The Legitimacy of the Modern Age*, pp. 312f.

19. Yet, as we have seen above, one of Augustine's favorite examples in introducing his usufructuary theory of reality is the extreme possibility of making "Mammon" into an idol; in short, the extremity of greed, where wealth becomes an end in itself and not just a means. "It is a perversion for people to want to enjoy money, but merely to make use of God. Such people do not spend money for the sake of God, but worship God for the sake of money." (*City of God* 11.25).

Heidegger is so ensconced in his "Christian facticity" at this time (note the Concluding Remark of WS 1920–21, chap. 2 above, p. 80) that he rarely ventures into comparative religion, as, e.g., Otto does. But one provocative comparison might be mentioned in this context: Hinduism identifies four legitimate ends of life in which the first two develop upon the Path of Desire, where we journey from sense pleasure to worldly success in its three forms, wealth, fame, and power. The enjoyments of curiosity are never mentioned. Is curiosity perhaps a peculiarly Western vice, as Heidegger's later accounts emphasizing its Greek oculocentrism will suggest, or do, for example, the cautions exercised by Theravada Buddhism against "idle speculations" which do not really contribute to achieving nirvana, like the questions of God's existence and the afterlife, involve a similar recognition?

20. Augustinus, *Opera Omnia*, vol. 3 (Migne, *PL* 35), pp. 1977–2062. Since these "Homilies on the First Epistle of John" provide Heidegger with several crucial texts, two reliable English translations might be noted: *Augustine: Later Works*, trans. John Burnaby, The Library of Christian Classics, vol. 8: (Philadelphia: Westminster, 1953?), pp. 251–348; *A Select Library of the Nicene and Post-Nicene Fathers of the Christian Church*, ed. Philip Schaff, vol. 7, trans. H. Browne and J. H. Myers, (New York: Christian Literature Co., 1888), pp. 459–529. Unfortunately, vol. 8 of this latter series, *Expositions on the Book of Psalms*, the only extant English translation of *Enarrationes in Psalmos*, is an abridged and uneven translation of an admittedly enormous text, which spans two volumes of Migne's PL, 36 and 37 (Aug. *Opera Omnia*, vol. 4).

21. That "peculiar dread, not to be mistaken for any ordinary dread," which constitutes a "perfect" fear of God, is discussed briefly in chap. 4 of Otto, *The Idea of the Holy*, pp. 13–15.

22. Recall Heidegger's reading program in the Psalms from 1917 (chap. 2, p. 87), which fused en route with a reading of Augustine's *Expositions on the Book of Psalms*.

23. I have not been able to locate the Latin text glossed by Heidegger, which apparently begins with the contrast of God and a robber (*latro*), but the flight from God's angry countenance to His becalmed visage (*a facie irati ad faciem placati*) is quite common in *En. in Ps.* (P.L. 36–37 = Aug. *Opera Omnia*, 4:235, 814, 953, 1217, 1791). Computer searches of the Augustinian Concordance made for me by Prof. Allan Fitzgerald, O.S.A., at Villanova University suggest that the contrast stems from Heidegger himself. (Whatever else might be said of the translation in BT of *Angst vor* as "anxiety in the face of," it is at least quite biblical!) In such searches, I have used the old *Index Generalis* for Augustine's *Opera Omnia* in PL 46, e.g., the many entries for "Timere" on pp. 635–7, where it became clear to me that Heidegger himself relied heavily on this index in his own researches on Augustine; see e.g., the entries for "Cura" and "Curiositas" on p. 204. So much for the ban on indexes foisted on us by Heidegger's literary executors even for translations of the GA!

At one point in his development of this important Augustinian (and not Kierkegaardian!) insight into the "concept of dread," Heidegger refers to Hunzinger's 1906 study on "The Problem of Fear in Catholic Doctrine from Augustine to Luther," but observes that "the interpretation of Augustine there is in need of essential revisions" (GA 20:394/285). At this late date, I am still not aware of any truly in-depth study of Augustine's conception of *timor castus*, especially in view of this new chapter in its *Wirkungsgeschichte*.

24. The formal indication thus generates a kind of "diagrammatology," calling unexpectedly for some computer graphics. I was not yet aware of these course diagrams when, in response to the pedagogical problem of expeditiously presenting the content of BT to beginning students, I developed a conceptual schematism of Dasein in its care and temporality along the intersecting axes of the world, self, and its lifetime, already with a strong sense that the formal indication, about which very little was known at the time, had a great deal to do with generating such diagrams. See my "Diagrammatic Approach to Heidegger's Schematism of Existence," *Philosophy Today* 28 (Fall 1984): pp. 229–241; "Professor Seigfried's Misreading of My Diagram and Its Source," *Philosophy Today* 55 (Spring 1986): 72–83.

The paradox of using representations to "destroy" representational thinking finds a kind of epitome in the schematism of the cross that Heidegger reaps from Augustine's texts, in order to transpose Christian factic life from images of objective content to those that tell us how to actualize it, in this case, by the example of the crucifixion which conveys the "magnitude" of the breadth of love, the length of perseverance, the height of hope, and the mysterious depth of grace.

PART II: CONFRONTING THE ONTOLOGICAL TRADITION

1. Pöggeler, *Denkweg,* p. 27/17.

5: What Did Heidegger Find in Aristotle? (1921–23)

1. Martin Heidegger, *Zur Sache des Denkens* (Tübingen: Niemeyer, 1969), pp. 86f.; Eng. trans. by Joan Stambaugh, *On Time and Being* (New York: Harper and Row, 1972), pp. 78f. Heidegger's letter to Richardson is in Wm. J. Richardson, S.J., *Heidegger: Through Phenomenology to Thought* (The Hague: Nijhoff, 1963), pp. x–xv.

2. This chronology is a very lean distillation drawn from a series of articles on Heidegger written by Pöggeler from 1977 to 1983: regarding phase 1), see esp. "Temporal Interpretation and Hermeneutic Philosophy," trans. T. Kisiel, in *Phenomenology: Dialogues and Bridges,* ed. R. Bruzina and B. Wilshire (Albany: SUNY Press, 1982), pp. 79–97, esp. p. 80 (the German version, written in 1977, has just been published in Pöggeler's *Neue Wege mit Heidegger* [Freiburg and Munich: Alber, 1992], pp. 115–141); this point seems to be an attempt to specify more precisely a line in Heidegger's *Zur Sache des Denkens,* p. 86 (78). Regarding 2), see esp. "Martin Heidegger: Zeit und Sein" (coauthored with F. Hogemann), *Grundprobleme der großen Philosophen,* ed. J. Speck (Göttingen: Vandenhoeck und Ruprecht, 1982), pp. 48–86, esp. p. 56. Regarding 3), see the above as well as "Zeit und Sein bei Heidegger," in *Zeit und Zeitlichkeit bei Husserl und Heidegger,* ed. E. W. Orth, *Phänomenologische Forschungen* 14 (1983): 152–191, esp. pp. 169, 155. Regarding 4), see "Heideggers Neubestimmung des Phänomenbegriffs," ed. E. W. Orth, *Phänomenologische Forschungen* 9 (1980): 124–162, esp. p. 131 and n. 3.

Heidegger at times apparently simply gave "1923" as the date for the break-through. Cf. *Denkweg*, the 1983 Postscript, pp. 351f./285, where Pöggeler also asks whether there was not a greater break in WS 1925–26, when the "scales fell from the eyes" of Heidegger upon reading Kant's texts on the schematism. One could go on, e.g., to 1929–30, in the Year of the Turn, when untruth as insuperable concealment first emerges. Under interrogation by his interlocutors about his accomplishments, the old Heidegger at times apparently could not resist going beyond the facts and indulging in a bit of exaggeration and self-romanticization. Can we possibly reproduce this insight into the question of Being and Time with the depth and force which moved Heidegger so drastically that he later sought to divide his works up to and away from the watershed year of 1923 into mere "juvenilia" and his authentic opus? One is reminded of Aquinas's judgment of his work after the mystical experience he underwent near the end of his life. But the dying Thomas then stopped writing.

For us, the importance of these conversations leading up to Pöggeler's defini-tive book on Heidegger's development is Heidegger's explicit support and sanc-tioning of the progression in which this book is laid out: the two dissertations with their still medieval sense of Aristotle were succeeded by a "completely new approach" developed on the one hand by a concern with Dilthey and on the other with early Christian eschatology and Luther. "Heidegger in fact emphasized that it was only when these two lines [hands] found each other that his authentic thought, the thought that still counts, began" (from a letter of Professor Pöggeler to me of July 31, 1991). Here we have, accordingly, what was lacking in the two more phenomenological accounts published by Heidegger during his lifetime: the overt sanctioning of the themes of the religion courses of 1920–21, within a hermeneutics of facticity, as a catalytic basis for the insights into truth and presence mediated by a rethought Aristotle, where these latter constitute the "decisive stroke of genius."

3. Note that the entire course manuscript itself bears the title "Einleitung" (GA 61:v, 201f.) and is referred to by that one-word title in the course itself (110, 112), the notes appended to it (182n, 183, 187f., 197), as well as in later courses (GA 63:47). After this proto-*Einleitung*, which predates the actual deci-sion to write a treatise on Aristotle (in the spring of 1922), the correspondence to Löwith records at least five more drafts of the *Einleitung*: September 1922 (the version read to Jaspers), October 1922, February-April 1923, July-Septem-ber 1923 (the version postponed by Niemeyer because of the Inflation), March 1924. Cf. Appendix B, n. 12, for further details.

4. But it is not called that until October 1922. The passage in GA 61:60 postdates the lecture course itself.

5. GA 61:38, 41ff., 56, 69; "hermeneutische Situation" on p. 3 postdates the lecture course itself. Since this distracting remark can easily be repeated *ad nau-seam* and multiply our footnotes like rabbits, the chronological unraveling of the published text of GA 61 is best left for another occasion. One needs only to inspect Heidegger's autograph of this course manuscript in Marbach—margin-alia of varying tints, textures, and styles piled upon marginalia up to six layers or so, most of which are worked into the edition without benefit of any separation

whatsoever, not even the break of a paragraph or a bracket—to see how "baroque" and chronologically compromised this edition is. Its first appearance attracted more attention than it deserved only because it was the first of the courses of the Early Freiburg period to be published, introducing the outside public for the first time to the wealth of insights to be found in the first steps taken by Heidegger toward BT.

6. Oskar Becker was so fond of this metaphor that he cited it repeatedly in his classes. It thus first appears in print in the 1963 book of his student, Otto Pöggeler: *Denkweg*, p. 70/54.

7. GA 61:92. The Brecht/Weiß transcript (on December 9, 1921) is somewhat more expansive in its parenthetical remark than the text in the published edition. It is worth citing, since this is Heidegger's first overt reference to the original meaning of οὐσία as "having." This practical sense is still operative in Aristotle while he overlays and so suppresses it with a more theoretical interpretation: "(Indication: that the concept οὐσία (Plato-Aristotle) denotes authentic being in the radically theoretical sense, yet at the same time also signifies belongings and property [*Habe*]; house-and-hold or real estate [*Hausstand*]; and so the power that comes with wealth and 'means' [*Vermögen*]: that in which I practically live.)"

8. The recently doctored Leo Strauss, passing through Freiburg in that semester, paused to sample Heidegger's by now famous teaching style. He later said to Franz Rosenzweig that, in comparison, Max Weber was but a "destitute waif" (*Waisenknabe* = "no comparison") in precision and probing and competence. And Werner Jaeger was simply outclassed when it came to the interpretation of the Aristotelian texts. See Leo Strauss, *The Rebirth of Classical Political Rationalism* (Chicago: University of Chicago Press, 1989), pp. 27f. I thank my colleague, Morton Frisch, for pointing out this reference.

The following paraphrase of this as yet unpublished course is based on the detailed transcript by Walter Bröcker typed by Herbert Marcuse (and so to be found in his archive in Frankfurt). But many passages in Helene Weiß's transcript provide an insightful counterreading, along with the dating. F. J. Brecht's partial transcript also has its moments. In presenting this course for the first time ever in an open forum since its initial presentation, I have likewise opted for a freer (albeit condensed), more idiomatic English presentation, to the degree that the matter is amenable to it.

9. Jaspers's book is discussed in some detail in the lecture of July 6. We now know that, at this time, course material and correspondence converge on the central point at issue, the need to "destroy" the Greek sense of "that it is" by way of Jaspers's "limit situation." Heidegger applies it in the course itself in his reading of Parmenides' poem. See the exchange of letters on June 27 and July 2, 1922, in the Heidegger-Jaspers *Briefwechsel*, pp. 26–32. We have already cited from the letter of June 27 (chap. 3, end) but the key lines are worth repeating in the present outburst of enthusiasm by Heidegger for Aristotle's ousio-logic to the point of introducing the language of *Habe* into many of his own conceptions. In observing that being alive and human is not something that a person has but is "and which *lives him*," Heidegger concludes: "Fundamentally, this means that there are matters which one does not have but 'is'; things whose What

rests simply in the 'That they are' " (pp. 26f.). In a philosophy of radical finitude, the classical ontological distinctions begin to waver and fail. This remark never-theless does not prevent Heidegger from continuing to give full amplitude in the coming months to the ousiological insight, "One is what one has."

10. See Theodore Kisiel, "The Missing Link in the Early Heidegger," in *Her-meneutic Phenomenology: Lectures and Essays* ed. Joseph J. Kockelmans (Washing-ton, D.C.: University Press of America, 1988), pp. 1–40, esp. pp. 6ff. With the discovery of the Missing Link (cf. n. 13 below), this full story can now be made fuller and modified in a few places. Let me point to one such modification in regard to Husserl's *Jahrbuch*. The decision to publish a book on Aristotle came too late for inclusion in vol. 6 of the *Jahrbuch*, which appeared in early 1923. With his heavy teaching load, Heidegger obviously needed more time, and so his monograph was scheduled for vol. 7 of the *Jahrbuch*, thus for the following year. "A great ground-laying work on Aristotle by Heidegger will appear in VII" (Husserl to Ingarden on Dec. 14, 1922). But in Sept. 1923, the Inflation caused Niemeyer to postpone publication, so vol. 7 first appeared in 1925, but without either Heidegger's "Aristotle" or his "Time," which by December 1924 replaced the former in the publication schedule. BT first appeared in vol. 8 of the *Jahrbuch* in 1927. See the "Chronology" of Appendix C.

11. "When I got back home, Husserl was waiting for me with the news that word had reached Marburg about my Aristotle courses etc., etc.: Natorp wants a concrete orientation on what I have in the works. So I sat myself down for three weeks and excerpted myself and thereby wrote an 'Introduction' " (Heidegger to Jaspers on November 19, 1922, pp. 33f.).

12. "The 'Time' is coming in the next volume [8, (1927)] of the Yearbook and in fact in the context in which it was worked out, as a ground for the destruc-tion of Greek ontology and logic" (letter to Löwith on March 29, 1925). Such remarks are not to be construed to mean that the historical is more important than the systematic, as a Derridean interpretation of Heidegger is inclined to do. For Heidegger at this time, these two aspects of phenomenological research belong together equally, they are "equiprimordial," and their separation is purely didactic. Cf. GA 20:9f./7 and the note to my translation, p. 7.

13. Martin Heidegger, "Phänomenologische Interpretationen zu Aristoteles (Anzeige der hermeneutischen Situation)," edited, with a Postscript, by Hans-Ulrich Lessing, *Dilthey-Jahrbuch* 6 (1989): 235–274. The Overview of *Nicomachean Ethics* Z is to be found on pp. 255–261 (29–39 of the typescript). This edition is based on the 51-page typescript of both the Introduction (through p. 28) and Overview recently discovered in Göttingen among the papers of Josef König, who was a student of Georg Misch, the first recipient of the document. In my paraphrase, I shall be referring to the pagination of this celebrated typescript (celebrated, e.g., by Hans-Georg Gadamer in his introduction to the above, pp. 228–234), which is also given in the English translation by Michael Baur, "Phe-nomenological Interpretations with Respect to Aristotle (Indication of the Her-meneutical Situation)," *Man and World* 25 (1992): 355–393. In addition, I shall be adding a few of the more telling handwritten marginal comments made by Heidegger in the months following its completion on his own carbon copy of

the typescript, still extant as a fragment up to p. 22 (cf. "The Missing Link," p. 22, n. 31). Square brackets in the body of this summary set off my own editorial amplifications, at times based on some of Heidegger's marginalia, along with my outline of the text into the parts suggested in the opening paragraph of the Introduction.

14. This sentence is Heidegger's handwritten addendum: "Die Unempfind-lichkeit und Sorglosigkeit gegenüber der eigenen und dabei oft verworrenen, zufällig aufgerafften hermeneutischen Situation legt man sich oft aus als Unvor-genommenheit."

15. This is Aristotle's *Ethics* ontologized. It is Heidegger's first attempt to translate the self-referential or circular movement of πρᾶξις—human action par excellence since it is action for its own sake, such that it constitutes for Aristotle both the ἀρχή and τέλος of φρόνησις—into the ontological terms later familiar to us in the analysis of Dasein as "ein Seiendes, dem es *in* seinem Sein *um* dieses Sein selbst geht": "a being which *in* its being goes *about* this being, is concerned *about* this being, *has* this being as an issue" (SZ 12 *et passim*). In BT, the phrase is first used to formally indicate the self-referential character of understanding. But in the early proto-context, the phrase introduces us to the genealogically more proximate biblical and Greek contexts, familiar to us from Heidegger's religion courses, connecting concern or *curare* with the philosophical cliché, "life is hard." This latter theme appears only indirectly in BT, in Everyone's "tendency to take things lightly and make things easy" (SZ 127f.; also GA 20:340/247).

16. This return to the title of the *Einleitung* reflects the transition in WS 1921–22 from the Second Part on "What Is Philosophy?" to the Third Part which outlines the "Basic Categories of Life." In this *Einleitung*, the systematic exposition of the problem of facticity develops the *Blickstand*, the position of sight, identified in the opening paragraph as the first facet (*ergo* our [1]) of the hermeneutic situation in need of explication. It is sometimes called *Blickhabe* or *Vorhabe*, the formal indication of "facticity," whereas in BT what is indicated is "existence."

The approach to the plurivocity of life in this new *Einleitung* is far more riddled with Aristotelian trail-markers than that of WS 1921–22 (GA 61:79ff.), which is more "modern" (out of the then current life-philosophies) and grammat-ical in its approach. The underlying framework is the same—the intentional correlation of caring with meaningfulness—but now the elaboration of the λόγος of life, how it is multiplied and organized, is clearly being guided by Heidegger's Aristotelian analyses of the genesis of the theoretical, the multiple "logic" of human motion, and the five ways of "taking into troth." Of prime importance from here on is the Aristotelian mindset which Heidegger is cultivating for himself.

17. Heidegger adds the following handwritten note: "recuratio: das Histo-rische! Darin die höchste Seinsverwahrung." ("care as restoration: the historical! This involves the highest form of taking Being in trust [i.e., "troth" as truth].") thus connecting care directly with his translation of truth (*Wahrheit*) as ἀληθεύειν (*Ver-wahr-ung*), the truth which is to be held in trust, safeguarded, shepherded, habituated by human virtuosity. To care is to take into troth and hold in troth,

the kind of having (e.g., of the world) involved in the habits of truth. "Every object has its own way of having, its way of access for taking into troth, and its way of falling into loss" (GA 61:23). Cf. the ensuing discussion of the "true-ing" virtues of *Nicomachean Ethics* Z below, where I shall maintain this "fiduciary" relation between care and truth as a holding in trust by way of the old English word for fidelity, "troth." The same associations are to be found in the original Christian sense of "being true" by "keeping the faith" (cf. chaps. 2 and 4 above).

A word here also about why Heidegger assumes without comment that ἀλήθεια can be translated as unveiling or unconcealment. It is simply the way the German dictionaries had been translating it since the early nineteenth century! See, e.g., Franz Passow, *Handwörterbuch der griechischen Sprache* (Leipzig: Friedrich Chr. Wilhelm Vogel, 1831), p. 81, where ἀλήθεια is translated not only as "Wahrheit" but also as "Unversrecktheit" and ἀληθής as "unverhohlen." (It may be noted, however, that Misch placed question marks on his copy of the *Einleitung* at the point where this translation first appears, whereas Natorp, who had been utilizing this translation in his courses at least since 1917, naturally accepts it without question.)

18. Here, Heidegger drops the fourth character of "annihilation" (*Vernichtung*) discussed in WS 1921–22 (GA 61:140,147f.) under the heading of "ruination" (here replaced by "fallenness"). From the preceding paragraph, we sense that fallenness assumes the proportions of de-pendence of an addiction. The related metaphorology of *Abfallen* (since SS 1920), a falling away from the self, develops it more as a moment of inertia or "drag" in human existence, a kind of existential "laziness."

19. In the only handwritten footnote to the typescript (thus probably inserted at the last minute in mid-October 1922), Heidegger now tries to restrict this broad term, which since SS 1920 ranged in meaning from passive "disquiet" to active "concern" and anxious "worry," to the more active choosing and seizing of the unique possibility of my existence, particularly in view of its questionability. Hitherto, this obviously middle-voiced term had been left to operate ambiguously between the extremes of "being troubled" and "troubling oneself." With its strict definition comes its demise. After Oct. 1922, *Bekümmerung* is no longer used as a central term, and gets displaced in this role by both "care" (already in SS 1921) and "angst" (first in SS 1923).

20. Heidegger later adds this marginal comment: "Zeitlichkeit – Tod – entscheidende Einmaligkeit! Dieses 'Einmal' ist radikal 'Alles' des Lebens. Zeitlichkeit nicht wie Quantitäten und solches Nacheinander, sondern existenziell faktische Sprünge. Die Kontinuität imgleichen *je* ein Sprung (προαίρεσις!), imgleichen das Wie des Erwartens." ("Temporality – death – decisive uniqueness! This 'one time' is the radical 'all' of life. Temporality is not at all like quantities, sequences, and the like, but existentielly factic leaps. The continuity is *in each instance* equally a leap of decision and the how of expectation.") It should be noted that προαίρεσις, which is consequent upon the insight of φρόνησις, means equally choice and anticipation.

21. Heidegger made plans for a course on Augustine in SS 1924, but at the last minute it was replaced by a course on Aristotle, in a final effort "to get the

book out" (see WS 1923–24 for more). One senses the content of such a course on Augustine precisely in these passages of Oct. 1922.

22. This outline of the projected book tallies with that in a letter from Heidegger to Gadamer, apparently in late 1922 (but perhaps in 1923). Cf. Hans-Georg Gadamer, *Heideggers Wege* (Tübingen: Mohr, 1983), p. 118. From the projected length of each part (16 galleys = 260 pages), one could presume that Heidegger intended to include his detailed translation paraphrases of the selections from Aristotle, along the lines of those of his course of SS 1922. Presumably, this book existed in manuscript form into 1926, when Heidegger labored over the projected Second Part of BT, according to a letter to Jaspers on April 24, 1926. The last mention of work on the *Einleitung* is found in a letter to Löwith on March 19, 1924: "The Introduction is still costing me a great deal of work. Up in the cabin in the last few days in the evenings, I sketched out a new structure in one stretch which now satisfies me the most. . . . In any event, I have now resolved to print the Aristotle, as far as I come. I have to get the thing off my back, probably by rewriting it once more while it is being printed." And on June 18, 1924, to Jaspers regarding an invitation to spend two years in Japan, "but only after my Aristotle is out." But with his "Time" lecture of July 1924 came the sequence of drafts that led instead to BT.

23. "I am almost staggered by the observation of how closely his entire view of Hellenism and its decisive influence on all of Western 'culture,' and of the unique position (in this culture and against it) of the *German mind—how this in Luther as well as, I think, in Kant*, positions itself *against* the past—comes to my own ideas and at once confirms them from many new sides" (Husserl Archive, R II Natorp 30. X. 22). See my "Missing Link," p. 14, n. 23, for further connections between the thought of the late Natorp and the early Heidegger, as well as for the further story of the *Einleitung* presented sketchily above, like the very different reaction to it by Georg Misch in Göttingen, pp. 12f.

6: Aristotle Again: From Unconcealment to Presence (1923–24)

1. Heidegger's lecture tour in early December 1924, as announced by the provincial group of Kant Societies banded together as the "West German Industrial Region," involved his giving the same lecture to six local groups according to the following schedule: Dec. 1 in Hagen, Dec. 2 in Elberfeld, Dec. 3 in Cologne, Dec. 5 in Düsseldorf, Dec. 6 in Essen, Dec. 8 in Dortmund. Cf. *Kant-Studien* 29 (1924): 626. In the following year's *Kant-Studien* 30 (1925), the local group in Dortmund reports that Heidegger had indeed given his lecture on "Dasein und Wahrsein nach Aristoteles" on (Monday) December 8, 1924 (p. 611). The group in Elberfeld-Barmen likewise confirms that the lecture was held (p. 612), but gives no date, while the group at Cologne reports that Heidegger held a lecture at their inaugural meeting on the campus of the university on December 4, 1924 (p. 616). On December 17, Heidegger writes to Löwith: "In Cologne, I spent 3 days with Scheler – stayed at his house." There is an unconfirmed report hinting that Heidegger went from Cologne straight to Essen, presumably skipping Düsseldorf: see Walter Biemel, *Martin Heidegger in Selbstzeugnissen und Bilddokumenten* (Hamburg: Rowohlt, 1973), p. 152.

I wish to thank Tom Sheehan for access to materials pertaining to this lecture.

The extant transcript puts the date of the talk in Cologne on December 2, 1924. For genealogical reasons, I shall here rely mainly on the formulations of the initial working manuscript of "1923–24," incomplete but already obviously too long for a single talk. But for the time being, it represents the earliest unequivocal identification by Heidegger of οὐσία with constant presence which can be documented. The more streamlined formulations of the delivered talk were nevertheless sometimes helpful in getting at the gist of this earlier text.

2. The reason given for the change was Heidegger's resolve finally to get the Aristotle book written and into print (letter to Löwith on March 19, 1924).

3. In SS 1922, however, Heidegger begins the course by noting that the "life and works" of the philosopher are presuppositions for the course, and to that end provides a list of reference works, including Zeller, Windelband, Gomperz, Brentano, and Sigwart's *Aristoteles und seine Weltanschauung* (1911). Cf. also below, chap. 8, n. 3, on Heidegger's concurrence with Dilthey's approach to philosophical biography. Also Theodore Kisiel, "Heidegger's Apology: Biography as Philosophy and Ideology," *Graduate Faculty Philosophy Journal* 14/2–15/1 (1991): 363–404.

In this section, the page numbers in parentheses will refer to citations from the detailed course transcript (134 pages of close elite type) for SS 1924 made by Walter Bröcker and typed by Herbert Marcuse. Copies of this typescript, replete with handwritten Greek, are located in the Marcuse Archive in Frankfurt and the Dilthey-Forschungsstelle in Bochum.

4. Heidegger is already exploiting, in this early course context, Aristotle's remark in *Metaphysics* 5.16. 1021b29 that death (τελευτή = end of life) as an "outermost" extremity is in a way a completion or perfection. Cf. SZ, § 48.

5. Oddly, Heidegger never pauses to examine closely this single instance of the use of the word καιρός in *Nicomachean Ethics* that relates most closely to his own usage, which he is carrying over more from his study of early Christianity.

6. *Rhetoric* 2.5. 1383a6. Heidegger makes strikingly frequent use of this quasi-religious Greek phrase in the remainder of the course. Thus he speaks of how virtue "saves the middle" and "God saves the sky – saving in the sense of maintaining it in Dasein, not permitting it to perish" (106). This note of salvation is dropped in Heidegger's application of this classic chapter on fear in the draft of SS 1925 (GA 20:394/285) but used in a suggestive way in WS 1925/26 (GA 21:261f.; cf. chap. 8 above). The fear/hope relation is alluded to in BT (SZ 345).

7. I am using the title found on all of the extant student transcripts of this course: "Interpretation platonischer Dialoge (Σοφιστής, Φίληβος)." The now-published German edition uses instead the title given in Richardson's list: *Platon, Sophistes* (Marburg Lecture Course of WS 1924–25), ed. Ingeborg Schüssler, GA 19 (Frankfurt: Klostermann, 1992). Here, I have worked only with the extensive transcripts of Hans Walter Loewald and Simon Moser.

8. Heidegger was impressed by the fact that Husserl as a phenomenologist, simply from the matters themselves, drew the same three distinctions as Aristotle in his intentional account of "Truth and Evidence" (LU VI, § 39; cf. chap. 1, n. 7). There is no real justification in Heidegger for my translating ἀληθεύειν as "trueing" except to suggest another nuance to this verb that is worth keeping

in mind. Heidegger typically translates it in the customary intransitive form of "being true," being interested especially in the old ontological problem of how we already find ourselves "in the truth," *ergo* truth understood as a "transcendental" (1915–16), a present perfect apriori (SZ 85). My intention is not to subjectivize the process of "making true" (Husserl above speaks of the "true-making thing") but to keep before us the fact that It is a process, an unconceal*ing* which we somehow take part in and "*go* along with."

9. Among Heidegger's early students, Oskar Becker, Walter Bröcker, and especially Hans-Georg Gadamer tell the story of Heidegger's equating of phronetic insight with the conscience in a seminar in Freiburg and not, as our doxographic record indicates, in this Marburg lecture course. Cf. esp. Hans-Georg Gadamer, *Philosophical Hermeneutics*, transl. and ed. David E. Linge (Berkeley, Los Angeles, London: University of California Press, 1976), p. 201.

PART III: THREE DRAFTS OF *BEING AND TIME*

1. Heidegger's card to Löwith, March 27, 1925. See Appendix C for the same citation in the original German. A month before, Heidegger had concluded his classes discussing the question of being as it is raised in Plato's *Sophist*, and is only now explicitly introducing this issue into his manuscripts on "The Concept of Time."

2. See Appendix C for the German text and source of this quotation, as well as for an account of the concurrent drafting of the two Parts of SZ.

7. The Dilthey Draft: "The Concept of Time" (1924)

1. "es ist wahrhaft existent . . ." This is the closest that Heidegger comes in the entire lecture to "existentialist" vocabulary. Recall also the comments in previous chapters regarding the differences between student transcripts and the published "Ausgaben letzter Hand," especially with regard to existentialist terminology, like the course of WS 1921–22. The same remark now applies to the forthcoming two first drafts of BT.

2. Heidegger to Löwith, June 30, 1925: "The theologians here are quite enterprising, the students divided and by and large grouped around Bultmann, who is careful and realistic in all things and sensibly distances himself from Barthianism and even more from Kierkegaardism. This last 'hurrah' is gradually becoming unbearable, the most incompetent people here have got into this dialectic and now have become so good at it that they at once also add, they don't really have to talk like that!!"

3. At his own request, Heidegger had received a review copy of the Dilthey-Yorck correspondence around Christmas of 1923 and by September of 1924 was busy writing a review of it in the larger context of comprehending historicality, the "common interest" of Dilthey and Yorck, in terms of temporality. See next section. There is even a hint that the lecture itself may have originally been intended more in this direction: "Today only the news that Heidegger's lecture 'History and Time' will take place on Friday the 25th in the evening" (Rudolf Bultmann to Karl Barth on July 4, 1924, in *Karl Barth–Rudolf Bultmann Briefwech-*

sel 1922–1966, ed. Bernd Jaspert ([Zürich: Theologischer Verlag, 1971], p. 16). Several days earlier, on July 1, Heidegger had proposed the following theme to the sponsors of his forthcoming Kassel lectures: "Geschichtliches Dasein und historische Erkenntnis (Einführung in Wilhelm Diltheys Forschungen)." Cf. n. 22 below.

4. Oskar Becker, "Mathematische Existenz," *Jahrbuch für Philosophie und phänomenologische Forschung* 8 (1927): 661–674.

5. The following is a synopsis of a story told in far greater archival detail in Theodore Kisiel, "Why the First Draft of *Being and Time* Was Never Published," *Journal of the British Society for Phenomenology* 20, no. 1 (January 1989): 3–22. This article also includes an earlier analysis of the text. A German edition of the correspondence which underlies this story is to be found in J. W. Storck and T. Kisiel , eds., "Martin Heidegger und die Anfänge der *Deutschen Vierteljahrsschrift der Literaturwissenschaft und Geistesgeschichte:* Eine Dokumentation," *Dilthey-Jahrbuch* 8 (1992).

6. *Briefwechsel zwischen Wilhelm Dilthey und dem Grafen Paul Yorck von Wartenburg 1877–1897*, Philosophie und Geisteswissenschaften, ed. Erich Rothacker, vol. 1 (Halle: Niemeyer, 1923).

7. The titles of these four sections are to be found in Klostermann's publisher's prospectus, which announces the forthcoming publication of the article itself as vol. 64 of the GA, thus the first volume of the series in the Third Division devoted to "Unpublished Treatises." Since the article is not yet published, my selective paraphrase will be somewhat more extensive than usual and, moreover, will take care in distinguishing the article as sent to Rothacker from later marginalia, some of which undoubtedly served to bridge this draft with the final draft of BT, like the addition of existentialist vocabulary. The article of November 1924 is, like the next draft of SS 1925, totally devoid of such terminology.

8. Georg Misch, "Vorbericht des Herausgebers," in Wilhelm Dilthey, *Gesammelte Schriften*, vol. 5 (Stuttgart: Teubner, 1924), pp. vii–cxvii. Cf. SZ 399n, where Heidegger notes that he can forgo a detailed discussion of Dilthey's work, begun in the 1924 draft, in view of Misch's thorough treatment of Dilthey's development.

9. Wilhelm Dilthey, *Einleitung in die Geisteswissenschaften*, vol. 1 of *Gesammelte Schriften* (Stuttgart: Teubner, 1922), "Vorrede," p. xvii.

10. This "event" (*Ereignis*) of the articulation of meaning in *Begegnis* and its disclosure of "truth" will reach virtually sublime heights of focus and concentration in the later Heidegger's *tour de force* in the German language when it is described as the "regioning" (*Vergegnis*) of the human being and at once the "conditioning" (*Bedingnis*) of things in the ultimate Region (*Gegend*, but esp. the more active old German *Gegnet*) or Place (*topos*) of Being which comes to meet (*entgegenkommt*) us. Of course, this entire meditation is intended, through a kind of pacifist reversal of human expectation (from *Erwarten* to *Warten*: the text stems from 1944–45), to offset the representational language of an object (*Gegen-stand*) objectified, through the power of human "transcendence," against the *horizon* of the present (*Gegen-wart*), which had seduced Heidegger in BT and its aftermath into vestigial metaphysical perspectives and activist attitudes. Cf. the dialogue

between the teacher, scholar, and scientist in *Gelassenheit* (English translation in *Discourse on Thinking*).

11. The passage thus reflects more the entropic factor of nature as such rather than the inertia of human nature, which Heidegger has already identified as the "pendency" and "decadence" of fallenness, which becomes an intrinsic element of human temporality. It thus approaches Aristotle's reflections on history as τύχη, chance. It may also be noted for what follows that the strange, alien, and exotic, in short, the Other understood impersonally, will recur in different contexts and so play different functions, e.g., in concern, in curiosity, and in the encounter with death.

12. An apparent exception occurs in WS 1921–22 among the categories of the relational sense of life. Being related to the world's meaningfulness includes being inclined *toward* it and at once a standing *before* it. This "inclination" and "distance" are made "equiprimordial" because the latter character is concealed, repressed, or "deflected" by the former into being "pulled down" into absorption and dispersion in the world. This distantiation is accordingly reduced to expressing itself implicitly in the form of rank and position *within* the world and life, in getting ahead, succeeding, putting on a show, etc. "Distance, which co-enables inclination, is swept along by it" (GA 61:102f.). But this domination of one character by another is but a refined development of the original heterothetical dynamics of identification and differentiation which lies at the heart of equiprimordiality, its subtle implications for the relations between Self and Other within the "with-world" of concern.

13. Heidegger to Löwith on November 6, 1924: "You'll be getting an offprint when the essay ["The Concept of Time"] comes out in January. Unfortunately, I had to leave out some important topics, in particular the 'formal indication,' which is indispensable for an ultimate understanding – I have worked essentially on this topic." Cf. the edition of letters by Storck and Kisiel, "Anfänge"; also Kisiel, "Why the First Draft . . . ," p. 9.

14. Passing remarks in Heidegger's letters to Rothacker in 1922-24—on philosophy as the "backbone" of intellectual history, on the influence of theological research on the human sciences (ibid.)—suggest that his interest in this new and somewhat hybrid journal at least stimulated, if not caused, Heidegger to focus his old thoughts on the "genesis of the theoretical" into a hermeneutic-phenomenological theory of the entire field of the sciences. This direction culminates in important statements on the "crisis" of the sciences in relation to philosophy (as "logic" as well as ontology) in 1925–27 (GA 20: § 1, GA 21: § 3, SZ: § 3, GA 25: § 2). The fact that the work on a Diltheyan history of literature by Rudolf Unger, who contributed to the inaugural issue of the *Deutsche Vierteljahrsschrift*, is singled out by Heidegger in the respective sections in GA 20 (p. 5) and SZ (p. 10), serves to support this connection. And in the section in GA 21 (p. 17), Heidegger observes that one of Dilthey's revolutionary accomplishments was "the transposition of historical research onto the foundation of what we nowadays call intellectual history, history *of* the human spirit."

15. Karl Jaspers, *Psychologie der Weltanschauungen* (Berlin: Springer, 1919, ⁶1971), pp. 274, 55.

16. Heidegger here is apparently responding to a remark subsequent to the July lecture from one of his Marburg colleagues (Natorp? Hartmann?) that the founder of the Marburg School of neo-Kantianism, Hermann Cohen, had already seen that the basic character of time is in the future. The location of the footnote, not carried over into BT, indicates that Heidegger considered this to be an insight into the inauthentic future: Cf. H. Cohen, *Logik der reinen Erkenntnis* (Berlin: Cassirer, ³1922), pp. 151ff., 226ff.; in the first edition, pp. 128ff., 193ff.

17. One is reminded of Kierkegaard's "knight of faith," who in outward appearance is indistinguishable from the proverbial "man in the street." Even the use of the Hegelian *Aufhebung* to describe this masking may be symptomatic of this connection. In a marginal comment to this passage, Heidegger remarks, "not moralizing!! – but rather existential."

18. One might cite, for example, the repeated return to a hyletic phenomenology in recent French philosophy. In Derridean imagery, the original field can be described as a diffuse vaginal enfolding rather than the phallocentric point which is being equated with monologocentrism. For more on this sort of translation of Heidegger, see my review of Mark Taylor's *Tears* in *Bulletin de la société américaine de philosophie de langue francaise* 2 (1990): 61–66. A later version is reprinted as a Discussion in the *Journal of the British Society for Phenomenology* 22, no. 2 (May 1991): 93–96.

19. Citing Heidegger's letter to Löwith on November 6, 1924. Cf. n. 13 above.

20. Kisiel, "Why the First Draft . . . ," p. 10: letter to Rothacker of November 18, 1924. For the German, see Appendix C.

21. Ibid., p. 11: letter to Löwith of March 27, 1925. See Appendix C.

22. Frithjof Rodi, "Die Bedeutung Diltheys für die Konzeption von 'Sein und Zeit': Zum Umfeld von Heideggers Kasseler Vorträgen (1925)," *Dilthey-Jahrbuch* 4 (1986–87): 161–177, esp. p. 165. Cf. n. 3 above. A transcript of the Kassel Lectures themselves is to be published in *Dilthey-Jahrbuch* 8 (1992).

23. Theodore Kisiel, "Heidegger's Apology: Biography as Philosophy and Ideology," *Graduate Faculty Philosophy Journal* 14/2–15/1 (1991): 363–404.

8: The Ontoeroteric Draft: History of the Concept of Time (1925)

1. By coining the term "eroteric," I have allowed myself a slight orthographic liberty with the usual English adjective "erotetic" (from ἐρώτησις, questioning) in order to suggest the close tie between *eros* and questioning that Greek etymology reflects. Especially in this phenomenological context, the quest for being first manifests itself on the preverbal erotic level, the pathos which gives rise to the question of being, before it reaches the verbal level of questioning.

2. This tacit phenomenological development in the course of SS 1925 and a number of other issues, including an explanation of my translation decisions of key terms in the course of SS 1925, like *Jeweiligkeit*, *Appräsentation*, and *Bewandtnis*, are discussed in my "On the Way to *Being and Time*: Introduction to the Translation of Heidegger's *Prolegomena zur Geschichte des Zeitbegriffs*," *Research in Phenomenology* 15 (1985): 193–226, esp. pp. 205f. This Translator's Introduction, following NEH guidelines, was originally intended for publication with the translation itself, but was forced under separate cover because of the paramilitary assaults on scholarship by Heidegger's literary executors.

3. Cf. chap. 2 above on Heidegger's own religious conversion out of the medieval lifeworld, and on his correspondence reflecting a growing consciousness of the relation between his own life and his thought. The issue of biography/ philosophy surfaces publicly only in passing in his early lectures until the second Kassel lecture weeks before SS 1925, where he presents a detailed "life of Dilthey, outwardly eventless," but with an "inner life" and "intellectual world" (*geistige Welt*) which must be regarded as "actual" (*gegenwärtig*), and made actual, if we wish to understand his works and writings as expressions of his life. Once again, the rehearsal of Dilthey's theological upbringing is in certain aspects reminiscent of Heidegger's own path (see chap. 7 and n. 23, above). It is yet to be estimated in what ways the young Heidegger's enthusiastic reading of Dilthey's two great philosophical biographies, *Life of Schleiermacher* and *The Young Hegel* (chap. 2), to be followed by his review of the Dilthey-Yorck correspondence (chap. 7), became central to Heidegger's orientation toward the life/thought issue. But as a beginning, see my "Heidegger's Apology." There, I pointed to the central role played by teacher/student parallelisms—Husserl to Heidegger as Heidegger to Kuki—in structuring the "Dialogue on Language with a Japanese Scholar." From the present passage, we can now backtrack to the Brentano/Husserl relation in the series of life/thought structuralisms that Heidegger is generating, at least partly consciously (e.g., the gift of Brentano's book from the fatherly Conrad Gröber). The parallel will touch the very core of Heidegger's philosophy in this chapter, as we witness Heidegger transforming the teacher-student relation into one of leadership and followership (not quite discipleship) in the matter of understanding being. The theme of teacher as *Führer* will then first surface publicly when Heidegger, as Husserl's "Nach*folger*," gives the *Festrede* on the occasion of Husserl's retirement in April 1929.

4. The prolific occurrence of the nondescript word "structure" and accordingly its guiding significance for Heidegger's formally indicative and schematizing approach did not dawn on me until I dug out my old index for this course, which was blocked at the last minute from appearing with the translation because of the undue interference of Heidegger's literary executors. With asinine arguments against indexes backed by authoritarian intimidation and threats, they in more than one way subverted the high scholarly standards mandated for the book by NEH funding. With my index to the translation now conspicuous by its absence, however, one might perhaps begin to appreciate how indispensable indexes are as research tools for an in-depth study of Heidegger's "Ways, not Works" in their chronology and genealogy, in short, in the way Heidegger meant them to be studied. This index has proved invaluable in my own work on the key concepts of this course in countless ways. As translator (and repairman of the German edition) of this text, I was surprised over how much of the text, which was once immediately present to me almost verbatim, had over the years lapsed into forgottenness.

5. Martin Heidegger, *Vier Seminare* (Frankfurt: Klostermann, 1977), pp. 111ff. For a more detailed discussion, see my "On the Way to Being and Time," pp. 202–204.

6. Addition of the hyphen to the "selbst-weltlich" (350) suddenly "develops," like a photographic plate, the underlined sentence into a configuration flashing back to 1919–20. For lack of a hyphen, the genealogical thread back to 1920 is almost entirely severed. The omission in the German resulted in a mistranslation in the published English translation.

7. This now-famous example from Nietzsche's everydayness occurs in the first draft in November 1924.

8. In the environmental analysis which in turn examines the basic terms of "being," "in," and "world," the first term is usually connected with the question "*Who* is in the world?" (SZ 53, 114, 117). Since this key word is subject to personalistic excesses, it should be noted that the very first formulation of this question was "How does 'Being' in a world look?" (GA 63:85), how does this most basic "activity" appear, what is its way-to-be, its self-showing How? The Who here really boils down to an activist How, a "style" of Being called "concern" and, at its best, "solicitude."

9. The *Aus-gabe lehrender Hand*, which often does not find accommodation in the *Ausgabe letzter Hand*, because the "handout" in 1919 or 1926 (i.e., no photocopiers, though we do have an occasional photograph) is on the blackboard, geared to the pedagogical occasion, *jeweilig*, and the note Heidegger had scribbled for himself before class has since gone astray. Student notes after all are "muddy sources," though they are often the only sources.

10. "On the Way to BT," pp. 214f. Having discussed this point at various international conferences, I have yet to find anyone who could admit to a "ready at hand" translation of *Bewandtnis* in his/her language.

11. This initial use (of three) of *Mitbefindlichkeit* in BT, in connection with "fearing for" the other, suggests a kind of emotional contagion that Aristotle's rhetor (cf. SS 1924) and, later, Hitler try to cultivate, naturally on the prior basis of already being co-disposed in mutual concern. Thus, the only other uses of the term in BT (SZ 162) speak of co-disposition as a "communication" and "discourse" that is far more basic than assertion. The only co-disposedness worked out in BT, without calling it that and so only by indirection, is the mood of averageness, "the undisturbed equanimity and the inhibited ill-humor of our everyday concern" (SZ 134), "the pallid lack of mood—indifference—which dominates the 'gray everyday' through and through . . . which is addicted to nothing and has no urge for anything, and which abandons itself to whatever the day may bring" (SZ 345). Clearly, the nature of *co*-disposition even here, and in all of its forms, is in need of fundamental clarification.

12. Cf. "On the Way to BT," p. 202 and n. 10.

13. Ibid., p. 197.

14. GA 20:144/104f., citing *Ideen I*, § 49. A comparison with Heidegger's version of world annihilation, the reification experiment in KNS (cf. chap. 1), would go a long way in contrasting these two phenomenologies at their very roots, as different itineraries for going back "to the things themselves." Husserl's thought experiment already operates from a mind/nature dualism and so manages to annihilate the world by means of a breakdown of our habitual regularities in experiencing it, dissolving the world into a chaos of sensations while leaving

the intentional consciousness intact. The world is thereby relativized and exposed in its full unstructured contingency, while the immanently self-reflective stream of *Erlebnisse* is left to define the absolute sphere ("world"!) of consciousness. Heidegger's reification experiment in KNS actually starts with a similar dualistic understanding of intentionality, by taking the vantage of a remote theoretical subject out to objectify all, which only succeeds in immobilizing all. For the objectifying tendency culminates, not in the relativistic softening of the world by dissolving it into the stream of experience (*Er-lebnis*) itself (Heraclitus), but in the objectivistic hardening of the encountered world into brute facticity, the mute unstructured (thus meaningless) givenness of "things," even when they are called the "facts of consciousness." Heidegger then turns about-face from this mute indifference of unstructured solidity (Parmenides) standing over against an equally indifferent ("no matter who") theoretical I, in order to return to the ordinary world of practical involvement and personal encounter (*Er-fahrung*) which precedes theory. The dual indifference of objectification is thereby replaced by the correlative "indifference" of the practical self's absorption in its meaningful environment: two contrasting senses of the "immediacy" of experience. (Sartre performs both thought experiments in *Nausea*—the gnarled solidity of the chestnut tree, mundane rhythm gone amok in cysts and ambulant meat—to come to the same conclusion: the "absurdity" of being, the muting and stilling of its sense or its dispersion in multiplicity. Each path operates under its own "laws" toward a common goal, the destruction of life.)

15. The last note suggested that there are implications in this "destruction" of Husserl begging further explication. Rudolf Bernet thus explicates what presuppositions or "theses about being" Heidegger could have drawn from the hidden ontology of Husserl's idealism at this point, presuppositions which work against a deeper grasp of intentionality. See his "Husserl and Heidegger on Intentionality and Being," *Journal of the British Society for Phenomenology* 21 (May 1990): 136–152, esp. pp. 145–147. In a genealogical context, one might ask whether this destruction of 1925 adds any new "constructive" element to Heidegger's own phenomenology which was not already established through his transformation of Husserlian phenomenology in 1919–20, e.g., by way of his triple-sensed schematism of intentionality.

16. Cf. Appendix C below on the factual chronology to BT. The two earlier occurrences of "existenzial" in WS 1925–26 (GA 21:151, 267) are from Heidegger's penciled emendations in his personal copy of the Moser transcript, and so postdate the course itself (cf. Appendix D on this term). I wish to thank Walter Biemel, who edited this volume for publication in 1976, for this information.

17. The course as given simply bore the title "Logik." To distinguish it from the course of SS 1928, "Logik (Leibniz)," which was also announced simply as "Logik," Helene Weiss entitled her transcript "Logik (Aristoteles)." This latter was the subtitle planned for the published edition of the course, according to the first two publisher's prospectuses (1974 and 1975) of the *Gesamtausgabe*, but in the end the subtitle was altered to "Die Frage nach der Wahrheit" at Heidegger's own request (according to Walter Biemel, in a private communication). It may well have been the very last editorial decision regarding the GA made by

Heidegger himself before his death in May 1976. We have already noted that Heidegger, in one of his lectures during the course, suggests the subtitle, "Das (Vom) Wesen der Wahrheit" (218), thereby connecting this course to a whole series of lectures from 1930 on—and even one as early as May 1926 (see Appendix B below)—as well as some later lecture courses bearing that title (beginning in WS 1931–32).

18. SS 1928, "Logik (Leibniz)" [GA 26: *Metaphysische Anfangsgründe der Logik im Ausgang von Leibniz*]; SS 1934, "Logik" [GA 38, proposed title: "Über Logik als Frage nach der Sprache"]; WS 1937–38 [GA 45: *Grundfragen der Philosophie. Ausgewählte "Probleme" der "Logik"*]; SS 1944, *Logik (Heraklits Lehre vom Λόγος)* [so titled in GA 55]. Recall also the course of WS 1916-17, "Grundfragen der Logik" (see Appendix B).

19. According to the development recorded in three letters to Jaspers during the course of that seminar, Heidegger was clearly fascinated by the first triad (Dec. 10, 1925), Being–Nothing–Becoming, especially in its implications for his own problem of formally indicating the concept of being, which is never a genus (Dec. 16). But he finally did manage to get into the second triad that departs from Becoming (Feb. 17, 1926), (Heidegger and Jaspers, *Briefwechsel 1920–1963*, pp. 57–61).

20. Ibid. The last class before the Christmas break, which announced the changeover to Kant, was held between the writing of these two letters, on December 14, 1925.

21. In WS 1927–28: GA 25:412. In 1929: *Kant und das Problem der Metaphysik*, §31; cf. Appendix to the 4th edition for the occurrence in the Davos Lectures, March 1929. One could readily infer that Heidegger also told the same story in Riga in September 1928. Cf. Appendix B, n. 29.

9: The Final Draft: Toward a Kairology of Being

1. This has been done from a translator's perspective in my "On the Way to Being and Time," pp. 221–226, which suggests the degree to which Heidegger had his copy of the Moser transcript of SS 1925 before him as he made the final draft of BT.

2. This relational formulation of the temporality of the question of being, which in its concreteness is the goal of BT, gives precedence to the future tense. In terms of the old schematism of intentionality, temporality as a whole is to be found in the fruition of enactment, in the temporalizing sense that brings together the relational, containment, and actualization sense.

We need not dwell here on § 2 in BT, "The Formal Structure of the Question of Being," whose importance is underscored by the amount of attention it has received in commentaries. Heidegger's handwritten note to the equivalent section (§16) in SS 1925 (GA 20:195/144f.), postdating the course itself, neatly organizes the basic terms of the question in preparation for an elaboration of its temporality: "Im *E*rfragten liegt das *Ge*fragte; im Gefragten liegt das *Be*fragte. [Also ist das Erfragte der] Horizont der Frage." "What is asked *for*, the sense of being, implies what is asked *about*, the being of entities; what is asked about implies what is interrogat*ed*, the entity itself [here the entity which excels in questioning, Dasein]. [The sense of being, for which the question is being asked, toward which the quest is directed, is thus the] horizon of the question." Time itself will now be regarded as the latent horizon, at once ontic and formal, of the quest for being, defining the scope and limit of its sense.

3. Cf. GA 20:200/148, 217/161, *268/197*, *279f./204*, 297/216, 335/243. All of these instances of the term "ontisch," excluding the two italicized, are Heidegger's handwritten insertions, postdating the course itself. Of the two that belong to SS 1925 itself, the first is the more telling, appealing to the "ontic" immediacy of the KNS-experience, and will be reiterated time and again in BT itself (first on SZ 15), and beyond: The self-evidence of our ontically immediate experience of being, "clear" as it is in its obviousness, is hardly transparent ontologically. Our "nearest reality" (*das allernächste Reale;* GA 20:268/197), the "nonobjective presence" of our being, is "in itself" at once the farthest removed from our minds, and philosophies. In SS 1925, accordingly, Heidegger does not yet openly broach the problem of founding all ontology, beginning with the "phenomenology of Dasein" (so in the paragraph later inserted on p. 200/148), upon the concrete "ontic fundament" of the ever-present background experience of our being, the "given" of already finding ourselves irrevocably caught up in life and under way in existence.

4. In a marginal note in his copy of the Moser-transcript of SS 1925 (GA 20: 206, line 11, Eng. trans., p. 153, line 22), which Heidegger followed in drafting the final version of BT. As an adverb modifying "to-be," "for a while" or "at its time" (*jeweilig*) not only distributively expresses the temporal individuation of the human situation, but at once indicates a how rather than a what. In the same note, accordingly, Heidegger poses the derivative problem of the "existential genesis of the what-question," the what of de-finition, from this more primary how of finitude.

5. The letter of August 20, 1927, cited *passim* since our Introduction, in Papenfuss and Pöggeler, *Zur philosophischen Aktualität Heideggers,* 2:33–38, esp. p. 36.

6. This point of priority in Heidegger's most fundamental assumptions needs underscoring: "Only on the ground of the understanding of being is existence possible" (Martin Heidegger, *Kant und das Problem der Metaphysik* [Frankfurt: Klostermann, [4]1974], § 41, p. 221; Eng. trans. by R. Taft, *Kant and the Problem of Metaphysics* [Bloomington: Indiana University Press, 1990], p. 155). This emphasis is all the more necessary since understanding itself, for all its ontic-ontological fundamentality, then gets taken up into the spiral of interpretation and is discussed in terms that appear to turn the relations of priority around. Thus, understanding as project "is not merely a kind of knowing but primarily a basic moment of existing in general" (ibid., § 42, p. 225/159).

7. The later Heidegger will never venture beyond this impersonal *Es gibt* in his response of gratitude for this gift, in the "Thanks" of Thinking It. In short, for all its dubious etymological plays, "fundamental thinking" will continue the formalization of ordinary language begun in these early texts.

8. At this interface of life and thought, to what extent is it licit to search for Heidegger's own predilections toward an "ontic ideal of authentic existence" lurking in the book itself, in its ontico-ontological hermeneutic situation whose

"deep structure" may reach into the deepest impulses of his own life? We are after all on the eve of the dramatic occasion in which Heidegger will "choose his own hero" (SZ 385), and the genealogical record leading up to BT already bears witness to the tragic heroics of an ascetic life of care on Greek-German *Boden*, in which the recurring ontic paradigm, both biblical and Aristotelian, is that "life is hard." And we now have Heidegger's letter of August 1921 in which he describes his unique facticity as a "Christian theo-logian" as at once definitive of his thought (see chap. 2). For an initial discussion, see Kisiel, "Heidegger's Apology." See also Karsten Harries's Introduction to the English translation of Günther Neske and Emil Kettering, eds., *Martin Heidegger and National Socialism* (New York: Paragon House, 1990), esp. pp. xxxii–xxxvii.

9. In WS 1929–30, Heidegger is far more unqualified in his praise of Kierkegaard's concept of *Augenblick*, the one concept which he takes directly from Kierkegaard. The purportedly Kierkegaardian concepts of *Angst* (SZ 190n) and *Existenz* (SZ 235n), on the other hand, come to him by a more complex and mediated path, by way of at least Paul, Augustine, Aristotle, and Jaspers, as our genealogical tracking has shown. Even for *Augenblick*, there is no archival evidence to indicate that Heidegger really studied a central text like *Philosophical Fragments* before he wrote BT. In 1929, it seems clear that he had, since he now gives voice to the revolutionary implications of its kairological sense of time: "What we are calling the Moment was in fact conceived by Kierkegaard for the very first time in philosophy. This conception launches the *possibility* of a completely new epoch of philosophy ever since antiquity" (GA 29/30:225).

10. Karl Löwith, *Mein Leben in Deutschland vor und nach 1933: Ein Bericht* (Stuttgart: Metzler, 1986), pp. 56; 33, 41.

11. Cf. chap. 8 above. As usual, the edition of SS 1925 includes premature early remarks, for example, on Dasein as "being-possible" (GA 20:185/136, 206/153), which postdate the lecture course itself.

12. This Index was of course not published with the translation. Cf. esp. GA 20:7/5, 15/14, 18/16 (Kantian horizon), 23/20 (medieval h.), 35/28, 93/68f. (*Fragehorizont*), 102/75, 106/78 (unified h.), 108/79 (*Problemhorizont*), 123/90, 127/93, 141/102 (*Betrachtungshorizonte*), 144/105, 164/119, 166/120, 183/135 (*Seinshorizont*), 186/137, 187/138, 193/143, 217/161, 358/259. The correlative to horizon, prefiguration, which also has its roots in Husserlian phenomenology, is frequently used in BT but too incidentally to be indexed in MacQuarrie and Robinson's outstanding Index for the English translation of BT. The French tradition of phenomenology has for decades applied the project-horizon correlation to various problems. See, e.g., Jean Ladrière's article of 1959, "Mathematics in a Philosophy of the Sciences," in *Phenomenology and the Natural Sciences: Essays and Translations*, ed. Joseph Kockelmans and Theodore Kisiel (Evanston, Ill.: Northwestern University Press, 1970), pp. 443ff. Finally, cf. "Horizont" in Appendix D.

13. Heidegger's critique of "horizon" is to be found in the "Conversation on a Country Path about Thinking," written in 1944. Cf. Heidegger's *Gelassenheit*, English translation under the book title of *Discourse on Thinking*. See n. 10 to chap. 7.

EROTETIC EPILOGUE

1. I owe a debt of thanks to Frau Antje Bultmann-Lemke for access to this important correspondence, in more ways than one, literally at the last minute of this project, and to the generosity of Dr. Klaus Müller, European curator of the Bultmann papers. See Rudolf Bultmann, "Heidegger, Martin," in *Die Religion in Geschichte und Gegenwart: Handwörterbuch für Theologie und Religionswissenschaft* (Tübingen: Mohr, ²1928), 2:1687f. For more references to the Bultmann-Heidegger relation, see Appendix B below, n. 20.

2. The term is about to be born, apparently in the context of review-discussions of BT. The earliest instance of the term "Existenzphilosophie" of which I am aware occurs in a letter from Jaspers to Heidegger on July 8, 1928: "But I was surprised to see that what I recently prophesied to you as a potential misunderstanding of your philosophy, was done by you yourself in the 'application' of existence-philosophy to 'primitive' folk" (*Briefwechsel*, p. 102). The reference is to Heidegger's 1928 review of Cassirer's *Philosophy of Symbolic Forms*, vol. 2, *Mythical Thought*. In this "application" of the existentials of BT to the *mana*-experience, however, Heidegger never even mentions the language of *Existenz*.

3. Georg Misch, "Lebensphilosophie und Phänomenologie: Eine Auseinandersetzung mit Heidegger," *Philosophischer Anzeiger* 3 (1928–29): 267–368, esp. pp. 267f. There are five more installments to this "article," which was then published in book form: *Lebensphilosophie und Phänomenologie: Eine Auseinandersetzung der Diltheyschen Richtung mit Husserl und Heidegger* (Bonn: Cohen, 1930; Leipzig: Teubner, ²1931). The recently discovered "Aristotle Einleitung" was really Misch's copy, passed on to one of his students, Josef König. See chap. 4 above. For Misch's remarks in 1922 concerning Heidegger's works, see my "The Missing Link in the Early Heidegger," pp. 1–40, esp. pp. 12f.

4. Ingeborg Bachmann, *Die kritische Aufnahme der Existentialphilosophie Martin Heideggers* (Munich and Zürich: Piper, 1985). The history of the reception of BT is a story worthy of being told in its own right.

5. Heidegger's letter to Löwith on August 20, 1927, is in *Zur philosophischen Aktualität Heideggers* 2:33–38, esp. pp. 36f. Cf. chap. 1 above.

6. Thomas Sheehan, in his work on the genealogy of the early Heidegger since the late seventies, has repeatedly underscored the importance of this conceptual development in SS 1928 which suddenly, and quite early, places us in the perspectives of the later Heidegger. See, for example, his "Getting to the Topic: The New Edition of Wegmarken," in *Radical Phenomenology*, ed. John Sallis (Atlantic Highlands, N.J.: Humanities, 1978), pp. 299–316. For a more complete treatment, see his "On the Way to *Ereignis*: Heidegger's Interpretation of *Physis*," in *Continental Philosophy in America*, ed. Hugh J. Silverman, John Sallis, and Thomas M. Seebohm (Pittsburgh: Duquesne University Press, 1983), pp. 131–164. This development will be carefully scrutinized in our Sequel: see Appendix D on "Ereignis."

APPENDIX B: HEIDEGGERS LEHRVERANSTALTUNGEN/ HEIDEGGER'S TEACHING ACTIVITIES, 1915–30

1. In presenting this list of Heidegger's teaching activities first in the German, we are following the excellent precedent established by the list composed by

Richardson, while improving upon it in the light of all the new evidence that has surfaced from the archives in the intervening years. See "Verzeichnis der Vorlesungen und Übungen von Martin Heidegger," in William J. Richardson, S.J., *Heidegger: Through Phenomenology to Thought* (The Hague: Nijhoff, 1963), pp. 663ff. Richardson's list was composed from university catalogues, ours balances this off with the evidence from other university records, student transcripts, correspondence, private sources, etc. As part of Heidegger's teaching activities, we have also included extracurricular talks (*Vorträge*) and, in the footnotes, some of the more informal seminars held outside of the regular university program and reported in the literature.

This is accordingly a search for the *title which Heidegger in fact gave to his course, seminar, or talk as he taught it or presented it*, or, when that is not forthcoming, for the most suitable, adequate, telling title in the historical context of Heidegger's development. *Was heißt ein Titel?* What can we learn from a title? In the case of Heidegger, usually quite a bit, even from the titles of his canceled courses. His titles are not always brief, especially for the seminars, but they are by and large carefully crafted: sometimes he would spend the opening period (the course of SS 1925), days, or even weeks (the course of WS 1920–21) carefully glossing every word of his chosen title.

2. This is the day on which Heidegger delivered his test lecture, "Der Zeitbegriff in der Geschichtswissenschaft" (FS 355–375), as the final requirement in the habilitation process. The text of the formal letter from the Philosophical Faculty to the Academic Senate requesting that the *venia legendi* (the license to teach in the German university system) be granted is to be found in both German and English in Thomas Sheehan, "Heidegger's *Lehrjahre*," in *The Collegium Phaenomenologicum: The First Ten Years*, ed. J. C. Sallis, G. Moneta, and J. Taminiaux (Dordrecht, Boston, London: Kluwer, 1988), pp. 77–137, esp. p. 81 and n. 11, pp. 120f. On August 5, the formal machinery of granting was completed and Heidegger officially became a *Privatdozent* (instructor).

3. Sheehan ("*Lehrjahre*," p. 82 and nn. 15 and 17) has pulled the various strands of evidence together regarding the title of this very first university course taught by Heidegger. Out of the record of the time, two witnesses (Heinrich Finke and Elfride Petri Heidegger) give the listed title, Heidegger in a letter of December 1915 speaks generically about his current course "on the history of ancient and scholastic philosophy," and the bursar's rolls (*Quästur-Journal*) list students for a course on "History of [Ancient] Philosophy." Heidegger is reported to have informed others that the manuscripts for all three of the courses he taught in 1915–17 were "destroyed" (*vernichtet*). Aber was heißt Vernichten? Heidegger had in fact relegated these notes to a 'scratch' paper bin, and some of these have resurfaced in the Deutsches Literaturarchiv in Marbach as the reverse side of notes added to the course manuscript of WS 1925–26. The numbered fragments thus found indicate that the young Heidegger in WS 1915–16 lectured at least from Pythagoras to Aristotle. Given the weight of these various shreds of evidence, the specialized title reported by Richardson from the university catalogue, "Über Vorsokratiker: Parmenides," cannot be the title of the course which was actually given. Finally, "two hours" in the extraordinary circum-

stances of the war years, with Landsturmmann Heidegger serving full time in the army in the capacity of military censor at the Freiburg Post Office, in fact meant that this course was taught every other week for four hours.

4. This is the title recorded in the bursar's rolls and in Elfride Petri's "Kollegiumbuch." See Bernhard Casper, "Martin Heidegger und die Theologische Fakultät Freiburg 1909–1923," *Freiburger Diözesan-Archiv* 100 (1980): 534–541, esp. p. 539 n. 14.

5. "Heidegger gave a course on 'Basic Questions of Logic,' drew a sizable audience from the secular faculties, but was not especially understood by the theologians, since he has a difficult terminology and the way he expresses himself is too complicated for beginners." This entry from Engelbert Krebs's diaries is cited in part by Casper, ibid. Heidegger in this semester was temporarily filling in for the position in Catholic philosophy, which was then occupied on a permanent basis in the following semester by Josef Geyser. But the seminar for this semester (whose title is not known) is apparently being funded by the secular side of the Philosophy Department (Husserl's Seminar I and not the Catholic Seminar II). Cf. the entry for October 10, 1916, in Karl Schuhmann's *Husserl-Chronik: Denk- und Lebensweg Edmund Husserls* (The Hague: Nijhoff, 1977), p. 207.

6. The formality conformed to university rules for maintaining the license to teach in the university system. Since Heidegger's remark at this point in Richardson's list, "Did not lecture, since drafted for frontline duty," has evoked some heated discussion, I have taken pains to outline what is known of Heidegger's military service in the last year of the war. For the supporting documents, cf. Sheehan, "*Lehrjahre,*" p. 121 n. 13, and Hugo Ott, *Martin Heidegger: Unterwegs zu seiner Biographie* (Frankfurt and New York: Campus, 1988), pp. 103–105. Heidegger's whereabouts in 1918 can also be traced through his correspondence with Husserl, Heinrich Ochsner, and Elisabeth Blochmann, as well as Krebs's diaries and incidental letters like Edith Stein to Roman Ingarden on June 8, 1918. The fact that Heidegger opted not to teach in his accustomed setting of Catholic philosophy in SS 1917 may also have been for reasons that go deeper than the academic politics of the Department. In his famous letter to Krebs on January 9, 1919, Heidegger opens with a summary of the two-year leave he had just taken from teaching: "In the past two years, in an effort to arrive at a fundamental clarification of my philosophical orientation, I have laid aside all particular scientific projects. This has led me to results for which I could not have preserved my freedom of conviction and academic freedom, had I any commitments beyond philosophy itself." The major result was a "transformation of my fundamental standpoint" which "made the *System* of Catholicism problematic and unacceptable to me." Cf. Casper, "Heidegger und die Theologische Fakultät," p. 541.

7. With this War Emergency Semester (= *Kriegsnotsemester* = KNS), we can also begin citing the published (or planned) edition of the course in Martin Heidegger's *Gesamtausgabe* (= GA) by its pertinent volume number; but not by the published title, which for various reasons is at times at variance with the title we are seeking to establish here, namely, the title given by Heidegger himself to his course or seminar at the time that he presented it.

The lectures in the extraordinary KNS were held from February to mid-April. Despite the extra burden of this "interim semester," Summer Semester (= SS) 1919 took place roughly at its traditional time, from May through July, while the subsequent Winter Semester (= WS) 1919–20 was held somewhat earlier than normal, from October through January. Typically, the Winter Semester in the German university calendar runs roughly from November through February, with a month off for the holiday period.

A letter from Heidegger to Elisabeth Blochmann on January 24, 1919, indicates that Heidegger also held a seminar in KNS. It was perhaps a colloquium on the course, but I have not been able to verify this, let alone establish its title. Cf. Martin Heidegger and Elisabeth Blochmann, *Briefwechsel 1918–1969*, ed. Joachim W. Storck (Marbach am Neckar: Deutsche Schillergesellschaft, 1989), p. 13.

8. Even though the two one-hour courses reported by Richardson from the university catalogue were combined into one two-hour course, with the cancellation of the course entitled "Die philosophischen Grundlagen der mittelalterlichen Mystik," it is worthy of note that Heidegger was in a position, and in fact did begin, to prepare a course with this content. The reason given for canceling it, pertaining to the pressures of an already overcrowded academic year, is to be found in Heidegger's letter to the Philosophical Faculty on August 30, 1919. Cf. Sheehan, "*Lehrjahre*," pp. 94f. and n. 81.

From Oskar Becker's transcripts, we find that Heidegger in WS 1919–20 held an additional seminar "in conjunction with the course 'Basic Problems of Phenomenology,'" apparently outside of the regular university program.

9. "Some time ago I was asked to speak for two hours on Spengler at a 'scientific week' in Wiesbaden. Other speakers include [Max] Born (Frankfurt) on Einstein's laws, [Hermann] Oncken (Heidelberg) on recent history, and Wolzendorf (Halle) on a juridical problem. . . . Perhaps I can repeat the lectures here [in Freiburg] in the summer" (Heidegger to Löwith, March 23, 1920). Oswald Spengler is first mentioned in Heidegger's courses toward the end of WS 1919–20 and treated in some detail in WS 1920–21 and SS 1923.

10. We get a glimpse of the direction this seminar takes from Heidegger's advice to Löwith on how to prepare for it: "For the 'Cogito,' *all of Christian philosophy* comes into question for me, since I want to see it *backwards*, look at it *in verso*, so to speak. It is only important that you know something of the other metaphysical treatises and the *Regulae*, so that the perversity of the epistemological resolution can be studied" (letter of September 13, 1920).

11. The university catalogue and bursar's rolls have Heidegger at this time regularly conducting the seminar entitled "Phenomenological Practicum for Beginners," and yet advanced students like Oskar Becker and Karl Löwith just as regularly enrolled for it, seemingly undermining the purpose of a seminar "for beginners" and serving to render the phrase meaningless. A glance at the Freiburg catalogues explains the real meaning of the distinction: the seminars entitled "Phenomenological Practicum" were regularly divided into an a) "for beginners" and a b) "for advanced students," where the b) section was invariably taught by Husserl and the a) section by his assistant, Heidegger! Hans Jonas, who came

to Freiburg in SS 1921 and so found himself enrolled in the "beginners" seminar on Aristotle given by Heidegger, later noted: "The rules . . . Husserl had introduced, made it so that young philosophy students were not allowed to begin by entering Husserl's seminars. First, they were sent to an introductory seminar, which was given by his young assistant Martin Heidegger. I therefore simultaneously had the double impact of these two powerful and very individual teacher personalities, thinker figures: Edmund Husserl and Martin Heidegger" (Neske and Kettering, *Heidegger and National Socialism*, pp. 197f.).

12. This three-part title is the full title given by Heidegger in the autograph to his course. The published edition drops the final title, "Einleitung." But the title recorded in the course transcript of Franz Josef Brecht speaks not of an *Einführung* but of an *Einleitung* to Phenomenological Research, and the subtitle in Helene Weiß's transcript is simply the single word "Einleitung." The addition of this third title is by no means as trivial and insignificant as it may seem (I have therefore italicized it), if it is put back into the context of the documentary story of Heidegger's development at this time. The editorial decision to use *Einführung* so unqualifiedly in the published title is not the responsibility of the Bröckers, who were the initial editors of the volume and in their Afterword likewise emphasize the importance of this keyword, since Heidegger identified the entire course manuscript as his "Einleitung" (GA 61:201f. and Table of Contents, p. v) and referred to it as such already within the course itself (110, 112) as well as the notes appended to it (182n, 183, 187f., 197) and in later references to this course (GA 63:47). For what we have here is the very first of several drafts of the "Aristoteles-*Einleitung*," of which the most famous, drafted in October 1922 in support of Heidegger's candidacy for a chair at Marburg and at Göttingen, was recently discovered in its entirety in the archives at Göttingen. This *Einleitung* to a projected book on Aristotle was the center of Heidegger's philosophical existence from early 1922 to early 1924, and in his struggles to compose a satisfactory version of it, he constantly referred to it in this way in his correspondence, for example, in seven letters to Löwith between 1922 and 1924: "Die Quasi Einleitung macht mir viel Arbeit . . . —sie ist nichts weniger u. mehr als meine 'Existenz' " (September 20, 1922); "Natorp, der Einl. u. Übers.[icht] zu Arist. hat, ist 'ergriffen' " (November 22, 1922); "Meine 'Einleitung' nimmt mich sehr mit" (July 30, 1923); "Die Einleitung macht mir noch viel Arbeit" (March 19, 1924). After this very last reference to the "Einl." to an Aristotle book, according to him the "most satisfying" draft, Heidegger gave the talk on "The Concept of Time" to the Marburg Theologians in July 1924; thereafter "Die Zeit" became the focus in the Löwith letters and in Heidegger's philosophical existence.

For an initial version of the story of this "Einl.," see Kisiel, "Missing Link," esp. pp. 23f. and n. 10, p. 16, on the problem of titles. The now discovered "missing link," the October 1922 version of the "Einl. u. Übers. zu Arist." recently found by Hans-Ulrich Lessing, is edited by him as Martin Heidegger, "Phänomenologische Interpretationen zu Aristoteles (Anzeige der hermeneutischen Situation)," *Dilthey-Jahrbuch* 6 (1989): 235–274. Michael Baur's translation of it is now published in *Man and World* 25 (1992): 355–393.

13. Note that Volume II of LU begins with the First Investigation entitled "Expression and Meaning" and includes a discussion of "occasional expressions" (§§ 26–28) like "I," "here," "now," "this," and *es gibt*, the components of what Heidegger at this time is already beginning to call "Dasein" (its "Jeweiligkeit," however, is first mentioned in the seminar of WS 1922–23). This seminar of 1921–22 thus became famous among students for its elaboration of precisely such indexical topics. Ludwig Landgrebe, for example, who heard accounts of this seminar when he first arrived in Freiburg in SS 1923, has mentioned this story often both orally and in print. Günther Stern (later Günther Anders), who took part in this seminar, will later do his doctoral dissertation on this topic under Husserl, while acknowledging Heidegger for the (then) unpublished ideas he obtained directly from lecture courses and seminars: "Die Rolle der Situationskategorie bei den 'Logischen Sätzen'" (Diss. Freiburg, 1924). Cf. also Günther Stern, *Über das Haben: Sieben Kapitel zur Ontologie der Erkenntnis* (Bonn: Friedrich Cohen, 1928), esp. chap. 7, "Satz und Situation."

The following semester will include a continuation of this seminar by a phenomenological interpretation of the Second Investigation of LU. Recalling this period, the old Heidegger also reports that "in addition to my lecture courses and regular seminars, I worked through the *Logical Investigations* weekly with advanced students in special study groups" (*Zur Sache des Denkens*, 87/79).

14. The title reported by Richardson from the university catalogue is not so much incorrect as it is cumbersome. We have therefore reported the more streamlined title which Heidegger announced to his class, as recorded in the extant student transcripts of Helene Weiss, Walter Bröcker, and Franz Josef Brecht. For one thing, it has the advantage of establishing continuity with the similarly worded title of the lecture course of WS 1921–22 as well as with one of the seminar titles of the coming semester. For *Phänomenologische Interpretationen zu Aristoteles* is likewise the title of the projected book that Heidegger is writing at this stage, and appears again as the overall title of the "Einleitung und Übersicht" which he wrote in October 1922 and dispatched to Marburg and Göttingen (see n. 12 above). Thus, the courses of WS 1921–22 and SS 1922 and the seminar of WS 1922–23 (continued in SS 1923) also give us glimpses into the contents of the Aristotle book that Heidegger was working on at this time.

15. This is the exact title found in Oskar Becker's transcript of the seminar, who observes that it was continued in SS 1923. It is the very first semester since the war in which Heidegger does not hold a lecture course (letter to Jaspers, November 19, 1922; to Löwith on September 20). He is presumably freeing time so that he can concentrate on his book: see Edmund Husserl, *Briefe an Roman Ingarden* (The Hague: Nijhoff, 1968), p. 25. But once again, the title of the canceled course, "Skepticism in Ancient Philosophy," is indicative of the kinds of issues that are troubling Heidegger at the time. The issue of skepticism is tied to the radical questionability of the philosophical endeavor, which prompts Heidegger to proclaim the radical "atheism" of philosophy and the peculiar "asceticism" of the scientific life (GA 61:195–199).

This peculiar constellation of themes was in part prompted by the posthumous publication of Franz Overbeck's *Christentum und Kultur* in 1919, and by 1922

Heidegger is deeply involved in an intensive study of all the works of this "atheistic" theologian and friend of Nietzsche. He will be raising such issues through his Marburg years with Bultmann and his circle.

16. We might perhaps get an idea of the upshot of this seminar from Julius Ebbinghaus, "Luther und Kant," *Luther-Jahrbuch* 9 (1927): 119–155. This joint colloquium developed from the habit that the two had since 1921 of spending one evening a week together to read the works of the young Luther and Melanchthon, mentioned by Ebbinghaus in *Philosophie in Selbstdarstellungen*, ed. Ludwig J. Pongratz (Hamburg: Meiner, 1975), 3:33f.

The continuation of the advanced seminar on "Phänomenologische Interpretationen zu Aristoteles" from the previous semester was perhaps held in SS 1923 outside of the official university program. On April 21, 1923, Heidegger writes to Löwith: "The Aristotle seminar will only be two hours in order to bring the study plan proposed in the winter to a conclusion. The seminar with Ebbinghaus will hopefully 'fizzle out.' The only one into which I shall put real effort is the Aristotle seminar for beginners on the *Nicomachean Ethics*." But whether official or unofficial, it was for Heidegger a single—and heavy—teaching load: "This semester I have a 1-hour lecture course and 3 seminars (6 hours)" (letter 16, to Jaspers, July 14, 1923, in Heidegger and Jaspers, *Briefwechsel 1920–1963*, p. 41). It should be noted that the edition of this vital correspondence continues to be plagued by errors of fact stemming from Richardson's list (e.g., n. 4 to letter 12, p. 227; n. 4 to letter 16, p. 229; n. 1 to letter 17, p. 230) and a lack of awareness of the story of the Aristotle "Einleitung" (p. 41 and n. 3 to letter 16, p. 229, and *no* note to letter 12, p. 34, line 3).

17. This is the title recorded in all of the extant student transcripts and in the bursar's rolls in Marburg (*Einnahme-Tagebuch und Dozenten Handbuch*). A month before the semester, Heidegger had two two-hour courses in mind, but obviously eventually managed to combine their contents into a single four-hour course: "I will lecture on 'Introduction to Phenomenology' two hours and two hours on Aristotle" (letter to Löwith on September 27, 1923).

Heidegger's appointment to Marburg came too late for him to submit a course title for their catalogue. On June 18, 1923, Heidegger wrote to the Dean there accepting the position of "Extraordinariat in philosophy with the rights and status of an Ordinarius." So I am a bit puzzled over the source of the title reported by Richardson, "The Beginning of Modern Philosophy (Descartes-Interpretation)." In its historical content, the course itself first examines Aristotle and Husserl in depth before getting around to Descartes.

18. Cf. SZ 51n. But cf. the similarly titled lecture of December 4, 1926, "Begriff und Entwicklung der phänomenologischen Forschung," announced for publication in the Klostermann prospectus; likewise the title given to the Preliminary Part of SS 1925, "Sinn und Aufgabe der phänomenologischen Forschung," and to Kassel Lecture No. V, "Wesen und Ziele der Phänomenologie." So the topic might be a bit premature for 1923, although Heidegger did cancel classes on December 6–7 in WS 1923–24. Clearly, further confirmatory archival evidence is required on this point.

19. This is the title recorded in the bursar's rolls and in the extensive transcript of Walter Bröcker (typescript by Herbert Marcuse); Helene Weiss's transcript varies only slightly: "Über einige Grundbegriffe aristotelischer Philosophie." The title alludes to the starting point of the course in Aristotle's philosophical lexicon of *Metaphysics* 5. Heidegger's selection of concepts for discussion will eventually be guided by the problem of speech (λόγος) and the passions (πάθη) in the *Rhetoric*, which in part accounts for the title in Löwith's transcript, "Aristoteles: Rhetorik," to which Richardson adds "II."

As early as July 30, 1923 (letter to Löwith), Heidegger had planned a four-hour lecture course on Augustine in SS 1924. During the course of WS 1923–24 he took more than one occasion to announce to his students that such a course would be concerned with the connection of "vita et veritas," with the nontheoretical character of the truth of faith as this is developed in the New Testament up to Augustine. Just before WS 1923–24 concludes, Heidegger spells out the projected content of next semester's course in some detail. In tracing the history of Christian theology, he would be concerned not only with the nontheoretical comportment connected with *verum* but also with that of *bonum*, the analogy between the two, and how truth itself came to be regarded as a "value" as well as certainty. "In my course on Augustine, I will have to elaborate this in connection with the Augustinian concepts of *summum bonum, perfectio, fides, timor castus, peccatum, beatitudo.* In a certain sense, Augustine becomes the focal point of the various possibilities which the problem of *bonum* as category of existence includes, from which its effects on the medieval and modern age then originate" (Weiß transcript, February 23, 1924). But several weeks later, Heidegger resolves, whatever the cost, finally to bring out the book on Aristotle. "So the Augustine gets dropped and I will lecture on Aristotle and hold only a medieval seminar. To the extent that I am able, I will hold an Augustine seminar *privatissimum* every two weeks" (letter to Löwith on March 19, 1924). There appears to be no evidence forthcoming to verify that an Augustine seminar was in fact held.

20. Martin Heidegger, *Der Begriff der Zeit. Vortrag vor der Marburger Theologenschaft Juli 1924*, edited, with a Postscript, by Hartmut Tietjen (Tübingen: Niemeyer, 1989). Now available in a bilingual translation by William McNeill, *The Concept of Time* (Oxford and Cambridge, Mass.: Blackwell, 1992). Heidegger may here have simply been taking his turn to speak, after sharply criticizing others in this Theological Society in which he took an active part from the very beginning of his stay in Marburg. His interventions in the postlecture debates of the Society, as well as his participation in Bultmann's seminars, have become legendary, and so are, in this context, in need of precise documentation. The evidence, though still fragmentary, is gradually coming to light. There are two transcripts (one by Wilhelm von Rohden) in the Bultmann Archive in Tübingen of Heidegger's contributions to Bultmann's seminar on "Paul's Ethics" in WS 1923–24 (on February 14 and 21). For a brief summary of their content, see Hermann Mörchen, *Adorno und Heidegger* (Stuttgart: Klett-Cotta, 1981), pp. 557f. Bultmann alludes to Heidegger's remarks on the lecture given by his colleague, Heinrich Hermelink, on Luther and the Middle Ages: Bernd Jaspert, ed. *Rudolf Bultmanns Werk und Wirkung* (Darmstadt: Wissenschaftliche Buchgesellschaft,

1984), p. 202. Eduard Thurneysen's talk on dialectical theology also took place in this first semester (on February 20, 1924), followed by Heidegger's Overbeckian intervention which Gadamer, in his repeatedly published article on "Heidegger and Marburg Theology," has in fact made legendary. Heidegger noted the occasion of the twentieth year of Overbeck's death, June 26, 1925, "which I at least celebrated," in an intervention to W. Heitmüller's talk, "On Interpreting the New Testament," given at the Society the next day (Heidegger's text is in Ernst Grumach's Nachlaß, DLA, Marbach). "[B]ut I expressed my skepticism clearly enough in a disputation which recently 'came off' on the occasion of a lecture by Heitmüller (Tübingen) on understanding and interpreting the New Testament" (letter to Löwith on August 24, 1925). Finally, there is an unconfirmed report that Heidegger took part in Bultmann's seminar in SS 1927 and gave a talk on Luther's Commentary on Galatians. Cf. Heinrich Schlier's remarks in *Erinnerung an Heidegger*, ed. Günter Neske (Pfullingen: Neske, 1977), p. 219.

21. In their program report of WS 1924-25 (see *Kant-Studien* 29 [1924]: 626), this regional group of the Kant Society announced a lecture series by Heidegger in six cities in the Rhine-Ruhr region from the 1st to the 8th of December, 1924, in which he would repeat a lecture bearing this title. In their report of the following year (*Kant-Studien* 30 [1925]: 611-616), three local groups reported that this lecture had in fact taken place: on December 1 or 2 in Elberfeld-Barmen, December 4 in Cologne, and December 8 in Dortmund. (Hagen, Düsseldorf, and Essen did not report.) In a letter to Löwith on December 17, 1924, Heidegger writes: "In Cologne I spent 3 days with Scheler and stayed at his house."

The Klostermann prospectus reverses the title—"Wahrsein und Dasein. Aristoteles, Ethica Nicomachea Z"—and indicates that the lecture was held in the "Kant-Gesellschaft Köln WS 1923-24." In view of the evidence just cited, I take this instead to be the period of composition of a first draft and presume that, because of the chaos caused by the rampant inflation in late 1923, the lecture itself was postponed and not in fact delivered until a year later.

22. Frithjof Rodi, "Die Bedeutung Diltheys für die Konzeption von 'Sein und Zeit': Zum Umfeld von Heideggers Kasseler Vorträgen (1925)," *Dilthey-Jahrbuch* 4 (1986-87): 161-177. A transcript of the Kassel Lectures is now being published in *Dilthey-Jahrbuch* 8 (1992).

23. Both WS 1925-26 and SS 1928 as presented by Heidegger at the time were entitled simply "Logik." To distinguish her two transcripts, Helene Weiß entitled them respectively "Logik (Aristoteles)" and "Logik (Leibniz)." And these were the planned publication titles announced in the first two GA-prospectuses during Heidegger's lifetime (October 1974 and November 1975). But then Heidegger, in perhaps the last editorial decision he made concerning his GA, suggested instead the eventual publication title of GA 21, "Logik. Die Frage nach der Wahrheit" (I report all this thanks to a private communication from its editor, Walter Biemel). As to SS 1928, its editor, Klaus Held, took his eventual book title from an internal title found within the course itself, as he explains in his Editor's Postscript of GA 26.

24. "The Hegel and Kant seminars are giving me an unusually great deal of pleasure, and I am glad that I am only now coming to these matters, at a time

when, at least relatively, there is the possibility of understanding something" (Heidegger's letter to Jaspers of December 10, 1925, *Briefwechsel*, p. 57). This unexpected delight of insight from the seminars impacts on the course when, immediately after the holidays, Heidegger abruptly plunges into his very first detailed analysis of Kant's Doctrine of the Schematism of the Understanding. The course of WS 1925–26, which at first could have been entitled "Logik (Aristoteles)"—it is in Weiss's transcript—thus becomes "Logik (Kant)."

25. There is an indication that Heidegger also held a seminar in conjunction with this course on Greek concepts. In this seminar, Georg Picht recalls, "he interpreted the first chapter of book 4 of Aristotle's *Metaphysics*. He discussed the *analogia entis*." [Was it perhaps the seminar of WS 1926–27?]. Cf. Neske and Kettering, *Heidegger and National Socialism*, p. 164.

26. Perhaps a harbinger of things to come, but more likely (as Walter Biemel speculates in his note) the "question of truth" as it arose in the course of WS 1925–26, presented at the Pentecost (!) celebration of this informal study group of twelve or so "volunteers" which Heidegger had a hand in running. Cf. Heidegger and Jaspers, *Briefwechsel*, pp. 57f., 64, 236. Such a talk may have also fallen back on the "truth" talk of December 1924.

27. Martin Heidegger, *Phänomenologie und Theologie* (Frankfurt: Klostermann, 1970); also GA 9:45–78. This publication is basically a revised version of the second presentation of the talk seven months later in Marburg under a variant title (see below). The first version is given a subtitle in Klostermann's prospectus: "I. Teil: Die nichtphilosophischen als positive Wissenschaften und die Philosophie als transzendentale Wissenschaft." From the 1970 Foreword, we can likewise presume a subtitle for the second version: "Die Positivität der Theologie und ihr Verhältnis zur Phänomenologie."

28. In a footnote to the typescript of this talk, Heidegger explains the change in title from the Tübingen talk: "Essentially the content of the second part of a talk, 'Phenomenology and Theology.' held at the invitation of the Evangelical Theologians' Society of Tübingen on 8 July 1927" (Heidegger and Blochmann, *Briefwechsel*, p. 141).

29. These data are drawn from a letter fragment of the Herder Society to Heidegger on August 10, 1928. The exact title of these lectures is not known, but as Heidegger reports in his Foreword to the first edition in 1929, the content bears upon the same themes as the book, *Kant and the Problem of Metaphysics*. It can, by chronological proximity, be connected with the course of WS 1927–28. For the circumstances surrounding the trip to Riga, and the "Rigenser Tage," followed by the obligatory pilgrimage to Kant's Königsberg, see Heidegger's letter to Jaspers of September 24, 1928, and especially to Blochmann of October 17, 1928, whom the Heideggers visited en route.

30. Max Müller, in this his first semester at Freiburg invited to attend the "upper seminar" by Heidegger himself, reports a different title: "Phänomenologische Übungen zu Aristoteles" (Neske and Kettering, *Heidegger and National Socialism*, p. 178). (Here, of course, I have reverted back to the title in the original German text of Müller's interview first published in *Freiburger Universitätsblätter* 92 [Juni 1986], p. 15).

31. This involved three lectures and several sessions of a working group, together with Ernst Cassirer, although he was ill during part of those ten days. Heidegger's summary of his three lectures and the disputation (compiled by Joachim Ritter and O. F. Bollnow) of this "Davos university course" are reproduced in the Appendix to Martin Heidegger, *Kant und das Problem der Metaphysik* (Frankfurt: Klostermann, [4]1973), pp. 243–268. For autobiographical details on the chronology and context of events, compare the Foreword to this edition with Heidegger's letter to Jaspers of December 21, 1928, and to Blochmann of April 12, 1929. A stenographic copy of the protocol of the disputation which was distributed at Davos, "Kontroverse in einer Arbeitsgemeinschaft" (Bericht, Davos, 25. 3. 1929, 25 pp.), is to be found in the Herbert Marcuse Archive in Frankfurt. "The high point of the conference for us students was the confrontation between Heidegger and Cassirer." So in one of two accounts of this three-week meeting in the Swiss Alps to be found in Guido Schneeberger, *Nachlese zu Heidegger: Dokumente zu seinem Leben und Denken* (Bern: private circulation, 1962), 1–9, p. 4.

32. This brief talk was first published in *Akademische Mitteilungen: Organ für die gesamten Interessen der Studentenschaft an der Albert-Ludwigs-Universität in Freiburg i. Br.*, Vierte Folge, IX. Sem., Nr. 3, 14. 5. 1929, pp. 46–47. Heidegger's essay, "Vom Wesen des Grundes," first appeared in Husserl's Festschrift, which made up an *Ergänzungsband* (supplementary volume) to that year's *Jahrbuch für Philosophie und phänomenologische Forschung, (Festschrift Edmund Husserl zum 70. Geburtstag gewidmet* [Halle: Niemeyer, 1929]).

33. There is a nine-page transcript of the opening hours of this short but important course, breaking new "aletheic" ground by an interpretation of Plato's Allegory of the Cave, in the Herbert Marcuse Archive in the City and University Library of Frankfurt. A complete transcript, albeit translated from Japanese back into German, is available in *Japan und Heidegger*, ed. Hartmut Buchner (Sigmaringen: Thorbecke, 1989), pp. 111–126. (Can we expect to see a transcript of it in an Appendix to GA 28?) In a letter to Maximilian Beck on May 9, 1929, the new student Marcuse gives his first impressions of Heidegger's courses and seminars of SS 1929 and of the typical "Heidegger student," along with a telling description of Heidegger himself, obviously in the throes of a radical transformation in his thought ("Lettre de Herbert et Sophie Marcuse à leurs amis Beck," in *Martin Heidegger*, ed. Michel Haar, L'Herne, no. 45 [Paris: L'Herne, 1983], pp. 163–165).

34. The Heidegger-Jaspers correspondence in June 1929 speaks of the phenomenon of Heidegger's "public existence" having begun after Davos, so he was now very much in demand: he repeated this inaugural lecture three more times in 1929: first, "beginning of October to a small group in Frankfurt" (letter to Blochmann on December 18, 1929), being invited there by Kurt Riezler (who was at Davos) from about the 9th to the 14th (to Jaspers, on October 8, 1929); 2) "4. Dezember in der Kant-Gesellschaft Karlsruhe" (to Blochmann, December 18); 3) "5. Dezember vor der Deutschen Fachschaft an der Universität Heidelberg" (to Jaspers, October 18, 1929), before it appeared in print around Christmas: *Was ist Metaphysik?* (Bonn: Friedrich Cohen, 1929), 29 pp.

35. But the GA-overseers insist on retaining *Einsamkeit*, which Heidegger never quite got around to changing to *Vereinzelung* in his manuscript, in the published subtitle, even though *Vereinzelung* was the clinching word in the subtitle announced on the bulletin board in Heidegger's own hand at semester's start (GA 29/30:537). This key concept already central in BT is then underscored in the opening hour as the third of the three pivotal concepts of the course (9), as well as at strategic turns throughout the course (120, 251). It is but one example of many of the strange and often inconsistent decisions generated by the posthumously interjected principle of an "edition of the dead hand," which our list seeks to offset by establishing the more vital title that Heidegger utilized and developed in his courses as he himself presented them.

36. The Klostermann prospectus is presently my sole source of evidence for these titles, as is the case for the titles of the talks on January 24, 1929, and October 26, 1930. I have already changed the title it reports for the Karlsruhe talk on December 4, 1929, on the strength of independent evidence (n. 32 above). Moreover, the archival evidence for this 1930 visit to Holland is at present quite slim (Heidegger's letters in the Pos Archive in Amsterdam have temporarily gone astray). In a letter to Blochmann of July 7, 1931, Heidegger writes: "On the first of August I am going to Holland, where I shall discharge a promise made during my first visit to lead a small group for a week in working through *Being and Time*." These two visits may be tied to the fact that Heidegger's student in WS 1922–23, Hendrik J. Pos, then became Professor of Philology at the University of Amsterdam and, in that capacity, had also lectured in the Davos University Courses of 1929.

37. Schneeberger, *Nachlese*, pp. 9–13. Also Heidegger's letter to Jaspers of July 15, 1930.

38. Heinrich Wiegand Petzet, *Auf einen Stern zugehen. Begegnungen und Gespräche mit Martin Heidegger 1929–1976* (Frankfurt: Societäts-Verlag, 1983), pp. 20ff. Also Heidegger's letter to Blochmann of September 20, 1930.

39. Heidegger's regular visits to the Benedictine monastery at Beuron, which date at least as far back as the war years and his association with Pater Engelbert Krebs and Heinrich Ochsner, assume for him a particular profundity in 1929–31. Cf. Heidegger and Blochmann, *Briefwechsel*, pp. 31ff., 34, 39f., 43ff., 53; cf. esp. pp. 39f. for his 1930 visit and a summation of WS 1930–31.

40. Data taken from a transcript of the lecture. The variant title suggests that Heidegger from the start adapted his oft-repeated lecture "On the Essence of Truth" to his context and audience. The connection between truth and "autochthony" (*Bodenständigkeit*) reportedly made when it was first delivered, to an audience purportedly receptive to 'Blubo' talk (see n. 37 above), may therefore not be too far from the "truth."

41. Data from Herbert Marcuse's transcript of the lecture, preserved in the City and University Library of Frankfurt. In the postscript to a 1945 letter, Heidegger asserts that he gave the lecture "twice in the winter of 1930 at the university here [in Freiburg]" (*Graduate Faculty Philosophy Journal* 14/2–15/1 [1991]: 554f.).

APPENDIX C: A DOCUMENTARY CHRONOLOGY OF THE PATH TO THE PUBLICATION OF *BEING AND TIME*, 1924–27

1. Martin Heidegger, *Zur Sache des Denkens* (Tübingen: Niemeyer, 1969), pp. 87f.; English translation by Joan Stambaugh, *On Time and Being* (San Francisco: Harper and Row, 1972), p. 80.

2. For the fuller story of this article intended for the *Deutsche Vierteljahrsschrift für Literaturwissenschaft und Geistesgeschichte*, see Theodore Kisiel, "Why the First Draft of *Being and Time* was Never Published," *Journal of the British Society for Phenomenology* 20, no. 1 (January 1989): 1–22. The originals of Heidegger's letters to Rothacker are in the Rothacker Archive at the University of Bonn. This correspondence is now published in "Martin Heidegger und die Anfänge der *Deutschen Vierteljahrsschrift für Literaturwissenschaft und Geistesgeschichte*: Eine Dokumentation," ed. Joachim W. Storck and Theodore Kisiel, *Dilthey-Jahrbuch* 8 (1992): 000–000. Note, in what follows, that 1 "galley" ("galley proof" or "signature" in printer's English) is equivalent to 16 pages of print.

3. I owe a debt of gratitude to Frau Ada Löwith for access to these letters and to Klaus Stichweh for help in deciphering them.

4. "Protokoll der 2. Kommissionssitzung für Neubesetzung des Philosophischen Ordinariats (Nachfolge Hartmann)," Hessisches Staatsarchiv Marburg, *Akten der Philipps-Universität Marburg: Philosophie und Pädogogie 1922–1943*, Accession 1966/10, Bestand 307d, Nr. 28, S. 74.

5. "Vorschläge für die Wiederbesetzung des Ordinariates für Philosophie," Hessisches Staatsarchiv Marburg, *Akten*, Accession 1966/10, S. 95.

6. Ibid., S. 100.

7. Heidegger and Jaspers, *Briefwechsel 1920–1963*, p. 61.

8. *Zur Sache des Denkens*, pp. 87f./80.

9. Hessisches Staatsarchiv Marburg, *Akten*, S. 103.

10. Ibid., S. 107. Cf. also Thomas Sheehan, " 'Time and Being,' 1925–27," in *Thinking about Being: Aspects of Heidegger's Thought* (Norman: University of Oklahoma Press, 1984), pp. 177–219, esp. p. 182.

11. The "Reinschrift" (both Divisions) and "Arbeitsmanuskript" (only of the extant Second Division) of *Sein und Zeit* were purchased from the Heidegger family in 1970 by the Deutsches Literaturarchiv, and so are open for public scrutiny in Marbach. I wish to thank F.-W. von Herrmann for a look at the corrected galleys of SZ in his possession. These end precisely at § 38, except for a few odd sheets from the later galleys of November-December 1926.

12. So in Malvine Husserl's letter to Roman Ingarden on April 16, 1926. Cf. Edmund Husserl, *Briefe an Roman Ingarden*, ed. Roman Ingarden (The Hague: Nijhoff, 1968), p. 37. The dedication page in *Sein und Zeit* drops the "grateful," but still cites the same place and date, "Todtnauberg i. Bad. Schwarzwald zum 8. April 1926."

13. Cf. Edmund Husserl, *Zur Phänomenologie des inneren Zeitbewußtseins (1893–1917)*, ed. Rudolf Boehm (The Hague: Nijhoff, 1966), p. xxiv.

14. R I Fritz Kaufmann 20. IV. 26, Husserl-Archief, Leuven.

15. Heidegger and Jaspers, *Briefwechsel*, p. 62.

16. Ibid., p. 64.

17. The sequence is inescapable, since the clean handwritten copy for these concluding sections of the First Division already incorporates in its footnotes the definitive page numbers in their internal reference to previous sections of SZ, whereas such internal page references in the first 11 galleys had been in their first instance necessarily left blank. But since there are no extant copies bearing printer's dates of galleys 12 to 15, as in the case of the first 11 galleys (into which several substantial, page-length, handwritten corrections were introduced), one can even doubt whether they were printed in time for dispatch to Berlin in mid-June. At any rate, the placing of footnote lists in the handwritten *Reinschrift* available in Marbach suggests that these concluding sections of the First Division were sent to the printer in three separate units: §§ 38–42 (SZ pages 175–196), followed by a half-page listing of 5 footnotes, 4 of which are internal references; §§ 42 & 43 (SZ 196–212), followed by a page listing 15 footnotes; § 44 (SZ 212–230), with a listing of 23 footnotes, several with late internal references, esp. n. 2 on SZ 221 and nn. 2 and 3 on SZ 223. This takes us through galley 14, with 5–8 additional pages needed to complete Division One. The old Heidegger recalls that 15 galleys, in duplicate, were sent to the Berlin ministry at the time: see *Zur Sache des Denkens*, p. 88/80.

18. "Auf das Schreiben vom 27. Januar 1926," Hessisches Staatsarchiv Marburg, *Akten*, S. 111.

19. Heidegger and Jaspers, *Briefwechsel*, p. 66.

20. Ibid., p. 67.

21. Copies of Heidegger's letters to Bultmann are to be found in the Bultmann Archive at the University of Tübingen. The originals have been transferred to the Heidegger Archive in Marbach. I wish to thank Frau Antje Bultmann-Lemke for access to this correspondence and Dr. Klaus Müller, European curator of the Bultmann Archive, for smoothing the way.

22. "Auf den Bericht vom 18. Juni d. Js.," Hessisches Staatsarchiv Marburg, *Akten*, S. 117; Heidegger and Jaspers, *Briefwechsel*, p. 69. The old Heidegger summarizes this particular turn of events in more clipped anecdotal fashion: "After a time, the page proofs were returned to the faculty with the remark: 'Unzureichend,' 'Inadequate' " (*Zur Sache des Denkens*, p. 88/80).

23. Heidegger and Blochmann, *Briefwechsel 1918–1969*, pp. 18f. Heidegger, perhaps by November 1, had already sent the clean copy of his (at least one possible) "transition chapter" (§ 83, SZ 436f) to the printer. This very last section of SZ is one of those rare sections in that clean copy (accessible in Marbach) that undergoes serious modification before it is finally published. These changes, however, were probably not finalized until after Heidegger's visit to Jaspers in the first January days of 1927.

24. Heidegger and Jaspers, *Briefwechsel*, p. 72. Galley 18 (§§ 56-58) ends on SZ 289 and galley 23 (§§ 69a-70) at the bottom of SZ 368.

25. Martin Heidegger, *Die Metaphysik des deutschen Idealismus* [the Schelling courses of 1941], ed. Günter Seubold GA 49 (Frankfurt: Klostermann, 1991), pp. 39f. Rilke died in a remote Swiss village on December 29, 1926, and, apparently because of the intervening holiday period (December 31 to January 2), the news was delayed in reaching Germany. This probably also accounts for the later Heidegger's faulty recall of the dates of his visit to Jaspers.

26. Heidegger and Jaspers, *Briefwechsel*, pp. 73f. The first edition of SZ was 438 pages in length. This is equivalent to 27 galleys plus 6 additional pages.

27. This terminal date is recorded on one of the galleys in F. W. von Herrmann's possession.

28. Heidegger and Jaspers, *Briefwechsel*, p. 77; *Zur Sache des Denkens*, p. 88/80.

29. Fritz Heidegger, "Ein Geburtstagsbrief" (Sept. 1969), in *Martin Heidegger zum 80. Geburtstag von seiner Heimatstadt Messkirch* (Frankfurt: Klostermann, 1969), p. 62. Cf. the above letter to Jaspers of April 18 for some variant dates on the duration of this visit to the deathbed in Meßkirch.

30. R I Heidegger 8. V. 27, Husserl-Archief, Leuven. The version of SZ in vol. 8 of Husserl's *Jahrbuch* appeared along with Oskar Becker's "Mathematische Existenz: Untersuchungen zur Logik und Ontologie mathematischer Phänomene," *Jahrbuch für Philosophie und phänomenologische Forschung* 8 (1927): 439–809. It seems as if the *Jahrbuch* version appeared after the separate work (*Sonderdruck*) of SZ began to be distributed.

31. R I Heidegger 24. V. 27, Husserl-Archief, Leuven. *Jahrbuch* 8 is now "out."

32. R I Heidegger 26. V. 27, Husserl-Archief, Leuven.

33. Heidegger and Blochmann, *Briefwechsel*, p. 20.

34. R II Reiner 14. VI. 27, Husserl-Archief, Leuven.

35. Much of this section of BT, the review of the Dilthey-Yorck correspondence (SZ 399/5–403/13), had already been drafted in the journal article of November 1924, and is lifted bodily from that early manuscript into the clean copy delivered to the printer in November 1926. Thus, among the white folio pages of the *Reinschrift* in Heidegger's hand, one at this point suddenly comes across several yellow legal-pad sheets written in 1924 in Elfride Heidegger's hand, only slightly retouched by Heidegger for the final rendition of BT.

36. Pending further archival evidence, we can tentatively concur with Pöggeler's estimate, made in his Postscript to the third edition of the *Denkweg* (1990). In accord with this estimate, the later Heidegger speaks of "the attempt made time and again since 1930 to raise the question of *Being and Time* in a more incipient way" (*Zur Sache des Denkens*, p. 61/55). In 1930, Heidegger began to give his public lecture, "Vom Wesen der Wahrheit," on a repeated basis (cf. Appendix B). On September 18, 1932, he writes to Elisabeth Blochmann: "People think, and even talk about it, that I am now writing SZ II. It is good that they do so. But since SZ I once was for me a *way* that led me in a certain direction, and since this path is now no longer being trodden and has already become overgrown, I can no longer write SZ II. I am not writing a book at all" (Heidegger and Blochmann, *Briefwechsel*, p. 54).

BIBLIOGRAPHY

This bibliography is restricted to already-published works and editions cited in this book. See Appendix B for a complete list of Heidegger's courses, seminars, and talks—published and unpublished—for the period of this study. The notes to Appendixes B and C make note of some of the as yet unpublished archive material.

WORKS BY MARTIN HEIDEGGER (followed by extant English translations)

A. Separate Works

"Anmerkungen zu Karl Jaspers *Psychologie der Weltanschauungen.*" In *Karl Jaspers in der Diskussion,* edited by Hans Saner, pp. 70–100. Munich: Piper, 1973. Also in GA 9, *Wegmarken,* edited by F.-W. von Herrmann, pp. 1–44. Frankfurt: Klostermann, 1976.

Der Begriff der Zeit: Vortrag vor der Marburger Theologenschaft Juli 1924. Edited with a Postscript, by Hartmut Tietjen. Tübingen: Niemeyer, 1989. Translated as a bilingual edition by William McNeill, under the title *The Concept of Time.* Oxford and Cambridge, Mass.: Blackwell, 1992.

Frühe Schriften. Frankfurt: Klostermann, 1972.

Gelassenheit. Pfullingen: Neske, 1959. Translated by John M. Anderson and E. Hans Freund, under the title *Discourse on Thinking.* New York: Harper and Row, 1966.

Kant und das Problem der Metaphysik. Frankfurt: Klostermann, 1929, ⁴1973. Translated by Richard Taft, under the title *Kant and the Problem of Metaphysics.* Bloomington: Indiana University Press, 1990.

Phänomenologie und Theologie. Frankfurt: Klostermann, 1970. Also GA 9:45–78.

"Phänomenologische Interpretationen zu Aristoteles (Anzeige der hermeneutischen Situation)." Edited, with a Postscript, by Hans-Ulrich Lessing. *Dilthey-Jahrbuch* 6 (1989): 235–274. Translated by Michael Baur, under the title "Phenomenological Interpretations with Respect to Aristotle (Indication of the Hermeneutical Situation)." *Man and World* 25 (1992): 355–393.

Sein und Zeit. Halle an der Saal (from 1949 in Tübingen): Niemeyer, 1927, [2]1929, [3]1931, [4]1935, [5]1941, [6]1949, [7]1953, [8]1957, [9]1961, [10]1963, [11]1967, [12]1972, [13]1976, [14]1977, [15]1979, [16]1986. 438 pages in the first six editions, 437 pages after resetting in 1953. The first edition appeared not only as a separate work but also as one of two "articles" (Oskar Becker's "Mathematische Existenz" was the second "article," pp. 439–809) in Husserl's *Jahrbuch für Philosophie und phänomenologische Philosophie*, Vol. 8 (1927): 1–438. The fifth edition in 1941 omits the dedication to Husserl. Translated by John Macquarrie and Edward Robinson, under the title *Being and Time*. New York: Harper and Row, 1962.

Unterwegs zur Sprache. Pfullingen: Neske, 1959. Translated by Peter D. Hertz, under the title *On the Way to Language*. New York: Harper and Row, 1962.

Vier Seminare. Frankfurt: Klostermann, 1977.

Was ist Metaphysik? Bonn: Friedrich Cohen, 1929.

Zur Sache des Denkens. Tübingen: Niemeyer, 1969. Translated by Joan Stambaugh, under the title *On Time and Being*. San Francisco: Harper and Row, 1972.

B. *Gesamtausgabe. II. Abteilung: Vorlesungen 1919–1944.* Frankfurt: Klostermann, 1975ff.

Vol. 19, *Platon: Sophistes.* Marburg lecture course of WS 1924-25. Edited by Ingeborg Schüssler. 1992.

Vol. 20, *Prolegomena zur Geschichte des Zeitbegriffs.* Marburg lecture course of SS 1925. Edited by Petra Jaeger. 1979, [2]1988. Translated by Theodore Kisiel, under the title *History of the Concept of Time: Prolegomena*. Bloomington: Indiana University Press, 1985.

Vol. 21, *Logik: Die Frage nach der Wahrheit.* Marburg lecture course of WS 1925–26. Edited by Walter Biemel. 1976.

Vol. 24, *Die Grundprobleme der Phänomenologie.* Marburg lecture course of SS 1927. Edited by F.-W. von Herrmann. 1975, [2]1989. Translated by Alfred Hofstadter, under the title *The Basic Problems of Phenomenology*. Bloomington: Indiana University Press, 1982.

Vol. 25, *Phänomenologische Interpretation von Kants Kritik der reinen Vernunft.* Marburg lecture course of WS 1927–28. Edited by Ingtraud Görland. 1978, [2]1987.

Vol. 26, *Metaphysische Anfangsgründe der Logik im Ausgang von Leibniz.* Marburg lecture course of SS 1928. Edited by Klaus Held. 1978. Translated by Michael Heim, under the title *The Metaphysical Foundations of Logic*. Bloomington: Indiana University Press, 1984.

Vol. 29/30, *Die Grundbegriffe der Metaphysik: Welt, Endlichkeit, Einsamkeit.* Freiburg lecture course of WS 1929–30. Edited by F.-W. von Herrmann. 1983.

Vol. 49, *Die Metaphysik des deutschen Idealismus.* On the Freiburg lecture courses of the First Trimester and SS 1941. Edited by Günter Seubold. 1991.

Vol. 56/57, *Zur Bestimmung der Philosophie.* The early Freiburg courses of KNS 1919 and SS 1919. Edited by Bernd Heimbüchel. 1987.

Vol. 61, *Phänomenologische Interpretationen zu Aristoteles: Einführung in die phäno-menologische Forschung.* The early Freiburg course of WS 1921–22. Edited by Walter Bröcker and Käte Bröcker-Oltmanns. 1985.

Vol. 63, *Ontologie: Hermeneutik der Faktizität.* The early Freiburg course of SS 1923. Edited by Käte Bröcker-Oltmanns. 1988.

C. Heidegger's Correspondence

"Brief Martin Heideggers an Elisabeth Husserl." Dated 24 April 1919; here with a note in Italian by its editor, Guy van Kerckhoven. *Aut aut* 223–224 (January–April 1988): 6–14.

Martin Heidegger and Elisabeth Blochmann. *Briefwechsel 1918–1969.* Edited by Joachim W. Storck. Marbacher Schriften. Marbach am Neckar: Deutsche Schillergesellschaft, 1989.

Martin Heidegger and Karl Jaspers. *Briefwechsel 1920–1963.* Edited by Walter Biemel and Hans Saner. Frankfurt: Klostermann; Munich and Zürich: Piper, 1990.

Letter to Engelbert Krebs on July 19, 1914. In Hugo Ott, *Martin Heidegger: Unterwegs zu seiner Biographie,* p. 83. Frankfurt and New York: Campus, 1988.

Letter to Engelbert Krebs on January 9, 1919. In Bernhard Casper, "Martin Heidegger und die theologische Fakultät 1909–1923," *Freiburger Diözesan-Archiv* 100 (1980): 541.

Hermann Köstler. "Heidegger schreibt an Grabmann." Letter of January 7, 1917. *Philosophisches Jahrbuch* 87 (1980): 104.

Letters to Karl Löwith on August 19, 1921 and August 20, 1927. In *Zur philosophischen Aktualität Heideggers,* edited by Dietrich Papenfuss and Otto Pöggeler. vol. 2, *Im Gespräch der Zeit,* pp. 27–38. Frankfurt: Klostermann, 1990.

Heidegger's correspondence with Erich Rothacker is to be found in "Martin Heidegger und die Anfänge der 'Deutschen Vierteljahrsschrift für Literaturwissenschaft und Geistesgeschichte': Eine Dokumentation," edited by Joachim W. Storck and Theodore Kisiel. *Dilthey-Jahrbuch* 8 (1992).

OTHER WORKS CITED

Arendt, Hannah. "Martin Heidegger zum achtzigsten Geburtstag." *Merkur* 10 (1969): 893. English version: "Martin Heidegger at Eighty." *The New York Review of Books,* October 21, 1971, p. 50. Also in *Heidegger and Modern Philosophy,* edited by Michael Murray, pp. 293–294. New Haven: Yale University Press, 1978.

Aristotle. *Physics, Metaphysics, Nicomachean Ethics, Rhetoric, De Anima, De Partibus Animalium,* etc. The Loeb Classical Library. Cambridge: Harvard University Press.

Augustine of Hippo. *Opera Omnia,* vols. 1–12 = Migne, *Patrologia Latina,* vols. 32–46.

———. *Expositions on the Book of Psalms.* An abridged and uneven translation of *Enarrationes in Psalmos* (PL, vols. 36–37). Vol. 8 of *A Select Library of the Nicene and Post-Nicene Fathers of the Christian Church.* Edited by Philip Schaff. New York: Christian Literature Co., 1888.

———. "Homilies on the First Epistle of John." Translation of *In Epistolam Joannis ad Parthos* (PL, 35.1977–2062) by H. Browne and J. H. Myers. In *A Select Library of the Nicene and Post-Nicene Fathers of the Christian Church*, edited by Philip Schaff, 7:459–529. Also *Augustine: Later Works*, translated by John Burnaby, pp. 251–348. The Library of Christian Classics, vol. 8. Philadelphia: Westminster, 1953?

———. *Letters*. Vol. 3 (131–164). Translated by Sister Wilfrid Parsons, S.N.D. Vol. 11 of *Writings of St. Augustine*. New York: Fathers of the Church Inc., 1953.

———. *The Trinity*. Translated by Stephen McKenna, C.SS.R. The Fathers of the Church, vol. 45. Washington, D.C.: Catholic University of America Press, 1963.

———. *The Works of Saint Augustine: A Translation for the 21st Century*. Edited by John E. Rotelle. Translated with notes, by Edmund Hill. Part 3. *Sermons*, Vol. 3. Brooklyn, N.Y.: New City Press, 1990.

Bachman, Ingeborg. *Die kritische Aufnahme der Existentialphilosophie Martin Heideggers*. Munich and Zürich: Piper, 1985.

Barash, Jeffrey Andrew. *Martin Heidegger and the Problem of Historical Meaning*. Dordrecht, Boston, Lancaster: Nijhoff/Kluwer, 1988.

———. "Les sciences de l'histoire et le problème de la théologie à partir du cours inédit de Heidegger sur Saint-Augustin." In *Histoire et politique: Heidegger dans la perspective du vingtième siècle*. Paris: Editions Aldines, 1991.

Bast, Rainer A. *Der Wissenschaftsbegriff Martin Heideggers im Zusammenhang seiner Philosophie*. Stuttgart–Bad Cannstatt: Frommann-Holzboog, 1986. Chap. 2, pp. 43–51, on Heidegger's review of Jaspers.

Beaufret, Jean. *Dialogue avec Heidegger*. Vol. 3: *Approche de Heidegger*. Paris: Minuit, 1974.

Becker, Oskar. "Mathematische Existenz: Untersuchungen zur Logik und Ontologie mathematischer Phänomene." *Jahrbuch für Philosophie und phänomenologische Forschung* 8 (1927): 439–809.

Bernard of Clairvaux. *Sancti Bernardi Opera*. Vol. 1, *Sermones super Cantica Canticorum*. Rome: Editiones Cistercienses, 1957. Translated by Kilian Walsh, OCSO, under the title *On the Song of Songs*. Spencer, Mass.: Cistercian Publications, 1971.

Bernet, Rudolf. "Husserl and Heidegger on Intentionality and Being." *Journal of the British Society for Phenomenology* 21 (May 1990): 136–152.

Biemel, Walter. "Zum Briefwechsel Jaspers/Heidegger." In *Zur philosophischen Aktualität Heideggers*, edited by Dietrich Papenfuss and Otto Pöggeler, vol. 2, *Im Gespräch der Zeit*, pp. 71–86. Frankfurt: Klostermann, 1990.

———. *Martin Heidegger in Selbstzeugnissen und Bilddokumenten*. Hamburg: Rowohlt, 1973.

Blumenberg, Hans. *The Legitimacy of the Modern Age*. Translated by Robert M. Wallace. Cambridge Mass., and London: MIT Press, 1983.

Bousset, Wilhelm. *Kyrios Christos: Geschichte des Christusglaubens vor den Anfängen des Christentums bis Irenaeus*. Göttingen: Vandenhoeck und Ruprecht, 1913.

Buchner, Hartmut, ed. *Japan und Heidegger*. Sigmaringen: Thorbecke, 1989.

Bultmann, Rudolf. "Heidegger, Martin." In *Die Religion in Geschichte und Gegenwart: Handwörterbuch für Theologie und Religionswissenschaft* 2:1687f. Tübingen: Mohr, [2]1928.

Caputo, John D. *Heidegger and Aquinas.* New York: Fordham University Press, 1982.

———. *The Mystical Element in Heidegger's Thought.* Athens, Ohio University Press, 1978.

———. "Phenomenology, Mysticism and the 'Grammatica Speculativa': Heidegger's 'Habilitationsschrift.' " *Journal of the British Society for Phenomenology* 5 (1974): 101–117.

Casper, Bernhard. "Martin Heidegger und die theologische Fakultät Freiburg 1909–1923." *Freiburger Diözesan-Archiv* 100 (1980): 534–541.

Cohen, Hermann. *Logik der reinen Erkenntnis.* Berlin: Cassirer,[3] 1922.

Cohn, Jonas. *Religion und Kulturwerte.* Philosophische Vorträge der Kantgesellschaft. Berlin: Reuther und Reichard, 1914.

Deissmann, Gustaf Adolf. *Die neutestamentliche Formel "in Christo Jesu."* Marburg: Elwert, 1892.

———. *Paulus: Eine kultur- und religionsgeschichtliche Skizze.* Tübingen: Mohr, 1911. Translated by William E. Wilson, under the title *Paul: A Study in Social and Religious History.* New York: Harper and Row, Harper Torchbooks, 1957.

Dilthey, Wilhelm. *Einleitung in die Geisteswissenschaften.* Leipzig: Duncker und Humblot, 1883. Also *Gesammelte Schriften*, vol. 1. Stuttgart: Teubner, 1922, [7]1973. Translated by Ramon J. Betanzos, under the title *Introduction to the Human Sciences.* Detroit: Wayne State University Press, 1988.

———. *Die Jugendgeschichte Hegels.* Berlin: Reimer, 1905.

———. *Leben Schleiermachers.* Berlin: Reimer, 1870; Berlin: de Gruyter, [2]1922.

———. *Weltanschauung und Analyse des Menschen seit Renaissance und Reformation.* Vol. 2 of his *Gesammelte Schriften.* Göttingen: Vandenhoeck und Ruprecht, 1914.

Dilthey, Wilhelm, and Paul Yorck von Wartenburg. *Briefwechsel zwischen Wilhelm Dilthey und dem Grafen Paul Yorck von Wartenburg 1877-1897.* Philosophie und Geisteswissenschaften, edited by Erich Rothacker, vol. 1. Halle: Niemeyer, 1923.

Ebbinghaus, Julius. "Julius Ebbinghaus." In *Philosophie in Selbstdarstellungen*, edited by Ludwig J. Pongratz, 3:30–34. Hamburg: Meiner, 1975.

———. "Luther und Kant." *Luther-Jahrbuch* 9 (1927): 119–155.

Ficker, Johannes, ed. *Luthers Vorlesung über den Römerbrief 1515/1516: Die Glosse.* Leipzig: Dieterich und Weicher, 1908.

Gadamer, Hans-Georg. *Heideggers Wege.* Tübingen: Mohr, 1983.

———. *Philosophical Hermeneutics.* Translated and edited by David E. Linge. Berkeley, Los Angeles, London: University of California Press, 1976.

———. "Wilhelm Dilthey nach 150 Jahren." In *Dilthey und die Philosophie der Gegenwart*, edited by E. W. Orth., p. 159. Sonderband der *Phänomenologischen Forschungen.* Freiburg and Munich: Alber, 1985.

Haar, Michel, ed. *Martin Heidegger.* L'Herne, no. 45. Paris: L'Herne, 1983.

Harries, Karsten. Introduction to the English translation of Günther Neske and

Emil Kettering, eds., *Martin Heidegger and National Socialism: Questions and Answers*, translated by Lisa Harries. New York: Paragon House, 1990.

Hegel, Georg Wilhelm Friedrich. *Hegels theologische Jugendschriften*. Edited by Herman Nohl. Tübingen: Mohr, 1907. Translated by T. M. Knox, under the title *On Christianity: Early Theological Writings*. New York: Harper and Row, Harper Torchbooks, 1961.

Heidegger, Fritz. "Ein Geburtstagsbrief." In *Martin Heidegger zum 80. Geburtstag von seiner Heimatstadt Messkirch*, pp. 58–63. Frankfurt: Klostermann, 1969.

Hunzinger, A. W. "Das Furchtproblem in der katholischen Lehre von Augustin bis Luther." *Lutherstudien*, 1. Abteilung, 2. Heft, 1906. Regarding this essay, Heidegger in GA 20:394/285 observes that "the interpretation of Augustine there is in need of essential revisions."

Husserl, Edmund. *Briefe an Roman Ingarden*. The Hague: Nijhoff, 1968.

———. *Ideen zu einer reinen Phänomenologie und phänomenologischen Philosophie, Erstes Buch = Jahrbuch für Philosophie und phänomenologische Forschung*, vol. 1, part 1. Halle: Niemeyer, 1913. Translated by Fred Kersten, under the title *Ideas Pertaining to a Pure Phenomenology and to a Phenomenological Philosophy, First Book: General Introduction to a Pure Phenomenology*. The Hague, Boston, London: Nijhoff, 1982.

———. Ibid., *Zweites Buch*. Edited by Marly Biemel. Husserliana IV. The Hague: Nijhoff, 1952. Translated by Richard Rojcewicz and Andre Schuwer, under the title *Ideas Pertaining to a Pure Phenomenology and to a Phenomenological Philosophy. Second Book: Studies in the Phenomenology of Constitution*. Dordrecht, Boston, London: Kluwer, 1989.

———. *Logische Untersuchungen*. Halle: Niemeyer, 1900–1901. Translated by J. N. Findlay, under the title *Logical Investigations*. New York: Humanities, 1970.

———. *Phänomenologische Psychologie*. Edited by Walter Biemel. Husserliana IX. The Hague: Nijhoff, 1962. Translated by William Scanlon, under the title *Phenomenological Psychology*. The Hague: Nijhoff, 1977.

———. "Philosophie als strenge Wissenschaft". *Logos* 1 (1910–11): 289–340, therefore called the "*Logos* essay." Available as a reprint, ed. Wilhelm Szilasi, in the series *Quellen der Philosophie*, ed. Rudolph Berlinger, no. 1. Frankfurt: Klostermann, 1965. Translated by Quentin Lauer, under the title "Philosophy as Rigorous Science," in E. Husserl, *Phenomenology and the Crisis of Philosophy*, pp. 71–147. New York: Harper and Row, Harper Torchbooks, 1965.

Jaspers, Karl. *Notizen zu Martin Heidegger*. Edited by Hans Saner. Munich and Zürich: Piper, [2]1978.

———. *Philosophische Autobiographie*. Munich and Zürich: Piper, [2]1977.

———. *Psychologie der Weltanschauungen*. Berlin: Springer, 1919, [6]1971. Paperback edition: Munich and Zürich: Piper, 1985.

Jaspert, Bernd, ed., *Karl Barth–Rudolf Bultmann Briefwechsel 1922–1966*. Zürich: Theologischer Verlag, 1971.

———. *Rudolf Bultmanns Werk und Wirkung*. Darmstadt: Wissenschaftliche Buchgesellschaft, 1984.

Jülicher, Adolf. *Der religiöse Wert der Reformation*. Marburg: Elwert, 1913.

Kant-Studien 29 (1924): 624ff.; 30 (1925): 611ff. Annual reports of activities of the local groups of the Kantgesellschaft, here the West German Industrial Group.

Kisiel, Theodore. "Diagrammatic Approach to Heidegger's Schematism of Existence." *Philosophy Today* 28 (Fall 1984): 229–241. Supplemented by "Professor Seigfried's Misreading of My Diagram and Its Source." *Philosophy Today* 55 (Spring 1986): 72–83.

———. "Edition und Übersetzung: Unterwegs von Tatsachen zu Gedanken, von Werken zu Wegen." In *Zur philosophischen Aktualität Heideggers*, vol. 3, *Im Spiegel der Welt: Sprache, Übersetzung, Auseinandersetzung*, edited by Dietrich Papenfuss and Otto Pöggeler, pp. 89–107. Frankfurt: Klostermann, 1992.

———. "Das Entstehen des Begriffsfeldes 'Faktizität' im Frühwerk Heideggers." *Dilthey-Jahrbuch für Philosophie und Geschichte der Geisteswissenschaften* 4 (1986–87): 91–120.

———. "The Genesis of *Being and Time*." *Man and World* 25 (1992): 21–37.

———. "Heidegger (1907–1927): The Transformation of the Categorial." In *Continental Philosophy in America*, edited by H. J. Silverman, J. Sallis and T. M. Seebohm, pp. 165–185. Pittsburgh: Duquesne University Press, 1983.

———. "Heidegger and the New Images of Science." *Research in Phenomenology* 6 (1977): 162–181. Reprinted in *Radical Phenomenology: Essays in Honor of Martin Heidegger*, edited by John Sallis. Atlantic Highlands, N.J.: Humanities, 1978.

———. "Heidegger's Apology: Biography as Philosophy and Ideology." *Graduate Faculty Philosophy Journal* 14/2–15/1 (1991): 363–404.

———. "Das Kriegsnotsemester 1919: Heideggers Durchbruch in die hermeneutische Phänomenologie." *Philosophisches Jahrbuch* 99, no. 1 (1992): 105–122.

———. "The Missing Link in the Early Heidegger." In *Hermeneutic Phenomenology: Lectures and Essays*, edited by Joseph J. Kockelmans, pp. 1–40. Washington, D.C.: University Press of America, 1988.

———. "New Philosophies of Science in the USA: A Selective Survey," *Zeitschrift für allgemeine Wissenschaftstheorie* 5 (1974): 201–233.

———. "On the Way to Being and Time: Introduction to the Translation of Heidegger's Prolegomena zur Geschichte des Zeitbegriffs." *Research in Phenomenology* 15 (1985): 193–226.

———. Review of Mark Taylor's *Tears. Bulletin de la Société américaine de philosophie de langue française* 2 (1990): 61–66. A later version is reprinted as a "Discussion" in the *Journal of the British Society for Phenomenology* 22, no. 2 (May 1991): 93–96.

———. "War der frühe Heidegger tatsächlich ein 'christlicher Theologe'?" In *Philosophie und Poesie: Otto Pöggeler zum 60. Geburtstag*, edited by A. Gethmann-Siefert, 2:59–75. Stuttgart: Fromann-Holzboog, 1988.

———. "Why Students of Heidegger Will Have to Read Emil Lask." In *Emil Lask and the Search for Concreteness*, edited by Deborah G. Chaffin. Athens: Ohio University Press, 1993.

———. "Why the First Draft of *Being and Time* Was Never Published." *Journal of the British Society for Phenomenology*, 20, no. 1 (January 1989): 3–22.

————. See also under Storck, Joachim W.

Kovacs, George. "Philosophy as Primordial Science (*Urwissenschaft*) in the Early Heidegger." *Journal of the British Society for Phenomenology* 21 (1990): 121–135.

Krell, David Farrell. "Toward *Sein und Zeit*: Heidegger's Early Review of Jaspers' 'Psychologie der Weltanschauungen.' " *Journal of the British Society for Phenomenology* 6 (1975): 147–156. Reprinted as "From Existence to Fundamental Ontology" in Krell's book, *Intimations of Mortality*, pp. 11–26. University Park, Pa., and London: Pennsylvania State University Press, 1986.

Ladrière, Jean. "Mathematics in a Philosophy of the Sciences." In *Phenomenology and the Natural Sciences: Essays and Translations*, edited by Joseph Kockelmans and Theodore Kisiel, pp. 443ff. Evanston, Ill.: Northwestern University Press, 1970.

Lask, Emil. *Gesammelte Schriften*. Edited by Eugen Herrigel. 2 vols. Tübingen: Mohr, 1923.

Löwith, Karl. *From Hegel to Nietzsche*. Garden City, N.Y.: Anchor, 1964.

————. *Mein Leben in Deutschland vor und nach 1933: Ein Bericht*. Stuttgart: Metzler, 1986.

Luther, Martin. "Heidelberg Disputation." In *Luther's Works*, edited by H. T. Lehmann, vol. 31, *Career of the Reformer: I*, edited by H. J. Grimm, pp. 40–54. Philadelphia: Muhlenberg, 1957.

Misch, Georg. "Lebensphilosophie und Phänomenologie: Eine Auseinandersetzung mit Heidegger." *Philosophischer Anzeiger* 3 (1928–29): 267–368. This lead article and its five subsequent installments became a book: *Lebensphilosophie und Phänomenologie: Eine Auseinandersetzung der Diltheyschen Richtung mit Husserl und Heidegger*. Bonn: Cohen, 1930; Leipzig: Teubner, [2]1931.

————. "Vorbericht des Herausgebers." In Wilhelm Dilthey, *Gesammelte Schriften* 5:vii–cxvii. Stuttgart: Teubner, 1924.

Mörchen, Hermann. *Adorno und Heidegger: Untersuchung einer philosophischen Kommunikationsverweigerung*. Stuttgart: Klett-Cotta, 1981.

Mulert, Hermann. *Schleiermachers geschichtsphilosophische Ansichten in ihrer Bedeutung für seine Theologie*. Gießen: Töppelmann, 1907.

Natorp, Paul. *Allgemeine Psychologie nach kritischer Methode*. Tübingen: Mohr, 1912.

————. *Deutscher Weltberuf: Geschichtsphilosophische Richtlinien*. Jena: Diederichs, 1918.

————. *Hermann Cohens philosophische Leistung unter dem Gesichtspunkte des Systems*. Berlin: Reuther und Reichard, 1918.

Neske, Günter, ed. *Erinnerung an Heidegger*. Pfullingen: Neske, 1977.

Neske, Günter, and Emil Kettering, eds. *Martin Heidegger and National Socialism: Questions and Answers*. Translated by Lisa Harries. New York: Paragon House, 1990.

Nohl, Herman. *Die Deutsche Bewegung: Vorlesungen und Aufsätze zur Geistesgeschichte von 1770–1830*. Edited by O. F. Bollnow and F. Rodi. Göttingen: Vandenhoeck und Ruprecht, 1970.

Norden, Eduard. *Agnostos Theos: Untersuchungen zur Formengeschichte religiöser Rede*. Leipzig and Berlin: Teubner, 1913.

Ochsner, Heinrich. *Das Mass der Verborgenen: Heinrich Ochsner 1891–1970 zum*

Gedächtnis. Edited by Curd Ochwadt and Erwin Tecklenborg. Hannover: Charis, 1981.

Oesterreicher, John M. *Walls Are Crumbling: Seven Jewish Philosophers Find Christ.* New York: Devin-Adair, 1952. An English summary of Adolf Reinach's "The Absolute" is on pp. 123–126.

O'Meara, Thomas F., O.P. "Heidegger and His Origins: Theological Perspectives." *Theological Studies* 47 (1986): 205–226.

Ott, Hugo. *Martin Heidegger: Unterwegs zu seiner Biographie.* Frankfurt and New York: Campus, 1988.

———. "Zu den katholischen Wurzeln im Denken Martin Heideggers: Der theologische Philosoph." In *Akten des römischen Heidegger-Symposions* (1992).

———. "Martin Heidegger—Mentalität der Zerrissenheit." *Freiburger Diözesan-Archiv* 110 (1990): 427–448.

Otto, Rudolf. *Das Heilige: Über das Irrationale in der Idee des Göttlichen und sein Verhältnis zum Rationalen.* Stuttgart: Gotha, 1917. Translated by John W. Harvey, under the title *The Idea of the Holy: An Inquiry into the Non-rational Factor in the Idea of the Divine and Its Relation to the Rational.* New York: Oxford University Press, Galaxy Books, 1958.

Papenfuss, Dietrich, and Otto Pöggeler, eds. *Zur philosophischen Aktualität Heideggers.* Vol. 2, *Im Gespräch der Zeit.* Vol. 3, *Im Spiegel der Welt: Sprache, Übersetzung, Auseinandersetzung.* Frankfurt: Klostermann, 1990, 1991.

Passow, Franz. *Handwörterbuch der griechischen Sprache* . Leipzig: Friedrich Chr. Wilhelm Vogel, 1831.

Petzet, Heinrich Wiegand. *Auf einen Stern zugehen: Begegnungen und Gespräche mit Martin Heidegger 1929–1976.* Frankfurt: Societäts-Verlag, 1983.

Pfeiffer, Franz. *Deutsche Mystiker des Vierzehnten Jahrhunderts.* Vol. 2, *Meister Eckhart.* 1857. Reprint Göttingen: Vandenhoeck und Ruprecht, 1906.

Pöggeler, Otto. *Der Denkweg Martin Heideggers.* Pfullingen: Neske, 1963, ²1983, ³1990. Translated by Daniel Magurshak and Sigmund Barber, under the title *Martin Heidegger's Path of Thinking.* Atlantic Highlands, N.J.: Humanities, 1987.

———. *Heidegger und die hermeneutische Philosophie.* Freiburg and Munich: Alber, 1983.

———. "Heideggers Neubestimmung des Phänomenbegriffs." Edited by E. W. Orth. *Phänomenologische Forschungen* 9 (1980): 124–162.

———. *Neue Wege mit Heidegger.* Freiburg and Munich: Alber, 1992.

———. "Oskar Becker als Philosoph," *Kant-Studien* 60 (1969): 298–311. Reprinted as "Einspruch gegen Panhermeneutik: Oskar Becker" in Otto Pöggeler, *Heidegger und die hermeneutische Philosophie,* pp. 365–388.

———. "Philosophie und hermeneutische Theologie." Düsseldorfer Akademie-Vortrag, 1989. To be published shortly (Opladen, 1993).

———. "Temporal Interpretation and Hermeneutic Philosophy." Translated by T. Kisiel. In *Phenomenology: Dialogues and Bridges*, edited by R. Bruzina and B. Wilshire. pp. 79–97. Albany: SUNY Press, 1982. The German version, written in 1977, has just been published in Pöggeler's *Neue Wege mit Heidegger,* pp. 115–141. Freiburg and Munich: Alber, 1992.

———. "Zeit und Sein bei Heidegger." In *Zeit und Zeitlichkeit bei Husserl und Heidegger,* edited by E. W. Orth = *Phänomenologische Forschungen* 14 (1983): 152–191.

Pöggeler, Otto, and F. Hogemann. "Martin Heidegger: Zeit und Sein." In *Grund-probleme der großen Philosophen*, edited by J. Speck, pp. 48–86. Göttingen: Van-denhoeck und Ruprecht, 1982.

Pohlenz, Max. *Vom Zorne Gottes: Eine Studie über den Einfluss der griechischen Philo-sophie auf das alte Christentum*. Göttingen: Vandenhoeck und Ruprecht, 1909.

Realencyklopädie für protestantische Theologie und Kirche 6:674–682, s.v. "Glaube." Leipzig: Hinrichs, ³1899.

Reinach, Adolf. "Bruchstück einer religionsphilosophischen Ausführung. Das Absolute." In *Sämtliche Werke*, edited by Karl Schuhmann, 1:605–611. Mun-ich: Philosophia, 1989. The section on "Das Absolute" was first published in Conrad Martius's Introduction to Adolf Reinach, *Gesammelte Schriften*, pp. xxxi–xxxvi. Halle: Niemeyer, 1921.

Reitzenstein, Richard. *Die hellenistischen Mysterienreligionen*. Leipzig and Berlin: Teubner, 1910.

Die Religion in Geschichte und Gegenwart. vol. 2, edited by F. M. Schiele and L. Zscharnack, cols. 1425–61, s.v. "Glaube." Tübingen: Mohr, 1910.

Richardson, William J., S.J. *Heidegger: Through Phenomenology to Thought*. The Hague: Nijhoff, 1963.

Rodi, Frithjof. "Die Bedeutung Diltheys für die Konzeption von 'Sein und Zeit': Zum Umfeld von Heideggers Kasseler Vorträgen (1925)." *Dilthey-Jahrbuch* 4 (1986–87): 161–177.

Schettler, Adolph. *Die paulinische Formel "Durch Christus"*. Tübingen: Mohr, 1907.

Schleiermacher, Friedrich. *Aus Schleiermachers Leben, in Briefen*. Edited by L. Jonas and W. Dilthey. 4 Volumes. Berlin: Reimer, 1858–63.

———. *Der christliche Glaube*. Berlin: Reimer, ⁶1884. English translation edited by H. R. Mackintosh and J. S. Stewart: *The Christian Faith*, vol. 1. New York: Harper and Row, Harper Torchbooks, 1963.

———. *Über die Religion. Reden an die Gebildeten unter ihren Verächtern*. In Schleier-macher's *Sämmtliche Werke*. 1. Abt., "Zur Theologie," 1:133–460. Berlin: Re-imer, 1843. Translated from the 3d German ed. by John Oman, under the title *On Religion: Speeches to Its Cultured Despisers*. New York: Harper and Row, Harper Torchbooks, 1958.

Schneeberger, Guido. *Nachlese zu Heidegger: Dokumente zu seinem Leben und Denken*. Bern: private circulation, 1962.

Schuhmann, Karl. *Husserl-Chronik: Denk- und Lebensweg Edmund Husserls*. The Hague: Nijhoff, 1977.

Sheehan, Thomas. "Getting to the Topic: The New Edition of *Wegmarken*." In *Radical Phenomenology: Essays in Honor of Martin Heidegger*, edited by John Sallis, pp. 299–316. Atlantic Highlands, N.J.: Humanities, 1978.

———. "Heidegger's Early Years: Fragments for a Philosophical Biography." In *Heidegger: The Man and the Thinker*, edited by Thomas Sheehan, pp. 3–19. Chicago: Precedent, 1981.

———. "Heidegger's 'Introduction to the Phenomenology of Religion,' 1920–21." *The Personalist* 55 (1979–80): 312–324. Reprinted in *A Companion to Martin Heidegger's "Being and Time,"* edited by J. J. Kockelmans, pp. 40–62. Washington, D.C.: University Press of America, 1986.

————. "Heidegger's *Lehrjahre*." In *The Collegium Phaenomenologicum: The First Ten Years*, edited by J. C. Sallis, G. Moneta, and J. Taminiaux, pp. 77–137. Phaenomenologica, vol. 105. Dordrecht: Kluwer, 1988.

————. "On the Way to *Ereignis*: Heidegger's Interpretation of *Physis*." In *Continental Philosophy in America*, edited by Hugh J. Silverman, John Sallis, and Thomas M. Seebohm, pp. 131–164. Pittsburgh: Duquesne University Press, 1983.

————. " 'Time and Being,' 1925–27." In *Thinking about Being: Aspects of Heidegger's Thought*, edited by Robert W. Shahan and J. N. Mohanty, pp. 177–219. Norman: University of Oklahoma Press, 1984.

Spranger, Eduard. "Zur Theorie des Verstehens und zur geisteswissenschaftlichen Psychologie." In *Festschrift Johannes Volkelt zum 70. Geburtstag dargebracht*, presented by P. Barth, B. Bauch, E. Bergmann, *et al.*, pp. 357–403. Munich: Beck, 1918. Also in Spranger's *Grundlagen der Geisteswissenschaften*, vol. 6 of his *Gesammelte Schriften*, edited by Hans Walter Bähr, pp. 1–42. Tübingen: Niemeyer, 1980.

Stein, Edith. *Briefe an Roman Ingarden 1917–1938*. Introduction by Hanna-Barbara Gerl. Notes by Maria Amata Neyer O.C.D. Freiburg, Basel, Vienna: Herder, 1991.

Stern, Günther. "Die Rolle der Situationskategorie bei der 'Logischen Sätzen.' " Diss. Freiburger, 1924.

————. *Über das Haben: Sieben Kapitel zur Ontologie der Erkenntnis*. Bonn: Friedrich Cohen, 1928.

Stewart, Roderick M. "Signification and Radical Subjectivity in Heidegger's Habilitationsschrift.' " *Man and World* 12 (1979): 360–386.

Storck, Joachim W., and Theodore Kisiel, eds. "Martin Heidegger und die Anfänge der *Deutschen Vierteljahrsschrift der Literaturwissenschaft und Geistesgeschichte*: Eine Dokumentation." *Dilthey-Jahrbuch* 8 (1992).

Strauss, Leo. "An Introduction to Heideggerian Existentialism." In Strauss, *The Rebirth of Classical Political Rationalism*, p. 27–46. University of Chicago Press, 1989.

Süskind, Hermann. *Christentum und Geschichte bei Schleiermacher: Die geschichtsphilosophischen Grundlagen der Schleiermacherschen Theologie*. Tübingen: Mohr, 1911.

Teresa of Avila. "First Mansions." In *Complete Works of St. Teresa of Jesus*, translated by E. Allison Peers, 2:201–212. London: Sheed and Ward, 1946.

Troeltsch, Ernst. "Die Zukunftsmöglichkeiten des Christentums." *Logos* 1 (1910–11): 165–185.

Walther, Gerda. "Zur Ontologie der sozialen Gemeinschaften." *Jahrbuch für Philosophie und phänomenologische Forschung* 6 (1923): 1–158.

Wehrung, Georg. *Der geschichtsphilosophische Standpunkt Schleiermachers zur Zeit seiner Freundschaft mit den Romantikern*. Strassburg: Müh, 1907.

Weinel, Heinrich. *Biblische Theologie des Neuen Testaments: Die Religion Jesu und des Urchristentums*. Tübingen: Mohr, [2]1913.

Weiß, Johannes B. *Das Urchristentum*. Göttingen: Vandenhoeck und Ruprecht, 1917.

Windelband, Wilhelm. *Präludien: Aufsätze und Reden zur Philosophie und ihrer Geschichte*. Tübingen: Mohr, [5]1915. Esp. "Das Heilige" (1902), pp. 295–332.

INDEX OF NAMES

INDEX OF SUBJECT MATTER

INDEX OF GREEK TERMS

INDEX OF LATIN TERMS

Indexes have been compiled by Michael Brezinsky, Tom Elkins, Kevin Friesen, Bob Kinkead, Marie Kisiel, Theodore Kisiel, Don Ringelestein, and Jim Williamson.

Designer: U.C. Press Staff
Compositor: Maryland Composition
Text: 10/12 Baskerville
Display: Baskerville
Printer: Thomson-Shore
Binder: Thomson-Shore